READINGS
IN PAKISTAN
FOREIGN POLICY
1971–1998

READINGS
IN PAKISTAN
FOREIGN POLICY
1971–1998

Edited by

MEHRUNNISA ALI

OXFORD

UNIVERSITY PRESS

Issued under the auspices of
The Pakistan Institute of International Affairs, Karachi.

OXFORD

UNIVERSITY PRESS

Great Clarendon Street, Oxford OX2 6DP

Oxford University Press is a department of the University of Oxford.
It furthers the University's objective of excellence in research, scholarship,
and education by publishing worldwide in

Oxford New York

Athens Auckland Bangkok Bogotá Buenos Aires Cape Town Chennai
Dar es Salaam Delhi Florence Hong Kong Istanbul Karachi Kolkata
Kuala Lumpur Madrid Melbourne Mexico City Mumbai Nairobi
Paris São Paulo Shanghai Singapore Taipei Tokyo Toronto Warsaw
with associated companies in Berlin Ibadan

Oxford is a registered trade mark of Oxford University Press
in the UK and in certain other countries

© The Pakistan Institute of International Affairs 2001

The moral rights of the authors have been asserted

First published 2001

ISBN 0 19 579393 5

Printed in Pakistan at
Mueid Packages, Karachi.
Published by
Ameena Saiyid, Oxford University Press
5-Bangalore Town, Sharae Faisal
PO Box 13033, Karachi-75350, Pakistan.

Contents

Contributors

Dr Khurshid Hyder (Late) was (in 1972) Associate Professor in the Department of International Relations, University of Karachi.

Zubeida Mustafa worked as Research Officer at Pakistan Institute of International Affairs (PIIA), Karachi. She is Assistant Editor, *Dawn*, Karachi.

Mehrunnisa Ali is former Professor of Political Science at the University of Karachi. She worked as Research Officer at PIIA, Karachi.

Khalida Qureshi (Late) was Research Officer at PIIA, Karachi.

Dr Nazir A. Mughal was (in 1976) Director of International Studies, Edinboro Staff College, Edinboro, USA.

Col. Ghulam Sarwar was (in 1981) Library Officer at National Defence College, Rawalpindi.

Safia S. Mohammadally is a writer on international affairs.

Naveed Ahmad was (in 1981) Research Officer at PIIA Karachi. She is Director, Area Study Centre Europe, University of Karachi.

Dr Mujtaba Razvi (Late) was (in 1982) Associate Professor in the Department of International Relations, University of Karachi.

Dr Hasan-Askari Rizvi was (in 1983) Research Fellow at the University of Illinois, USA. He is Professor of Political Science and former Chairman of the Department of Political Science, University of Punjab.

M. Raziullah Azmi was (in 1983) senior fellow in the Area Study Centre for Africa, North & South America, Quaid-i-Azam University, Islamabad.

Rashid Ahmad Khan was (in 1984) Associate Professor in the Department of Political Science, University of Punjab. He is currently Chairman, Department of Political Science, University of Punjab.

Zafar Iqbal Cheema was (in 1986) Assistant Professor, Department of Defence and Strategic Studies, Quaid-i-Azam University, Islamabad.

Mehrunnisa Iqbal is a writer on international affairs.

Dr Mohammad Ahsen Chaudhri is former Chairman, Department of International Relations and former Dean, Faculty of Arts, University of Karachi.

Dr Pervez Iqbal Cheema was (in 1988) Chairman, Department of International Relations, Quaid-i-Azam University, Islamabad.

Hamid H. Kizilbash was (in 1989) Associate Professor, Department of Political Science, University of Punjab.

Dr Mohammad Uzair is a leading economist.

Anees Jillani is an advocate and writer.

S. Amjad Ali (Late) was a senior journalist and former Editor of *Pakistan Quarterly*.

Marvi Memon was (in 1994) Research Officer at PIIA, Karachi.

Thom A. Travis was (in 1994) Professor of Political Science & International Relations at Bucknell University, Lewisburg, USA.

Vyacheslav Ya Belokrenitsky was (in 1995) Professor & Head of The Near & Middle East Department of the Institute of Oriental Studies, Moscow, Russia.

Farzana Shakoor was (in 1998) Senior Research Officer at PIIA, Karachi.

Preface

The seventies has been an epoch making era in the history of international relations, for it marked a significant recession in the cold war, the beginning of the Soviet-American détente and the Sino-American rapprochement having far-reaching implications for the world in general and the third world in particular. For Pakistan, however, the seventies was an era of formidable challenges. Covering a period of the last three decades, the anthology starts with the year 1971 due to a number of reasons as mentioned below.

The year 1971 has been a turning point in Pakistan's history. The East Pakistan crisis, provoking international ramifications, was followed by war with India in 1971 eventually resulting in the break-up of the country. The emergence of Bangladesh also had its bearing on Pakistan foreign policy. One visible direct impact was that Pakistan stopped identifying itself as a South East Asian state. A policy reappraisal was initiated. Accepting the new realities that had emerged in the region in the aftermath of the war, Pakistan's leadership decided to reduce tension with India by concluding the Simla pact resolving the issues ensuing from the war.

Pakistan withdrew from SEATO—the US sponsored multilateral defence pact—in the seventies not only due to its disillusionment with the US but also because of the loss of East Pakistan. From thence onwards, Islamabad policy became more Middle East oriented with less identification with South Asia.

The seventies also marked the beginning of a new era in the new Pakistan, the unique feature of which was the assumption of power by the first directly elected government in Pakistan, and the adoption of the 1973 constitution with a broad national consensus.

A new policy approach of bilateralism in foreign relations was initiated with a distinct thrust towards the third world and the Muslim countries. Pakistan emerged as a leading champion espousing the cause of the third world and the Muslim states.

The seventies also heralded the beginning of a nuclear Pakistan. The introduction of nuclear technology, besides being a new phenomena in Pakistan security and defence, created some problems— chief being the tension with the US affecting Pakistan's political and economic situations. The political crisis in the country ultimately resulted in the fall of Pakistan's first democratically elected government and the imposition of a third Martial Law.

Another significant development of far-reaching international repercussions in the close vicinity of Pakistan was the Soviet military intervention in Afghanistan, creating a host of problems for Pakistan on the border and within the country as well. Despite the Soviet disengagement from Afghanistan in 1989, Pakistan continues to feel the impact of the fallout from the Afghan war. Drug trafficking, arms smuggling, terrorism, and ethnic tension between the locals and the Afghan refugees are some of the problems affecting the country's internal and external position.

Comprising twenty-eight articles drawn from various issues of *Pakistan Horizon* and an introduction, the book starts with 1971, encompasses significant events pertaining to Pakistan foreign policy of the cold war era of the eighties, and concludes with the post-cold war period of the nineties focusing on the new challenges posed by the present day unipolar world. The introduction briefly points out the policy traits of the last fifty years, exposes the weaknesses of the policy, and suggests to opt for a less risky course.

As for the selection of twenty-eight articles out of several published in *Pakistan Horizon* during 1971–98, apart from the quality research, in-depth analysis, and maturity in style quite conspicuous from some of the articles, the collection could be categorized as (i) geographically relevant, (ii) crisis related, (iii) issue-oriented, (iv) region directed, and (v) era-wise policy reviews. This categorization as a matter of fact constitutes the criteria for the present selection.

Bounded by India, Iran, Afghanistan and China, Pakistan's geographical environment is a major determinant of its foreign policy. Any work on foreign policy would be incomplete without an exposition of the nature of problems and ties Pakistan has with its neighbours. The country's geostrategic location explains the rationale for the inclusion of articles dealing with India, Iran, Afghanistan and China. The article on Turkey finds a place in the work on account of Turkey's association with Pakistan in the US sponsored defence pact CENTO (liquidated in the seventies), in the RCD (now renamed and expanded as ECO) and its being the only Muslim European member country in NATO.

A developing country of the third world depending on big powers' good will for economic aid, arms, and technology transfer, Pakistan's relations with the major powers, particularly with America, always occupy a place of prominence in its foreign policy making process. The policy pursued by Pakistan till the sixties is well reflective from the big powers' attitude towards the East Pakistan crisis. The first four articles fit in the category of crisis related work exposing the friendly or unfriendly posture of major powers towards the East Pakistan crisis and the 1971 India-Pakistan war.

Articles on Kashmir, the nuclear programme, the security, the Afghan crisis, and foreign debt could be classified as issue-oriented. Providing a broad spectrum of foreign relations in the regional context are the papers on the Middle East, Western Europe, South Asia, and Central Asia. Era-wise foreign policy reviews relate to the cold war and post-cold war periods.

The first four articles dilate on the major powers' posture during the India-Pakistan war of 1971. Analysing the US stance, Khurshid Hyder (late) describes Pak-US relations in 1965–71 as 'correct and cordial' but not 'intimate and friendly'. Talking about the future she avers that resurrection of the past pacts or formulation of a new one would invest our policy with inflexibility such as that of the fifties. Her observation remains relevant to the present day unipolar world.

As for the USSR's role, Zubeida Mustafa considers Russian attitude in the initial pre-war phase as ambivalent. 'Publicly the USSR upheld the territorial integrity of Pakistan but covertly it worked to destroy the unity of Pakistan' (p. 23). She opines that direct involvement by the USSR (open support to India) forced America and China to take a positive stand in favour of Pakistan leading to a polarization of power in South Asia.

Concerning China's diplomacy during the war, Mehrunnisa Ali asserts that China supported Pakistan as much as was possible for it to do so. The Indo-Soviet treaty and the fear of Soviet intervention prevented direct Chinese involvement in the war (pp. 43–4). The fifth article is an exposition of the British role during the conflict. Khalida Qureshi (late) calls British policy 'unprincipled' and its support to India in contravention of international law and the UN charter. The succeeding article provides a detailed comparative study of the Simla and Tashkent pacts focusing on Kashmir and the problems ensuing from the wars. It explains why Bhutto, despite his claim to fight India a thousand year war sought peace with Delhi, and how a politically strong and militarily powerful Mrs Gandhi was persuaded to sign the Simla deal.

Zubeida Mustafa points out the trends in Pakistan's policy towards the Middle East in the mid-seventies. Islamabad exploited fully its 'Middle East option' (p. 91) by intensifying its efforts to foster closer ties with Iran, Turkey, and the Arab countries taking into account the geostrategic changes in the region after the 1973 Arab-Israeli war. Nazir Mughal focuses on the India-Pakistan 'fragile relationship' which 'fluctuated between cold war to hot war from 1948 to 1971' (p. 110). Noting the beginning of a 'cautious détente' between the two since 1972, the writer states that the 'century old enmity cannot disappear from the minds of the people of both countries in a short period of time' (p. 121). Article nine reviews Pakistan's foreign policy in the context of the global and regional developments of the seventies—the 1978 Afghan *coup*, the revolution in Iran, and the Soviet-American equation.

The next paper briefly outlines the geostrategic importance of the Muslim world and suggests measures for promoting Muslim unity. The writer proposes that Pakistan should further strengthen its ties with the Muslim states in order to combat the threat to its security posed by the Soviet military presence in Afghanistan. Article eleven undertakes a survey of Pak-Iran relations during 1947–79. According to the writer common heritage and geostrategic position of both account for their steady cooperation and cordiality over these years.

Article twelve is a narrative survey of Pak-Turkey relations from the fifties to the seventies. Besides the economic and trade ties, the paper highlights Ankara's stand on Kashmir and Islamabad's on Cyprus. Mujtaba Razvi (late), in his paper, avers that Pakistan is security conscious because of its unique geographical features. There is no defence depth, and all its major cities are border outposts (p. 184).

Article fourteen is an exposition of the determinants of the country's defence policy. Defence requirements enjoyed top priority due to Pakistan's geostrategic location in the region and the pattern of relationship with its neighbours. Summing up his analysis, Hasan Askari Rizvi asserts that Pakistan would continue to assign top priority to its defence requirements in the coming years (p. 219).

Article fifteen is a study of Pakistan-US relations in historical perspective. Of the four quoted vulnerabilities in their relationship, i.e. the India factor, the nuclear issue, human rights, and narcotics, Raziullah Azmi believes that the people and government in Pakistan feel very strongly on the first two, i.e. the India factor and the nuclear question. Rashid A. Khan in his paper 'Pakistan, India, and Regional Cooperation in South Asia' concentrates on divergent perceptions of the two countries which he considers as one of the most important causes of slow progress under SAARC.

Article seventeen examines the policy trends in the eighties taking into account the geopolitical changes in the region and superpowers' involvement in the Afghan quagmire. Recommending a balanced policy approach to meet the new challenges, the writer emphasizes the urgency to stay out of the superpowers' conflict, to mend fences with Moscow, and improve understanding with neighbours (p. 265).

Pakistan's case for a nuclear security guarantee has been tackled by Zafar I. Cheema against the background of India's nuclear explosion. The writer considers the nuclear security guarantee under the UN resolutions incredible on various grounds and calls for developing an independent national capability to counter the likely threat (p. 281).

Article nineteen recounts Pakistan's political, economic, trade, and cultural ties with Western Europe during 1975–86. The Russian military presence in Afghanistan and the influx of Afghan refugees in Pakistan evoked Western Europe's sympathetic attitude towards Islamabad.

Article twenty deals with Pakistan-China relations in political, military, and nuclear spheres with special reference to China's role during the last two India-Pakistan wars. Mohammad Ahsen Chaudhri delves into the military dimension of their ties in the light of the convergence of interest and common perception of both on the Afghan crisis. The succeeding paper studies the impact of the Afghan war on Pakistan's political, economic, social, and strategic conditions. Pervez Cheema opines that direct and indirect Soviet pressure on its western border pushed Pakistan closer to the US.

Writing on the superpowers and SAARC, Hamid Kizilbash remarks that the superpowers have not behaved as outrageously in South Asia as in other parts of the world and that they have not interfered in the politics of the states in the region. While one may contest his viewpoints, one could hardly disagree with the author's assertion that the basic difference in the behaviour of the two superpowers is that while Moscow has given complete and unwavering support to its ally, this has not been possible for Washington (p. 358).

Mohammad Uzair tackles the issue of foreign aid by dividing the period into two phases: the period up to 1970, and 1971–1991. The writer contends that countries get good results in economic development during dictatorships and undisturbed continuity of the system. However, when there is too much of democracy or 'parody of democracy', and intense politicking, economic progress suffers (p. 370).

Anees Jillani briefly recounts Pak-Afghan relations during 1958–88, highlighting various ups and downs in their bilateral ties with reference to their respective stand on the Durand Line and Pakhtunistan.

S. Amjad Ali examines the prospects of Pakistan's cooperation with the Central Asian republics in the light of the inducements for and impediments in the way of cooperation with these states. Some of the impediments as pointed out by the writer include internal rivalry and competition amongst the Central Asian states, the Afghan problem, the civil war in Tajikistan, and economic dependence of these states on Russia.

The impact of the post-cold war era on Pakistan foreign policy is the content of Marvi Memon's paper. She opines that the geostrategic regional environment with neighbours continues to remain the obvious constraint. Noting an increase in the constraints in the post-cold war period, she emphasizes the need for policy reorientation through increased regional involvement in Central Asia and regional organizations like SAARC and ECO.

Thom Travis discusses the advantages and disadvantages of the post-cold war era with reference to Pakistan. The author envisages less global power of the third world states than what they enjoyed in the past. While one may have strong reservations about his averment that the US will not often resort to warfare in the post-cold war period, his observation would sound relevant to many that in the unipolar system the UN Security Council will operate mainly as an instrument of the G-7 powers, particularly the US, Britain, and France.

V. Y. Belokrenitsky throws light on the importance of Central Asia for Russian and Pakistani policy planners. The writer opines that while

Russia has all the geographic-cum-infrastructural advantages in Central Asia, the same is not the case for Pakistan. The last article briefly outlines the impact of nuclearization of South Asia on the Kashmir dispute. Farzana Shakoor emphasizes the need to bolster Pakistan's defence capability in nuclear terms and to initiate a tripartite conference on Kashmir involving the three parties to the dispute—India, Pakistan and the Kashmiris.

One of the objectives of this anthology is to peep into the past in order to learn from the committed follies. In the light of past experiences and consequences of omissions and commissions of acts one can avoid pitfalls in future. Why was a particular stance under what compulsions pursued? Did it prove risky or less risky in terms of consequences? Without an objective study into these queries, one can hardly suggest a correct or a less risky course for the future.

Besides, this endeavour also seeks to assist the postgraduate students in comprehending the various facets of Pakistan foreign policy. Keeping in view their requirements, this anthology is prepared so that students can find all relevant material concerning important phases of foreign policy in one book. An attempt has been made to make the collection as concise and thematic as was humanly possible.

The articles included in this book were published in different issues of *Pakistan Horizon*. Except for a few changes deemed essential for editing purposes, the articles have been reproduced in their original form. The writers, whose articles have been included in the collection, are of diverse academic discipline and had been working in different capacities at various places. The views expressed in the papers are those of the authors. The editor gratefully acknowledges the cooperation of the Pakistan Institute of International Affairs, Karachi, in granting permission to reprint from the Journal. I am also grateful to Yasmeen Qureshi for her cooperation regarding this endeavour. Thanks are particularly due to Ameena Saiyid of OUP whose initiative made this work possible.

I am also indebted to Mehrunnisa, Farzana, Iqbal, and Rasool for their assistance in proofreading.

I am thankful to Oxford University Press for publishing the book.

Mehrunnisa Ali
May 1999
Karachi

Introduction

Mehrunnisa Ali

A penetrating survey of the last fifty years of Pakistan foreign policy would reveal certain distinct constants which permeate the entire gamut of Pakistan's relations with the external world. The first trait which can be easily discerned is the pre-eminence accorded to the US by Pakistan policy planners to ensure the country's security against the perceived threat from outside. Notwithstanding the changes in regional and global scenarios, maintenance of special ties with Washington has always remained the basic motto of the ruling elites. Beginning in the early years of independence with Liaquat Ali's decision to visit America, bypassing Moscow's invitation at a time when Pakistan had not yet aligned itself with either of the superpowers, the trend became an inherent part of foreign policy in the subsequent years of total and then conditional alignment. Despite various ups and downs in Pakistan-US relations and Islamabad's membership of the NAM, the country's foreign policy has remained US-tilted.

The other foreign policy constant is the primacy given to the Kashmir dispute. Pakistan's stance towards India revolves around Kashmir. Causing two wars in the past, the dispute remains the major irritant in India-Pakistan relations, consistently driving both to massive arms build-ups, conventional as well as nuclear. Another trait is the aid-oriented nature of Pakistan's policy. The need for external economic assistance in the initial years of inception was real when Pakistan was beset with grave problems. However, with the passage of time, the dependence on foreign aid also increased. Heavy reliance on external loans has now assumed such an alarming form that it determines the tenure of the party in power. Stability and survival of the governments now depend on the continuous flow of funds from the IMF and the World Bank. Any suspension or stoppage of aid is construed as a weakness of the government and sets the seal on its fate. Hence the object of each government has been to ensure the uninterrupted flow of aid even at the cost of freedom of action in foreign policy.

Beyond the above constants, Pakistan's policy has been mostly reactive towards other matters of regional and international import. The questions arise: Did the alliances with America secure Pakistan against external aggression? Has the policy thrust on the Kashmir issue brought its solution nearer in sight? Has foreign aid made Pakistan economically strong and self-sufficient and free from the need for further loans? A quick glance at the recent past would provide answers to the above queries.

Faced with a hostile powerful India and an unfriendly Afghanistan on the borders, the planners sought to protect Pakistan through a policy of alliances with America. However, the past fifty years bear testimony to the fact that special relations with the US did not protect Pakistan against external aggression. An alliance between unequal partners of varying strength, with divergent interests and threat perceptions often proves more beneficial for a powerful partner as it renders a small ally vulnerable to the former's pressure. Same was the case with the US-Pakistan alliance. Washington never shared the ruling elite's threat perception about India. Likewise, Pakistan did not view China and the former Soviet Union from the US angle. For Washington, CENTO (formerly the Baghdad pact) and SEATO were a part of its global strategy to counter and contain communist expansion in the region, while Pakistan construed the pacts as a guarantee against external aggression. That the policy of defence alliances failed to guarantee Pakistan's security and integrity against the powerful foe India is borne out by the breakup of the country in 1971. Not only that, the policy in the long run proved detrimental to its national interest. By acceding to the US sponsored anti-communist pacts, Pakistan incurred the Soviet wrath. Moscow retaliated by endorsing India's stand on Kashmir and siding with Kabul on the Pukhtunistan issue. Comparatively speaking, the Pakistan-US alliance was no match to the Indo-Soviet friendship insofar as the practical benefits accruing to the parties were concerned. The late sixties and the period that followed thereafter witnessed how Pakistan was endangered by the Indo-Soviet collaboration and how the 1971 Indo-Soviet treaty helped India inflict defeat on Pakistan forces in the former East Pakistan province.

Under the changed international situation marked by the Soviet-American détente and the Sino-American normalization in the seventies, military alliances lost their rationale and Pakistan formally abandoned the alignment policy. Nevertheless, even after Islamabad's exit from SEATO and CENTO, relations with the US continued to enjoy primacy. This proved advantageous for America when the Soviet forces entered Afghanistan in 1979. It used Pakistan as a conduit for arms supply to the Afghan resistance groups. Pakistan has to bear the brunt of the re-intensified Soviet-American rivalry in the region. The consequences of the Afghan war and its impact on Pakistan's security, politics, economic condition and ethnic composition are well-known but do not fall within the purview of this introduction.

After the end of the cold war and the disintegration of the Soviet Union as a superpower in the early nineties, Pakistan has lost its strategic importance for the US policy planners. However, it appears that the emerging new realities of the unipolar world have hardly brought about any significant change in the outlook of the ruling elites. The present leadership too seeks special ties with Washington. Talks of reviving the relationship of the fifties by the Nawaz government is a pointer to the persisting trend. Taking place after a period of twenty-five years, Nawaz Sharif's recent visit to Russia can hardly be considered a major indicator of any policy reshuffle. For one, Russia is no more a superpower. It is passing through severe economic crisis; economically its condition is not much different from that of Pakistan. However, Russia needs Pakistan's cooperation for the resolution of the Afghan issue to contain the Taliban meddling in some Central Asian states and for implementing its strategic partnership scheme. Nevertheless, given Moscow's special association with Delhi and the bitter experience of their 1971 friendship treaty, mending of fences with Russia would be in accord with Pakistan's security imperatives and help serve its long term policy objectives in the region.

As for the Kashmir-oriented approach, suffice it to say that the policy of dialogue and dualogue has not served the purpose. Despite the past two wars on Kashmir, several parleys held between the two states from time to time and their recently conducted nuclear tests, the resolution remains as distant as ever. Firmly adhering to their respective stance, Delhi and Islamabad do not appear to have moved an inch towards the settlement of the conflict. That the recent India-Pakistan normalization drive set off by the Lahore Declaration and the starting of a Lahore-Delhi bus service is accompanied by the missile tests by both indicates that dialogue or no dialogue, both continue to doubt one another's motives. The issue can not be solved unless any of these eventualities occurs: (i) under internal compulsions or external pressures India changes its stance; (ii) the major powers exert adequate effective pressure on Delhi to grant the right of self-determination to the Kashmiris; (iii) the intensified freedom struggle in Kashmir saps India's resources and exhausts it (the way Vietnam exhausted America, of course with China's strong material support), compelling it to accede to a plebiscite; (iv) Pakistan-India and Kashmiris reach an accord on the future status of Kashmir. Again this needs a change of heart on the part of Delhi. Till the occurrence of any of these possibilities, Pakistan has little option except to keep extending its moral and diplomatic support to the Kashmiris and publicizing the issue at all international forums. Any other course (intervention or settlement over the heads of Kashmiris) would be fraught with danger having ominous portents on security, peace and stability in the region. Given its own domestic compulsions, Pakistan has to first put its house in order. The approach should be inward-looking aiming at protecting and preserving the present Pakistan by making it economically strong and politically viable. Without forsaking the Kashmir cause, the policy has to be realistic and futuristic to meet the eventuality of an unfavourable outcome of a plebiscite. In view of the prevailing state of affairs in the region, the majority of Kashmiris may opt for independence in the event of a free and fair plebiscite.

As for the priority assigned to foreign aid in policy making, as long as Pakistan does not come out of the present economic mess, the policy will remain aid-afflicted and the planners will continue to please the aid-giving agencies by accepting their conditionalities attached to the delivery of loans. It goes without saying that wrong economic policies, mismanagement of foreign aid, and official corruption at high levels have increased the country's dependence on the IMF and the World Bank, so much so that not only its freedom of action in external matters has been compromised, but the government has to yield to the dictates of the donors even in matters of purely domestic concern. Can Pakistan come out safely from the staggering external debt of $ 29.7 billion in the next millennium? Only time can tell.

What the country needs is good governance to rescue it out of this economic morass.

The persistence of old issues apart, the emergence of unipolarism poses new formidable challenges to the strategists. The bipolar world was much safer and beneficial for the third world nations. For, it not only offered opportunities to small states to use superpower rivalry to their advantage, it also provided them protection against the adventurist designs of one superpower. In the bipolar era, the two superpowers used to contain one another's struggle for power and expansionist drive in the areas of strategic importance. With the collapse of the Soviet Union as a superpower, the balancing force in the international arena has disappeared. Major challenges now faced by Pakistan or for that matter the entire third world are of three types. One is their greater vulnerability to the dictates of one superpower. Second, the undisputed pursuit of policy ambitions by one power involves grave implications for small countries. The US, as an unrestrained superpower, could be legitimately perceived as a threat by small nations. Current history is replete with examples of US air strikes and bombing of small countries on one pretext or another. Third, as a result of the changed role of the UN in the present day unipolar world, small states are now exposed to the US dominated UN. The world body has now become a tool in the hands of the US and its coalition partners of the West. The Gulf War and the continued sanctions against Iraq provide one example of how the UN has been used by America to further its own economic and strategic interests in the region. Another matter of grave concern is the increased religious fanaticism in the region, be it the extreme form of Hindu nationalism in India, the rise of Taliban type Islam in Afghanistan, or the growing influence of seminaries in Pakistan.

In addition to the above, Pakistan has to reckon with the new realities of the changed regional scenario. The policy formulators can hardly be oblivious of the security implications involved in the continued armed struggle in Afghanistan, differences with Iran, the Sino-Indian patch-up and the increasing Indo-Russian collaboration. An improved understanding with Russia is one step in the right direction. A change in Pakistan's Afghan policy of supporting one group would help mitigate the grievances of other combatant Afghan groups as well as the regional states.

The adherence to the above mentioned traits in the last fifty years has exposed the weaknesses of the policy in realizing the goals of security, resolution of the Kashmir dispute, and economic self-sufficiency. A policy reappraisal as such is long overdue. There is no denying the fact that in the ever-changing world of real politik there is no risk-free policy approach, nevertheless, one can strive for a less risky course if one is fully aware of the past failures and successes.

A policy of peace and cooperation with neighbours, greater collaboration with China, and increased economic links with the Muslim states in the vicinity could help tackle the challenges of the new era. A successful policy is one which keeps the enemy farther and friends nearer which is rational, fully cognizant of the exigencies of real politik, dynamic to adjust to the changing regional and global situations and reflective of long term national interest.

2

United States and the Indo-Pakistan War of 1971*

Khurshid Hyder

US-Pakistan relations have undergone wide fluctuations in the last twenty-five years. The amorphous cordiality of the early years gave way to unqualified alignment in the fifties based on a series of bilateral and multilateral treaties. In a bipolar world marked by active rivalries between the communist and non-communist powers, with the 'third world' trying to steer clear of these rivalries under the cover of non-alignment, Pakistan's policy of alignment reflected a deliberate decision on her part to link her policies with the West and more particularly the United States. In the sixties, the exigencies of the internal and external developments led to a gradual erosion of the cohesive links of the fifties and ushered in the third phase in her relationship, the period of 'qualified alignment'.

Pakistan's relations with America have been motivated primarily by a set of political and economic factors. Politically, Pakistan expected the alliance with America to provide security against India and large-scale military aid which she considered to be necessary to ensure a power equilibrium in the subcontinent. Added to it, was the desire to get enhanced economic and technical assistance to accelerate the process of economic development. Pakistan was thus drawn into the vortex of alliances with America till she acquired the questionable distinction of being the most allied ally of the United States in Asia.

---

* Vol. xxv, No. 1, 1972.

But the policy of alignment in the heyday of non-alignment visibly strained her relations with the communist countries, particularly the Soviet Union—who became openly hostile and also isolated her in the 'third world'. It also gave India the formal excuse to unilaterally renounce her international commitments on Kashmir. As against this, it brought Pakistan large-scale military aid and considerably enhanced economic assistance. These were substantial material gains. But in terms of security against India, or even diplomatic backing in the disputes with India, she was sorely disappointed. The United States did not consider it politic to alienate the most important country in South Asia to gratify Pakistan. Thus while Pakistan became America's most loyal ally in Asia, the latter refused to be her patron against India. The US reservation to the SEATO Treaty in 1954, clearly bore this out. It was further underlined in 1959, when Pakistan signed the bilateral agreement of cooperation with the United States. Under the terms of this agreement, the United States was required, in certain circumstances, to assist Pakistan if she became the victim of aggression. India demanded and, according to Mr Nehru, received, a specific assurance from Washington that this agreement could not be used against India. Shorn of sophistry, this demand amounted to seeking an assurance that if India should commit aggression against Pakistan, the United States would not come to her assistance under this agreement.[1]

To the United States, on the other hand, Pakistan's relevance was only in the context of the global strategy to contain communism. With the crystallization of the spheres of influence in Europe by the end of the forties the focus of attention shifted to Asia in the early fifties. The establishment of a communist government in China, the Korean War followed by the French debacle in Indochina, all made Asia the theatre of cold war politics. Mr Dulles was firmly convinced of the reality of the communist threat in Asia. Accordingly, he decided to adopt the strategy in Asia, which had been vastly successful and yielded spectacular results in Europe viz., Marshall aid programme and NATO. Therefore, the search for allies. The refusal of the Arab states to be drawn into a Western sponsored defensive arrangement in the Middle East focussed attention on Pakistan as a possible alternative. She thus became associated with the 'northern tier' defence system, consisting of the countries directly contiguous to the Soviet Union. Similarly, the refusal of India, Burma, Ceylon, and Indonesia to join the SEATO, inevitably pointed towards Pakistan, which, by virtue of her eastern half, could be considered as a South East Asian power as well.

Though America signed the mutual security agreement with Pakistan and also got allied with her through SEATO, the alliances were never too popular in the United States. India was regarded as the pivotal country in South Asia; a policy which led to estrangement with her was widely criticized particularly by the Democrats. Besides, there was the more general criticism that the alleged communist threat in Asia was primarily political and therefore military alliances were altogether superfluous. They tended to give a military image to the Western presence in Asia and were likely to evoke popular resentments. It was further pointed out that since there was no underlying harmony in the security interests of the signatories, as in the case of NATO, the pacts in Asia could not acquire any lasting cohesion.

In the post-Dulles era, there was a marked change in American policy towards the aligned and the non-aligned countries. Alignment was de-emphasized and non-alignment was given official approval. This ineluctably reacted on Pakistan's relations with the United States because among the countries directly affected by the change of policies were the two rival neighbours—one aligned and the other non-aligned. The Sino-Indian war of 1962 further stimulated the change in attitudes towards India and Pakistan respectively. It forthwith created an informal alliance between Delhi and Washington on the one hand, and Peking and Rawalpindi on the other. In the years following the Sino-Indian war of 1962, this new pattern of relationships superseded the alignments of the fifties.

It is in this context of changed relationships that US policy in the Indo-Pakistan war of 1965 should be evaluated. America not only refused to come to Pakistan's assistance but suspended military aid to both the countries. As Pakistan was almost exclusively dependent on American weapons, the arms embargo had a serious impact on Pakistan's war efforts and was deemed by her as an unfriendly act. It was also widely—though wrongly believed at that time—that America had instigated India into attacking Pakistan to chastise her for the pro-China policy. Washington also appeared chary of playing any mediatory role in the war of 1965. President Ayub's plea for mediation to Johnson did not evoke any response from the White House. It involved the difficult task of maintaining a delicate balance between a formal and an informal ally. The United States wriggled out of this predicament by abstaining from an active mediatory role. Its diplomatic moves were restricted to dissuading China from interfering in the Indo-Pakistan war through its ambassador in Warsaw and supporting the ceasefire resolution in the Security Council. Consequently, the 1965 war led to a sharp decline in American influence in the subcontinent and Soviet ascendancy in the region. Throughout the war, the Soviet Union was diplomatically active and offered its good offices. After the end of the war, it successfully mediated between the contending neighbours at Tashkent.

Consequently, from 1965 to 1970, Pakistan's relations with America were 'correct and cordial' but not 'intimate and friendly'. Prospects for the renewed intimacy of the fifties appeared bleak. The suspension of military aid and its total discontinuance in April 1967, weakened the rationale of the alliance with America.[2] Pakistan's relations with China and America's developing ties with India also erected impediments in the way of closer friendship. There was no disposition on the part of Pakistan to revert to the policy of unqualified alignment. The American alliance had not provided security against India; thereby it had taken away the *raison d'etre* of alignment. Besides, the suspension of military aid compelled Pakistan to look to the Soviet Union for the fulfilment of her defence requirements. This, in turn, drew Pakistan further away from America and prompted the decision in 1968 not to renew the lease of the communication base at Badebar.

It should perhaps be emphasized here that in the post-1965 period, because of mounting American involvement in the Vietnam war and pre-occupation with internal problems, there was a steadily declining interest in the happenings in South Asia.[3] The Vietnam war shifted the focus of interest from South to South East Asia. It also gave rise to widespread neo-isolationist sentiment among influential groups in America. According to Senator Barry Goldwater, the trend towards 'isolationism is increasing in direct ratio to public frustration with the war in Vietnam and intensified agitation for all kinds of multi-billion dollar social engineering and improvement projects on the domestic front'.[4]

All these factors have worked towards the limitation of American influence in South Asia. The Nixon Doctrine, elaborated in February 1970, envisages a formal re-orientation of American policy in Asia. It is predicted on the belief that the age of American global supremacy has come to an end. In keeping with the changes in the world power structure, it states that treaty commitments will be maintained but 'perhaps re-defined, allied states will be granted military and economic assistance against non-nuclear aggression provided they take primary responsibility for their own defence and a nuclear shield will be provided if a vital area or allied nation is threatened by nuclear power'. The Nixon Doctrine is based on the assumption that a series of power centres can be created to supplement, or even to replace, the existing situation of American pre-eminence. It was felt that America had overstretched its military involvement in Asia and in view of the narrowing gap in the power balance, it should renounce the role of the world's sheriff and instead concentrate on areas absolutely vital to the security of American interests.

Against this reassessment by America of its role and commitments in Asia in the seventies, amounting to a conscious curtailment of both, there has been a formidable increase in Soviet military power accompanied by an ever-widening sphere of diplomatic activity thereby re-enlivening the dangers of a confrontation between the two superpowers. The phenomenal growth in Soviet naval power represents by far the most significant development. It has virtually released Russia from its former geographical confinement. It is now a naval power in the Mediterranean, in the Red Sea, and the Indian Ocean. This has enormously augmented its diplomatic manoeuverability as well as its capacity to pose a multi-dimensional threat to Western interests. America's projected military disengagement from Asia has encouraged the Soviet Union to reinforce and stretch its influence there. As in 1950, Acheson's exclusion of Korea from the American defence perimeter invited North Korean attack on South Korea, similarly the announcement of the American intent to limit and curtail its role in Asia, has emboldened Moscow in making a bid for a dominant position in South Asia in general and the Indian Ocean in particular. American policy makers since last year have evinced marked uneasiness at the steady growth of Soviet military power and political influence. In his State of the World Address to Congress on 25 February 1971, President Nixon stated that 'certain Soviet actions in the Middle East, Berlin and Cuba are not very encouraging. Taken against a background of intensive and unrestrained anti-American propaganda, these actions inevitably suggest that intransigence remains a cardinal feature of the Soviet Union.' He further stressed the enormous increase in the Soviet 'strategic arsenal'. This was one of the many factors which prompted America to make an overture to China with a view to normalizing relations, or at least, renouncing the policy of confrontation.

This is the diplomatic backdrop against which the American role in the Indo-Pakistan war of 1971 has to be assessed. From the onset of the trouble in East Pakistan, direct and far-reaching Indo-Soviet involvement became quite manifest. As the crisis in East Pakistan deepened, the Soviet Union cast aside its earlier role of an 'honest broker' between India and Pakistan and decided, instead, to back unreservedly Indian policy towards East Pakistan. To Moscow the secession of East Pakistan appeared inevitable; the Kremlin, therefore, concluded that Pakistan minus its eastern half was not important enough to warrant a carefully balanced policy towards the two countries. Moreover, friendship with India has always been the overriding objective of Soviet policy in Asia. In the framework of its policy of countering Chinese influence in Asia and establishing its sway in the Indian Ocean, close understanding with India appeared indispensable. And when President Nixon's projected visit to Peking was announced in July, the Soviet Union promptly formalized its special relationship with India by signing the Treaty of friendship and cooperation with her in the following month. The underlying aim of the treaty was to neutralize possible Chinese role in the impending Indo-Pakistan conflict and to make the Soviet Union the arbiter of affairs in Asia.

America throughout viewed with concern the deepening crisis in East Pakistan and the extent of Soviet and Indian involvement in it. In view of the earlier American policy of the containment of China, India assumed American endorsement of her political aims in East Pakistan. But the unexpected change in American policy towards China forced a hurried reappraisal of non-alignment in favour of the Soviet Union by means of a defensive alliance with it.

The attitude of the United States towards Pakistan in the unfolding trouble in East Pakistan may generally be termed as sympathetic. This, notwithstanding the fact that in the initial stages, it was widely believed that the United States had inspired and encouraged the secessionist movement in East Pakistan.[5] So long as America, like India and the Soviet Union, followed the policy of containment towards China, an independent East Pakistan may have seemed a feasible proposition. But long before July, when Nixon's visit to Peking was announced, there were straws in the wind, pointing to a possible change in US policy. Among these one can refer to the lifting of restrictions on travel by Americans to communist China, the visit of the American table tennis team, lifting of some trade restrictions and permitting the use of American ships to carry Chinese cargoes, easing of currency restrictions, reducing the Taiwan Straits patrol and stopping of military reconnaissance flights over Chinese territory. All these moves heralded a redefinition of American policy towards China. It simultaneously removed one of the major irritants in US-Pakistan relations and brought to an abrupt end parallelism in the Indo-Soviet and American policies towards Peking. Notwithstanding the détente in Soviet-American relations, and some progress in the SALT, a marked increase in Soviet naval and military strength forced America to abandon her earlier policy which made China the 'Hypostatized enemy' and Russia an ally in maintaining a *status quo* in Asia as it did not correspond to realities of the power pattern in Asia. The waxing Soviet power in the Mediterranean and the Indian Ocean could acquire menacing dimensions. It was in view of this creeping apprehension that the US Defence Department announced in April 1971 that US Pacific Fleet had sent an aircraft carrier, four destroyers and submarines into the Indian Ocean for 'exercises'.

Because of these inter-locking factors and changes, the United States was not inclined to favour the secessionist movement in East Pakistan. Therefore, soon after the army action in East Pakistan, a State Department spokesman told newsmen in Washington that the United States viewed developments in Pakistan as an internal matter. However, as the scope of military action in East Pakistan expanded, the United States, to mollify India and the public opinion at home, stopped the issuing and renewing of licences for military shipments to Pakistan and put a hold on arms that had been committed before and new commitments for economic development loans were not made. Here it should be emphasized that while the American administration evinced a great deal of understanding about the very difficult internal situation with which Pakistan was faced, which had been made more intractable by the espousal of the secessionists' cause by India, Congressional and public opinion was virulently hostile. Only a one-sided version of the happenings was reported. The American newspapers did not publish the Pakistan government's side of the story of events in East Pakistan. The US Congress was generally critical of the policies of Yahya's government in East Pakistan. The Senate Foreign Relations Committee passed a resolution calling for the suspension of US assistance to Pakistan until the conflict in East Pakistan was resolved. Earlier, ten Republican and Democratic senators had asked Secretary of State

William Rogers to suspend aid to Pakistan unless Pakistan allowed Red Cross officials to coordinate relief measures.

As the situation in East Pakistan failed to normalize and both India and Pakistan were caught up in the rising spiral of tensions, with the risk of war, the United States tried its utmost to preserve peace and contain the dangers of war. President Nixon tried to bring about a political settlement in East Pakistan. It was with this end in view that he wrote to President Yahya on 28 May 1971, urging him 'to restore conditions in East Pakistan conducive to the return of refugees from Indian territory as quickly as possible', and to exercise restraint along the borders with India and in general relations with that country. A similar appeal was addressed to India in which Nixon stressed, *inter alia*, that 'as one of Asia's major powers, India has a special responsibility for maintaining the peace and stability in the region'. The United States also contributed substantially to the relief programme within the framework of the United Nations.

It was at American suggestion and under pressure from Washington that President Yahya agreed to an international relief presence in East Pakistan, replacement of General Tikka Khan by Dr A.M. Malik and a general amnesty for all who had been convicted of various crimes. It is quite obvious in the light of reports which have appeared since the war, that Yahya's policies to a very large extent were dictated and determined by the State Department. The American government also established contact with the Awami League representatives in Calcutta and successfully prevailed upon President Yahya Khan to agree to negotiate with them with a view to working out a mutually acceptable settlement of the East Pakistan crisis.[6] Thus America, far from being a passive or neutral observer in the difficult and confused months before the war, played a vital role which shaped the direction of Pakistan's policy in East Bengal.

But America's efforts to persuade India to explore the possibilities of a peaceful resolution of the East Pakistan crisis were altogether unsuccessful. Whereas Pakistan accepted most of the proposals emanating either from Washington or from the United Nations, India refused to consider any of them. President Nixon's Foreign Policy Report to the Congress outlining the various American moves to prevent an Indo-Pakistan war, clearly brings this out. According to him, 'as the tension along the border intensified in the fall, the United States proposed that both Indian and Pakistan troops pull back from the borders. Pakistan accepted this proposal; India turned it down. UN

Secretary-General U Thant placed his good offices at the disposal of both. Pakistan responded favourably and, in addition, suggested the despatch of UN observers to both sides of the border. India refused the Secretary-General's offer and declined to accept the UN observers. The United States then proposed to Pakistan that it pulls its forces back from the borders unilaterally, as a first step towards a mutual pull back. Pakistan accepted this idea, provided India would give some assurance that it would eventually reciprocate. India would not.'[7]

In the same report, President Nixon has pointed out that the United States remained in constant touch with the Soviet Union so that both powers could jointly ensure peace in the subcontinent. With a view to restraining India from starting the war, Secretary of State Rogers informed the Indian ambassador, as early as August, that America would not continue economic assistance to a nation that started a war.

In early November, the United States cancelled export licences for $3.6 million worth of military equipment to Pakistan. This action affected the remainder of the arms 'pipeline' material contracted for but not shipped. This step was taken primarily to please India, who had been insisting on a complete embargo on the shipment of military equipment to Pakistan. Charles Bray, State Department spokesman, however, denied, that the timing of the cancellation had anything to do with representations from the Indian government.[8] In a subsequent statement, Secretary of State Rogers explained that it was done because the shipments were 'not understood' by some members of the Congress and were exaggerated in the minds of most Indians.

As tension continued to mount ominously in East Pakistan, Assistant Secretary of State, Joseph Sisco, urged both India and Pakistan to take such steps as they believed they could to defuse the situation and both refrain from any actions which could exacerbate the situation.[9] In a statement on 13 November, Secretary of State Rogers stated that the United States was making every effort to prevent India and Pakistan from going to war and if a conflict occurred on the Indian subcontinent, America will stay out. 'United States values good relations with both nations and has no intention of joining either side in the event of war.'[10] And when on 22 November 1971, India launched a full scale military attack against East Pakistan, the Secretary of State Rogers promptly urged military disengagement between India and Pakistan and a mutual withdrawal of both countries' forces from the frontier to keep the situation from escalating. The State Department spokesman,

Mr Bray, told correspondents that 'American diplomats are working quietly in various capitals to defuse the India-Pakistan situation.'[11]

Since the United States' efforts to urge restraint and de-escalation on India proved altogether abortive, it took a number of other steps. It requested an urgent session of the UN Security Council to consider a resolution for an immediate ceasefire and mutual withdrawal of troops. Unfortunately, this resolution was vetoed by the Soviet Union. At American initiative the matter was then taken to the General Assembly which passed the ceasefire resolution by 104 to 11 votes with 10 abstentions. As India did not heed the General Assembly resolution, another emergency session of the Security Council was convened. The United States took the stand that with East Pakistan virtually occupied by the Indian troops, a continuation of the war, could take on increasingly the character of armed attack on the very existence of a member of the United Nations, and urged upon the members to vote for its resolution calling for an immediate ceasefire and the withdrawal of troops to pre-war positions. The resolution was again vetoed by the Soviet Union.

While the various organs of the United Nations deliberated ineffectively on the Indo-Pakistan war, the United States announced a number of measures with a view to halting Indian aggression. In the beginning of December, it stopped licencing of arms shipments to India. According to the State Department spokesman, the action was taken because the Indian military forces had crossed the border to fight in East Pakistan. On 7 December 1971, the United States suspended $87.6 million worth of general economic assistance to India. On 15 December, it was reported that the nuclear aircraft carrier *Enterprise* and seven other US naval vessels, which had been operating off the Vietnamese coast, in the Gulf of Tonkin, had been ordered to proceed towards the Bay of Bengal. The purpose of the diversion of the naval vessels was not too clear. Was it to pressurize India into agreeing to a ceasefire in West Pakistan, or was it to impress upon the Soviet Union that its presence in the Indian Ocean would not be allowed by the United States to go unchallenged?

In the meantime, according to disclosures made later by President Nixon in numerous policy statements, the United States received convincing evidence that India was seriously contemplating the seizure of Pakistan-held portions of Kashmir and the destruction of Pakistan's military forces in the West. To quote President Nixon, 'We could not ignore this evidence. Nor could we ignore the fact that when we repeatedly asked India and its supporters for clear assurances to the contrary, we did not receive them.'[12] The United States then sought to influence India via Moscow. And it was, perhaps, through the Soviet Union that President Nixon succeeded in forcing India to agree to a ceasefire on 17 December 1971.

Thus it becomes clear that both the superpowers had a crucial role to play in the war. The Soviet Union's military and political support to India after last year's friendship treaty was the prime factor which encouraged India to attack Pakistan and to ignore the General Assembly resolution calling for a ceasefire. The Soviet Union by its threatening statements and military moves was able to neutralize China's role in the war. It also immobilized the Security Council by its use of the veto. As against this, the part played by the United States was positive and constructive. It sought to involve the United Nations actively in the dispute and to mobilize support for its ceasefire resolutions in the Security Council and in the General Assembly. Thus, unlike the 1965 war, in which the two superpowers' objectives were the same viz., to prevent Chinese intervention and bring about a cessation of hostilities, in last year's war their policies were conflicting and incompatible with each other which placed them on opposite sides of the fence. The Soviet Union actively supported India in its designs against Pakistan and successfully frustrated all UN efforts to bring about a military disengagement in the subcontinent till India had completed the military conquest of East Pakistan. The United States, on the contrary, worked for a ceasefire and withdrawal of forces to their pre-war positions. Its policy was fully backed and supported by China. The Soviet-American compact of 1965 to forestall Chinese intervention in the Indo-Pakistan war gave way last year to Sino-American collaboration with a view to countering Indo-Soviet designs against Pakistan. This is reflective of a profound and far-reaching change in American policy in Asia. It has moved from confrontation against to cooperation with China to balance the rising Soviet ambitions and power in Asia. If the Soviet involvement in the Indian policy towards East Pakistan had not been so deep and extensive, it may not have provoked an American riposte against Indian aggression. It was the unqualified support of the Soviet Union to East Pakistani secessionists and to India in her move to disintegrate Pakistan, which invested the happenings in East Pakistan with ominous implications as regards the power balance in South Asia. The underlying aim of the

American policy was not so much to restrain India, as to inhibit the growing Soviet influence in South Asia.

Since the downfall of Khrushchev, the Soviet Union has unobtrusively and effectively expanded its political influence in the eastern Mediterranean, the Middle East, South Asia, and the Indian Ocean in the best tradition of great power politics. The pattern of that expansion has been constant: Russia has moved into the spaces left by the British and the French after the liquidation of their empires, thereby bringing close to consummation the Tsarist aspirations which, during the better part of the nineteenth century, had pitted Russia against Great Britain over the Eastern Question.[13] The Soviet Union has furthermore taken full advantage of the American involvement in and preoccupation with the Indochinese war, to seek, acquire, and consolidate its influence in South Asia without any challenge or opposition from Washington. Consequently, ever since Tashkent which established Russia as the supervisory power in the subcontinent, its influence has been on the increase. It is very anxious to acquire a presence in the Indian Ocean. British announcement in 1968 to withdraw her forces from the east of Suez by the end of 1971, held out tempting opportunities to Russia to establish a controlling position which will enable it to influence the policies of Asian and African littoral states. It is here that relations with India acquire transcendent importance. Soviet navy to operate in the Indian Ocean on a long-term basis needs adequate air support and shore maintenance facilities. The Soviet fleet has no aircraft carriers in operation, which makes it highly vulnerable to missile-armed warplanes like the ones carried by American aircraft carriers. The need for bases thus becomes imperative. Kremlin is, therefore, keen to acquire a port and air facilities in the area and India can fulfil this need. India has already granted to the Soviet Union some bunkering and other facilities in the Andaman and Nicobar Islands. The Soviet Union has also been permitted to set up a supply depot and training mission at Visakapatnam for naval aid to the Indian navy in the eastern half of the Indian Ocean. A Soviet naval radio station and ammunition depot have been established at Socotra, at the entrance to the Red Sea. In the United States, there has been a belated realization of the threat posed by the phenomenal increase in Soviet strength in the Indian Ocean, which will enable it to outflank communist China and to open a bridgehead into all of South East Asia. That partly accounts for the despatch of the nuclear powered *Enterprise* and other supporting vessels during the Indo-Pakistan war to the Bay of Bengal.

In order to meet the Russian threat on a long term basis, the United States has decided to build a naval communications centre on the island of Diego Garcia, 1100 miles south of India. It has also entered into an agreement with the newly independent government of Bahrain to maintain a permanent naval station on the Persian Gulf island and take over a portion of the British base there which the United States has used as a home port for the small three-ship Indian Ocean permanent force. The United States has further extended its naval power in the Indian Ocean by ordering Seventh Fleet warships to patrol the region more frequently. Full responsibility for the Indian Ocean theatre has been given to the Pacific Fleet commander who previously shared duties with the Atlantic Fleet. Finally, in addition to these, the United States has a huge supply harbour complex at Sattahip in southern Thailand.[14]

American policy towards Pakistan is conditioned by its determination to prevent the Indian Ocean from becoming a 'Russian Lake'. With India acting as the spearhead of Soviet designs in Asia, the continued viability of West Pakistan acquires special significance in terms of US policy aims in South Asia. It becomes an integral part of the 'northern tier' defence system outlined by Dulles. In the sixties, when the Soviet-American relations seemed to be evolving from détente into *entente*, the pacts of the Dulles era were treated with derision and publicly downgraded. But the Brezhnev Doctrine, Soviet intervention in Czechoslovakia in 1968, its policy in the Middle East, alliance with India as part of a determined effort to acquire a commanding position in the Indian Ocean, and espousal of a security pact in Asia covering much of South Asia including Ceylon, Afghanistan, Burma, Malaysia, and even Pakistan, have all underlined the need for a more positive policy in South Asia. With the formal change in Indian policy from non-alignment to alignment with the Soviet Union, relations with Pakistan have acquired enhanced importance.

Finally, the United States' emerging and evolving dialogue with the People's Republic of China should also be taken into account in assessing US policy in the Indo-Pakistan war. Washington felt that 'the war in South Asia was bound to have serious implications for the evolution of the policy of the People's Republic of China. In the words of President Nixon that country's attitude towards the global system was certain to be profoundly influenced by its assessment of the principles by which this system was governed—whether force and threat ruled or whether restraint was the international standard.'[15] Earlier Sino-Pakistan relations had strained Pakistan's relations with America. Now they may help to reinforce the bonds between the countries. China, Pakistan, and the United States, it is adumbrated, have a shared interest in restraining Soviet ambitions in South Asia. To quote President Nixon, 'the Soviet Union in 1970s is projecting a political and military presence without precedent into many new regions of the globe....It would be dangerous to world peace, if our efforts to promote a détente between the superpowers were interpreted as an opportunity for the strategic expansion of Soviet power. If we had failed to take a stand, such an interpretation could only have been encouraged, and the genuine relaxation of tensions we have been seeking could have been jeopardised.'[16] This sums up the reasons behind US policy in the Indo-Pakistan war of 1971 and also provides the *leit motif* for closer US-Pakistan relations in the seventies. The role of the United States in the war was direct and decisive; it helped to bring about a ceasefire in West Pakistan and checkmated Indo-Soviet designs against Pakistan.

The future course of American policy towards Pakistan will largely be determined by two interacting factors viz., the extent of Soviet involvement in India and the latter's ability, or inability, to have a balanced relationship with the two superpowers. In case New Delhi decides to strengthen its alliance with Moscow, then Washington may feel impelled to cultivate closer relations with Islamabad. Alternately, if India plays down the implications of last year's Treaty of Friendship with the Soviet Union and successfully maintains an equipoise in her relations with the superpowers,—an unlikely eventuality given the current trend in her foreign policy and her military dependence on the Soviet Union—America may reciprocate and avoid any special relationship with Pakistan. At present there is no prospect of either the re-activation of the mutual security agreements of the fifties or the resumption of military aid on an extensive scale. Secretary of State Rogers has made this abundantly clear.

Pakistan should not press for a security pact either. Should the United States consider the security of Pakistan vital to its interests in Asia, it will assist Pakistan irrespective of a security agreement. But if Pakistan's continued viability is not considered vital to American national security policy then, despite security agreements and pacts, assistance may not be forthcoming. The Kennedy administration rushed emergency aid to India during its war with China in 1962, notwithstanding the fact that India was non-aligned and had directly provoked the war by its forward policy in the borderland with China, because America did not want any disturbance in the *status quo* in Asia. As against this, despite our numerous treaty links with America, it did not come to our aid in the 1965 war with India, because a change in the Indo-Pakistan power balance was considered inconsequential as it was not likely to have a distruptive impact on its interests in South Asia. The nature and source of a future threat will also condition American attitude. If in the threat to Pakistan inheres the danger of an unfavourable shift in the larger power balance, then American assistance may be forthcoming. But in the eventuality of a conflict with a neighbouring country like India involving adjustments in the regional power pattern only, American policy will at best be uncertain. Resurrection of the past pacts or formulation of a new one will not, therefore, be purposeful. It may exacerbate our relations with other countries, invest our policy. with inflexibility such as that of the fifties, precondition our response, and inhibit permutations in our policy in consonance with the shifts and changes in the global power environment.

NOTES

1. Mohammad Ayub Khan, *Friends, Not Masters*, Karachi, Oxford University Press, 1967, p. 130.
2. Later a limited amount of non-lethal weapons were supplied and at one time the sale of some military equipment was allowed in 1970.
3. Cf. Norman D. Palmer, 'Alternative Futures for South Asia and United States Policy', *Orbis*, Philadelphia, Pennsylvania, Vol. XV, 1971; 'The United States knows little of the real conditions in South Asia. She is not enamoured with the leaders and policies and orientation of these States and regimes; she feels that her present efforts including billions of dollars, have not been sufficiently effective or appreciated; she is increasingly appalled by the magnitude of problems facing the South Asian countries...and she is disturbed that their leaders spend so much time and waste so much of their limited resources on internal rivalries and political manoeuvering (in the case of India and Pakistan, in prolonged hostilities), showing little evidence of willingness to foster real regional cooperation. From the point of view of American national interest...South Asia represents level two and not level one interest.' pp. 378–9.
4. Barry Goldwater, 'The perilous conjuncture: Soviet Ascendancy and American isolationism', *Orbis*, Vol. XV, 1971, p. 55.

5. The late Khwaja Nazimuddin, a former Governor-General and Prime Minister of Pakistan, had stated in 1962 that a foreign power giving economic and other aid to Pakistan, wanted to divide Pakistan and was instigating the people of East Pakistan by various methods to secure secession from Pakistan and set up an independent sovereign state of Bangladesh. Pointing out the American design, in February 1971, retired Air Marshall Asghar Khan asserted that it was in the global interests of the United States to weaken and divide Pakistan. It has also been asserted that the United States was supplying funds to the Awami League. Some foreign diplomats were reported in the Pakistan Press to have been engaged in a whispering campaign aimed at bringing about the secession of East Pakistan. Mr John Rhode, a SEATO official in East Pakistan, after the November cyclone, openly set himself as the champion of Bengali nationalism. Mehrunnisa Ali, 'East Pakistan Crisis: International Reactions,' *Pakistan Horizon*, Karachi, Second Quarter, 1971, pp. 43–4.

6. *New Approaches to Peace*, US President Richard Nixon's Foreign Policy Report. A Panorama Supplement, Karachi, Vol. XXIV, No. 2, 1972, p. 15.

7. Ibid., p. 16.

8. *USIS News Release*, Karachi, 9 November 1971.

9. Ibid., 12 November 1971.

10. Ibid., 13 November 1971.

11. Ibid., 25 November 1971.

12. *New Approaches to Peace*, op. cit., p. 17.

13. Hans Morgenthau, 'Changes and Chances in American-Soviet Relations', *Foreign Affairs*, New York, Vol. 49, No. 3, 1971, p. 435.

14. 'Show Down in the Indian Ocean', *US News and World Report*, 24 January 1972, reproduced in *The Mirror*, Singapore, 21 February 1972.

15. *New Approaches to Peace*, op. cit., p. 19.

16. Ibid., p. 18.

3

The USSR and the Indo-Pakistan War, 1971*

Zubeida Mustafa

The role played by the USSR in the Indo-Pakistan war of 1971 had a great impact on the pattern of politics in South Asia. It was primarily responsible for imparting to the conflict an international dimension by drawing the subcontinent into the vortex of big power rivalries. In the months preceding the war, the USSR's attitude towards the crisis in East Pakistan was on the whole ambivalent. On the one hand, the Soviet Union repeatedly stressed that it upheld the territorial integrity of Pakistan and it carefully refrained from giving overt support to the insurgents, but on the other hand, Moscow adopted a posture of hostility towards Islamabad. At a time when Indo-Pakistan relations had reached their nadir, the Soviet Union extended full diplomatic and military support to India. Without tacit support from the Kremlin, it is unlikely that Mrs Gandhi's government would have sustained, since its inception, the guerrilla movement in East Bengal and pursued its policy *vis-a-vis* 'Bangla Desh' with its underlying danger of a military conflict. Publicly the USSR upheld the territorial integrity of Pakistan, but covertly it worked to destroy the unity of Pakistan by extending assistance by proxy to the insurgents. In fact it is generally believed that India not only launched the attack on East Pakistan with Moscow's knowledge but with its specific approval.[1]

---

* Vol. xxv, No. 1, 1972.

I

When the war broke out, the Soviet Union cast aside all pretentions of neutrality and non-partisanship it had fostered since the Tashkent meeting of January 1966. During the Indo-Pakistan war of 1965, the Soviet leaders had sought to promote accommodation between the two parties. But in 1971, operating in the context of nuclear parity with the United States and superiority in conventional land forces, the Russians were in no hurry to terminate the fighting since their interest was better served by the continuation of hostilities leading to an Indian victory. Soviet policy was directed towards the attainment of this goal and to this end it provided an umbrella under which the war could run its course. The factors which decisively determined the outcome of the war were: first, Soviet military assistance to India; second, the USSR's role in the UN Security Council; and third, Russian strategy to prevent a direct Chinese intervention in the war.

The Soviet Union first emerged as a major supplier of arms to India in 1962 with the conclusion of the MIGs deal. But it was in the period following the Indo-Pakistan war of 1965 that the USSR and its East European allies by sharply expanding their military aid to India acquired a predominant position in the area. They furnished over 730 million dollars worth of tanks, combat aircraft, artillery, surface-to-air missiles, submarines, missile boats, and other heavy equipment to India.[2] In the wake of the Indo-Soviet treaty of friendship signed in August 1971, there was a further airlift of sophisticated Soviet missiles and weapons to India. In early November 1971, it was reported in the foreign press that twelve Soviet transport aircraft carried military equipment, mainly advanced versions of SAMs to New Delhi and Bombay. The equipment arriving by air was primarily meant for training purposes and was reported to have been accompanied by Russian military instructors.[3] Meanwhile, a Russian consignment of 250 tanks, forty 120mm rockets, and a large number of radio sets and other equipment were dispatched as negotiations were initiated for the supply of supersonic medium bombers, medium reconnaissance aircraft, and MIG-23 fighters.[4] This resulted in a positive shift in the military balance in the subcontinent in favour of India, thus removing all restraint upon India from resorting to the use of force against Pakistan. Furthermore, it is alleged that during the war the Russians rendered active assistance to the Indians. The Reuter news agency reported that Soviet personnel were manning Indian missile boats and flying military planes inside Indian territory.[5] Although the Soviet government denied these reports, the allegations of active Soviet assistance were later repeated by the Chief of the Pakistan Air Force in a press conference.[6]

Of equal significance was the Soviet role in the debates of the Security Council which was convened to discuss the India-Pakistan conflict. For the first time in many years the Soviet Union disassociated itself from the mainstream of international opinion by rejecting the proposition that in an armed conflict priority be given to the imposition of a cessation of hostilities. Moscow's position was that a ceasefire was inconceivable without a political settlement in East Pakistan. As Indian forces moved on Dhaka, the USSR used its veto twice on 4 and 5 December 1971 to prevent the Council from adopting a resolution calling for a ceasefire on the ground that it did not take into account the fundamental cause of the war. Expressing views identical with those of the Indian government, the Soviet representative first vetoed an American draft resolution proposing that the Security Council should call upon India and Pakistan to cease fire immediately, to withdraw their troops from each other's territory to their own sides of the border and to exert their best efforts towards the creation of a climate conducive to the voluntary return of refugees to East Pakistan. At the next meeting the USSR again exercised its veto to prevent the adoption of an eight-power draft resolution which also called for an immediate cessation of hostilities, withdrawal of forces and urged that efforts be intensified to bring about conditions necessary for the voluntary return of the East Pakistan refugees to their homes.[7] Thus the Russians effectively blocked all international diplomatic pressures on India giving it time to bring its military operations in the East to a successful conclusion.

In the General Assembly, where the issue was transferred[8] under the Uniting for Peace Resolution, the Soviet Union voted against a draft resolution calling upon India and Pakistan to cease fire and withdraw their forces.[9] The resolution was adopted by the Assembly out of whose total membership of 131, 104 states voted for it. Despite this mandate from an overwhelming majority of the world community, the USSR vetoed for the third time in the Security Council a draft resolution drafted on similar lines as the previous ones.[10] It was only after the Indian occupation of Dhaka that Moscow dropped its obstructive approach.[11]

The USSR also expressed explicit support for 'Bangla Desh'. In the first place, the Soviet delegate insisted that representatives of 'Bangla Desh' be given a hearing in the Council. Secondly, he introduced a draft resolution in the Council calling 'for a political settlement in East Pakistan which would inevitably result in a cessation of hostilities' and asking the Pakistan government 'to take measures to cease all acts of violence by Pakistani forces in East Pakistan which have led to a deterioration of the situation.'[12] This draft resolution was rejected by the Council, but these delaying tactics employed by the Russians prevented the quick mobilization of world opinion in favour of a ceasefire.

The Russian attitude *vis-à-vis* China also proved to be vital in the war. For the Indian government, the major deterrent to resorting to armed forces against Pakistan would have been the fear of direct Chinese intervention across the Himalayas. This flank was secured through the Indo-Soviet Treaty of friendship of August 1971. Furthermore, India launched a full-scale attack on Pakistan only after winter had set in and the northern passes were blocked with snow. But most significant was the report that Soviet leadership assured the Indians that it would make military moves against China if the threat of Chinese intervention materialized.[13] This would not have involved a major military manoeuvre as the USSR had deployed more divisions on its eastern frontier with China than in East Europe.

Throughout the duration of the war, the Soviet attitude towards Pakistan was, generally speaking, 'unfriendly'. In November 1971, when Indian forces crossed the East Pakistan border, the USSR chose to remain silent. Its first public official reaction to the fighting came twelve days later when fighting had escalated to the West Pakistan borders. On 4 December, a Soviet spokesman disclosed that Mr Kosygin did not plan to mediate between India and Pakistan as he did in 1965–6, since the Indo-Soviet Treaty precluded him from doing so.[14] The following day the Soviet government issued a statement warning Pakistan about its 'grave responsibility' in 'following this dangerous course'. Asserting its interest in the developments which 'are taking place in direct proximity of the USSR's borders and therefore involve the interests of its security', the Soviet government called 'for the speediest ending of the bloodshed and for a political settlement in East Pakistan on the basis of respect for the lawful rights and interests of its people'.[15] Relations between the USSR and Pakistan, which had considerably cooled since April 1971, thenceforth deteriorated rapidly.

The Russian government suspended its economic aid to Pakistan and the Russian experts working on various projects left the country. The Soviet import organization advised the Afghan Bank-i-Milli not to permit any movement of Pakistani goods into Afghanistan which serves as the overland transit route for Pakistan-USSR trade. Sea trade was also suspended and after November 1971 no Soviet ship came to pick up cargo from Karachi.

II

In the period following the Indo-Pakistan war, Soviet policy has been directed towards consolidating its influence in the subcontinent. It is likely that the price Moscow will extract from New Delhi for its support during the war will be in the form of Soviet bases on Indian territory. There is no denying the fact, as a critical observer remarks, that 'arms aid, a treaty of alliance and Russian vetoes in the United Nations during the war with Pakistan have raised Moscow's influence to an all-time high in India'.[16]

Russian efforts to establish a foothold in Dhaka have not gone unnoticed. By adopting an ambivalent attitude towards the crisis in East Pakistan in the initial phases and by extending full diplomatic support to the 'Bangla Desh' movement in the later stage, the USSR hoped to gain a predominant influence in East Bengal. At first the Soviet Union implemented this policy through the Indian government, since it anticipated 'Bangla Desh' to be a client state of India. In October 1971, Peter Hazelhurst of *The Times* reported that India was making vigorous efforts to transform the movement in East Pakistan into an organization which would eventually align itself with Moscow. Thus in September 1971, the Awami League was forced to form a broad-based consultative committee with mainly pro-Soviet Bengal communists to direct the Liberation Front. Later, the Provisional government was pressurized to alter the composition of its delegation to the United Nations to include the communist leader, Professor Muzaffar Ahmed, and exclude the pro-West, Khondkar Mushtaque Ahmed.[17] The Russians also showed a keen interest in the orientation of the non-Marxist government in East Bengal and during the war when the fall of Dhaka seemed imminent, a Russian delegation headed by the First Deputy Foreign Minister Kuznetsov arrived in New Delhi to work out the organization of the 'Bangla Desh Government'. It could not be coincidental that soon after the war, Khondkar Mushtaque Ahmed, who had pro-West leanings, was removed from the important post of Minister of Foreign Affairs of 'Bangla Desh'.

After the Soviet Union had extended recognition to 'Bangla Desh' on 24 January 1972, it offered extensive economic aid to the new state. It reportedly expressed its willingness to help in the restoration of communications, to train and equip the 'Bangla Desh' air force and navy and to rebuild the naval base at Chittagong. In March 1972, the Bengali leader, Sheikh Mujibur Rehman, visited the USSR where he conferred with the Russian leaders mainly on economic topics. The two sides reached agreement on Soviet aid in the construction of a 'Bangla Desh' thermal power plant, radio stations and an electrical engineering plant. Russia would also help the new state in the reconstruction and development of the merchant marine and sea fisheries. 'Bangla Desh' would also be assisted by the Soviet Union in the reconstruction of railway transport and the USSR would also supply helicopters for interior communications. Aid would also be rendered in the training of national cadres for industry and agriculture.[18] These agreements are of great importance as they will enable the Soviet Union to establish a foothold in this region. Thus, the seemingly innocuous fishery agreement is in line with the Soviet method of penetration by means of the fishing fleet which operates in conjunction with the growing Soviet fleet of ocean-going submarines. Soviet offer to develop the naval base at Chittagong and supply a squadron of MIGs to the 'Bangla Desh' air force, when viewed in the context of Russian strategic aims in the Indian Ocean, acquire great significance. Moscow's influence in the new state has been further enhanced through the India-'Bangla Desh' treaty of friendship concluded in March 1972. With India already aligned with the Soviet bloc, this treaty brings 'Bangla Desh' formally into the Indo-Soviet equation in South Asia.

A survey in the *US News and World Report* correctly pointed out: 'Bangla Desh is receiving so much Soviet attention that some European diplomats already are convinced that Russia, not India, will be the dominant foreign influence there within a few months. Traditional Moslem-Hindu and Bengali-Indian rivalries, these experts explain, will speed the spread of Soviet influence. So will the vastly greater capability of Russia and the East European satellites to provide economic aid, weapons and other assistance sought by the new nation...By the time Bangla Desh is really independent—when the

Indians pull out—the country will be part of the Soviet economic bloc.'[19]

As the balance of power in South Asia is undergoing a process of realignment, the Soviet Union has not lost the opportunity to regain some of its lost influence in Pakistan. In the first place, it shrewdly did not crow over its triumph in the India-Pakistan war but exercised great restraint. Moscow extended recognition to 'Bangla Desh' more than a month after the fall of Dhaka. Secondly, Soviet recognition followed that of four other communist states, viz. East Germany, Mongolia, Poland, and Bulgaria. This gave the Pakistan government time to reassess the situation. Initially it reacted by implementing in a limited way a Hallstein Doctrine of its own. But when the USSR recognized the new state, Islamabad did not break off diplomatic ties with Moscow.

In the meantime, the climate of public opinion in Pakistan gradually became more conducive to the normalization of relations with the USSR as a school of thought started gaining ground demanding a fundamental change in the foreign policy of the country. In January 1972, President Bhutto paid a surprise visit to Kabul and it was reported in the press that 'Pakistan is no longer averse to the idea that she should cooperate in the possible arrangement for allowing easy flow of traffic on the Asian Highway and open her borders with Afghanistan and India for the purpose'.[20] This idea was linked with the Russian proposal for an Asian security system. Though a spokesman of the Foreign Office denied reports that Pakistan was backing a regional security pact to maintain some links with East Pakistan, there was no denial in respect of economic arrangements. It is significant that the announcement regarding the resumption of shipment of Soviet machinery was made just after the Kabul visit. Furthermore, the USSR expressed its willingness to initiate bilateral talks between India and Pakistan for an overall peace settlement. Russia's keenness to preserve its ties with Pakistan has been generally noted. David Loshak reported in *The Daily Telegraph*, 'Moscow is anxious...that neither India nor other countries should presume from the close links with India that the Soviet Union does not wish to have good relations with Pakistan'.[21] The USSR's desire to normalize its relations with Pakistan was clearly manifested by a letter written by an APN commentator to the local newspapers in which he set out to explain and justify the Soviet role in the December war.[22]

It is obvious that despite its growing influence in 'Bangla Desh', the Soviet Union would not like to revert to its previous policy of concentrating on India to the exclusion of Pakistan. Moscow's policy is directed at re-establishing its influence in Islamabad in order to use it as a counterpoise in its relations with New Delhi, and to counteract the growing Sino-American influence in Pakistan. Furthermore, Pakistan is a vital link in the cordon sanitaire which the USSR hopes to establish around China. This was borne out by Mr Kosygin's remark at a luncheon in honour of the visiting Afghan Premier that a system of collective security in Asia would contribute towards the consolidation of peace in the area. Coming on the eve of President Bhutto's visit to Moscow, this remark was a meaningful one. In March 1972, President Bhutto during his talks with Soviet leaders, agreed to the restoration of trade, economic, scientific, technological and other ties though there was a wide area of disagreement on the political situation in the subcontinent of South Asia.

III

Soviet policy towards South Asia should be viewed in the perspective of its global strategy. It would be difficult to disassociate the Indo-Pakistan conflict from the triangular relationship between the USSR, China, and the US. The war brought into sharp focus the strategic significance of the Indian Ocean and big power rivalry to gain control of it. The Soviet Union is determined to win supremacy over the entire area in order to outflank China and open a bridgehead into South East Asia. By controlling the Indian Ocean and its littoral states in South Asia, Moscow can isolate Peking on the mainland, leaving it to face Russian troops on its northern and western frontiers, Russian influenced neighbours to the south, and to the east another ocean it does not control. The introduction of the Soviet navy in the Indian Ocean could also be intended as a pre-emptive move to prevent the deployment of US Polaris submarines in this area. With the introduction of the Polaris A3 missiles with a range of 2500 nautical miles, hitherto inaccessible targets such as Soviet Central Asia, can be reached not only from the Eastern Mediterranean but also the Arabian Sea.[23] Thus the north-western portion of the Indian Ocean is likely to become an attractive deployment area which would in due course be utilized by the American navy. To deny unrestricted freedom of the seas to the US in this potential deployment area, the Soviet Union has adopted the strategy of introducing its own naval presence in the Indian Ocean.

But the Soviet Union is handicapped by its lack of shore bases anywhere between Vladivostok and the Red Sea and the lack of air cover for its fleet as it has no big aircraft carrier in operation. In order to furnish shore-based air cover for Russian combat ships and port facilities for fuel, supplies, and maintenance, Russia has sought to establish a network of naval and air bases in the Indian Ocean. It has, therefore, gained access to the islands of Mauritius and Socotra in Southern Yemen, has secured bunkering and other naval facilities in the Andaman and Nicobar Islands, and has established a supply depot and training mission at Visakapatnam. In addition, over fifteen Soviet vessels now operate in the Indian Ocean. The Soviet fleet is reported to comprise five missile-carrying cruisers and destroyers, six supply ships, six electronic ships, one amphibion landing craft, and three or four submarines, one of them nuclear.

The Russain move to establish its hegemony in the Indian Ocean region has led to counter moves by the Western powers. The United States began construction of a communications centre at Diego Garcia, south of the Maldives, and signed a pact with Bahrain for securing a naval station there. The danger of a direct confrontation first came to the forefront during the Indo-Pakistan war. On 14 December 1971, a US naval task force of nine vessels headed by the nuclear-powered aircraft carrier *Enterprise* entered the Indian Ocean as a symbolic show of support for Pakistan and to discourage the Indian government from concentrating its full military might on the Western front. The Soviet reaction was quick and hardly had the American ships cleared the Strait of Malacca when a Soviet force headed by a Kresta-class guided missile cruiser sailed into the Bay of Bengal. Another Russian cruiser arrived in early January. The US force left for the South China Sea on 10 January 1972 after carrying out routine manoeuvres in the region. It was disclosed that thenceforth the Seventh Fleet would operate more frequently in the Indian Ocean and shadow the Soviet ships there. As for the Russian fleet which arrived during the war, it is expected to remain there. This marks the beginning of active big power rivalry in the Indian Ocean.

The Soviet policy in the region has been primarily responsible for the reintroduction of big power involvement in the subcontinent. For the last few years, South Asia had remained virtually insulated from the global rivalries of the US, the USSR, and China by virtue of the balance of power in the region which was tacitly recognized by them. But by supplying New Delhi with a large quantum of arms and providing it with big power protection in the war against Pakistan, Moscow helped in destroying the *status quo*. Direct involvement by the USSR forced the US and China to take a positive stand in favour of Pakistan, leading to a polarization of power in South Asia. By imparting this new international dimension to the situation in the subcontinent, the USSR has once more exposed the region to big power rivalries as each of them strives to expand its sphere of respective influence while the politics of South Asia, following the Indo-Pakistan war, is still in a state of flux.

NOTES

1. Henry Branden reported that this view is strongly held by high officials in Washington. *The Sunday Times*, London, 19 December 1971.
2. Reported by President Nixon in his Foreign Policy Report to the American Congress on 9 February 1972.
3. *The Times*, London, 6 November 1971.
4. *Dawn*, Karachi, 4 November 1971.
5. Ibid., 10 December 1971.
6. *The Daily Telegraph*, London, 28 December 1971.
7. See proceedings of Security Council meetings of 4, 5, and 6 December 1971. *UN Monthly Chronicle*, New York: Office of Public Information, January 1972, pp. 4–25.
8. Resolution 303 (1971) of 6 December 1971.
9. Resolution 2793 (XXVI) of 7 December 1971.
10. See proceedings of Council meetings of 12 and 13 December 1971, *UN Monthly Chronicle*, op. cit., pp. 27–36.
11. On 21 December 1971, the Council adopted Resolution 307 (1971) demanding that a durable ceasefire be observed by the parties.
12. *UN Monthly Chronicle*, op. cit., p. 4.
13. President Nixon's Report to Congress, loc. cit.
14. *Dawn*, Karachi, 5 December 1971.
15. Statement released by TASS on 5 December 1971.
16. 'Showdown in the Indian Ocean?' *US News and World Report*, 24 January 1972. Reproduced in *The Mirror*, Singapore, 21 February 1972.
17. *The Times*, London, 7 October 1971.
18. USSR-'Bangla Desh' joint communique published by TASS, 4 March 1972.

19. *US News and World Report*, loc. cit.
20. *Dawn*, Karachi, 12 January 1972.
21. *The Daily Telegraph*, London, 30 December 1971,
22. *The Sun*, Karachi, 22 February 1972.
23. Geoffry Jukes, 'The Soviet Union and the Indian Ocean', *Survival*, London, November 1971, p. 371.

4

China's Diplomacy during the Indo-Pakistan War, 1971*

Mehrunnisa Ali

The outbreak of the East Pakistan crisis in March 1971, gave rise to certain political issues of international importance such as those of separatism, East Pakistani displaced persons, foreign intervention, and external armed aggression. These issues because of their serious nature and repercussions on the situation in the subcontinent, had to be considered by China or for that matter any other country in the light of its foreign policy objectives. Therefore, the nature and extent of China's support to Pakistan during the crisis and the ensuing war must be considered in the light of these issues and the relative Chinese stance towards them.

The Chinese official attitude towards the crisis and the issues arising out of it, was made public for the first time on 12 April, in a message[1] by Mr Chou En-lai to President Yahya Khan. A close study of this letter shows the Chinese point of view regarding the crisis: (i) China considered the 'happenings in Pakistan' as 'a purely internal affair' to be settled by the Pakistani people without 'foreign interference'. This adherence to the principle of non-intervention could also be seen in China's protest Note to India of 6 April 1971; (ii) China opposed the separatists as was reflected in the expression: 'the unification of Pakistan and the unity of the people of East and West Pakistan are the basic guarantees' for Pakistan's prosperity and strength; (iii) China considered the separatists to be in a minority, 'a handful of persons

---

* Vol. xxv, No. 1, 1972.

who want to sabotage the unification of Pakistan'; (iv) As regards the means for settling the problem, China's preference for negotiations can be easily discerned in the expression that 'through the wise consultation and efforts' of the government and 'leaders of various quarters in Pakistan', the situation would be restored to normal; (v) Taking note of the 'gross interference' by India in the affairs of Pakistan, China considered the USSR and the US guilty of collusion with India. In its protest Note of 6 April also China had accused India of flagrantly interfering in the internal affairs of Pakistan; (vi) China's firm support to Pakistan was assured if 'the Indian expansionists dare to launch aggression against Pakistan;'[2] (vii) The message made no mention of the 'refugee' problem as emphasized by India.

Throughout the period of the crisis and the ensuing Indo-Pakistan war, China consistently followed the policy it had adopted in April. The principles of this policy were reiterated and the pledge of support to Pakistan was reaffirmed in November when Mr Bhutto visited Peking as the personal representative of President Yahya Khan. The decision to send an eight-man delegation under Mr Bhutto's leadership to Peking was no doubt influenced by five factors: (i) Deployment of Indian troops[3] on the East Pakistan border had created an alarming situation for Pakistan; (ii) The guerrillas who were aided, trained, and armed by India[4] had stepped up their activities. Exchange of fire between the Indian and Pakistani troops and shelling of border towns in East Pakistan had increased the danger of direct confrontation between the two; (iii) After signing the treaty with India in August 1971, USSR had increased the supply of arms[5] to India; (iv) Indian Prime Minister, Mrs Gandhi's tour of Western countries to mobilize world opinion in favour of India had forced Pakistan, as a counter-move, to rally its friends; (v) The US decision to stop the supply of arms to Pakistan, with effect from 25 March 1971, and the revocation on 8 November of licences for the export of $3.6 million worth of military equipment, while massive Russian arms supply to India continued, had widened the existing military imbalance between India and Pakistan. In this situation Pakistan was in need of strong diplomatic and military aid. China seemed to be the only country which was able to provide it and to whom Pakistan could turn with confidence. China did not disappoint Pakistan although no joint communique was issued at the end of Mr Bhutto's visit, which might be due to the fact that Mr Bhutto was not at that time holding an official post in the government. However, the Chinese viewpoint regarding the crisis was stated in a speech by Mr Chi Peng-fei, Acting Foreign Minister, which was later endorsed by Premier Chou En-lai. China reiterated its previous pledge that 'should Pakistan be subjected to foreign aggression', China would 'resolutely support the Pakistan Government and people in their just struggle to defend their State sovereignty and national independence'.[6] The view that the secessionists were a 'handful of persons' was expressed by Chi Peng-fei who also asserted that the 'broad masses of Pakistan are patriotic and want to safeguard the national unity and oppose internal split and outside interference'.[7] China emphasized that 'disputes between States should always be settled through consultation and not by resorting to force'.[8] Interference and subversive activities by India in East Pakistan were slated on the basis of China's adherence to the principle of nonintervention into the affairs of other countries. This time China discreetly avoided repeating the allegation of the United States colluding with India, no doubt in view of President Nixon's intended visit to Peking in February. The visit was described a 'complete success' and it was claimed that 'more tangible and concrete' results would follow which would be 'deterrent to aggression'.[9] Both President Yahya and Mr Bhutto indicated the possibility of China's intervention[10] in case of an Indian invasion of Pakistan. That this was only a distant possibility because practical considerations weighing heavily against intervention was not generally realized in Pakistan. In fact, China had not pledged more than continued diplomatic and military support to Pakistan and had given no assurance of physically intervening or resorting to diversionary action[11] on the Sino-Indian border.

During the Indo-Pakistan war, which began on 22 November, when the Indian army crossed into East Pakistan, China remained in constant contact with the government of Pakistan, reaffirming its support to Pakistan and denouncing India and the Soviet Union on various occasions, such as at the receptions on the Albanian Independence Day, on the Tanzanian National Day, the banquet in honour of the Sudanese delegation and the UN forum. After the outbreak of the war, the Chinese criticism of India and the Soviet Union became sharper. This was because of India's admission of crossing the East Pakistan border for 'self defence' which convinced Peking that India had been the aggressor. China's objection to the Soviet Union's role stemmed not merely from its differences with Moscow, but also from its opposition to the big power's interference and diplomatic expansion in Asia. The Soviet Union was, for the first time, singled out as the power 'fanning the flames' in the subcontinent by 'supporting and encouraging' Indian 'subversive activities' and 'military provocation' against Pakistan.[12] When 'Bangla Desh' was recognized by India, Peking denounced it as 'a New Delhi farce' and a puppet regime 'forcibly imposed' upon the East Pakistani people by India and a 'handful of...bad elements of Pakistan'.[13] The Soviet Union was accused of being 'the real director of the "Bangla Desh" farce.'[14]

China's support to Pakistan and the denunciation of Indo-Soviet collusion became more pronounced during the war. This was apparent also from the speeches made in the United Nations. While extending support to Pakistan, China consistently emphasized the principles to which it adhered. At the same time China repeatedly recalled what the Soviet Union had done in Czechoslovakia, and India in Tibet and Kashmir. The debates held in the Security Council and the General Assembly on the Indo-Pakistan conflict also revealed the growing Sino-Soviet differences. The bitter verbal dual between the Soviet and the Chinese representatives and their charges and counter-charges against each other did not help to improve the situation. Of course, their hostility to each other incapacitated the Security Council, but it is hard to hold China responsible for this. China 'at least had moral justification for condemning the cynicism of invoking the right of self-determination for the Bengalees and of refusing the same right to the people of Czechoslovakia.'[15] On the other hand, Moscow was 'actively encouraging New Delhi to occupy the territory of another State'[16] and, to that end, it had repeatedly used the veto to 'give India time to present the world with a *fait accompli*: an occupied East Pakistan.'[17] Presumably, one of China's motives in condemning and 'exposing' the Soviet Union in the UN, was to lower Moscow's prestige in the third world nations who saw a dangerous precedent in the dismemberment of Pakistan.

China's support to Pakistan was not confined to verbal criticism of the Indo-Soviet role but was also practically demonstrated in the UN. China moved a draft resolution (which it later withdrew) which condemned India, asked the warring parties to withdraw their troops, and called upon 'all States to support Pakistan' in its struggle to resist 'Indian aggression'.[18] China voted for the General Assembly resolution of 7 December and the Security Council resolution of 21 December calling for a ceasefire and withdrawal of troops. However, it expressed its dissatisfaction with the resolution in that it did not condemn India and support Pakistan against the Indian aggression.[19] It expressed its solidarity with Pakistan by strongly opposing the Soviet proposal to invite a 'Bangla Desh' representative to take part in the UN debate and by vetoing the Soviet resolution that called for a ceasefire without withdrawal. Had China not been a permanent member of the Security Council, the Soviet resolution of 5 December which secured two affirmative votes of Moscow and Poland with twelve abstentions, would have been passed. Thus China's presence in the UN proved a source of strength for Pakistan.

It is worth noting that after the outbreak of the war there was, between China and the United States, a great deal of identity of views and cooperation on the Indo-Pakistan conflict, stemming as much from their common apprehension of the growing Soviet influence in Asia as from President Nixon's desire not to risk his coming visit to Peking. Like China, the US also accused India of aggression[20] and Moscow of blocking 'international action until the capture of East Pakistan was a *fait accompli*'.[21] It also believed that the treaty with the Soviets had encouraged India in its aggressive designs against Pakistan and that 'with support from India a guerrilla movement developed in East Pakistan'.[22] The US also noted the 'strategic expansion of Soviet power'.[23] Both voted for the same resolutions in the General Assembly and the Security Council. In their joint communique issued on 27 February in Peking, both had called for the observance and implementation of the Security Council resolution of 21 December. Both so far, have not recognized 'Bangla Desh'. However, the use of the term 'East Bengal' for East Pakistan in the Foreign Policy Report and the assertion that the US had 'never been against the aspiration'[24] of East Pakistani people clearly showed the direction of the wind in the days ahead. Similarly, China, in the said joint communique, supported Pakistan's sovereignty and independence, observing a discreet silence on the territorial integrity of Pakistan.

The last important official statement made by China on the Indo-Pakistan war came on 16 December. Although it was issued on the day on which the Pakistan forces surrendered in East Pakistan, from the expression that the 'Indian Government is...moving massive troops to press on the capital of East Pakistan, Dhaka',[25] it appears that at the time of issuing the statement, China did not know about the surrender. China's stand on the basic issues involved, i.e. non-intervention, Indian aggression, and the Soviet role in the war, remained the same. Apart from that there were some significant points pertaining to the situation in the statement. 'Bangla Desh' was considered a 'puppet regime', 'manufactured' and 'inserted...into East Pakistan' by India with the help of force. But there was also recognition, on the part of China of the existence of a nationality problem in East Pakistan, for which the Chinese said Pakistan was willing 'to seek a political solution...in the spirit of understanding and cooperation'. China, for the first time, officially took note of the East Pakistani refugee problem and asserted that the problem should be settled by India and Pakistan 'through consultation', without resorting to force. Be it recalled that neither Premier Chou En-lai in his message of 12 April nor Chi Peng-fei in his speech on 7 November had made any mention of the 'refugee' problem. However, the Chinese representative in the UN had likened the problem with the Tibetan refugee problem, as having arisen out of the Indian interference in Pakistan's affairs. In contrast with the previous statements, now it was openly declared that China was not only supporting the Pakistani people politically but that it would 'continue to give them material assistance'. There was also a warning to India about the future consequences of its aggression, the statement said: 'Henceforth there will be no tranquility...on the South Asia subcontinent...The Indian expansionists will surely eat the bitter fruit of their own making'. Another interesting point to note in the statement was China's advice to the South Asian friendly countries 'to strengthen their defence capabilities' so as 'to hit back' when attacked.[26]

China's reaction to the occupation of Dhaka by the Indian army was reflected in Premier Chou's meaningful remark that the 'fall of Dhaka is...the starting point of endless strife on the South Asian subcontinent and of their (the Indians') defeat'.[27] That this was a reassertion of the 16 December statement shows how and with what purpose China was looking at the changed situation in the subcontinent.

It is evident from the statement of 16 December that China's support was not only moral and diplomatic but practically it comprised material assistance also. After the suspension of arms supply to Pakistan by the US and other Western countries, Pakistan had no alternative but to lean heavily on the Chinese source. Since the US embargo, China had been Pakistan's main supplier in the period 1966–71, during which it had provided Pakistan with 133 million dollars worth of arms.[28] After the crisis, China supplied 'all the weapons and ammunition' that Pakistan needed.[29] Not only that, but some were supplied free.[30] The US Defence Department disclosed on 4 November that Pakistan was about to receive arms shipments from China and Rumania. Later reports,[31] and the closure of the Northern areas bordering China on 31 November, show that the Chinese arms were pouring into Pakistan. Besides arms delivery, China helped Pakistan in other ways also. It was disclosed by an Indonesian military spokesman that China had sent 200 instructors to Pakistan to train Pakistani troops in counter-guerrilla warfare.[32] China also offered to equip two divisions being raised in West Pakistan to replace those sent to East Pakistan.[33] During the last days of war in East Pakistan, when it seemed certain that the Pakistan army could not hold on for long because of the difficult situation created by the naval blockade and lack of air protection, it was reported[34] that China's rescue ships had been assembled in the Ganges delta for the evacuation of Pakistani forces in East Pakistan. While it cannot be said for certain that the Chinese submarines and other ships were assembled for the purpose of evacuation of Pakistani troops, keeping in view the press reports and Moscow's advice[35] to India to keep off from attacking the Chinese ships, it can be certainly said that the Chinese armada was in the Bay of Bengal during the war.

China's posture remained friendly after the surrender of Pakistani forces in the East and ceasefire in the West. There were various friendly gestures. Despite the letters of Bhashani to Chairman Mao and Premier Chou urging them to recognize 'Bangla Desh' and similar appeals by Mujib, China's silence over the matter shows that it understands Pakistan's viewpoint about the whole issue. Some of the gestures of Chinese goodwill for Pakistan at this stage were the closure of the Chinese consulate in Dhaka, criticism of the Indian and the rebel troops for 'savagely slaughtering the innocent people of Pakistan'[36] in East Pakistan and the letters to the Security Council, urging the UN to end the killing of Pakistanis in 'Bangla Desh'. A Sino-Pakistan joint communique issued on 2 February at the end of President Bhutto's visit also shows that China supports Pakistan's sovereignty and territorial integrity. To help Pakistan tide over its economic difficulties, China converted four loans into grants and extended the repayment period of another loan to twenty years.

Analysis

Despite being a revolutionary country, champion of the right of oppressed people, supporter of wars of liberation and upholder of the rights of the Indo-Chinese and the Palestinians, why did China support Pakistan against the 'war of liberation' launched by the 'people' of

East Pakistan? This question has puzzled many. The following analysis might help understand the rationale of the Chinese policy towards Pakistan.

Theoretically China's solidarity with Pakistan was based on principles of non-intervention, peaceful coexistence, opposition to foreign aggression, and the use of force, which were repeatedly emphasized in all the statements and speeches made by China in this regard. The Indo-Pakistan war was considered a 'struggle between aggression and anti-aggression, between division and anti-division and between subversion and anti-subversion'.[37] Support to Pakistan, however, did not mean that China had approved of military action in East Pakistan. Considering it an internal matter, China had never commented on it. But a 'friendly advice' to the Pakistan government for negotiations could be found in all the Chinese statements. China condemned India because it was violating the Bandung principles, to which China adhered. Moreover, China had not forgotten the case of Tibet and the border war with India.

As for the 'war of liberation' in East Pakistan, two points needed to be determined: was it a genuine war? and was it launched by the broad masses of the people of East Pakistan? China did not endorse the 'liberation war' theory about it. First, because according to the Chinese standard it was not a genuine guerrilla war fought by peasants and workers of that province. It was a separatist movement launched, not by the 'broad masses' of East Pakistan, but by a 'handful of persons' who wanted 'to sabotage the unity' of Pakistan.[38] It should be recalled here that China had also condemned Chi-Guevarist JVP in Ceylon and declared its support for Mrs Bandaranaike. Secondly, the true nature of the war was also revealed by the fact that those 'handful of persons' were being aided financially and militarily by a foreign power which aimed at the 'dismemberment'[39] of the whole of Pakistan. It has always been the Chinese policy that guerrillas must fight their own war without the aid of an outside power. Thirdly, China could not have looked approvingly at the Awami League's policy and leadership. The Awami League stood for improved relations with India, and Mujib was known to be a pro-American. Therefore, it seemed doubtful that after coming into power, the party would work for the workers and peasants. Finally, it would be wrong for China to support separatist movements in other countries when it was seeking the unification of Taiwan with itself and opposing the idea of an independent state for that island.

Apart from these theoretical considerations there were some solid practical factors that could have influenced Peking's attitude towards Pakistan. Problems with the Soviet Union on the one hand, and past difficulties with India on the other, demanded the continuance of China's friendly relations with Pakistan. In the wake of the prevailing Moscow-Delhi cooperation, signing of the Indo-Soviet treaty in preceding August came as a contributing factor confirming China's support to Pakistan. There is no denying the fact that the treaty played a decisive role in hardening the Chinese attitude towards India and bringing the former closer to Pakistan. With the flow of Russian arms to Delhi in pursuance of the treaty, China's moral and material help to Pakistan also became more pronounced and active.

The reason for China's opposition to 'Bangla Desh' was its apprehension that its creation as an independent state near its border under Soviet influence would weaken its security on its western and southern frontiers. That 'Bangla Desh' is increasingly becoming a zone of Soviet influence is apparent from the presence of pro-Soviet elements in its government under the pressure of Moscow, and its recent agreements—economic and other—with Moscow. In the wake of massive Russian military strength along its northern border, China, logically, cannot be pleased with the existence of a Soviet protegé to its south. Moreover, the growing naval presence of the USSR in the Indian Ocean, which is directed mainly against China,[40] has also been a cause of concern to China. After securing naval facilities at the port of Visakapatnam and Chittagong, the USSR would be able to further strengthen its naval presence in the Ocean. That explains why China favours making the Indian Ocean a peace zone.

Another reason for China supporting Pakistan is the border agreement signed in 1963, which is provisional and according to which Pakistan ceded some 1300 sq. miles of Azad Kashmir to China. Peking has since then linked up the old Silk Route Highway from Sinkiang to Gilgit with the all-weather road running to the northern region of Ladakh near the ceasefire line. Occupation by India of Azad Kashmir, will thus, make the Chinese position vulnerable. Though this apprehension did not materialize, there was great possibility of Chinese intervention if the Indian troops had got anywhere near China's highway. The reports about the Chinese moves on the northern borders[41] indicated that possibility. That China had promised to join the fight if Azad Kashmir was menaced was indicated by some Pakistanis at the UN.[42] The fear of China's intervention was thus one of the reasons that deterred India from launching a large-scale offensive against Azad Kashmir.

Not content with verbal declarations, China also made certain moves. Undoubtedly, the alertness of Chinese troops in Tibet,[43] the passing of weather data for locations in Tibet and along the Sino-Indian border, and the assurance to Pakistan as revealed by President Yahya that within seventy-two hours they would move towards the border,[44] created concern in India, as was apparent from the statements of its leaders.[45] However, in view of the assurance to Delhi by Moscow that it would start a diversionary action in Sinkiang in the event of Chinese intervention[46] and Mr Bhutto's remark rejecting the possibility of Chinese diversionary moves,[47] India presumed that China would not intervene on Pakistan's behalf. India acted on that presumption by moving its mountain divisions from its border with China to East Pakistan. Similarly, China's protest Notes to India against border violations by its troops on the China-Sikkim border did not bring any effective pressure on India because they were not timely. The text of the first protest Note[48] shows that the intrusion was made on 10 December and the protest was lodged on 16 December, i.e. six days after the intrusion. Similarly, the second protest[49] was lodged on 27 December, twelve days after the second border violation on 15 December. The demand made in the first Note to 'immediately stop the activities of intrusion into Chinese territory' was repeated in the second Note. But in none of these Notes was there a stern warning to India of 'grave consequences', such as was given in 1965. These Notes compared to the stern and timely protest Note of 1965, were mild in effect. Several questions arise. Why was China lukewarm this time? Why was its help limited? None other than Premier Chou En-lai admitted on 31 January 1972 that China's help 'in the past has remained limited' and that China 'could not do more'. The joint appeal made on 14 December by the UCP (United Coalition Party) leaders of Pakistan to China and the US for urgent practical help was another indication of limited Chinese help. Before analysing the factors that exercised a restraining influence on China's part in the Indo-Pakistan conflict, it should be borne in mind that nowhere in their statements had the Chinese ever indicated the possibility of their involvement in the war.

The major factor that prevented direct Chinese involvement in the war was the existence of the Indo-Soviet treaty. Article 9 of the treaty provides for holding mutual consultations and 'taking appropriate effective measures,' in case any of the parties 'is attacked or threatened with attack.' The treaty, on the one hand, strengthened China's support to Pakistan; on the other, it confirmed the Soviet entry into the war on India's side, in case of China's intervention. 'India could not have liberated Bangla Desh (without) the treaty of friendship with the Soviet Union.'[50]

Next, China could not help more actively because it had always opposed the use of force to settle disputes. Even its disputes with the USSR and the United States it wants to settle by pacific means on the principle of peaceful coexistence. All Chinese statements and speeches about the Indo-Pakistan dispute carried an appeal for negotiations and its peaceful settlement. When in its own matter of Taiwan, China did not resort to force, how could it be expected that it would embark on a military adventure in support of Pakistan against India that was backed by a military power, i.e. the USSR.

In China different groups have advocated different approaches to foreign policy, one favouring rapprochement with the US while the other advocating close relations with the USSR. True, Chairman Mao and Premier Chou have succeeded in maintaining the upper hand, as indicated by the recent disappearance of Lin Pao and the purge of a number of Chinese officials on the charges of collusion with the Soviets. However, in view of the leftists' pressure, who wanted to support the 'revolutionaries' in Ceylon and Pakistan, China had to follow a moderate course in regard to the Indo-Pakistan war.

Another major deterrent was the fear of Soviet intervention, the possibility of which was apparent from the USSR's warning to other countries to stay out of the conflict, and its assertion that the 'Soviet Union cannot remain indifferent to the developments...taking place in the direct proximity of the USSR's borders and therefore, involve the interests of its security'.[51] That the USSR was prepared to come to India's help, in case of China's entry into the war, was evident from the reported massing of USSR troops on the Soviet-Afghan border and its promise to India to start a diversionary action in Sinkiang against the Chinese in case of the latter's intervention in Ladakh.[52] Besides, China had not forgotten the happenings in Czechoslovakia. The presence of 44 Russian divisions along the Chinese border[53] in the north figured prominently in China's eyes as did its own relatively weak defence capability.

Weather has often been described as a factor restraining the Chinese movement in the north. True, winter snow had closed the Himalayan passes. But there were other routes available including the all-weather road through which the Chinese supply was reaching Pakistan.

One other reason referred to by some in this regard is the absence of a defence pact between China and Pakistan. Much cannot be said about this because of lack of information regarding the Chinese views on such a pact. It is not known, at least publicly, whether the idea of such a pact was mooted during Mr Bhutto's visit to Peking in November, and if it was, what the Chinese reaction was to it. Although it had been stated that China had offered to enter into a defence pact with Pakistan in 1965 and also in November 1971, this was however, denied by Mr Bhutto.[54]

To sum up, it must be said that China supported Pakistan as much as was possible for it to do so. The extent and nature of the support varied according to the prevailing situation. The support was friendly but cautious in the initial period of the crisis, stronger and more practical, though short of physical intervention, in its final phase. That China will continue to be a helpful friend of Pakistan is evident from the Sino-Pakistan and Sino-American joint communiques. With the Indian occupation of East Pakistan, the balance of power in Asia has been upset. China now faces two adversaries, to its north the USSR and to its south India, that is heavily depending upon Soviet arms to maintain its dominance in the subcontinent. The USSR, most likely to use this dependence to encircle China, is also making moves towards Tokyo for this purpose. Time will show the Chinese reaction to this new development. It is not without significance that there has been an increase in the activities of the Naxalites, who are believed to be ideologically akin to the Chinese.

NOTES

1. See the text of the letter in *Pakistan Horizon*, Karachi, Second Quarter, 1971, pp. 153–4.
2. Ibid.
3. *The New York Times*, New York, 22 October 1971; in an article published in *Washington Post*, the American columnist Joseph Alsop said that even before Mrs Gandhi's tour to Western countries Indian divisions on the East Pakistan frontier began to be reinforced to make a total of 12. *Washington Post*, Washington, 26 November 1971.
4. See *The Times*, London, 17 and 19 July 1971; also see *The Economist*, London, 17 July 1971, p. 25.

5. It was disclosed by *The Times* that 'at least 12 Soviet transport aircraft have landed at Bombay and Delhi during the past few days loaded with military equipment'. *The Times*, London, 6 November 1971.
6. Mr Chi Peng-fei's speech in *Peking Review*, Peking, 12 November 1971, p. 5.
7. Ibid.
8. Ibid.
9. See Mr Bhutto's statements in *Dawn*, Karachi, 8 and 9 November 1971.
10. President Yahya in an interview to CBS said that China would intervene if India attacked Pakistan. Ibid., 9 November 1971. See also Mr Bhutto's statement in ibid., 13 November 1971.
11. It is significant to note here that when asked by a foreign correspondent whether China would resort to diversionary action, Mr Bhutto replied that diversionary action was a 'superficial method'. Ibid., 9 November 1971.
12. See the *NCNA* commentaries in ibid., 1 and 6 December 1971.
13. *The Daily Telegraph*, London, 8 December 1971.
14. The *NCNA* commentary in *Dawn*, Karachi, 12 December 1971.
15. *Le Monde*, (English Edition), Paris, 11 December 1971, p. 13.
16. *The Guardian Weekly*, London, 22 January 1972, p. 12.
17. *Le Monde* (English Edition), Paris, 11 December 1971, p. 13.
18. The draft resolution in *Peking Review*, Peking, 10 December 1971, p. 10.
19. See Huang Hua's speech in the UN in ibid., 31 December 1971, p. 4.
20. See the US Ambassador, Mr George Bush's speeches on 5 and 7 December in the Security Council in *Dawn*, Karachi, 7 December and *USIS News Text*, Karachi, 8 December 1971.
21. Nixon's Foreign Policy Report, *USIS News Text*, Karachi, 9 February 1971, p. 11.
22. Ibid., p. 14.
23. Ibid., p. 3.
24. Ibid.
25. The statement of the government of People's Republic of China in *Peking Review*, Peking, 17 December 1971.
26. Ibid.
27. Premier Chou En-lai's speech in ibid., 24 December 1971, p. 9.
28. *USIS News Text*, Karachi, 9 February 1972.
29. President Yahya's interview, *Newsweek*, New York, 8 November 1971, p. 19.
30. Ibid.
31. The Associated Press reported that the Chinese in the final days of war, gave more than 200,000 rounds of tank and anti-aircraft ammunitions to Pakistan. *New Times*, Moscow, No. 2, January 1972, p. 10.
32. *Dawn*, Karachi, 25 November 1971.
33. *The Economist*, London, 13 November 1971, p. 13.

34. *The Daily Telegraph*, London. 13 and 14 December 1971.
35. *Dawn*, Karachi, 14 December 1971.
36. *The Daily Telegraph*, London, 29 December 1971; Also see *Peking Review*, Peking, 31 December 1971.
37. The statement of the government of People's Republic of China, op. cit.
38. Premier Chou En-lai's letter, op. cit.
39. See the statement of the government of the People's Republic of China. op. cit.
40. This was stated by the West German Defence Minister, *The Daily Telegraph*, London, 1 December 1971.
41. *New Times*, Moscow, No. 52, December 1971, p. 9.
42. *The Economist*, London, 18 December 1971, p. 32.
43. *The Observer*, London, 12 December 1971.
44. *The Daily Telegraph*, London, 10 January 1972.
45. See Mrs Gandhi's speech in ibid., 13 December 1971.
46. Ibid., 10 January 1971.
47. See *Dawn*, Karachi, 9 November 1971.
48. See the text of the Note in *Peking Review*, Peking, 24 December 1971. p. 4.
49. See the text of the second Note in ibid., 31 December 1971, p. 4.
50. *The Times of India* quoted in the *Mirror*, Singapore, 10 January 1972, p. 3.
51. *Tass* statement quoted in *Dawn*, Karachi, 7 December 1971.
52. *The Daily Telegraph*, London, 10 January 1972. President Nixon in his Foreign Policy Report stated that the Soviet Union was willing to 'make military moves to deter China on India's behalf'. *USIS News Text*, Karachi, 9 February 1972, p. 16.
53. 'The Strategic Survey 1971', published by the British Institute of Strategic Studies quoted in *The Times*, London, 2 May 1972.
54. *Dawn*, Karachi, 14 January 1972.

5

Britain and the Indo-Pakistan Conflict over East Pakistan*

Khalida Qureshi

With the announcement of its decision, on 30 January 1972, to terminate its membership of the Commonwealth with immediate effect, Pakistan broke off one of its oldest international ties. Pakistan took this decision in view of the declared intention of Britain, New Zealand, and Australia to recognize 'Bangla Desh'. The Pakistan government had been informed by these countries of their intention to do so. In Pakistan's view their decision was an unfriendly act which struck at the very root of the principles of the Commonwealth association and respect for the sovereignty of its members on which it was founded. It amounted to the approval, encouragement, and legitimization of an act of aggression by one member of the Commonwealth against another.[1] Subsequently, Australia and New Zealand recognized 'Bangla Desh' on 31 January while Britain announced its recognition on 4 February 1972.

Whilst Pakistan's decision to quit the Commonwealth and Britain's recognition of 'Bangla Desh' did not create any great stir, what certainly caused some surprise was why Britain had delayed the recognition so long. For it was evident to any observer of the affairs of the Indo-Pakistan subcontinent, especially since March 1971, which way Britain's sympathies lay. In fact, it would not be an exaggeration to say that Britain played an important role not only in the creation and promotion of the secessionist movement in East Pakistan, but also

---

* Vol. xxv, No. 1, 1972.

in the establishment of what came to be known as 'Bangla Desh'. A review of the conduct of British policy in the region, before, during, and after the India-Pakistan war of 1971 would substantiate this contention.

During the period before the war Britain's interests in the area were confined to the following: The promotion of the cause of 'Bangla Desh', the projection of the Indian viewpoint, the conducting of an unfavourable propaganda campaign against West Pakistan and the Pakistan government, the exerting of diplomatic and economic pressures on Pakistan and persuading others to do the same, refusing to utilize the UN and the Commonwealth which could have played an important role in defusing the East Pakistan situation, and projecting an image of Britain as a country willing to mediate in the crisis. The British government, social organizations, members of political parties both Labour and Conservative, parliamentarians, the press, television, the BBC and other news media, with a few exceptions, all played an important role in promoting these interests.

By granting facilities on British soil to the leaders of the 'Bangla Desh movement' and by allowing them to carry on subversive activities against the legally constituted government of Pakistan, Britain greatly assisted the secessionist movement. Rebels and insurgents, defected Pakistani diplomatic personnel, and fugitives from Pakistan's justice, found sanctuary in Britain and were allowed time and facilities on the television and radio. London became a centre of anti-Pakistan activities and Britain the sole European base for 'Bangla Desh' activities. Britain also permitted its colonies, for example Hong Kong, to be used as bases for launching subversion aimed at the territorial integrity of Pakistan.[2]

A 'Bangla Desh Mission' was set up in London in August 1971 and a 'Bangla Desh' newspaper was allowed to be published from Britain. On 26 July 1971, a former Labour minister launched 'Bangla Desh' postage stamps from British Parliament premises with the object of getting international recognition for 'Bangla Desh' covertly, through the seemingly innocent device of the postage stamp.[3] All this was done with the British government's knowledge and it seems with its approval and encouragement. The Pakistani government's protests against these hostile actions and the partisan attitude of the British government, were all to no avail.[4]

The British Parliament and political parties also lent strong support to the 'Bangla Desh movement'. Pakistan's internal affairs were the subject of several debates in the British Parliament, whose members generally upheld the cause of 'Bangla Desh', expressed sympathy for India and denounced Pakistan. MPs called for British intervention through economic sanctions.[5] They issued appeals covering full pages of newspapers calling for the recognition of 'Bangla Desh'. Ten former ministers and 211 MPs, mostly belonging to the Labour Party, signed a resolution in the House of Commons which condemned Pakistan army action in East Pakistan and called on the British government to press for a 'ceasefire' in East Pakistan.[6]

While a 'Bangla Desh' lobby already existed in the House of Commons, on 3 December 1971, an all-parties pro-secessionist parliamentary group was set up which was led by professional secessionists such as John Stonehouse and Hugh Fraser who were earlier involved in the advocacy of secessionism during the Nigerian civil war.[7] As for the British parliamentarians who visited Pakistan, they expressed divergent views about conditions in East Pakistan. Whereas some like Mrs Jill Knight, Mr James Tinn, and Mr John Osborne gave a factual account of the East Pakistan situation, stating categorically that they saw no evidence of atrocities committed by the Pakistan army during their extensive tour of the area, their truthful appraisal did not accord with British political susceptibilities.[8] The BBC distorted Mrs Knight's statement at which she protested. In fact the highly exaggerated, biased, and unfavourable to Pakistan account given by the official parliamentary delegation, led by Mr Arthur Bottomley, was more in line with British thinking.[9]

Besides such pressure tactics and moral support, British MPs and social organizations rendered material and moral aid as well. They joined hands to raise funds for 'Bangla Desh'. Money was not only collected for humanitarian purposes, for example, for the East Pakistan refugees in India, but also to meet the expenses of the 'Bangla Desh Mission', for propaganda purposes and to buy arms for 'Bangla Desh' guerrillas in order to enable them to carry on subversive activities against Pakistan. These funds must have been huge to pay for the numerous appeals in support of 'Bangla Desh' which appeared in the British press, for it was reported that a full page advertisement cost £500.[10] It was also revealed, by a 'Bangla Desh' leader in Geneva, that these funds were kept in the Jewish Hambrose Bank of Bishop Gate, London, and because the leading London banks had refused to open an account in the name of 'Bangla Desh', the account was jointly operated by Abu Saeed Choudhry (now 'President of Bangla Desh'), Mr Stonehouse and another British MP.[11]

As for the British information media, it also played a significant role. A perusal of the British press of those days, and a review of the BBC and British television programmes would illustrate their pro-India and 'Bangla Desh' bias and their hostility to Pakistan. From the very outset they imparted a romantic hue to the 'Bangla Desh movement'. Bengal's desire for independence and guerrilla activities were highlighted. Press reports sometimes incited the East Pakistanis against the army, gave directions to the 'Bangla Desh movement' and produced fear among the population of the area. British correspondents played up the possibility, even the inevitability of secession.[12] Earlier too, during the cyclone in East Pakistan and the Pakistan elections in 1970, the British press had accentuated the differences between the two wings of Pakistan. The BBC and the British press which are widely heard and read in the Indo-Pakistan subcontinent and all over the world, greatly misguided people in East Pakistan as elsewhere. It demoralised other Pakistanis too and thus helped the cause of 'Bangla Desh' and India.

British information media also waged a clever propaganda campaign against Pakistan. Often, it reported not facts, but produced fantasies, such as the report about the death of the Pakistani General, Tikka Khan.[13] Newspapers printed false stories about Pakistan army atrocities in East Pakistan, conveniently forgetting Ulster and the British army's atrocities there. The problem of the East Pakistan refugees was blown up out of all proportion. The press refused to publish anything contrary to its anti-Pakistan policy. For example, *The Times* refused to publish a letter written by a Conservative MP, Sir Frederick Bennet, in which he had accused the paper of deliberately presenting a cockeyed version of the happenings in East Pakistan.[14] The Pakistan side of the story was either ignored or not given any prominence. The object it seems was to create an opinion so adverse against Pakistan that it would be isolated, and if later military operations against it were undertaken, they would have less grave repercussions.

While it painted Pakistan black, the British news media depicted India as the injured party. The rapidly inflating Indian figures about East Pakistan refugees in India[15] were faithfully reproduced by the British press.[16] India's dilemma and the necessity for it to take action were emphasized. The idea of an Indo-Pakistan conflict was promoted. Public opinion favourable to India was created which eased India's task and paved the way for Indian aggression against Pakistan. This was necessary, for world opinion generally sides with the victim of aggression and not the aggressor, especially if the victim happens to be a small power and the aggressor a bigger country.

What comes to mind is why the British information media acted the way they did. Opinions vary as to whether the bias arose from ignorance or malice. While some argue that because Pakistan sent back foreign correspondents at the beginning of the crisis,[17] those that remained in India came under Awami League and Indian influence and gave one sided accounts of events. The other view is that Jewish and Indian vested interests coloured these accounts. The British press, BBC, and other news media acted as the Information Department of the Indian government and their correspondents, especially Peter Hazlehurst, who felt at home in the Indian External Affairs Ministry, played the part of publicity agent for India.[18] Then there are others who feel that this happened because the British press and BBC traditions have generally deteriorated. *The Daily Telegraph* complained recently that the BBC had forgotten of late its duty to put truth, fairness, and objectivity before sheer entertainment value.[19] Perhaps the British information media's attitude was the product of all these factors.

It should, however, be remembered that not all Britishers misrepresented the truth. There were occasional articles, reports, and letters that were factual. Individuals, e.g. Mrs Knight, Mr Osborne, Mr Rushbrook Williams and others upheld the truth and drew attention to the British press's unbalanced presentation of happenings in East Pakistan.[20] But their voices were lost in the noise of the multitude. Their anguish is aptly described by Mrs Knight: '...usually I feel as though I am a little voice shouting against the volume of lies and this is something which distresses me desperately. I don't want to be partial to one side or unfair to the other, all I'm asking for is the truth and that we haven't so far had...'[21] As it happened the British press and BBC showed a slight change when, in November 1971, India openly aggressed against East Pakistan and when the war broke out in December 1971. Doubts were expressed then about Mrs Gandhi's good intentions, BBC commentators stated that the Indian attack on East Pakistan was not defensive. *The Daily Telegraph* and *Guardian* wrote that India was showing belligerence towards Pakistan. After the war ended some stories appeared about the atrocities committed on the

Bihari minority in 'Bangla Desh'. But by then it was too late, the damage had already been done.

Economic pressures were also exerted against Pakistan by the British government in order to promote India's cause and the secessionist movement. Britain suspended its development aid to Pakistan and declared that no further aid would be given. The resumption of aid was made conditional to a political solution acceptable to the people of East Pakistan. The British Foreign Secretary, Sir Alec Douglas-Home, and the Minister for Overseas Development, Mr Richard Wood, made statements to this effect in the House of Commons.[22] The British Export Credit Guarantee Department ceased covering further transactions of exports to Pakistan and the British government's contribution to the World Bank Aid-to-Pakistan Consortium was also made conditional. Britain urged others, especially Consortium countries, to take joint action to pressurize Pakistan through aid into accepting India's and the secessionists' demands.[23] The British Director of the World Bank, Peter Cargill, played an important role in this connection. He led a team of World Bank observers to East Pakistan in June 1971, and prepared and placed before the Consortium a highly tendentious and politically motivated anti-Pakistan report.[24] This was later leaked out to the British and American press. Although controversial portions of the report were later expunged from the World Bank's official records by orders of its President, Mr McNamara, the damage had been done. British correspondent Peter Hazlehurst was not making empty boasts when he wrote that Britain had taken stronger steps than India to bring President Yahya Khan to his senses.[25]

Britain's strong measures certainly hit Pakistan hard because of the prevailing economic situation in the country and Pakistan's dependence on aid. Around a third of Pakistan's foreign exchange or about $400 million is obtained through aid.[26] Pakistan had been facing a balance of payments problem and its reserve position was bad even before the East Pakistan cyclone in 1970 and the events of March 1971. Since then, the economic situation had worsened and Pakistan was on the verge of bankruptcy. In these circumstances Pakistan could perhaps absorb the shock of the loss of British aid of about £10 million or more as President Yahya Khan and his Economic Adviser, Mr M. M. Ahmed, stated,[27] but joint action certainly it could not bear. It made a damaging impact on Pakistan's economy. Whilst it cut off its aid to Pakistan, Britain increased its assistance to India and continued it even during the war. Thus it contributed to India's military capability because with increased British aid India could divert its own resources to buying arms to use against Pakistan.

Britain served India and 'Bangla Desh' in another way also. It refused to utilize the UN and the Commonwealth to prevent the East Pakistan crisis from escalating. While taking no positive action it posed as a power anxious to mediate and settle the dispute. These tactics served India and the cause of 'Bangla Desh' admirably. Britain is a medium-sized power but with considerable world-wide influence, it is an important Commonwealth member, one of the big five of the Security Council and Pakistan's partner in the Commonwealth, SEATO, and CENTO. It could certainly have intervened in a more positive manner. Earlier in the case of the Nigerian civil war, the Commonwealth had acted jointly. Britain had earlier taken a stand on the question of Kashmir and had mediated in 1965 the Rann of Kutch dispute between India and Pakistan. During the recent crisis the UN Secretary-General, U Thant, had pleaded with the great powers of the Council to act and defuse the explosive situation. Mr Stewart, Britain's ex-Foreign Minister, and the Secretary-General of the Commonwealth, Mr Arnold Smith, had called for Commonwealth mediation.[28] Mr Rushbrook Williams had supported the Australian suggestion to convene a Commonwealth Prime Ministers' Conference. Although Britain made much noise about messages to President Yahya Khan and consultations with India and Pakistan, it made no real effort to stop the situation from getting worse. In fact by condemning Pakistan, Britain forfeited its influence over Pakistan and made itself unacceptable to it as a mediator.[29] On the other hand it was not willing to displease India in any way. For example, when Britain encountered Indian opposition to the proposal of the posting of UN observers on the India-East Pakistan border, instead of using its undeniably great influence over India to make it agree to this reasonable suggestion, Britain preferred to pursue the matter no further. Thus Britain by its actions belied its own claims that it was non-partisan and neutral during the crisis. In fact its attitude was pro-India and anti-Pakistan.

When war broke out between India and Pakistan in December 1971, Britain helped India and 'Bangla Desh' by obstructing the work of the UN and by supplying arms to India. Since the end of the war Britain's endeavours on behalf of India and 'Bangla Desh' can be summed up as follows: to begin with, Britain has helped in the establishment and consolidation of 'Bangla Desh' by persuading the international community to recognize it, by providing it with aid, by getting economic benefits for it from others', by working on Pakistan to accept the 'reality of Bangla Desh' and settle its problems with it, and by being useful generally to 'Bangla Desh' e.g., on the question of prisoners of war. Britain has also projected an image of India as the dominant power of the region and is trying to build a collective security system with India. Britain realizes that to achieve this objective it is necessary that Pakistan be prevailed upon to accept 'Bangla Desh' and end its confrontation with India, hence it is making diplomatic efforts to initiate talks between India, Pakistan, and 'Bangla Desh'.

While discussing Britain's recent role in the UN, Lord Caradon, Britain's Permanent Representative at the UN until 1970, wrote: 'We see an attempt by the British Government not to make greater use of the instrument (UN) but to take the lead in preventing its effective use'.[30] Britain's role at the UN during the recent India-Pakistan conflict was indeed a shameful one. The Security Council had met on 4 December 1971 to consider the conflict at the request of nine powers including Britain.[31] During three meetings held on 4, 5, and 6 December eight draft resolutions were introduced, four were brought to vote, and one was adopted. As a result of an impasse in the Council the matter was then transferred to the General Assembly where meetings were held twice on 7 December and a resolution was adopted. At the United States' request the matter was brought back to the Council where seven meetings were held between 12 and 21 December during which nine resolutions were introduced, two were put to vote, and one adopted.[32] Britain abstained on all votes except the final one. It abstained in the Council on the US draft resolution of 4 and 12/13 December and the 8-power resolution of 5 December, all of which called for an immediate ceasefire and withdrawal of forces.[33] Eleven powers had voted each time in favour of these resolutions which were vetoed by the Soviet Union. Britain abstained with eleven others on the USSR draft resolution of 4 December which called for a political settlement.[34] While the USSR and Poland had voted for this resolution, China had cast a negative vote. Britain also abstained on the 6-power Council resolution adopted on 6 December which transferred the matter to the General Assembly.[35] When, on 7 December, the Assembly adopted a 34-power resolution which called for an immediate ceasefire, troop withdrawal and return of refugees by a vote of 104 in favour to 11 against and 10 abstentions, Britain abstained on this too.[36] Later, Britain with France introduced a draft resolution in the Council on 15 December (not voted upon) calling for a ceasefire in both East and

West Pakistan, the withdrawal of troops, the conclusion of a comprehensive political settlement based on realities, UN Secretary-General's good offices for refugee rehabilitation and the observance of Geneva Conventions.[37] But this was done only when the surrender of Pakistani troops in East Pakistan was a foregone conclusion. When Britain finally agreed to cast an affirmative vote on the 6-power Council resolution of 21 December,[38] which called for a durable ceasefire, troop withdrawals, observance of the Geneva Conventions and the UN Secretary-General's good offices for the solution of humanitarian problems, Pakistan forces had surrendered in the East and both India and Pakistan had agreed to a ceasefire.

Throughout the debates Britain declared that unanimity and consensus were essential. Britain's representative at the UN said there was no practical advantage in supporting resolutions which had no chance of success. Tactics to delay the work of the Council were adopted e.g., adjournment for consultations. Much was made about Britain's behind-the-scene activities,[39] though even India later, according to reports, belittled Britain's contribution to a ceasefire.[40] In this manner though the majority of the UN members wanted a ceasefire and withdrawals, the Council was made ineffective and their voices were silenced. Later Britain's inactivity was explained as 'studied non-partisanship' and the object, it was said, was that at a later date Britain could act as a mediator between India, Pakistan, and 'Bangla Desh'. But Pakistan's President, Mr Zulfikar Ali Bhutto's explanation seems more plausible that Britain instead of using its influence to change the course of affairs abstained in order to play a role.[41] It wanted the fall of Dhaka and the defeat of Pakistan's forces in the East so that it could then accept the *fait accompli*. It is not surprising that Britain's relations with India improved greatly as a result of Britain's cooperative stand at the United Nations.

During the recent crisis Britain augmented India's military might by supplying it with arms even when the war was going on. 'British factories worked night and day to supply arms to India.'[42] Chartered Air India Boeings were airlifting missiles and spares for aircraft, tanks and naval equipment.[43] The British press revealed that Britain was supplying Tigercat low-level ground-to-air missiles in accordance with a secret deal signed between India and the British firm, Shorts, of Belfast. The deal was negotiated when the East Pakistan crisis began and the British government was reported to have been closely involved in the deal, being the controlling shareholder in Shorts. Britain had also helped the Indians to finance the order.[44] When Pakistan protested at Britain's policy, the British Foreign Secretary was told by the Indian High Commissioner to keep in mind Britain's economic and political interests in India and 'Bangla Desh' while reviewing the question of arms sales to India.[45] Sir Alec obliged by declaring in the House of Commons, on 13 December 1971, that there were long-standing contracts with British commercial firms for supplying military equipment to India and that there were no prospects of an embargo on sales of arms to India and Pakistan.[46] The reference to Pakistan was unnecessary as Britain had not been a regular supplier of arms to Pakistan for many years. Since the war ended, the British press has reported that India would buy 50 Jaguar attack planes built jointly by British and French concerns to make up for its losses in the recent war with Pakistan.[47] Reports said that Britain would also be willing to sell sophisticated weapons to India in order to reduce its reliance on Soviet arms.[48] The possibility of Britain assisting India in building up its navy has also been mentioned.[49] Having so recently been subjected to Indian aggression, such reports naturally created apprehension in Pakistan and raised doubts about Britain's motives.

Britain not only recognized what Sir Alec called the reality of 'Bangla Desh' but helped 'Bangla Desh' in acquiring a legal status through international recognition. That pressure was used by Britain on Commonwealth states for this purpose was stated by the Maltese Prime Minister, Mr Dom Mintoff, on 24 February 1972.[50] The British Prime Minister, Mr Edward Heath, was also reported to be persuading the European countries to jointly recognize 'Bangla Desh' and his diplomatic efforts succeeded when, on 4 February 1972, eight European states simultaneously accorded recognition.[51] Concerted action was sought so as to make it difficult for Pakistan to take any retaliatory measures. These tactics, according to reports, had been agreed upon when Sheikh Mujibur Rehman (now 'Prime Minister of Bangla Desh') had met Mr Heath and the Commonwealth Secretary-General, Mr Arnold Smith, in London, after his release in January 1972.[52] The timing of Britain's recognition on the eve of President Bhutto's departure for Peking was also considered important. It was meant to discourage him from getting too close to China.[53] But Pakistan was not intimidated and broke off relations with the Commonwealth. Incidentally this action was approved of by the Chinese Prime Minister, Mr Chou En-lai.[54]

In Pakistan, the decision to terminate Commonwealth ties won popular acclaim. The press generally approved of it,[55] though a few newspapers did disapprove and called it 'a petulant gesture'.[56] Pakistan's decision to quit the Commonwealth was in accord with the desire of the people of Pakistan who had raised the demand in the past also. It was neither a departure from Pakistan's past policies nor did it cause any serious difficulties to Pakistan. Pakistan had already delinked its rupee from the pound sterling in September 1971 and its trade had been diversified some time ago. The Commonwealth tariff preferences, through which Pakistan derived economic benefits, were to end when Britain entered the ECM in 1973. Britain's Commonwealth attachments that had already weakened would then fall away.[57] The British government later announced (to assuage Pakistan's feelings perhaps) that the status of about 235,000 Pakistanis in Britain, which was regulated by the British Nationality Act of 1948, would not be affected by Pakistan's decision.[58] Both Britain and Pakistan have also decided to continue their bilateral relations. However, Pakistan did encounter some difficulties recently because of Britain's unfair and politically motivated decision to place restrictions on Pakistan's textile exports to Britain.[59]

Besides helping 'Bangla Desh' on the recognition issue Britain assisted it in other ways too. Britain's official contribution to aid to 'Bangla Desh' refugees in India had totalled £14.75 million, and for relief in East Pakistan, £2 million, before the war. In January 1972, Britain gave a further £1 million, thus bringing the total to £3 million. On 26 February 1972, Britain and 'Bangla Desh' signed an agreement under which Britain gave 'Bangla Desh' £4,835,000 worth of interest-free commodity loans, repayable on easy terms, for buying goods and services from Britain.[60] Later British officials confirmed that aid to 'Bangla Desh' would increase. British communication experts were also sent to 'Bangla Desh' for reconstruction purposes. 'Bangla Desh', which acquired Commonwealth membership on 18 April 1972[61] and had decided to join the sterling area, was offered Commonwealth assistance by the Commonwealth Secretary-General as well.[62] It was reported that Britain would assist, when the time came, in sorting out financial relations between Pakistan and 'Bangla Desh'.[63] The British government was also reported to be making efforts for the early establishment of an Aid-to-'Bangla Desh' Consortium under the aegis of the World Bank. As for the question of the trial of Pakistani prisoners of war for 'war crimes' by the 'Bangla Desh government', it was reported that the British Secretary of the International Commission of Jurists in Geneva was seeking to associate the Commission in their trial.[64] Sir Alec, during his press conference at Lahore, had evaded the issue. Britain's unconditional aid and other assistance to 'Bangla Desh', however, contrasted sadly with its attitude to Pakistan. For example, on 14 February 1972, the British Minister for Aid stated that new development aid to Pakistan would be conditional on the reorganization of Pakistan's economy and an agreement on debt servicing moratorium, including presumably foreign debts incurred for East Pakistan.[65]

Since the war ended, Britain has also been busy projecting an image of India as a potential great power, capable of being 'stronger than China',[66] which accords with India's own ambitions to dominate Asia. Britain's object, it seems, is to put forward the idea of a western oriented collective security system for South Asia and the Indian Ocean,[67] as a counterpoise to the Soviet proposal for an Asian security pact. As Sir Alec stated in New Delhi, Britain hopes that India could become the 'foundation and basis' of this security system,[68] and would like to assist India in this. But to make this plan feasible, it is necessary that Pakistan be made to accept the new situation arising out of the war and end its confrontation with India. Sir Alec stated that Britain was ready to help to achieve a reconciliation between India, Pakistan, and 'Bangla Desh'. Britain considered an early meeting between Mrs Gandhi, President Bhutto, and Sheikh Mujibur Rehman essential and London was offered as a meeting place.[69] In order to initiate reconciliation talks, Sir Alec visited India in February 1972, Pakistan in March and 'Bangla Desh' in June. When in Pakistan, Sir Alec stated that he wished to see an independent and prosperous Pakistan. But what Britain either fails to realize or purposely ignores is the fact that Indian hegemony in the region spells danger for Pakistan as well as for other smaller countries of the region. During the recent conflict also, Britain erroneously held the view that India was not out to annex West Pakistan and Mr Heath disagreed with President Nixon on this question at their Bermuda talks.[70] Britain should realize that by following such a policy it is making India's desire to dominate Asia possible[71] and is also endangering the safety of the smaller countries of the region.

Historical, economic, and strategic considerations motivated British policy towards the conflict. To begin with, Britain's traditional close friendship with India and its antipathy towards Pakistan conditioned this policy. At the root of this British-Indian affinity lies Britain's pro-

Hindu and anti-Muslim bias. For it was the Muslims of the subcontinent who resisted British rule and suffered the most as a result, whereas the Hindus made an alliance of convenience with the British and gained great advantages for themselves. Therefore, when the partition of India was forced upon the British by the Muslims of the subcontinent, they reluctantly accepted the creation of Pakistan and did their best to accentuate and weaken this Muslim state. The pro-India machinations of the last British Viceroy of India, Lord Mountbatten, and the unfair and illogical boundary alignments drawn by Sir Cyril Radcliffe had but one object—to make Pakistan unviable.[72] The longstanding British strategic and economic interests in India further cemented Indo-British relations and this factor conditioned the British politicians' attitudes in the recent conflict. That British politicians would go to any length to please India had been demonstrated earlier when the Labour Party leader, Mr Harold Wilson, retracted his statement made in 1965 in which he had accused India of aggression against Pakistan. In the recent conflict too, when American aid to India was stopped, Mr Wilson advocated India's case with the US and also promised help to 'Bangla Desh'.[73] Britain's Jewish controlled press also, motivated by hatred for Pakistan, supported India. In view of all this it is easy to understand why the British government, politicians, and the press sided with India.

The economic factor, despite Sir Alec's disawovals,[74] also affected British policy in the recent conflict, for the British are a nation of traders. British assets in India are reported to be worth about £8,000 to £10,000 million and their size approaches the largest single block of British investments abroad in Australia and New Zealand (£12,000 million or over).[75] British trade as well as its aid to India are also considerable. India is the largest recipient of British development aid since 1952. From 1958 to 1971 the disbursement of official British aid to India had totalled £421.6 million.[76] Loans have often been free of interest and repayable on easy terms. British investments in Pakistan and its trade with Pakistan by comparison are negligible. Britain has been the third largest importer of Pakistan's goods after the US and West Germany. While exports from UK to West Pakistan in 1970-71 came to Rs 188.261 million plus re-exports of Rs 4.142 million, those to East Pakistan for the same period amounted to Rs 129.645 million.[77] According to Sir Alec, British investment in West Pakistan is also higher than it is in East Pakistan.[78] But the important fact remains that Britain imports mostly cotton, textiles, skins, and tobacco from West

Pakistan for which it can find alternative markets, but East Pakistan is its main source of supply of raw jute on which British industry, especially the factories in Dundee, depend.[79] British investments in 'Bangla Desh' are also substantial, amounting to over £100 million in jute, tea, petroleum, chemicals, tobacco, engineering and shipping.[80] For these reasons Britain desired good relations with 'Bangla Desh' and India, for it could ill afford to jeopardize its jute trade with the former and its trade and investments with the latter. India took full advantage of Britain's weakness and at a time when it sensed that Britain might modify its policy, the Indian Prime Minister, Mrs Gandhi, and Foreign Secretary, Mr Kaul, did not hesitate to remind Britain of its assets in India and 'Bangla Desh' and the repercussions that might follow if it persisted in any such folly.[81] Britain's sacrifice of principles at the altar of economic necessity certainly fetched good dividends for it. India rewarded it by an increase in trade which grew from Rs 18 crore 80 lakh to Rs 24 crore 95 lakh. Britain also benefitted from the discontinuance of US aid to India.[82] As for 'Bangla Desh', eternally grateful for Britain's support, it too promised good prospects for future British trade and investment.

In the formulation of recent British policy towards the region, another predisposing factor was Britain's fear of Soviet domination in the Indian Ocean area and its littoral states. Britain feared that if any single power dominated the region it would disrupt the sea lanes and would adversely affect British and Western trade and their oil supplies from the Persian Gulf.[83] Soviet penetration in the area had been referred to by Mr Heath at the Singapore Conference of Commonwealth Prime Ministers in January 1971. Sir Alec's statements and the British Defence White Paper published on 16 February 1972[84] also drew attention to this fact. Britain's modification of its earlier policy to withdraw east of Suez was also the result of this fear. But what increased the fear enormously was the change in the region resulting from America's decision to withdraw from Asia, the recent phenomenal growth of Soviet naval power in the Indian Ocean, and the recent boost Soviet influence received in the area from its treaty with India (August 1971) and its role in the India-Pakistan conflict. Britain was afraid that India and 'Bangla Desh' fearing a Pakistan-China-US axis might lean more on the Soviet Union and fulfil its longstanding desire by giving it bases in the region. Britain was also aware of the existence of pro-Moscow factions in the Indian Foreign Office[85] and in the 'Bangla Desh government' that desired close relations with the

USSR. It wanted to diminish and neutralize this growing Soviet influence in India and 'Bangla Desh' by keeping intact some Western influence in these countries. Perhaps what it desired was Indo-British coordination in the region with the USSR looking on in a friendly fashion.[86] And because a Pakistan, with its two zones united, did not fit in with the British scheme of things, Britain was willing to sacrifice it. Britain felt that a strong Pakistan might not acquiesce to British plans, but a reduced and weak Pakistan would neither have the capacity nor the will to resist. This explains Britain's hostility to Pakistan and its support to India and 'Bangla Desh'.

Britain's unprincipled policy during the conflict created bitterness among the people of Pakistan. Both Presidents Yahya and Bhutto called it hostile. India and 'Bangla Desh', however, greatly appreciated it and Britain derived economic and political benefits as a result from these countries. But Britain's policy is bound to have far-reaching and grave repercussions. Britain's support to India in its contravention of International Law and the UN Charter, will weaken the rule of law and the world organization. The help rendered to India in the dismemberment of Pakistan will make Britain suspect in the eyes of Afro-Asian nations. What is more, the breakup of Pakistan, which marks the beginning of endless strife in the region, will, in the long run, endanger Britain's own interests in the area.

NOTES

1. Pakistan government announcement of 30 January 1972, *Pakistan News Digest*, Karachi, 15 February 1972, p. 3.
2. *Dawn*, Karachi, 1 September 1971.
3. Ibid., 28 July 1971.
4. Pakistan's verbal protests and notes to Britain of 27 March, 5 and 7 July, 28 and 30 August 1971.
5. *British Review*, Karachi, 22 May 1971.
6. *The Observer*, London, 2 May 1971 and *Dawn*, Karachi, 21 August 1971.
7. *Dawn*, Karachi, 5 December 1971.
8. For the expression of their views see 'British MPs' views on Pakistan', *The Pakistan Society Bulletin*, London, Winter, 1971, pp. 25–41.
9. *Pakistan News Digest*, Karachi, 1 August 1971, p. 3.
10. *Morning News*, Karachi, 31 August 1971.
11. *The Pakistan Observer*, Dhaka, 18 November 1971,

12. For the role of the British news media see Hasan Zaman (ed.) *East Pakistan Crisis and India*, Dhaka 1971, pp. 34–111, and *Pakistan Economist*, Karachi. 28 August–3 September 1971, pp. 5–8.
13. During the Indo-Pakistan war of 1965 the BBC had also wrongly reported the fall of Lahore.
14. *Dawn*, Karachi, 2 August 1971.
15. B. L.C. Johnson, 'Bangla Desh: A Chronolgy', *Australia's Neighbours*, Victoria, November 1971–January 1972, pp. 2–3.
16. Later British correspondents, e.g. Clare Hollingworth expressed doubts about the veracity of Indian figures. *Morning News*, Karachi, 2 February 1971.
17. They later returned to Pakistan.
18. N.C. Chaudhri in *Hindustan Standard* of 6 June 1971, reproduced in Hasan Zaman, *East Pakistan Crisis and India*, op. cit., pp. 64–5.
19. *The Daily Telegraph*, London, 9 July 1971.
20. See 'British MPs views on Pakistan', *The Pakistan Society Bulletin*, op. cit., pp. 25–41 and Hasan Zaman, *East Pakistan Crisis and India*, op. cit., pp. 289–92.
21. 'British MPs' views on Pakistan', *The Pakistan Society Bulletin*, op. cit., p. 40.
22. *Survey of Current Affairs*, London, COI, 1971–72, p. 322.
23. *Dawn*, Karachi, 1 August 1971.
24. Excerpts in *The Times*, London, 14 July 1971, see also *Pakistan News Digest*, Karachi, 1 August 1971,
25. *The Times*, London, 29 July 1971.
26. *The Economist*, London, 15 May 1971, p. 73.
27. *The Guardian Weekly*, London, 3 July 1971, p. 24.
28. Ibid., 3 July 1971, p. 24 and *Morning News*, Karachi, 3 February 1972.
29. *The Daily Telegraph*, London, 22 July 1971.
30. Lord Caradon, 'Britain's Shameful UN Role', *The Guardian Weekly*, London, 8 January 1972, p. 9.
31. Letter to the President of the Security Council dated 4 December 1971, S/10411.
32. For proceedings of the Security Council and General Assembly debates see *UN Monthly Chronicle*, New York, UN Office of Public Information, January 1972, pp. 3–46, 89–91.
33. Security Council draft resolutions Nos. S/10416, S/10446 and Rev. 1, S/10423.
34. Draft resolution S/10418.
35. Security Council resolution S/RES/303 (1971).
36. General Assembly resolution A/RES/2793 (XXVI).
37. Draft resolution S/10455.
38. Security Council resolution S/RES/307 (1971).
39. *The Times*, London, 20 December 1971.

40. *The Daily Telegraph*, London, 30 December 1971.
41. President Bhutto's speech in the Security Council of 15 December 1971, *Pakistan News Digest*, Karachi, 1 January 1972.
42. President Bhutto's statement in *The Daily Telegraph*, London, 20 December 1971.
43. *Dawn*, Karachi, 9 December 1971.
44. *The Sunday Times*, London, 19 December 1971.
45. *Morning News*, Karachi, 9 December 1971.
46. Ibid., 14 December 1971, and *Dawn*, Karachi, 15 December 1971.
47. *The Daily Telegraph*, London, 2 March 1972.
48. *The Economist*, London, 12 February 1972, pp. 40–41.
49. *The Daily Telegraph*, 8 February 1972.
50. *Dawn*, Karachi, 25 February 1972.
51. *The Pakistan Times*, Lahore, 6 February 1972.
52. *Dawn*, Karachi, 12 January 1972.
53. *Pakistan News Digest*, Karachi, 15 February 1972.
54. *Dawn*, Karachi, 1 February 1972.
55. *Morning News*, Karachi, 31 January 1972 and *The Pakistan Times*, Lahore, 1 February 1972.
56. *Dawn*, Karachi, 1 and 5 February 1972.
57. *The Times*, London, 16 October 1971.
58. *Morning News*, Karachi, and *The Pakistan Times*, Lahore, 7 February 1972.
59. *Dawn*, Karachi, 1 April 1972.
60. *Survey of Current Affairs*, op. cit., 2 February 1972, pp. 62–3.
61. *Morning News*, Karachi, 19 April 1972.
62. *Dawn*, Karachi, 25 February 1972.
63. *The Daily Telegraph*, London, 9 February 1972.
64. *Dawn*, Karachi, 27 March 1972.
65. Ibid., 21 April 1972.
66. Sir Alec's statement, in New Delhi, ibid., 14 February and 9 March 1972.
67. *The Economist*, London, 12 February 1972, pp. 40–41.
68. *The Daily Telegraph*, London, 9 February 1972.
69. *The Times*, London, 21 March 1972 and Sir Alec Douglas-Home's press conference in Lahore of 20 March 1972, *Press release*, British Information Services, Karachi, 22 March 1972.
70. *The Pakistan Times*, Lahore, 22 December 1971.
71. *The Economist*, London, 26 February 1972, p. 33.
72. See Shahid Hamid 'Squint in the British eye is not new', *The Pakistan Times*, Lahore, 3 October 1971, Razi Wasti 'British policy towards Indian Muslims immediately after 1857', *The Journal of History and Political Science*, Lahore, 1971–72, pp. 78–97, and Kemal A. Faruki, 'Britain Empoverished Bengal', *Pakistan Economist*, Karachi, 28 August 1972, pp. 13–16.

73. *Morning News*, Karachi, 9 January 1972 and *Dawn*, Karachi, 11 December 1971.
74. Sir Alec's press conference at Lahore of 20 March 1972, op. cit.
75. 'The Subcontinental crisis-1971, The role of Britain', *Pakistan Economist*, op. cit., p, 6.
76. *'Overseas Development'*, London, September 1971, p. 6.
77. *Dawn*, Karachi, 15 February 1972.
78. Sir Alec's press conference at Lahore, op. cit.
79. *The Economist*, London, 19 June 1971, p. 76.
80. *The Daily Telegraph*, London, 30 December 1971.
81. Ibid., 7 December 1971.
82. Report in *Jang*, Karachi, 14 March 1972.
83. British Defence Statement in *Survey of Current Affairs*, op. cit., March 1972, p. 101.
84. *The Daily Telegraph*, London, 17 February 1972 and *Survey of Current Affairs*, op. cit., pp. 71–2.
85. *The Daily Telegraph*, London, 30 December 1971.
86. *Dawn*, Karachi, 14 February 1971.

6

The Simla and Tashkent Agreements*

Mehrunnisa Ali

Pakistan sought to maintain peace with India despite the fact that it has never reconciled to the concept of Pakistan, has committed aggression against it in the recent past and dismembered it by sheer physical force, defying the UN Charter and the Bandung principles on the pretext of helping the people in achieving their right of 'self-determination'—a right that it has been denying to the people of Kashmir. The reasons for the recent somersault in the government's attitude towards India are many and of varying nature.

First, peace was sought as a measure of last resort. In the changed situation, the policy of confrontation with India did not seem to be in accord with the national interest. Pakistan was a defeated country without any effective bargaining power. India had torn it asunder. It held Pakistan's 93,000 POWs in captivity and large tracts of its land. Therefore, it was in a position to negotiate with Pakistan from its vantage point as the military victor. India's assertion that it would not talk with Pakistan from a position of strength[1] did not positively change the existing situation.

The second factor that could not be overlooked was the considerable accretion in India's prestige at home and the resulting improvement in its internal political atmosphere. India's victory over Pakistan had brought about a euphoria and a sense of confidence in Indian nationhood all over the country. Moreover, Congress's overwhelming

* Vol. xxv, No. 3, 1972.

success in the state elections in March and the defeat of the Marxist Party in West Bengal had further strengthened Mrs Gandhi's position *vis-à-vis* President Bhutto.

The third important consideration was that of Soviet military and diplomatic backing—the bitter fruit of which Pakistan has already tasted in the recent past. The existence of the Moscow-Delhi axis formalized by the Indo-Soviet treaty and the supply of sophisticated weapons by Moscow in pursuance of the treaty, together with India's capability of producing its own arsenals were the factors that heavily weighed against Pakistan's relatively weak military position. While factories in India had been manufacturing tanks and aircraft, Pakistan, was not in a position to do the same. Extensive military aid from the United States in the near future seemed a distant possibility. American assistance will be forthcoming if Pakistan's security is considered vital to US strategic interests in Asia. Chinese arms no doubt had filled the gap but they were no substitute for the Soviet sophisticated weapons delivered to India.

Fourthly, Pakistan was beset with manifold internal problems of a complex nature, such as labour and language controversy. Its economy had been virtually at a standstill for the past two years. The crisis in East Pakistan which culminated in the war with India had caused widespread disruption in economic activity.[2] Politically it had to evolve a federal democratic framework acceptable to all the provinces. In the midst of this situation, the wise course for Pakistan was to divert its energies and pool its resources to put its house in order. Therefore, Pakistan had to gear all its efforts to prevent another showdown with India unless it was forced upon it. Its past experience of wars with India proved that they solved no problem. Thrice in the past Pakistan had been at war with India without securing a solution of the Kashmir problem.

Finally, it was not a question of Pakistan's choosing a way with India and 'Bangla Desh'. Soviet interest, as was evident from its revived notion of an Asian Collective Security scheme following the 1971 India-Pakistan war, was exerting decisive influence on the happenings in the subcontinent. Moscow's desire for peace and stability in the region was well reflected in Premier Kosygin's offer to help in the settlement of 'disputable issues',[3] and his advice to President Bhutto to recognize 'Bangla Desh'.[4] Of vital importance to Moscow's scheme is the normalization of relations between the states of the subcontinent. Continued enmity between India and Pakistan and the latter's friendship with China are the two major impediments to the realization of the scheme which is primarily designed as a bulwark for containing Chinese influence in South Asia and consolidating the Kremlin's position there. For a long time, the Soviet Union has been anxiously looking for an overland trade route to India. Not only that, it is also seeking to shorten its access to the Indian Ocean. In view of these Soviet aims, Pakistan's adamant posture *vis-à-vis* India would have been deprecated. And one need not recall here the past consequences of incurring Soviet displeasure. Pakistan has certain 'sensitive' areas where internal dissensions can be fomented with foreign assistance. It would not be out of place to mention what Mr Kosygin said during President Bhutto's visit to the Soviet Union. While justifying the Soviet role in the East Pakistan crisis, he remarked: 'If history were to be repeated, we would take again the same stand'.[5]

It was under these prevailing circumstances that Pakistan was compelled to come to terms with India. If peace with India was a pressing need of the time, so was a just and honourable settlement based on the principles of sovereign equality and territorial independence of nations. Any further humiliation in the form of an unequal peace settlement with Delhi could not be acceptable to the Pakistani masses. The press,[6] the political parties and different pressure groups were vocal and emphatic in their assertions that national honour should not be compromised at the forthcoming summit. There is no denying the fact that the task for President Bhutto in the days ahead at Simla were formidable and challenging. A person who once followed a policy of confrontation with India was now compelled by the force of circumstances and the prevailing objective conditions to initiate talks with that country. In an unequal position with no political leverage, President Bhutto was to negotiate with his Indian counterpart who held all the cards. He was fully aware that if he failed at Simla in reaching an agreement with India, it would be made an issue by his political opponents at home. Before his departure for Simla, he undertook a tour of fourteen Muslim and African countries to consolidate his position against India and win diplomatic backing from the third world for his stand on the issues of 'Bangla Desh' and POWs. At home, his position was no doubt strengthened by the support he received from all sections of the people irrespective of their party affiliations and policy differences. Nevertheless, the support was not unqualified. President Bhutto had time and again assured the people that he would not barter away the interests of Pakistan for the sake of peace with India.[7]

As for the reasons for India's acceptance of Pakistan's offer, a number of internal and external considerations could have prevailed with the Indian decision-makers. Till the end of January 1972, India was talking as a victorious power, laying down preconditions for talks such as the recognition of 'Bangla Desh',[8] the adjustments on the CFL in Kashmir,[9] and an overall settlement of disputes.[10] It was after mid-February that a change occurred in the rigid stance and Delhi expressed its willingness for direct talks 'at any time at any level and without preconditions'.[11] India firmly rejected the charge that it wanted to negotiate with Pakistan from the position of a victor to impose a humiliating settlement.[12] As a matter of fact India moved from its position not because of goodwill for Pakistan but for certain considerations and mental reservations about the future.

One of the considerations that might have influenced India was the prevailing unfavourable international opinion against India's illegal intervention in East Pakistan.[13] The UN resolutions of 7 and 21 December 1971 made India realize that it was fast losing international support and that it must mend its ways before it was too late. Even the British press that had generally upheld the Indian cause before and during the war was now suggesting to Mrs Gandhi to mend the fences with Pakistan. With the United States and China on Pakistan's side, Delhi had now the blessings of Moscow which, because of its own strategic reasons, was not in favour of continued confrontation between India and Pakistan.[14] It was reported that during the war, Moscow exerted pressure on Delhi to cease fire on the Western front[15] when the latter was out to destroy West Pakistan.[16] Following the war also, the Soviet Union continued to call for peace in the subcontinent. The Sino-American rapprochement, coming in the wake of the changed situation in the subcontinent, also had the effect of softening Delhi's bellicose mood. It is not without significance that India's announcement on 19 February expressing its willingness to enter into talks without preconditions came on the eve of Nixon-Chou negotiations in Peking.

Apart from the exigencies of the international situation, India was motivated to negotiate with Pakistan because of India's desire for a confederation as was reflected in its suggestion for an economic union between India, Pakistan, and 'Bangla Desh'. Putting forward the idea, the Indian Foreign Secretary, Mr T. N. Kaul, said that the new union could subsequently be extended to cover Nepal and other countries of the region.[17] No less meaningful was Mrs Gandhi's call to the Asian countries to take a lesson from the European countries to forge cooperation and friendship.[18] Of equal significance was the Indian Defence Minister's proposal that 'India, Bangla Desh and Pakistan should jointly resist any outside interference in the affairs of the subcontinent'.[19] These statements and suggestions well indicate the direction in which Indian strategy was moving step by step. After having dismembered Pakistan, India has obliterated the threat to its dominance and emerged as a strong country whose authority in the region is now indisputable. The Chinese challenge could be countered with Soviet backing. With a mutilated Pakistan reduced in size and population and a protegé, 'Bangla Desh', India would easily maintain its hegemony in the confederation scheme. Therefore, to realize the objective, Pakistan was to be appeased by a show of leniency in the initial period. By agreeing to talk without preconditions, India actually expected gains out of its modified approach. It was calculated that a pacified and friendly Pakistan would be less dependent on China, thus China's influence in the region that poses a threat to India's future scheme could be easily done away with.

Another cause of India's softened attitude was Pakistan's weak position. A dismembered, defeated, militarily and economically weak Pakistan was least likely to pose a threat to India's security. Hence the settlement of disputes with it would serve a double purpose: it would improve India's image in the world community and create an atmosphere conducive to the realization of its long-term planning. Besides, India must have considered that in the event of Pakistan going off the track, its 93,000 POWs and large territory under Indian occupation could be used as a lever to extract concessions. The breakdown of the dialogue would leave Pakistan's crucial issues unsettled and President Bhutto's position exposed to danger at home.

Another weighty factor was the question of Kashmir which India sought to settle once and for all. While Pakistan's immediate objectives in matters of priority were to secure the withdrawal of Indian troops from its territory and the release of its POWs, India's major concern was Kashmir. With time in its favour and all cards in its hands, India could not afford to miss the chance of exploiting the situation to its benefit. What India actually wanted was the conversion of the CFL with certain adjustments into an international border. This was well evinced in the Indian Defence Minister's repeated assertions[20] that

India would not withdraw from Pakistan's territory until a border settlement was reached with it and that India wanted the CFL to be adjusted and made into an international frontier. Thus, long before the Simla Agreement, troop pull-out was tied up with border adjustments in Jammu and Kashmir.

Soviet pressure could also have been at work persuading Mrs Gandhi to normalize relations with Islamabad. Although Premier Kosygin's offer of help in the settlement of disputes did not receive a favourable response from India, where it was reported to have been described 'as premature if not superfluous',[21] the Soviet Union was working behind the scenes to persuade both the feuding parties to come to the negotiation table. President Bhutto in an interview to the *Guardian* (London) on 29 February disclosed that the initiative for talks with India had been taken through the Soviet embassy in Islamabad. That at Simla, India succumbed to Soviet pressure was the accusation levelled by the Jan Sangh Party leader, Mr Vajpayee.[22] Keeping in view Moscow's close alliance with Dehli, its role in shaping the course of events in the subcontinent and its revived interest in the Asian Collective Security scheme, it can be presumed that its influence has had a bearing on India's subsequent softened attitude towards Pakistan.

With these motivations, India decided to meet Pakistan at the negotiation table. The 'modalities' of the forthcoming summit were 'settled' and 'the subjects to be discussed' were 'defined'[23] at the meeting of the India-Pakistan emissaries, held on 30 April 1972. Although the time for the summit fixed by the emissaries was the end of May or the beginning of June, due to preoccupation of both the leaders, the summit could not be held until 28 June 1972.

It was the first India-Pakistan dialogue at the highest level since the Tashkent meeting. The two leaders met with diametrically opposite views. India wanted to settle all disputes, particularly Kashmir in one go, while Pakistan emphasizing the step by step approach sought to hold it up for the time being till the major issues of POWs and withdrawal were satisfactorily settled. The meeting lasted for five days. Despite the fact that the subjects to be discussed were agreed upon in the preceding April, the question of agenda was raised again by the Indian officials. And at a time when it appeared that the summit would end in fiasco, both the leaders decided to meet without an agenda. After much argumentation by both sides and exchange of drafts between the two, an agreement was reached on 2 July, both sides 'making eleventh hour concessions when a communique admitting their agreement to disagree was already being drafted'.[24] The Agreement provided *inter alia* for the withdrawal of forces to the India-Pakistan border and the maintenance of *status quo* in Jammu and Kashmir. The reaction to the Agreement in both the countries was generally favourable. With the exception of the Jan Sangh Party and a few socialist members, the accord was generally acclaimed in India. The NAP and the JUI in Pakistan hailed the agreement. The NAP welcomed it because it was in accord with its party manifesto. However, other smaller but influential right-wing parties were not happy with the accord.[25] It has been decried as a 'no-war' pact, a surrender worse than Tashkent, which solved no basic issues. Before examining the soundness of the objections in the light of a comparative analysis of the provisions of the Simla and the Tashkent Agreements, it is pertinent to examine the background of both.

The Tashkent and the Simla pacts were signed in entirely different circumstances. India, after having accused Pakistan of sending 'infiltrators' in Kashmir, crossed the CFL on 24 August 1965. This was admitted by the Indian Defence Minister. And the same day it seized two posts of Azad Kashmir in the Titwal sector and later overran the Haji Pir pass. Not content with these gains, Indian troops advanced, on 6 September, 'across the frontier towards Lahore and towards Sialkot'.[26] In 1965, fighting was limited to West Pakistan, whereas the 1971 war engulfed both the wings and resulted in the separation of the eastern wing. Both in 1965 and in 1971, India crossed the international border using different excuses.

As for the position of the two parties at Tashkent and Simla, Pakistan met India at Tashkent as an equal. It was not a vanquished country in 1965. Pakistan had, under its occupation 1617 sq. miles of Indian territory as against its 446 sq. miles under Indian occupation.[27] Pakistan had suffered less casualties and captured more POWs. More important was the fact that Pakistan was one united country. This situation had put President Ayub in a favourable position to talk on equal terms with his Indian counterpart. The Indian Prime Minister, Mr Shastri, who had succeeded the late Mr Nehru was no equal to his predecessor in popularity and statesmanship. Besides, the Indian army had failed in achieving its military objective i.e., capture of Lahore. On the other hand, while President Ayub had no direct mandate from his people, he was constitutionally more powerful than the late Mr Shastri. Pakistan came to Simla as a loser, reduced in size and population and deprived of four divisions of its army and large areas of its territory. Although President Bhutto was an elected leader, the existing circumstances had adversely affected his bargaining capacity.

The agreement at Tashkent was made possible because of the Soviet efforts to bring the warring parties to the conference table. By so doing Moscow sought, on the one hand, to offset the growing Chinese influence, and on the other, to upgrade its own prestige in that region. That Moscow exerted pressure on the Indian Prime Minister, Mr Shastri, who had earlier ruled out the possibility of any talks over Kashmir is borne out by Clause I of the agreement which said that Jammu and Kashmir was discussed by both the sides. The shift in Moscow's stand on Kashmir did not go without criticism by a section of the Indian press which accused it of being partial.[28] It was reported that before the Tashkent meeting, the Indian Foreign Minister, Mr Swaran Singh, was summoned to Moscow because the latter was irked at the statements of the Indian leaders that Kashmir was not a matter for discussion and they did not expect much to come out of the Shastri-Ayub meeting.[29]

Since the post-Tashkent era, there had been significant changes in the political equation in Asia. With China emerging as a superpower on its north, having growing nuclear capability and Pakistan responding unfavourably to the proposed Asian Security scheme, Moscow decided to discard its pre-Tashkent neutral stance and establish close relations with Delhi. In a brief span of five years, Soviet policy towards India and Pakistan was completely overhauled and later in 1971 it was transformed into forthright support to India. With all the big powers taking side of either of the parties in the 1971 war, none had a leverage left in either of the countries. Hence the direct negotiations at Simla. Despite the reorientation of the Soviet policy, its major objective in the subcontinent remained the same, that is, normalization of India-Pakistan relations—a prerequisite to the realization of its security scheme.

Therefore, the Agreements should be studied in the light of this prevailing state of affairs in the subcontinent. Instead of undertaking a clause by clause comparison of the two, an attempt is made to analyse the provisions under different titles, which are the writer's own and given for sorting out the matter under study.

Normalization of Relations

The prime objective of the Tashkent and the Simla accords was, as stated in their respective preambles, to normalize relations between India and Pakistan so that the two countries should work for the progress and welfare of their people. At Tashkent both the parties declared their 'firm resolve to restore normal and peaceful relations between their countries',[30] the Simla accord makes an advance on its precursor by declaring the intent of the two governments to 'put an end to the conflict and confrontation'[31] and to live in 'peaceful co-existence'.[32] To realize this common purpose both countries pursued different approaches. Pakistan's stand at Tashkent was that since Kashmir was the basic cause of conflict, it should be settled first and the relations should be normalized subsequently. India, on the other hand, held that normalization should precede the solution of the problem. That India's step by step formula prevailed at Tashkent was evident from the document itself. Clauses V and VI of the Agreement called for the restoration of diplomatic, economic and trade relations, whereas the 'matters of direct concern' were to be discussed at future meetings of both 'at the highest and other levels'.[33] Simla witnessed a complete reversal of the attitudes of both. Because of the changed situation Pakistan gave up its previous approach in favour of a settlement on a piecemeal basis. Conversely, India, considering the time opportune, sought a package deal on Kashmir. However, it was Pakistan's approach that gained ground. Para III of the Simla accord calls for different steps, excluding the resumption of diplomatic relations, to 'normalize relations between the two countries step by step'. Like Tashkent, the Simla accord also left the settlement of basic issues for future negotiations between the two. This was described as President Bhutto's major 'accomplishment' in 'breaking her (Mrs Gandhi's) resolve to wrap up all outstanding issues in a package deal.'[34] However, the latest Indian tactics of making the withdrawal dependent on the completion of delineation in Kashmir indicate that what was conceded at Simla, now appears to be coming to a naught. Before the relations return to normal and the POWs are repatriated, India will seek to settle Kashmir according to its own liking.

Insofar as steps towards normalization are concerned, both Agreements expressed the intent of the two parties to restore economic and trade relations, communication and cultural exchanges. While at Tashkent both countries decided to restore diplomatic relations, the

Simla accord puts off the matter for future meetings of the two countries. In pursuance of the Tashkent provisions, diplomatic, trade, economic relations and communication were resumed, whereas the Simla accord still awaits its implementation.

Bilateralism

Despite the fact that the Tashkent Declaration was signed under Soviet auspices and Moscow was a witness to it, the Agreement neither provided for the mediation of a third party in future India-Pakistan talks nor did it preclude Pakistan from raising the issue at the UN. Under it Pakistan had made no commitments of that kind.[35] Clause IX called for continued meetings between the two countries on 'matters of direct concern to both'. Whereas under Clause II (para II) of the Simla accord both parties are specifically committed to 'settle their differences by peaceful means through bilateral negotiations or by any other peaceful means mutually agreed upon between them'. The Clause has raised much apprehension in Pakistan. It has been contended that the UN role in Kashmir is by-passed and that it amounts to a waiver on the part of Pakistan of all the UN resolutions[36] on Kashmir. Commenting on the Agreement and its possible repercussions in the subcontinent, *The Times* (London) in its editorial on 4 July 1972, expressed that 'Kashmir will cease to be an international question...when a Kashmir boundary has been finally settled the UN might be asked to the final ceremony to pronounce a blessing'. Expressing similar opinion, *The Guardian* (weekly) said that in response to Mrs Gandhi's concession to withdraw from the occupied areas, 'Mr Bhutto has removed the Kashmir issue from international surveillance; which is the first step towards obliterating it as a source of strife'.[37] This interpretation of the Clause has been officially repudiated. President Bhutto in his speech to the National Assembly on 14 July 1972 said that the accord did not prevent Pakistan from reagitating Kashmir in the UN. On another occasion he pointed out that the Clause does not contain the phrase 'exclusively' bilateral negotiations[38]—a word that India feverishly attempted[39] to include in the Clause—therefore, Pakistan is not restrained from re-exploring the possibilities of the settlement in the UN. In pursuance of these averments, the Pakistan government has not withdrawn Kashmir from the UN and it has apprised the UN of its intention to retain the UN observers in Kashmir.

Pakistan's interpretation of the Clause certainly did not fit in with the Indian strategy of taking the issue out of the UN. Continued presence of Kashmir on the UN agenda causes India much embarrassment and exposes its double standard policy. It also belies India's claim that Kashmir is its internal matter. Therefore, with conditions in its favour, India, since the end of the December war, has been actively moving step by step towards its ultimate objective. Its first step was the denial of the existence of the CFL in Kashmir and refusal to hold flag meetings on truce violations 'in the presence of the UN observers'. This was followed by getting recorded the principle of bilateralism in the Agreement. And finally with the desired end in sight, India has now asked for the removal of the UN observers. Disagreeing with Pakistan's contention, Mrs Gandhi said: 'We agreed to bilateralism as far as every issue is concerned.'[40] Since 'every issue' includes Kashmir also, therefore, the UN 'observers have no role to play',[41] as such they should be recalled from the area. Later speaking in the Parliament on 31 July, the Indian Foreign Minister highlighted the bilateral aspect of the Agreement.

The acceptance of the principle of bilateralism was one of the major concessions that Mrs Gandhi won at Simla.[42] But was it really India's 'major diplomatic victory' as has been contended?[43] No doubt, the UN principles shall govern the relations between the two countries (Clause I, para II) and the commitment of both to bilateralism, is well within the meaning of Article 33 of the UN Charter which provides *inter alia* for 'other peaceful means' of parties' choice. True, the phrase 'exclusively bilateral' is not used in the Clause and the phraseology of the Agreement does not specifically prevent Pakistan from reagitating the issue at the UN. Also there is no denying the fact that the UN has failed to settle the matter and therefore there is no harm in exploring other unattempted means. But the UN at least provides a forum for exposing India's intransigence and emphasizes the international character of the dispute. Pakistan's resorting to the UN would mean failure of bilateralism. It might be argued that so long as the Simla accord subsists Pakistan is precluded from raising the matter in the world body. As has been declared by President Bhutto, if 'bilateral negotiations fail; then there is nothing to stop us from the process of going to the United Nations'.[44] Viewed in this light, the Clause augurs well for India's plan to prevent Pakistan from reopening the issue in the UN. However, the Clause does not make it obligatory on Pakistan to withdraw the case from the UN or to ask that body to remove its team of 45 observers from Jammu and Kashmir. At the most the Clause will keep the matter dormant in the UN as long as bilateral negotiations continue under the Simla provisions.

Principle of Non-Interference

The principle of non-intervention as stated in the Tashkent and Simla Agreements seems at first glance, to be merely a formal expression which usually finds its place in other bilateral and multilateral agreements. In view of Article 2(4) of the UN Charter, such protestations in pacts would appear to be a reaffirmation of the parties' existing obligations unless they are studied in the background of the existing conditions and the prevailing attitudes of the parties concerned. The Clauses in the Tashkent and the Simla accords relating to non-intervention derive their importance from the existing situation and the relative stance of the two parties towards each other. Clause III of the Tashkent Declaration which laid down that India-Pakistan relations 'shall be based on the principle of non-interference...' would be without significance if not read with its Clause I which states *inter alia* that 'Jammu and Kashmir was discussed and each of the sides put forth its respective position'. India's position on Kashmir was that it considered it a part of its territory and hence its internal matter. According to this Clause India could interpret Pakistan's acts of assistance to the Kashmiri freedom fighters as interference in its 'internal affairs'. Insofar as the observance of this provision by India is concerned, hardly a month had passed after the signing of the Tashkent Agreement, when India reverted to its old policy of intervening in Pakistan's affairs by declaring support to 'the principle of a separate State for the Pukhtoons'.[45]

At Simla, the objective condition was that India intervened in the internal matters of Pakistan, first by assisting, arming, and training East Pakistan's secessionists, and then by resorting to military action in that area. After having achieved its aim of separating East Pakistan, India could conveniently agree to adhere to the principle of non-interference and respect for what was left of Pakistan's territory. Does the commitment 'to respect each other's national unity, territorial integrity, political independence and sovereign equality' mean that

India has reconciled to Pakistan's existence as a separate independent nation and that it has no further political or military designs against what is left of Pakistan? True, the intent of the parties to the Agreement gives reality to their pronouncements. But of much importance are the intent and action of the stronger party insofar as the observance of declared principles is concerned. Significantly, the Simla accord by recognizing the existence of the question of Jammu and Kashmir has placed the problem outside the purview of the application of the principle of non-interference.

Renunciation of Force

Under both the Tashkent and the Simla Agreements, force as a means of settling disputes was renounced by the signatories. In contents and meaning, Article I of the former is similar to Clause VI (para II) of the latter. Both were described as 'no-war pacts' and subjected to strong criticism in the country. Their relevant stipulations do not convey the meaning that the parties are entering into a no-war pact. Both are merely agreements declaring the intention of the parties to refrain from the use of force. They cannot be termed as contracts or treaties creating obligations binding the contracting parties. It might be argued that renunciation of force in settling disputes is as good as a no-war pact. But it is one thing to state an already existing obligation as under the UN Charter, to which both parties are signatories, and quite another to enter into a bilateral no-war treaty. The phraseology of the provisions of both well indicates that force is renounced in accordance with the UN Charter, whose Article 51, nevertheless, recognizes the right of self-defence.

Clause I of the Tashkent Declaration laid down that the parties 'reaffirm their obligation under the Charter not to have recourse to force and to settle their disputes through peaceful means'. This was 'far from the no-war declaration' that could 'have assured the Indians that Kashmir was closed to future violence'.[46] There is no denying the fact that India aimed at a no-war pact. Indicative of this was the Indian Prime Minister Shastri's speech on 4 January 1966 at the opening of the summit in which he emphasized the need for a no-war agreement and the draft proposed to that effect which was rejected by Pakistan.[47] The ink had hardly dried on the Declaration when India began giving its own interpretation of the Clause, claiming that

Pakistan, by agreeing to renounce force, had virtually signed a no-war pact. Needless to, that Pakistan firmly rejected India's interpretation and declared that the Agreement did not preclude Pakistan from espousing the cause of the Kashmiris.[48]

Likewise at Simla, India had come out with humiliating terms. It was reported that India submitted drafts with such terms as reduction in Pakistan armed forces in proportion to its population and regular supervision by India of Pakistan's ordnance factories.[49] Despite Indian pressure, what Pakistan agreed to at Simla was the abstention from the use of force in accordance with the UN Charter. Clause VI (para II) stipulates: 'That in accordance with the Charter of the United Nations, they will refrain from the threat or use of force against the territorial integrity or political independence of each other'. This obviously means that the commitment is made under the UN Charter which also recognizes the right of self-defence. This Clause appears to be a logical product of the preceding Clauses I and II. If the relations between the two countries are to be governed in accordance with the UN principles and the outstanding disputes are to be settled peacefully through bilateral negotiations then it naturally follows that the parties 'will refrain from the threat or use of force.'

Return of the POWs

At Tashkent the release of the POWs was one of the side issues which was resolved by the agreement between the two parties 'to carry out the repatriation of the prisoners of war'.[50] Accordingly about 1000 POWs held by both sides[51] were released by the end of January 1966. With the forces withdrawn to their respective sides of the border and the POWs set free, the consequences of the war were removed. While at Simla, the return of 93,000 POWs was one of the basic issues, the settlement of which was procrastinated until the future summit, which was delayed because of Pakistan's alleged backout[52] on the recognition of 'Bangla Desh'.

In clear violation of the Geneva Conventions and the Security Council resolution of 21 December, India is protracting the incarceration of the POWs, and it will continue to do so unless its two preconditions are fulfilled. The first oft-repeated one is the recognition of 'Bangla Desh' by Pakistan. It is contended that Pakistan forces in the eastern sector surrendered to the Joint Command of India and

'Bangla Desh' forces, therefore, 'Bangla Desh's' approval to their repatriation is essential. And to that effect India had assured Sheikh Mujib that it would not release the POWs until Pakistan had accepted the reality of 'Bangla Desh'. Not only that but India would cooperate 'in holding trials of those persons who had committed crimes against the people of Bangla Desh'.[53]

From the legal point of view India's argument does not hold good. At the time when fighting broke out in East Pakistan between the Indian and Pakistani forces, 'Bangla Desh' was actually not in existence at all. The Pakistan army was fighting on its own territory and not on that of 'Bangla Desh'. Not a single country had recognized the existence of 'Bangla Desh' or for that matter its 'liberating forces'. Even the Indian recognition came on 6 December i.e., two days after the war had escalated into West Pakistan. Before 16 December the Indian General Manekshaw repeatedly appealed[54] to the Pakistan army to surrender to the Indian forces. Subsequently India manipulated the surrender document to its advantage by inserting in it provisions of its own liking.

The reasons for India's insistence on the recognition of 'Bangla Desh' are obvious. After having lost much for the creation of a client state, India cannot alienate the goodwill of that 'state'. India and 'Bangla Desh' consider the POWs as an effective lever to extract recognition from Pakistan. The Chinese veto on 'Bangla Desh's' entry in the UN has further raised the importance of Pakistan's acceptance of the Dhaka 'government'. Another reason stronger than the first is India's persistent and constant attempts to frustrate the ideological basis of Pakistan. India considers that Pakistan's formal acceptance will strike a total blow to the two-nation theory.

In fact what India actually seeks, besides the recognition of 'Bangla Desh', is a settlement of the Kashmir dispute; Kashmir is India's major concern, therefore, the issue of the POWs is tied up with its settlement. Illustrative of this is Mrs Gandhi's statement: 'the return of prisoners of war depends on the establishment of peace'.[55] Also before the Agreement she had made it clear that she would not release them without firm assurances that 'they will not be used to attack us again.'[56] Having secured the assurances in the Agreement on bilateralism and renunciation of force India now wants frontier adjustments in Kashmir. Criticizing Mrs Gandhi's attitude, a leading British daily editorialized: 'It is, of course, quite wrong that she should relate the question of prisoners of war to her ambitions in Kashmir.

The frontier adjustments that she seeks would extend the Indian frontier beyond its 1971 line. Kashmir is written on her heart...'[57] Given such Indian designs, there is no guarantee that Pakistan's recognition of 'Bangla Desh' will bring forth the release of its POWs.

Withdrawal of Troops

In both the Tashkent and the Simla Agreements, there are provisions for troop pull-outs, but with certain fundamental differences: (i) The former called for the withdrawal of 'armed personnel' while the latter for the pull out of 'India-Pakistan forces'; (ii) Under Clause II of the Tashkent Declaration withdrawal 'to the position held prior to 5 August 1965' was to take place in all sectors including Jammu and Kashmir. The Simla Agreement, for the time being, limits it to the international border of India and Pakistan; (iii) The former fixed a deadline i.e., 25 February 1966, for the completion of that task, whereas the latter sets a limit of 30 days to commence from the period of its ratification.

The reasons for this difference recline in the situation that prevailed at the time the two Agreements were signed. The use of the phrase 'armed personnel' instead of armed forces or troops in the Tashkent Declaration was an endorsement of the Indian version of the cause of conflict—the alleged 'infiltration' by Pakistani armed personnel into Kashmir. Although the UN Security Council has used the same expression in its resolution of 20 September 1965, its use in the Declaration, nevertheless, signified, besides the acceptance of India's demand for the disengagement of the alleged infiltrators, an oblique recognition that there had been 'armed infiltration' in the disputed area. Despite this, the Tashkent Agreement 'offered the chance of disengagement with some semblance of honour.'[58] India, by agreeing to mutual withdrawal, was to move back from territory across the 1949 CFL in Kashmir which it had firmly said it would not give up. That the disengagement materialized before the set deadline was the only major achievement of the Tashkent Declaration. One may argue that both countries, according to the rules of International Law and the Security Council resolution of 20 September 1965, were under an obligation to move back to their pre-war position. But principles of International Law and the UN resolutions are honoured more in their non-observance and violation. And Pakistan's past experience with India in this regard was certainly not a happy one. Soon after Tashkent, it became evident that India was resiling from its commitments. In clear violation of the provisions, it refused to withdraw from three points in the Sialkot sector; it continued to describe Kashmir non-negotiable; and it reverted to its policy of support to 'Pukhtunistan'.

As for the Simla accord, withdrawal was to take place to the India-Pakistan border excluding the CFL in Jammu and Kashmir. The reasons are pretty obvious: Pakistan's relatively weak position at Simla and the distinct difference of territorial gain and loss of each in the 1965 and 1971 wars. In 1965 Pakistan was in possession of 1617 sq. miles of Indian territory including 340 sq. miles in Chamb area, as against the loss of 446 sq. miles including 182 in Azad Kashmir. These figures were contested by India which claimed that it was in possession of 740 sq. miles of Pakistan's territory as against the loss of 210 sq. miles.[59] Without denying the possibility of exaggeration from both sides, the fact remains that Pakistan had successfully resisted the Indian attack and in Kashmir it was in a fairly advantageous position. At Simla the positions were reversed. It was India that had made significant gains across the international border and the CFL in Jammu and Kashmir. Pakistan had lost to India a vast tract of 5139 sq. miles in the west wing and 479.96 sq. miles in Kashmir. Whereas Indian loss was minimal: 69 sq. miles of its territory and 52.57 sq. miles in Jammu and Kashmir.[60] Forty strategically important mountain outposts around Kargil were also under Indian occupation.[61]

Obviously, India had a good opportunity to exploit this situation to its benefit. After having lost the chance of annihilating West Pakistan's military strength, Mrs Gandhi could not let this opportunity slip out of her hands. Acting on the strong conviction that reoccupation of the lost territory was Pakistan's main concern, she made it a point to exploit Pakistan's weakness in order to achieve as much political and strategic gains in Kashmir as was possible under the circumstances. India cleverly manipulated the upcoming events at Simla: First, by public pronouncements that every new war will create a new CFL implying thereby to obliterate the UN presence in the disputed area; then by protracting the Simla talks on the question of the previously agreed agenda; and finally by agreeing willy-nilly to withdraw from Pakistan's territory after securing Pakistan's acceptance to 'respect the line of control in Jammu and Kashmir resulting from the ceasefire of December 1971'. No doubt by agreeing to withdraw, Mrs Gandhi 'has made a big concession to Mr Bhutto',[62] but in return she 'won two major concessions,' a promise to respect the CFL and an agreement to settle disputes bilaterally.[63]

That India signed the Agreement with certain mental reservations is borne out by its subsequent delaying tactics on troop pull-outs. Having made it a point not to withdraw without securing tactical gains in Kashmir, India linked the withdrawal to the delineation of the entire line of control in the disputed area. This was a preconceived and well thought out manoeuvre. Long before the Agreement India had related the issue to border adjustments in Jammu and Kashmir.[64] Neither the Simla accord nor the subsequent Delhi agreement makes the disengagement dependent on the marking of the line of control. The withdrawal which was to be effected before 4 September, was first postponed to 15 September and now is delayed till the 'entire line will be delineated'.[65] Actually before the start of the next summit for the final settlement of Jammu and Kashmir, India aspires to finish off the task of territorial adjustment in Kashmir to include the control of the Kargil area in order to block Pakistan's road link with China. So that at the next summit, India can present Pakistan with a *fait accompli*: a partitioned Kashmir on the basis of delineation of its choice.

Kashmir

Insofar as the settlement of the dispute was concerned, Pakistan visibly gained nothing at Tashkent. The Tashkent Agreement because it 'entailed no betrayal of Indian interest in Kashmir appeared as a triumph for Indian diplomacy'.[66] The Agreement relegated the Kashmir issue. The purpose of reactivating and internationalizing the issue, that was achieved by the war, was lost at Tashkent.

Clause I of the Tashkent Declaration stated: '... that Jammu and Kashmir was discussed and each of the sides put forth its respective position.' This shows: (i) that the Agreement recorded that discussion on Jammu and Kashmir had taken place at Tashkent; (ii) that the Declaration did not recognize Jammu and Kashmir as a dispute, for there is no indication of it; (iii) and that the discussion ended without any agreement between the two sides or any concessions from either side to the other. Pakistan stuck to its position that Kashmir was a disputed area and India remained firm in its stand that Kashmir was India's internal matter and, therefore, non-negotiable.

It might be argued in defence that a country does not discuss its internal matters with a foreign state. India, which had been persistently refusing to talk about the issue, had to agree at Tashkent not only to discuss the matter with Pakistan but to have it recorded in the Declaration. Although none of the Clauses specifically provided for future talks on Kashmir, Clause IX calling for the meetings of both 'on matters of direct concern' cannot be interpreted as excluding Kashmir.[67] Accordingly, India was bound to talk and as a matter of fact it did not refuse to discuss Kashmir; what it actually denied was the acceptance of it as a dispute. This was clearly borne out at Tashkent and in the post-Tashkent era. The first meeting of the Foreign Ministers of India-Pakistan in March 1966 ended without making any significant progress towards the settlement of the dispute. The Indian attitude remained unchanged: its sovereignty over Jammu and Kashmir was not negotiable.[68]

Despite all the inferences and interpretations of the vague Clause, the fact remains that the Agreement neither resolved the basic issue nor did it make a start towards its settlement. The non-recognition of the existence of the Kashmir problem and the conspicuous omission of the word problem or question in the Clause consolidated India's position and enabled it to interpret Pakistan's future assistance to the people of Kashmir as interference in its internal matter. Kashmir was thus relegated, but Pakistan made no commitments under the Declaration.

The questions raised by some people about the Simla accord are: Is there any undertaking by Pakistan regarding Kashmir? Was there a secret agreement between President Bhutto and Mrs Gandhi on the fate of Kashmir? It has been repeatedly asserted by President Bhutto that he has not entered into any secret deal with India.[69] Besides, both being elected leaders of their respective countries, they must have realized that secret agreements in a democratic era seldom create binding obligations on the parties. As for the first question, Pakistan has made commitments not on the future of Kashmir, but on the method of resolving the dispute about it. Throughout the conference India insisted on a package deal on Kashmir. With that purpose, it proposed to make the CFL in Kashmir an international border.[70] Pakistan, however, resisted Indian pressure and the summit ended by holding the issue in abeyance till the next meeting of the two.

The last para of the accord makes a mention of Jammu and Kashmir as one of the 'questions' for the 'final settlement' of which both have agreed to 'meet again at a mutually convenient time in the future...' The para thus takes a step forward on Clause I of its precursor by: (i) describing Jammu and Kashmir as a question; and (ii) calling for future meetings for its final settlement. This was Pakistan's major achievement since 'India has conceded publicly that Kashmir is, in fact, in dispute'.[71] This was, however, contested by the Indian officials who held that the Agreement did not speak of any dispute and that Pakistan should vacate the occupied areas of Kashmir.[72] By signing the Agreement India did not move an inch from its previous stand on Kashmir. Illustrative of this is the Indian Foreign Minister's statement on 31 July 1972 that the accession of Kashmir to India 'is complete and final' and that India's sovereignty over Kashmir is 'not negotiable'. Speaking in terms of Clause II (para IV), India's position affects neither Pakistan's stand nor the internationally recognized status of Jammu and Kashmir.

However, the importance of the last para is considerably affected by Clause II (para IV) which reads: 'In Jammu and Kashmir the line of control resulting from the ceasefire of 17 December 1971, shall be respected by both sides without prejudice to the recognized position of either side...' This means: (i) That the India-Pakistan forces will not withdraw to the CFL in Jammu and Kashmir; (ii) That the *status quo* shall not affect the stand of either of the parties; (iii) That the line of control shall not be unilaterally altered by force. The consequences following the implementation of the Clause will be: (i) Pakistan will retain Chamb in Kashmir; (ii) India will continue to control the Kargil area; and (iii) India will get back the two strategic posts in the Lipa valley which were recaptured by Pakistan after the ceasefire. The posts being fifteen miles away from Muzaffarabad, the capital of Azad Kashmir, are considered to be strategically important for the defence of that area.

With the purpose of obliterating the UN presence in Kashmir, India has manipulated to get the above-stated provision recorded in the Agreement. The Clause is not in conformity with the Security Council resolution of 21 December 1971 which called upon both parties to return to the positions that 'fully respect the Ceasefire Line in Jammu and Kashmir...' Accordingly India has come out with the claim that the resolution has now been superseded by the Simla Agreement. As a matter of fact the UN resolutions remain valid unless and until they are repealed, modified or annulled by subsequent UN resolutions.

It is contended that the provision to maintain the *status quo* and the use of the term 'line of control' strengthen India's case against the continued presence of the UN. Strictly speaking in the context of the said Clause the line is to be respected 'without prejudice to the recognised position of either side.' Pakistan's *locus standi* on the CFL and Kashmir is internationally known and accepted. The UN resolutions on Kashmir are evidence of the fact that Kashmir is a disputed territory and the CFL is a temporary border in Kashmir between India and Pakistan pending the final settlement of the issue. Therefore, the expression 'without prejudice to the recognised position of either side' coupled with Pakistan's refusal to recall the UN observers from the disputed area has considerably frustrated India's efforts to write off the UN role. The Clause does not prescribe any time limit for the continuance of the *status quo*. Nevertheless, the limit can be inferred from Clause II (para II) which states: '...Pending the final settlement of any of the problems between the two countries, neither side shall unilaterally alter the situation...' This means that the present line is to be respected till the final settlement of Jammu and Kashmir. Therefore, in the event of delay in the settlement, the prolonged continuation of the *status quo* might stabilize the present line in place of the CFL and the line of control might, through usage, acquire the status of an international boundary.

As a matter of fact conversion of the present line into an international border has always been India's purpose. Illustrative of this design are the pre-summit statement of the Indian Defence Minister on 2 February and the Indian proposal during the summit to make the present line a permanent border between India and Pakistan. With this object in view India insisted on delineating the entire line of control while the war had disturbed the CFL only at some places, leaving 90 per cent of the line intact. Of late, India has declared that it harbours no such designs about the line of control.[73] Definitely India will not be satisfied with the present line but will seek to further extend the Indian border in Kashmir. Indicative of this are the various post-Simla statements made by the Indian officials from time to time. Soon after the Agreement Mrs Gandhi claimed Azad Kashmir as part of India.[74] This was followed by another assertion that in future negotiations with Pakistan, India would ask for 5000 sq. kilometres of Kashmir territory, allegedly ceded by Pakistan to China under the 1963 border agreement.[75] It will not be out of place to mention that the veteran Kashmiri leader, Sheikh Abdullah, has strongly rebuffed the idea of partition of Kashmir.[76]

Insofar as the right of self-determination of the people of Kashmir is concerned, the Agreement makes no mention of it. Nevertheless, it does not restrain Pakistan from upholding their cause. Speaking in the National Assembly President Bhutto declared that Pakistan had not withdrawn its support to the Kashmiris and 'if the people of Kashmir start a freedom movement we will be with them, no matter, what the consequences'.[77] After having tried the UN, fought two wars on the dispute, and lost half of the country, the only desirable course for Pakistan is to continue efforts to settle the dispute peacefully without abnegating its support to the Kashmiris. It is high time for the people of Kashmir to intensify their struggle for freedom. Apparently the Agreement does not specifically restrict Pakistan's freedom of action in this regard. However, one cannot overlook the implications of the expression contained in Clause II (para II) that 'pending the final settlement of any of the problems...both shall prevent the organisation, assistance or encouragement of any act detrimental to the maintenance of peaceful and harmonious relations.' In the event of Pakistan's active practical support to the people of Kashmir, India can conveniently invoke this Clause and interpret Pakistan's assistance 'as an act detrimental to the maintenance of peaceful and harmonious relations'.

Summing up the preceding analysis, it can be said that like the Tashkent Declaration, the Simla accord also puts off the basic disputes for future negotiations. Insofar as Kashmir was concerned, the Tashkent Agreement was not a step forward 'but a sharp retreat to the pre-war situation.'[78] The Simla accord, on the other hand, is a step towards a new direction. Despite certain basic differences, 'both Agreements contain almost identical undertaking on peace and harmony between the two countries; both foresee steps being taken to normalize relations and most critical of all, both leave the Kashmir dispute unresolved.'[79] The Tashkent Declaration after having fulfilled its objectives became more or less void for all practical purposes. The Simla accord has yet to prove its credence. It appears from recent developments that the fate of the accord is in the balance. The events illustrating this are: troop movements by India in the disputed area as indicated by President Bhutto on 2 October 1972; unprovoked firing on Pakistani posts in the Kotli sector of Jammu and Kashmir; repeated incidents of inhuman firing on the Pakistani POWs held in the Indian camps; and India's delaying tactics in withdrawal. Despite these incidents it seems most likely that India will eventually withdraw its troops because of its interest in Kashmir and the important area of Hussainiwala, East Punjab, India, presently under Pakistan's occupation.

NOTES

1. Mrs Gandhi's press conference in Prague, *Dawn*, Karachi, 21 June 1972.
2. See the summary of the annual report of the State Bank of Pakistan in *Dawn*, Karachi, 11 September 1972.
3. Ibid., 15 March 1972.
4. *The Daily Telegraph*, London, 4 September 1972.
5. *Dawn*, Karachi, 18 March 1972.
6. See for instance editorials of the *Jang* (Urdu daily), Karachi, 29 June 1972 and *Dawn*, Karachi, 22 June 1972.
7. President Bhutto's interview to ABC and his speeches, *Dawn*, Karachi, 15 May, 25 and 28 June 1972.
8. Mrs Gandhi's statements on 31 December 1971 and 21 January 1972.
9. The Indian Defence Minister's statement on 2 February 1972.
10. Mrs Gandhi's interview to ABC. Text released on 14 May 1972.
11. This was stated by the Indian Representative to the UN on 19 February 1972.
12. This was stated by Mrs Gandhi at her press conference in Prague on 20 June 1972.
13. A study of the events in East Pakistan, recently published by the ICJ, held that India's action in East Pakistan was illegal and could not be justified on the grounds of humanitarian intervention. See *The Events in East Pakistan*, 1971, International Commission of Jurists, Geneva, 1972.
14. Addressing the fifteenth Congress of the Soviet Trade Unions, CPSU, General Secretary, Leonid Brezhnev, said that his country stood 'for the promotion of the closest possible relations with Asian States' and that it was the Soviet 'aim to help strengthen peace in Asia...' *New Times*, Moscow, No. 13, March 1972, p. 11.
15. 'Victors of Bangla Desh' in *The Sunday Times*, London, 19 December 1971, p. 6.
16. President Nixon in his third Annual Foreign Policy Report disclosed that 'India was seriously contemplating...the destruction of Pakistan's military forces in the West'. See the extracts in *Pakistan Horizon*, Karachi, First Quarter, 1972, pp. 168–75.
17. *Dawn*, Karachi, 18 January 1972.
18. Ibid., 2 July 1972.
19. Ibid., 2 June 1972.
20. The Indian Defence Minister's statements in ibid., 18 January and 3 February 1972.
21. Ibid., 17 March 1972.
22. Ibid., 12 July 1972, *The Daily Telegraph*, London, 1 August 1972.
23. Joint statement of India-Pakistan emissaries, *Pakistan Horizon*, Second Quarter, 1972, p. 139.

24. *The Economist*, London, 8 July 1972, p. 16.
25. Council Muslim League, Pakistan Democratic Party, Jamiatul Ulema-e-Pakistan, Jamaat-e-Islami and Tehrik-e-Istiqlal have opposed the Agreement. See for their reactions *Dawn*, Karachi, 4 and 5 July 1972.
26. *The Economist*, London, 11 September 1965, p. 973.
27. Pakistan government statement of 24 September 1965 published in *Dawn*, Karachi, 6 October 1965.
28. See for the reaction *The Pakistan Times*, Lahore, 5 January 1966.
29. *Dawn*, Karachi, 2 January 1966. Also see *The Economist*, London, 15 January 1966, p. 166.
30. The Tashkent Declaration (text), *Pakistan Horizon*, Karachi, First Quarter, 1966, pp. 97–100.
31. The Simla Agreement (text), *Dawn*, Karachi, 4 July 1972.
32. Ibid., Clause III (para II).
33. Clause IX of the Tashkent Declaration, op. cit.
34. *The Economist*, London, 8 July 1972, p. 16. See also *The Times*, London, 4 July 1972.
35. Pakistan's Foreign Minister, Mr Z.A. Bhutto's speech in the National Assembly, *Morning News*, Karachi, 16 March 1966.
36. See for the reaction of different opposition groups, *Dawn*, Karachi, 4–5 July 1972. Similar opinion was expressed by an English weekly, *Outlook*, Karachi, 8 July 1972.
37. *The Guardian* (weekly), London, 8 July 1972, p. 10. See also *The Economist*, London, 8 July 1972, p. 16.
38. President Bhutto's speech on 31 July 1972.
39. It was stated by the Pakistan officials at Simla that they successfully resisted Indian pressure to use the phrase 'exclusively bilateral'. *The Daily Telegraph*, London, 13 July 1972.
40. *The Times*, London, 13 July 1972.
41. Ibid.
42. *The Economist*, London, 8 July 1972, p. 16.
43. *The Times*, London, 3 July 1972.
44. President's speech in the National Assembly, *The Pakistan Times*, Lahore, 19 July 1972.
45. The Indian Foreign Minister's statement in the Parliament, ibid., 23 February 1966.
46. *The Times*, London, 11 January 1966.
47. This was stated by the former President Ayub Khan in his speech on 14 January 1966.
48. Pakistan's Foreign Minister's speech in the National Assembly, *The Pakistan Times*, Lahore, 16 March 1966.
49. *Jang*, Karachi, 7 July 1972.
50. Clause VII of the Tashkent Declaration, op. cit.
51. *The Times*, London, 24 January 1966.

52. It was reported in *The Times of India* of 12 August 1972 that President Bhutto had given a 'clear indication' at Simla that he would recognize 'Bangla Desh' to facilitate tripartite discussion on the POWs.

53. *Dawn*, Karachi, 15 September 1972.

54. See *Daily Mirror*, London, 8 December 1971, *The Guardian*, London, 9 December 1971 and 'The War of 700 million' in *The Sunday Times*, London, 12 December 1971, p. 7.

55. Mrs Gandhi's press conference, *The Times*, London, 13 July 1972.

56. *The Economist*, London, 1 July 1972, p. 34.

57. *The Daily Telegraph*, London, 5 September 1972.

58. Micheal Edwardes, 'Tashkent and After', *International Affairs*, London, July 1966, p. 381.

59. *Keesings Contemporary Archives*, Bristol, 1965–66, p. 21108.

60. *Dawn*, Karachi, 6 August 1972.

61. *The Daily Telegraph*, London, 8 July 1972.

62. *The Times*, London, 4 July 1972.

63. *The Economist*, London, 8 July 1971, p. 16.

64. See the Indian Defence Minister's statement in *Dawn*, Karachi, 18 January 1972.

65. The Indian Foreign Minister's speech in the UN General Assembly, ibid., 5 October 1972.

66. Michael Edwardes, 'Tashkent and After' op. cit., p. 383.

67. *The Economist*, London, 15 January 1966, p. 166.

68. The Indian Foreign Minister's statement on 4 March 1966.

69. President Bhutto's statements, *Dawn*, Karachi, 13 July and 7 October 1972.

70. *The Times*, London, 3 July 1972.

71. Ibid., 4 July 1972.

72. *Dawn*, Karachi, 4 July 1972.

73. The Indian Foreign Minister's statement on 7 October 1972.

74. Mrs Gandhi's press conference in *The Times*, London, 13 July 1972.

75. The Indian Defence Minister's statement, *Dawn*, Karachi, 9 August 1972. See also *Dawn*, 18 August 1972.

76. See Sheikh Abdullah's statement in *The Times*, London, 1 August 1972.

77. President Bhutto's speech in the National Assembly, *The Pakistan Times*, Lahore, 19 July 1972.

78. Micheal Edwardes, 'Tashkent and After' op. cit., p. 382.

79. *The Daily Telegraph*, London, 11 July 1972.

7

Recent Trends in Pakistan's Policy towards the Middle East*

Zubeida Mustafa

In the post-Bangladesh period, one of the most significant developments in Pakistan's foreign policy has been the special relationship it has forged with the countries of the Middle East. This by no means implies that Pakistan's efforts to foster close ties with the region constitute a new development. In fact, since its inception, Pakistan has enjoyed friendly ties generally with most of the Arab countries and specifically with the northern tier states, viz., Turkey and Iran. But in the years following the secession of Bangladesh, Islamabad has exploited fully its 'Middle East option'. Today its policy towards the various countries of the Middle East is more concerted and coordinated within the framework of a calculated strategy than it has ever been before.

 Two important forces have been at work simultaneously which have had a profound impact on Pakistan's relations with the Middle East: first, the emergence of this region as a powerful force in international politics; and second, the fundamental changes that have taken place in Pakistan's geopolitical features.

* Vol. xxviii, No. 4, 1975.

I

The Middle East, which broadly speaking comprises the region stretching from the Maghreb countries of North Africa in the west, to Pakistan in the east, and from Turkey in the north to the Indian Ocean in the south has always enjoyed a special importance in world affairs by virtue of its strategic location.[1] This area has served for centuries as a bulwark against Russian advance southwards to the warm waters of the Indian Ocean. Until the end of the Second World War it had never come under Russian influence. Moreover, it has also served as a vital centre of communications between the East and the West. All the land, air and sea routes (via the Suez Canal) connecting Asia, Europe, and Africa pass through the Middle East. But since the advent of the seventies, this region has acquired unusual significance because of its oil wealth. It is the largest reservoir of oil and its control over this vital source of energy has enabled the Middle East to wield unparalleled influence in world affairs. The petrodollars the Middle Eastern countries have acquired, have also made it possible for them to make their presence felt on the international scene. This has also led to a shift in emphasis in the world economic order and as such for the first time the oil producing countries of the Middle East have assumed the role of major economic aid donors and they are now in a position to play a more positive and assertive role in world affairs. This gives a new dimension to the relationship the Middle East forges with other countries such as Pakistan, not only in the bilateral context but also on a wider plane.

As for the changes in Pakistan, the country which emerged in the aftermath of the December 1971 war has found itself placed in a more vital position *vis-à-vis* the Middle East. Previously, its two wings flanked either end of the subcontinent and as such they were obliged to face inwards. Hence it had come to be established firmly as a South Asian power with its policy oriented towards the subcontinent. Although it had links with Southeast Asia as well as the Middle East by virtue of the location of its two wings, Pakistan's focus tended to be in South Asia. Now that is no longer the case. It is still deeply concerned and affected by developments in India and Bangladesh but its policies are no longer tied down to this region exclusively. By virtue of the cultural orientation of its people, Pakistan tends to look towards the Middle East. Of equal importance is the position Pakistan has come to occupy in the Middle East strategic thinking. This region and South Asia have emerged as two major zones in Asia[2] whose interaction will, in the long run, make a profound impact on Asian politics. Pakistan's significance lies in its location in both zones. Hence as such it plays the sensitive role of a transitional zone which has to cushion the pressures from either sides.[3] Were Pakistan to prove unequal to this function due to internal weakness or external pressures it would bring great instability to the region. This should explain the interest shown by some of the Middle East states, especially neighbouring Iran, in the territorial integrity of Pakistan.

II

Pakistan's relations with its Middle Eastern neighbours have generally been close and cordial, except for a few exceptions, since 1947.[4] Great emphasis has been placed by the government as well as the people on the religious solidarity, ethnic bond, and common cultural and historical heritage which have served to cement the friendly ties between Pakistan and a number of these states. Broadly speaking, the Middle East countries might be classified into the non-Arab northern tier states and the Arab powers to the south.

With the northern tier states, viz., Turkey and Iran, Pakistan has consistenlty enjoyed close and friendly ties. Even before 1955, when they were formally linked together in a defence alliance—the Baghdad Pact which later became CENTO—these three countries had developed a pattern of cooperation which was partly responsible for their decision to enter into a military arrangement. In the years following 1955, Iran, Turkey, and Pakistan forged close economic and defence cooperation which went much further than the framework of their formal military alliance. Thus during the Indo-Pakistan wars of 1965 and 1971, CENTO as a defence organization proved quite ineffective due to the political strategy of the big powers. But both Turkey and Iran extended material and logistic support to Pakistan. When these countries decided to set up the Regional Cooperation for Development in 1964 they simply underlined their disappointment with CENTO and their need to institutionalize the close cooperation they were trying to forge among themselves on a regional basis. Hence the RCD not only bypassed the big powers, it also went much further in its aims and objectives than what had been envisaged by CENTO.

Pakistan's relations with the Arab states in the period prior to 1971 were not as uniformly cordial, although three salient features of its Middle East policy had a favourable impact on its ties with the Arabs. In the first place, Pakistan has consistenly extended steadfast and undivided support to the Arabs in their struggle against Israel. When the Palestine issue was first being debated in the UN in 1947, Pakistan's Foreign Minister Sir Mohammad Zafrulla Khan, became a brilliant advocate of the Arab point of view. Since then Pakistan has given unequivocal diplomatic support to the Arab cause and has not extended diplomatic recognition to Israel. Islamabad has given monetary assistance to the Arabs displaced from Palestine and has very strongly condemned Israeli acts of aggression against the Arabs. Secondly, Pakistan unhesitatingly took up the Arab cause in the decolonization struggle. It was in the forefront in demanding the independence of Libya, Morocco, Tunisia, and Algeria. This inevitably led to friction with the colonial powers but Pakistan clearly indicated its priority for the Arab cause. Finally, Pakistan has scrupulously tried to adhere to the policy of non-involvement in inter-Arab disputes and it has by and large succeeded in adopting a non-partisan profile. Only on two occasions has Pakistan failed to keep up this image and has been alleged of partisanship. In the Yemen war, Pakistan was charged with involvement in favour of Saudi Arabia. Again in the Jordanian-Palestine crisis of 1970, it was alleged that Pakistan was throwing its weight behind the Jordanian government.

However, Pakistan's membership of the military pacts had a profound effect on its relations with the Arabs. It alienated completely the radical Arabs led by Gamal Nasser. But Pakistan's relations with the pro-Western conservative monarchies such as Jordan and Saudi Arabia remained consistently cordial.

III

In the post 1971 period, important changes have taken place in the Middle East power pattern which have proved to be favourable for Pakistan.

With the British withdrawal from the east of Suez, new centres of power have come up in the region. Previously weak and divided, the trucial states have come together in a new union known as the United Arab Emirates which, with its newly discovered oil wealth and strategic location on the Gulf, is now regarded as an important power in the Middle East. Another state which has come up as a significant force to be reckoned with is Iran. It has assumed a new and dynamic role for itself as a military power to fill in the vacuum in the Gulf created by the British withdrawal. The rise in oil prices in the seventies has facilitated Iran's military spending. The Iranian government has used its petrodollars to purchase sophisticated arms worth $3 billion annually, with which it hopes to build up its military potential to such an extent as to exclude all foreign influence from the Gulf region. Exercising control over the Hormuz Straits which constitute the entry to the Gulf and through which 85 per cent of the non-communist world's crude oil passes, Iran enjoys much strategic importance and is likely to emerge as a powerful force in the Gulf region.

With the changes in the concept of national power and the growing emphasis on oil resources, Saudi Arabia has emerged as another centre of power in the Middle East. Possessing large resources of oil, Saudi Arabia has come to occupy a vital position in the area which has been further enhanced by the special status it enjoys by virtue of being the spiritual fountainhead of the Islamic world.

But the most important development in the Middle East which has had a profound impact on Pakistan's policy has been the advent of the era of reconciliation between the various states. This has led to the erosion of the politico-ideological and ethnocentric differences between the radical and the conservative Arab states and between the Arabs and the non-Arabs. This trend began in 1967 in the wake of the Arab defeat in the June war after which circumstances proved to be conducive to a major realignment of forces. The Yemen war which was a major source of friction between Cairo and Riyadh ended in 1967. After President Nasser's death in 1970, the two countries moved closer to each other and spearheaded a détente in inter-Arab relations. As a result of this rapprochement, the Arabs displayed greater solidarity in the Ramazan war of 1973 and even the small Arab states played a more meaningful role in the conflict against Israel.

A number of longstanding disputes among the Arab states have been resolved or are in the process of being settled. Thus Saudi Arabia has agreed to give up its claim to Bureimi in exchange for an additional corridor to the Gulf where it plans to build a new port and a refinery. Kuwait and Iraq have also settled their differences by agreeing to give Iraq a wider access to the Gulf. Moves are on to bring about a settlement between Oman and South Yemen on the issue of aid to the Dhofar rebels and between Syria and Iraq on the sharing of the waters of the Euphrates. Although the second Sinai agreement on Israeli troops withdrawal has given rise to differences, efforts are being made to contain them.

Of equal significance is the Arab-Iranian détente. Baghdad and Teheran have come to terms on their border dispute and the Kurdish problem. This has helped to ease the confrontationist approach adopted by the Arabs on the west bank of the Gulf and Iran on the east bank.

On account of these changes, which have enabled the Middle East states to manifest greater independence in their dealings with the big powers, Pakistan has been able to forge a pattern of relationship with the Middle East which is not directly interrelated with its own links with the superpowers. Pakistan's policy has been determined by its own political, economic, and strategic interests.

IV

In early 1972, the Pakistan government turned towards the Middle East to strengthen its hand on the vital issues it faced *vis-à-vis* India. Militarily vanquished and dismembered, diplomatically isolated and politically weakened, Pakistan was faced with gigantic problems. In the diplomatic sphere, the major issues confronting the Pakistan government were the release of the 93,000 POWs held in Indian camps and the evacuation of Indian troops from Pakistan's territory occupied during the war. Moreover, the question of the recognition of Bangladesh and the normalization of relations with Dhaka and New Delhi had also to be taken up.

It is significant that during the critical period which followed, Pakistan decided to explore its Middle East option fully. Mr Zulfikar Ali Bhutto, who took over as President in December 1971, effectively employed personal diplomacy as an instrument of foreign policy and succeeded in winning political and diplomatic support from the countries of the Middle East for Pakistan's stand on the unresolved issues emanating from the war of December 1971. In January 1972, he visited eight countries in the region in order to apprise their governments of Pakistan's stand on the issues facing the subcontinent and to elicit their support. This was followed by another whirlwind tour of fourteen capitals in May-June of the same year.[5]

Mr Bhutto succeeded by and large in winning the support of the Middle East states, as is indicated by the joint communiques and statements issued by the various governments. Those countries with whom Pakistan enjoyed close and cordial ties[6] specifically called for: (a) an early withdrawal of the troops of Pakistan and India to their own sides of the border and in Jammu and Kashmir in accordance with the resolutions of the United Nations General Assembly and the Security Council of 7 December and 21 December 1971, respectively; (b) the repatriation of the prisoners-of-war in accordance with the Geneva Conventions to which both Pakistan and India are signatories; and (c) a durable and honourable settlement of the complex disputes between the two countries that would safeguard peace and security with honour for their peoples.[7] Other governments whose attitude was more non-committal[8] expressed the view that 'every effort should be made for the success of the summit talks to be held between the President of Pakistan and the Prime Minister of India in accordance with the resolutions of the United Nations.'[9]

This support proved to be quite decisive in helping Pakistan to come out of its diplomatic isolation. It also found its hand strengthened in its negotiations with India and this ultimately enabled it to successfully secure the repatriation of the prisoners-of-war and the evacuation of occupied territory without ostensibly making any major concession. Even in the case of Bangladesh these countries adopted a constructive approach. None of them extended recognition to the secessionist state which would have jeopardized Pakistan's interest.[10]

In March 1972, the conference of Foreign Ministers of Islamic countries decided to send a delegation comprising representatives from Tunisia, Iran, Morocco, Algeria, Somalia, Malaysia, and Mali to Islamabad and Dhaka to bring about conciliation between them. However, the conference made its loyalties clear when it declared 'its support for Pakistan, its territorial integrity, national sovereignty and independence'.[11]

Iraq was the first country in the Middle East to recognize Bangladesh in July 1972 after the initial Indo-Pakistan deadlock had been broken at Simla. Moreover, Iraq's attitude towards Pakistan was governed by its own relations with Iran. On account of Baghdad's differences with Teheran (which were sorted out in 1975), and Iran's close ties with Pakistan, Baghdad entertained certain reservations *vis-a-vis* Islamabad. However, other governments of the Middle East extended recognition to Bangladesh in 1973 after the process of normalization in the subcontinent had set in and a number of them consulted Pakistan before taking the decision. A number of countries in the region, such as Iran, Turkey, the UAE, Saudi Arabia, Libya, and Jordan displayed their solidarity with Pakistan by not recognizing the breakaway state until Islamabad had taken the first step in that direction. It was the mediatory efforts of the Middle East states which ultimately helped in breaking the deadlock and effecting a smooth recognition of Bangladesh by Pakistan on the eve of the Islamic Summit in February 1974.

A major factor which could have worked in Pakistan's favour indirectly was that of Soviet influence in the Middle East and India. By early 1972 the Soviet Union had established its presence in these regions through treaties of friendship and non-aggression with New Delhi, Cairo, and Baghdad. This influence served as a common denominator in linking the Middle East and the subcontinent together. Moreover, the climate of opinion in the Middle East was in favour of Pakistan and this must have surely been noted by Moscow. As such it would not be too far-fetched to believe that Moscow's own approach towards South Asia might have been modified under the impact of the Arab world's policy *vis-à-vis* this region. This could have also brought pressure on India to change its hard-line approach.

In the post-1971 period, the Pakistan government has steadily worked to consolidate its ties with the Middle East through frequent exchange of visits at the highest level. Personal diplomacy has been widely resorted to and the proximity of the Middle East to Pakistan has enabled the leaders of the various states to undertake very brief visits to discuss important issues personally rather than entrust them to subordinate officials or even special emissaries. The importance attached by Pakistan as well as the Middle East governments to direct high level contacts is underlined by the frequency of official visits paid by the heads of governments of these countries to each other's capitals.[12]

On two occasions the political links between Pakistan and this region have come into focus prominently. In October 1973, when the fourth Arab-Israeli war broke out, the Pakistan government extended full diplomatic support to the Arab cause and showed greater involvement in it than it had ever done before. Mr Bhutto undertook brief visits to Iran, Turkey, and Saudi Arabia to coordinate their diplomatic efforts. Medical teams were also dispatched to Egypt and Syria while fighting was still taking place. Again, in February 1974, at the initiative of Saudi Arabia, Pakistan played host to the Islamic Summit Conference. Although essentially an organization of Muslims from all over the world, the Islamic Summit tends to be oriented towards the Middle East whose problems it mainly projects. Pakistan's willingness to host this conference and the subsequent strengthening of its diplomatic posture represented a major shift in its foreign policy orientation from South Asia to the Middle East.

V

Pakistan's strategic link with the Middle East is one of the most important bonds holding the two regions together. Pakistan occupies a vital position in the strategic planning of Iran, on the one hand, and the Arabs on the other.

In the wake of the 1971 crisis, Pakistan has emerged as an area of special interest for Iranian security. Even previously the two countries regarded each other as a vital flank in their respective defence plannings. During times of crisis when Pakistan has been threatened by India and Afghanistan, and Iran's northern and western flanks have been exposed to Russian and Iraqi threats, Islamabad and Teheran have stood by each other. Iran extended unequivocal support to Pakistan on all vital issues, such as the Kashmir dispute and the 'Pakhtunistan issue' with Afghanistan. During the wars of September 1965 and December 1971, Iran gave substantial material and logistic support to Pakistan. In 1966, the Iranian government supplied some Sabre jets to Pakistan. Coming at a time when the American arms embargo had cut off Pakistan virtually from its major source of sophisticated weapons, the Iranian assistance was highly appreciated. Last year it was reported that Iran has also agreed to supply F-5 jet fighters to Pakistan to help it replace the outdated F-86 Sabre jets.[13]

Since 1971, Pakistan's strategic importance has been considerably enhanced. Lying between two important zones, viz., the Persian Gulf area where Iran is emerging as a major power, and the subcontinent where India holds a preponderance of power, Pakistan has come to enjoy a special strategic position. Iran's foremost concern has been to preserve the territorial integrity and political independence of Pakistan. Teheran feared that if the events of 1971 were to generate forces and pressures which would lead to the further disintegration of the country, Iran would be adversely affected. In an interview in Washington the

Shahinshah spoke very candidly. 'The integrity of Pakistan is vital for us. If it were threatened and some separatist movement started, this would create an absolutely intolerable situation for our eastern frontiers'.[14] The Shahinshah reiterated these fears in July 1974, although the situation in Pakistan had achieved a certain measure of stability. He declared that he would 'intervene militarily' if the situation became intolerable.[15]

Three major compulsions have determined Iran's strategic interest towards Pakistan. First, the instability and unrest generated by the pro-autonomy National Awami Party in Balochistan was likely to have adverse repercussions in Iran. Faced with a similar problem from the nationalists in Iranian Balochistan, the Shahinshah had a direct stake in the political stability of Pakistan's western province, which is geographically and ethnologically an extension of Iranian Balochistan. As such, the Shahinshah has repeatedly reiterated his interest in Pakistan's territorial integrity and independence.

Secondly, Iran's own tense relations with its Arab neighbours on the Gulf until 1975 caused it to adopt a cautious attitude towards Pakistan's policy of systematically cultivating these Arab states, especially the UAE and Saudi Arabia. Iran's own historic and ethnocentric rivalry with the Arabs was responsible for its sensitiveness towards close defence arrangements between the Arabs and a third power which it regarded as a threat to its own security. Hence despite its close ties with Pakistan, in late 1973 Teheran initiated a policy of détente with New Delhi which had so far viewed with suspicion the close links between Pakistan and Iran. In December 1973, the Iranian Foreign Minister visited India, inaugurating a new pattern of relations between the two countries. Later they signed an economic agreement providing for a $370 million Iranian loan for Indian economic development. This process of reconciliation continued thenceforth. In 1974, Mrs Gandhi, the Indian Prime Minister, paid a visit to Iran and the Shahinshah went to New Delhi on a state visit. This has helped to broaden Iran's power base in the region.

Thirdly, Iran's concern with Pakistan's territorial integrity rises from its own need to safeguard the sea-lanes leading up to the Gulf. It is building a naval base at Chahbahar, a few miles from the borders of Balochistan to protect its lines of communication.

Iranian interest in the region coincides with Pakistan's own interest to maintain stability and peace on its western and southern flanks. While it withdrew from SEATO in 1973, Pakistan has strengthened its links with CENTO. Under the present government, it has upgraded its representation in this pact to the ministerial level after having been represented by an ambassador for several years. In 1974, it played host to the CENTO naval exercise, 'Midlink' in the Arabian Sea, which was the largest exercise ever conducted by CENTO. However, the CENTO has not proved to be a militarily effective organization. As a matter of fact its Asian members have forged significant defence cooperation amongst themselves outside the framework of CENTO.

Iran and Pakistan have shown greater interest in the sphere of defence within the framework of the RCD, although it is basically oriented towards economic cooperation. In November 1975, when the Shahinshah visited Turkey he declared in a press interview, 'We desire to become self-sufficient in armaments. A joint arms industry may be considered on both a bilateral basis between Turkey and Iran or a tripartite basis to include Pakistan as well'.[16] Earlier in October 1975, during the Turkish President's visit to Pakistan the leaders of the two countries had also shown a keen interest in setting up a joint arms industry. If such a project does materialize, it would increase military cooperation between the RCD members by standardizing their weapons and making interchange feasible.

While Iran's security is directly linked with Pakistan's stability, the Arab states of the Middle East have found their strategic interest in Pakistan to be of a different nature. In the wake of the British withdrawal from the region in 1971, the Gulf states have been working systematically to build up their indigenous power base. In this effort, they have found that cooperation with Pakistan can prove to be fruitful. Their newly acquired petrodollars have undoubtedly facilitated the purchase of expensive and sophisticated weapons, but for training and maintenance facilities the Arab states have also turned to outside help. Pakistan has extended full cooperation in this field. It is estimated that until 1974, 4000 Saudi soldiers and airmen had been trained in Pakistan in a contract worth $10 million a year. The scheme was later extended to cover Saudi seamen too.[17] It has also been reported that Pakistan has supplied combat pilots to Saudi Arabia, the UAE, Kuwait, and other states which are experiencing a shortage of trained personnel.[18] It has also been reported that a tripartite arms deal between France, Pakistan and the Gulf states has been under consideration for quite some time. It would, if it materializes, provide for setting up a Mirage plant in Pakistan with Gulf finance and French expertise.[19] Prime

Minister Bhutto's press statement[20] expressing interest in joint defence production with the Gulf states gives some substance to the reports of a trilateral deal.

The Arab states' interest in Pakistan stems from three factors: first, defence cooperation with Pakistan entails no political strings or commitments. Secondly, Pakistan has a number of arms from the same sources from which the Arabs are now purchasing their military equipment. Thus Pakistan already possesses the Mirage planes which have been acquired by Saudi Arabia, the UAE, and Libya. As such, Pakistan has traded personnel and servicing facilities. Finally, since there is no basic clash of interest between Pakistan and the Arabs, the feeling is generally strong in the Middle Eastern capitals that Pakistan can be relied upon for steadfast and consistent support which will not be withdrawn in times of crisis to exert pressure on them.

Finally an important strategic compulsion which has brought Pakistan and the Middle Eastern states together is the threat of the proliferation of nuclear weapons and big power rivalry in the region. Broadly speaking, Pakistan as well as the other states of the Middle East favour the creation of a peace zone in the Indian Ocean, of which they are all littoral states. This would, *inter alia*, envisage the exclusion of all foreign powers from the region. But Pakistan has simultaneously proposed the establishment of a nuclear weapon free zone in South Asia, which has been vigorously opposed by India, which exploded a nuclear device in 1974. Iran has also sponsored a proposal for a nuclear weapon free zone for the Middle East. These proposals underline the sensitivity of most of these countries to big power competition and rivalry as well as their fear of a local power establishing its hegemony in the area. Pakistan and the Middle East states have repeatedly expressed their common interest in preserving the stability of the region by creating nuclear weapon free zones.

VI

Pakistan's economic ties with the Middle East have expanded phenomenally in the last few years. Previously, apart from the commercial links, economic contacts between Pakistan and the Arab countries were minimal. However, with the RCD countries, Pakistan enjoyed a reasonable degree of economic cooperation although the RCD had envisaged much more when it was founded in 1964.

By 1972–3, the economic picture of the Middle East had changed completely. The energy crisis and the rise in oil prices left the oil producing states with more money than their developing economies could absorb. Moreover, they lacked in expertise and trained personnel. Hence, they resorted to importing the services of foreign skilled workers and in supplying economic assistance to the non-oil producing developing states. As a result, the pattern of foreign economic assistance received by Pakistan has undergone a change and its overwhelming dependence on Western aid is gradually giving way to economic aid from the Middle East. Because of its manpower, expertise, and technical know how, Pakistan has been able to secure a special position in the Middle East. Already there are 170,000 Pakistanis working in the region. (For country-wise break-up see Table C.)

Pakistan has set up joint commissions with six Middle Eastern states to facilitate and expedite economic cooperation viz. Iran, Libya, UAE, Saudi Arabia, Egypt, and Turkey. It enjoys the maximum economic cooperation with the first four of these countries.

Economic cooperation between Iran and Pakistan has made steady progress over the years. Since May 1973, when the Iranian-Pakistan Joint Commission was established, economic collaboration has received further impetus. In 1974, Iran agreed to provide Pakistan a loan of $580 million spread over a period of three years. The credit is repayable over eight years with a grace period of three years bearing an interest rate of 2.5 per cent per annum. Although the terms of this loan are not as favourable as soft loans provided by a number of Western countries, it would go a long way in meeting Pakistan's need for capital. The Iranian loan is designed to finance a number of projects, such as the 100,000-spindle capacity textile plants, the 300,000-ton capacity cement plant, an agro-livestock complex, and a 516,000-ton fertilizer plant.

In addition to this loan, which is the largest Iran has extended to a developing country after Egypt, it has also agreed to provide $63 million for joint industrial and technical projects, besides engineering and medical colleges in Balochistan. A new field, in which the two countries have agreed to collaborate, is that of nuclear energy. In the joint communique issued at the conclusion of the Shahinshah's last visit to Pakistan in March 1976, the leaders of the two countries while reaffirming the need to halt the spread of nuclear weapons, expressed their conviction that mankind would benefit from the development of nuclear energy for peaceful purposes. Hence they stressed the need for mutual cooperation in this field.[21]

With the UAE, Pakistan has concluded an agreement for the expansion of a fertilizer plant at Multan at a cost of $102 million. It has also planned to set up an oil refinery in Multan as a joint Pakistan-UAE project with a 560 mile pipeline to Karachi. The two countries are also to establish a large-scale agricultural and cattle farm as a joint venture at Thatta. The project is estimated to cost $30 million, excluding the cost of the 25,000 acres of land on which it will be set up. Comprising 20,000 acres of cattle farm and 5000 acres of agricultural farm, the joint venture is to be export oriented and is designed to supply farm and meat products to the UAE and other neighbouring countries.

Saudi Arabia is another country of the Middle East with which Pakistan's economic ties have expanded considerably. Riyadh has provided Islamabad a credit of $100 million, out of which $50 million will be utilized in setting up a fertilizer factory at Mirpur Mathelo. Two cement plants are to be expanded at a cost of $17 million each and $10 million has been allocated for the setting up of a polyester plant at Karachi. Saudi Arabia and Pakistan have agreed to set up a Saudi-Pakistan Bank, *Al Jazeera*, with an authorized capital of 10 million Saudi rials.

Libya has also developed closer economic and cultural ties with Pakistan. Though this collaboration is not on such a wide scale as with some of the other countries of the region, it is still considered important. The major projects agreed upon are a joint investment banking corporation, a joint shipping company, an Islamic centre, and a multi-lingual printing and publishing house in Karachi.

These projects are helping to interlink the economies of the Middle Eastern countries and Pakistan even though the joint ventures are not on an extensive scale. The oil producing states have been providing the credit needed while Pakistan has supplied the skilled manpower. This interdependence has helped to bring these countries closer together. Moreover, the oil rich nations have gradually taken over the role of major donors of economic aid. Thus in 1974–5, members of the Organization of Arab Petroleum Exporting Countries (OAPEC) gave a credit of $49 million to Pakistan. Again in January 1975 when an earthquake struck the northern regions of Swat, Pakistan received cash donations worth $48 million from abroad. Of this sum $40 million was provided by the Muslim countries of the Middle East.

Libya was the largest donor with a donation of $16 million, Saudi Arabia gave $10 million, the UAE $8 million, Kuwait $5 million and Iran $1 million.

Trade between Pakistan and the Middle East had shown a set pattern until recently when the increase in oil prices changed the trends. Pakistan's imports and exports to this region account for nearly a fifth of its total trade. It is a major market for Pakistan's exports, as a result of which until 1974–5, the balance of trade with the Middle East was in Pakistan's favour (see Table D). Another change which has come about has been in the relative volume of Pakistan's trade with the RCD members and the Arab states. In 1969–70 its trade with the RCD partners accounted for one quarter of its total trade with the Middle East but, in 1974–75, it accounted for only one-eighth. The importance of Pakistan's trade with the Middle East lies in the fact that this region is its oil supplier. Saudi Arabia and Kuwait are the two major sources of Pakistan's petroleum, in 1974–75 oil imports from these two countries amounted to $320 million. Although the oil exporting countries have made it clear that they will not make any concessions in oil prices for the third world, they have provided substantial credit and deferred payment facilities.

Over the years, the Middle East will emerge as one of the most important regions in Pakistan's foreign relations. The strategic and economic interrelationship is bound to increase.

TABLE A

Recognition of Bangladesh by some of the major governments of the Middle East	
July 1972	Iraq
January 1973	Afghanistan
July 1973	Morocco, Algeria, Tunisia
September 1973	Syria, Egypt
November 1973	Kuwait
February 1974	Pakistan, Iran, Turkey, Libya, Jordan
March 1974	UAE
August 1975	Saudi Arabia

TABLE B

Exchange of official visits between Pakistan and
other countries of the Middle East

Date	Visiting dignitary	Country of visit
January 1972	Shah of Iran	Pakistan
" "	President Bhutto	Afghanistan
" "	Crown Prince of Jordan	Pakistan
" "	President Bhutto	Iran, Turkey, Morocco, Algeria, Tunisia, Syria, Libya, Egypt
May 1972	President of UAE	Pakistan
May–June 1972	President Bhutto	Abu Dhabi, Kuwait, Iraq, Jordan, Lebanon, Saudi Arabia, Sudan, Turkey, Iran
December 1972	President of UAE	Pakistan
January 1973	Shah of Iran	Pakistan
May 1973	President Bhutto	Iran
October 1973	Prime Minister Bhutto	Iran, Turkey, and Saudi Arabia
December 1973	Prime Minister Bhutto	Kuwait
" "	Prime Minister Bhutto	Bahrain, Abu Dhabi, Dubai, Qatar
February 1974	Islamic Summit	Pakistan
" "	President of Libya	Pakistan
March 1974	President of UAE	Pakistan
" "	Prime Minister Bhutto	Iran
July 1974	Ruler of Dubai	Pakistan
October 1974	Prime Minister Bhutto	Iran
January 1975	Ruler of Dubai	Pakistan
February 1975	Shah of Iran	Pakistan
" "	President of UAE	Pakistan
September 1975	Prime Minister Bhutto	Saudi Arabia
October 1975	Prime Minister Bhutto	Iran
" "	President of Turkey	Pakistan
March 1976	Shah of Iran	Pakistan

TABLE C

Pakistani nationals living and working in the Middle East*	
Country	Number
Abu Dhabi	20,000
Bahrain	7,000
Dubai	25,000
Iraq	5,000
Kuwait	25,000
Libya	8,000
Qatar	45,000
Saudi Arabia	35,000
Total	170,000

* Figures given by Manpower Division of the Government of Pakistan, cited in *Dawn*, Karachi, 12 February 1976.

NOTES

1. Afghanistan has not been included in this paper because its relations with Pakistan fall in a category of its own. Afghanistan calls for separate treatment.
2. The Middle East has been divided into two sub-zones; the Persian Gulf area and the area of the Arab-Israeli conflict. Pakistan, on account of its contiguity, is more directly related to the Gulf area.
3. Pakistan has been described as a 'historical shatterbelt' by some writers. See E.L. Tepper, 'Pakistan's Search for a New Identity', *International Perspectives*, Ottawa, November/December 1973, p. 9.
4. For a detailed account of Pakistan's relations with the Middle East till 1965, see Khalida Qureshi, 'Pakistan and the Middle East', *Pakistan Horizon*, Second Quarter, 1966, pp. 156–66.
5. See Table B.
6. The countries which were more explicit in their support were the UAE, Kuwait, Jordan, Sudan, Saudi Arabia, Turkey, Iran.
7. Pakistan-Kuwait Joint Communique of 29 May 1972, *Pakistan Horizon*, Karachi, Third Quarter, 1972, pp. 135–7.
8. Such as Iraq and Lebanon.
9. Pakistan-Iraq Joint Communique of 31 May 1972, *Pakistan Horizon*, Karachi, Second Quarter, 1972, p. 137.
10. See Table B.

11. *Dawn*, Karachi, 5 March 1972.
12. See Table B.
13. *Washington Post*, 8 March 1975.
14. *Kayhan International*, Teheran, 25 October 1973.
15. *Le Monde*, Paris, 1 July 1974.
16. *The Middle East*, London, January 1976, pp. 29–11.
17. *The Sunday Times*, London, 3 February 1974.
18. *Indian Express*, Bombay, 13 August 1973.
19. *Washington Post*, Washington, 10 January 1974.
20. *Dawn*, Karachi, 10 December 1973.
21. *Dawn*, Karachi, 13 March 1976.

8

Inching Together or a Mile Apart: India and Pakistan towards Détente* ·

Nazir A. Mughal

The term détente is a relatively new word to be used in a political sense in South Asia. The word originally comes from the old French word *destendre*—to release or loosen. However, détente is widely viewed in South Asia as the end of the cold war or, at the very least, a substantially tempered phase of it.[1]

In view of the mutual distrust and antagonistic competition between India and Pakistan (which has existed since 1947), one should think of détente as a movement away from cold war, but this will not necessarily imply that the total relationship has become harmonious. If conflicts erupt at some point along the spectrum, this will not necessarily mean that détente has been totally replaced by cold war between India and Pakistan. By the same token, the signing of a new treaty by the two countries such as the Simla Agreement of 1972, does not ensure that all potential for conflict has been forever driven away from their relationship. There is a gradual thaw in India-Pakistan relations, but much time and energy are needed to bring the two governments towards an era of negotiation and understanding. Indeed, the necessary efforts towards tension reduction can be readily halted or even destroyed by a variety of forces. One authority has aptly described the situation that détente is like a flower—'complicate to nurture' and 'easy to trample'.[2]

---

* Vol. xxix, No. 3, 1976.

This paper will focus attention on the fragile relationship which existed between India and Pakistan, from 1947, and continues to the present day—the relationship which fluctuated between cold war to hot war from 1948 to 1971, and since 1972, is marked by a cautious détente. What factors, then, generated and sustained Pakistan's cautious détente with India?

Underlying Factors

Historical

The motive forces impelling both India and Pakistan towards détente cannot be explained without the historical note. Since the partition of India, the two major countries of the region—India and Pakistan— have been in a state of perpetual cold war. This cold war evolved from the conflict over Kashmir in 1947, closing of the canal waters flowing from India to Pakistan, India's conquest of the princely state of Junagadh in 1947, through the hostilities of 1965, to the final round over East Pakistan in 1971. These outbursts between the two countries increased the tempo of the cold war and transformed it into hot war.

The regional cold war was not conducted in a vacuum. Elements of global politics as well as the geostrategic location of the Indo-Pakistan subcontinent brought about the involvement of three external powers. These powers played important roles in the subcontinent. As is well known, prominent among the major powers involved in Asia were those that had an interest in the three dominant sets of conflict in the international system—viz., the Soviet-American, the Sino-Soviet, and the Sino-American. The involvement of these major powers in the subcontinent was sometimes related directly to their interests in the region, but more often resulted from their larger interests in international competition and domination.

The major factor which brought the two countries towards cautious détente was the catastrophe of 1971, which culminated in the defeat of Pakistan and the birth of a new country at the expense of Pakistan. It was a major victory for India, not so much from a military point of view but more so from the psychological—the satisfaction that India's historical enemy, Pakistan, had been forced, for the first time, to kneel before its arch enemy, India.

The hate and fear relationship has existed between the two countries from the days of the British Raj in India. Thus, the basic reason underlying their hostility is to be found in their historical experience. Many Pakistanis believe that India has never accepted the concept of the 'two nation theory', thus undermining the existence of Muslim Pakistan. To the Indian elite, on the other hand, the establishment of Pakistan represents a tragedy as well as 'the vivisection of the body' of mother India. The Prime Minister of India, once remarked that the idea of a separate Muslim nationhood was absurd and mischievous, and 'hardly worth considering'.[3]

Pakistan has been deeply conscious that influential sections of Indian opinion have resented the mere fact of its existence,[4] and have made no secret of their belief that the entire subcontinent will one day be reunited under New Delhi. Pakistan, with its two wings, on either side of India, had become an anathema to Indian leaders. Pakistani leaders' efforts at projecting the ideological character of the Pakistani state was also disliked by India. It meant, above all, the portrayal of Pakistan as the 'Bastion of Islam' in the subcontinent, in perpetual conflict with Hindu India. The depiction of such a conflict-relationship with India, naturally became a *raison d'etre* for Pakistan, since it served both to justify the creation of Pakistan and to unite Muslim Bengal with West Pakistan. In the light of 1971 events, the Indian leaders were quick to announce that the concept of the 'two nation theory' was based upon false foundations.[5]

Military Balance

The events of 1971 also solved another major point of confrontation between India and Pakistan—the question of power parity. The fear of survival had pushed Pakistani policy-makers towards gaining military parity with India. Pakistani leaders wanted to project their country's image in the international arena as an equal of India in military terms, and wished to redress the subcontinental power balance. To accomplish this, Pakistan joined forces with the major powers in military alliances. Thus, despite the dissimilarities between the two countries in size, population, and resources, Pakistan was able to keep India in check and maintain a military stalemate during the wars of 1948 and 1965. This power parity which was maintained by Pakistan for a decade became an anathema to the leaders of India. In 1971, however, this equilibrium was disturbed. The growing chaos in East Pakistan provided the opportunity to India—with Soviet assistance—to effect a restructuring of the power balance in South Asia. Thus, the emergence of Bangladesh as an independent nation created a new order of power in South Asia that gave India a more dominant position than before.

The events of 1971 also had beneficial effects on India's domestic as well as external environments. Domestically, India's victory was mainly psychological. The Indian view was that the break-up of Pakistan had proved that the Congress-Muslim League rivalry had ended in favour of the Indian National Congress which had opposed the partition of India on communal lines. The Bangladesh crisis, according to an Indian spokesman, also provided India with the 'opportunity of the century' to destroy its enemy number one, Pakistan.[6] With Pakistan cut to size, it became possible for the average Indian and for the Indian policy-makers to get rid of their obsession with Pakistan.

India's success in the war of 1971 suddenly brought into focus the guidelines that Nehru had set for India's foreign policy—his vision of India in world affairs. Nehru's dexterous handling of India's post-independent foreign policy had made his country a leader of the newly emerging Afro-Asian states, i.e., the third world. In this fashion, Nehru had projected India's image as a separate force in Asia, capable of exercising leverage upon the major power blocs. Moreover, the Indian Prime Minister wanted his country to play an important role in the settlement of Asian problems. He also considered Western involvement in Asia as an encroachment in the domestic affairs of Asian countries.[7] The call for Pan-Asianism[8] as well as the occasional outbursts of Indian leaders against the US involvement in Vietnam were the expression of those feelings prevailing in India during the 1950s and 1960s.[9]

The war in 1971 seems to have fulfilled these aims for India. India emerged as a dominant power in South Asia, with no formidable competitor in sight. With the political support of the Soviet Union, India gained a 'military victory' over Pakistan, psychological victory over China, and political and moral success against the United States. Thus, Indian prestige and military power acquired a new vision among Asian and African countries. For the first time, after 1971, India could take a relatively relaxed view of Indo-Pakistan relations.

Pakistan began its post-1971 phase with a crisis of new identity and a series of political, economic, and psychological problems.

Pakistan saw a part of its territory (East Pakistan) emerging as a new sovereign Muslim state (Bangladesh), and experienced the transfer of power from military dictatorship to an elected representative government (after thirteen years of military rule). It faced numerous problems: 91,000 Pakistani prisoners-of-war under detention in India, 5000 sq. miles of Pakistani territory in the western region occupied by the Indian army, and a badly mauled economy. In addition to these Pakistan lacked the sympathy of world public opinion, and its relations with the major powers were under a strain (the exceptions being the People's Republic of China and, to an extent, the United States with its psychological 'tilt' towards Pakistan).

Knowing well that all the trump cards were in India's hand, Mr Z.A. Bhutto, the new elected leader of truncated Pakistan, realized that he had to play his cards well and with great finesse. In his speeches at public meetings he warned India that a one-sided settlement would lead to a 'dictated peace' and continued instability in the subcontinent. He indicated that he desired to establish a new relationship between India and Pakistan based on equity and justice. Subsequently, the traditional cold war pattern of relationship changed and the two countries moved towards a cautious détente. Beginning with the Simla Agreement of 2 July 1972, the process continued through the agreement of 28 August 1973 regarding the repatriation of Pakistani prisoners-of-war, recognition of Bangladesh by Pakistan, the Indo-Pakistan trade agreement of 23 January 1975, the shipping protocol of 15 January 1975, and the commercial and communication agreements of 13 January 1976 and 14 May 1976 respectively.

Normalization Process at Simla

The spirit of accommodation between the two countries was manifested at the Simla conference in June-July 1972 in which both governments resolved to 'put an end to the conflict and confrontation' that had hitherto marred their relations, and further asserted their determination that 'the principles and purposes of the Charter of the United Nations shall govern the relations between the two countries'.[10]

The willingness on the part of both countries to withdraw their armed forces and to discuss the repatriation of their armed personnel,[11] the Pakistani acceptance of a postponement of the prisoners-of-war issue, and, above all, the compromise on the line of control in Kashmir demonstrated the willingness on the part of the political leaders of both countries to work out a post-war settlement which would be as equitable as possible in the then prevailing circumstances. The fact that at Simla both parties had compromised in order to accommodate each other's point of view was borne out by the criticism levelled at the agreement by domestic opposition forces in India and Pakistan.[12]

The agreement called for prevention of hostile propaganda directed against each other; resumption of various forms of communications; promotion of travel facilities for the nationals of each country and cooperation in the socio-economic field. In addition to this, both parties agreed to refrain from the threat or use of force in violation of the line of control in Kashmir, and to solve the issues that had bedevilled relations between the two countries for the last twenty-five years by peaceful means, through negotiations in the future on a 'bilateral basis'. From India's point of view, the Pakistani acceptance of the principle of bilateralism was a victory for India which had all along insisted on the exclusion of third party interference in Indo-Pakistan problems. Thus, the incorporation of this principle at Simla was in a way an 'ideological vindication of India's past stand'.[13]

However, in the past, India had accepted the role of outside powers in three major crises between the two countries, namely the Soviet Union's mediatory role at Tashkent in 1966, international arbitration over the Rann of Kutch issue in 1965, and the Indus Waters Treaty of 1960.

At Simla both countries jointly pledged to uphold the principles of peaceful coexistence, respect for each other's territorial integrity and sovereignty, and non-interference in each other's internal affairs. They also agreed to respect each other's national unity, territorial integrity, political independence, and sovereign equality. From Pakistan's point of view, this was taken as a public admission by India that West Pakistan would continue to exist as a separate Muslim nation. Thus, tacitly, India acknowledged the existence of the 'two nation theory' in the Indo-Pakistan subcontinent, and pledged that it would not interfere in Pakistan's internal problems such as the Pakhtunistan issue.

Accord on Kashmir

The most dramatic manifestation of the thaw in the cold war between the two countries was their mutual accommodation on the question of

Kashmir. India, after the 1971 war, had adopted a tough attitude and was trying to secure the final settlement of the Jammu and Kashmir problem on the basis of 'existing realities'. India demanded that the cease-fire line of 17 December 1971 (CFL) in Jammu and Kashmir be transformed into the international boundary between India and Pakistan, thus solving once and for all the problem of Kashmir. Pakistan's position was that India should go back to the 1949 CFL in Kashmir (which was supervised by the UN) and suggested to leave out the Kashmir question till a more opportune moment.

Finally, at Simla, the line of actual control in Jammu and Kashmir resulting from the cease-fire (of 17 December 1971) was accepted which 'shall be respected by both sides without prejudice to the recognized position of either side', and it was agreed that the representatives of the two governments would meet preparatory to the next summit meeting, to discuss, among other things, 'a final settlement of Jammu and Kashmir'.[14]

This compromise gave India the satisfaction of delinking the new line from the old unsupervised CFL and also permitted it to keep alive its technical and legal claims to the Pakistani-controlled portion of the disputed state, i.e., Azad Kashmir. From Pakistan's point of view, the Simla Agreement admits the existence of the Jammu and Kashmir dispute. Moreover, Pakistan derived the satisfaction of having resisted Indian efforts to solve the Kashmir issue on Indian soil.

Even more important than the agreement at Simla are the parallel events that have taken place, since then, on both sides of the line in the two parts of Kashmir. These events have strengthened the accommodative stands of both India and Pakistan on the question of Kashmir. The developments on the part of Pakistan include its systematic efforts to evolve constitutional links between Muzaffarabad and Islamabad, pending the settlement of the wider Kashmir issue with India. Eventually, a formula was evolved by which an Azad Kashmir and Jammu Council consisting of fourteen members was set up to coordinate all arrangements between Azad Kashmir and Pakistan. In addition to this, an all-Pakistan party emerged on the Azad Kashmir political scene and the local dominant party—the Muslim League Conference—soon made its decision to merge with the existing political party in power, the Pakistan People's Party (PPP).[15]

The elections were held in Azad Kashmir in May 1975 which brought into power the PPP. The coming to power of the PPP in Azad Kashmir was the first step towards Azad Kashmir's 'representation in the parliament of Pakistan',[16] and this directly cut across Mr Bhutto's plea for self-determination in Kashmir. It was this action which was severely criticized by the President of the Muslim League Party in opposition.[17]

About the same time, New Delhi broke the twenty year stalemate with Sheikh Mohammad Abdullah, the leader of the Plebiscite Front in occupied Kashmir and as a result of this, Sheikh Abdullah was installed as the Chief Minister of the Indian-held Kashmir on 25 February 1975.

New Delhi probably realized that the time was ripe to reopen a dialogue with Sheikh Abdullah. The protracted negotiations carried on with the Sheikh at the highest level were themselves indicative of the fact that, so long as the Sheikh and his followers remained sulking in their tents, it was not possible to expect real stability in Kashmir. Indeed, Kashmir had no other leader who could be compared with the towering personality of Sheikh Mohammad Abdullah. So long as he remained out, or was left out, the problem of Kashmir could never be solved. New Delhi also seemed to have realized that even if it denied that there was a problem of Kashmir to which Pakistan was a party, it would be highly unrealistic to deny that there was no problem in Kashmir, as long as significant elements in the valley had not been assimilated willingly into the system. Sheikh Abdullah had also realized by then that they could no longer use the Pakistan factor in order to gain greater concessions from India. The changed balance of power in South Asia had left India in a position of relative prominence. Consequently, India conceded the trappings of autonomy to the state of occupied Kashmir and left the substance of accession with India intact. Indian leaders realized that a reconciliation with Sheikh Abdullah would put India in a stronger position *vis-à-vis* Pakistan at the negotiating table. Sheikh Abdullah would then naturally espouse India's cause and would oppose the idea of self-determination for the people of Kashmir.

New Delhi's acceptance of Sheikh Abdullah's demands were based on the conditions that he would dissolve the Plebiscite Front and would not renew his old demand for a plebiscite in Kashmir or some other form of self-determination.[18] The Indira-Abdullah accord, however, was vigorously criticized by the Indian right wing Jan Sangh leader, Rishi Kumar Kaushal and Sheikh Abdul Rahman of the *Bharatiya Lok Dal*.[19] Mr Bhutto also was obviously not pleased with the accord. He gave a call for *hartal* (strike) across the border in the state of occupied Kashmir which was indeed effective.[20]

With the Kashmir issue moving, the outlook for Indo-Pakistan détente in the not-too-distant future becomes all the more favourable. It does not mean that all Indo-Pakistan problems will be automatically settled once the *status quo* in Kashmir is maintained by both parties. There is no denying the fact that conflicts of interest in the political and economic spheres will continue to emerge in Indo-Pakistan relations but, there is a good chance now that attempts would be made on both sides to isolate such disagreements and conflicts so that they do not threaten the embryonic process of détente between the two countries.

Indo-Pakistan Stalemate

Soon after the signing of the Simla Agreement and the initiation of the normalization process, a rift appeared in India-Pakistan relations. India refused to release the prisoners-of-war and used the issue to extract political advantages from Pakistan. New Delhi demanded that 'in order to secure their release Pakistan must first recognize Bangladesh'.[21] Pakistan was constrained to take the matter before the International Court of Justice. Finally, an agreement was concluded in New Delhi on 28 August 1973, which resolved a major part of this humanitarian problem.

The relations between India and Pakistan became less accommodative, once again, when India exploded a nuclear device in May 1974. The Indian atomic explosion inevitably introduced a new and significant factor in the Indo-Pakistan strategic balance. Pakistan reacted strongly to the Indian nuclear explosion. Prime Minister Bhutto declared that India was in an 'expansionist mood'.[22] When Mr Bhutto approached the United States government for lifting of the embargo on arms supplies to Pakistan, the Indian Prime Minister, Mrs Gandhi, was quick to comment that the sale of arms amounted to 'Pakistan's new belligerency' over India's settlement of the Kashmir issue.[23]

But despite these obstacles, both countries have been strictly following the terms of the Simla Agreement. Practical implementation of the agreement, however, has proceeded very slowly. Nevertheless, for the first time in a decade, goods are being exchanged, e.g., Pakistani cotton for Indian engineering products, and perhaps Indian coal for

Pakistan natural gas in the future. Rail and air links between the two countries were also restored in July 1976.[24] Propaganda against each other through the radio, television, and newspapers has been at a low ebb since 1972.

These changes in the regional environment of the subcontinent have, to some extent, gone unnoticed because of the past performance of the two governments, as well as due to the post-war rhetoric in which the leadership on both sides has indulged, in order to please certain sections of their respective domestic constituencies. However, one is apt to find a greater willingness on both sides to accommodate, within certain limits, the other party's point of view.

Regional Strategic Intentions and the Interest of the Major Powers

As already stated, Pakistan's strategic purpose since independence has been dominated by its demands for territorial restitution from India and consequent military anxieties. Subsequently, Pakistan sought a variety of coalition arrangements with extra-regional actors over the years—through CENTO and SEATO, bilateral security arrangements with the US (since 1954), and in a nebulous relationship with the People's Republic of China since the 1960s. These arrangements were beneficial to Pakistan inasmuch as they provided it with some military hardware. These extra-regional relationships, however, did not provide Pakistan with any long-term gain *vis-à-vis* India. Specifically, these relationships did not compensate for India's over-reaching strategic capabilities.

In strategic terms, India offers greater gains to global actors and poses a greater threat of system disruption if India's interests are jettisoned in favour of Pakistan. This was evident in the crisis of 1971 when, through swift intervention, India challenged a twenty-five year US commitment to create a military balance between India and Pakistan without permanent damage to India's own relationship with the US. Similarly, Soviet-American irritation with India's nuclear explosion has not broken the latter's links with either superpower. In the future, Indian nuclear capabilities may provide a parallel interaction with the People's Republic of China, insofar as its policies concern subcontinental relations. Pakistan's strategic anxieties need to be viewed in this context and its external dependence re-evaluated.

The United States' policy towards South Asia in the post-1971 period has been a relatively low profile one. The importance of South Asia in American policy has been downgraded for much of the last decade. In future, American policy towards Pakistan will be shaped by the latter's proximity to the oil-rich Gulf and its capacity to enhance American interests in that strategic region. However, it does not mean that the US would be completely averse to Pakistan playing the role of an irritant to India in South Asia. The foreign policy experts believe that such a Pakistani role could probably increase the American leverage with India to some extent in certain situations.

The other extra-regional actor who has taken a keen interest in the region has been the People's Republic of China. Peking has been the main supplier of arms to Pakistan after 1965 and has consistently supported Islamabad's disputes with New Delhi, both before and after the Bangladesh crisis and the war of 1971. The change in the international environment following the thaw in the Sino-American cold war, also reinforced Pakistan's calculations that it could now use both China and the USA as counter-weights to India and to growing Indo-Soviet cooperation in South Asia.

Peking's involvement in the subcontinent may be judged *vis-à-vis* Soviet designs in this region. India looms large in Chinese thinking primarily because it has become the king-pin of Soviet policy in South Asia. As long as India continues to bolster Soviet interests in the area, one can argue that China will give unequivocal support to Pakistan against India. However, Peking will act with caution for it would not like Pakistan to risk another head-on military collision with India, since a collision might cripple Pakistan's military machine. If that happens the Soviet Union, as far as China is concerned, will grab the opportunity for its own political expansion. As such, China is bound to have a vital stake in Pakistan's territorial integrity as well as its political stability. On this account alone, it would seem essential to Peking that Indo-Pakistan tension be kept within manageable limits. China has to balance its policy of using Pakistan as an irritant or counter-weight to India, and its desire to see that an Indo-Pakistan confrontation does not get out of hand and prove counter-productive as far as the Chinese vital interests are concerned.

Iran has emerged as a third extra-regional nation whose growing power has to be reckoned with. Iran's bid to take Britain's place as the 'Gulf policeman' with the latter's formal withdrawal in 1971 was widely publicized, as was Iran's ensuing interest in building up its military capabilities. Soon after the British withdrawal, Iranian policy-makers '...suddenly saw divisions crossing international borders, the dismemberment of Pakistan, (and) the mass media applauding...'.[25]

Iran's growing interest in the South Asian subcontinent coincides in part with the greater opportunities perceived for influence there rather than in building upon the Arab-Gulf states competition. Particularly significant are the uncertainties about US commitments to Pakistan's integrity.

The Iranian regime has repeatedly affirmed its interest in maintaining Pakistan intact. Pakistan now has little territorial depth in the event of hostilities with India in the future. A determined Indian onslaught in the event of a war would lead to the severing of Pakistan's north-south lines of communication at a number of places. Pakistan's strategic depth, in fact, lies only with Iran. That such a possibility exists is a major reason for considering the Iran-Pakistan-India relationship in geostrategic terms.[26] Iran has expressed a direct interest in the future territoriality of Pakistan. Iranian-Pakistan anxieties about India's interest in relation to Pakistan's territoriality are allied to an independent concern about Pakistan's ability to maintain its cohesion against disruptive movements, supported by outside elements, in certain regions of Pakistan. Thus, Pakistan's domestic conditions and relations provide incentives for military collaboration with Iran.[27]

As far as the Soviet Union's policies in the region are concerned, it has, since 1950, adopted a pro-Indian stance. Soviet support for India in its regional cold war with Pakistan was the result of Pakistan's political and military alliance with the US. With the successful outcome of the 1971 war, in which the Soviet Union supported the victor—India—and as a result of Pakistan's new policy which has been moving from the Western network of alliances to a positive neutrality, there seems to be no reason for the Soviet Union to interest itself in preventing the emergence of a détente in Indo-Pakistan relations. The reduction in the cold war pattern between the two superpowers has also helped Moscow to develop the above line of approach in the subcontinent.

Conclusion

The future prospects of the rapprochement between India and Pakistan seem bright. However, one has to guard oneself against the charge of being overly optimistic and complacent about the future development of Indo-Pakistan relations. The development of a new power equilibrium, which resulted out of the violent conflict of December 1971, has to be understood by both India and Pakistan. The century-old enmity cannot disappear from the minds of the people of both countries in a short period of time.

Pakistani leadership has taken a pragmatic view of the post-1971 power structure in the subcontinent. However, there are certain elements of the Pakistani elite—intellectual, political, and military—who are advocating a power parity with India. If both parties, i.e., India and Pakistan keep before them as an example the Shanghai Communique, issued by the United States and China, which stresses the sovereign equality of nations,[28] then there is a strong possibility of continuous development of the normalization process between India and Pakistan. The normalization between the two countries should not be based upon the perpetuation of inequity and the *status quo*.[29] Peaceful development between the two countries must be without hegemony of one nation over the other.

In view of the present power realities in the subcontinent, the domestic problems facing both countries, and the limited capabilities of external powers to intervene in such a fashion as to decisively transform the power equilibrium in the region, the prospects of an Indo-Pakistan détente are not at all bleak. The recent rapprochement between Pakistan and Afghanistan, the suggestion that India should join the Regional Cooperation for Development (RCD), and other normalization processes at work, clearly indicate that a new era is at hand for the people of the Indo-Pakistan subcontinent.

NOTES

1. For a detailed meaning of the term, see the *Meaning of* Détente, State Department Publication 8766, Washington D.C., US Government Printing Office, June 1974.
2. W.C., Clemens Jr., *The Super-Powers and Arms Control: From Cold War to Interdependence*, Lexington, Mass, Die Health, 1973, p. 21.
3. Jawaharlal Nehru, *Towards Freedom*, New York, John Day & Co., 1941, p. 292; V.P. Menon, *The Transfer of Power in India*, Calcutta, Orient Longmans and Co., 1957, p. 384.

4. Pran Chopra (ed.), *The Challenge of Bangladesh: A Special Debate*, New York, Humanities Press, 1973, p. 19; also see V.P. Menon, op. cit., p. 384.

5. See issues of *Monthly Public Opinion Surveys*, New Delhi, Indian Institute of Public Opinion, 1972.

6. *Hindustan Times*, New Delhi, 1 April 1971. Speech by Mr K. Subrahmanyam, Director, Indian Institute of Defence Studies and Analyses, at the symposium organized by the Indian Council of World Affairs on 31 March 1971.

7. R.A. Scalapino, *Asia and the Major Powers*, Washington, D.C., American Enterprise Institute for Public Policy Research, 1972, p. 36.

8. Based upon the principle of *Pancha Shila*.

9. For a study of Indian attitudes and policy on the Vietnamese question see Desai Sar, *India's Foreign Policy in Cambodia, Laos and Vietnam, 1947-64*, Berkeley, University of California, 1968.

10. Text of the Simla Agreement, *Pakistan National Assembly Debates*, 5, September 1972.

11. On the Western front the prisoners-of-war captured were 600 Indian and 160 Pakistanis. Whilst India had occupied 5000 sq. miles of Pakistani territory, Pakistan had occupied 100 miles of Indian territory.

12. See Wali Khan's speech in *Dawn*, Karachi, 15 July 1972; the right wing parties in both India and Pakistan also opposed the Agreement. As late as the year 1976, the President of Pakistan Muslim League, Pir Pagaro, accused the Bhutto government of sellout of Pakistan at Simla, for details see *Morning News*, Karachi, 7 June 1976.

13. K.P. Misra, 'Trilateralism in South Asia', *Asian Survey*, Berkeley, California, July 1974, Vol. XIV, p. 630.

14. Embassy of Pakistan, Washington, *Pamphlet on the First Five Hundred Days: A Background Report*, 1973.

15. For a detailed analysis of political developments in Azad Kashmir see *The Pakistan Times*, Lahore, 29 June 1976.

16. Ibid.

17. See Pir Pagaro's statement in the *Morning News*, Karachi, 7 June 1976.

18. See editorial of the Indian weekly journal, *Janta*, 19 October 1975, and *The New York Times*, 27 February 1976.

19. *The Overseas Hindustan Times*, 13 February 1975, Jan Sangh leadership has consistently advocated its refusal to negotiate with Sheikh Abdullah. Mr Rahman also advised New Delhi not to negotiate with Sheikh Abdullah since he did not represent all the three regions of the state of Kashmir and should, therefore, seek a mandate from the people before reaching any settlement with the Indian government.

20. Ibid.

21. Z.A. Bhutto's speech before the UN General Assembly, on 20 September 1973.

22. *The New York Times*, 13 May 1974.

23. Ibid., 27 February 1976.

24. See *Dawn*, Karachi, 20 July 1976.

25. *Newsweek*, New York, 21 May 1973, p. 17.

26. *Kayhan International*, Teheran, 8 November 1975.

27. R.M. Burrell and Alvin J. Cottrell, *Iran, Afghanistan, Pakistan: Tensions and Dilemmas*, Beverely Hills, California, Sage Policy Paper, *The Washington Papers*, 20, Vol. II, 1974.

28. '...neither should seek hegemony in the Asia-Pacific region and each is opposed to efforts by any other country or group of countries to establish such hegemony...'

29. Z.A. Bhutto's address to the Foreign Policy Association and Asia Society, New York, 21 September 1973.

9

An Overview of Pakistan's Foreign Policy in Recent Years*

Zubeida Mustafa

Since July 1977, when the military government took over in Islamabad, Pakistan's foreign policy has been increasingly subject to the stresses and strains generated by international politics in the region of which Pakistan is a part. It has, like other small third world powers with extremely limited resources, formulated a foreign policy which is based not so much on initiatives as on a set of responses to an evolving situation. With little, if any, capacity to change the course of events in international politics, Pakistan has found its foreign policy options drastically limited. This trend has been further accentuated in the last few years during which the economic, political and strategic compulsions that determine the country's foreign policy have become stronger in view of its growing economic dependence on outside powers and the vicissitudes of its domestic politics.

Here we shall first pinpoint the developments which have had a direct bearing on the foreign policy of Pakistan.

Changes in Afghanistan

The April 1978 coup in Kabul which brought the *Khalq* Party of Nur Mohammad Tarahki into power changed entirely the geographical

* Vol. xxxii, No. 4, 1979.

dimensions of international politics in Central and South Asia. The new government was not only socialist in orientation but it also had very close ideological and political links with Moscow. As such the Saur revolution was widely regarded as having ended the so-called 'buffer status' of Afghanistan which since the days of the British Raj in India has enabled Kabul to maintain a tenuously independent existence between two big powers. Even after Britain's departure from the subcontinent, Afghanistan's independent and neutral status had continued to be informally recognized by the big powers. The 1978 putsch and the Treaty of Friendship and Cooperation concluded the same year by Kabul and Moscow firmly threw Afghanistan in the Soviet orbit. The Soviet involvement in this Central Asian country has continued to grow, culminating eventually in December 1979 in the induction of Russian troops on a large scale (there were estimated to be over 30,000 of them in December 1979) into Afghanistan. In fact the Soviet military presence was used reportedly to bring into power the regime of Babrak Karmal, known to have close leanings towards Moscow.

Developments in Afghanistan since 1978 and the direct Soviet military intervention there have had far-reaching implications for Islamabad. In the first place, they have spelt the virtual end of the stability in Pakistan-Afghanistan relations and the prospects of reconciliation between them which the normalization process begun in 1976 was expected to lead to. In other words, the tension and turbulence which marked the north-western border of Pakistan in the fifties were revived in their entirety and with their full implications for the domestic politics of Pakistan, especially in its western provinces. Secondly, the beginning of the insurgency in Afghanistan which was triggered off by the Tarahki government's socio-economic reforms and anti-Islamic stance, and the resulting influx of refugees into Pakistan, has had a direct bearing on Islamabad since it has provided the regime in Kabul and its supporters in the Kremlin with grounds to attack the Pakistan government allegedly for its policy of assisting, training, and providing a sanctuary to the insurgents. Thirdly, the Afghan situation has also had a profound impact on Islamabad's ties with Moscow.

Revolution in Iran

Another major development in the area which has had far-reaching implications for Pakistan is the revolution in Iran, which toppled the pro-Western monarchy of Reza Shah Pahlavi. This has had a bearing on Pakistan in two ways. First, it changed radically the power balance in the Persian Gulf, and the predominance the US enjoyed in the region by virtue of its massive military presence in Iran, was brought to an abrupt end with the departure of the ex-Shah from Teheran. Within a month of taking over power, the revolutionary government announced its withdrawal from CENTO, which changed the strategic and political environment in the Gulf area. Secondly, this had far-reaching implications for the special relationship Pakistan and Iran had forged over the years in the broader context of the international politics of this region.

Changes in India

The defeat of the Congress party in the March 1977 elections in India and the coming into office of the *Janata* Party had a profound impact on India's ties with Pakistan. Mrs Indira Gandhi's successors introduced a positive shift in orientation in India's foreign policy in an attempt to make it 'truly non-aligned'. While Mr Morarji Desai's government sought to improve relations with the United States, it also adopted a more conciliatory attitude towards its smaller neighbours, and relations with China came under review. This not only created a climate of détente in the subcontinent and lowered tension in the region, it also led to the resolution of some of those disputes which had bedevilled India's relations with the states in its vicinity.

Changes in China

Political developments in China following the death of the architects of the Chinese revolution, Mao Zedong and Chou En-lai, also brought a shift in foreign policy. The power struggle in Beijing resulted in the emergence of Deng Xiaoping as the most powerful leader. Deng's programme of modernization created the compulsion for China to forge closer economic and political links with the United States and the

West European states. Chinese diplomacy *vis-à-vis* the West and developments in South East Asia and Afghanistan have led to an intensification of the Sino-Soviet rivalry. Although the two powers have also opened normalization talks, the broad trends in their mutual relations have remained unchanged. The ramification of China's new opening in the West and its unabated conflict with Moscow have been profound for Pakistan's foreign policy.

Big Power Relationships

Finally, another major factor which has had an impact on Pakistan's foreign policy is the big power equation which has recently emerged. While China and the US have come much closer politically and economically (diplomatic ties were established in 1979 and Deng paid a visit to the United States the same year), relations between the Soviet Union and the US have not been equally smooth. The two superpowers have confronted each other on different issues such as Afghanistan, Cuba, and the Horn of Africa and détente has come under severe strain. Although SALT-II was signed in June 1979 by President Jimmy Carter and Mr Leonid Brezhnev, tension between them has been quite marked on different occasions. It is quite evident that the triangular relations between the US, the USSR, and China have not been on an equal plane. The identity of interests that has emerged between the US and China and the growing tensions between Washington and Moscow, and between China and the Soviet Union have made the US-China side of this triangle rather short.

When seen against this backdrop, Pakistan's foreign policy acquires new dimensions. Broadly speaking its relations with outside powers might be divided into three categories: relations with the big powers, relations with its neighbours, and its position in the Islamic Conference and the third world.

Pakistan's Relations with Big Powers

Despite the fact that Pakistan's relations with the United States have undergone major fluctuations in the last few years, it is significant that this did not affect its ties with other powers and in essence the broad pattern of its relationship with China and the USSR remained unchanged, at least until the Soviet action in Afghanistan.

For over three years, Pakistan-US ties remained under great stress on account of Washington's opposition to Pakistan's nuclear programme. Islamabad's quest for a nuclear reprocessing plant, for which a deal had been concluded with France in early 1976, evoked a strong reaction in Washington. Ostensibly on grounds of the American position on nuclear non-proliferation, Mr Henry Kissinger, the American Secretary of State, had at that time bluntly demanded that the deal be called off. In fact sharp differences on the nuclear reprocessing plant, which Pakistan claimed was not being acquired for military purposes, had led to a steady deterioration in Pakistan-US relations during the last days of the former Prime Minister of Pakistan Mr Z.A. Bhutto. When the military regime took over in Islamabad in July 1977, relations with the US showed no improvement mainly because Islamabad's stand on its nuclear programme remained unchanged. The Pakistan government consistently took the plea that its nuclear programme was entirely designed to fulfil its need for energy for economic development. It agreed to accept all international safeguards laid down by the IAEA, but refused to accept any inspection or full-scope safeguards on a discriminatory basis. Its plea was that it would accept all conditions so long as they were universally applicable.

The US position on the issue was rigid and at times not easily explained. In the first place, it never quite accepted Pakistan's assurances and voiced its opposition on the ground that the acquisition of a nuclear reprocessing plant by Pakistan could lead to nuclear proliferation. Even after the reprocessing plant deal went into cold storage in 1978, the United States wanted more categorical assurances from Islamabad that it would not try to acquire nuclear technology even indigenously. Hence, it also opposed Pakistan's plan for a uranium enrichment plant. It appears that the US was fully convinced that Pakistan was seeking to manufacture a nuclear bomb which it would place at the disposal of its Muslim allies. The acquisition of such an 'Islamic Bomb', it was feared in Washington, would tilt the balance of power in the Arab-Israeli context.

Pakistan's protests notwithstanding, the US adopted a firm and even unfriendly attitude and brought pressure to bear against Islamabad. On two occasions (in August 1978 and April 1979) the nuclear issue was used as a pretext to announce suspension of economic aid under the Symington Amendment.

But despite the outbursts of angry emotion on both sides which brought relations to a low ebb, neither of the two countries appeared to have decided to abandon the other altogether. These irritants in its relations with Washington notwithstanding, which often led to the suspension of American economic aid (military assistance having been ended many years back), Pakistan showed a notable reluctance to downgrade its ties with the United States in any way. Thus in 1978 the Presidential Adviser on Foreign Affairs, Mr Agha Shahi disclosed that Pakistan's membership of CENTO was under review.[1] Earlier, President Ziaul Haq had also stressed the need for a reappraisal.[2] But no positive decision could be taken until the Iranian revolutionary government quitted the military alliance, facilitating Pakistan's exit from the pact. That the decision to leave CENTO was in effect a response to the Iranian initiative rather than a calculated move on the part of Pakistan, is not much in doubt. That no qualitative change in policy *vis-à-vis* Washington was intended is all the more evident from the fact that the US-Pakistan Mutual Defence Treaty of 1959 was not revoked. This was clearly demonstrated in November 1979 when after the burning down of the American embassy in Islamabad by an angry mob, both governments played it cool. Soon thereafter, the entry of Soviet troops into Afghanistan evoked a similar response from both Islamabad and Washington. Due to basic similarity in outlook, it did not prove too difficult for the two governments to work towards an understanding on the issue. It goes to underline the similarity in orientation between the two countries that despite all differences President Carter could venture to offer military assistance to Pakistan and the latter gave due consideration to the American position on the issue.

Given the international equations in the region, Pakistan's close ties with China did not impinge upon its friendship with the US. Although Sino-Pakistan friendship was forged much earlier in the sixties, by the end of the seventies its international context changed. In the sixties, China's close ties with Pakistan were conceived more directly in the context of their respective relations with India. True, they had repercussions on Islamabad's ties with the other big powers, especially the US, but the foremost impact of the Sino-Pakistan friendship was on the subcontinent, where it helped to balance India's claim to predominance. But in view of the easing of tensions in Sino-Indian and Indo-Pakistan relations, Pakistan's relations with China have acquired a new meaning. The completion of the Karakoram

Highway linking the two countries together, closer cooperation in the economic sphere and more frequent consultation on defence matters ensured for Beijing an ally in an area where it could otherwise have been outflanked by Moscow. For Pakistan, its friendship with China meant that it was not left diplomatically isolated at critical periods when its relations with the US were at a low ebb and not many links existed with Moscow. But conversely Pakistan's ties with Beijing had serious implications for Pakistan's relationship with Moscow.

During the last two or three years Islamabad's relations with Moscow have been officially correct and economic cooperation has continued on a low key. But no close understanding could be reached between the two governments. Thus Pakistan's withdrawal from CENTO, the alliance Moscow had bitterly attacked at its inception in the fifties, had no impact on the Russians whose attitude showed no softening towards Pakistan whatsoever.

Relations between Islamabad and Moscow were also affected by the Soviet Union's forward policy in Africa, Middle East, and Southeast Asia. This policy threw the USSR in confrontation with countries with which Pakistan enjoys a close equation such as Somalia in the Horn of Africa, Saudi Arabia in the Arabian Peninsula, and China in Southeast Asia, all of which had a stake in the *status quo* in these regions, which the USSR was seeking to change.

In such circumstances it was not inevitable that with the Afghan *coup* of December 1979 and the induction of Russian troops into Afghanistan, Pakistan-USSR relations would reach a new low and become an area of concern. The events in Afghanistan could lead to a revival of the cold war of the fifties, with the chances of Pakistan being sucked in appearing quite real.

The Pakistan government based its position on the premise that Soviet troops had been inducted into Afghanistan to determine the outcome of the political crisis there. It insisted the Russians had no legal basis to maintain a military presence in Afghanistan.[3] Islamabad condemned in no uncertain terms the Soviet military intervention as a violation of the principles of peaceful coexistence and non-intervention. The question of moral, legal, and religious principles aside, the military and strategic implications of the Soviet intervention were also weighed and caused grave concern. Moreover, it also expressed the fear that the Islamic identity of Afghanistan was under threat. This had serious ramifications for the Muslim world. However, Pakistan's identity of interests with China and the United States was quite significant in view of the fact that both Beijing and Washington perceived the Russian intervention as a military invasion which was a prelude to its 'southward thrust' to the Indian Ocean and the sea-lanes there. Whether Islamabad officially subscribed to this theory was not immediately known, but this could not be ruled out in view of the positive interest shown in strengthening the security and defence of the country by acquiring arms from the West.

Relations with Neighbours

In recent years, the international politics of South Asia has proved to be conducive to peace and détente which has enabled Pakistan to develop more amicable ties with its neighbours in the subcontinent. The policy of friendship with Bangladesh which was initiated after the fall of Sheikh Mujibur Rehman was further consolidated and economic ties with Dhaka were strengthened. President Ziaur Rahman paid a goodwill visit to Islamabad in late 1977 and economic, commercial, cultural and other non-political ties developed at a steady pace.

With India, there was a perceptible effort on both sides to keep relations on an even keel although the traditional pattern of relations between them did not undergo a fundamental change. Thus the Kashmir dispute, communal riots in India, arms deals which either of the two governments concluded with third powers and their nuclear programmes provided occasion for an exchange of polemics from time to time. But this was carried out more through the press rather than at the government level. Due to the continuing pattern of suspicion and hostility, differences on some basic issues could not be resolved although an agreement was reached on some other questions which were not of a fundamental nature such as the Salal Dam. But the Kashmir dispute, the nuclear weapon free zone in South Asia and the question of determining the arms ratio between the two countries continued to evade a settlement. Yet India under the *Janata* did not pose a security problem for Pakistan, although the normalization process did not proceed any further after a certain stage.

Among its neighbours, Pakistan found its relations with Afghanistan the most eventful. On at least three occasions in recent years it appeared that the two countries were on the verge of a breakthrough in their relations which would have altered the pattern of politics in the area. But invariably a change of government in Kabul foiled whatever progress could be achieved in the normalization of relations between them. Under Sardar Daud the Afghan government opened a dialogue with the Pakistan government and an agreement was also reached on the framework within which negotiations were to be conducted. But before any progress could be made Sardar Daud was overthrown. With the new government of Nur Mohammad Tarahki which came into power in Kabul in April 1978, Afghan foreign policy orientation underwent a marked change. There was initially some tension in relations between the two countries on the 'issue of the rights of the Pashtun and Baluch' as the Afghan government now prefers to term what it previously called the 'Pakhtunistan dispute'. But subsequently another issue emerged as the major irritant between them. The socio-economic reforms, the anti-Islam bias of its policy and the strongly pro-Moscow line introduced by the ruling *Khalq* party gave rise to a reaction among the people affected by them and an insurgency broke out in some areas of Afghanistan.

Although the insurgents were divided among themselves, their Islamic orientation proved to be a common denominator among them. This also won for them the sympathies of Muslim states. The insurgency was also accompanied by an influx of refugees into Pakistan who were estimated to number nearly 400,000 in January 1980. These refugees became a source of tension in Kabul-Islamabad relations. The Afghan government alleged that many of these refugees were subversive elements being trained in camps on Pakistani soil from where they were infiltrated back into Afghanistan to carry on the insurgency. This was denied by Islamabad. When President Ziaul Haq met President Tarahki at Havana in September 1979, it was anticipated that a dialogue would be initiated once again. But soon thereafter Tarahki was overthrown and killed. When the new government of Hafizullah Amin came round to fixing a date for a visit by the Pakistan Adviser for Foreign Affairs to Kabul, the Afghan regime was once again ousted from office in a *coup* backed by Soviet forces. The induction into power of the government of Babrak Karmal in December 1979 with active military assistance from Moscow and the entry of Russian troops into Afghanistan has had a direct impact on Pakistan-Afghanistan relations which deteriorated rapidly thereafter.

With the revolution in Iran began a new phase in Pakistan-Iran relations, which could, until then, be described as extremely friendly and cordial. In the wake of the revolution, Iran tended to be inward-looking and its foreign policy lacked the dynamism it had previously displayed. Secondly, the anti-Shah thrust of revolutionary Iran's policies meant that all previous connections came under review. Thus after leaving CENTO, Teheran also sought to terminate the RCD, describing it as a 'by-product of CENTO'. Pakistan reaffirmed its close relationship with Iran and the Iranian leadership reciprocated the sentiments expressed, but it was obvious that Iran was no longer the stabilizing force on Pakistan's western flank.

Position in Third World and Islamic Countries

Relations with the Islamic countries and the third world continued to be friendly and close. However, in view of the general lack of political dynamism shown by the Islamic Conference, Pakistan's role also tended to be on a low key. It adhered to its long-standing position of upholding Islamic and Arab causes, such as demanding the return of Jerusalem and other Israeli-occupied Arab territories and espousing the rights of Muslims in other parts of the world.

But the divisions among the members of the Islamic Conference made Pakistan's position all the more difficult. Islamabad got round this difficulty by adopting a policy of going along with the moderate leadership provided by the Saudi Arabian government on the Arab-Israeli question and other issues of concern to the Islamic world. This saved it from making a difficult choice between supporting the radicals such as Libya, Syria, Iraq, and Algeria or the openly pro-Western states such as Egypt, Sudan, Oman and Somalia which had expressed themselves in favour of negotiations with Israel.

Moreover, closer ties with Saudi Arabia helped Pakistan in maintaining a balance in its Middle East policy, especially when in the last few years there was a shift away from the very close ties Islamabad had previously forged with some Arab states such as Libya and the UAE.

However, the single major development in Pakistan's foreign policy was its debut in the Non-Aligned Movement (NAM). For nearly a decade Pakistan was known to have sought entry into this expanding club of third world countries. Islamabad's membership of CENTO had precluded its admission into this movement, as the basic criterion of membership had been laid down as early as 1961 to be the non-membership of military alliances conceived in the context of big powers' rivalry. Although Pakistan terminated the American base at

Badebar near Peshawar in 1969 and for nearly two decades it had held identical positions on world issues as NAM, its membership of CENTO was used as a pretext by some interested countries, notably India, to exclude it from NAM.

In July 1978 this opposition had weakened sufficiently to enable Pakistan to attend, as a guest, the Belgrade Foreign Ministers' conference. Withdrawal from CENTO in March 1979 paved the way for Pakistan's entry into NAM. But this development was not free from complexities for Islamabad since at this juncture NAM was poised at a difficult phase in its history. At the Havana summit, a confrontation between Cuba and Yugoslavia was barely averted on the question of defining non-alignment and the direction the movement was to take. Yugoslavia prevailed in steering the middle course and keeping the movement strictly non-aligned. Pakistan threw its weight behind President Tito. But on specific issues it displayed no consistency in its orientation. While it sided with the radical Arabs on the question of Egypt's membership of NAM, it went along with the conservative anti-Soviet lobby on Kampuchea opposing recognition of the Vietnam-backed Heng Samrin regime.

Pakistan's entry into NAM, however, was not expected to make any significant difference in the general trend of the country's foreign policy since CENTO had ceased to be an effective strategic or military force. This assessment was confirmed by President Ziaul Haq in a statement at Islamabad airport on his return from Havana.[4] Yet Pakistan's membership of NAM was not without importance for the country. In the first place, by being excluded from a major third world forum Islamabad ran the risk of being excluded from the mainstream of third world politics. Secondly, it often found itself denied the opportunity to formulate its position in its defence against the attacks launched by some countries which were also members of NAM. Thirdly, by remaining outside NAM, Islamabad could always be vulnerable to charges of aligning itself too closely with one or the other big power. In this context, Pakistan found its hand considerably strengthened after Havana.

NOTES

1. Mr Agha Shahi's statement in Karachi, *Dawn*, Karachi, 18 October 1978.
2. Ibid., 15 September 1978.
3. Statement of the Pakistan government of 29 December 1979, *Dawn*, Karachi, 30 December 1979 and the statement of the Permanent Representative of Pakistan in the UN Security Council, *Dawn*, Karachi, 6 January 1980.
4. *Dawn*, Karachi, 11 September 1979.

10

Pakistan and the Muslim World*

Col. Ghulam Sarwar

An Overview

The latest changes that have taken place across our Western frontier are full of grim portents for Pakistan. Dominance of the Soviet Union in Afghanistan has considerably influenced the political geography of the region. Pakistan's geographic location in the strategic zone of the Middle East oil and the Afro-Asian ocean is of considerable importance. In the context of its global strategy, the Soviet Union has vital strategic, political, and economic interests in the region. As such, it is incumbent upon Pakistan to be vigilant at all times, and adopt a pragmatic and rational approach towards its neighbours.

The impending threat to Pakistan's security calls for a serious reappraisal of the whole situation. Pakistan has now become more vulnerable to Soviet pressures than ever before. The buffer which the British had tried to build up in Afghanistan as a bulwark against Russian expansionism has now disappeared all too suddenly. With Soviet borders moving from the Amu River to Spinbaldak, the Gawadar port of Pakistan on the Arabian Sea is only 300 miles away.

In order to combat this threat, it is proposed that the religious and cultural ties that bind Pakistan with the Muslim world should be further strengthened. The focal point of Pakistan's diplomatic activities should

* Vol. xxxiv, No. 1, 1981.

be to foster still closer relations with all Muslim countries, especially those located in the Middle East. On the diplomatic front, Pakistan should convince the Muslim world that its survival is in the interest of the entire *Ummah*. Pakistan must convince Muslim states that it is the spirit and compulsions of renascent Islam that can save the situation. For this, the Organization of Islamic Conference must realize its duty to forge a united front and mobilize the Muslim states' collective resources. They should demonstrate complete solidarity with Pakistan to ensure its independence.

Having spelt out the problem in brief terms we now propose to discuss in detail the geostrategic importance of the Muslim world, insofar as it relates to Pakistan.

Geostrategic Importance of the Muslim World

The Muslim world stretches over a vast area of the globe from Indonesia in the east to Morocco in the west. It embraces a variety of national and ethnic groups which are divided by geographical distances as well as by different languages and interests. The commonality of religious belief, however, provides a natural platform for the cultivation and development of inter-state relations. The Muslim world enjoys a unique strategic importance in the global context. For instance, as master of the Bosphorus and the Dardanelles, Turkey occupies a very strategic position. It stands on the gateway of the Mediterranean from the north. The Mediterranean sea is more than 60 per cent a Muslim lake. Its eastern gateway is controlled by Egypt and on the western end of the Mediterranean, Tangier (Morocco) is also under Muslim control. Also, the Red Sea is a Muslim lake, being controlled on either side by Muslims. Likewise, the Gulf is a Muslim lake. In Southeast Asia, Indonesia not only stands out as the outpost of the Muslim world in the Pacific Ocean, but also serves as the stepping stone for one who intends to cross over to the West. From the southwestern borders of Russia stands a solid bloc of Muslim countries. The coastal region of East Africa is almost entirely Muslim. East to west from Eritrea across the whole continent, the whole bloc consists of Muslim countries. Then from Mauritania down south and east with the exception of Liberia and Ghana, it is entirely a bloc comprising majority Muslim areas. This throws ample light on the strategic importance of the Muslim belt in the world.[1]

As compared to the state of Muslims in the last century, we note with satisfaction that they are now far happily placed. We see that mid-way through the last century, the West had occupied or dismembered the entire Muslim world, from the parched deserts of North Africa to the steamy jungles of Indonesia. In 1940, there were only seven independent Muslim states. Now there are more than forty and all are free from colonial rule. After years of political subjugation, stagnation, and poverty during the long era of their decline, Muslim states now have the means to turn the tables on former colonial powers—oil.

Conflicting Interests of the Muslim World

Although the Muslim family shares a number of basic values, regrettably, it also suffers from lack of unity. North Yemen versus South Yemen, Morocco versus Algeria in the Western Sahara, Egypt versus Libya, Iran versus Iraq, and Syria versus Iraq are some of the sore points threatening the solidarity of the *Ummah*. Other inter-Islamic disputes have featured Libya and Tunisia, Iraq and Kuwait, etc. Lately Anwar Sadat, President of Egypt, the most populous Arab country, incurred the wrath of most Islamic states by concluding a peace pact with Israel.

In view of these divergent views and conflicting national interests, it will be rather idealistic to aspire for a joint defence of the Muslim world. This will amount to talking in abstractions. What can possibly be achieved under the circumstances is the mutual assistance which Muslim countries can offer to one another without jeopardizing their own interests. Since Pakistan enjoys good relations with all Muslim countries, it can look towards the Muslim world for assistance, both moral and material, in this grim hour of its existence.

Strategic Spectrum of Pakistan

Pakistan is an ideological state whose geopolitical stature has come to occupy a position of importance in the Muslim world's strategic thinking. It is likely to be drawn into the conflicting interests of the super and major powers surrounding it. This is a very sensitive situation that calls for extreme vigilance while framing Pakistan's national policies.

Pakistan's peculiar strategic location gives it an internationally important position among the Muslim nations. It is linked with the Muslim countries of South West Asia, which are grouped together under the title of Middle East countries. These are primarily oil rich countries. Further west, lie the Arab countries of North Africa, so that there is one continuous bloc of Muslim countries from the Indus basin to the Atlantic. Pakistan is, thus, a bridge between the Middle East and Southeast Asia. It is a bridge from the north Arabian Sea board to the heart of the USSR and also to the southwestern part of the People's Republic of China.

Steps towards Muslim Unity

It is suggested that independent of US, USSR, and China alignment, Pakistan should establish economic and political links with the Islamic bloc, commencing with an alliance of the Gulf states. This has certain long-term advantages, e.g. economic benefits and escape from superpower rivalry. Economic benefits will enable Pakistan to make itself militarily strong. Also a neutral posture towards superpowers will extricate Pakistan from many difficult situations.

After strengthening its ties with the Gulf states, Pakistan should next establish a significant partnership with fraternal Islamic states located in the Middle East. This will lead to unity of purpose in multi-dimensional spheres of regional and international cooperation. In addition, Pakistan should strive towards the establishment of a more influential bloc for accelerating the pace of development among Muslim states. Fostering deeper relations with regional Islamic states through maximizing cultural and economic cooperation must receive Pakistan's urgent attention. Steps towards ensuring mutual technical assistance and incentives for multiple joint ventures, particularly in defence production and technology, must merit serious attention.

In addition to its contacts with Gulf states and the Middle East, Pakistan must aim at the establishment of closer multi-dimensional relations with Iran and Turkey. The RCD should be strengthened and possibilities for expanding this arrangement to include Gulf states should be sought.

Over the years, Iran-Pakistan relations have been characterized by extreme cordiality. They have built up a tradition of mutual consultation and cooperation. It is hoped that despite Iran's internal problems, good understanding and cooperation towards Pakistan will be enhanced in view of the Islamic resurgence in both these countries. Moral support of Iran at this juncture will be of great value to Pakistan.

As regards Pakistan's relations with Turkey, it is in the cultural and political fields that both countries feel more strongly motivated to act together with unified policies. This is likely to remain the solid base for their collaboration in future as well. It is heartening to know that having remained distant for a considerable time, Turkey is now moving closer to the Arab Muslim states and Pakistan's assistance in the further development of such relations would strengthen the existing ties between Turkey and Pakistan. Turkey's support for Pakistan in international forums will also considerably strengthen the latter's hands.

And now a word about Pakistan's relations with the Middle East. As already mentioned, common cultural experiences, close geographic proximity, and deep religious feelings bind Pakistan emotionally and psychologically to the Muslim countries of the Middle East. The psychological aspiration of the people of Pakistan to be a member of the Pan-Islamic expanse is innate and historical. Also, Pakistan's search for friends and supporters from the beginning made Pakistan look towards the Arabs. The historic-cultural ties have been constantly employed and appreciated by both sides to establish close relations. Lastly, oil revenues have placed massive assets at the disposal of the Arabs, creating a situation that offers many economic possibilities for Pakistan. These possibilities include the Arab capability of direct financial assistance to Pakistan, Pakistan manpower employment in the Middle East, and the likelihood of joint industrial ventures. The Middle East also presents an expanding and affluent consumer market which could accommodate a good deal of Pakistan's trade.

In short, the Middle East is emerging as one of the most important regions in Pakistan's foreign relations. It provides unparalleled economic opportunities which Pakistan can gain and exploit by virtue of its geographic proximity, abundance of exportable manpower, and its established diplomatic presence in the region.

Defence Potential of the Muslim World

In this connection, the following few suggestions are offered for consideration:

(a) Muslims should aim at creating a better understanding of the Islamic defence concepts and discuss ways and means whereby Muslim countries, individually and collectively, could develop effective defence capabilities

(b) A concerted effort is required to undertake coordinated research so that advanced technology could be acquired by the Muslim world in all the fields without any loss of time. Our technological dependence on the advanced countries must come to an end. Urgency of the problem calls for an objective appraisal of the state of science and technology in the Muslim world and a plan for strengthening the technological base in all contemporary fields of development. If we decide to pool our manpower and material resources, we can accelerate our growth and move towards greater self-reliance.

(c) Muslim countries must aim at self-reliance in defence preparedness. This will serve as a deterrent against any encroachment upon their territorial integrity and their Islamic way of life which they cherish so dearly.

(d) Muslim countries must share their resources ungrudgingly and selflessly for the security of every Muslim country and for the economic, social, and technological development of the Muslim world as a whole.

(e) They should cooperate in the pursuit and advancement of knowledge and technology and in the eduction and training of their peoples.

(f) They should set up joint industrial ventures in the field of defence production for the attainment of collective self-reliance. The establishment of the Islamic Institute of Defence Technology is a step in the right direction. Muslim countries must cooperate with the Institute to strengthen its activities.

(g) Muslim countries must intensify their efforts to acquire defence technology from wherever it is available at the best terms.

(h) A committee of military experts should be formed. They should be fully qualified in the field of Islamic studies to prepare a comprehensive study of the above issues and the possibilities of their realization.

(i) Muslim countries must take up the exploitation of their national resources in their own hands. If foreign assistance is inevitable, it should be taken, as far as possible, from other Muslim countries and not from non-Muslim states.

(j) Every Muslim country should have before it a clear-cut, practicable and adequate programme for providing necessary defence arrangement internally. Ordnance factories and heavy machinery for producing necessary defence equipment should be set up immediately according to local needs. Help in procuring necessary raw material for putting up steel plants and other basic units should be freely obtained from Muslims rather than non-Muslim countries. This question of defensive armament should be given top priority in every national budget. Steps should be taken by richer Muslim countries to develop nuclear energy, because without advances in nuclear equipment, no country is really safe these days. Our emphasis should be on self-development, self-reliance, and internal strength. Whenever there is a necessity for augmenting this, Muslims should depend upon other Muslims and not on any superpower.

This brief narrative should convince everyone that Muslims are in a position to finance their defence measures. Setting up of basic industries, heavy machinery complexes, armament factories, and even development of nuclear energy for peaceful purposes is financially possible. Pakistan possesses the requisite technical know-how and a well-oriented military. It is up to the affluent Arab world to finance Pakistan, attain the requisite status in the field of science and technology and equip its armed forces on the most modern lines. Pakistan is passing through the most crucial period of its existence and the call of the hour is that the Muslim world should generously finance all projects which could ensure a viable status for Pakistan in the comity of nations.

NOTE

1. Dr Inamullah Khan, *World Muslim Gazetter,* Karachi, 1975, p. 28.

11

Pakistan-Iran Relations (1947–1979)*

Safia S. Mohammadally

Inter-state behaviour can exhibit three types of group relations, namely, conflict, competition and cooperation.[1] While the majority of situations reflect 'competition', it is remarkable that Pakistan-Iran relations have had a steady undertone of cooperation and cordiality. At all levels of interaction, local, regional, and global, the two countries have by and large, through the years, been able to identify common interests. Common interests overlapping with shared heritage have made cooperation a predictable feature of their mutual relationship.

Challenges and demands of regional politics as well as those of the global environment have influenced the policies of both countries in a similar manner. In the early phase of their relationship, both countries faced problems of consolidation compounded by security needs and both aligned themselves with the United States in the cold war era. Later, both grew disenchanted with their common ally and turned to mutual cooperation at the regional level. During the seventies the security needs of a dismembered Pakistan and regional ambitions of an economically powerful Iran altered the fundamental equation of relationship by creating a dependency of the former on the latter. Notwithstanding this, the two countries were brought in closer cooperation. At present, the special relationship has found yet another *locus standi*; a growing quest for identity and policy in the region.

---

* Vol. xxxii, No. 4, 1979.

A great deal of the cordiality owes its origin directly to the common heritage[2] of the two countries. This heritage that encompasses the whole spectrum of cultural, ethnic, linguistic, and religious affinities dates back centuries. 'From the time of the first sustained Muslim influences', writes Horward Wriggins, 'the models for political structures and processes, as well as religious inspiration and cultural influences came from Iran and the Arab Middle East.'[3] Ethnically, the people of both Iran and Pakistan belong to the same Aryan stock. Persian, the language of Iranians, has had strong influence on most of Pakistan's languages. This is so because Persian, along with Arabic, was the court language of the Mughals throughout their seven-century rule over the Indo-Pakistan subcontinent.

Another important factor, external to the overall period of Pakistan-Iran relations, is the geostrategic position of Pakistan. The good neighbourly relations also owe their origin to the geographical location of both Iran and Pakistan in an area criss-crossed by regional and global rivalries and competition. Pakistan is a Middle Eastern and a South Asian power, and 'South Asia is a strategic transitional zone between West Asia and Southeast Asia...Events in South Asia have considerable impact on neighbouring areas'.[4] Additionally, Pakistan itself plays the role of a 'transitional zone'[5] by virtue of being both a South Asian and a Middle Eastern power. Thus Pakistan's stability is linked with the stability of the entire region.

Because of Pakistan's geographic location, its destiny has been linked historically with that of 'northern tier' countries. All calculations, at regional and global levels, concerning strategy and geopolitics have made Iran and Pakistan constant partners. Furthermore, these calculations have drawn Iran and Pakistan into the vortex of superpower rivalry. It is interesting to note that despite the transition in international politics from a bipolar system to a more flexible balance of power system, Pakistan and Iran found themselves, throughout the changes in superpower relations, on the same side of the fence. Both looked to the West in their period of consolidation and were linked by the Baghdad pact in 1955, later known as CENTO. Both sought to follow a normalization policy *vis-à-vis* the Soviet Union in the mid-sixties as disillusionment with the West set in. In the early seventies both looked to the West again for reassurance, Pakistan more so than Iran. The Nixon Doctrine matched perfectly with Iran's bid for regional leadership. This in turn fulfilled Pakistan's cardinal need for some sort of guarantee of its territorial integrity.[6] Towards the end of the decade Iran and Pakistan's relations with the West became tenuous. Attention centered on domestic upheavals which finally resulted in change of governments in both countries.

In the current phase both have emphasized developing relations with the non-aligned countries in general and the Muslim world in particular. A concomitant desire to be free from all sorts of domination of the superpowers is also common to both.

Pakistan-Iran Relations 1947–1970

Raymond Aron observes that a small power restricts its ambition to physical survival and preservation of its legal independence.[7] In 1947 both Pakistan and Iran were faced with hostile neighbours and hence their desire for survival was acute. Formed on the basis of Islamic ideology, Pakistan, in the years following independence, turned to the Muslim world, 'especially the Muslim countries of the Middle East for understanding, friendship and support'.[8]

Pakistan received such support from Iran and the two countries signed a treaty of friendship to initiate trade relations in February 1950. In March of the same year, the Shah of Iran became the first head of state to visit the new member of the international community, Pakistan. While Iran backed Pakistan's entry into the UN and its stand on Kashmir, Pakistan lent its support when Iran nationalized British oil companies in 1951. The friendship of Iran in those lean, early years in the life of the Pakistani nation was truly valuable, given the attitude of other Muslim countries to Pakistan. Since its independence, Pakistan had sincerely and with considerable enthusiasm taken upon itself the task of consolidating and unifying the Muslim world, but its efforts were misunderstood as a bid for leadership.[9]

Pakistan, Iran and Baghdad Pact (1955)

In the 1950s the cold war was at its peak and Iran's physical proximity to the Soviet Union aggravated its security needs. Thus the threat of communism, the memories of the occupation of Azerbaijan as well as the knowledge of the American role in bringing this occupation to an end,[10] decided the Iranian choice *vis-à-vis* the Baghdad pact. Pakistan on the other hand, with a hostile India and not too amiable Afghanistan as neighbours, was also occupied with a quest for security. Pakistan carefully cultivated the friendship of the United States and joined the Western alliance system in the hope of securing arms for its defence needs. The United States on its part was receptive as it had itself embarked on a search for allies for its policy of containment of communism.

Following the Iraqi revolution in 1958, the Baghdad pact was renamed CENTO. In 1959 both Pakistan and Iran signed defence agreements with the United States on a bilateral basis. It must be noted that the Soviet Union had offered Iran a fifty year non-aggression pact. Iran rejected this offer, choosing to stand by its allies after the direct appeal, from the leaders of Pakistan, Turkey, and Britain.[11] The common alignment with the US served to promote warmer ties and closer contact between Pakistan and Iran. During the Suez crisis in 1956 for instance, Iran and Pakistan, along with other Muslim members of the Baghdad pact jointly condemned the Israeli, British, and French aggression against Egypt.[12] Again, during the 1967 Arab-Israeli war, Pakistan and Iran supported the Arabs in and outside the United Nations.

Formation of the Regional Cooperation for Development (RCD)

The Iraqi revolution (1958) and the U-2 incident (1960) created similar apprehensions for both Iran and Pakistan. Pakistan absorbed the shock more quickly and began developing relations with the People's Republic of China. The dangers of partisanship in foreign relations became apparent to Iran as well. Consequently it was announced in 1962 that Iran would not allow the stationing of American nuclear missiles on Iranian soil.[13] This had the positive effect of a noticeable reduction in the hostile Soviet propaganda and of the emergence of a détente in Iran-Soviet relations. Thus both Iran and Pakistan began to cultivate a regional outlook in dealing with their respective problems. Sustaining this mood, Pakistan sought to normalize its relations with Afghanistan. Iran also favoured this normalization, and suggestions for some sort of a confederation of Afghanistan, Pakistan, and Iran came to be mooted publicly.[14] The President of Pakistan, General Mohammad Ayub Khan, himself suggested collaboration between Pakistan, Iran, and Afghanistan at a public meeting in Quetta in August 1962.[15] But these proposals evidently did not meet the approval of the Afghan government and were consequently shelved. However, a more benign and less bold organization was set up by Pakistan and Iran together with Turkey in 1964—the RCD.

The RCD was created by its members in part because of their disenchantment with CENTO's role and 'as a consequence of their dissatisfaction with its inherent unresponsiveness to any conflict other than the one with the Soviet Union. Turkey was dissatisfied with it over the Cyprus problem, Pakistan over the Kashmir dispute and Iran over the conflict with Iraq'.[16] The RCD partners were also aware of a relaxation of tension between the US and the USSR, reducing the value of military pacts. They sought to institutionalize close cooperation among themselves in all fields through the RCD. However, throughout the 1960s the gap between promise and performance remained piteously unabridged. RCD never developed into an organization exploiting its potential.

Iran as Friend and Mediator

On a number of occasions Iran's mediation helped ease out tense relations of Pakistan with other countries. In intra-regional disputes especially, Pakistan found in Iran a steadfast friend. In 1963, Iran's mediation helped restore diplomatic ties between Pakistan and Afghanistan after a break of two years. King Zahir Shah of Afghanistan was coaxed to tone down his support for the 'Pakhtunistan' issue. In 1965, Pakistan once again reposed its trust in Iran when it chose Mr Nasrollah Entezam, an Iranian diplomat, as its nominee on the tribunal appointed to arbitrate the Rann of Kutch dispute between India and Pakistan.

In the 1965 Indo-Pakistan war, Iran aided Pakistan both diplomatically, and materially. An Iranian government statement labelled the Indian attack on Pakistan as 'aggression'.[17] While Iran could not respond positively to Pakistan's request for aircrafts due to the constraints of its arms policy *vis-à-vis* the United States, it did provide Pakistan with jet fuel and gasoline.[18] Iran's diplomatic support was particularly valuable in offsetting the feeling of isolation in Pakistan—a feeling that was the direct result of the neutralist attitude of its ally, the United States of America.

Relations during the Seventies (1971–1979)

Throughout the earlier phase of their relationship, there was a tremendous amount of goodwill, but Pakistan stood out as the more dynamic partner, especially in the fifties and early sixties. This was so firstly, because of Iran's non-assertive foreign policy. 'The overriding concern of the state was internal survival and repression and there was little room for a coherent, active foreign policy'.[19] Good-neighbourly relations apart, Iran was mostly tied down to internal consolidation, domestic reforms, and suppression of internal uprisings. Fear of Soviet expansionism and Arab radicalism also kept the regime of the Shah fully occupied. All these factors robbed Iran of a dynamic role on the regional or global levels. In contrast Pakistan, the largest Muslim nation with a growing industrial base and an enviable military establishment since 1959, was more dynamic.[20] But from the mid-sixties, and more definitely in the seventies began the period that saw a general resurgence of Iran in world affairs.

In the late sixties Pakistan experienced widespread domestic upheavals which finally culminated in the crisis of 1971 and the dismemberment of Pakistan. Iran, on the other hand, having achieved a measure of political and economic stability, was in a better position to play a more active role in world affairs. Britain's east of Suez withdrawal policy also brought about a major change in the region. Following the British withdrawal from the Arabian peninsula and the Gulf,[21] and Iran's ambitious bid to substitute Britain's responsibilities in the region, the Pakistan-Iran relationship became fundamentally altered. The emergence of Iran as the more dynamic and dominant partner was further confirmed when following the 1973 oil embargo and the subsequent increase in oil revenues, Iran began to aspire for regional supremacy. It began an assertive foreign policy towards the attainment of this goal. As regards foreign policy of the new Pakistan, it was given a new orientation—towards Muslim states of West Asia and the Middle East. In the years following 1971, Iran's friendship became invaluable and developed into the cornerstone of Pakistan's resurgent security needs.[22]

In wider regional terms, the relationship became less ambiguous in the seventies. By 1968 it was hard to assess which region, the Middle East or South Asia, was more influential in relation to each other and within the broader global system. The period extending from 1971 to 1973, however, removed all doubts. The Middle Eastern-Iranian area directed substantial influences towards South Asia, receiving no reciprocal influences in response.[23] Interpreted in terms of Pakistan-Iran relations, this meant the virtual dependence of Pakistan on Iran's goodwill and sustained guarantee of Pakistan's territorial integrity.

Iran's dominance and intrusion in South Asia was expressed even through its economic relations with all the principal South Asian countries. As far as the Middle East was concerned, Iran began to build up its position as a regional power. It simply tried to replace the British as the keeper of the Gulf. Iran began to utilize its petrodollars for its military and economic build-up and technological advancement. By 1975 the pattern of its activities suggested that while the Gulf would remain the principal region of concern, Iran's influence was to extend to the entire Middle East, South Asia and the Indian Ocean areas as well. An increased stabilizing role of Iran in South Asia, and more generally in the Indian Ocean region, in view of Soviet and Indian dominance in the wake of the 1971 Indo-Pakistan war, was more than welcomed by Pakistan. Thus the change in the regional power pattern in favour of Iran suited Pakistan.

Both Pakistan and Iran needed each other in this phase of their relationship. Pakistan, dismembered and dispirited, militarily and politically weakened, was faced with the task of rebuilding and redefining its relationship with India, Bangladesh, and the Soviet Union. Iran in turn needed Pakistan as the focus of its South Asian policy. But the relationship was to be an unequal one. Iran helped Pakistan with all its problems. It helped in the normalization of Pakistan's relations with its neighbours and it provided Pakistan with military, economic, and diplomatic support at a crucial time. In the Iranian view, a weak and disintegrated Pakistan would seriously threaten Iran's south-western frontier region. In an exclusive interview to the chief editor of Le Monde, the Shah of Iran reiterated that in case of an attempt aimed at further dismemberment of Pakistan, Iran would 'certainly intervene'.[24] Such assurances amounted to guaranteeing Pakistan's territorial integrity.

There were also other factors involved in Iran's concern regarding Pakistan's territorial integrity, these being Iran's relations with Arab countries and the question of the safety of sea-lanes.[25] Until 1975 when Iran normalized its relations with several Middle East Arab states, Pakistan served as a useful medium in improving these ties. Similarly, the importance of the coast of Mekran was not lost on Iran, as, in unfriendly possession it could create havoc for the flow of Iranian oil to 85 per cent of the non-communist world. Moreover, Pakistan's military weakness in the post-1971 period[26] was a direct threat to Iran's own national security interests as perceived in Teheran. 'A fundamental tenet of Iranian security policy has long been the territorial integrity of Iran's Muslim but non-Arab neighbours, i.e., Turkey and Pakistan'.[27]

Pakistan tried to make up for its military vulnerability by developing a diplomatic option; strengthening and cementing relations with powerful Muslim states, such as Iran, who could be depended upon in any future conflict with India. Iran's interest in Pakistan as an indispensable buffer state between itself and India—its prospective regional rival—was fully realized by Pakistan. The two states with overlapping interests increased their collaboration. Economic relations were vastly expanded and CENTO and RCD were revitalized to serve the new needs of old friends. In 1974 Pakistan played host to the largest CENTO naval exercise, *Midlink*, in the Arabian Sea.[28]

Economic Relations

In the economic field, Iran came forth to help Pakistan resolve its difficulties, aggravated due to the loss of the domestic market of East Pakistan and inflated oil bills. In the 1970s the volume of trade between the two countries increased tremendously. From 1970 to 1973 the trade balance though in favour of Iran was progressively narrowed, and in the post-1973 period it was wholly in favour of Pakistan.[29] Apart from such beneficial trends in Pakistan-Iran trade, Iran provided Pakistan with generous credit to finance a number of development projects and to offset the oil price increases. Under an agreement signed on 12 June 1974 and another signed on 18 April 1976, Iran pledged loans to Pakistan worth $580 million and $150 million respectively.[30] Additionally, Iran financed several joint industrial and technical projects. The loan of $580 million was the largest that Iran had forwarded to any country except Egypt. The repayment on this loan was scheduled to begin in 1979 but the new government of Iran, on Pakistan's request, extended the original grace period of 3 years to 5 years. It also reduced the annual repayment burden to almost half of its original installment, from $58 million to $22 million.[31] However, it is clear that since the foreign policy goals of the Islamic Republic of Iran are more realistic, less ambitious than those of the Shah, and its own economy is currently disorganized, it would not be able to assist Pakistan in the near future with any substantial economic aid.[32] Nevertheless, this changed position would have no adverse effect on the excellent relations existing between the two Islamic countries.

RCD in the 1970s

The RCD had been set up in the hope of providing yet another instrument of economic cooperation. At the Izmir Summit held in 1976 it was given a new orientation, and a call was made for removal of tariffs in order to expand intra-regional trade. A number of ambitious projects were also outlined. According to the treaty of Izmir, the member states were to adopt measures for the establishment of an RCD-Free Trade Area within a period of ten years.[33] A review of the RCD performance, however, shows that it did not live up to its promise or potential. In the 1960s, the RCD failed to fulfil its aspirations because of the commitments of its members to other organizations, such as Turkey's association with the EEC and Pakistan's membership of the Commonwealth. Most of these impediments were removed by the mid-seventies,[34] but even then intra-regional exports of RCD countries, compared to their exports with the rest of the world, remained miserably low throughout the seventies. In fact intra-regional trade was halved from 2.2 per cent in 1960 to 1.1 per cent in 1977.[35] The protocol of trade to establish the Free Trade Zone in accordance with the Izmir treaty is yet to see the light of day. The Izmir treaty laid down the political will essential to make the RCD operative, but among other things, it was the question of the enlargement of RCD's membership that stunted its growth. While Iran under the Shah wished to enlarge the RCD membership by including initially India and Afghanistan, Pakistan objected to this. Pakistan favours regional cooperation amongst countries that are at the same level of development.[36]

Iran's Impact on Pak-Afghan Relations

Even in the earlier phase, in the sixties Iran's mediation had helped normalize Pakistan's relations with Afghanistan. In the 1970s one objective of Iran's South Asian foreign policy was reduction of the growing Soviet influence in the region. To achieve this objective, Teheran initiated an active diplomatic offensive to normalize the relations of Pakistan with India, Bangladesh and Afghanistan.[37] As it happened, Iran's policy objectives coincided with those of the United States, and throughout the seventies, Iran played the role of a 'stable state which is willing and apparently able to defend both itself and parallel American interests in a vitally strategic area.'[38]

In 1973 Pak-Afghan relations deteriorated with the ascendancy of hardliner Sardar Mohammad Daud to power in Afghanistan. However, Iran improved its own relations with Afghanistan, and this had a favourable influence on Pak-Afghan relations. Economic and development aid amounting to $2 billion was also utilized by Iran to increase its influence in Afghanistan. An atmosphere was created in which normalization of Pak-Afghan relations seemed imminent. It became possible for the heads of the two states to exchange visits in 1976. In 1978 Pak-Afghan relations became cordial and talks began on normalization of relations between the two countries. President Daud, from all accounts, seemed inclined to remove the impasse over the recognition of the Durand Line as an international frontier, but he was overthrown in a bloody *coup*. Two succeeding Afghan marxist governments made attempts to continue the dialogue with Pakistan, but were not allowed to do so and were overthrown. Iran's policy of drawing away Afghanistan from Moscow's influence failed and this failure was particularly regretted by Pakistan.

Relations since the Revolution in Iran

Pakistan was the first country to recognize the Islamic Republic of Iran. The immediate effect on Pakistan-Iran relations of this change in Iran and the withdrawal of the two countries from CENTO, is indicated by the closeness that has developed between the two countries. Iran's foreign policy objectives and attitudes have changed. Iran is no more a US ally; it has been neutralized. Besides, as one writer observed: 'The revolutionary government has no intention to play the big brother towards its neighbours.'[39]

Even as the revolution in Iran continued and consolidation came only gradually, new directions in foreign policy were adopted. Having disassociated itself from American interests in the Gulf and in the Middle Eastern-South Asian region, Iran joined the non-aligned movement in 1979.[40] As Pakistan too moved in this direction following its withdrawal from the CENTO in March 1979, the two countries' area of identification broadened. Another effect of the revolution in Iran was a temporary economic and military setback for Pakistan. Militarily Iran is no longer a strong ally, and it would be unrealistic for Pakistan to depend on military aid from Iran in case of a conflict situation involving Pakistan with any of its neighbours. Such immediate setbacks notwithstanding, Pakistan can look forward to a fruitful relationship with Iran. Pakistan's hopes that Iran's foreign policy develops with an Islamic bias have largely been satisfied. Dr Yazdi stated that because of Islam there will have to be 'close and deep relations between Iran and the rest of the Muslim world'.[41]

The RCD issue that came up at this stage between Pakistan and Iran indicates the new direction in Iran's foreign policy. The revolutionary government of Iran was initially in favour of reorganizing the RCD as a possible component of a larger economic pact of Muslim countries, including some Middle Eastern oil producing ones.[42] Later, Iran seemed inclined to dissolve the RCD altogether because it was an instrument of 'superpower influence in the region'[43] and a 'by product of CENTO'.[44] Pakistan, on the other hand, resorted to active diplomacy to save the RCD. President Ziaul Haq's Foreign Affairs Adviser explained that RCD and CENTO were separate from each other.[45] Pakistan also proposed a meeting of the RCD Ministerial Council to review all outstanding questions relating to RCD and to persuade Iran to review its RCD policy. The seventies thus ended with the fate of the RCD hazardously suspended in an ambiguous position.

Pakistan's reactions to recent developments in Iran are also worth noting. Following large anti-US demonstrations in Teheran, members of the American diplomatic mission were held as hostages by a group of revolutionary students. Pakistan has adopted a correct and balanced position on the hostage issue. It has emphasized a peaceful resolution of the crisis and a need for quiet diplomacy. The Pakistan government has advised the United States to refrain from issuing threats of using force against Iran. Pakistan announced that it would not be a party to any economic sanctions that the US and its allies may impose on Iran. However, Pakistan has also called for the observation of international diplomatic conventions.[46] Pakistan has supported the fact-finding mission of the UN Secretary-General to Teheran, but so far mediation efforts made by several personalities and states have not been successful in diffusing the crisis.

In December 1979 Iran adopted a constitution and it is expected to go to the polls in early 1980. With a constitutional, representative government in power, there will be greater coherence and continuity in Iran's foreign policy. The Islamic criteria in Iran's foreign relations, however, will continue to be emphasized and this alone, if nothing else, guarantees sustained warm and brotherly ties between Iran and Pakistan. Islam will be the basis on which the two countries will collaborate effectively in future.

TABLE 1

Pakistan-Iran Trade Flow
(Million Rupees)

Year	Pakistan Imports	Pakistan Exports	Balance
1951-52	18.7	0.6	− 18.1
1961-62	115.1	8.1	−106.8
1962-63	140.9	17.8	−123.1
1963-64	167.8	9.7	−158.1
1964-65	66.9	12.1	− 54.8
1965-66	28.9	13.6	− 15.3
1966-67	124.3	17.3	−107.0
1967-68	157.3	21.1	−136.2
1968-69	123.9	24.1	− 99.8
1969-70	120.6	25.7	− 94.9
1970-71	102.8	18.8	− 84.0
1971-72	63.8	20.7	− 43.1
1972-73	97.9	60.0	− 37.9
1973-74	221.4	329.2	+107.8
1974-75	116.8	594.2	+477.4
1975-76	62.8	176.2	+113.4
1976-77	30.6	879.1	+848.5
1977-78 (July-March)	46.8	316.1	+269.3

Source: *Pakistan Economic Survey, 1963–64*, p. 61; *1965–66*, pp. 32-5; *1970–71*, p. 66; *1977–78*; pp. 84–6, Islamabad, Government of Pakistan, Economic Adviser's Wing, Islamabad.

NOTES

1. Joseph Frankel, *International Relations*, London University Press, 1969, p. 71.

2. In their diplomatic exchanges the two countries consistently refer to their common heritage. For example, in their recent exchange of letters both President Ziaul Haq and Ayatollah Khomeini have stressed the historical, cultural and Islamic ties of Iran and Pakistan. See *Dawn*, Karachi, 14 February 1979.

3. Horward Wriggins, 'Changing Power Relations between the Middle East and South Asia', *Orbis*, Philadelphia, Fall 1976, p. 787.

4. Leo. E. Rose, 'The Superpowers in South Asia: A Geo-strategic Analysis', *Orbis*, op. cit., Summer 1978, p. 399.

5. Zubeida Mustafa, 'Recent Trends in Pakistan's Policy towards the Middle East', *Pakistan Horizon*, Karachi, Fourth Quarter, 1975, p. 2.

6. See Rouhollah K. Ramazani, 'Emerging Pattern of Regional Relations in Iranian Foreign Policy', *Orbis*, op. cit., Winter 1975, pp. 1046–47.

7. Cited in ibid., p. 1050.

8. Khalida Qureshi, 'Pakistan and Iran: A Study in Neighbourly Diplomacy', *Pakistan Horizon*, op. cit., Third Quarter 1968, p. 34.

9. *See* 'Pakistan's relations with the Islamic States,' A Review by the Ministry of Foreign Affairs, Government of Pakistan, 21 February 1977, published in Documents Section, ibid., First Quarter, 1977, pp. 217–36.

10. President Truman threatened to use the atomic bomb on the Soviet Union in the event of failure of the evacuation of Soviet troops from Iran. See *Time*, New York, 28 January 1980.

11. Rouhollah Ramazani, *Iran's Foreign Policy, 1941-1973*, Virginia, University Press of Virginia, 1975, p. 282. Also see *Dawn*, 13 February 1959.

12. This was expressed in joint communiques issued on 8 November 1956 in Teheran and on 22 November 1956 in Baghdad. See Khalida Qureshi, op. cit., p. 36.

13. R. K. Ramazani, 'Iran and the Arab Israeli Conflict', *Middle East Journal*, Washington D.C., Autumn 1978, p. 416.

14. On 20 January 1962 the Iranian Ambassador to Pakistan, Mr Hasan Arafat, said in Karachi that 'the best solution of Afghan-Pakistan problems would be to have an Iran-Afghanistan-Pakistan confederation'. See Chronology in *Pakistan Horizon*, op. cit., First Quarter, 1962, p. 78.

15. See Chronology in ibid., Third Quarter 1962, p. 248.

16. Rouhollah Ramazani, *Iran's Foreign Policy 1941-1973*, op. cit., p. 354.

17. Khalid Qureshi, op. cit., p. 39.

18. See S. M. Burke, *Pakistan's Foreign Policy: An Historical Analysis*, Karachi, Oxford University Press, 1973, p. 305.

19. Fred Halliday, *Iran: Dictatorship and Development*, Harmondsworth, Middlesex, Penguin Books Ltd., 1979, pp. 250–51.
20. Shirin Tahir Kheli, 'Iran and Pakistan: Cooperation in an area of conflict', *Asian Survey*, Berkeley, California, May 1977, p. 477.
21. This began in 1961 with the independence of Kuwait. The British then withdrew from South Yemen in 1967 and in 1971 from the Emirates, Bahrain and Qatar. In 1977 it withdrew from Oman as well.
22. Shirin Tahir Kheli, 'Foreign Policy of New Pakistan', *Orbis*, op. cit., Fall 1976, pp. 733–59.
23. See Howard Wriggins, op. cit., p. 790.
24. *Dawn*, 2 July 1974.
25. See Zubeida Mustafa, op. cit., pp. 9–12.
26. For Pakistan's inferiority *vis-a-vis* India see, Anwer H. Syed, 'Pakistan's Security Problems: A Bill of Constraints' in Wriggins, *Pakistan in Transition*, Islamabad University Press, Islamabad, 1975, p. 253.
27. A. J. Cottrell, 'Pakistan: Internal Unrest and Military Weakness' in Burrell and Cottrell, *Iran, Afghanistan, Pakistan: Tensions and Dilemmas, Washington Papers*, Vol. II, California, 1974, p. 57.
28. Zubeida Mustafa, op. cit., p. 10.
29. See Table 1.
30. *The Muslim*, Islamabad, 11 August 1979.
31. *The Pakistan Times*, Lahore, 18 October 1979.
32. Iran has stopped financial grants to foreign governments and institutions. Recipients of grants included Pakistan. Ibid., 12 July 1979.
33. See *Pakistan Economic Survey 1976-1977*, Islamabad, Government of Pakistan, Finance Division, Economic Advisers Wing, p. 120.
34. See *The Muslim*, 20 July 1979.
35. Ibid., 10 August 1979.
36. Pakistan was, however, in favour of including new members from Muslim countries, in case of expansion of the RCD. See Chronology in *Pakistan Horizon*, op. cit., Second Quarter, 1976, p. 84.
37. See Pakistan-Iran joint communique issued at the conclusion of the Shah of Iran's visit to Pakistan in March 1976, ibid., Second Quarter, 1976, pp. 178–9.
38. Shirin Tahir Kheli, 'Foreign Policy of New Pakistan', op. cit., p. 754.
39. Shameem Akhtar, 'The Impact of the Islamic Movement in Iran on the Region', *Pakistan Horizon*, op. cit., First and Second Quarters, 1979, p. 91.
40. The then Foreign Minister of Iran Dr Yazdi announced at the UN that his country had joined the 'anti-colonial, anti-imperialistic and anti-Zionist force'. See *Dawn*, 6 October 1979.
41. In an interview to *Impact International*, London, 26 October–8 November 1979.

42. Vice Premier Mr Amin Entezam's interview with the Turkish daily *Milliyet*, reported in *Morning News*, Karachi, 20 April 1979.

43. The Iranian Minister of Foreign Affairs, Karim Sanjabi's interview with French newspaper *Le Monde* quoted in *Dawn*, 13 March 1979.

44. Iranian Foreign Minister, Dr Ibrahim Yazdi's interview with PTV correspondents in Havana reported in ibid., 8 September 1979. Dr Yazdi talked of a new arrangement including India and Bangladesh as members.

45. Ibid., 1 October 1979.

46. Ibid., 21 December 1979.

12

Pakistan-Turkey Relations*

Naveed Ahmad

The Muslim nationalist movement in South Asia, which gave birth to Pakistan, was vitally concerned with the fate of Muslims in other parts of the world, particularly the Middle East. But even before this movement took shape the religious and political elites of the Indian Muslim community possessed a lively awareness of the condition and the problems of the Muslims of north-east Africa. As an heir to this tradition Pakistan proudly acknowledges its close kinship with Muslims in lands far and near and upholds the ideal of Islamic solidarity.

The sentiments of brotherhood that Pakistanis have for people of Turkey have their roots in history. The institution of *Khilafat* has occupied a very important place in the history of the Islamic peoples. After the sack of Baghdad in AD 1258 the *Khilafat* passed into the hands of the Fatimid rulers of Egypt and finally into those of the Ottoman sultans in the first half of the sixteenth century.

The Mughal rulers of India did not recognize the Ottoman sultans as their spiritual head. Instead, they got the *Khutbah* read in their own name. After the disintegration of the Mughal empire, however, there occurred a change, and the name of the Ottoman caliph was extensively used in the sermon from the pulpit at Friday prayers in India. This had little political significance but it showed that sizeable sections of the Muslim community in South Asia regarded the caliph as the symbol of Islamic unity and a source of spiritual inspiration.

---

* Vol. xxxiv, No. 1, 1981.

In 1905 there arose a controversy over the attitude the Muslims could adopt in case hostilities broke out between England and Turkey. One school of thought held that the Muslims owed their allegiance and loyalty to the sultan of Turkey, because he was the caliph of Islam, while the other group insisted that Muslims should not annoy and alienate the British by supporting their adversary. Besides they thought that the Muslims, like all other Indians, owed their allegiance to the British rulers.

This was the period when the process of the decline and erosion of the Turkish empire was being hastened by the designs of the imperialist powers. France had already seized the Ottoman provinces of Algeria and Tunisia and was moving to take over Morocco. The British were firmly entrenched in Egypt. Now the Italians sought European support for their claim on Tripoli and Cyrenaica. Having been duly encouraged, they began their invasion in 1911. This led to war between Italy and Turkey and touched off the Balkan wars of 1912–13, which in turn merged with World War I. The effect of the World War, in which the Ottomans found themselves on the side of the central powers, was the final distintegration of the Turkish empire and the division of its territories as spoils of war between the victors—the British and the French. The plight of the Turks distressed the Indian Muslims deeply. The news of inhuman atrocities perpetrated on innocent Turkish civilians, the conquest and desecration of the holy places of Islam, the French occupation of Morocco, and the hangings of the Meshad *ulema* by the Russians, deeply grieved the Indian Muslims. They blamed all these sufferings upon the British, who they thought were out to destroy the last bastion of Muslim supremacy. Leaders of great repute, like Maulana Mohammad Ali, Shaukat Ali, Abul Kalam Azad, and Shibli N'umani condemned in unequivocal terms the brutalities perpetrated on the Turks by the aggressors. A number of new newspapers like the *Al Hilal*, *Comrade*, *Hamdard*, and *Zamindar* appeared which passionately supported the Pan-Islamic movements. The Aga Khan and Syed Ameer Ali, Presidents of the All-India Muslim League and the London Branch of the League respectively, made earnest appeals to the British government to save Turkey from total disintegration.

The campaign of the *Khilafat* movement resulted in the collection of huge funds for the support of the Turks. Branches of the Red Cresent were formed all over India and a medical mission was organized and despatched to the scene of the war under the leadership of Dr Mukhtar Ahmad Ansari.

In 1915 a secret agreement was made between the British government and Hussein Ibn Ali, the Grand Sharif of Makkah, under which Britain pledged to recognize and uphold the independence of the Arabs over certain agreed territories in return for an Arab rising against the Turks under Hussein's leadership. Hussein carried out his part of the bargain, and by 1917 Turkish rule over Hijaz had been ended.

Among those Muslim leaders who warned the British government against the consequences of its interference with the future of the *Khilafat* was Mr Mohammad Ali Jinnah. He urged the government to take into consideration the feelings and sentiments of the Indian Muslims with regard to Turkey while formulating the policies of the empire. The Muslims hoped that their strong expression of support for Turkey would persuade the British not to be too harsh in their treatment of a defeated foe.

Turkey signed the armistice on 3 November 1918. Immediately after that the British forces marched into Mosul. Constantinople was officially occupied by the Allies, mainly by the British. Finally on 15 May the Greek armies, at the instance of England, entered Smyrna. The British government paid no heed to the numerous appeals made by the Muslims from all over India to spare Turkey. As Muslim hopes were dashed they were driven into a confrontation with the British rulers.

On 17 October 1919, the All India *Khilafat* Committee observed the *Khilafat* day. The first session of the *Khilafat* Conference in New Delhi decided on 23 November that Muslims will not participate in the official rejoicing over victory in the war and that if their demands were not accepted, they would boycott British goods and would not cooperate with the government. A Muslim delegation under the leadership of Maulana Mohammad Ali Jauhar went to England. The Muslim demands were presented to the British Prime Minister, Lloyd George. His blunt reply was that all vanquished states would be treated alike and there would be no exceptions. One consequence of the British stand was a decision by groups of Muslim militants to migrate from British India which was declared *Dar-ul-Harb*.

While the Indian Muslims were making heavy sacrifices for Turkey, the Ottoman Sultan, Wahid-ud-Ain, accepted the Treaty of Sevres. This treaty was never enforced, as the Turks rallying around Mustafa Kemal, had established a nationalist government in Angora (Ankara). They inflicted a crushing defeat on the occupying Greek forces and expelled them from Anatolia.

On 8 July 1921, Maulana Mohammad Ali presided over a session of the *Khilafat* Conference in Karachi, in which he warned the British government: 'if the British Government fought the Angora Government, the Muslims of India would resort to civil disobedience, proclaim complete independence and hoist the flag of the Indian Republic at the Ahmedabad session of the Indian National Congress'.[1]

This resulted in the arrest and trial of the Ali brothers along with other Muslim leaders in September 1921. Thus what began as a movement for the preservation of the *Khilafat* was transformed into a passionate defence of the Turkish Republic under Kemal. It was the first time that an eastern people had challenged Western imperialism and succeeded in vindicating its national sovereignty. In 1903 Japan had exploded the myth of European superiority and invincibility by inflicting a crushing defeat on Czarist Russia. But that conflict was the product of imperial rivalry and did not involve the issue of independence in Asia. What Turkey managed to do was to beat off imperialist attempts at domination and dismemberment of national territory. 'The news of this struggle had its repercussions throughout Syria and Egypt, as far as Persia, India and even China. Here surely was the prototype for others to emulate, of the Eastern Nationalist Revolution.'[2]

Materially, Kemal's strongest support came from the Indian Muslims, who saw nationalist Turkey as the only independent Muslim nation. The *Khilafat* Committee in Bombay started a fund to help the Turkish nationalist struggle, establishing contact with a representative of Kemal in Constantinople who received constant letters of encouragement. Part of the Indian Muslim fund, which eventually amounted to some £125,000 was used to pay the army. But most of it was kept and later devoted to the construction of a new parliament building in Angora (now Ankara), and the foundation of the first Nationalist Bank.

Pakistan-Turkey Relationship since the Inception of Pakistan

When after independence, Pakistan thought of establishing diplomatic relations with foreign countries, one of the foremost lands to which its thoughts turned was Turkey.

Quaid-i-Azam Mohammad Ali Jinnah told the first Turkish ambassador to Pakistan on 4 March 1948:

Turkey has been in our thoughts constantly and has drawn our admiration for the valour of your people and the way in which your statesmen and leaders have struggled and fought almost single-handed in the midst of Europe for your freedom and sovereignty which have been happily maintained...I can, therefore, assure your excellency that the Muslims of Pakistan entertain sentiments of affection and esteem for your country, and now Turkey and Pakistan both as free, sovereign and independent countries can strengthen their ties more and more for the good of both.

We hope that with your Excellency's assistance and cooperation we may be able to build up closer political and cultural ties with your state, and thus contribute our share to the attainment of peace and prosperity throughout the world.[3]

On 2 April 1954, Pakistan and Turkey signed an agreement for friendly cooperation. After noting in the preamble the desire of the two countries for greater mutual cooperation deriving from the sincere friendship existing between them, the agreement provided that: 'They will consult on international matters of mutual interest, and taking into account international requirements and conditions, cooperate to the maximum extent' (Art. 2). In the agreement the two parties pledged to promote cultural exchanges and bring about greater cooperation in the economic and technical fields, 'if necessary by concluding other agreements' (Art. 3).

The agreement's provisions pertaining to defence envisaged endeavours to meet, as far as possible, the requirements of the parties in the production of arms and ammunition and determination of the manner and extent of cooperation which might be effected between them, in accordance with Article 51 of the UN Charter should an unprovoked attack occur against them from outside.[4] The agreement, though naturally proceeding from close bonds of friendship, has to be viewed in the context of the similarity of the foreign policy orientations of Pakistan and Turkey in the early fifties.

Turkey was firmly in the Western camp and fully shared the West's apprehensions regarding a possible southward expansionist thrust on the part of the Soviet Union. On the other hand, a combination of internal and external factors was inexorably driving Pakistan towards total reliance on the West. Pakistan faced serious political instability after the assassination of its first Prime Minister. The current of provincial sentiment was running strong and the feudal West Pakistan leadership was worried about controlling and neutralizing the democratic pressures from the then East Pakistan.

This combined with the perceived external threat from a hostile India and a not-too-friendly-Afghanistan as well as serious mistrust of the communist colossus to the north, produced an acute sense of insecurity. This seemed to call for an active policy of long-term affiliation to the powerful West. The threat of famine in Pakistan in 1953 was averted through the US gift of 610,000 tons of wheat. An effete political leadership incapable of securing the support of the people for a policy of national independence also found itself overwhelmed by the strain of financing our defence requirements from out of very limited foreign exchange reserves. By withholding Pakistan's share of military stores from the undivided subcontinent, India had managed to keep Pakistan's armed forces poorly equipped. The Kashmir dispute was still unresolved, and the direction it could take was unpredictable. The force of these circumstances had to be weighed against Pakistan's natural anxiety to retain its freedom of action in the external field. Pakistan had already shown a pronounced Western sympathy when the late Mr Liaquat Ali Khan paid a visit to the United States. The leadership which took over in 1954 was quick to resolve the dilemma. It opted for a Western, or more specifically, an American connection. In May 1954 a military aid pact was signed by Pakistan and the United States.

The Western powers, anxious to link the defence of West Europe to that of the Middle East proposed the establishment of the Middle East Defence Organization in March 1953. This was stoutly opposed by the Egyptian leadership under Nasser and no Arab country, except for Iraq under Nur al-Saeed, was found to be enthusiastic. The proposal therefore fell through and Western strategists began to concentrate on the 'northern tier', comprising Turkey, Iraq, Iran, and Pakistan.

In April 1955, Iraq and Turkey signed a pact of mutual cooperation. On 2 July 1955, the Pakistan Prime Minister, Mr Mohammad Ali Bogra, announced Pakistan's decision to accede to the Baghdad pact.

On 22 September 1955, Pakistan formally joined the Baghdad pact, bringing the total number of adherents to four, the others being: Iraq, Turkey, and the UK. Iran joined the pact later. In November 1955, the Prime Minister of Pakistan led his country's delegation to the Permanent Council of the Baghdad pact powers. The US announced that it would establish military and political liaison with the nations of the Baghdad pact.

On 24 February 1956, celebrating the first anniversary of the signing of the pact, the Prime Minister of Pakistan stated: 'The Baghdad pact is purely defensive in character. It threatens no one and merely represents an attempt to strengthen the mutual defensive capacity of the member states in an area of the world where it is clearly needed.' The final communique issued after the Baghdad pact council meeting in Teheran in April 1956 also tried to explain the peaceful intentions of the pact and declared that its aims and purposes had been clearly misunderstood by the world at large. Thus the Baghdad pact powers hoped 'that as these purposes become better known, these criticism will give way to sympathetic and active cooperation, and that the Baghdad pact will become, as it is intended to be, a unifying factor among peoples in the region who wish to preserve a free and democratic way of life'.[5]

On 15 July 1956, President Iskandar Mirza of Pakistan arrived in Ankara on a state visit. In the joint communique issued at the conclusion of the visit, Pakistan and Turkey exchanged solemn assurances that Turkey would support Pakistan in the settlement of disputes with India and Afghanistan and Pakistan would support Turkey over the Cyprus issue.

In July 1958 a military coup overthrew the pro-Western monarchy in Iraq. The leader of the revolution immediately denounced the Baghdad pact and Iraq ceased to be a member. Soon after the change in Iraq, Prime Minister Menderes of Turkey, Premier Eghbal of Iran, and Premier Feroze Khan Noon of Pakistan attended the Baghdad pact Ministerial Council meeting in London in July 1958. At first all that was achieved in London, was a standstill agreement which meant that they agreed that no major policy decision was to be announced. After Iraq's defection, the adherents pinned their hopes on the possibility of America joining the pact as a full member. However, for fear of antagonizing Israel, Washington refused to associate itself directly with the pact. But to boost the morale of its members, the US Secretary of State offered to sign separate defence pacts with each one of them, although it was not explained why new bilateral pacts were necessary when each member was already linked to the US by various treaties.

With the solitary Arab member of the pact out of it, militant Arab critics of the pact who maintained that it was designed to sow discord among the Arabs lost their main argument, but President Nasser and his Arab supporters continued, in the wider regional context, to view the grouping with suspicion.

The July 1958 meeting of the Baghdad pact council in London, decided that another defence organization should take the place of the defunct Baghdad pact. The new organization came to be known as the Central Treaty Organization or CENTO.

When the President of Turkey, Mr Celal Bayar, arrived in Karachi on 22 September 1958 there was speculation among diplomatic circles that the Turkish President, while in Kabul, had tried to probe the possibilities of a closer friendly alliance between Turkey, Pakistan, Afghanistan, and Iran. Certain Western circles were toying with the idea of the formation of a confederation between these countries. The idea began to be talked about on a wider scale after the revolution in Iraq. Of course this could not materialize because of Afghanistan's strict neutrality and the Russo-Iranian treaty. However, the Turkish President's visit to Pakistan was officially described as 'a purely courtesy visit' without any political significance. In the course of his earlier visit to Afghanistan, Mr Bayar was generally believed to have discussed with Afghan leaders proposals for greater cooperation among the four Muslim nations.

The Shah of Iran welcomed this idea in a statement on 28 September 1958. Following public criticism of the idea of a confederation (in the National Assembly, etc.) Pakistan's President Iskandar Mirza categorically denied that he was engaged in furthering such a plan, and the Premier declared that all he had in mind was closer economic ties and easier travel conditions between Pakistan and its neighbours.

On 18 November 1959, President Ayub Khan arrived in Ankara, on a state visit. His talks with the Turkish leaders in Ankara were in continuation of those held at Teheran on 17 November 1959, among the Shah of Iran, the President and the Premier of Turkey. During his talks in Teheran and Ankara, President Ayub had the occasion to discuss with the two heads of state the crucial importance of CENTO for the security and strength not only of the partners but also of regions far beyond the frontiers of the three countries. The need was keenly felt for concerting more effective military measures. With Iraq out of the picture, there was an increase in the alliance's cohesion and Iran, Turkey, and Pakistan felt brotherly regrets over Afghanistan's unwillingness to join the alliance.

By January 1960, work began on the construction of the Ankara, Teheran, Karachi radio micro-wave link, so that the three countries could be linked by a rapid communication system. The US committed $1,837,000 to this CENTO project for engineering and equipment.

Pakistan and Turkey were involved in an unpleasant incident with the Soviet Union in May 1960. An American U2 reconnaissance plane which had allegedly taken off from the American base at Peshawar was shot down in the Soviet Union. Soviet authorities on 13 May handed to the Pakistani and Turkish ambassadors in Moscow notes of protest from the Soviet government, saying that it had been established that the plane took off from the American-Turkish air force base of Incirlik, near Adana. On 27 April it had flown to the Peshawar airport. The note warned that if such actions were repeated, retaliatory measures would be undertaken.

Meanwhile spectacular political changes took place in Turkey. The pro-American government of Adnan Menderes was overthrown in May 1960, in a *coup d'etat* and General Gursel took over power. Though Pakistani newspapers and political leaders expressed concern over the fate of the ousted leader, the Pakistan government recognized the new government on 30 May.

In the early sixties, the Turkish leaders and public opinion showed keen appreciation of Pakistan's point of view in regard to the Kashmir dispute. For instance in February 1962, the *Yeni Istanbul*, a widely circulating daily of Turkey, in an article, supported Pakistan's 'right stand' on the Kashmir issue and said that Kashmir possessed the same powerful weapon of nationalism which Mr Nehru had used while occupying Goa. It added that if the world considered the occupation of Goa normal and supported India in this case, on the plea of nationalism, the Indian Premier should have accepted Pakistan's right over Kashmir and acted with greater understanding.[6]

The Sino-Indian border war in 1962 and the West's hurried despatch of arms to 'neutralist' India put the American-sponsored defence pacts, CENTO and SEATO, into a new perspective. The sudden surge of enthusiasm for a non-ally, India, in the Western capitals made Turkey and Pakistan feel that the position of the West's allies in SEATO and CENTO had been downgraded. A country could avoid binding obligations under an alliance and could still make demands upon the Western countries provided its policy orientation at a given time had the West's approval. On the other hand, the alliance which carried the serious risk of annoying rival powers, could often be taken for granted. A curious aspect of the alliance was that its members could be called upon by America to part with their equipment in favour of an anti-pact country if that country was supposed to be engaged in a conflict with a communist country.

In connection with this clause of the CENTO, the Turkish Foreign Minister Feridim Cemal Erkin said that Turkey had reached no decision yet on India's request for weapons against China. He said: 'We will study both the requests and the legal situation...A decision will be taken later'.[7]

Soon it was revealed that Turkey had postponed a decision on an offer of arms to India following a vigorous protest by Pakistan. According to the *Times* of London (5 November 1962) Turkey had agreed, the previous week, to provide some fairly old mountain howitzers to India for use against the Chinese invasion. An aircraft containing the first consignment of Turkish arms for India was already waiting at Ankara airport when the Pakistani ambassador to Turkey conveyed his government's protest to the Turkish Foreign Minister.

In July 1964, President Ayub Khan visited Turkey. The Pakistani President disclosed later that during his meeting with Turkish leaders, they had expressed grave concern over the Cyprus situation. Therefore he had promised to convey the Turkish concern to the forthcoming Commonwealth Prime Ministers Conference in London. The President added that just as the Pakistani Muslims were concerned over the difficulties faced by the Turkish Cypriots, Turkey had likewise shown concern over the trials and tribulations of the people of Kashmir and the Indian Muslims.

Meanwhile, the Western media, noted that there was a new 'line-up' between Turkey, Iran, and Pakistan outside the framework of CENTO. As one British newspaper commented: 'It is also significant, in the light of recent anti-Western feeling in Turkey over Cyprus, that Turkey should be taking part in talks with Iran and Pakistan, which have in recent years adopted a more flexible policy towards the Soviet Union and China.'[8]

Foundations of RCD

Pakistan and its western neighbours, Afghanistan, Iran, and Turkey are bound together by geographical contiguity, a common religion and marked cultural affinities. These are held to constitute good grounds for bringing about a certain measure of inter-dependence and for defining specific areas in which such cooperation can be practicable and rewarding. Although the relations between Iran, Pakistan, and Turkey had been cordial during the last seventeen years, cooperation had been confined mainly to defence. And the basis of even this cooperation had been the military pact which was not entirely regional in its origin and inspiration.

Pakistan's experience of the opportunism of its allies on the question of Kashmir and of arms aid to India, and Turkey's disillusionment with the West caused by its allies' lack of concern over the fate of the Turkish Cypriots, bore witness to the need for such reorientation. For nearly two generations, Turkey had been not only pro-Western but had claimed to be in fact a European nation—being a member not only of the Atlantic pact but also of the Council of Europe and later even linked with the EEC. Many pro-European Turks had no wish whatever to impair the Western connection by getting involved in a new bloc with two unmistakably Asian countries. Therefore, Turkey was rather reserved about the idea of a regional alliance. Later, however, public opinion in Turkey became more congenial to the idea. In Iran, too, there was in evidence a trend towards national assertion, and the country had sought to lessen its embroilment in the Russo-American conflict. There was little doubt that it suited the interests of all the three countries concerned to bring a practical and down-to-earth approach to bear on the development of their mutual relations.

The summit talks between the three countries, held in Istanbul in July 1964, reflected a new, grand concept which not only brought the three countries closer but played a significant part in furthering the idea of cooperation among all Muslim countries. The historical Istanbul Summit recorded the belief of the heads of state that regional cooperation was essential for accelerating the pace of material development and for the maintenance of peace and stability. Accordingly they resolved that appropriate ways and means should be adopted to enlarge and develop further cooperation in the existing relations in all fields.

The summit participants evidently thought that though tripartite defence cooperation had a logic of its own, it had to have an economic underpinning if it was to prove to be a stable factor. They realized that cordial diplomatic relations and shared security concerns were not enough to lay the basis for a strong and durable regional alliance. Accordingly, they proposed a machinery which would work for the success of the newly proclaimed Regional Cooperation for Development. The summit decided to set up a permanent Ministerial Council to execute joint plans, a regional Planning Committee to accelerate the pace of development, and a Secretariat to serve these organizations. Equally notable was the agreement to promote free movement of goods through trade pacts, promote collaboration among Chambers of Commerce and draw up plans to reduce postal rates, float a joint international airline and a maritime line, integrate rail and road links, abolish visa formalities for travel purposes, encourage tourism within the region, and provide technical exchanges on an extensive basis.

RCD was to be wholly independent of CENTO, but it was seen to be a parallel set up. The sponsors of the new alliance had made it very clear that they were not seeking uniformity or identity of views on all issues. This explained why they were not rushing into a hasty political federation. The Ministerial Council of the RCD which met in Teheran in October 1964, decided that the inter-regional postal and telegraph rates between Turkey, Iran, and Pakistan be reduced to the level of internal rates and that the charges for telephone calls between the countries of the region be substantially reduced. As a step towards promoting cooperation among the three states Iran, Turkey, and Pakistan also signed an agreement on 16 October 1964 for the abolition of visas amongst them.

India-Pakistan Wars and the Kashmir Problem

Relations between the US and Pakistan came under severe strain when, following the Sino-Indian border war, Pakistan and China signed a number of agreements in rapid succession. The beginning of 1965 saw a serious deterioration in the relations between India and Pakistan. In July 1965, the United States and its allies announced that the Consortium aid to Pakistan had been postponed. The Turkish Foreign Minister, Mr Hassan Isik, told newsmen on 23 July 1965, that Turkey was as unhappy as Pakistan over the reported postponement of Consortium aid to Pakistan.

The outbreak of the Indo-Pakistan war on 6 September 1965 constituted a major test of the friendship of Pakistan's regional allies. The Turkish Premier, Mr Urugplu said that the Turkish government hoped that efforts by the UN Secretary-General U Thant to achieve a ceasefire would prove successful. He also said that India had aggravated the crisis by taking the conflict beyond Kashmir into Pakistan and by bombing Pakistani towns. He further observed: 'The dangerous crisis which has been developing recently between the two countries is a direct result of the failure in finding a just solution to the Kashmir problem.' Official Turkish support to Pakistan was thus expressed in unequivocal terms. At the same time spontaneous expressions of public sympathy in Turkey, for Pakistan, were widespread.

On 10 September 1965, Turkey and Iran in a joint statement called for an immediate ceasefire, the withdrawal of Indian forces from Pakistani territory and the despatch of a UN peace force to the frontiers to supervise the ceasefire. The communique concluded: 'The Governments of Turkey and Iran reaffirmed the solidarity which links Turkey-Iran and Pakistan, and declared that they are ready to support Pakistan, a brother country and an ally.' The Turkish Premier announced that Turkey would send five million dollars worth of Turkish-made arms and ammunition to Pakistan under the terms of an existing trade agreement.

Pakistan was deeply touched by Turkey's sympathetic attitude and President Ayub made a short visit to Turkey in December 1965 and met President Cemal Gursel of Turkey. He thanked President Gursel for the moral and material support Turkey gave to Pakistan during the Indo-Pakistan war and briefed him on the latest Indo-Pakistan situation.

Turkey's support for Pakistan's efforts to seek a Kashmir solution continued to be expressed after the war ended and in all subsequent visits exchanged between the heads of state of the two countries, Turkey reiterated its steadfast support to Pakistan on the Kashmir question. In October 1966, the Turkish Foreign Minister made an impassioned plea before the UN General Assembly for an early solution of the Kashmir problem in the light of the Security Council resolutions.

With the Indo-Pakistan war of 1971 and the civil strife preceding it, came another test of Pakistan-Turkish friendship. On this occasion, as on that of the 1965 war, the Turkish government adopted a sympathetic and helpful attitude. In October 1971, speaking in the UN General Assembly on the question of the refugees who had crossed the East Pakistan border into India, Mr Osman Olcay, the Turkish Foreign Minister, said that his country shared the deep sorrow felt in Pakistan following the tragic civil strife. He called for greater efforts by the international community to assist in the humanitarian problem of the displaced persons.

When the Indo-Pakistan war began in December 1971, the Turkish Premier, Nihat Erim, called for the immediate withdrawal of Indian troops and observed: 'The principles of respect for independence and territorial integrity and non-interference in the international affairs of others should constitute the basis of international life.'

In June 1972, the President of Pakistan, Mr Zulfikar Ali Bhutto, paid a visit to Turkey. In a joint statement issued after his talks with the Turkish President Cevdet Sunay, the two leaders expressed the hope that the planned summit between the Pakistani president and the Indian premier would lead to a durable and honourable settlement of the dispute between their two countries. They pointed to the necessity for an early withdrawal of Pakistani and Indian troops to their respective territories in accordance with the December 1971 UN resolution. They also called for the repatriation, without further delay, of prisoners-of-war from the Indo-Pakistani conflict in accordance with international conventions.

At the beginning of 1972, Pakistan's friends faced the ticklish question of whether or not they should extend recognition to Bangladesh, Pakistan's former eastern province. As a result of a vigorous diplomatic offensive conducted by India and the Soviet Union in favour of recognition, the leaders of a number of countries friendly to Pakistan found themselves on the horns of a dilemma. They did not wish in the least to embarass Pakistan. But they felt and argued that whatever the means and mode of Bangladesh coming into existence, that was all a matter of history, while Bangladesh was a reality; and if Pakistan's friends did not step into the diplomatic vacuum, its adversaries would, which again would work to the detriment of Islamabad. Pakistan, in turn, argued that if the fruits of aggression were recognized in a hurry, it would set a dangerous precedent and prove detrimental to the sovereignty and territorial integrity of small countries.

With thousands of Pakistani prisoners-of-war still held by India, Pakistan found it necessary to plead with its friends to put off recognition. Pakistan continued to keep them fully informed of new developments at its end. For if Pakistan took the lead in recognizing Bangladesh, these countries would be placed in a very embarrassing position vis-à-vis Dhaka, New Delhi and Moscow, and their subsequent recognition of Bangladesh would mean nothing to the Dhaka authorities. It was vigorous lobbying by Pakistan which dissuaded several Muslim countries from rushing into recognition.

On 4 October 1972, the Turkish Foreign Minister, in a speech before the UN General Assembly, made a strong plea for the release of Pakistani prisoners-of-war held in India since December 1971. A debate in the UN General Assembly on the question of the entry of Bangladesh into the UN was delayed and consultations between the various delegations were going on. Iran, Turkey, Somalia, Morocco, Algeria, and some other third world countries had agreed to sponsor a parallel resolution on the implementation of the Security Council resolution on the Indo-Pakistan war. Thus the UN General Assembly on 29 November 1972 adopted two independent resolutions which made Bangladesh entry into the UN conditional on the full implementation of the Security Council resolution on the Indo-Pakistan war. Pakistan recognized Bangladesh on 22 February 1974, with Iran and Turkey also extending recognition at the same time.

Pakistan and Cyprus

Pakistan had lent consistent and unqualified support to Turkey in defence of Turkish Cypriot rights. In 1954 when the Cyprus question was discussed in the UN General Assembly, the Pakistan delegation supported Turkey's position on the island. Again, in 1959, the Pakistan delegation at the United Nations urged the world body for the fulfilment of the human rights and legitimate aspirations of the Turkish Cypriots.

Cyprus achieved independence in 1960 under the treaty of Zurich signed by Turkey, Greece, and the UK. The constitution provided the Turkish minority with broad rights in communal affairs and an absolute veto on important governmental matters. However, the majority community's bad faith in the implementation of the constitution was bound to destroy inter-communal harmony. Archbishop Makarios, the leader of the Enosis movement[9] and the President of Cyprus, proposed certain changes in the constitution where it affected the safeguard of the Turkish community's guaranteed rights. The Turkish Cypriots reacted promptly and in December 1963 trouble started. Communal friction culminated in open conflict and the matter was referred to the UN, and a resolution of the Security Council brought a UN peace-keeping force to the island.

At the start of trouble in 1963, the Pakistan Foreign Minister expressed the concern of his government and people. He said: 'The Agreements which brought about the settlement of the problem of Cyprus will have to be respected as they are solemn international commitments. We are with Turkey in her moment of crisis and whatever cooperation may be needed from Pakistan will be extended in the fullest measure.'

The Turkish government time and again expressed gratitude to Pakistan for the unfailing support Pakistan had extended to Turkey on the Cyprus problem. The Turkish Prime Minister, Mr Suleyman Demirel, expressed appreciation of Pakistan's stand on Cyprus. On his visit to Pakistan in April 1967, he said: 'When Turkey was faced with a threatening situation in Cyprus, when she had to do her utmost to save the Turkish community of the unhappy Island from subjugation, when she had the opportunity of judging the sincerity of several countries, Pakistan was unswervingly on the side of peace, freedom and justice.' The communal situation again deteriorated in July 1974. The then Pakistan Prime Minister, appealed to the people of Pakistan to demonstrate their sympathy and support for Turkey.

A dangerous situations was created on the island when Greek officers who controlled the Greek national guards, an unconstitutional organization, and the Greek contingent stationed on the island staged a coup. This jeopardized the independence of the island. The Turkish government was forced to land its forces on the island in pursuit of its obligations under clause 4, paragraph 2 of the Guarantee Treaty, in order to safeguard the existence of Cyprus as an independent state. Pakistan lent unequivocal support to the Turkish action. Thus Pakistan had always been keenly interested in the present and future of the Turkish Cypriot community, and this involvement has found ample expression in diplomatic moves, on international forums and in the articulation of popular support by the press.

During the UN General Assembly debate on the Cyprus question in November 1974, the Pakistan delegate expressed the hope that the current initiatives, both inside and outside the UN, would help resolve the Cyprus problem on the basis of equality of the Turkish and Greek communities. Again in the General Assembly debate on Cyprus in November 1976, the Pakistan delegate called for a 'just settlement' that would guarantee the rights of both sides in ethnically divided Cyprus. The Pakistan delegate also regretted the emotional statement by the Cypriot Foreign Minister describing the Turkish intervention as an act of aggression by Turkey; the intervention was an obligation on Turkey, being one of the guarantor powers.

When President Ziaul Haq visited Turkey in November 1977 the two sides exchanged views on matters of mutual interest. Prime

Minister Demirel and President Zia took note of the traditional friendship which provided an excellent basis for the further development of cooperative relations between Turkey and Pakistan. Premier Demirel thanked Pakistan for its sincere interest in and keen understanding of the Cyprus question.

Attitude towards the Middle East Problem and the Islamic Bloc

Turkish and Pakistani perceptions of the Middle East question have not always been identical. Turkey's relations with the Arabs in general have, in consequence of past interactions, involved an element of complexity, while the thrust of Pakistan's policy has been to cultivate very good relations with the Arab states. Turkey has maintained diplomatic relations with Israel, Pakistan has never even dreamt of it. And yet over the years the two countries have found it possible to agree on ways of promoting a Middle East solution.

Thus during President Ayub's visit to Turkey in October 1967 which had been a crucial year in the Middle East, the two countries' leaders recognized the dangers inherent in the situation. Expressing their opposition to the use of force as a means of securing territorial gains, they asked for the withdrawal of Israeli forces from the Arab territories to the positions held before the June 1967 war. They were also critical of the measures taken by Israel to alter the status of Jerusalem and stressed the need for the implementation of the resolution of the UN General Assembly on the question. In numerous subsequent meetings between the leaders of the two countries, Turkey and Pakistan called for the implementation of UN Security Council resolution 242 of November 1967.

During the 1973 Middle East war, a very significant development was the refusal of Turkey, a member of NATO, to allow its American bases to be used for an airlift of arms to Israel. It is a well-known fact that the Turks keep their religion and politics apart. But on the question of Jerusalem, the Turkish government, despite the constitutional difficulties, had courageously responded to the strong feelings of the people. Thus the Turkish President did not hesitate in joining the heads of states of Iran and Pakistan in demanding that the status of Jerusalem must stay unaltered.

After Turkey found itself forced to intervene in Cyprus, its ties with Europe were subjected to a severe strain. The period also witnessed a severe crisis in Turkey's relations with the US, and its confidence in its Western allies received a jolt. At this juncture, Turkey and the Arab countries came closer, and the Islamic countries began to show a greater appreciation of Turkey's principled stand on the Cyprus question. Turkey's participation in the Islamic Foreign Minister's Conferences became a regular feature. Its participation in the Islamic Summit Conference held at Taif in January 1981 showed that Ankara had shed whatever reservation it might have had earlier on the question of its association with the Organization of Islamic Conference (OIC).

The joint communique issued at the conclusion of President Ziaul Haq's visit to Turkey in January 1981, reflected an agreement of opinion between the two countries on all international issues discussed—Afghanistan, the Iran-Iraq conflict, and the Palestine question. Both sides reiterated their desire for a political settlement in Afghanistan, for a speedy and mutually acceptable resolution of the Iran-Iraq crisis, for the restoration of the Arab status of Al-Quds-al-Sharif and for the restitution of Palestinian national rights.

Trade and Economic Relations

In the mid-fifties, Pakistan had a smaller volume of trade with the Baghdad pact countries than with some other Middle Eastern countries, such as Afghanistan, Saudi Arabia, Egypt, and Bahrain. In the late fifties, among the Baghdad pact countries, Iran's trade with Pakistan was the largest of all, with Iraq and Turkey occupying the second and third places respectively.

Trade relations among the Baghdad pact countries failed to offer rich possibilities and the volume of trade never rose to a respectable level. The reason for this was the absence of significant elements of economic interdependence. All the countries imported capital equipment and investment goods which were available only in the advanced countries. The next important item of imports was essential consumer goods which again were imported from outside the region.

However, by the beginning of the sixties, the two Baghdad pact countries, Pakistan and Turkey, began searching for avenues of expanded trade. A Turkish trade team arrived in Karachi in October 1959. A joint communique announced that there were 'possibilities of development of trade' between Pakistan and Turkey and further official meetings were expected to take place in the near future 'for achieving some positive results' in this respect. As the Pakistan Commerce Minister noted with regret at a press conference in Istanbul on 15 October 1959, trade between the two countries was negligible with a balance of about two million rupees in favour of Pakistan. However, he foresaw an increase in volume with the contemplated purchase of Turkish cement and coal and the sale to Turkey of tea, paper, newsprint, bicycles, and tyres and tubes. In the sixties, jute manufactures formed about 85 per cent of the total Pakistan exports to Turkey. The remaining 15 per cent covered such items as henna powder, raw hides, pressure lamps, glycerine, etc.

The Turkish Foreign Minister, Ihsan Sabri Caglayangal noted in November 1975 that the possibilities of trade between the brotherly countries of Turkey and Pakistan had not been tapped. Pakistani exports to Turkey, which mainly comprised jute and its products, received a setback after the jute-producing eastern province seceded from Pakistan in 1971. At that point a reappraisal of commercial exchanges between the two states was essential. Besides until sometime ago, Turkey was dependent on other countries for its requirements in textiles, pharmaceuticals, automobiles, trucks, tractors, tyres, refrigerators, chemicals, and a variety of other goods. Today it is in a position to export a wide range of these goods.

The need to institutionalize Pakistan-Turkish trade was fulfilled with the establishment of a Pakistan-Turkish Joint Commission for Economic and Technical Cooperation in November 1975. Bilateral cooperation was expected to reinforce the tripartite partnership in the framework of the RCD.

When various avenues for increased Pakistan-Turkish trade were explored, it was found that Turkish traders were interested in importing from Pakistan, items like surgical instruments, caustic soda, glycerine, castor oil, and products of stainless steel. Pakistani importers, on the other hand, were keen to buy chemicals and textile auxiliaries among other goods from Turkey.

During a session of the Pakistan-Turkish Joint Commission for Economic and Technical Cooperation, held in Islamabad in March 1977, the two governments had been able to identify a number of areas of cooperation, including agriculture and food. Interest was shown in launching joint ventures in the fields of commerce, industry and transportation. On 28 March 1977, Pakistan and Turkey signed a protocol in Islamabad, providing for increased cooperation in the fields of trade, industry, agriculture, and technical exchanges. The Joint Commission favoured an increase in the volume of trade, envisaging frequent exchange of trade delegations, and agreed in principle, on joint participation in appropriate international fairs.

In the field of agriculture, Turkey agreed to provide technical assistance to Pakistan in the cultivation and marketing of olives, development of rain-fed agriculture, sunflower cultivation, and the production of quality cotton seeds.

In the next meeting of the Joint Commission held in Ankara in May 1978, it was noted that an increase in trade had taken place during the last financial year. The increase was accounted for by the addition of an entirely new item of Pakistan export, fuel oil, and a virtual doubling of the export of Pakistani rice to Turkey, during the year. The rising trend, however, could not be maintained. The total volume of trade which amounted to Rs 301 million in 1977–78 came down to Rs 242 million in 1978–79. Pakistani exports to Turkey had tapered off from Rs 244 million in 1977–78 to Rs 160 million in 1978–79.[10]

There are certain obvious factors which inhibit a rapid growth of bilateral trade between the two countries. The most significant one relates to the existence of a narrow margin of complementarity between the two economies. Both are heavy importers of capital equipment and durable goods from the advanced countries, and of Petroleum Oil and Lubricants (POL) products from the OPEC countries. They do not have very much to sell to each other.

Transportation presents another difficulty. Even though both countries possess modest merchant fleets of their own, they have to rely on Western lines to carry their trade. The RCD rail and road projects show no sign of being completed. The Turkish and Iranian railway systems have been linked, but a big gap in the Iran-Pakistan rail link rules out the movement of goods by rail. Similarly, the RCD highway's Pakistani section is still incomplete. Yet another factor is the meagre commercial information each has about the other.

Since the October 1973 Middle East war, the non-oil-producing countries have been brought virtually to the edge of bankruptcy. Both Turkey and Pakistan have suffered from the effects of the world-wide inflationary trend and of the oil price increase. Both carry a heavy burden of external debt and face a chronic problem of payments imbalance. Both are facing a population explosion of major proportions. Both have a large expatriate labour force working abroad.

Economic Cooperation under RCD

The RCD began to address itself to the possibility of some very ambitious projects. In October 1964 the Ministerial Council of the RCD meeting in Teheran called for the preparation of a preliminary report on the setting up of a joint airline. The project was pursued for a long time but it proved a non-starter. Another RCD project related to the establishment of a conference arrangement between Iran, Pakistan and Turkey for pooling their traffic and ships on specific and agreed routes as a first step towards the establishment of a joint maritime line. The RCD shipping services which started operation on intra-regional routes in May 1966 provided a direct sea link between Pakistan and Turkey and made a visible impact on regional trade.

TABLE 1
Pakistan-Turkey Balance of Trade

Year	Imports	Exports	In Million Rs. Balance
1959-60	15.7	0.4	- 15.3
1960-61	0.1	0.1	-
1961-62	0.2	0.1	- 0.1
1962-63	0.1	0.2	+ 0.1
1963-64	1.0	0.3	- 0.7
1964-65	4.2	0.2	- 4.0
1965-66	0.7	0.6	- 0.1
1966-67	8.2	0.8	- 7.4
1967-68	1.6	1.1	- 0.5
1968-69	1.4	0.5	- 0.9
1969-70	1.0	1.6	+ 0.6
1970-71	2.3	1.5	0.8
1971-72	9.4	1.2	- 8.2
1972-73	54.8	1.4	- 53.4
1973-74	20.3	3.2	- 17.1
1974-75	21.0	6.1	- 14.9
1975-76	16.3	83.6	+ 67.3*
1977-78	57.3	243.9	+ 186.6
1978-79 (July-March)	71.1	158.6	+ 87.5

* *Pattern of Foreign Trade of Pakistan*, a statistical compilation by Chamber of Commerce and Industry, Karachi, Royal Book Company, 1977, p. 261. The remaining figures have been taken from *Pakistan Economic Survey, 1978–79*, Govern-ment of Pakistan, Finance Division, Economic Advisors Wing, Islamabad, p. 113.

A joint airline project was originally conceived by the Regional Planning Council in March 1965. Not long afterwards the RCD Committee on air transport began to establish regular airlinks and the first RCD flight of Pakistan International Airlines (PIA) linking Karachi with Teheran and Istanbul started on November 1966. Iran Airlines followed this up by starting a jet service to Europe via Istanbul.

On 6 July 1967 an RCD joint venture for printing bank notes was inaugurated in Karachi. It was the first industrial project in which all three RCD countries had collaborated. The new factory was sponsored by the Pakistan Security Printing Corporation. The agreement on the RCD union for multilateral payments arrangements was signed in Ankara in April 1967. This was an important step toward the expansion of intra-regional trade. The RCD Insurance Centre was established in Karachi to promote a study of measures which could facilitate cooperation in this field. The centre published the RCD Insurance Manual in 1967. The three RCD insurance pools functioned effectively and several national companies joined the pools.

Government efforts to promote intra-regional trade proved unequal to the task of overcoming the formidable obstacle that discouraged trade expansion. For instance in 1969 the percentage of goods exchanged among Pakistan, Iran, and Turkey stood at the level of 1, 1.9, and 0.5 per cent respectively of their total trade. Thus about 99 per cent of the region's foreign trade was still conducted with the rest of the world. It was partly to expand their potential and diversify the exchanges that the RCD Regional Planning Council decided to set up joint purpose industries. Until 1969, fifty-five joint purpose enterprises had been either established or approved in principle.

At the RCD Ministerial Council meeting held in Pakistan in January 1976 the three member states resolved to take measures to strengthen and revitalize the RCD. This clearly reflected an awareness that the organization had not been able to achieve all that it set out to achieve. At the Izmir RCD Summit held in April 1976, the then Pakistan Premier called for the removal of intra-regional trade barriers to pave the way for the establishment of a free trade area. In March 1977, the RCD states signed the Izmir treaty, which among other things provided for the establishment of an RCD investment and development bank for initiating, promoting and financing projects of a regional character.

Closer cooperation in aviation was the theme of a meeting of the representatives of the three national airlines held at Teheran on

16 January 1978. The three airlines decided to take necessary steps for increasing their inter-lines cargo business on both inter-regional and international routes. The national airlines also decided to give 50 per cent discount to students of the three member countries travelling within the region. This cooperation was seen to be vitally important for promoting free movement of goods and people within the region.

The Present Phase of Turkey-Pakistan Relations

CENTO was established in the context of the cold war, and the impulse for its formation was at least partly provided by the Western perception of the security of states of the region. As long as it lasted, it had limited use in affording the three governments useful opportunities of contact with one another. But as the cold war subsided, the non-regional members' enthusiasm for the organization also abated. They were often unable to comprehend the significance, intensity, and long-term effects of regional crises. Their understanding and interpretation of the regional security arrangements did not coincide at such a moment, with those of the regional countries. On the Cyprus question, Turkey felt very badly let down by its Western friends. Twice CENTO failed to come to the aid of Pakistan when it faced external aggression. By the late seventies a large segment of opinion in both Pakistan and Turkey had come to favour a policy of non-alignment.

Thus when the Turkish Foreign Minister Gunduz Okcun visited Pakistan in July 1978, an intensive review of foreign policy was undertaken. Islamabad and Ankara, which had each been maintaining close contacts with the non-aligned nations, were hopeful of getting admission as guest participants in the Non-Aligned club. Another subject which was discussed by the two Foreign Ministers concerned the future of CENTO. Pakistan was known to be having second thoughts about its CENTO ties and now even Turkey was reappraising its CENTO links. The Ankara-Moscow friendship treaty which had been signed earlier was an additional factor of great significance, and Pakistan was briefed by the Turkish Foreign Minister on the rationale of the development.

Pakistan was busy considering the question of withdrawing from CENTO when the Shah of Iran was overthrown by a popular upheaval led by Ayatollah Khomeini. The triumphant revolutionaries lost no time in denouncing CENTO. This was also when Pakistan decided to quit the pact. It joined the Non-Aligned Movement in 1979 and attended the Movement's summit conference at Havana in September of the same year. The demise of CENTO did not have to involve the automatic liquidation of the RCD, but Iran took the view that the latter was an offshoot and by-product of the former. Consequent upon Iran's decision to take no part in the work of the RCD, the economic grouping has virtually ceased to exist. It thus remains for the three former partners to salvage their relationships from the wreckage of the tripartite alliance.

While the nature of the Iran-Pakistan relationship is to a certain extent still an open question, there is no doubt that the ties between Turkey and Pakistan remain fully intact and capable of further development. Turkey-Pakistan friendship was put to a test when the UN General Assembly adopted a resolution on 20 November 1979 demanding the immediate withdrawal of all foreign armed forces from Cyprus and asking the UN Secretary General to continue to provide good offices for the negotiation between the representatives of the two Cypriot communities. The draft was approved by a vote of ninety-nine in favour to five against and thirty-five abstentions. Pakistan along with four other Muslim countries voted against it. Pakistan supported the Turkish contention that the provision was designed to internationalize the issue which should be settled through negotiation between the two communities in the island.

Following the military takeover in Turkey in September 1980, the Turkish ambassador to Islamabad immediately stated that Turkey's relations with Pakistan would 'continue to be most cordial and friendly' inspite of a change of government in Ankara.

NOTES

1. Syed Razi Wasti, *The Political Triangle in India (1850-1924)*, Peoples Publishing House, Lahore, 1976, p. 233.
2. Lord Kinross, *The Rebirth of a Nation*, Wiedenfield and Nicolson, London, 1964, p. 297.
3. *Quaid-i-Azam and the Muslim World, Selected Documents 1937-1948*, compiled and edited by Atique Zafar Sheikh and Mohammad Riaz Malik, Royal Book Company, Karachi, 1978, p. 284.
4. *Pakistan Horizon*, Karachi, Vol. VII, No. 3, September 1954, pp. 163–4.
5. *Pakistan Horizon*, Karachi, Vol. IX, No. 2, June 1956, p. 107.

6. Quoted in *The Pakistan Times*, Lahore, 23 February 1962.
7. *Dawn*, Karachi, 4 November 1962.
8. *The Times*, London, quoted in *Dawn*, 9 July 1964.
9. Movement for the union of Cyprus with Greece. The Turkish and Greek Cypriots have always lived as separate entities and have never intermixed. The Greeks are afraid of partitioning the island, while the Turkish minority fears Enosis.
10. *The Pakistan Times*, Lahore, 24 December 1979.

13

Pakistan's Geopolitical Environment and Security*

Mujtaba Razvi

Geography controls the political environment of a country. There is no escape from one's geography and from its impact on one's policies. It has often been said, one can choose one's friends or allies but seldom gets an option to choose one's neighbours. They are there and one has to cultivate correct relations if not a cordial one; it is unfortunate to have incorrect or bad relations with neighbours. According to the Napoleonic dictum, 'Geography determines a nation's history—the political significance of an area bears a well defined relations to its climate, land forms and natural resources'. Ideologies can change, socio-political systems can change, but a state must retain a territorial personality. The security of a state depends largely on a vigilant policy towards its neighbours, which postulates a sound frontier policy. It was Lord Curzon, who said: 'Frontiers are indeed the razor's edge on which hang suspended modern issues of war or peace, of life or death to nations'.[1]

Pakistan has the unique distinction of being surrounded by three of the world's largest nations, i.e., the Soviet Union, China, and India. The 'geographical pivot of history' and strategically the most critical zone in Eurasia is formed by those states which lie along the periphery of the great continental powers of Asia, the USSR, and the People's Republic of China. As a Southwest Asian peripheral state, Pakistan's security is linked with the Indian Ocean/Arabian Sea and the Gulf

* Vol. xxxv, No. 3, 1982.

region. It must find an equation with big neighbours and with the USA, which has global interests. Traditionally, Pakistan has shared a common destiny with its two Muslim neighbours, Afghanistan and Iran. Afghanistan with its high mountain ranges and legendary passes (the Khyber and Bolan) guards the strategic pathway of the Indo-Gangetic plains of the subcontinent and no one has reached them without getting control of Kabul. Despite the air age, the triangle of land, wedged strategically between Iran, remains the gateway to the subcontinent. The Pakistan/Iran/Afghanistan region provides a land-corridor to any power to the warm waters of the Arabian Sea and the Indian Ocean. The events of the Horn of Africa and West Asia may look like distant problems for Pakistan, but their repercussions have a destabilizing effect on Southwest Asia as a whole (of which Pakistan is a part). The Straits of Hormuz, characterized as the 'international oil highway' which connects the world's largest site of oil reserves and production with world markets and the hub of international oil tanker traffic is 250 miles off the naval complex of Iran at Chah Bahar, which is about fifty miles west of the Pakistan border, thus linked with the crucial geopolitical problems of the 'life line' sea-lanes.

The circumstances of Pakistan's origin and composition, as well as the unique geographical features (especially from 1947-1971) makes it a particularly security-conscious country. There is no defence depth, all its major cities are border outposts. Any army crossing the Kyber Pass or the Punjab border could seek to cut right across Pakistan, disrupting the whole communication system and thus bringing about a political and economic chaos in which survival of the state would hang in a precarious balance. (An attempt of such nature was made from the Punjab border in 1965.) Thus, Pakistan's foreign policy, in the last thirty-five years, has very largely revolved around the problem of defining and defending its territorial personality, and it may continue to be so.

The crisis over Afghanistan is having immediate geopolitical effects. There has been a shifting of the area of superpowers' struggle eastward from West Asia towards South Asia. Though the fact remains that after Israel's Sinai withdrawal Americans will be posted on Tiran Island in the Tiran Strait, which leads from the Suez and the Red Sea into the Gulf of Aqaba. Tiran is still formally Saudi territory leased to the President Nasser in 1954. Sharm al-Shaikh and Tiran have been assigned to American Rapid Deployment Force. This can bring China, (already linked with Pakistan through the Karakoram Highway) more directly in the game. There is the Indo-Soviet treaty of 9 August 1971, article 9 of which contains a stronger guarantee for India than the promise of assistance provided in the NATO convention. Chinese efforts to block Soviet expansion may prompt a parallel expansion of the Indian-Soviet relationship. The spectre of the Soviet Union and India looms large, a threatening perception for the small states. In the words of Olaf Caroe, 'Russia is so tender in central Asia, that it cannot afford the "polarization" of alliances which could bring China in support of Pakistan's right into Kashmir'.[2]

The Soviet intervention has its impact on Southwest Asia. 'Improved Soviet ability to project power, the erosion of northern-tier barrier to Soviet access to the region, the Soviet foothold along the periphery of the area and the growing naval presence in the south, all fundamentally affected the security calculus of the states.'[3] President Zia pointed out on 15 January 1980: 'If you visualise the map of the region and if you extend the hammer and sickle over Afghanistan and then see from there onwards, which are the areas that are likely to come under the influence. Where is Iran, where is the Gulf and where is the Strait of Hormuz and where is Saudi Arabia and the rest of the Muslim world...and if the recent events because of the Soviet intervention have changed the environment, then Pakistan deserves attention'.[4] 'The presence of troops in Afghanistan may have put the Soviets so near to the Gulf in geographic terms, that not for many years had Moscow been so far from influencing events in that region.'[5]

The geopolitical perception may be that Moscow is seeking to close gaps in its arc of influence stretching from the Horn of Africa to Central Asia. One end of this arc is anchored in Ethiopia where Col. Mengistu's government puts Moscow in a position to control the Red Sea and the Suez Canal. The Soviet Union is boosting its influence in the Seychelles archipelago, which is situated 1170 miles from the coast of Kenya, and occupies a strategic position on the route used by all freighters bound for the US and Western Europe. The Russians see Seychelles as strategically located and feel the island can be effectively used to balance the US naval base of Diego Garcia. Some analysts believe that Moscow is moving to encircle the Gulf of Aden-Persian-Arabian Sea region. South Yemen, a pro-Soviet state, flanks Saudi Arabia and controls the Arabian Sea approaches of the Red Sea. *The Financial Times* observed: 'The Soviet foothold in Aden, now reinforced, could hardly be more strategic...progress toward Yemen unity is halted, Saudi Arabia will be more convinced that the encirclement is speeding up'.

Hence, the Russian control of Afghanistan is regarded by some analysts as the first step towards warm water ports or to control the immense wealth of the Gulf states either through Iran or Pakistan, since the Russians have aspired to control the south of their territory in the direction of the Indian Ocean, the Arabian Sea, and the Gulf region. The ethnic ties between Pakistan and Iran with Afghanistan make this country an ideal place for subversion against them.

The Indian Prime Minister, Mrs Indira Gandhi, is quoted as having told a French correspondent on 8 January 1980 that the Soviet intervention in Afghanistan was a threat to India, although one for which the US was basically responsible. Moreover, Pakistan was showing the signs of a prolonged strain under the pressures emanating from Afghanistan, Moscow, and New Delhi. Though various efforts to open genuine negotiations on Afghanistan proved abortive, Western and Pakistani persistence, in pursuing them may well have suggested to Moscow that it really had little fear. After the UN move, and the EEC's peace initiatives, Diego Cordovez, the UN Secretary-General's personal representative is having negotiations with Islamabad, Kabul and Teheran to bring about a political solution of the Afghanistan issue.

However, it is becoming fashionable these days to refer to Afghanistan as 'Moscow's Vietnam'. In Washington, this seems to excuse the blunders and miscalculations of American policy in the last thirty years—a policy which effectively threw Afghanistan into Soviet hands on 27 December 1979 by transforming US misjudgements into a shrewd Soviet policy. Washington's warnings and 'sanctions' (hardly implemented) against Moscow have not earned credibility of American policy either in the third world or West Europe. There is no indication that Washington is ready to back-up the warnings with any security muscle. In such circumstances, if the Afghan freedom fighters should succeed, it would be the first time that Russian territorial expansion has been stopped and turned back by one of the nations it sought to swallow.

The United States has yet to define its Indian Ocean/Gulf posture. This posture cannot be articulated in a policy vacuum with increasing Arab/Muslim disenchantment with Washington's patronage of Israel. A multinational approach to a common Western problem (maintenance of secure supplies of raw materials from the Indian

Ocean/Gulf region) sought to mitigate some of the political sensitivity that the deployment of American forces in the region arouse among the littoral states. Problems of independence and security in the third world are by no means for unilateral American action. The Afghan invasion is clearly related to the problem of continuing access to oil from the Middle East. The revolution in Iran, itself a product of deep political, economic, social and religious forces, affords a unique opportunity for Soviet exploitation. So does ethnic ferment there and in the neighbouring countries. Soviet activities in the Horn of Africa, the Arabian peninsula and along the shores that the Middle East follows en route to Europe, Japan, and the US give further opportunity for trouble-making. During the last three years, American policy-makers have rediscovered the Indian Ocean. With this re-evaluation, the United States has increased its forces in the Indian Ocean/Gulf region. The fall of the Shah in January 1979 and the Soviet intervention in Afghanistan in December of that year lent new urgency to American efforts to secure the flow of Persian Gulf oil to the West. Former President Carter, declared in his 23 January 1980 State of the Union message that the Persian Gulf was vital to US interests and that the United States would use military force to protect it, if necessary. Now, the Reagan administration has stressed its perception that there is a 'strategic consensus' among nations in the area threatened by the Soviet Union and the US policy must be guided by that perception.

The US problem of containing Russian influence is most difficult in Southwest Asia; this is because of special commitment to Israel. The steady extension of Israeli settlements in the West Bank and Gaza convinced many observers that Begin's intention was annexation, which would foreclose any Palestinian settlement. Israel's annexation of Syria's Golan Heights in December and Begin's retort to US criticism and suspension of the pact for military cooperation seemed to prove the dream of an Arab-Israeli accommodation even further from reality. Thus in the diplomatic sphere, the debate revolves around the policy of the Reagan administration's priorities.

'The Reagan foreign policy thus far consists of little more than an ill-coordinated series of ideologically motivated gestures. Above all, there has been virtually no attempt by Washington to start talking seriously to Moscow, even though this administration views almost all world problems through the prism of Soviet-American rivalry...questions connected with Afghanistan being discussed together with questions of Gulf security.'[6] What has really provided the Soviet Union with an opening in Southwest Asia has been the United States's inept handling of the situation in the region. In the first place, its unqualified and open-ended commitment to Israel has proved to be a negative factor in the evolution of Washington's ties with the Arab/Muslim world. Secondly, President Reagan's policy of strengthening relationships with some governments in order to promote American strategic interests *vis-à-vis* Moscow has produced a backlash. Thus, the Gulf Cooperation Council's repeated affirmation of its desire to keep the area free from the presence of outside powers obviously springs from its members' concern over the US plans for the Rapid Deployment Force. Similarly, the treaty of friendship signed by Libya, Ethiopia, Syria, and South Yemen is pointedly directed to be against American military activity in the Indian Ocean and the Gulf. 'The Saudi ambivalence towards the United States is nowhere more apparent than on the issue of a US military presence in the Persian Gulf area. The official Saudi position is that the superpowers should stay out of the region militarily and no foreign bases should be allowed in the area...The Saudis are gradually responding to Soviet overtures and are talking of the possibility of opening some form of diplomatic contacts. The Soviets from time to time pass messages through intermediaries such as the PLO.'[7] Critics say that the Russians are moving because they have seen the weakness of the United States. They do not believe that the Americans will fight if they move into Pakistan or Iran, whereas the US reply is that they have strengthened their alliance with NATO to contain Russia. The American security perception in Asia should be through Sino-US strategy to contain the Soviet Union. For this the Reagan Administration has to find some formula to recognize the Chinese interests over Taiwan.

'Moscow doggedly attempts to push an "Asian Collective Security" coalition which will give the USSR access to the area and constrain Chinese and American power. Its efforts are reinforced by growing Soviet naval air deployments to the Asian theatre and the opportunistic establishment of bilateral political ties and security treaties.'[8] But Washington shows lack of clear perception about Asian security or a clear regional security. A western multinational approach to a common western problem of securing supplies of raw materials from the Indian Ocean/Gulf region has not been successful, as the Soviet capabilities appear to be extending to more distant regions of the globe, and the Western alliance system has become increasingly archaic. 'Reagan's remark in conversation that the exchange of tactical weapons against troops in the European field would not inevitably mean a commitment of the full might of the US to the defense of Europe'[9] has further damaged NATO. The study, prepared by the Congressional research service said there was a belief in Europe that US leadership was no longer contributing effectively to Western security. A similar study was released by the Senate Foreign Relations Committee: Europeans see our attitude as careless...(and) are preoccupied by desire to avoid war. We tend to see the current European attitude as weak-kneed. The Reagan administration's policies have aggravated differences with Europeans over nuclear issues and the role of arms control. There seems to be rising trend of neutralism in Europe in the US-USSR conflicts. The Europeans ravaged by two world wars, regard war as something that will happen in their backyard, while Americans are accustomed to thinking of war as happening 'over there'. In the final analysis, however, fundamental questions must be addressed, and the key question is how the alliance will proceed in the decade of the 1980s. In testimony before the Senate armed services, on 31 January 1980, former US Defence Secretary, Harold Brown said: 'We can't assure that we could win a war there (Gulf-West Asian region), but to cast doubt on our ability to deter or fight...is damaging to US security'.

Now the Russians are at the borders of Pakistan and within striking distance of warm-water ports they have sought so long. From the all-weather Kandahar airport in southern Afghanistan they are only 720 kilometers from the Arabian Sea, where they are within striking range of Western shipping and communications (especially the US naval forces assembled there to protect the Gulf of Oman), the Straits of Hormuz and the Gulf. In Kandahar, they are also near Quetta, and the heart of Balochistan. 'Should the Soviets secure their presence and lines of communication (LOCs) within the country and also construct bases in southwest Afghanistan, their ability to project power to the Straits of Hormuz and the entrance to the Gulf would be greatly enhanced. As a result, the Soviets could provide aircover for the insertion of airborn elements into Bandar Abbas or Chah Bahar, in addition to reducing the ground forces that might go overland along the Helmand river-Zahidan Bandar Abbas or Zahidan-Chah Bahar with them, a Soviet combat air and bomber presence in Afghanistan.'[10]

Pakistan remained associated with the United States in intimate bilateral and multilateral military ties for about sixteen years, but felt cheated by the authorities in Washington when it was locked in its battle for survival against India in 1965 and 1971. Pakistan's motives in joining the alliances were explained by the then Foreign Minister, late Mohammad Ali Bogra: 'Our main and only purpose was to safeguard the safety and security of Pakistan and we needed support from the like-minded and peace-loving nations. We never made any secret of the fact that we apprehended a threat to our security from India.'[11] For this reason, Pakistan made fruitless efforts in September 1954 at the Manila conference to induce the United States to commit itself to the defence of Pakistan against all types of aggression, communist or non-communist, whereas, Secretary of State Foster Dulles, appended a note to the text of the SEATO that United States 'commitments would apply only to communist aggression'. 'Neutralist doctrine, hostility to Pakistan, fear of China, and a determined policy of accommodation with Peking all reinforced Indian opposition to an American alliance system.'[12] Replying to US criticism of Sino-Pakistan friendship, President Ayub had said on 21 February: 'The object of SEATO and CENTO is that war should be prevented from coming to these regions. Well, if this freedom for the area can be obtained through good offices between neighbours, the object of SEATO and CENTO is being achieved.' Pakistanis convincingly argued that if the solidarity of the Western world was said to remain unimpaired after the America-Russia détente or the Anglo-American-Soviet Test Ban Treaty (1963) how, by the same token, could a relationship with China jeopardize Pakistan's relations with the United States? But in September 1965, the United States suspended all military and economic aid to Pakistan, followed by an announcement of the complete stoppage of military assistance to Pakistan on 12 April 1967. After the dismemberment of Pakistan, a supposedly pro-Pakistan Nixon administration encouraged India to be the 'security manager of South Asia'.

In a broad sense, both the Democratic and Republican parties of the USA do not appear to be markedly different; both agree on India's pre-eminent position in the subcontinent. Under-Secretary of State Warren Christopher made a statement in New Delhi in July 1977, that the US had decided to look towards India as the leader of South Asia. Earlier, in late March 1977, the Foreign Assistance subcommittee of the Foreign Relations Committee recommended that the measures adopted by the Congress in July 1974 in reaction to India's nuclear explosion, requiring the US representative to the World Bank to vote against low-interest loans to India by the Bank's affiliate, the International Development Association should be revoked. Recently, India got massive aid from the World Bank (which is now highly subscribed by Saudi Arabia). Since 1947 India has been receiving economic aid from the US. In the wake of the Sino-Indian clash 'a non-aligned' India got more lavish arms aid than 'aligned' Pakistan. The Carter Administration stopped all aid to Pakistan in April 1979. Pakistan became the first victim of the US non-proliferation policy, whereas India received Washington's assistance in its nuclear programme. Apparently, there has been an amendment in the Symington laws in favour of Pakistan to receive economic aid and to purchase arms but this stick can at any time be used against Pakistan. The Senate passed legislation to cut off $3.2 million in promised military aid if the country explodes a nuclear device. Senator Alan Cranston said the opening of a fuel fabrication plant meant Pakistan had cleared the final technological hurdle in its weapons programme.[13] Dr Lewis A. Dunn of the Hudson Institute who has written a book on nuclear proliferation, in a special interview to *Dawn*'s correspondent, said on 31 March 1981: 'I believe, and that is my personal view, that Pakistan is seeking the capability to make a device, but hasn't decided whether or not to do so. It is, however, acquiring the knowledge and technicality...I think the whole US-Pakistan relationship currently is undergoing a review and is being reassessed. What it will lead to, I cannot say. Pakistan's insistence on the peaceful uses of nuclear energy is endorsed by the absence of complaints from the International Atomic Energy Authority. It has allowed inspection of safeguard facilities in PINSTECH and KANUPP. On the other hand, the US is in favour of signing the NPT. Pakistan has called for a nuclear weapon free zone in South Asia and the Indian Ocean.

The American leadership has reviewed South Asia with a sense of equanimity. The assumption has been that nothing is likely to happen in South Asia that will seriously affect US vital interests elsewhere in Asia. The United States—because of the narrow, unimaginative approach adopted by successive administrations and the propensity in Washington's view to see South Asia from every perspective but that of the region itself—has rarely been able or willing to use the substantial economic and ideological advantages it has enjoyed in South Asia. The revolution in Iran is considered by many as the greatest setback for American interests in West Asia, in the post-war era. The United States administration's appalling lack of understanding of Asian problems is a great tragedy for the Americans themselves. No Soviet move has undercut the effectiveness of the American policy as its lack of perception and isolationist trend in the wake of Vietnam and Watergate. The strategic balance changed in Asia after the Americans' retreat from Vietnam. The Soviet-supported Vietnamese occupation of Kampuchea has alarmed both communist China and the non-communist Southeast Asian nations (ASEAN). The Chinese believe that the Soviet Union is the 'greatest threat' to world peace and this can only be contained by the combined efforts of Washington, Peking, Tokyo, and the West Europeans. The Karakoram Highway is of major importance to China, being its only access route (through Pakistan) to the Arabian Sea–Indian Ocean. In any crisis in which Pakistan is involved, it is the geopolitical interest of China, apart from a firm friendship with Pakistan, that may induce China not to remain a silent spectator. Therefore, Pakistanis look to China as a neighbour favourably inclined to assist than a distant United States.

There is a natural tendency for American defense planners to concentrate on the Southwest Asian contingencies in terms of Soviet-US balance and to worry if the United States will support the regional nations. These constraints are not real, and it is not certain that the United States will be able to see the anti-Soviet coalition with Southwest Asia that it would like to see. The Soviet intervention in Afghanistan challenged the perceptions of the American policy-makers in regard to Soviet intentions, calling into question the Soviet interpretation of détente and its strategic ends with respect to the third world. On 28 December 1979 (the day following the Soviet intervention) former President Carter telephoned President Zia to say that he was reviewing ways that could help counter the Soviet threat to Pakistan. Two days later, the then US National Security Adviser, Zbigniew Brzezinski, reaffirmed a 1959 bilateral agreement (SEATO & CENTO ended in 1972 and 1979 respectively) under which the United States would take appropriate action, including the use of force to protect Pakistan if it was attacked. The then Secretary of Defence, Harold Brown, visited China (first visit of its kind since 1949) and discussed how the United States and China might work 'in parallel' to assist Pakistan. Islamabad's response to Washington was that of caution and restrain. When the US Deputy Secretary of the time visited Islamabad, he was told that Pakistan was not entirely happy with Brzezinski's public invocation of the 1959 bilateral agreement without advance consultation. Pakistan was not unmindful of the fact that this agreement could not be of any use to Pakistan to check Indian aggressions in 1965 and 1971 whereas, the Indo-Soviet treaty of 1971 put India in a position to intervene militarily and dismember Pakistan.

Washington knew about the signing of such a treaty on 31 July (ten days before). Moreover, Warren Christopher said that the 1959 agreement covers aggression on Pakistan by the Soviet Union or by a country in the control of the Soviet Union (impliedly, he excluded India). When Brzezinski visited Islamabad, he concentrated much more on analysing the nature of the problem that this region was confronted with, particularly the threat to Pakistan on the long term basis as if he had nothing to do with the immediate security of Pakistan, rather he laid stress that the US wanted to minimize the chance of conflict in the region between India and Pakistan to enhance the security of this region which was constantly threatened from the north. The question has been raised as to how eager Pakistan is to get the protective umbrella of the United States when the US, according to ex-Secretary of State Edmund Muskie wanted, as early as 1980, to press ahead for the ratification of Strategic Arms Limitations Talks (SALT-II), despite the Soviet presence in Afghanistan.

The illustrious American journalist, Harrison says: 'Examined in the cold light of local realities, however, the US decision to embrace Pakistani President Mohammad Ziaul Haq emerges as a monumental self-defeating blunder that could enable Moscow to make major diplomatic and political advances in Southwest Asia without direct military involvement. Indeed, Reagan's policy is likely to fan the fires of anti-Americanism in both Pakistan and India, accelerate the process of the national disintegration underway in Pakistan, and stimulate a new arms race between Islamabad and New Delhi that could eventually explode in a nuclear war.'[14] The present American ambassador to Pakistan, Ronald Spiers, listed in Karachi on 20 April 1982 four vulnerabilities: (i) the concern in the US that a positive relationship with Pakistan will be misunderstood as anti-India; (ii) the Human Rights problem has been a source of continuing reservation among important sectors of opinion in the US about the Martial Law. It is not for the Americans to advise on its internal political structures, but for many Americans one of the basic human rights is the right to participate in the political process; (iii) and a more serious threat is the issue of narcotics; about 70 percent of the heroin in American streets is now coming from Southwest Asia, much of it from or through Pakistan; and (iv) the final shadow on the horizon of US-Pakistan relations is the nuclear issue and any explosion whether labelled 'peaceful' or not would probably jeopardize our renewing ties with Pakistan. It is alleged by Indian writers that the US is not concerned primarily with Pakistan's security *vis-à-vis* the Soviet Union but with the safety of 'sea lanes' of the Gulf region, and Pakistan also fears another 'Yalta' between the US and the USSR over the spheres of influence in this region.

India has been on the threshold of acquiring arms from America. The recent exchange of visits between top officials of the countries indicate that the US may sell arms to India to neutralize the Russian influence over the Indian government. K.P. Menon had gone on a 'goodwill mission' to the USA and Canada. The visit by Menon, in fact, was a culmination of a move to buy some sophisticated American arms which was initiated by C. Subrahmaniam as the Defence Minister in the Charan Singh government. India launched its eight billion dollar five-year defence programme in May 1980, which was made before Pakistan and the US had entered into arms negotiations. India has made a deal with Moscow for Soviet arms worth 1.28 billion roubles, on the Soviet credit at 2.5 per cent per annum, repayable in seventeen years. The exact nature of the military hardware, to be supplied by the Russians under this agreement, has not been disclosed by the Soviet Union. But according to press reports, these include missiles, rockets, anti-tank weapons, and electronic equipment. Furthermore, the purchase of 100 tanks will be followed by the production of 690 more tanks in India under Soviet licence. Russians are reported to have offered MIG 23s, MIG 25s, MIG 27s, MIG 29s, MIG 24 helicopters, and T72 tanks. India has also made deals with West European countries such as Britain, France and West Germany to purchase Jaguars, Mirage 2000s, and submarines. According to a report published in *Dawn* (Karachi) of 21 March 1982, India has apparently agreed to share more closely the Soviet global strategic concerns in return for the USSR's agreeing to establish more sophisticated arms production plants in India. Bhabani Sen Gupta, the director of the Indian Research Centre, said that the Soviet Union had adequate congruance of strategic and political interests in the development of India's real defence capability. The Ustinov visit put the seal on expanding Indo-Soviet collaboration in defence production (Soviet Defence Minister, Marshal Ustinov's visit to India disrupted a planned tour of Europe of the heads of India's army and air force). Subrahmanyam said in Bombay, on 20 December 1980 that India at some cost which is not unmanageable, can take care of the hardware likely to be transferred to Pakistan by the US, and the Indian forces can defeat the Pakistanis in battle.

K. N. Ramchandra wrote in *Hindustan Times*, New Delhi, 19 April 1981: 'It is indeed time—there is no need to shy away from it—that we had intervened in 1971 to create Bangladesh under the framework of an integral South Asian security system from the Durand Line to the border of Burma, including Bhutan and Nepal.' Another Indian writer, Ajit Bhattachari, in his article, 'India and Neighbours', *Indian Express*, New Delhi, 5 December 1981, observed: 'Indian policies and postures are creating an atmosphere of insecurity...the fact cannot be hidden behind a smoke-screen of self-righteous denunciation of others...though linked with India more closely than any other country by ties of common culture and history, Nepal's fears could not be completely obscured by diplomatic jargon and the brave speeches made by Mr Narasimha Rao during his recent visit there.' Like the North, Pakistan is also exposed to possible attack from a Soviet ally, India. It may be that Pakistan needs blanket security from the US against Indian aggression. *The Economist* (London) wrote on 5 December 1981: 'The stable commodity on the South Asian subcontinent today is distrust. Contrary to geopolitical logic, it is in largest supply in the largest country, India. Surveying its surroundings from the most heavily armed, heavily industralized and heavily populated country in the region, India sees threats and pressures on every hand.' It also observed 'India insists that Pakistan should accept the centripetal pull of the subcontinent rather than look to the fellow Muslim to the West. All these amounts to "Bhutanisation".'

In the context of the changed security environment, Pakistan's arms deal with the US is not a massive one as is made out by the Indian Prime Minister, Mrs Indira Gandhi. It is the height of exaggeration to say, as Mrs Gandhi does, that an arms race is being triggered by Pakistan. If there is any race at all, it is a race being triggered by India. Pakistan insists on a more satisfactory and durable relationship with the United States, it seems to underline guarantee, against the recurrence of the previous experience of American attitudes towards Pakistan in case of any Indian aggression. It is known to the world that the Soviet leaders once urged former Indian Prime Minister, Morarji Desai 'to do something to Pakistan to teach the neighbour a lesson'.

Pakistan has been showing the signs of prolonged strain under the pressures emanating from Afghanistan, Moscow, and New Delhi. Though all efforts to open genuine negotiations over Afghanistan proved abortive, Western and Pakistani persistence in pursuing them may well have suggested to Moscow that it really had little to fear.

Consistent with the expression of the will of the world community, Pakistan has taken further initiatives on the problem on the basis of four principles: (a) withdrawal of Soviet troops from Afghanistan; (b) observance and respect for the non-aligned and independent status of that country; (c) the reaffirmation of the right of the Afghan people to determine their own political and socio-economic system free from coercion and outside interference; (d) and the return of the Afghan refugees (numbering now over 2.7 million) to their homes in safety and honour. The UN Secretary-General's representative, Diego Cordovez has trilateral talks with Islamabad, Kabul, and Teheran, Pakistan is quite hopeful of a political solution of the Afghan problem.

The visit of Nikolai Firyubin, Deputy Foreign Minister of the Soviet Union to Islamabad, in September 1981, at Pakistan's request was the biggest diplomatic event in recent years, a gesture that Pakistan must live with peace and amity with its superpower neighbour, with whom Pakistan has developed strong economic ties. Former Foreign Minister of Pakistan Mr Agha Shahi, took considerable pains to stress that Pakistan was determined not to tie itself with American strategic plans for the Persian Gulf. 'We just cannot have a strategic accord with the United States', he affirmed, 'our position on the Middle East crisis is the reverse of Americans.' Both the United States and the Soviet Union have put forward security and peace plans for the Gulf. We have supported the regional security concept of the Gulf countries without any external intervention. He stressed the point that Pakistan had turned down Washington's offer to sell weapons at a token rate of interest but had deliberately given in for credits at 14 per cent interest. However, many Pakistanis resent the US aid package because it can only prolong Pakistan's dependence on the United States. On the no-war pact offer to India, Nehal Singh observes: 'Let us assume that Pakistan's interest in the non-aggression pact stems from its desire to build up its military arsenal and perfect the nuclear bomb in undisturbed peace...Even so, how does India lose in signing a non-aggression pact?'

Whatever might have happened in early January 1980, in the second half of 1981 or the first half of 1982, Pakistan's perception of the Afghan solution has vastly changed. Instead of talking in terms of global crisis demanding global solution, Pakistani authorities have maintained dialogue with Moscow and the Russians seem to have assured them that they have no plan or intention to send troops into Pakistan. The Soviet Union no longer accuses Pakistan of being the 'principal actor in external intervention in Afghanistan'. As *Pravda* made it clear in an editorial on 25 September 1981, the Soviets regard the United States as the main aggressor in Afghanistan. Though Pakistan does not recognize the Karmal regime, it is willing to have negotiations with Babrak Karmal as the leader of the political force that rules in Afghanistan.

Pakistan now takes a more or less regional view of the Afghan crisis. It has on the whole accepted the Soviet proposal that the problem should be settled through direct negotiations between Afghanistan, Pakistan, and Iran. The political stability in Iran and an Iran-Pakistan approach (in the wake of Vilayeti-Ishaq exchange of visits) may bring more diplomatic pressure on Moscow to solve the problem, thereby snatching initiatives from the superpowers.

Pakistan left CENTO when it was virtually on a collision course with the United States over the nuclear programme in 1979. Surely the US view of the matter is going to be a far bigger determinant than what Pakistan thinks are the limits of its commitments. Pakistan does not like to be an instrument in worsening the security environment by allowing military bases on its soil. If Pakistan gets sucked deeper and deeper into the American framework, the Russians are not going to sit quiet. Pakistan realizes that if it is going to take a role in the US-Soviet confrontation, then at some point in time there is the possibility that the Soviets might decide to take retaliatory measures. The internal political situation in Pakistan is such that it offers considerable scope for destabilization and turmoil by external exploitation. Pakistan is also vulnerable to America; if it thinks that Pakistan is not sufficiently responsive to its strategic objectives it could decide to destabilize Pakistan. It should avoid being a 'cockpit' of superpower rivalry in the context of geostrategic developments in the region. Pakistan cannot court disaster by another round of war with India.

NOTES

1. Lord Curzon of Kedleston, *Frontiers, The Romanes Lecture*, 1907, London Clarenden Press, 1908, p. 4.
2. Olaf Caroe, *Soviet Empire*, London, Macmillan, 1967, p. 49.
3. Denis Rose, 'Considering Soviet threats to the Persian Gulf', *International Security*, Cambridge, Fall 1981, pp. 159–81.
4. *The Pakistan Times*, Lahore, 16 January 1980.

5. Karen Dawisha, 'Moscow's Moves in the Direction of the Gulf - So Near and So Far', *Journal of International Affairs*, New York, Spring 1981, p. 219.
6. Gwynne Dyer, 'The Foreign Policy Vacuum in Washington', *Dawn*, Karachi, 31 May 1981.
7. William B. Quandt, 'Riyadh Between The Superpowers', *Foreign Policy*, Washington, Fall 1981, pp. 38 & 52.
8. Richard H. Solomon, ed., *Asian Security in The 1980s*, Massachusetts, 1980.
9. Walter Laqueur, 'Reagan and the Russians', *Commentary*, January 1982, p. 22. See also his article 'A New State in European Neutralism', ibid., August 1981.
10. Denis Ross, op. cit., p. 177.
11. *Dawn*, 23 Novemebr 1962.
12. Fred Greene, *US Policy and the Security of Asia*, London, McGraw-Hill Co., 1968, p. 109.
13. Norman D. Palmer. 'Indo-American Relations: The Politics of Encounter', *Orbis*. Philadelphia, Pa., Summer 1979, pp. 403–20.
14. Selig Harrison, 'Fanning Flames in South Asia', *Foreign Policy*, Washington, Winter 1981, p. 84.

Pakistan's Defense Policy*

Hasan-Askari Rizvi

There has been a general realization amongst the scholars of International politics and diplomats for the last two decades that the defense and foreign policies of the 'small' and 'weak' states do contribute to shaping regional and international politics. This is the outcome of the subtle changes which have taken place in the international system during the twentieth century. From a Europe-centric and then, Europe-North American centric international system, it came to be dominated by two superpowers in the post-World War II period. There were a number of states which endeavoured to stay aloof from the superpower rivalry and maintained a non-aligned posture but the most outstanding characteristic of this period was the cold war. The superpowers' impact on international politics was so profound that the other forces shaping world politics appeared secondary and dependent. This bias in favour of the superpowers and their major allies made it difficult to give due recognition to the role of other actors in the international system. The behaviour-pattern of other actors (state as well as non-state) was often studied with reference to, or from the standpoint of, the superpowers' policies.

The hierarchical pattern of the international system with two superpowers at its apex, pulling the strings of international politics, could not sustain itself over a long period of time. The two superpowers continued to maintain their preponderance in military power including

* Vol. xxxvi, No. 1, 1983.

nuclear weapons technology, but there emerged cracks in both the blocs. New regional power centres began to emerge. These included Western Europe, Japan, China, and the Non-Aligned Movement. None of the new actors in the international system could displace the two superpowers from their positions of eminence, but these actors made it increasingly difficult for the superpowers to dominate the international system the way they used to do in the period immediately after the conclusion of World War II. This transformation contributed to multipolarity or what was sometimes described as bi-multipolarity, in the international system.[1]

The polycentric trends in the international system were reinforced by the increase in the number of actors in the international system. This was mainly due to the process of decolonization which brought into being a large number of independent and sovereign states in Asia, Africa, and the Middle East. These new nations crowded the major international organizations, created several new ones, and revived others from the state of dormancy. The activism of the 'small' and 'weak' states received an impetus by the successful enforcement of the 1973–74 oil embargo by the OPEC, the substantial rise in oil prices since then, the growing interdependence of the actors in the international system, and the decline of American power beginning with its withdrawal from Indo-China in 1975. The change in the character of the international system can be identified by the fact that only five Asian and no African states participated in the Hague Conferences of 1899 and 1907. The League of Nations had only seven Afro-Asian states as original members. In the case of the UN only twelve original members came from Asia and Africa.[2] Now, almost two-thirds of UN members are ex-colonial and third world states. They dominate the proceedings of the General Assembly and most of its organs (except the Security Council) and the specialized agencies.[3]

The overthrow of the Pahlavi dynasty in Iran (1979) in the wake of a mass upsurge led by the Ayatollahs despite the fact that the former Shah was a staunch ally of the US, showed that there was a limit to what a superpower could do in the third world. Similarly the two superpowers were unable to bring an end to the Iraq-Iran war (1980–82). These events demonstrated that many issues and conflicts had their regional and local dynamics which could not always be manipulated by the superpowers to their satisfaction because the international system had become polycentric, multilayered, and complex. There emerged numerous discontinuities in the international system which made it imperative to examine the role of actors other than the superpowers to fully appreciate the dynamics of international politics.

The late sixties and the seventies witnessed a gradual shift in the focus of study i.e., from the superpower orientation to a multi-targeted perspective. Some devoted attention to regional sub-systems as an important unit of international politics, its relationship with the international system and the dynamics of regional politics.[4] Others examined relationships between the weak and the powerful states.[5] Still others examined the factors which made a state a regional power or a middle power. They also endeavoured to identify several states which, in their estimation, qualified to be known as the middle powers.[6]

A good number of studies now focus on the policy-outputs of the 'small' and 'weak' states in the international system.[7] These studies recognize the fact that the small and weak states are not always on the receiving end of the international system. Their policies cannot be dismissed simply as reflexes to the policies of the super/major powers. The experience of the last decade suggests that the policy-outputs of the 'small' and 'weak' states merit a detailed examination because these states have not only become quite active in international politics but have also collectively attempted to make the international system more responsive to their demands and concerns. Their goals and aspirations; strengths and vulnerabilities; human and material resources; patterns of interaction with other small states, the middle powers and the superpowers; and the roles the power elite perceive for their states in the international system are interesting facets of international politics. The study of behaviour patterns of the 'small' and 'weak' states is useful for another reason. There are enumerable ethnic, dynastic, ideological, territorial, and economic disputes amongst these states. These sources of tensions have a profound impact on their domestic politics as well as external policies.

An important aspect of the behavior pattern of a small state in the international system is its defense policy. This becomes an interesting aspect of a small state's posture in international politics because of the limited human and material resources at its disposal and the numerous systemic constraints under which it has to formulate policies to protect its sovereignty and territorial integrity, reinforce its foreign policy strategies and improve its bargaining position in dealings with other states, especially the middle powers and the states in the immediate neighbourhood.

Numerous factors shape a country's defense policy. The major among these include geostrategic location of a country, nature of its territorial boundaries, and pattern of relations with its neighbours. Though there have been revolutionary changes in means of communication, geography still plays quite an important role in influencing decisions on strategic options. Natural resources, i.e., minerals, power, energy and food production, do have a bearing on a country's defense policy. In addition to these factors, industrial development and the nature of military establishment (quantity and quality of manpower, weapons and equipment) are also important determinants of defense policy.

Geostrategic Milieu

The geostrategic milieu has caused serious defense concerns for Pakistan as it is situated in the region described as the fulcrum of Asia[8]—a region where the Soviet Union, China, India and Pakistan meet. The politics of this region is characterized by several discontinuities, intra-regional conflicts based on discrepancies in ideology, national objectives, territorial disputes, and political rivalries. The superpowers also maintain direct and indirect interest in the region and its politics. While devising its defense and foreign policy, Pakistan has to take into account the geostrategic realities and intra-regional discontinuities as well as the policy postures of the superpowers towards the region.

Pakistan shares an approximately 1400 mile long border with India,[9] running from the Rann of Kutch on the Arabian Sea to the state of Jammu and Kashmir in the north east. In addition to this there is a long ceasefire line in the state of Jammu and Kashmir which divides the state into Pakistan and Indian-held Kashmir. There are no natural barriers on most of the Indo-Pakistan border which makes it convenient for troops and heavy armour of either side to cross the frontiers.

The Pakistan-Afghanistan border (the Durand line) has a mountainous terrain and is about 1200 miles long. It runs from the Sharikal range of the Pamirs in the north to the Iranian border at the Koh-i-Malik Siah. The main transit and trade routes between Pakistan and Afghanistan are through a number of passes in the mountain ranges dividing the two countries. These passes are also strategically important as military movement across the Durand line has traditionally taken place through these passes. One of the passes, the Khyber pass, was the traditional invasion route to India. All foreign troops, except those of Europeans, primarily used the Khyber pass route.

Pakistan has about 590 miles of common frontier with Iran which stretches from the Koh-i-Malik Siah (where the Afghanistan, Pakistan, and Iranian frontiers meet) to Gwader in the Arabian Sea. In the south, Pakistan is bound by about 450 miles of coastline of the Arabian Sea stretching from the Rann of Kutch/Indian border to Iran in the west. Pakistan does not share borders with the Soviet Union but at one point in the north (Wekhan area) the Durand line is about 25-30 miles from the Soviet border. Pakistan has a common frontier of about 400 miles with China in the Kashmir-Xinjiang region. It stretches from the tri-junction of Afghanistan, Pakistan, and China to the Karakorum pass.

Pakistan was faced with a generally hostile strategic environment because of the pattern of its relationship with India and Afghanistan. There were periods during the last 35–36 years when Indo-Pakistan relations could be described as 'correct and cordial' but generally their relations were characterized by mutual distrust, hostility, and serious disagreements on regional and international political issues. This was partly due to the legacy of the pre-independence period and partly due to the compounding impact of the developments immediately before and after independence in 1947. The distrust and hostility that developed between the Muslim League and the Congress Party leaderships in the last phase of the struggle for independence transformed into hostility between the two states after independence. Several disputes concerning the process of partition further spoiled their relations. These disputes included, *inter alia*, the influx of refugees, communal riots, the problem of minorities, the distribution of assets of the Indian government and the former Indian military, the canal water dispute, the evacuee property issue, the concentration of Indian troops on the Punjab border in 1950–51, and the unilateral suspension of trade by India in 1950.[10] It was generally believed in Pakistan that India did not want to solve these problems amicably in order to 'strangle' the new state of Pakistan soon after its inception. This perception of India's intentions was reinforced by the war in Kashmir (1947–48) and India's 'military action' in Junagadh and Hyderabad. Many in Pakistan interpreted India's 'military action' as a warning that the same might happen to Pakistan in the future.

Pakistan's relations with Afghanistan have mostly been far from cordial. When the Afghanistan government came to know in 1947 that the British had finally decided to wind up their rule over India and that the state of Pakistan would be created, they laid claims on North-West Frontier province and parts of Balochistan. This claim, though never clearly spelled out by Afghanistan,[11] has continued to be the major irritant in Pakistan-Afghanistan relations. On more than one occasion Pakistan and Afghanistan reached the brink of war on this issue in the late fifties and early sixties. Twice they severed diplomatic relations. Afghanistan was able to obtain Soviet support for its claims on Pakistan's territory.[12] This made the Afghan government more vocal in its demands. India also pampered Afghanistan by extending support on the 'Pakhtunistan' issue.[13] This was bound to cause serious concern in Pakistan. A large section of public opinion as well as the government circles feared a two-front war, i.e. armed clashes erupting simultaneously on the Pakistan-India and the Pakistan-Afghanistan borders.

What intensified Pakistan's feeling of insecurity *vis-à-vis* its neighbours, especially India, were a number of security handicaps Pakistan had to face. Pakistan's territory lacked depth and the main communication line ran parallel to the Indo-Pakistan border. A number of major cities were so close to the border that India's troops had to be confronted at the border. This required a well-equipped, highly mobile and hard-hitting army. Pakistan lacked all this in its formative years. It inherited a small, weak, and loosely organized military which hardly had the necessary arms and equipment. India declined to transfer a good part of Pakistan's share of armament and equipment of the former British Indian army. There was no ordnance factory in Pakistan at the time of independence.[14] India, on the other hand, inherited a stronger and larger military, all ordnance factories, and quite a substantial quantity of arms and equipment. India, thus, had a clear military edge over Pakistan.

Objectives of Defense Policy and Defense Strategies

The unfavourable geostrategic environment and the security concerns developed in the early years of independence shaped Pakistan's world view. It was characterized by a deep sense of insecurity inspired by external threats to its independent existence. The major goal of

Pakistan's defense policy has, therefore, been the search for security. This practically meant two things. First, the augmentation of security of Pakistan against 'threats' primarily from India and secondarily from Afghanistan. Second, the offsetting of India's military superiority in South Asia by strengthening Pakistan's defense arrangements and, at times, by using diplomacy as a countervailing measure.

Defense requirements enjoyed the top priority in Pakistan. Each successive government has allocated a large part of the national budget to defense. Pakistan had civilian governments during 1947–58 and 1971–77 by different political parties. The leaders of these governments often criticized their predecessors but all of them attached equal importance to the maintenance of strong defense. Pakistani governments whether led by civilians or military officials, allocated the maximum possible resources to the military. The national legislature, whenever it was allowed to function, generally underlined the need for maintaining a strong defense posture and supported the high budgetary allocations for defense.

Pakistan's defense expenditure has ranged from about 73 per cent to 34 per cent of total expenditure during 1947–83. On average it was 53.48 per cent. The 1982–83 budget has provided Rs 22,095.3 million for defense services. This is the highest defense allocation made so far. It comes to 47.1 per cent of total expenditure for 1982–83, and shows a 12.8 per cent rise over the revised defense expenditure for 1981–82. The details of defense expenditure in Pakistan since 1947 have been given in table 1.

It must also be pointed out here that, in addition to the overt allocation for defense, some expenditure on defense and security, i.e. defense-related projects come under other heads, i.e., civil works, roads and highways, law and order. To this we should also add the military hardware and equipment which Pakistan has obtained as a part of aid arrangements with a number of countries, especially the US.

Special attention was given to the reorganization and modernization of the armed forces. Reorganization of the three services of the military was undertaken in the first couple of years after independence. Their modernization was, however, an on-going process. Reorganization was necessitated due to the division of the former Indian military at the time of independence in 1947. The regiments with common traditions, recruiting areas, and class composition were amalgamated. The gaps were filled by fresh recruitments. The competent officers were given accelerated promotions. A reasonable number of non-commissioned officers of the three services were promoted to the commissioned ranks. Moreover, the personnel released from the military during the last few years were given a choice to rejoin the service. A good number of them availed this offer. All releases from the three services were stopped except in special cases. The qualified personnel of the military of the princely states acceding to Pakistan were also absorbed in the Pakistan army.

The modernization of the armed forces is a continuous process in an age of rapid technological advancement. A nation having a smaller and weaker military than its neighbouring adversary will have to make serious and repeated endeavours to improve the quality of its fighting forces so that its numerical handicap can be overcome by the superior quality of manpower as well as equipment. There were three major aspects of modernization of the Pakistan military. First, while the process of reorganization was underway Pakistan got involved in the first Kashmir war (1947–48) with India. This made it imperative for Pakistan to speed up the process of reorganization and modernization, meet with the immediate needs of armament, and take steps to meet with the long-range requirements of weapons and equipment. Second, in order to provide the necessary training, Pakistan established new training schools, including the Military Academy at Kakul, to replace the institutions lost to India at the time of independence. A number of selected officers were sent to England, the US and some of the Commonwealth countries for specialized and technical training. After Pakistan's participation in the West-sponsored security arrangements, American military experts were based in Pakistan to provide necessary training and technical advice to Pakistani officers in Pakistan. Since the late 1960s Pakistani military personnel were also sent to France and China for training.

Third, modernization also involves the provision of arms and ammunition in necessary quantity and quality. Pakistan was especially handicapped in this field as it did not inherit a single ordnance factory and most of its share of arms and ammunition belonging to the British Indian army was withheld by India after the outbreak of the Kashmir war.[15] Pakistan speeded up a plan to erect an ordnance factory and by the end of 1951, the first ordnance factory was inaugurated at Wah. Pakistan also obtained arms, equipment, aircraft, and naval ships and communication gear from abroad. Part of it was purchased on cash or against loans, and the rest was obtained as aid. Pakistan relied heavily on Western sources of supply, especially the US and Great Britain.

Later it diversified its sources of supply by purchasing defense equipment from France, West Germany and arms markets in Europe. It also secured arms and military hardware including helicopters, tanks, and aircraft from the Soviet Union (1968–70) and China.

The desire to enhance Pakistan's security was one of the major reasons[16] that Pakistan joined the West-sponsored security arrangements in 1954–55. Pakistan and the US signed the Mutual Defense Assistance Treaty in May 1954. Under this treaty, the US agreed to provide military equipment and training to Pakistani armed forces. This was followed by the establishment of the South East Asian Treaty Organization (SEATO) in September 1954. Besides Pakistan, this organization included Thailand, the Philippines, USA, United Kingdom, France, Australia, and New Zealand. One year later Pakistan also joined the Baghdad Pact.[17]

Pakistan and the US were operating from two different perspectives. For the US the underlying considerations were global; for Pakistan regional consideration was important. For the US the major concern was the containment of the Soviet Union and China; for Pakistan, India was the major adversary. The US was obsessed with communism and it wanted to contain its impact on Asian countries. Pakistan wanted to offset India's military superiority by obtaining military and economic assistance from the West.

Pakistan obtained over $900 million worth of military equipment under the Mutual Defense Agreement, the CENTO, and SEATO.[18] This included tanks and other small arms and transportation equipment, aircraft including F-104, B-57, F-86, and C-130 aircraft, equipment for the navy, radar and other communication equipment. An American advisory mission was set up in Pakistan to help Pakistani senior commanders in their endeavours to modernize the armed forces and improve their overall disposition and efficiency. The US-Pakistan cooperation during the 1950s and the early 1960s proved very useful for making up considerable deficiencies in the defense arrangements of Pakistan. It accelerated the modernization process and enabled the air force and the navy to improve its efficiency and acquire valuable experience by participation in CENTO's joint exercises. Though the overall balance of power in South Asia still remained in favour of India, these security pacts gave Pakistan the much needed confidence that it could now withstand India's military and diplomatic pressures. The American aid also strengthened the position of the military in the domestic political system as it had, in addition to having substantial domestic resources at its disposal, got external aid which made it the most modernized segment of society characterized by cohesion, hierarchy, discipline, and *esprit de corps*.[19] The US also benefited from this relationship. It obtained the support of the second largest non-communist Asian state. The US also enjoyed communication, intelligence gathering facilities, and related services in Pakistan. These were useful for America's global strategy against the Soviet Union.

Changes in the Defense Policy

The basic goal of Pakistan's defense policy, i.e., the provision of security against external threats, did not change but the strategies to achieve this goal were revised in the late 1960s and 1970s. Three major developments in this period made the defense planners review their defense strategies. These were the supply of arms to India after the 1962 Sino-Indian border conflict, the September 1965 Indo-Pakistan war, and the war on the Bangladesh question between India and Pakistan in November-December 1971.

India was provided with substantial military assistance by the US, the UK, Canada, and Australia in the aftermath of the Sino-Indian border conflict, 1962. The assistance programme included the supply of arms and ammunition, aircraft and communication equipment. Several Western military missions visited India in order to appraise India's long term defense requirements and provide necessary advice to refurbish its defense arrangements.[20] The Indian air force also held joint air exercises with the air forces of the US, the UK, and Australia. Throughout this period India was also obtaining weapons and aircraft from the Soviet Union. For some time it appeared as if the western countries and the Soviet Union were competing with each other for the supply of weapons to India, ostensibly to fight China.

There was a clear shift in India's domestic economic priorities. More resources were made available for defense by diverting these from economic development. This re-ordering of the priorities was clearly visible from the defense allocations in the national budget which registered a rapid increase during 1963–72 decade. India also embarked on a five year defense plan for the comprehensive modernization of the three services and defense production programme. This plan was revised and updated several times later or was financed partly from domestic resources and partly from the help and cooperation of the Western countries and the Soviet Union.[21]

India's military build-up in the 1960s accentuated Pakistan's security anxieties because it widened the already existing military disparity in South Asia to the detriment of Pakistan. The ruling elite of Pakistan seemed convinced that India would use its newly acquired military power against Pakistan. They claimed that India had no intention of fighting China but was simply using the China 'bogey' to amass sophisticated weapons from the West.[22]

Pakistan, upset over the extensive military assistance to India by the US and other western powers, gradually revised its defense and foreign policy to deal effectively with the growing military imbalance in South Asia. It started playing down its membership of the West-sponsored defense pacts and improved its ties with the countries of the socialist bloc. The defense planners started thinking in terms of diversifying the sources of supply of defense hardware and weapons. Before they could really do this, a war broke out between India and Pakistan in September 1965. The US imposed an arms embargo on India and Pakistan. This decision seriously undermined Pakistan's combat effectiveness because its defense procurement was primarily America-oriented. Pakistan's air force was equipped almost entirely with American aircrafts. One Pakistani writer commented that the American embargo had 'serious repercussions on Pakistan's defence capability and was one of the factors which contributed to its dismemberment in 1971'.[23] In March 1966, the embargo was partly eased by America's decision to allow the sale of non-lethal military equipment (i.e. trucks, medical and engineering supplies and communication items). One year later the embargo was further eased by the American decision to sell spare parts for military equipment supplied in the past. No new combat equipment was allowed to be sold to either country. Pakistan was provided with some arms and equipment during 1970–71 as a 'special one-time exception' extended by President Nixon. All supplies and provision of non-lethal equipment were suspended after the outbreak of the civil war in East Pakistan in 1971. It was not earlier than February 1975 that embargo on the sale of lethal arms was lifted and South Asian countries were allowed to purchase arms and equipment on 'cash and carry' basis.[24]

The American embargo of 1965 compelled Pakistan to procure arms and equipment, including aircraft, tanks, and submarines, radar and communication equipment, from several non-American sources.

China was the most important source of supply of weapons in the post-1965 war period. Pakistan also obtained weapons through Iran and Turkey. Later it secured weapons from the UK, West Germany, France, Italy, and the international arms markets in Europe. The Soviet Union also supplied military equipment including helicopters and tanks to Pakistan during 1968–70.[25]

A negative implication of the earlier supply of Western arms aid to Pakistan was that a low priority was assigned to indigenous production of arms and weapons. As Pakistan was getting arms and equipment of sufficient quality and quantity from the West in the late 1950s, the pace of development in the field of defence production was rather slow. In the late 1960s, more so in the 1970s, self-sufficiency in arms and ammunition became a popular theme with defense and economic planners. A defence production division was set up in the Ministry of Defence in 1973 to encourage the indigenous production of arms and ammunition. The Wah Ordnance Factory was expanded and modernized. Three new ordnance factories were set up around Wah. By the mid-seventies Pakistan became self-sufficient in several types of small arms. Technical and financial assistance was sought from China and the Soviet Union to set up a heavy mechanical complex and a steel mill respectively. A Mirage rebuild and overhaul factory was set up under permission from France. Similarly, a F-6 rebuild complex and a tank rebuild factory were set up with the cooperation of China. Plans were underway to produce tanks, aircraft, frigates, and other sophisticated equipment locally to make Pakistan as self-sufficient as possible. It will be several years before all these projects become fully operational.

Establishment of Bangladesh and Security of Pakistan

The establishment of Bangladesh, no doubt, relieved Pakistan of the security responsibilities of what was hitherto East Pakistan, but this did not bring about a significant change to the advantage of Pakistan (West Pakistan) in the overall strategic environs. In fact, the defense problems were aggravated in several respects. As Bangladesh was created with the support and cooperation of India, the troops India used to deploy on the East Pakistan borders during 1947–71 could now be moved to the Pakistan-India border when, and if, needed; thereby increasing military pressure on Pakistan. Even after the August and November 1975 coups in Bangladesh and the end of the Indo-Bangladesh 'honeymoon' period, India did not need to concentrate so many troops on that border as was the case when the eastern wing of Pakistan had not seceded. The Bangladesh military was too weak to pose any serious threat to India.

Pakistan's military debâcle in East Pakistan and the establishment of Bangladesh with India's active support confirmed India's military and political preponderance in South Asia. India wanted to give permanence to the power structure which emerged out of the 1971 war in South Asia. It, therefore, continued with its efforts to strengthen its military muscle by obtaining weapons of all kinds, including aircraft, tanks, warships, submarines, missiles, radar and communication equipment from the Soviet Union as well as Western countries. It also accelerated the pace of defense production in the country. By the early eighties India had one of the strongest defense and defense-oriented industrial bases in the third world. It was producing locally, *inter alia*, tanks, armoured cars, and aircraft of different types, frigates, electronic and communication equipment.

India's decision to explode a nuclear device in May 1974, described as Peaceful Nuclear Explosion (PNE) by the Indian government, had far-reaching implications for South Asia. India not only made a 'gate crash' entry into the 'nuclear club' but also injected new variables in the politics of regional security. It made the policy planners of other South Asian states, especially Pakistan, perceive of a scenario wherein India was brandishing its nuclear 'sword' to force the non-nuclear states of South Asia to abide by India's priorities in regional politics.

Pakistan responded to the political and security environment and the power structure in South Asia in the post-1971 period by adopting a two-pronged strategy. The first was meant to deal with the problems relating to the outcome of the 1971 war. These included the return of Pakistani POWs, recovery of the territory lost to India on the (West) Pakistan-India front, and the rehabilitation of war affected areas and people. A process to solve these problems was set in motion when the former Pakistani Prime Minister and Indian Prime Minister Indira Gandhi met at Simla in July 1972 and signed a peace document, popularly known as the Simla accord.[26] These efforts were accompanied by steps to deal with the long term defense and security issues. Pakistan was not aiming at parity with India; rather it wanted to muster enough military and diplomatic clout that would discourage India from using its military preponderance to restrict Pakistan's policy options. It was not, therefore, surprising that the pattern of high defense expenditure, the purchase of defense equipment from abroad, and efforts aiming at improvement of mobility and striking power of the military continued unabated. The numerical strength of the military was increased by fresh recruitment and special attention was given to their training at the time of induction into the service and during the subsequent years so that a very high level of efficiency could be maintained. Modern weapons were obtained from diverse sources on cash and against loans. Some funds for the purchase of military hardware were made available by a number of friendly Arab states.

So far as the additional defense worry, i.e., India's nuclear explosion, was concerned, Pakistan adopted a three-point strategy to counter what it described as India's nuclear 'threat'. First the programme for peaceful uses of nuclear technology was expanded. More funds were made available for this purpose in the backdrop of India's nuclear explosion. Pakistan, however, made it clear that it wanted to use nuclear technology for peaceful purposes and that it had no intentions of embarking on a nuclear weapons programme. Pakistan's plea of pursuing a peaceful nuclear programme is rejected by India and other nations are also sceptical about the Pakistani profession, because of reports about Pakistan's efforts to obtain reprocessing technology in bits and pieces from Europe and North America after France refused to supply the promised nuclear reprocessing plant. Secondly, Pakistan sought international guarantees through the UN for the non-nuclear weapons states against any possible nuclear 'threat' so that small states could live in peace and would not need to acquire directly or indirectly nuclear weapons for their security. Thirdly, Pakistan put forward a proposal at the UN General Assembly that South Asia should be declared a Nuclear Weapons Free Zone. Since 1974 this proposal had been endorsed by the General Assembly several times.[27]

Pakistan's diplomatic efforts, i.e., guarantees for the non-nuclear weapons states and the concept of a nuclear weapons free zone, stemmed from the belief that if the international community did not dissuade India from pursuing its so-called PNE programme and, if adequate safeguards were not provided to the non-nuclear states, these states might be tempted to follow India's example. The environment of uncertainty and insecurity could induce the small and weak states to divert their peaceful nuclear programmes to non-peaceful purposes.

The Afghanistan Crisis

The direct Soviet military intervention in Afghanistan in December 1979 was a highly disturbing development for Pakistan because it worsened its security and defense problems. Pakistan was uneasy ever since the April 1978 coup in Afghanistan which brought Nur Mohammad Tarahki to power. This government had strong Marxist orientations and it revived Afghanistan's irredentist claim on Pakistani territory. The Soviets had stormed Afghanistan with around eighty thousand troops, killed the incumbent President (Hafizullah Amin) and installed Babrak Karmal as President.[28] These developments added several new dimensions to Pakistan's defense and security environment.

First, no doubt, the Tarahki and Amin governments were Moscow-oriented and a reasonable number of Soviet military and civil advisers were attached with these two governments, but, never in the past, had Soviet troops marched south across the Soviet-Afghan border in such a large number. The continued Soviet presence in Afghanistan brought the Soviet Union practically to the Pak-Afghan border. Afghanistan now ceased to serve as a buffer between Pakistan and the Soviet Union.

Second, the Soviet participation in counter-insurgency measures against the Afghan insurgents (*Mujahideens*) proved counter-productive. Instead of containing the conflict it gave greater determination to the Afghan resistance groups to take up arms against the Soviet-installed Kabul regime. As these guerrilla groups had ethnic, linguistic, cultural and ideological linkages in Pakistan, especially in the tribal areas of Pakistan, their resistance activities evoked a positive popular response there. The government of Pakistan also made no secret of its sympathies for these resistance groups. This further strained the already chilled Pakistan-Soviet relations.

Third, the influx of 2.8 million Afghan refugees into Pakistan has caused serious economic, social, and political problems. International relief agencies and individual states extended assistance for meeting with the expenses of refugees. This assistance comes to about half of the total expenditure on refugee maintenance. Out of the daily expenditure of Rs 10 million, Pakistan is spending Rs 5 million from its domestic sources for extending humanitarian assistance to these refugees.[29] The economic cost of the maintenance of refugees will increase in the future because there are as yet very little prospects of an early settlement of the internal strife in Afghanistan—the major cause of their flight to Pakistan.[30]

Fourth, the Soviet and Afghan authorities suspect the bona-fides of the refugee camps and relief operations in Pakistan. They maintain that there is a deep connection between the insurgent activities in Afghanistan and refugee camps in Pakistan. They also accuse Pakistan of providing sanctuary, military training, and supply of weapons to the nationalist and Islam-oriented Afghan resistance groups. Pakistan's denial of these charges hardly convinces the Soviet authorities. They retaliated in the past by encouraging the Afghan troops and aircraft to intrude into Pakistan and attack refugees camps. There were sixty-two violations of Pakistani territory by Afghan soldiers and 415 instances of air space violations by the Soviet supplied aircraft of the Afghan air force since April 1978 after the first marxist coup. Nine persons, mostly refugees, were killed and several more were injured during these attacks.[31] If the present insurgency intensifies in the future the Soviet and Afghan authorities might be tempted to resort to border skirmishes with Pakistan and air-raids on refugee camps more often. This would widen the scope of the internal strife in Afghanistan and, thus, intensify military pressure on Pakistan.

A large number of people and the political elite in Pakistan regard the Soviet intervention in Afghanistan as a watershed. The South Asian region as a whole is now vulnerable to Soviet penetration.[32] It is seen as a part of the Soviet 'grand design' to reach the warm waters of the Indian Ocean and oil resources of the gulf region.[33] There are those who look at the Soviet presence in Afghanistan in the backdrop of the history of this region. They claim that in the past whichever power emerged from the Central Asian region and consolidated its hold over Kabul, did not stop there. They also came down to the Indian sub-continent and held sway over it, if the Soviet Union was not dissuaded from consolidating its position in Kabul, it is argued, history can repeat itself and, then, nobody in Iran and South Asia will be able to withstand the onward march of the Soviet Union.[34] At times the Soviet intervention in Afghanistan is interpreted as a threat by communism to Islam, and could pose a serious threat to the future of Islam in the international system.[35] There are only a small number of people who view the Soviet intervention as a defensive move; protection of Soviet security interests in Afghanistan and a response to the stepped-up presence of the US in the Indian Ocean and Persian Gulf area.

Leaving aside the merits and demerits of these explanations advanced in Pakistan—the grand design strategy, the prospects of repetition of history or an ideological war—when we examine the Soviet intervention in Afghanistan in the context of the history of Pak-Soviet relations, the Soviet role in the Bangladesh crisis, and the improved ties between the Soviet Union and India, what emerges with crystal clarity is that Pakistan's security dilemma has become extremely acute.

The Soviet intervention in Afghanistan was interpreted by the US as a clear threat to American interests in the Persian Gulf and the Indian Ocean. More so, because this came about within less than one year of the fall of the Shah in Iran, whose was the staunchest pro-American regime in the region. These two developments were seen as the major extra-regional and intra-regional threats respectively to the security and stability in the Persian Gulf.[36] The US not only put forward the Carter Doctrine (1980) but also decided to set up the Rapid Deployment Force to give 'teeth' to the Carter Doctrine and reassure the pro-American Gulf states that the US was capable of coming to their rescue at the time of crisis.[37] The US also decided to shore up defenses of the states exposed to potential Soviet penetration. As Pakistan share a long border with the Soviet-occupied Afghanistan, Pakistan acquired geopolitical relevance in America's global strategy.[38] The US also felt that Pakistan could be useful for its policy-goals in the Persian Gulf due to Pakistan's proximity and linkages with the region. Pakistan was, therefore, now considered a frontline state in the new geopolitical strategy and firm security assurances were made to Pakistan against any Soviet incursions into its territory.[39] The US agreed to provide a $3.2 billion package of economic assistance and military sale credits spread over a period of five years 1982-83 to 1987-88. Under this arrangement Pakistan would purchase tanks, armoured personnel carriers, missiles, helicopters, and other military equipment from the US. In addition to this Pakistan would get forty F-16 fighter-bomber aircraft. This reversed the pattern of US-Pakistan relations characterized by strains due to the serious differences on the nuclear question, the stoppage of all American economic assistance in spring 1979, and the burning down of the American embassy at Islamabad in November 1979.

The renewed cooperation between Pakistan and the US in the military field does not really solve Pakistan's defense problem.[40] The assistance package has been spread over five years with the renewal of Congress approval every year. One is not sure if this assistance programme will run smoothly through the next five years. Even if it proceeds without any serious snag, the military equipment secured by Pakistan under these arrangements will not cause a significant change in the existing balance of power in the region. Given the military sales by the Soviet Union to India over the last couple of years, procurement of sophisticated aircraft and other military equipment from other sources, and the expanding indigenous production of arms and equipment, India will continue to maintain a comfortable and safe margin over Pakistan. So far as the Soviet 'threat' to Pakistan is concerned, it will be naïve to think that the procurements of weapons from the US will enable Pakistan to withstand any direct Soviet military intervention in Pakistan.

Instead of a full-fledged invasion of Pakistan or stepping-up attacks on refugee camps or border skirmishes, the Soviet Union has another option available to pressurize Pakistan to reduce its support to the *Mujahideen* in Afghanistan. It can cultivate the dissident elements in Balochistan. If the Soviets decide to extend active political and military support to disgruntled elements in the province, Pakistan's security and integrity will come under heavy stress.

The Indian Ocean Question

It was not until the late sixties that the Indian Ocean acquired salience in Pakistan's defense policy. This was mainly due to the decision of the British government—a friendly government—to gradually reduce their presence east of the Suez, and the desire of the two superpowers and a few littoral states either to step into the British shoes or, at least, assume a dominant position in the region.

The US and the Soviet Union gradually increased their presence in the Indian Ocean in the sixties and the seventies and competed with each other to bring more and more states in their orbit of influence. The superpower conflict in the Indian Ocean and the Persian Gulf region became sharper than ever in the aftermath of the Iranian revolution (1979), the Soviet intervention in Afghanistan (1979), and the US decision to develop new security relations with some states of the region and to setup the Rapid Deployment Force.

In addition to this, a few relatively powerful states—the middle powers—especially India and Indonesia, showed a deep interest in the post-British withdrawal power structure in the Indian Ocean. They undertook a series of steps to expand and modernize their naval forces so as to assume the role of powers of regional significance.

Pakistan holds the view that the increased presence of the superpowers and their mutual rivalry will increase tension in the region. This will not only have adverse implications for the peace and tranquillity of the area but will also restrict the policy-options of the smaller littoral and hinterland states. Pakistan also maintains that any attempt by a regional power to establish its dominance in the Indian Ocean or a part of it, will be as dangerous as the superpower rivalry. This will promote mutual distrust and directly threaten the security of other smaller states which do not want, or cannot afford, to enter the power struggle in the Indian Ocean.[41]

Pakistan's concern over the assumption of a dominant role by a littoral state of the Indian Ocean stems from a strong belief that India is making a bid for becoming a regional influential in the Indian Ocean area. This belief, shared by some other states of the area and a number of military experts and scholars, is sustained by India's massive efforts to modernize and expand its navy in the post-British withdrawal period. By the mid-eighties India will have the strongest naval force amongst the littoral states falling in the category of the third world. Pakistan is perturbed by this development because it feels that India will use its naval superiority (along with its powerful army and the air force) to bring the smaller states of the region under its influence. This will breed tension and conflict in the area as all the small states will not necessarily accept India's *diktat* on regional and international problems.

A country like Pakistan which has a strong aversion to the idea of India's domination because of the factors discussed in the earlier sections of this article, is bound to express strong opposition to the efforts of any littoral state (especially India) to become a power of eminence in the Indian Ocean region.

Pakistan took several steps to enhance its defense and security in the Indian Ocean. It embarked on a modest programme of modernization of its navy. This part of the Pakistan armed forces was relatively neglected in the past. This policy was revised in the early 1970s and more resources were made available for the expansion and modernization of the navy, though the army and the air Force still obtained the larger share of funds allocated for defense. Pakistan used diplomacy at the international level and mobilized international support for the provision of security for the weaker and smaller states *vis-à-vis* the superpowers and the middle level powers or the regional powers. It joined hands with other small states in their efforts to designate the Indian Ocean a Zone of Peace and a Nuclear Weapon Free Zone.[42]

While supporting the peace zone concept for the Indian Ocean, Pakistan did not limit its criticism to the superpower presence in the region. It also underlined the dangers posed to the small states by the efforts of some littoral states to make the Indian Ocean an area of their exclusive influence. Pakistan proposed on several occasions that, in addition to the exclusion of the superpowers from the Indian Ocean, there should be some equilibrium of naval forces of the littoral and hinterland states. These states should respect each other's sovereignty and territorial integrity, and settle their disputes through amicable means.[43] Pakistan has adopted the position that until the possibilities of some powerful regional state acquiring a hegemonial or near hegemonial position are not excluded and, unless there develops mutual trust and confidence amongst the littoral and hinterland states, the mere exclusion of the superpowers will not make the Indian Ocean a zone of peace.

Defense and Security in the Eighties

Pakistan's defense policy can be described as the search for security by a 'small' and 'weak' state in a world characterized by the unequal distribution of material resources, technology, power, and influence. No doubt, Pakistan's survival is not at stake the way it was in the first couple of years after independence but the overall security environment has not improved very significantly during the last 35–36 years.

Pakistan's major concern in the eighties will continue to be India. After establishing its military primacy in South Asia in 1971, India continued to work towards enhancing its military power in all its dimensions. This has increased military disparity between India and Pakistan reinforcing Pakistan's fears of India. It has been predicted that this military imbalance is going to increase in the future and Pakistan will be facing an extremely powerful India by the end of this decade. Pakistan will, therefore, constantly search for political and military ways and means to allay its sense of insecurity *vis-à-vis* India.

The Soviet military intervention in Afghanistan, the intense civil strife that followed the intervention, and its ramifications on regional and international politics will be another set of problems needing serious attention in this decade. Whatever happens in Afghanistan—whether the Soviets withdraw completely, reduce their presence, or Soviet military presence continues on its present scale with continuing civil strife—all these possibilities will have bearings on Pakistan's defense and security. Despite the strained relations between the Soviet Union and Pakistan mainly due to the Afghanistan crisis, there is no evidence to suggest that the Soviet Union will either play the 'Balochistan card' or invade Pakistan in the near future. But, if the civil strife intensifies in Afghanistan, border skirmishes between Pakistan and Afghanistan or raids by the Soviet-supplied Afghan gunships (helicopters) on Pakistani territory become more frequent and intense, it will complicate Pakistan's security situation. Pakistan will, then, have to revise its defense strategy. Instead of the Indo-Pakistan border, the Durand Line might, in such a situation, become the most serious security concern. A graver security problem can arise if India, on its own or on the advice of the Soviet Union, starts applying military pressures on Pakistan and/or clashes on the Durand Line coincide with tension on the Indo-Pakistan border.

Pakistan will continue to assign the top priority to its defense requirements. The present trend of high budgetary allocations for defense will continue in the eighties and, perhaps the nineties. Pakistan will endeavour to maintain a credible defense posture so as to increase the cost of an invasion on Pakistan or border skirmishes to a high level for the adversary. The emphasis will be on the quality of manpower, military technology, greater mobility, and strike power so that it quickly responds to any security threat either on the Indo-Pakistan border or on the Durand Line. This will also require more attention to the improvement of means of communication and transportation to enable Pakistan to quickly shift and switch its troops from the Indo-Pakistan border to the Pakistan-Afghanistan border and vice versa in case such a need arises. At the moment the main communication link is on the east of the Indus river. In addition to the improvement of this route and other roads and railways, the proposal approved and partly implemented by the government, to establish a new south-north road link west of the Indus river, needs to be reactivated so that there is a relatively safe alternate route to the present road link from Karachi to the northern areas.

Pakistan will have to give more attention to the expansion and modernization of the navy in the future. The growing naval activity in the Indian Ocean region by the extra-regional as well as regional powers underlines the importance of strengthening naval forces in order to protect Pakistan's maritime interests, including coastal defense. Besides improving the naval defense arrangements at Karachi and Port Qasim, Gwader can be developed into a naval base. This can play a useful role in the naval defense of the country as well as play a role in enhancing the security of the Gulf region. A massive allocation of funds will be required to turn Gwader into a functional port/naval base and establish road and air links with Quetta and Karachi.

Pakistan has asserted time and again that its nuclear programme is peaceful but if Pakistan's security situation worsened from what it is at present, and Pakistan faces serious difficulties in obtaining weapons and military equipment from external sources, or if Pakistan begins to feel that the international community is incapable of providing it with security guarantees, it may be constrained to exercise the 'nuclear option'.

Pakistan's experience suggests that the acquisition of weapons from one major external source can give leverage to the supplier-state over the recipient which it may use for its political convenience. Pakistan's defense capability was seriously undermined when, during the Indo-Pakistan wars of 1965 and 1971, one major source of arms supply imposed an arms embargo. Therefore, the policy of diversification of sources of supply, undertaken since the first embargo in 1965, could be pursued more effectively in the eighties.

More important than the diversification of sources of procurement of weapons is their indigenous production. Efforts should also be made to set up more defense oriented industries in Pakistan with necessary technological and financial cooperation from international sources. Once strong defense oriented industrial enterprises are established, these will contribute to Pakistan's industrial development as well as reduce, if not eliminate, Pakistan's over-reliance on external sources of arms procurement.

A small country like Pakistan will also have to continuously employ skilful and patient diplomacy at the bilateral, multilateral, and international levels to offset its military inferiority *vis-à-vis* its powerful adversaries. The existing international and regional organizations, i.e., the UN, the OIC, NAM, need to be strengthened and their forums persistently used to ensure defense and security. A skilful use of diplomacy can also reduce tension and facilitate amicable settlement of contentious problems. It is in this context that the improved economic ties between India and Pakistan in the early eighties, travel facilities to each other's citizens, and the efforts during 1982–83 to evolve a framework for a no-war pact appear meaningful. Given the long history of conflict and distrust and a wide discrepancy in their outlook on regional and international issues, it may be too optimistic to suggest that the 1980s will see the transformation of the Indo-Pakistan subcontinent into an arena of perpetual peace and tranquillity. The improved ties between these two countries can, however, generate goodwill and identify areas of cooperation. This will ease tension and contribute to reducing some security pressures on Pakistan.

Efforts continue to find a negotiated settlement of the Afghanistan crisis. The first round of indirect talks between Afghanistan and Pakistan were held in June 1982 in Geneva under the auspices of the UN Secretary-General's representative. The thread of these talks was picked up during Pakistan's Foreign Secretary's visit to Moscow in September 1982 and, then, during the regular session of the General Assembly in the fall of 1982. The major goal of these diplomatic efforts is to identify common grounds for negotiating a settlement of the internal war in Afghanistan and the return of Afghan refugees to their homes. Only a negotiated settlement can ensure Pakistan's security on the Durand Line and protect the Soviet Union's legitimate security interests on its southern flank. Any intensification of the internal strife in Afghanistan will not only compound Pakistan's already complex security problems but will also result in a heavy diplomatic, military, and financial cost for the Soviet Union, including a threat of the stepped up involvement of the other superpower in the civil strife in Afghanistan.

TABLE 1
Defense Expenditure of Pakistan : 1947–48 to 1982–83

In million Rs.

Year	Defense Expenditure	Total Expenditure met from Revenue	Defense Expenditure Percentage of Total Expenditure
1947-48	153.8	236.0	65.16
1948-49	461.5	647.0	71.32
1949-50	625.4	856.0	73.06
1950-51	649.9	1,266.2	51.32

1951-52	779.1	1,442.3	54.01
1952-53	783.4	1,320.1	59.34
1953-54	653.2	1,108.7	58.91
1954-55	635.1	1,172.6	54.16
1955-56	917.7	1,433.4	64.02
1956-57	800.9	1,330.7	60.18
1957-58	854.2	1,521.8	56.13
1958-59	996.6	1,956.5	50.93
1959-60	1,043.5	1,846.5	56.51
1960-61	1,112.4	1,894.2	58.72
1961-62	1,108.6	1,986.8	55.79
1962-63	954.3	1,795.3	53.15
1963-64	1,156.5	2,337.2	49.48
1964-65	1,262.3	2,736.2	46.13
1965-66	2,855.0	4,498.1	63.47
1966-67	2,293.5	3,765.5	60.09
1967-68	2,186.5	4,077.1	53.62
1968-69	2,426.8	4,371.0	55.52
1969-70	2,749.1	5,109.4	53.80
1970-71	3,201.5	5,751.3	55.66
1971-72	3,725.5	6,303.8	59.09
1972-73	4,439.6	7,480.7	59.34
1973-74	4,948.6	11,724.6	42.02
1974-75	6,914.2	16,139.6	42.83
1975-76	8,103.4	17,613.5	46.00
1976-77	8,120.6	18,161.5	44.71
1977-78	9,674.5	22,781.9	42.46
1978-79	10,167.6	29,851.8	34.06
1979-80	12,654.8	34,845.1	36.31
1980-81 Revised	15,283.9	39,592.5	38.06
1981-82 Revised	19,592.9	38.090.0	51.43
1982-83 Budget	22,095.3	49,910.0	47.01

Average Annual Percentage of Defense Expenditure: 53.48

Source: Compiled from *Pakistan Econmic Survey,* an annual publication of Government of Pakistan, Ministry of Finance, Islamabad.

NOTES

1. R.N. Rosecrance, 'Bipolarity, Multipolarity and the Future', in J.N. Rosenau, (ed.), *International Politics and Foreign Policy*, revised edition, Free Press, New York, 1969, pp. 325–35.
2. Bull Hedley, 'The Third World and International Society', *The Year Book of World Affairs, 1979*, The London Institute of World Affairs, London, 1979, pp. 15–31.
3. For a study of the role of the Third World States in the UN, see J. Rosen, 'How the Third World Runs the UN', *Times*, New York, 16 December 1979.
4. W.R. Thompson, 'The Regional Subsystem', *International Studies Quarterly*, Maldine, March 1973, pp. 89–117.
5. M. Singer, *Weak States in a World of Powers: The Dynamics of International Relationship*, New York, The Free Press, 1972.
6. S.P. Cohen, 'Toward A Great State in Asia', in O. Marwah, and J.D. Polack, (eds.) *Military Power and Policy in Asian States: China, India, Japan,* Boulder, Westview, 1980, pp. 9–41.
7. A.T. Mugomba, 'Small Developing States and the External Operational Environments', *The Year Book of World Affairs, 1979*, The Institute of World Affairs, London, 1979, pp. 201–216.
8. Bhabani Sen Gupta, *The Fulcrum of Asia*, Peagasus, New York, 1970.
9. It may be pointed out that before the establishment of Bangladesh in 1971, East Pakistan also shared a border with India. East Pakistan was surrounded by India from three sides which caused additional defense problems. We are not discussing the security problem arising out of the geographic location of East Pakistan during 1947–71.
10. For an extended study of these disputes, see, G.W. Choudhury, *Pakistan's Relations with India 1947-66*, Pall Mall, London, 1978; Chaudhri Mohammad Ali, *The Emergence of Pakistan*, Columbia University Press, New York, 1967.
11. Mujtaba Razvi, *The Frontiers of Pakistan*, National Publishing House, Karachi, 1971, pp. 145–63; S. Tahir-Kheli, 'Pakhtoonistan and its International Implications', *World Affairs*, Winter, 1974-75, pp. 233–45.
12. S.M. Burke, *Pakistan's Foreign Policy, An Historical Analysis*, Oxford University Press, Karachi, 1973, pp. 206–207.
13. Ibid., p. 75.
14. Fazal Muqeem Khan, *The Story of the Pakistan Army*, Oxford University Press, Karachi, 1963, p. 34; Hasan-Askari Rizvi, *The Military and Politics in Pakistan*, Progressive Publishers, Lahore, 1976 (rev. edn.), pp. 36–7.
15. Ibid., pp. 38–40.
16. Economic consideration also compelled Pakistan to enter into defense arrangements with the US. Pakistan was facing economic crisis, especially

grain shortage, during these years. The American willingness to make grain available to Pakistan created goodwill which facilitated Pakistan's entry into the defense pacts.

17. Burke, op. cit., pp. 164–70.
18. W.H. Wriggins, 'The Balancing Process in Pakistan's Foreign Policy', in L. Ziring, R. Braibanti, and W.H. Wriggins, (eds.), *Pakistan: The Long View*, Centre for Commonwealth and Comparative Studies, Duke University, Durham, NC, 1977, p. 312.
19. For an analysis of the US-Pakistan alliance system, see N. Houghton Mifflin, Boston, D. Palmer, *South Asia and United States Policy*, 1966. W.J. Barnds, *India, Pakistan and the Great Powers*, Praeger, New York, 1972.
20. For a summary of Western military assistance to India in the post-Sino-Indian border conflict, see Hasan-Askari Rizvi, *South Asia and Indian Military Build-up*, Progressive Series No. 14, Progressive Publishers, Lahore, 1973, pp. 9–10, 15–16.
21. Ibid., pp. 11–12.
22. Mohammad Ayub Khan, *Friends Not Masters*, Oxford University Press, Karachi, 1967, pp. 135, 136, 143. See also Ayub Khan's interview, *The Sunday Times* (London), 20 October 1963. Ayub Khan's press conference, *Dawn*, Karachi, 23 February 1964.
23. Khurshid Hyder, 'Pakistan's Foreign Policy in the Early Seventies', in Masuma Hasan, (ed.), *Pakistan in a Changing World*, Pakistan Institute of International Affairs, Karachi, 1978, p. 106.
24. For details, see, S.P. Cohen, 'U.S. Weapons and South Asia: A Policy Analysis', *Pacific Affairs*, Spring, Vancouver, 1976, pp. 49–69.
25. A valuable source of information on arms supplies to Pakistan is *The Arms Trade Register*, published by Stockholm International Peace Research Institute (SIPRI). See also another publication by the same Institute, *World Armaments and Disarmament*, *Sipri Yearbook*.
26. For a detailed study of the Simla Accord, see the special issue of *Pakistan Horizon*, Vol. XXV, No. 3, Third Quarter, 1972.
27. There has been a proliferation of literature on the nuclear question in the South Asian context since the Indian detonation of a nuclear device in May 1974. For more information on the issues raised in this study, Zalmay Khalizad, 'Pakistan: The Making of a Nuclear Power', *Asian Survey*, Berkeley, June 1976, pp. 580–92. Akhtar Ali, 'Indian Nuclear Alibi', *Pakistan and Gulf Economist*, Karachi, 10–16 April 1982, pp. 8–17. Safdar Akhund and M. Ahmed, 'Nuclearization: The Politico-military and Economic Case for Pakistan', *Pakistan Economist*, Karachi, 24 November 1979, pp. 14–25. Hasan-Askari Rizvi, *Politics of the Bomb in South Asia*, Progressive Series No. 23, Progressive Publishers, Lahore, 1975.
28. For internal developments in Afghanistan, see L. Dupree, 'Afghanistan Under the Khalq', *Problems of Communism*, July–August 1979,

pp. 34–50. Kuldip Nayar, *Report on Afghanistan*, New Delhi, Allied, 1981. K.P. Misra, (ed.), *Afghanistan Crisis*, Vikas, New Delhi, 1981.

29. Statement of Chief Commissioner for Afghan Refugees, *The Muslim* (Islamabad), 16 May 1982.

30. For a detailed study of the Afghan refugee problem in Pakistan, see Hasan-Askari Rizvi, 'The Afghan Refugees', *The Muslim*, 19 March 1982. 'Search For a Solution', *Pakistan and Gulf Economist*, Karachi, 3–9 April 1982, pp. 10–24.

31. Daily *Jang* (Lahore), 11 December 1981. Daily *Nawa-i-Waqt* (Lahore), 13 September 1981. *Dawn*, 11 February 1982.

32. A.R. Siddiqi, 'Afghanistan: A Geopolitical Wastershed', *Defence Journal*, Karachi, June-July 1982, pp. 1–8. M.B. Naqvi, 'Pakistan's Dilemma over Afghanistan', ibid., pp, 23–7.

33. K.M. Azhar Khan, 'Threats and Dangers Faced by Pakistan.' *MAG Weekly*, Karachi, 7-13 May 1981, pp. 4–5. Sultan Muhammad Khan, 'Pakistan Geopolitics: The Diplomatic Perspective', *International Security*, Cambridge, Summer, 1980, pp. 26–36.

34. See for example, Fateh Naseeb Chaudhury, 'Islamabad our Delhi Ka Mahafaz: Kabul'. (Urdu), *Qumi Digest*, (Lahore), October 1981, pp. 130–40. See also Lt.-General Fazle Haq's (Governor NWFP) interview, ibid., p. 30.

35. Lt.-General Fazle Haq (Governor NWFP)'s statements, *Dawn*, 26 September 1981. See the letter of Maulana Tufail Mohammad, Leader of the Jamaat-i-Islami of Pakistan published in *Afghan Majahid*, Vol. I, No. 4, October 1980. (A publication of a Pakistan based Afghan resistance group in the Urdu language. This ceased publication after some time.)

36. Many in the West regard the ideology of the Iranian Revolution as a greater immediate threat to the Persian Gulf than the direct Soviet military intervention in the region. To them the security of the Persian Gulf also means the preservation of the conservative and pro-American regimes *vis-à-vis* Iran's anti-West and radical Islamic ideology.

37. The Pentagon's Guidance Document says, 'Our principal objectives are to assure continued access to Persian Gulf oil and to prevent the Soviets from acquiring political-military control of the oil directly or through proxies'. The reliable sources assert that the RDF will also strengthen the friendly nations 'politically and militarily'. This will include 'security assistance, such as the sales of weapons and equipment, response to requests for training and advice, and a military construction'. *The New York Times*, 25 October 1982.

38. In an interview with a Pakistani weekly, the U.S. ambassador to Pakistan, Ronald I. Spiers, said, '...Our major interest and pre-occupation is to prevent an extension of Soviet power ... The Soviet move in Afghanistan has changed the strategic environment in this part of the world. Pakistan

is now a frontline state, under direct threat from the Soviet Union'. *MAG Weekly*, Karachi, 18–24 February 1982, p. 4.

39. See President Carter's address to the nation *The New York Times*, 5 January 1980.

40. See, for example, Pervaiz Iqbal Cheema, 'Pakistan's Security Dilemma - 111'. *The Muslim*, 24 May, 1982.

41. For a detailed discussion, see Hasan-Askari Rizvi, 'Pakistan and the Indian Ocean', *Strategic Studies*, Islamabad, Summer 1981, pp. 30–42.

42. For an extended analysis of the concept of Peace Zone, see S. Chawla and D.R. Sardesai, (eds.), *Changing Patterns of Security and Stability in Asia*, Praeger, New York, 1980, pp. 179–91.

43. Hasan-Askari Rizvi, 'Superpowers, India, Pakistan and the Indian Ocean', *Defence Journal*, Karachi, September 1981, pp. 7–16.

15

Pakistan-United States Relations: An Appraisal*

M. *Raziullah Azmi*

Pakistan's relations with the United States have had a chequered history. National interests and socio-economic and political differences occasionally exacerbated by diplomatic ineptitude, as well as the problems inherent in relations between a superpower and a developing country, have all combined to make it so, while geo-political realities and strategic compulsions on both sides have tended to bring the two countries closer. An attempt will be made in these pages to appraise Pakistan-US relations in their historical perspective.

Generally speaking, the subcontinent has evoked only 'peripheral interest'[1] from the US. It was not until the Second World War that the US evinced any interest at all in the affairs of this region which economically has not held much promise for its policy-makers. And unlike the USSR and China, the US does not share common borders with any of the regional states and has no territorial interests here. As Leo Rose has pointed out, 'for the most part; the American leadership has viewed South Asia with a sense of equanimity, even when developments have conflicted with US objectives in surrounding areas'.[2] Consequently, South Asia has figured in US foreign policy only in the context of its relations with the other superpower—the Soviet Union.

---

* Vol. xxxvi, No. 3, 1983.

I

Within a few years of achieving independence, Pakistan gradually moved to the American camp for a number of reasons, the most important being its pressing need for support in consolidating its security and in economic rehabilitation and development. However, many in the US viewed Pakistan as a country without a basis in logic. Adlai Stevenson referred to it as a 'tragic outcome of the senseless conflict between blood brothers', while Chester Bowles, one-time US ambassador to India, referred to it as an unfortunate product of religious fanaticism.[3]

The Pakistan-US alliance in the fifties was the result of US policy directed towards the containment of international communism, although it was very clear from the outset that Pakistan did not subscribe to the American assessment of the threat from the north. India's non-aligned stance further enhanced Pakistan's importance for the US strategists. 'Pakistan was the point at which the alliance systems geographically converged and thus was a linch-pin in their continuity.'[4] And while the US gained base facilities in Pakistan for reconnaissance flights over the Soviet Union and China—'significant privileges in the era before spy satellites'[5]—Pakistan, for its part, sought to enhance its own security vis-à-vis India through membership of SEATO (1954), Baghdad pact (1955), which was later renamed CENTO and the bilateral agreement with the US in 1959. Pakistan made an unsuccessful attempt to include a clause covering 'all types of aggression' in SEATO's defence perimeter. In the view of an American scholar, for the United States, the alliances served 'the primary purpose of expanding the scope of the policy of containment, for Pakistan it serves primarily the purpose of increasing the political, military and economic potentials vis-à-vis her neighbours'.[6] Because of this divergence in mutual perceptions, during the Korean war, Prime Minister Liaquat Ali Khan reportedly declined to accept the US offer to equip an entire division of the Pakistan army in return for the dispatch of a token Pakistan force to Korea to fight against the communists.[7] Nevertheless, by joining the two alliances, namely, SEATO and CENTO, Pakistan irretrievably identified itself with their aims which 'from the outset...were those of the donor (US), rather than in the interest of the recipient'.[8]

On 5 March 1959 the United States and Pakistan signed a bilateral agreement according to which 'the USA...will take such appropriate action, including the use of armed force, as may be mutually agreed upon...in order to assist the Government of Pakistan at its request' and it reaffirmed its support for the 'national independence and integrity' of Pakistan.[9] However, as if to underline the divergence in the perception of the two signatories, the very next day the US ambassador to India called on the Foreign Office to give assurances that '...the defensive agreement signed yesterday was limited to communist aggression...'. On 13 March, Prime Minister Jawaharlal Nehru revealed in the Indian Parliament that he 'had been specifically assured that this agreement cannot be used against India'.[10] This was not viewed with favour in Pakistan because it had made no secret of the fact that from Pakistan's point of view the threat to its security and integrity emanated from its eastern border. Popular sentiment in Pakistan was correctly projected in a remark of the then Prime Minister, Mr Feroze Khan Noon, made before the National Assembly on 8 August 1958 that if Pakistanis were 'to choose between Hindu domination and Communism, it is Communism they would choose'.[11] It is thus evident that the two countries were at cross-purposes from the moment they entered the alliances. The border clashes between Pakistan and Afghanistan in September 1961, during which Pakistan used some of the American-supplied military equipment, also revealed the tenuous nature of their alliance. President Ayub Khan reportedly 'resented' US enquiries about the use of American weapons and reaffirmed that Pakistan would without hesitation use these arms in the event of any threat to itself.[12]

The Pak-US alliance suffered a tremendous setback when the US decided to provide India with military aid in the aftermath of the Sino-Indian war in 1962, of which Pakistan took very serious exception. Even apart from the impetus which the Sino-Indian conflict provided for the development of Indo-American collaboration, the US had always taken particular care to foster and promote strong economic and cultural ties with India. Between 1949 and 1964, India received from the US nearly ten times greater economic assistance than did Pakistan.[13] In the fifties, the US leaders had proclaimed India as a model for developing countries in opposition to China, but President John F. Kennedy caused greater annoyance in Pakistan by urging Prime Minister Nehru 'to extend his leadership' in the region.[14]

For all practical purposes, the alliance was now a dead letter, notwithstanding President Ayub Khan's apt statement describing Pakistan as the United States' 'most allied ally' in Asia. The crunch, however, came during the Indo-Pakistan war in 1965. The US attitude of treating an ally and a non-aligned country on the same footing by suspending arms supplies to both—a step which hurt Pakistan much more than India—put an end to any illusions that might have been nurtured in Pakistan with regard to its 'special relationship' with the US. As pointed out by a Pakistani writer 'the special relationship which had begun to wane rather early, had now lost all its flavour'.[15]

Symptomatic of the waning United States interest in the region was its total acquiescence to Soviet mediation between Pakistan and India at Tashkent. Its interest in Pakistan had shrunk to such an extent that this country did not even figure in the comprehensive Senate hearings in 1969–70 on American security commitments overseas.[16]

In 1971, Pakistan was to suffer even greater disappointment. Its eastern province was invaded by India and the country dismembered with overt Soviet support while the US remained, for all practical purposes, a silent spectator, with or without the much publicized tilt of the Nixon administration towards Pakistan. In 1971, the Pakistan government tried to invoke the 1959 bilateral security agreement with the US but, according to Dr Henry Kissinger, the then National Security Adviser to President Richard Nixon, the 'State Department found it hard to follow the White House strategy (which favoured some action in support of Pakistan) or to break with three decades of sentimental attachment to India'.[17] There was some controversy regarding whether the 1959 bilateral agreement committed the United States to defend Pakistan against a non-communist aggressor. Dr Kissinger suggests that it did, while the State Department thought otherwise. But, as Kissinger points out, 'the image of a great nation conducting itself like a shyster looking for legalistic loopholes was not likely to inspire the allies...The fact was that over the decades of our relationship with Pakistan, there had grown up a complex body of communications by the Kennedy and Johnson administrations, going beyond the 1959 pact, some verbal, some in writing whose plain import was that the US would come to Pakistan's assistance if she was attacked by India'.[18]

US policy towards South Asia has gradually shifted from a balance of power model in the fifties and sixties to a position of 'greater recognition of India's pre-dominance' since 1971.[19] During the seventies the US seemed more eager to appease an increasingly recalcitrant India than to meet Pakistan's security needs. It would appear that the 'India factor' as a constraint in US relations with

Pakistan rose in proportion to India's increasing fraternization with the other superpower, the Soviet Union. Pakistan's frantic appeals for security guarantees in the aftermath of the Indian nuclear explosion in 1974 failed to evoke any meaningful response from the United States and even the promised supply of A-7 fighter planes in 1976 was linked to Pakistan's renunciation of the nuclear option. The 1976 Democratic Party platform went so far as to state that 'India has now achieved a considerable hegemony over the subcontinent...(and) future American Policy should accept this fact'.[20]

In 1976, the Ford administration put immense pressure on Pakistan to renounce the reprocessing plant it had contracted to purchase from France with the approval of the International Atomic Energy Agency (IAEA). Failing in that, the US persuaded Canada to terminate all assistance to Pakistan in the nuclear field in contravention of bilateral and trilateral commitments.[21] Pursuing the same line even more vigorously, the Carter administration brought to bear its whole diplomatic weight on France forcing it to renege from its commitment to sell to Pakistan a duly safeguarded reprocessing plant.[22]

According to Lawrence Ziring, the Carter administration had 'concluded that India's hegemony in South Asia is unquestioned and must be adapted to rather than challenged'.[23] By conspicuously avoiding to pass even a few hours in Pakistan while making an official visit to India in January 1978, President Carter may perhaps have made his own contribution to the consolidation of India's hegemonistic ambitions.

The Carter administration confirmed Pakistan's worst fears when in April 1979, it added insult to injury by suspending all development aid to Pakistan on the unsubstantiated allegation that this country was manufacturing a nuclear device. It is a pathetic reflection on US treatment of Pakistan that the same administration 'gave in when the Indian Prime Minister remained pretty adamant'[24] on the nuclear issue and, later, the Reagan administration persuaded France to provide India with nuclear fuel to circumvent US laws which prohibited this.

Thus, in about three decades Pakistan-US relations had gradually reached a stage where the one-time most allied ally had been transformed into a veritable pariah. And, generally speaking, the strategic and military importance of South Asia (including Pakistan), had seriously declined.

II

The Soviet armed intervention in Afghanistan in December 1979, coupled with the revolution in Iran and India's pro-Soviet stance, once again turned Pakistan into a 'strategic' state for the United States. Prompted therefore not so much by the threat to Pakistan's security as by its 'potential role as an important element in the defence of the Persian Gulf region', the Carter administration in February 1980 offered $400 million to Pakistan, equally divided between security and economic assistance. In March 1980, Secretary of State Cyrus Vance reaffirmed the US commitment to the 1959 agreement on cooperation with Pakistan. While Pakistan was anything but eager to resuscitate a treaty relationship with the US, the offer of $400 million was promptly rejected by President Ziaul Haq as 'peanuts' because it would entangle this country in superpower rivalry without bolstering its security to any appreciable degree.

Pakistan's rejection was viewed as 'a startling development which is an ominous indication of the degree to which Washington's perceived reliability, effectiveness and steadfastness have been put in doubt by the chaotic drift in American foreign policy'.[25] In the post-1979 perspective, Pakistan, since the defection of Iran was the most qualified country in the new American strategy to prevent a further southward Soviet thrust threatening Western access to Gulf oil (Carter Doctrine). Hence, rejection of the US offer was interpreted as one of the most ignominious blunders in post-war American diplomatic history.[26] Pakistan's rejection of the offer precisely when it needed it the most was the result of very rational thinking, given the chequered history of Pakistan-US relations, the US propensity to appease India and the general record of US failures to fulfil its commitments. It was felt, with some justification, that the Carter offer met short-term American objectives rather than promoting Pakistan's long-term security interests.

The Reagan Administration exhibited a better appreciation of Pakistan's needs and sensibilities. On 12 November 1981, Under-Secretary of State James Buckley called Pakistan 'an essential anchor of the entire Southwest Asia region'. Secretary of State Alexander Haig called for the creation of a 'strategic consensus' from Turkey to Pakistan, the latter being dubbed as a 'front-line state'. However, in view of America's credibility gap and Pakistan's credibility as a non-aligned country, a more practical bilateral agreement based on a proper appreciation of its economic, political and security needs, was in Pakistan's interest.

Admiral Robert Long, the Commander of US Pacific fleet who visited Pakistan, said in a Congressional testimony that 'Pakistan's strategic location requires us to strengthen our security relationship'. On 24 March 1981, Jane Coon, Deputy Assistant Secretary of State for South Asia, testified before the Senate Foreign Relations Committee: 'The invasion of Afghanistan, the turmoil in Iran and the increasing Soviet presence in the Indian Ocean have had profound implications for our relations with the countries of South Asia. These developments have greatly enhanced the importance we attach to the area. We consider it the eastern flank of a region in which vital interests of the US are at stake.'[27] Richard Burt, Director of the State Department's Bureau of Politico-Military Affairs, during Congressional testimony on 23 March said that arms transfers would promote America's national security interests. 'We are seeking to forge a policy that will ensure that arms transfers contribute directly to US security interests.'[28]

In an interview with *Newsweek*, President Ziaul Haq categorically stated that 'we are not resurrecting the past military aid relationship'.[29] As a result of negotiations held from April to June 1981, a $3.2 billion five-year aid package, divided almost equally between economic and security assistance to Pakistan, was announced on 15 June 1981. The package included the sale of forty F-16 aircraft, which the US government was not too keen to provide owing to stiff opposition from the Indian and Jewish lobbies. The Reagan Administration made it clear 'totally' and 'without a doubt' that a nuclear explosion by Pakistan would result in an immediate termination of the aid package.[30]

As the deal was awaiting Congressional approval, it was reported that the Indian and Jewish lobbies were closely collaborating to prevent its going through.[31] However, after the administration put its weight behind it, with Secretary of State Alexander Haig calling it 'vitally important to the national interest of the United States', the Senate on 20 October approved a six-year waiver for Pakistan of the law which had blocked US assistance since 1979. An amendment was, however, passed which envisaged a cut-off of US aid to any recipient (not a member of the nuclear club) which exploded a nuclear device, although it was obvious, as Senator McClure pointed out, that this provision would, in practice, never apply to Israel.[32]

Meanwhile, public opinion in Pakistan was apprehensive of 'the levels of commitment sought and commitment given'. (*Muslim*, 11 December 1981). A US Congressional study mission which visited both India and Pakistan in October 1981, reported that 'there is no evidence to substantiate an Indian perception that the US arms package is actually a first step towards American military bases in Pakistan'. Its report to the Congress also stated that 'India's reaction to the proposed US package is driven by its determination to maintain its position as the dominant power in the region'.[33]

President Zia quashed all rumours and fears by categorically stating, on 3 April 1982, that while signing the aid package Pakistan had made it clear that she would not provide any bases as a *quid-pro-quo*. *Dawn* in its editorial on 5 April 1983 welcomed the announcement as 'both timely and unequivocal' for it was considered of 'supreme importance that the country firmly adheres to its non-aligned policy...and jealously guards its independence in foreign policy'.

III

It is perhaps indicative of the fragility of Pakistan-US relations as well as of the constraints of the US executive that, twice within a few months, Pakistan faced the threat of a reduction in aid. In May 1982, it was reported that the package was 'in serious jeopardy' owing to 'two blows' dealt by the Jewish lobby. Firstly, Senator Cranston proposed that the $125 million increase in the economic aid to Israel be made up by deducting at least $75 million from the $175 million economic support fund earmarked for Pakistan for the fiscal year 1983. Secondly, Senator John Glenn circulated an amendment suggesting that the previous year's waiver on aid to Pakistan be rescinded if Islamabad 'engages in the reprocessing of spent nuclear fuel'. This was a departure from his earlier stand that the embargo be reimposed only if Pakistan actually 'exploded a nuclear device'.[34] The threat, however, receded as a result of 'a coincidence and compromise': Israel got the extra money at El Salvador's expense. However, again in October, a cut in the US assistance to Pakistan for the fiscal year 1983 was feared because of Congress failure to approve the 1983 budget and its passing of a 'continuing resolution' which would have meant that in 1983 Pakistan would receive the same amount as it did in 1982 which was $150.6 million in contrast to $525.8 million promised for

1983.[35] Fortunately, the Reagan Administration initiated emergency measures to stave off this eventuality.[36]

A month later, it was reported that the aid package to Pakistan could be adversely affected as a result of changes in the composition of the House Foreign Affairs Committee in favour of Democrats.[37] President Zia complained, in an interview with UPI, of discriminatory US policy towards Pakistan on the nuclear issue and declared that his country will 'resist' the 'pressure'.[38] President Zia's decision to resist American pressure for the acceptance of safeguards not applicable to other countries with a nuclear potential was lauded as 'a principle stand on which no compromise can be made.'

Barely a few days before President Ziaul Haq's official visit to the United States beginning on 6 December 1982, a dispute developed over the US refusal to equip the F-16 aircraft to be delivered to Pakistan with the latest electronic equipment which form an integral part of the Fighting Falcons. Pakistan took a very strong stand on the issue[39] and later the US Secretary of Defence Casper Weinberger revealed that it had been received 'happily', implying that Pakistan would, after all, get the F-16s equipped with ALR-69 which it had insisted upon.[40]

In March 1983, the US allocation for Pakistan for fiscal 1984 under the package deal came up for hearing before the Congress. It was reported that the 8 March hearing in the Congress 'was not a very smooth affair. For Pakistan came under some rough questioning and criticism...'[41] And in May the Senate Foreign Relations Committee slashed 75 million dollars from the allocation for 1984.[42]

IV

It is clear that the American commitment to Pakistan's security 'is rather ambiguous and tenuous ... The deal itself is hostage to the whims of the Zionist-influenced Congress and every year Pakistan has to furnish a "certificate of good behaviour" on its nuclear programme.'[43] Given the nature of the US commitment, the constraints of the US executive and the divergences in their mutual perception, Pakistan can ill-afford to place too much reliance on this relationship even under an American administration and a regional geopolitical environment which greatly favours a stable relationship between the two countries such as at present. Pakistan is now seen as 'commanding the sea-lanes from the oil-rich Gulf into the Arabian Sea and 'blocking access to the warm waters of the Indian Ocean'.[44] Mr Howard B. Schaffer, Deputy Assistant Secretary in the State Department underlined Pakistan's current significance for US strategic thinking when he told the Senate sub-committee that South and Southwest Asia is a region of critical strategic importance to the US and Pakistan lies at the heart of this region.[45]

But even common threat perceptions do not provide a stable and durable basis to bilateral relations between states. A number of factors as well as the history of their relationship, 'provide a poor basis for extensive cooperation, even in the pursuit of mutual interests, between the United States and Pakistan'.[46]

Ironically, just before this American rediscovery of Pakistan's strategic value, relations between the two erstwhile allies had reached their lowest ebb. And since the renewed American interest in Pakistan's security was the direct result of the Soviet intervention in Afghanistan, it must not be viewed in isolation from the so-called Carter doctrine and the Rapid Deployment Force.

These relations, therefore, depend, in addition to other factors, on (1) continued Soviet presence in Afghanistan, (2) prolonged US-Soviet competition in the Southwest Asia region, and (3) the persistence of Iranian hostility towards the US and the Indian ambivalence on Afghanistan.

The nature of American interest in Pakistan being what it is, Pakistan should be careful not to identify itself too closely with the US strategic planning which has the Soviet Union as its target of hostility. Because, while Pakistan looks at this relationship strictly in the context of its own security, the US gives priority to the imperatives of its long-term global strategy. In any contingency, Pakistan might come under pressure from the US to provide facilities, if not bases, to the RDF, and the United States would assess the value of its bilateral cooperation with Pakistan in that context. Mr Agha Shahi, the then Minister of Foreign Affairs, had stated in the *Majlis-e-Shoora* on 15 January 1982 that 'Pakistan would not be expected to align itself with the US in a regional strategic consensus'. Throughout the negotiations leading to the aid package, Pakistan had taken meticulous care not to accept any offer which could impinge upon or inhibit Pakistan's non-aligned policy or commitments within the Organization of Islamic Conference. For this reason, Pakistan refused to accept concessional credit terms and opted instead for loans on market-related interest rates with the greater burden that they entailed.

Unfortunately, as an American writer has pointed out, US assistance 'has not always been rendered in the most graceful manner'.[47] If in the early days anti-communism was the criterion for American patronage, now Pakistan's nuclear programme has come under pressure. In an important speech in Karachi on 20 April 1982, the US ambassador to Pakistan, Ronald Spiers, had mentioned 'four vulnerabilities' in Pakistan-US relations, viz., the India factor, the nuclear issue, human rights, and narcotics.

Of the four 'vulnerabilities' referred to by Ronald Spiers, the people and government in Pakistan feel very strongly on the first two—the India factor and the nuclear question. A segment of opinion would be prepared to forego American assistance rather than yield on basic principles.

When President Zia complained of US pressure on Pakistan on the nuclear issue, it was reported that the US Administration had persuaded France to supply India with nuclear fuel which the US law prohibited it from providing. One may recall that the Carter Administration had successfully pressurized France into reneging on its commitment to sell Pakistan a duly safeguarded reprocessing plant. India not only got away with its nuclear explosion but what was worse, Pakistan was caught in the whirlwind of India's making.

The India factor has always played a decisive and crucial role in the formulation of US policy in this region. Indeed, American efforts to appease India have often resulted in the latter exercising a virtual veto over US policy towards Pakistan. It was with considerable diplomatic manoeuvring that the Reagan Administration succeeded in surmounting Indian opposition to the aid package. A Rand study has suggested that in the present circumstances, 'the US can afford to be a bit less solicitous of Indian opinions that it has been in the past'.[48]

It would be wishful thinking to expect that India would cease to figure, as prominently as hitherto, in Pakistan's security considerations in the foreseeable future. As an American scholar, Leo E. Rose, pointed out in his paper at the First Bilateral Conference on Pakistan-US Relations (7–10 June 1981), 'no American Administration can or would provide an unconditional security commitment that would include India—or, at least, one upon which Pakistanis could place any great reliance'. In any case, American spokesmen have made it quite clear that Pakistan should not expect any support from the US in any future Indo-Pakistan conflict.

Moreover, Pakistan cannot absolutely rule out the possibility of a tacit American-Soviet understanding involving the withdrawal of US support to the Afghan resistance in return for Soviet concessions in areas of more vital interest to the former. Given its security dilemma in the regional context, it would be in Pakistan's long-term interests not to bow to foreign pressure. However, Pakistan should work for a non-proliferation regime being uniformly applied on a non-discriminatory basis to all the countries of South Asia. At any rate, Pakistan cannot foreclose the nuclear option before obtaining adequate security guarantees from the superpowers.

Another factor that Pakistan can overlook only at its own peril is the fact that 'while there may be a Republican commitment to the security of Pakistan, it is not really a national commitment'.[49] Dr Zbigniew Brzezinski, former President Carter's National Security Adviser, has warned that US policy is not bipartisan, 'Pakistan will have problems on the Hill, and little can be done about it.'[50]

In conclusion, it needs to be emphasized that the chequered history of Pak-US relations, the nature and the constraints of the US commitment to Pakistan's security, the shifting emphasis and the changing proclivities of the US administrations and public, all make it absolutely essential for Pakistan to take every step with the utmost care. Even while promoting cooperation with the United States, Pakistan should continue to take an active part in the Organisation of Islamic Conference and the Non-Aligned Movement and strive to enhance understanding with India and the Soviet Union and defuse tension in the region. In the words of an American scholar, 'Islamabad must understand that US policy on security issues (in the region)...would probably rebound to Pakistan's advantage currently, but certainly not on all occasions in the future, as there are hard choices ahead for both Washington and Islamabad on basic strategic issues.'[51]

NOTES

1. Stephen P. Cohen, 'Security Issues in South Asia', *Asian Survey*, Berkeley, March 1975, p. 207.

2. Leo E. Rose, 'The Superpowers in South Asia: A Geostrategic Analysis', *Orbis*, Philadelphia, Summer, 1978, p. 395.
3. Quoted in M. Ahsen Choudhry, 'Pakistan and the United States' in Rais Ahmad Khan (ed.), *Pakistan-United States Relations, Proceedings of the National Symposium held at Islamabad, August 28-30, 1982*, Area Study Centre, Islamabad, 1983, p. 11.
4. Rodney W. Jones, 'Mending Relations with Pakistan', *The Washington Quarterly*, Spring 1981, p. 20.
5. Ibid.
6. Quoted in S. Adil Hussain, 'Politics of Alliance and Aid : A Case Study of Pakistan (1954–1966)', *Pakistan Horizon*, Karachi, first & second quarter 1979, p. 11.
7. Rashid Ahmed Khan, 'Security in the Gulf: Pakistani Perspective', in Khan (ed.), *Pakistan—US Relations*, p. 160.
8. Sattar Baber, *United States Aid to Pakistan: Case Study of the Influence of the Donor Country on the Domestic and Foreign Policies of the Recipient*, Pakistan Institute of International Affairs, Karachi, 1974, p. 113.
9. For full text, see, Department of State Historical Office, Bureau of Public Affairs, *American Foreign Policy, Current Documents*, 1959, Arno press, New York, 1971, pp. 1020–22.
10. Sattar Baber, op. cit., p. 90.
11. Quoted in Mehrunnisa Ali, 'Pakistan-US Threat Perceptions', in Khan (ed.), *Pakistan-US Relations*, p. 188.
12. W. Norman Brown, *The United States and India, Pakistan, Bangladesh*, Harvard University Press, Massachusetts, 1972, p. 400.
13. Shaheen Irshad Khan, *Rejection Alliance? A Case Study of US-Pakistan Relations (1947-1967)*, Ferozsons, Lahore, 1972, table 4.1, p. 68.
14. Ibid., p. 79.
15. Nazir Kamal, 'American Policy Towards Pakistan', *Muslim*, Islamabad, 12 June 1979.
16. Ibid.
17. Henry Kissinger, *The White House Years*, Weidenfeld and Nicolson and Michael Joseph, London, 1979, p. 892.
18. Ibid., p. 895.
19. William L. Richter, 'Strategy for Peace & Security in South Asia: View of a Superpower'. Paper read at First International Conference on Strategy for Peace and Security in South Asia, *Strategic Studies*, Islamabad, Winter/Spring 1982/83, p. 43.
20. Norman D. Palmer, 'The Carter Administration and South Asia', in Lawrence Ziring (ed.), *The Subcontinent in World Politics: India, its Neighbour and the Great Powers*, Praeger Publishers, New York, 1978, p. 199.

21. See M. R. Azmi, *Pakistan-Canada Relations, 1947-1982: A Brief Survey*, Area Study Centre, Islamabad, 1982, pp. 105–113.
22. Ibid., pp. 115–16.
23. Lawrence Ziring, 'South Asian Tangles and Triangles', in Ziring (ed.), *Subcontinent in World Politics*, p. 24.
24. Shirin Tahir-Kheli, 'Pakistan's Nuclear Option and US Policy', *Orbis*, Summer 1978, p. 366.
25. 'Pakistan: The Rising Soviet Threat and Declining US Credibility', *Backgrounder,* Heritage Foundation, Washington D.C., 4 June 1980, pp. 7–8.
26. Ibid., p. 12.
27. Quoted in Mushahid Hussain, 'Pakistan-America Relations: The Shahi Visit', *Muslim*, 28 April 1981.
28. Quoted in Mushahid Hussain, 'Pakistan America Relations: Divergence or Convergence of Interests?', *Muslim*, Islamabad, 29 April 1981.
29. *Dawn*, Karachi, 11 June 1981.
30. Bernard Gwertzman, 'Pakistan Blast Could End Aid', *New York Times*, 17 September 1981.
31. *Dawn*, 6 October 1981.
32. *Dawn*, 23 October 1981.
33. *Dawn*, 14 December 1981.
34. *Dawn*, 28 May 1982.
35. *Dawn*, 25 September 1982.
36. *Muslim*, 13 October 1982.
37. *Muslim*, 6 November 1982.
38. *Dawn*, 24 November 1982.
39. Bernard Gwertzman, 'Pakistan Rejects F-16s without Advanced Gear', *International Herald Tribune*, Paris, 1 December 1982.
40. *Dawn*, 9 December 1982.
41. Ijaz Hussain, 'US Aid to Pakistan: Congressional Perspective', *Muslim*, 31 March 1983.
42. *Muslim*, 12 May 1983.
43. Mushahid Hussain, 'Pakistan's Foreign Policy: An appraisal', *Muslim*, 21 February 1983.
44. *Dawn*, 28 November 1982.
45. *Dawn*, 27 April 1983.
46. Norman D. Palmer, 'The US and Pakistan: A Tortured Relationship'. Paper read at the 1st Bilateral Conference on Pakistan-US Relations, Arlingion (Virginia), 7–10 June, 1981, p. 20.
47. W. Norman, op. cit., p. 409.
48. Francis Fukuyama, *The Security of Pakistan: A Trip Report*, Rand Note, N-1584-RC, September 1980, p. 38.
49. Salman A. Ali, 'Alternative Futures for US-Pakistan Relations' *Nawa-i-Waqt*, Rawalpindi, 1 March 1983.

50. A.T. Chaudhry, 'Interview with Brzezinski: The US Interest in Pakistan', *Dawn*, 26 February 1983.
51. Leo E. Rose, 'Pakistan's Role and Interests in South and South-West Asia'. Paper read at the 1st Bilateral Conference on Pakistan-US Relations, Arlington, Virginia, 7–10 June, 1981, p. 6.

16

Pakistan, India, and Regional Cooperation in South Asia*

Rashid Ahmad Khan

Relations between Pakistan and India carry crucial importance for efforts aimed at achieving regional cooperation in South Asia. It is so, because these two countries enjoy the status of big states in this area (India, of course, being the biggest) in terms of size, population, resources, and potential. Any discussion of the problems of regional cooperation in South Asia inevitably boils down to the issues, controversies, and divergence of perceptions of these two neighbouring countries and their mutual relations. Progress in the field of SAARC (South Asian Association for Regional Cooperation) cannot be thought of unless there is improvement in relations between Pakistan and India. Unfortunately, Indo-Pakistan relations have not yet moved beyond normalization; and it may take them a lot of effort and time before they enter the stage of cooperation. SAARC is being much talked about and desired but judging from the results so far achieved, the process of regional cooperation in South Asia is slow paced. There may be a number of reasons for the slow progress in this direction, but one of the most prominent causes of delay in this endeavour is the sharp divergence of perceptions between Pakistan and India on regional cooperation in South Asia.

The history of this divergence dates back to the history of the idea of regional cooperation in South Asia itself, indeed, even before the

* Vol. xxxvii, No. 3, 1984.

emergence of Pakistan and India as independent nations in South Asia. For example, when, just before independence, Nehru convened the first Asian Relations Conference in New Delhi, the All India Muslim League refused to participate in it and denounced it as an attempt by the Congress to spread its influence in other parts of Asia. After independence this divergence found its expression in the policies of these two countries regarding regional as well as international issues. The founder of Pakistan Quaid-e-Azam Mohammad Ali Jinnah had, no doubt, expressed his desire for good will and understanding between India and Pakistan but it implied the recognition, on the part of India, of certain principles which are fundamental to the process of meaningful and mutually beneficial cooperation among independent states. These principles are respect for sovereignty, independence, and territorial integrity of the states, recognition of their equal status as sovereign nations and non-interference in their internal affairs. Unfortunately, India has always considered the division of South Asia as artificial[1] and partition of the subcontinent the result of British machinations. In his book *Discovery of India*, Nehru again and again refers to the cultural influence of ancient India on an area extending from the Persian Gulf to Indo-China and much before independence, had advocated the federation of India and Ceylon. However, when there appeared resentment in Ceylon over his idea, he modified his stand and declared his readiness to welcome and accept Ceylon as an independent sovereign state. But in spite of the fact that India recognizes the existence of separate and independent states in South Asia, there is the apprehension so frequently expressed by the leaders of smaller South Asian nations that India strives to exert its role of pre-eminence in this region with a view to turning the cultural sphere of influence into a political sphere of influence.

The Indian mind on regional cooperation in South Asia has been framed by the doctrines propounded by Nehru and K.M. Panikar. According to Nehru, the obstacles placed by a long colonial rule in the way of intra-regional relations must be removed by free and independent states of South Asia. Together they should work for the creation of an environment where there is almost complete identity and unanimity of views on major issues of world politics, so that South Asia could speak with 'one voice'. For the countries of South Asia this means that India's neighbours should toe her line in their external policies. Any attempt by the smaller countries of South Asia to develop relations with outside powers, particularly major powers, is viewed by India as a threat to the stability and peace of the region. This explains why India opposed Pakistan's entry into an American sponsored military pact in the 1950s. It is also with this objective in view that India has chosen to express its reservations about Nepal being a Zone of Peace.

The Indian perception of its role in regional cooperation in South Asia is based, apart from historical and cultural factors, upon the sheer size and potential of her resources. India's population is three times the combined population of all the other regional states. It has virtually 100 per cent of the total resources of the region in respect of uranium, iron ore, bauxite, copper, gold, lead, manganese, silver, tungsten, zinc, asbestos, and diamonds. It has more than 90 per cent of the resources in coal, crude petroleum, chromium, magnesite, and salt.[2] Under the impact of British rule, the Indian middle class was, in comparison with other parts of South Asia, at a higher level of educational and cultural development at the time of independence. The Indian nationalist movement under the leadership of Congress was supported and financed by the middle class. After independence all the Indian governments have acted as promoters of the interests of the middle class both inside and outside the country. Over the last thirty-seven years India has succeeded in obtaining substantial economic interests in not only South Asia but in such regions as Africa, Middle East, Persian Gulf, and even South East Asia. In the Middle East, India's economic interests have been growing steadily. The large number of Indian workers in the Gulf have become a substantial source of revenue for the Indian government, not only by sending back money to their families but also by investing in India. It has also been getting an increasingly large number of contracts in the Arab world, especially for consultancy. According to the Indian Trade Ministry, Indian contracts in the Arab world in 1981 amounted to about US$5 billion. There has also been a substantial increase in the volume of trade between India and the Middle East since 1969–70. In 1976, the Middle East had become India's biggest trading partner.

It was this expanding economic activity of the Indian bourgeoisie that compelled India to move in the direction of seeking regional cooperation in the area 'extending from Iran to Indo-China'. 'The objective of this policy was to serve India's national interests by building an infrastructure for regional co-operation', commented an Indian analyst.[3] In terms of political advantages it was thought, by the

Indian policy makers, that such regional cooperation would enable the South Asian countries to remain free from outside influence and internal tensions. It (South Asia) would command a unique weight in the counsels of the world and, as the former foreign minister of India, Mr Vajpayee put it '...we can be a powerful group of nations contributing to international stability'.[4]

It was therefore, in pursuit of this objective that India in the mid-1970s, indicated its desire to join the RCD. The Indian desire of joining the RCD was expressed after the former Shah of Iran had proposed an economic community comprising Iran, Afghanistan, Pakistan, India, and Bangladesh. After Pakistan's refusal to join such an economic community and its objection to India's joining the RCD, the Indian government reportedly requested a transit trade route between India and Iran. According to Mr K. Subrahmanyam, the People's Party government had agreed to provide such a transit trade route to India.[5] It was believed so because the former Shahinshah of Iran had helped a great deal for the reconciliation between Pakistan and India after 1971 and the restoration of diplomatic relations between these two nations in 1976 was reportedly brought about through his efforts,[6] and he, it was thought, might have put pressure on Pakistan. However, it remained doubtful whether any such facility became factually operational because the then Pakistan ambassador to India, Mr Fida Hassan categorically denied the existence of any such facility.[7]

One of the prominent features of the Indian perception of regional cooperation in South Asia is that while the neighbours of India want strategic issues to be resolved along with those of regional cooperation, India keeps these two sets of issues separate, although expressing the hope that cooperation in non-strategic and non-political areas would ultimately lead to the resolution of strategic and political issues. India has differences with almost all its important neighbours concerning regional as well as international issues and with Pakistan it has a longstanding dispute over Kashmir. Indo-Nepal relations are strained over the issues of transit trade, Zone of Peace for Nepal and Nepal's growing relations with China and the West. Similarly Bhutan has been irked by the Indian refusal to allow it to trade with West Asia. Likewise, India has territorial and ethnic problems with Bangladesh and Sri Lanka. The public opinion in these countries is, therefore, less enthusiastic about regional cooperation because of the lack of progress in the resolution of these issues. Another aspect of Indian perception on South Asia is that its approach to regional cooperation is bilateral rather than multilateral. The logic in adopting the bilateral approach in intra-regional relations is obvious. Regional cooperation in South Asia is still at the stage of infancy, and there has not evolved an institutional arrangement whereby collectively taken decisions could be enforced. Moreover, India has no wish to forsake its predominant position in the region by submitting its will to a forum where much smaller but majority nations could take decisions inimical to the interests of India.

Thus, according to Indian logic, regional cooperation in South Asia is a device through which the region can be turned into a region of peace free from tension; and an end can be put to poverty, economic backwardness, and a solution can be found of other pressing problems such as energy, technological advancement, agricultural development, etc. This is a pre-condition for such an objective. Economic underdevelopment is, according to India, the root cause of much of the tension in South Asia manifest in the form of the influence of 'external powers' and friction between India and her neighbours. Poverty and backwardness create political instability in these countries. Unstable political conditions produce such regimes in these countries which can only thrive on either taking a strong anti-India line or leaning heavily on outside powers for economic assistance. As a result, India says, the 'strategic discord' between India and its neighbours has widened. In order to convert South Asia into a zone of peace, it is necessary to expel the influence of big states to give first priority to the issues of economic development. Since a long period of economic association of these states with developed states had created only dependent economies in these countries, with ever worsening economic conditions, the need for a self-reliant economy is very obvious. India considers itself a useful model of a self-reliant economy; the countries of South Asia, India thinks, should learn from the Indian example. The objective of a self-reliant economy can be expedited through regional cooperation in economic, commercial, and technological areas. Once the countries of South Asia take the road to self-reliant economies, there will be a climate of political stability and less chances of coming under the influence of outside powers.

For India, the removal of so-called external influence from South Asia is an important policy objective and it is one of the important compulsions in Indian initiative for regional cooperation, especially cooperation with Pakistan. Because, as Subrahmanyam has stated, India has always regarded Pakistan as an instrument for external intervention in the subcontinent to countervail India. He goes on to say that India is not unduly concerned with Pakistan *per se*, but India has to worry about superpowers or great powers, whose influence and intervention Pakistan brings into the subcontinent because of its obsession with India's size and potential.[8]

To the Indian mind Pakistan has always sought to secure parity with India, although the latter is many times larger than Pakistan in size, population, and resources. This gap has been greatly widened after the separation of East Pakistan. But Pakistan, India thinks, is still in the search of elements which could support its claim to parity with India. This desire of Pakistan, Mr Subrahmanyam asserts, is a hangover from pre-partition days when the Muslim League sought parity with the Congress with the support of the British. He alleges that after independence, Pakistan's leadership still attempts to lean on the United States or China to secure parity with India. 'The real issue is not India's dominance but whether Pakistan has reconciled itself to coexist in the subcontinent with India, without being able to claim an artificial parity with India.'[9] In the South Asian context Pakistan is seen making every effort to realign as many peripheral nations in South Asia as possible against India.[10]

The Indian dominance is, therefore, taken for granted in India's perception of the South Asian cooperative relationship. The dominance is no doubt there as a geographical fact and owing to the vast gap in economic, and strategic capabilities of India and its small neighbours. It is this dominance which is responsible for the historic fear among India's neighbours, acting as one of the major constraints on efforts for real détente in South Asia. Although India is a major trade partner of most of the South Asian states, intra-regional trade in South Asia is less than 1 per cent of the entire foreign trade of the region.[11] Almost the same condition prevails in the trade relations between Pakistan and India. Pakistan renewed its trade relations with India in 1975 after a lapse of ten years, yet Indian imports from Pakistan come to just half a per cent of the total Indian imports.[12] These figures are enough to illuminate both the scope and limited possibilities of regional cooperation in South Asia.

Pakistan, though much smaller than India in terms of size, population, and resources, is, nevertheless a major country in South Asia. Apart from its importance derived from its geostrategic location, there is a lot of potential both in material and human resources that can entitle it to be a major trading partner not only with smaller states of South Asia but also with India itself. Pakistan has already established trade links with such South Asian countries as Nepal, Sri Lanka, Maldives, and Bangladesh; and these trade links are steadily growing. For example, in the last decade the trade turn out between Pakistan and Sri Lanka has increased manifold. In the beginning of the 1970s Sri Lanka imported goods from Pakistan worth Rs 3 million only; in 1981–82 the imports from Pakistan rose to Rs 75 million. Commenting on the potential of trade between Sri Lanka and Pakistan, Sri Lanka's Minister of Trade Mr Labith Athulabmudali, during an official visit to Pakistan in March 1982, said, '...there is a great scope for increasing trade and economic relations between the two countries'. He even suggested a legal framework to increase the establishment of trade further. During his visit, the 1985 trade agreement between Pakistan and Sri Lanka was replaced by a new one.[13] The expansion of commercial and economic relations between Pakistan and Bangladesh has been more spectacular; especially during the last seven or eight years.

In addition to fostering economic, cultural, and technological links with smaller countries of South Asia, Pakistan has also succeeded in achieving what can be termed as 'Strategic Accord' with such countries as Nepal, Sri Lanka, Maldives, and Bangladesh. There have taken place a number of official visits, many at the highest level between Pakistan and these countries. Pakistan's President General Ziaul Haq has had an opportunity to interact with the heads of these states at the Non-Aligned and OIC conferences. As a result of growth in bilateral relationships both in economic and political fields, these countries hold similar views on such strategic issues in South Asia as a Nuclear Free Zone in the Indian Ocean and a Zone of Peace for Nepal and Afghanistan.

However, it is with India that Pakistan's relationship continues to suffer from a lack of satisfactory growth, especially in the political field. As for the economic and trade sectors, although the two countries signed a trade agreement in 1975 and a number of visits have been exchanged between the two countries for promoting mutual trade, Pakistan-India trade still remains at a low level. But it is the continued existence of strategic discord between Pakistan and India which casts a dark shadow not only on the prospects of bilateral cooperation but is also the most important element for shaping Pakistan's perceptions on regional cooperation in South Asia.

The relations between Pakistan and India, which were at the lowest ebb in 1971 were normalized in 1972, when the two countries signed the historic Simla Agreement. Ever since the Simla Agreement has remained a mutually acceptable framework for the promotion of bilateral relations. In 1976 the two countries restored diplomatic relations and over-flights. As a result of President Zia's meeting with Mrs Indira Gandhi at New Delhi in November 1982, these relations received further impetus and the two countries even established a joint commission for further expansion of relations in various fields. A meeting of the sub-commission of this joint commission has recently been held and it looks as if relations between the two countries are developing smoothly. But despite the fact that there is a great scope and potential for increase in trade and economic relations between Pakistan and India, Pakistan's relations with its neighbour have not, since 1972, progressed beyond the stage of normalization. A fundamental principle of peaceful coexistence is the non-interference in the internal affairs of other states. Both Pakistan and India have accused each other of interfering in the internal affairs of each other.

A major reason behind the lack of progress in the development of Pakistan-India relations is the unresolved dispute over Kashmir. In 1976, when the two countries restored diplomatic relations, Pakistan offered to move further, provided there was a settlement of the Jammu and Kashmir dispute. The then Prime Minister of Pakistan, in a banquet speech in Beijing in May 1976 said: 'With the steps that we have recently taken towards completing the process of normalization and in the reestablishment of diplomatic relations, Pakistan has been able to bring its relationship with India to the level that existed before the war of 1965 over Jammu and Kashmir ... We on our part are willing to advance from the stage of normalization to peaceful coexistence in accordance with the five well known principles pertaining to inter-state relations. Clearly however this relationship can be achieved only after a settlement of Jammu and Kashmir dispute in accordance with the United Nations resolution which had been accepted by both India and Pakistan. For, it must be clearly understood by all concerned what normalization means in scope and content.'[14]

In the mid-1970s, Iran, under the Shah, was advocating the formation of a common market comprising Iran, Pakistan, and Bangladesh. Pakistan refused to join such an organization and held the position that the Simla Agreement precluded any regional association for it provided in the first instance, 'a bilateral step by step approach'. In 1976 there were rumours that Pakistan had agreed to provide India transit facility to directly trade with West Asian countries at the request of the former Shah of Iran. There was a sharp reaction to this suspected move by the government, even from the opposition parties in Pakistan. Pir Sahib of Pagara, President of the Pakistan Muslim League (now defunct) issued a lengthy statement criticizing the government on seeking friendship with India at all costs. Commenting on the report that India was interested in having a land route through Pakistan to trade with Afghanistan he said: 'An overland link through Pakistan would give India access to the frontiers of the Soviet Union and undermine the strategic importance of this country', the government of Pakistan had to categorically deny the existence of any such facility.[15]

The question of transit trade again appeared in early 1978 when the then Indian Foreign Minister Atal Behari Vajpayee was about to embark upon an official visit to Pakistan. It was reported, just prior to Mr Vajpayee's departure, that he was expected to offer a comprehensive proposal to be agreed upon between the two countries for providing transit facilities for Pakistani trade goods bound for Bangladesh and Nepal and for similar facilities to India so that it would find a route for its goods bound for Afghanistan and Iran.[16] However, an official spokesman in Islamabad issued a statement saying that the Indian Foreign Minister was bringing no specific package proposals and Pakistan did not expect him to raise any substantial issue like transit trade or the common market.[17]

On the issue of a common market the position of Pakistan was the same as it was in 1976. An official statement issued by the government of Pakistan on the eve of A.B. Vajpayee's visit to Pakistan made it clear that Pakistan had no interest in joining the proposed common market in South Asia. The official spokesman of the Pakistani government said that Pakistan had clear cut views on the matter (common market). Pakistan did not think that the setting up of the common market at that stage by countries having different economic patterns would serve any useful purpose. The spokesman said that Pakistan held the view that India had a population of 600 million people, a strong industrial base and advanced technology; India would, therefore, dominate the common market if created, with adverse effects on Pakistan's industry.[18] The apprehension of Indian dominance is a recurrent theme not only in the context of multilateral arrangements but also with regard to a bilateral trade relationship between the two countries.

With the advent of the decade of 1980s, Pakistan showed its willingness to not only enter into a multilateral association like the organization of South Asian Regional Cooperation but also took significant steps in the direction of improving its bilateral relationship with India; yet the perception of Pakistan on regional cooperation in South Asia remained fundamentally different from that of India. Explaining the factors that shape Pakistan's perception in this regard, the former Foreign Minister of Pakistan, Mr Agha Shahi said in an address before the seventh meeting of the Committee on Studies for Cooperation Development in South Asia (22 April 1982) that India's population is 77 per cent of the total population of South Asia; it has 72 per cent of the total area and 78 per cent of the national product. Since it constitutes three quarters of the region, its massive economy would tend to dominate the smaller economies, unless adequate safeguards are designed to protect the interests of participating countries and ensure balanced interdependence. He further stated:

> Intra regional disputes and differences, conflicting responses to geo-political challenges, divergent foreign policies, not to speak of incongruence of economic interests resulting from disparities and disadvantages of size, population, location and levels of economic development, pose obstacles to harmonious cooperation, which is a *sine qua non* for the formulation of strategies of development on a basis of national and collective self reliance.[19]

The major fillip to South Asian cooperation was provided by the meeting that took place between President Zia and Prime Minister Indira Gandhi at Delhi in November 1982. President Zia himself indicated this during his South East Asian tour and said that his talks with the Indian Prime Minister would hopefully lead to the formation of a South Asian Organization on the lines of the Association of South East Asian Nations (ASEAN).[20] That Pakistan is committed to regional cooperation, however, does not mean that Pakistan will meekly accept hegemonic tendencies in the region and agree to be dominated by any power either within the region or outside the region.

There is, therefore, a great divergence of perceptions between Pakistan and India on regional cooperation in South Asia. This divergence stems from historical, social, and cultural cleavages between the two countries. The Indian perception is basically based upon its self image of mother country treating South Asia as its cultural domain which can be turned into its political domain as well, through economic collaboration. India thinks that regional cooperation must proceed even without removing strategic discord between the South

Asian nations. Pakistan, like other South Asian nations, is fearful of Indian dominance because of its overwhelming superiority in economic patterns, size, population, and resources. In Pakistan's view, regional cooperation means not only cooperation in trade, commerce, and technology, etc., but is inseparable from the solution of those problems which have set the countries of South Asia against each other for the last thirty-seven years.

NOTES

1. Buddhudasa R. Kirthisinghe, 'An Economic Community for South Asia', *The Economic Times*, New Delhi, 2 November 1978.
2. M.L. Qureshi, *Survey of Economy—Resources and Prospects of South Asia*, Marga Institute, Colombo, 1981, pp. XIX-XX quoted in Samina Ahmed, 'South Asian Regional Cooperation', *Regional Studies*, Institute of Regional Studies, Islamabad, Summer, 1982.
3. S.D. Muni, 'India's Beneficial bilateralism in South Asia', *India Quarterly*, New Delhi, October–December 1979, p. 418.
4. Ibid.
5. K. Subrahmanyam, 'India and the Security of the Sub-Continent', *India Quarterly*, July-December 1980.
6. Indian press reports quoted in *The Pakistan Times*, Lahore, 17 May 1976.
7. *The Pakistan Times*, 3 October 1976.
8. K. Subrahmanyam, op. cit.
9. Ibid.
10. P.K. Mishra, 'Determinants of Intra-regional relations in South Asia', *India Quarterly*, January-March, 1980.
11. Ibid.
12. Statement by Mr A.K. Jain, leader of the Indian businessmen's delegation that visited Pakistan in February 1983. According to Mr A.K. Jain, total Indian imports were Rs 13,500 crores, out of which India imported goods from Pakistan worth about Rs 70 crore in 1981–82. *The Pakistan Times*, 22 February 1983.
13. *The Pakistan Times*, 31 March 1982.
14. Ibid., 31 May 1976.
15. Ibid.
16. Ibid., 4 August 1976.
17. Ibid., 26 January 1978.
18. Ibid., 5 February 1978.
19. Ibid., 4 February 1978.
20. A.T. Chaudhury, 'Détente through Trilateralism', *Dawn*, Karachi, 15 May 1982.

Pakistan Foreign Policy: Trends and Challenges of the Eighties*

Mehrunnisa Ali

Other implications and ramifications apart, the new US aid package envisaging $4.02 billion of military-cum-economic assistance for the post-1987 period indicates that Pakistan's policy in the coming years would not be much different from what it had been in the recent past. As long as the present government remains in power, the Afghanistan issue remains unresolved, and Moscow continues to exert pressure on Islamabad, there is not the least likelihood of any significant shift in Pakistan's foreign policy** stance in the post '87 period. As a matter of fact alignment with the US, notwithstanding its varying degrees of total and conditional, has remained the most stable feature of Pakistan's policy since the mid-fifties. Despite its professed adherence to non-alignment, Islamabad's posture on regional and international issues continued to be conditioned by the US global and regional considerations.

Officially it has been claimed that the package involves no *quid pro quo*, that Pakistan has secured the deal at concessional rates without bartering away its freedom of action and that it has not compromised its stand on nuclear technology nor has it surrendered to

---

* Vol. xxxix, No. 1, 1986.
** See Mehrunnisa Ali, 'Constraints in Soviet-Pakistan Relations', in A.A. Kadeer and Naveed Tahir (eds.), *Pakistan-Europe Ties—in Contemporary Setting*, Area Study Centre for Europe, University of Karachi, Karachi, 1988 (Editor).

US dictates on base facilities. The facts and developments, however, tell a different story. At the time of the conclusion of the $3.2 billion package in 1981, similar assertions were made regarding the non-existence of a *quid pro quo*. However, an incisive sight at Islamabad's stance would reveal a close meshing of Pakistan-US policies. Pursuing an Afghan policy of US liking, it had to act as a conduit for arms supply to the Afghan rebels.[1] Washington's pressure was reportedly at work[2] behind the breakdown of the third round of the Geneva talks in April 1983. It is no more a secret now how Washington's arm twistings and warnings slowed down Pakistan's drive for the acquisition of a nuclear reprocessing plant. Without mincing words President Reagan in his letter of 12 September 1984 warned General Zia that Pakistan's nuclear activities could undermine the existing $3.2 billion aid and security relationship. This being the recent past, Pakistan's future course of action could hardly be free from restraints. Certain developments already indicate future eventualities. The first ever call on the Karachi port of the US nuclear powered aircraft carrier *Enterprise* in mid March 1986 in the wake of negotiations over the package could be a beginning to an eventual forced acquisition of docking facilities for US nuclear armed ships at Pakistan's ports. Equally significant is the Reagan administrations decision[3] to give *Stinger* surface-to-air missiles to Afghan fighters, which implies the continued use of Pakistan for arms supply to the resistance groups.

As for the acquisition of nuclear technology, even if it is accepted that Pakistan has not compromised its stand, given the strong opposition of the Congress to its nuclear programme it cannot go nuclear during the deal period, for any move in that regard would result in Congress scrapping the aid bill. Moreover, in the event of Congress refusal to extend the waiver of the Symington Amendment, which is going to expire in October 1987, Pakistan might be compelled to sign the NPT.

Viewed against this backdrop the package obviously implies a halt to Pakistan's nuclear advance. India would be the major beneficiary of this prevailing nuclear imbalance in the region. Not being a signatory to the NPT, India would be free to further augment its nuclear strength. Having reportedly accumulated enough plutonium to produce at least fifteen atomic bombs in a year, it could use that superiority to establish its hegemony in the region. In view of its occupation of the Siachen Glacier and its recent renewed toughness towards Pakistan coupled with the US unwillingness to intervene on behalf of Pakistan in any future armed conflict with India, a nuclear Pakistan could not only be an effective deterrent to India's future adventurist designs but could also guarantee regional peace and security. There is no denying that Pakistan's peaceful nuclear device would evoke Washington's political as well as economic retaliation. It can nevertheless survive without US aid by slashing administrative and non-development expenses. In view of their support to Pakistan's nuclear programme, friendly Arab states would not mind extending a helping hand in tiding over its economic hardship. Without going into the economic aspect of the arguments advanced for and against the US aid,[4] it could be safely asserted that given the sharp rise in the loan repayment with interest and the debt servicing cost, the economic benefits would be much less than what has been claimed to accrue.

Moreover what makes the package uninnocuous is the fact that a sizeable part of the $4.2 billion assistance will be advanced on concessional terms. Seldom being an unmixed blessing, superpowers' aid entails concessions which vary in nature and degree according to the amount and nature of the aid. Being one of the five major recipients of US aid after Israel, Egypt, South Korea, and the Philippines, which have strategic ties with the US, Pakistan could also be forced to concede facilities of a strategic nature. That Pakistan is expected to serve US interests is indicative from the US Secretary of State, George Shultz's testimony before the Congressional investigation committee on 9 February last in which he bracketted the former with South Korea and Oman.

One of the concessions which Pakistan could be compelled to make is to keep the Afghan issue alive to suit Washington's global strategy. Notwithstanding its support to the UN-sponsored indirect Geneva talks, it seeks to continue the Afghan stalemate for a number of reasons. By keeping the Soviet forces engaged, it diverts or releases Soviet pressure from other strategic places. The issue also provides it an opportunity to admonish Moscow at every international forum. Since the Soviet intervention has tarnished its image in the third world, the US would do everything possible to block the process of rehabilitation of that image. Realizing that Moscow would not advance towards the Gulf without risking direct confrontation, it feels no urgency to expedite the process of a settlement. It would particularly prevent a solution which it deems detrimental to its interest in the region. With this end in view, it has been playing up the Soviet danger against Pakistan, alleging it of nurturing designs to control Pakistan, Iran, the Gulf, and the Indian

Ocean.[5] Its avowed willingness lately conveyed to the UN Secretary-General to act as a guarantor of a settlement by no means reflects its eagerness for a speedy solution. The latest increase in the CIA aid to Afghan insurgents which reached $250 million in 1985 and Reagan's decision to supply them *Stinger* missiles speak of a different intention.

Since the aid package is an outcome of Soviet intervention in Afghanistan, its full utilization depends *inter alia* upon the continuation of that crisis. Coming in the wake of the Shah's downfall, Soviet intervention in Afghanistan was perceived by the Pentagon as a prelude to its eventual putsch towards the Gulf to control the Western oil supply routes. Under the changed geopolitical situation arising out of the emergence of an anti-American government in Iran and the presence of Soviet forces in Afghanistan, Washington had little political options but to revive friendship with Islamabad with whom it had been at odds on the nuclear plant issue. Due to its proximity to the Gulf and contiguity to Afghanistan, Pakistan was considered as the first line of defence to be protected in order to safeguard the vital oil supply lines. In the military regime of Pakistan, Washington found a willing supporter of its policy goals in the region. Faced with hostile neighbours in the vicinity and lacking a popular power base, the Zia regime seized the opportunity created by the Afghanistan crisis to consolidate itself internally and externally.

Since Washington's interest in Pakistan emanates from its concern over the Soviet presence in Afghanistan which is deemed a threat to the Gulf oil supply lines, its security commitments to Pakistan against the possible Soviet onslaught as well as its aid programme are obviously linked to that issue. In the event of any material change in the prevailing situation arising out of the solution of the Afghan problem either through the UN sponsored Geneva talks or through a Yalta type deal between the superpowers, the package could hardly remain intact. Although very little is known as to what transpired between Reagan and Gorbachev at their Paris summit last year and what motivated the former to express his willingness in December 1985 to act as a guarantor, given their consensus about avoiding a direct confrontation and Washington's preference for a status quo, Pakistan cannot rule out the possibility of Washington bargaining Afghanistan's fate in exchange for guarantees for the Gulf oil routes or a free hand in Central America.

Furthermore, US commitments to Pakistan could be invoked only in the event of a Soviet attack, the possibility of which has been ruled out not only by Soviet officials but by President Zia himself. Fear of US intervention would prevent Moscow from launching a direct offensive against Pakistan. It could, however, penalize Pakistan through its friends in Delhi and Kabul, if its pressure tactics fail to stop Islamabad's alleged interference in the Afghan affair. As for the question of Delhi's response, it has made no secret of its opposition to the US supply of sophisticated arms to Pakistan. It also resents the prospects of Pakistan becoming nuclear. There is a lobby in India which still cherishes the prospects of Pakistan's extinction. Much, however, depends on Moscow's *modus operandi*, Rajiv's ability to withstand Soviet pressure and the state of India-Pakistan relations in the days ahead. If tension between the two countries increases again, Delhi might decide to oblige Moscow. In the event of India's onslaught, US reaction would not be much different from what it has been in the past. When posed with a challenge of choosing between India and Pakistan, Washington has always shown a clear preference for the former. Pakistan, due to its small size, its weak internal infrastructure, and its political instability is a weak, dispensable ally. While India, owing to its size, political stability, working democracy, and ability to withstand Soviet pressure, could play a vital role in counteracting Soviet penetration in the region. This being the perception, Washington has been lately trying to mend fences with Delhi as is evident from its recognition of India as a major power and from its agreement for the sale of a supercomputer along with sophisticated arms to India. Pakistan, on the other hand, though important for the recently formed US unified command, but in relation to India, ranks low in the US estimation.

As a result of the Moscow-Kabul-Delhi aversion to Pakistan's growing collaboration with the US, tension has increased on the borders. Their resentment to the development of an 'Islamabad-Washington axis' had dangerously exposed the frontiers to foreign designs. The Indian occupation of the Siachen Glacier and a sudden rise, of late, in the incidents of clashes between Pakistan and the Indian border security forces could not be viewed as isolated events. How insecure and violable the western border has become is evident from the increasing number of border transgressions and air raids by the Soviet aided Afghan MiGs, frequent bombing of Pakistani areas, the presence of a Soviet militarized fort along the Pak-Afghan border,[6] and the operation of Soviet mobile units within 32 km of Pakistan's frontier. The situation on the border will continue to remain tense as long as the Afghan issue remains unresolved and the refugees continue to inhabit Pakistan's soil.

By incurring Moscow's wrath, by compromising its non-aligned posture, and by conditioning its freedom of action, Pakistan has paid a heavy price for its identification with the US. Moscow perceives this association as anti-Soviet and anti-Kabul. It considers US arms supply as an American bid to turn Pakistan into a major military base in South Asia.[7] Despite Islamabad's repeated denials, the Kremlin leadership keeps accusing it of granting Washington the right to the Mekran coast. Radio Moscow in a broadcast on 11 February 1985 alleged that Washington has under a secret accord secured rights to use military, naval, and air bases in Pakistan.

Not only that, Moscow also views with concern the recently reinforced Pakistan-China ties. Under the changed pattern of power alignment brought about by the growing convergence of Sino-American interests in the region and their identity of views on Afghanistan, Moscow appears to be apprehensive of the consequences of these countries' close relations with Pakistan. Moscow's repeated allegations against Beijing about training the insurgents, helping Pakistan to explode a nuclear device in China to prevent its detection and its adverse comments on the opening of the Khunjerab pass in the Karakorum[8] clearly manifest its resentment against the growing Pakistan-China amity.

This being the perception, Moscow cannot but express its disapprobation of Islamabad's approach towards the Afghan crisis. Without mincing words it has denounced Pakistan's alleged involvement in the Afghan war. One of the three main obstacles in the Soviet-Pakistan ties, as pointed out by the former Soviet envoy Smirnov, is the latter's support to the counter-revolutionaries.[9] Resorting to various pressure tactics ranging from overtures, persuasions and warnings to mild retaliation, Moscow has been trying since 1985 to desist Pakistan from supporting the rebels' armed struggle against the Kabul regime. To induce Pakistan to come to some arrangement about the Afghan issue, it offered economic aid, assistance in the nuclear field, and cooperation in 100 projects. At the same time, it missed no chance to show its displeasure. It arranged the postponement of Niaz A. Naik's visit to Moscow in July 1984 and cancelled the visit of a high level Soviet delegation last year. Apart from mounting pressure on the border, it has expressed its indignation through protests and warnings; some of the instances of which are its protest over the Matani incident on 27 April 1985,[10] Gorbachev's warning to Zia during his last journey to Moscow about the consequences of persisting interference in the Afghan affairs, and Smirnov's remarks hinting at the possibility of a joint Soviet-Afghan action against Pakistan.[11] Admitting the escalated Soviet military and diplomatic pressures, Pakistan Foreign Minister, Sahabzada Yaqub Khan pointed at the frequency and intensity of the cross border raids, air violations, and artillery barrages.[12] Moscow's growing desperation with Pakistan could prove hazardous for the country. It is high time that Islamabad should review its approach towards the Afghan issue. The longer the problem lasts, the weaker will be its negotiating position. Washington and Moscow would not mind continuing the stalemate as the issue has not materially hurt them much. The delay in the settlement, however, costs Pakistan much in terms of strategic, political, economic, and social effects of the problem. Hence the need for a change in the posture, which except for bringing in US aid, has otherwise led to grave consequences.

Strategically, the stance, by failing to diffuse tension on the border, has not served well the cause of national security. With the Soviet forces operating in the proximity, the danger on the border has been further augmented. Pakistan's identification and growing military collaboration with the US has diluted its non-aligned status. By incurring Soviet fury Islamabad has enhanced its dependence on the US and thereby has severely restrained its freedom of action. Apart from the economic burden of feeding and sheltering over 2.5 million Afghan refugees, their social impact on the peoples of Balochistan and the Frontier province is tremendous. The refugees have not only changed the demography of the two provinces but have adversely affected their ethnic harmony too. The locals resent their purchase of properties and their competition for jobs. Apart from the incidents of clashes between the locals and the refugees, no less dangerous for internal peace and security is the latter's involvement in gun-running, drug-trafficking and the country's internal politics. Moreover, the two border provinces stand exposed to the activities of infiltrators, who have, as officially acknowledged, entered the country posing as refugees.

What further necessitates a policy modification is Moscow's strategy and the insurgents' ability to hold on. In view of the political and strategic importance of Afghanistan, Moscow would not pull out without firmly consolidating itself and without seeking guarantees of non-interference in that country. Having vital interest to protect there, it is unlikely to budge an inch from its known stand. Although it has repeatedly indicated its desire to withdraw,[13] it is in no hurry to disengage its forces. The prolonged war has, as a matter of fact, benefitted Moscow as it has, besides giving it a justification to stay there, enabled it to strengthen its position. Neither the increased American aid to the resistance groups nor the resultant intensified fighting has blocked its consolidation drive. That it has tightened its grip is apparent from its increased armed strength in that country, the development of military communications facilities in the areas adjoining Iran and Pakistan and the reported building of airfields at two places near the Pakistan-Iran border. Thus its disengagement from Afghanistan, like that of its past pull-out from Finland and Austria would neither be unconditional nor premature (i.e. prior to the realization of its objectives). It would withdraw its forces but in phases, after seeking firm guarantees of non-interference and reserving the right to return in the event of any perceived threat or danger to its interest there.

As for the insurgents' ability, they have, at the most, by their continued fighting prevented the stabilization of the Karmal regime and have kept the forces under pressure. However, they could hardly, on their own, drive the Soviet forces out of the country. Being ideologically divided, politically disorganized and materially ill-equipped they can neither dislodge the Kabul regime nor can they oust the Soviet forces. With the passage of time their resistance will get feeble and so will Pakistan's bargaining position. If Moscow decides to launch a full scale offensive, they will not hold on for long without massive external support which is unlikely to come. Apparently tired of six years of protracted fighting, the new leadership in the Kremlin seems set to expedite its end. Making various political and diplomatic moves in that regard it has of late intensified its drive against the resistance movement. The two major offensives launched at Barikot and Khost last August and its reinforcements on the border outposts speak of Moscow's intention. Hence the urgency of a negotiated solution before the time runs out, depriving Pakistan of its limited leverage. Islamabad has to reframe its posture in the light of these factors. That it has reconsidered its position to a certain extent is evident from its flexible stance on the issue of direct talks with the Kabul regime.

Since there will be no eighth round,[14] the Geneva VII* scheduled on 5 May will be the decisive, 'make it or break it' round. Having principally agreed on three basic points of non-interference, international guarantees, and the return of refugees, the most crucial issue the parties have to tackle at the seventh round is to link these with the time-frame for Soviet pull-out. A major breakthrough in the deadlock over the format which wrecked the Geneva VI had been achieved during Cordovez's visit in March when both accommodated each other's viewpoint on the matter. Pakistan agreed to enter into direct talks with the Kabul regime after the finalization of Instrument IV pertaining to the timetable for Soviet withdrawal. Kabul, in return, consented to continue its participation in the proximity talks.[15] The most crucial problem besetting the parties at the Geneva VII will be the time limit of pull-out and its relation to non-interference. Kabul seeks to extend the time to 18 months or probably more, whereas Pakistan would prefer a speedy pull-out.[16] Cordovez had already indicated that the period could extend over two years. Given its desire to stabilize itself, Kabul is likely to insist on an extended time frame alongwith the immediate stoppage of outside interference.

In the event of the breakdown of the parleys, Pakistan would be the main loser. For one, it would possibly take the issue out of the purview of the parties concerned and brighten the prospects of a superpowers' deal. For another, it would provoke Soviet retaliation which may take any form, such as the stepping up of hot pursuit drive, bombing the rebels' sanctuaries, destabilizing Pakistan through the Afghan agents' subversive activities,[17] or resorting to 'gun and gold' strategy to incite the tribes in the border areas.[18] In both these eventualities, Islamabad's options are limited. Given the country's disturbed political scene, vulnerability of the sensitive border provinces to foreign influence, involvement of Afghan agents in terrorist activities in the country, and the lately renewed tension with India, Pakistan cannot afford to prolong the present stalemate nor can it be the permanent abode of the refugees. The presence of refugees on Pakistan's soil has made it a suspect in Moscow's eyes and a constant target of its fury. As such it has to give top priority to their speedy return.

---

* For a detailed analysis of the Geneva Accords. See Mehrunnisa Ali, 'Geneva Accords and the Superpowers', *Pakistan Horizon*, Karachi, Third Quarter, 1988. (Editor).

An accord on the Afghan problem would help in minimizing Pakistan's reliance on the US, salvage its non-aligned status and above all soften Moscow's stance. However, the question of relevance in this regard is how far Pakistan can go at the seventh round without getting a green signal from Washington. The package has indeed restrained the regime's options. It cannot go ahead on its own without displeasing America. In the event of Islamabad going off the track, Washington could resort to arm-twisting by stopping arms supply and aid as it did in the mid-sixties and seventies. Suffice it to say that the US armoury has not forestalled external invasion in the past nor can it now avert a Soviet sponsored attack, the possibility of which exists as long as the Afghan issue continues to bedevil Pakistan-Soviet relations. Washington may also choose a different course, given the past history of its interventionist policies in the third world,[19] particularly the Muslim countries (as lately revealed by the Teheran Documents),[20] possibility of Washington toppling a 'deviant' regime of Pakistan cannot be ruled out. Thus Washington's intolerance to Islamabad's 'deviation' could be risky for the regime, but more hazardous for the country's security and survival would be Moscow's retaliation to Pakistan's 'obduracy'. When assessed in the context of the enhanced possibility of Moscow's offensive in the event of Geneva VIIs failure, Pakistan's *entente cordiale* with the US ceases to be a less risky course.

Lacking in parity of strength and usefulness, an association between a superpower and a small state proves disadvantageous for the latter as there always exists a possibility of the big power using the weak for its own benefits. The link could be more unequal and unnatural if it lacks common objectives and perceptions. Pakistan-US threat perceptions[21] do not converge at global and regional levels. America perceives the USSR as its real ideological and political rival posing a threat to Western security. Pakistan does not look at the Soviet Union from the US-projected angle. Although Soviet intervention in Afghanistan has forged an identity of views, both governments observe the development from different perspectives. The Pakistan government deems the presence of Soviet forces dangerous for the country's security. The US, on the other hand, perceives Soviet intervention as a threat to Western economic and security interests in the Gulf. Pakistan views the crisis in the context of its impact on its own security, while the US looks at it from the global perspective in the context of its competition and rivalry with Moscow.

The divergence is visible on a regional plane also. For Pakistan, India has been and will continue to be a security threat. The US neither shares Pakistan's fear nor is willing to support it against that threat. Besides their different cognition of the Middle East issue and Israel, both do not share one another's perception about the Iranian revolution. Washington considers Iran's revolution a threat to its own interest as well as to the stability of pro-American Arab regimes in the Gulf. It has made no bone about its intention to undo it. Given the US designs against the Khomeini regime and its support to Iraq in the Gulf War, Washington could seek Islamabad's 'collaboration' for any adventurist move against Iran. Coming in the wake of Teheran's recent thrust in the Gulf War and its advance towards the mouth of Shatt-ul-Arab; the movement of the US fleet around the Strait of Hormuz and in the Gulf, preceded by its latest air strikes against Libya, are ominous portents for Pakistan. Owing to its special relationship with the US, Islamabad could be forced to be a party to an American offensive against Iran. The extent of freedom Islamabad enjoys in foreign policy matters was lately instanced when it refrained from condemning the US attack on Libya.

These being the compulsions, the sooner Pakistan balances its obvious leanings towards the US, the better it is for its long term national security interests. A negotiated settlement of Afghanistan would indeed help lessen Pakistan's reliance on the US. However, of particular significance in this regard would be Moscow's positive role. By softening its stance towards Islamabad, it could induce the latter to gradually lower its special links with Washington. Since it cherishes the prospects of Pakistan's 'exit' from the US 'camp' it can, by restraining its wrath, make that 'exit' possible. For the tougher it gets towards Islamabad, the closer it pushes it towards Washington. Mindful of this, it has so far restrained its reaction to prevent the crystallization of a US-Pakistan-China axis in the vicinity. However, Moscow's continued restraint depends on the Pakistan government's behaviour. That it would not indefinitely tolerate Islamabad's persistent 'adamancy' is allusive from a Soviet official's remarks. Accusing Pakistan of taking unfriendly actions against his country one after another, he averred: 'In fact we have carefully refrained from taking any action that might have even indirectly destabilised Pakistan....They can't expect us to remain friendly if they do not reciprocate.'[22] Hence the rationale for an accommodation with Moscow. Besides easing tension on the border, it would go a long way in minimizing Pakistan's need for US support. A patch-up with Moscow would not affect Pakistan's amity with China. For one, Beijing itself being engaged in the normalization process with Delhi and Moscow, would not mind such a move. Since the presence of Soviet forces in the Wakhan strip has exposed its borders to Soviet danger, it would welcome any accord that leads to Soviet disengagement from Afghanistan. Besides, Moscow has never objected to the Pakistan-China friendship the way it has to the former's solidarity with the US. It is in the context of the Afghan quagmire that it looks askance at the Islamabad-Beijing collaboration. Despite its rift with China and its aversion to the Sino-American convergence of interest, Moscow perceives America and not China as its real adversary.

As for the fear shared in a few quarters that an improved understanding with the Soviet Union would facilitate its ideological expansion and pave the way for an Afghan-type revolution, it might be clarified, in the first place, that Pakistan does not have to replace the friendship of one power with the cordiality of an other. Instead of closely associating with one superpower, it should work for an equation with both. Moreover, owing to the dissimilarity in Pakistan and Afghanistan situation, consequences of an Islamabad-Moscow accommodation can hardly be the same as those ensued from the Soviet-Afghan friendship. Moscow worked in Afghanistan for years overtly and covertly involving itself in its economic development and in the organization and training of its armed forces. Taking advantage of the Western neglect of Afghanistan, it eventually succeeded in planting its roots there. Given the training and orientation of Pakistan's armed forces and civil bureaucracy over whom Soviet influence is not strong, Pakistan is less exposed to such Soviet penetration in the near future. If India, or for that matter Iraq and Syria, despite their close ties with the USSR could remain non-marxist, so could Pakistan, provided it puts its house in order. An ideology, for its expansion, knows no geographical bound nor does it require a foreign sponsor. Having their genesis in the peoples discontent with the prevailing socio-economic order, revolutions start from within. By ensuring socio-economic justice and equal participation of the federating units under a democratic framework, Pakistan can protect itself against the foreign machination be it of Moscow or of Washington.

There is no denying that in this militarily bipolar world dominated by two superpowers competing for influence, a small strategically located state cannot have a risk-free course. There are less or more dangerous courses. Since the policy of friendship with the US, having its own pitfalls, is not at all less risky, Pakistan should adopt a policy which is least hazardous. Instead of becoming a party to Washington's global and regional plans for checkmating the Soviet influence, it should ensure its security by staying out of the superpowers' conflict, mending fences with Moscow and improving understanding with neighbours. A relaxed atmosphere in the region brought about by resolution of major conflicts would go a long way in guaranteeing Pakistan's security and stability.

NOTES

1. See article published in *Time* (Weekly), New York, 9 December 1985, Pakistan's Minister of State for Foreign Affairs described the article as 'Irresponsible'. *Dawn,* Karachi, 3 February 1986.
2. See, *South* (London), March 1985, p. 20. Soviet envoy Smirnov accused America of torpedoing the Geneva talks, *Dawn*, 30 May 1983.
3. *The Washington Post* report of 30 March in *Dawn*, 31 March 1986. *Pravda,* on 2 April, criticized the US decision. Ibid., 3 April 1986.
4. *Dawn*, 13 March 1986 and *Dawn Economic and Business Review*, 8–14 March and 29 March–4 April 1986.
5. Jean Kirkpatrick's statement, *The Pakistan Times,* Lahore, 13 March 1985.
6. *Dawn*, 2 June 1985.
7. *Pravda* quoted in *The Muslim,* Islamabad, 22 November 1984.
8. See Mehrunnisa Ali, 'Pakistan Soviet ties since the Afghanistan crisis', *Asian Survey,* Berkeley, September 1983, pp. 1025–42.
9. *The Pakistan Times*, 19 November 1984.
10. Moscow accused Pakistani forces of killing twelve Soviet soldiers at Matani on 27 April 1985. This was denied by the Pakistan Government; see for Soviet protest and Pakistan denial *Dawn*, 10, 15, and 21 May 1985.
11. *The Muslim,* 4 February 1984.
12. Ibid., 18 July 1985.
13. A Soviet high official has said, 'Taking our troops out of Afghanistan... is one of our top priorities', *Dawn*, 17 November 1985; see also *Economist,* London, 31 August 1985.
14. Cordovez statement, *Dawn*, 18 April 1986.
15. *Dawn*, 7 April 1986.
16. Official circles in Islamabad were once speaking of a time-frame of six months, ibid., 18 April 1986.

17. Arbab Mohammad Jehangir Khan, Chief Minister of NWFP alleged that sabotage activities in Peshawar (bomb blasts) were carried out by infiltrators 'coming from across the border', ibid., 28 January 1986.
18. A Pakistan border official said that during the current year 500 rifles were given by the Afghan Government to the supporters of tribal leaders, Wali Khan Kukikhel who recently led the Khyber insurgency, ibid., 2 November 1985. It was also reported that 400 Soviet officers had entered the Khyber Agency. The Pakistan Government, however, denied the report, ibid., 20 January 1986.
19. Thomas L. Brewer, *American Foreign Policy*, Prentice Hall Inc., New Jersey, 1980, see chapter 10, pp. 212–30.
20. Document No. 45 of the *Teheran Documents* (seized from the American embassy in Teheran by the Iranian students) deals with US involvement in Pakistan's politics during 1977–79.
21. See Mehrunnisa Ali, 'Threat perception by the US and Pakistan' in Rais Ahmed Khan (ed.), *Pakistan-United States Relations*, Area Study Centre for Africa, North and South America, Islamabad, 1983, pp. 183–201.
22. Soviet Deputy Foreign Minister's interview in New Delhi on 1 September 1984, partly published in *The Muslim*, 6 September 1984.

18

Pakistan's Case Study for a Nuclear Security Guarantee*

Zafar Iqbal Cheema

In the past few years Pakistan has undergone intense pressures to thwart its determined efforts, aimed at building up a modest nuclear programme for peaceful purposes.

Pakistan happens to be the most directly and adversely affected country by the development of nuclear capability by India. The Indian nuclear explosion in May 1974 exacerbated the politico-strategic imbalance in South Asia and added immensely to Pakistan's predicament, making its security dilemma more complex and acute. Expressing Pakistani fears, Zulfiqar Ali Bhutto, the then Prime Minister of Pakistan, said: 'A more grave and serious event has not taken place in the history of Pakistan'.[1]

After initial exclamations, Pakistan attempted to adjust to the new realities by dispassionately probing into a few but viable policy options. These options which meant to neutralize the nuclear threat or blackmail from India, included: working on a diplomatic pursuit to contain the transformation of India's nuclear capability into a nuclear weapons capability by securing South Asia a Nuclear-Weapon-Free-Zone (NWFZ) through the UN General Assembly; or seeking the umbrella of a nuclear security guarantee of bilateral or multilateral character from the Nuclear Weapon States (NWS); or else, to develop a nuclear potential, though peaceful, but convertible into a military one, if its aforesaid diplomatic options fail to materialize. Pakistan's case for the

* Vol. xxxix, No. 4, 1986.

availability and the feasibility of a nuclear security guarantee is explored in the succeeding paragraphs.

Soon after the Indian nuclear explosion, Pakistan's Prime Minister stated that the country would prefer to seek a nuclear umbrella of all the five permanent members of the UN Security Council; or failing that, at least from one of them. There are, however, some important questions to be answered in this respect. First, are security guarantees against a nuclear threat or attack feasible under the current global circumstances? We are no longer living in the era of cold war, in which after the first Chinese nuclear explosion at Lopnor in 1964, the US President declared: 'the nations that do not seek national nuclear weapons, can be sure, if they need our strong support against some threat or nuclear blackmail, then they will have it'.[2] For extending a security guarantee to a Non-Nuclear Weapon State, a nuclear power has to keep in mind many other considerations of international politics. Second, a question arises about the form and credibility of a nuclear security guarantee and how would it materialize in case of an actual nuclear attack on a Non-Nuclear Weapon State (NNWS)? Third, can a security guarantee be available to a country like Pakistan which has not yet signed the NPT and under what conditions? The answers to some of these questions would determine whether such a policy option is practicable for Pakistan or not.

The concept of nuclear security guarantee to the NNWS by a Nuclear Weapon State (NWS) against a nuclear threat or attack encompassed the international non-proliferation efforts which began in the mid-1960s. During the NPT negotiations, the NNWS stressed that if they were to forego the right to equip their defence with national nuclear weapons, they should be 'compensated' by other measures that would ensure their security against a nuclear attack or threat.[3] This compensation was to be given in the form of a security guarantee through the UN Security Council by the NWS, party to the NPT. The NPT by itself does not include any provision incorporating a security guarantee to the NNWS who would sign the treaty, and therefore relinquish the right to manufacture or acquire nuclear weapons. The three depositary states of the NPT i.e., USA, USSR, and UK, pledged to provide such a guarantee through the UN Security Council as was visualized in the NPT negotiations. On 17 June 1968, five days after the NPT text was endorsed by the UN General Assembly, the three depositary states made identical but unilateral declarations in the Security Council, offering security guarantees to the NNWS, parties to the NPT, against an aggression with nuclear weapons or a threat of such an aggression.[4] In these unilateral declarations, each of the depositary states undertook to act immediately through the UN Security Council in case of a nuclear aggression or threat, to ensure that the Security Council would give immediate help to the victim in accordance with the UN Charter. The declarations confirmed the natural right of self-defence, individual or collective, as provided in Article 51 of the UN Charter. These declarations were supplemented by UN Security Council Resolution 255, adopted on 19 June 1968, which undertook to provide or support immediate assistance to NNWS, party to the NPT, that faced a nuclear aggression or threat. Security Council Resolution 255 recognized that:

> The aggression with nuclear weapons or the threat of such aggression against a NNWS would create a situation in which the Security Council and above all, its NWS (Permanent members) would have to act immediately in accordance with their obligations under the UN Charter.[5]

The resolution welcomed:

> The intention expressed by certain states (USA, USSR and UK) that they would provide or support immediate assistance, in accordance with the Charter, to any NNWS party to the NPT, that is a victim of an act or an object of a threat or aggression in which nuclear weapons are used.[6]

The resolution also reaffirmed in particular:

> The inherent right, recognized under Article 51 of the UN Charter, of individual or collective self-defence if an armed aggression occurs against a member of the UN until the Security Council has taken measures necessary to maintain international peace and security.[7]

The resolution was passed by ten votes in favour (Canada, Denmark, Ethiopia, Hungary, Paraguay, Senegal, Taiwan, the UK, the USA, and the USSR). The following five abstained: Algeria, Brazil, France, India, and Pakistan.[8]

Now the fundamental question arises once again: Is the security guarantee contained in UN Security Council Resolution 255 and the three-powers' declarations a 'compensation' credible enough on the basis of which the NNWS like Pakistan are required to sacrifice their inherent right to equip their defence with nuclear weapons, if it becomes absolutely imperative? In the first instance, there is no precise form in which the security guarantee contained in the UN Security Council Resolution 255 is available to the NNWS against nuclear aggression or a threat of that. It is not specified in these documents as to who would provide the security guarantee and how it would be provided in case of a nuclear aggression or threat of that, nor is it mentioned whether the guarantee is multilateral or unilateral in nature. There is no automatic procedure in which the guarantee is to be realized in practice. UN Security Council Resolution 255, while recognizing that a nuclear aggression would create a qualitatively new situation in which the Security Council and its permanent members would have to act in accordance with their obligations under the UN Charter, welcomed the intention expressed by certain states (UK, USA, and the USSR in their unilateral declarations) to provide or support immediate assistance to the NNWS and reaffirmed their right of self-defence.

It is to be recalled here that Chapter VII Article 51 of the UN Charter has already recognized the right of self-defence by any state, individually or collectively, till the UN Security Council provides for collective measures to prevent or remove the threat to international peace and security. However, under the Charter, the assistance to the country attacked is not contingent on the nature of the aggression; whether nuclear or conventional, in fact it may mean both. So, UN Security Council Resolution 255 does not envisage a new eventuality nor does it accompany any new commitment or a specific duty undertaken to forestall nuclear aggression against NNWS. The views expressed from time to time by the US official spokesmen as well as the Congressmen are worth noting in this respect. It is insisted that the guarantee given by the US in the UN Security Council for the protection of the NNWS against a nuclear aggression or threat, implies no new duties or promise for the US except perhaps, the duty to inform the Security Council if the possibility mentioned in Resolution 255 were to become a fact.[9] In fact, the resolution has simply re-emphasized certain aspects already covered by Chapter VII of the UN Charter. The only new thing it contained is that it restricts the right of all UN members to benefit from the security guarantee, as it applies only to the NNWS party to the NPT.

Whatever little validity existed in the unilateral declarations of the three depositary states of the NPT has been lost by the interpretation of the depositary states. The declarations are not even recognized as 'unilateral'. Each of the states i.e. UK, USA, and the USSR made the declaration because the other two have made a similar one. In a hearing before the foreign relations committee of the US Senate, Mr Dean Rusk, forcefully insisted that the guarantee contained in the declarations given in the UN Security Council is not unilateral and that, it is limited by the right of veto.[10] Plainly speaking, the declarations which are meant to provide the security guarantee to the NNWS againt a nuclear aggression or threat, are only a type of implicit agreement concluded in an unusual form. They are without any binding obligations undertaken by the declaring states. The declaring states have only shown their desire to act through the UN Security Council but also in the normal way. Thus, any action taken by the UN Security Council under Resolution 255 is bound to have the consenting vote (affirmative) of its permanent members. Keeping in mind the past record of the UN Security Council and the practices regarding the exercise of veto power, one can work out the incredibility of the security guarantee provided in Resolution 255 and the tripartite declarations made in this respect.

What adds further uncertainty is the fact that France was not among the sponsors of the resolution and it even abstained from voting on the resolution. The PRC had not occupied its seat in the Security Council till then, although it had become a nuclear power. No UN decision concerning the security guarantee to the NNWS against a nuclear aggression or threat can be put into effect without the approval of these states. UN Security Council Resolution 255 and the unilateral declarations of the three depositary states have also not catered for a protracted conventional war between a NWS and a NNWS say, like the Vietnam war, which could have escalated and may have led to the use of nuclear weapons by the NWS (the US in this case).

The last but an important factor, which injects all the more incredibility in the UN security guarantee, is that the NWS parties to the NPT have not renounced the use of nuclear weapons against the NNWS. It reflects not only the insincerity but also the unreliability of the three depositary powers regarding the provision of a nuclear security guarantee by them. A 'negative security guarantee' by the nuclear-weapon-powers that they would not use nuclear weapons against NNWS, would have made the UN security guarantee system more acceptable to the NNWS in order to forego their right to develop or acquire nuclear weapons. A proposal for a negative security guarantee was presented by Switzerland and Romania in the NPT discussions, according to which the NWS were to undertake 'formally and solemnly' not to use the nuclear weapons against the NNWS party to the NPT. The proposal was rejected by the US who had long before officially stated (in a special message by the US President to the Congress on 28 March 1961), that it would take 'whatever action with whatever weapons are appropriate', in the event of an aggression which could not be countered by conventional forces.[11] On 1 February 1966, the Soviet Union proposed a modified version of the earlier proposal (Swiss and Romanian), generally known as the 'Kosygin formula'. Under this formula, the Soviet Union showed its willingness to accept a clause in the NPT forbidding 'the use of nuclear weapons against non-nuclear countries, parties to the NPT, and not having nuclear weapons on their own territories'.[12] The Soviet alteration was intended to exclude states like West Germany which did not possess but did have nuclear weapons on their territories. The Kosygin formula was widely acceptable except to the US and its NATO partners which had nuclear weapons on their territories under the command of NATO forces. Once again, on 9 May 1966, the PRC unilaterally made a solemn declaration that at no time and under no circumstances would it be the first to use nuclear weapons. However, the PRC invited other NWS to make identical declarations. The US, however, remained unwilling to relinquish the first use of nuclear weapons.[13]

The question of security guarantees once again figured in the NPT review conference in May 1975. There the proposal for the negative security guarantees in the form of legally binding undertakings was widely supported. A group of eleven NNWS suggested that an additional Protocol III to the NPT should be added under which the NWS states were to undertake that 'never and under no circumstances' would they use or threaten to use nuclear weapons against the NNWS party to the treaty whose territories were 'completely free from the nuclear weapons' and to refrain from the first use of nuclear weapons against the NNWS party to the NPT.[14] The proposal was rejected by the US taking the plea that such commitments, undertaken on a global basis, would not serve the purpose of non-proliferation and universal adherence to the NPT. According to the US, renouncing the option of the first use of nuclear weapons, would be equivalent to accepting a 'self-denying ordinance that weakens deterrence'. The US would therefore, be prepared to make use of nuclear weapons should it 'be faced with serious aggression likely to result in defeat in any area of very great importance...in terms of foreign policy'.[15]

In lieu of the US objections to the negative security guarantee, no common agreement could be concluded in this regard. It would have been much better if the three depositaries, or all the NWS, would have undertaken to provide security guarantees in the actual body of the NPT or in a separate multilateral treaty, including binding obligations with completely worked out means and procedures, to protect the NNWS from nuclear attack or threat. This would have enhanced the utility of the UN security guarantee system for the nuclear abstaining states.

For Pakistan to avail the benefits of an international nuclear security guarantee from the three depositary powers, collectively, as stipulated in UN Security Council Resolution 255 is a remote possibility. In the first instance, Pakistan has not signed the NPT and the security guarantee visualized in Resolution 255 can only be enjoyed by a NNWS, party to the NPT. To be more accurate, such a guarantee is a compensation to those states who undertake, by signing the NPT, to abstain from developing or acquiring nuclear weapons. Thus, for Pakistan to seek the nuclear umbrella of the UN Security Council requires a major policy change on its part, i.e. a willingness to sign the NPT. It is beyond doubt that Pakistan has never opposed the objective for which the NPT stands. Pakistan not only provides whole-hearted backing to the non-proliferation efforts but its nuclear power programme is subjected to the international safeguards exercised by the IAEA, except a small uranium enrichment plant at Kahuta. Pakistan refuses to sign the NPT because India has not signed it in the first place. Policies of both the states are thus interlinked in this connection.

After the Indian nuclear explosion of May 1974, it has become crystal clear that India opposed the NPT to make a breakthrough in nuclear military technology under the guise of principles. It made non-proliferation contingent upon disarmament and insisted that so long as the nuclear weapon powers did not stop 'vertical proliferation', they have no right to ask for 'horizontal non-proliferation'. An American delegate aptly told his Indian counterpart that, 'by making non-proliferation contingent upon disarmament, you are making sure that you get neither'.[16] It has now become certain that India will not sign the NPT under any circumstances. In fact, the former Indian Prime Minister, Mr Desai, stated that India has become a nuclear power and so there is no question of its signing the NPT but he stressed that Pakistan should sign it. The policies of Indira Gandhi, and now that of her son, Prime Minister Rajiv Gandhi, are no different from that. In fact, much of the unsafeguarded nuclear programme of India and its military potentiality was developed under Mrs Gandhi's stewardship. Mr Rajiv Gandhi is reportedly considering to openly unleash his country's nuclear military programme under the guise of alleged presumptions that Pakistan is likely to go nuclear.[17]

The fundamental question that arises at this point is: Should Pakistan sign the NPT in order to compensate itself with a security guarantee provided by UN Security Council Resolution 255 against a probable Indian nuclear attack, threat or blackmail? As a matter of rational policy, no sane statesman or strategist would expect Pakistan to trade its national security for an ambiguous, imprecise, incredible and non-committal security guarantee provided in the UN Security Council Resolution. As analysed earlier, the security guarantee given by the UN Security Council is not automatic. It is to be translated into an action plan when a nuclear threat or attack actually materializes, and that action plan has to come through the UN Security Council which remains paralysed too often because of the veto mechanism. Pakistan already has bitter experience of the veto system in the case of the Kashmir dispute and its tragic dismemberment in the 1970–71 crisis.

Hypothetically, even if none of the permanent members of the UN Security Council exercises a veto to pre-empt the materialization of the security guarantee under Resolution 255 the decisions of the Security Council are normally too delayed to effectively manage a conflict. Indecisiveness on the part of the Security Council would be increased in the case of a conflict where nuclear aggression or a nuclear threat is involved. The Security Council so far has no experience of how to handle such a situation. The greater the delay in the expected action to forestall a nuclear aggression, the more catastrophic would be the consequences. Finally, India is not a party to UN Security Council Resolution 255 which provides a security guarantee against nuclear aggression or threat as India was not a nuclear power at that time. Moreover, New Delhi has not shown any willingness to subscribe or respect the above security guarantee, nor has it renounced the option of the first use of nuclear weapons.

Pakistan did not receive a welcoming response from the nuclear powers, including India, when in 1976 it presented a draft resolution in the political and security committee of the UN General Assembly on strengthening of the security of the NNWS. The issue was once again taken up in the 1977 session of the UN General Assembly with no more encouraging results. The political and security committee of the UN General Assembly on 17 November 1977, adopted Pakistan's draft resolution by 86 votes in favour to none against with 36 abstentions.[18] Under the text of the draft resolution, the General Assembly was to affirm the provisions of the resolution, which requested the Nuclear-Weapon-States,

> to consider undertaking, as a first step towards a complete ban on the use or threat of the use of nuclear weapons, without prejudice to their obligations arising from treaties establishing nuclear-weapon-free-zones, not to use or threaten to use nuclear weapons against non-nuclear weapon states not parties to the nuclear security arrangements of some nuclear weapon powers.[19]

Presenting his government's argument, the Pakistan delegate took the plea that, since the NPT did not contain adequate assurance for the NNWS, the negative security guarantee was an essential element in the concept of non-proliferation of nuclear weapons.[20] The draft resolution could not get the expected support from the NWS. The PRC was the only nuclear weapon power which voted for Pakistan's resolution while all others abstained. Most of them took the argument that the idea behind Pakistan's resolution was good, no doubt, but they could not go along with its formulation. The US delegate, C.L. Flowerree, contended that assurances regarding the non-use of nuclear weapons against the NNWS would no doubt complement the global non-proliferation efforts, but a more satisfactory approach to the question of security assurances would be one which increased the confidence of all the nations that their security was adequately protected, promoting stability of the international system as a whole. The US delegate further stated that the proposed resolution did not fully meet the concerns of his government regarding the maintenance of the existing security arrangement, and that there were imprecisions in the formulation of the proposed resolution which made it difficult to accept.[21] The British representative said that the widest possible adherence to the NPT would provide the widest possible security for all the parties and so, his delegation abstained. The rest of the nuclear weapon powers also abstained, taking almost similar arguments. Pakistan promised to make the formulation of the resolution more precise in the next session.

Pakistan's resolution once again figured prominently in the 1980 session of the UN General Assembly. Under the Pakistan-sponsored text, the General Assembly reaffirmed the urgent need to reach an agreement on effective international arrangements to assure the NNWS against the use or threat of the use of nuclear weapons.[22] The Assembly appealed to all the states, particularly the NWS to show the political will to reach an agreement on a common approach which could be included in an international instrument of legally binding character and recommended that the committee on disarmament continue negotiations on the subject.[23] The resolution was approved by a vote of 121 in favour to none against, with 24 abstentions. The principal Western objection to the Pakistan resolution was that it prejudged the work of the committee on disarmament. Among the NWS only the USSR and the PRC supported Pakistan's resolution, whereas India along with the USA, the UK, and France abstained.[24] Since then Pakistan's proposal is regularly on the annual agenda of the UN General Assembly but without any concrete results. In a nutshell, Pakistan should not harbour a hope that on this basis it would be able to seek approval of the nuclear weapon powers to secure a nuclear security guarantee. They would not bind themselves in the UN General Assembly to renounce the option of the first use of nuclear weapons. At least India would not do so under any conditions. The impracticability of a credible security guarantee through the UN Security Council has already been explored in the previous paragraphs. So, for Pakistan, this part of the option is virtually closed.

However, the remaining part of the option can be explored, i.e. Pakistan's chances to seek a multilateral or a bilateral security guarantee directly from the NWS. It may be mentioned that such a security guarantee has to be definite, credible, absolutely clear with procedures and framework for the definition of a nuclear aggression, threat or blackmail and, of course, an unfailing method for its materialization into a workable deterrence or nuclear strike if deterrence were to fail. Now, let us see the possibilities of such a guarantee. Changes in the structural processes of international and regional politics, since the beginning of the 1970s, have rendered any chances of a multilateral security guarantee for Pakistan impossible. There is no possibility that either the US and the USSR would offer a joint security guarantee to Pakistan against a likely nuclear attack or threat from India or the US and the PRC would provide such a guarantee in concert with each other despite their rapprochement in recent years. There may be a chance if the US and the PRC assume identical positions in a future South Asian crisis as happened in 1970–71. But there is no possibility that they would enter into a written agreement incorporating a nuclear security guarantee for Pakistan. One should never consider a possibility in which France and Great Britain could be a party to a multilateral security guarantee to Pakistan, as none of these powers pursue global interests of such a nature in which Pakistan could fit. The only possibility, if any, is that of a security guarantee on a bilateral basis.

Once again, France and Great Britain would not, and Pakistan probably would never look to them to provide a bilateral security guarantee against a nuclear threat by India or anybody else. Pakistan has never had cordial enough relations with the Soviet Union to sustain such a burden. In fact, after the Soviet military intervention in Afghanistan, Pakistan is also exposed to the possibility of a nuclear threat, blackmail or intimidation from the Soviet Union itself. There are reports about the presence of Soviet nuclear weapons in Afghanistan as an integral part of the Soviet army divisions deployed there. There are only two possible alternatives to which Pakistan can look to seek a security guarantee directly against a likely Indian nuclear threat or attack, i.e., the US and the PRC. As a matter of principle, the US would not provide Pakistan with a security guarantee for a variety of reasons. Firstly, it is not definite that the US would extend a nuclear security guarantee beyond its existing commitments. This should be evident from a statement made in a White House debate by Hadley Bull. He contended:

> The United States is already over-committed, or at least would be over-committed if it added a blanket pledge to come to the rescue of any nation in the world which, while practicing nuclear abstention, becomes the victim of nuclear aggression or blackmail.[25]

As mentioned earlier, the US has even refused to accept the interpretation that the security guarantee provided in UN Security Council Resolution 255 creates any specific commitments for it on a unilateral basis. Under the United States' present bilateral and multilateral commitments given to its allies, the US would think hard to extend its deterrent guarantee to Pakistan in order to receive its signature on the NPT. On the other hand, Pakistan has not given any hint on the question of acceding to the NPT if the US provided it a security guarantee. Beyond this argument, there is neither a justification nor an incentive for the US to extend a security guarantee to Pakistan against possible nuclear aggression or blackmail by India. The history of the American involvement in South Asian affairs indicates that the US has always shown a preference for India rather than for Pakistan. In the mid-1950s, it went for the second best alternative (Pakistan), as it could not enlist the support of the biggest actor (India) of the region. At the outset of the Pak-US alliance, Washington knew well that Pakistan's major adversary is India, not communism or socialism. But when the crunch came, it tried to play the role of an honest broker rather than that of a committed ally. It has officially accepted the Indian hegemony in South Asia since Pakistan's dismemberment in the 1970–71 crisis and has quite often suggested to India that it should exercise a leading role in the region. So, the US would be unwilling to provide a security guarantee against India under the present conditions.

After the Soviet military intervention in Afghanistan, the geo-strategic importance of Pakistan has been revitalized in the US perceptions and a new mutuality of interests has developed. However, the $3.2 billion aid package, spread over a period of six years (1981–87) is primarily oriented towards the Soviet Union and falls short of a binding security guarantee for Pakistan. Besides, it also seeks to dissuade Pakistan from developing a nuclear military programme. Therefore, to think that the US would ever provide a security guarantee against India is just a fantasy.

Furthermore, there would be no credibility in the security guarantee provided by the US, even if available. The credibility of the US nuclear umbrella has been seriously diminished ever since Pierre Gallois expressed his fear in 1961 that 'America would never retaliate against Moscow just because she had invaded Europe' and suggested that an independent French retaliatory force was therefore, required.[26] It was the incredibility of the US security guarantee which animated France in the Gaullist era to develop an independent national nuclear deterrence. Since the fall of Vietnam and Cambodia (now Kampuchea), faith in the US guarantee has been severely shaken. If a superpower like the US cannot live up to its commitments in a limited conventional war, how can a state feel secure with its security guarantee in the event of a probable nuclear attack or threat which might escalate into a major war. If the US could abandon Indo-China to communism, which was the main obsession of its 'domino theory' and the 'containment doctrine', what is the surety that it would not abandon a state like Pakistan where its vital interests are not at stake? The credibility of a US guarantee is further reduced against a nuclear aggression or threat by India which is aligned to the Soviet Union with a treaty of peace, friendship and cooperation, which is a virtual defence treaty. It seems pertinent to mention here that the Soviet record of treaty observance with regard to its allies is far more impressive than that of the US. The Soviet alignment with India would inhibit the US to accept any interpretation of a given conflict-situation other than what would suit its own priorities and not the one which would put the US in an acid test to stand by its friend like Pakistan. So, once again the US security guarantee is no option for Pakistan, firstly because of its non-availability and secondly because of its unreliability, even if available.

Last remains the PRC and the extent to which Pakistan can look towards it to seek a security guarantee against a probable nuclear aggression or threat. After the separation of East Pakistan in 1970-71, the question of Pakistan's signing a defence pact with the PRC loomed large publicly. The arguments registered in favour of a viable Sino-Pakistan defence agreement were not just based on geographical contiguity but the entire range of a community of strategic and political interests. With India's explosion of a nuclear device in May 1974, the PRC came under strong pressure to demonstrate its prowess on behalf of its besieged friend. According to most of the South Asian experts, the PRC has no alternative under the present circumstances but to provide some kind of assistance or promise to Pakistan to wash away the psychological imprints of India's nuclear capability. In the words of J.E. Dougherty:

> If Peking abandons Islamabad, while the Soviet-Indian relationship thrives, the PRC will suffer a loss of political prestige in Asia. Sooner or later, China will either help Pakistan to match the Indian accomplishment or extend to Pakistan a guarantee or support comparable to that contained in the Soviet-Indian Friendship Treaty.[27]

According to a report appearing in the *India Quarterly*, Mr Bhutto's willingness to resume normalization talks with India after their interruption on the Indian nuclear explosion, was inspired by the fact that Pakistan had received a security guarantee from the great powers against any nuclear blackmail by India and that the implied security guarantee was provided by the PRC.[28] However, there were no official statements from the governments of Pakistan and the PRC on the question of a security guarantee given to Pakistan, nor were there any denials of the reports that such a guarantee has been worked out. Such a guarantee cannot be a child's play. Its implications would go far beyond the frontiers of the South Asian region.

The Indo-Soviet treaty of August 1971 was mainly concluded to counter any Chinese assistance to Pakistan in a South Asian conflict as was successfully demonstrated to Pakistan's detriment in the 1970–71 crisis. Because of its limited conventional and nuclear military potential as compared to the Soviet Union, the PRC could practically do nothing to save Pakistan from dismemberment, except giving wholehearted political and moral support. So long as India and the Soviet Union remain treaty partners, the PRC would think hard to extend a nuclear security guarantee to Pakistan against India. It is also to be kept in mind that the military pacts, conventional or nuclear, are not a part of the PRC's policy. On two occasions, the PRC took up arms (the Korean war and Himalayan war with India) only when its own frontiers were under direct threat. So, one cannot really conclude that the PRC would extend a nuclear shield to Pakistan against an Indian nuclear threat or Soviet nuclear blackmail and the nuclear shield provided by China would be credible enough to serve Pakistan's purpose. The only thing that the PRC could do is to provide nuclear expertise or other facilities to help Pakistan develop its own nuclear programme. There was some speculation in India in early 1975 that the PRC might support Pakistan to develop and test a nuclear explosive device. It was reported in the *Indian Express* that Mr Bhutto had requested the PRC to provide assistance in the nuclear field and Beijing had responded by dispatching a delegation of nuclear experts to Islamabad.[29]

Any international security guarantee to Pakistan against an Indian nuclear attack, threat of Soviet blackmail, provided by the US or the PRC, if any, should be made public so that none of the parties get locked into a position from which it would like to retreat in case of conflict. To make the adversaries cognizant of a likely deterrence or counter-deterrence and the extent to which it can be pursued, is one of the crisis management pre-requisites. It would reduce the eventualities in which the security guarantor would have to be called upon to honour the credibility of its promise. Pakistan has also to keep in mind that dependence on a security guarantee would restrict the independent course of its foreign policy. Independent pursuit of foreign policy implies not only avoidance of perpetual reliance upon outside help but a need to promote self-sufficiency in defence production and other related aspects. Since Pakistan is trying to follow a policy of non-alignment, it is incumbent to develop reliance on its own resources and capabilities. Pakistan's past experience has also shown that the small states have very little influence over the affairs of nuclear weapon powers. The membership of the regional defence alliances like SEATO and CENTO did not provide stipulated security in the event of crises faced by Pakistan. The NWS parties to these alliances interpreted the conflicts in the way that suited their priorities. It is but natural that in the event of a conflict-situation, each side first secures its own strategic interests and only then contemplates providing the degree of help it deems necessary at that time. The complex nature of international relations makes it uncertain that the guarantee would definitely materialize to the rescue of Pakistan. So, the best way to avoid the uncertainties of such a security guarantee is to develop an independent national capability, credible enough to counter the likely threat.

NOTES

1. The former Prime Minister, Z.A. Bhutto's statement in the National Assembly of Pakistan on 7 June 1974, quoted by Dilip Mukerjee, 'India's Nuclear Test and Pakistan', *India Quarterly*, New Delhi, XXX: IV (October–December 1974), p. 262.

2. James E. Dougherty and J.F. Lehman Jr. (eds.), *Arms Control for the Late Sixties*, D. Van Nostrand Company Inc., 1967, p. XXVI.

3. *IAEA, A Short History of Non-Proliferation*, International Atomic Energy Agency, Vienna, February 1976, p. 8.

4. George Fisher, *The Non-Proliferation of Nuclear Weapons*, Europa Publications, London, 1971, pp. 146–7.

5. J. Goldblat, 'The UN Security Council Resolution of 19th June 1968, and the Security of Non-Nuclear-Weapon States', *Nuclear Proliferation Problems*, The MIT Press, 1974, p. 240.

6. Ibid., pp. 240–41.

7. Ibid., p. 241.

8. Ibid., p. 237

9. George Fisher, op, cit., p. 148.

10. Ibid.

11. *World Armaments and Disarmament: SIPRI year book—1976*, Stockholm, p. 386.

12. Ibid.

13. R.B. Russel, *The United Nations and the United States Security Policy*, Brookings Institute, Washington, 1968, pp. 112–14.

14. *SIPRI year book—1976*, p. 384.

15. Ibid.

16. George Fisher, op. cit., p. 144.
17. *The Muslim*, Islamabad, 5 May 1985.
18. *Dawn*, Karachi, 19 November 1977.
19. Ibid.
20. *The Pakistan Times*, Lahore, 20 November 1977.
21. *Dawn*, 19 November 1977.
22. *The Muslim*, 14 December 1980.
23. Ibid.
24. Ibid.
25. Dougherty and Lehman (eds.), op. cit., p. 27.
26. George Quester, *The Politics of Nuclear Proliferation,* The John Hopkins University Press, Baltimore and London, 1973, p. 3.
27. James E. Dougherty, 'Nuclear Proliferation in Asia', *Orbis* (special issue), (Philadelphia), XIX: 3 (Fall 1975), p. 939.
28. Dilip Mukerjee, op. cit., p. 267.
29. *Indian Express,* New Delhi, 7 January 1975.

19

Pakistan and Western Europe (1975–86)*

Mehrunnisa Iqbal

The relations between Pakistan and Western Europe are largely determined by Pakistan's economic, social, and political conditions, and the attitude of Western Europe towards the third world countries. Another important factor influencing the outlook of Western Europe towards Pakistan is the Russian presence in Afghanistan, and Pakistan's decision to take on an enormous number of refugees.

With the end of the colonial empire in Southeast Asia, the political influences, power and interest of the colonial states in the area had also dwindled. Now, as such, none of the West European countries have a direct political ambition in this part of the world. Their interest in the area is primarily economic or in the context of East-West rivalry, and to some extent humanitarian.

Western Europe has acknowledged its dependence on the developing countries for its economic advancement. Nearly 40 per cent of its income comes from trade with this area. It needs dependable sources of energy and raw materials as much as outlets for its finished products.

A large number of West European entrepreneurs are concentrating on investments in the third world, since the European industries have reached a saturation point at home. Their future potential markets now profitably lie in the developing countries like Pakistan, who have a large population base.

* Vol. xxxix, No. 2, 1986.

Another important factor is that the period of economic depression is over in the West European countries and there has been a remarkable rise in their industrial output. Their foreign trade is moving ahead and the trade deficit is on the decline. Thus their economic growth, on the whole, is accelerating and they can now absorb larger amounts of imports than before.

It is being felt in the industrialized countries of Europe (the second world) that their interests are in growing contradiction with the first world (the superpowers). Therefore, it is felt among the second world countries that developing cooperation with the third world would be to the mutual benefit of both, and it could also be possible to bring about a new international economic order free from exploitation.

Pakistan, of all the Islamic bloc countries, is accorded special attention in Europe. According to Mr Claude Cheysson, the EEC Commissioner, 'Europe needs the goodwill of the Islamic country which has not chosen the path of fanaticism'.[1] Pakistan is basically an agricultural country, aiming at rapid economic development and improving the lot of the common man by eradicating poverty, disease, and illiteracy. It needs to acquire modern technology for modernizing the agricultural sector and to improve the necessary infrastructure to form the base for industrialization. Thus Pakistan seeks from the developed, technologically advanced European countries financial aid, technical assistance (and also cooperation for debt re-scheduling), transfer of technology, foreign investments, and favourable terms of trade.

Keeping in view the needs of Pakistan and the interest of Western Europe in the third world countries, the emphasis is more on the economic aspect of the relationship.

Financial Aid and Technical Assistance

West European assistance is made available to Pakistan, bilaterally, through the Aid-to-Pakistan Consortium, which has a majority of the West European countries as its members, and through other international bodies like the Asian Development Bank and the International Development Association.

Federal Republic of Germany

The Federal Republic of Germany (FRG) is the largest donor from Western Europe among the Aid-to-Pakistan Consortium countries. German aid is considered by far the 'safest' as Bonn's aid policy has a purely economic and humanitarian motivation with little or no political strings. Germany seeks no political advantages in the third world. The FRG favours actual development and its grants are for well-defined categories and projects and not for merely financing consumption. German assistance is made available by way of funds, soft term loans, commercial loans, and technical assistance. In the beginning, all German loans were untied, it was only much later that they became tied. The German interest rate is low at 0.75 per cent and re-payment time is fifty years whereas interest on export credit is nearly 11 per cent.[2]

German funds have been given in the fields basic for Pakistan's economic development, i.e. for infrastructure concerning energy, irrigation, transport, telecommunications, etc., and commodities supply like raw material and spare parts for industry. During the next couple of years, Germany will finance several multi-million DM projects only in the key sectors of energy, transport, and telecommunications.

Germany to date has assured funds amounting to more than 2.7 billion DM. Another 300 million DM has been earmarked for other forms of bilateral cooperation like aid for Afghan refugees and food and humanitarian assistance. General credit assurance given by West Germany amounted to nearly 2.5 billion DM. This is besides the funds made available for debt re-scheduling and 200 million DM for the Indus Basin Development Fund.[3]

Some of the important projects, past and present, for which the FRG has given fund assurances are the expansion of Faisalabad's and Quetta's gas turbine power stations, supplementary projects of Tarbela Dam and the construction of power stations, canals and wells under the salinity control and reclamation programme (SCARP), and the Ghotki irrigation programme. German assistance was made available in setting up of Pakistan Fauji Fertilizer plants and loans have been advanced to meet foreign exchange of two gas turbines for Kote-Addu power station and building power stations and power supply lines from Mardan to Peshawar and Dadu to Khuzdar. Loans have been extended to PICIC for re-financing of investment to be used in expanding the small and medium-sized sector and also to IDBP. Pakistan Railways is being modernized with German assistance and assistance for establishment of an elaborate digital telecommunication system has been pledged. Interest free assistance of 10.6 million DM is being provided for training of power engineers and technicians.

West German technical assistance has been afforded mainly for rural development, forestry, and vocational training. Some major German-assisted projects are a timber processing centre in Peshawar, Multan agricultural training and advisory project, provision of instructors to staff a training institute in Lahore, supply of labour and workshop equipment for staff training and assistance to the Pakistan Forestry Institute, Peshawar, and assistance in improving the telecommunication system in Rawalpindi. Technical assistance has been made available for producing quality crops in Kaghan Valley, planning of a low pressure hydro-electric power station, technical training centres in Quetta and Peshawar, training of technical staff in metal and electro-technical sectors, Faisalabad training institute of WAPDA and many other vocational and technical training centres in various fields. A German organization called the Pak-German Technical Co-operation (GTZ) has undertaken various developing projects in Pakistan. It has also given a Rs 8.2 million grant to cover foreign exchange costs of studies for the necessary schemes.[4]

Germany provides scholarships for training of Pakistani specialists and managerial personnel in that country. Under the cultural protocol of 17 April 1985, eight scholarships to Pakistanis for postgraduate studies will be provided for 1986–87. A Society for Pak-German friendship and cooperation was formed in Bonn to foster closer ties and greater economic cooperation. The society has undertaken to create partnerships between the towns of the two countries. This town partnership would help in arranging the flow of technology from Germany to Pakistan on town-to-town basis.[5]

United Kingdom

Since independence, Britain has extended substantial amounts of aid to Pakistan. The total grant extended to Pakistan during 1975–86 amounts to more than £76.421 million. British aid to Pakistan per capita is higher than per capita aid to India. In 1978, all British outstanding loans amounting to £76.421 million were converted into grants.[6]

Now all British bilateral aid is in the form of grants. British grants are mostly spent on social projects which directly helps the poor section and on projects to improve Pakistan's infrastructure. British aid is often tied for it is utilized by Britain for promoting its exports to the recipient countries and for maintaining jobs for its workers inside Britain. British financial assistance, besides bilateral grants, is available in the form of Consortium loans, export credits, ODFC, MGB loans, and loans from British financial institutions.[7]

An amount of £70 million was granted for the agricultural sector to improve the irrigation and drainage scheme. In addition a sum of £50 million was also given to WAPDA and KESC to build electricity sub-stations. In 1980, the British Foreign Secretary signed a £9.6 million grant for the purchase of three cargo vessels from UK for the Pakistan National Shipping Corporation.[8] According to Sir Geoffrery Howe, the Secretary of State for Foreign Affairs of UK, the British government had made extra provisions in its global aid budget to enable British firms to offer highly competitive financial packages when bidding for commercial contracts—which otherwise cannot be covered by bilateral aid programmes.[9] In 1986, Britain will provide £25 million in development aid. This fund will be utilized for projects under joint consideration of the governments of Pakistan and Britain mainly in the field of agriculture, irrigation, power generation, health, and education.[10]

Britain has given Pakistan valuable technical assistance and transfer of technology to Pakistan's industry was initially from the UK. Now Britain is prepared to enter into joint ventures in the industrial sector of Pakistan for providing technical collaboration, imparting technical know-how, and guidance in marketing and supply of machinery. British experts were the first to strike oil in Pakistan. English consultants have also made contributions in the Kalabagh Dam, surface drain in Sindh, the Karachi airport, mineral development, and rural electrification.[11]

Britain also supplied machinery, chemicals, and transport which contributed to the development of Pakistan's industrial base. For the heavy engineering complex at Taxila, Britain agreed to supply gas turbine generators. The British government has also given approval to the Commonwealth Development Congress to extend its operation to Pakistan, and Britain has extended educational aid for Pakistani students. By far the largest amount of students are in Britain, nearly 23 per cent. They are not only trained in education but in the fields of agriculture and engineering. An amount of £1.5 million was given for study purposes.[12] The Cambridge University has decided to take ten Pakistani students every year for post or undergraduate studies and it will bear the tuition fee.[13]

Italy

As a founding member of the Consortium, Italy has consistently and significantly contributed to the development process in Pakistan. Italian cooperation has been more in the form of aid than trade. Since 1960, Italian loans carry an interest rate of 7 per cent and has a short amortization period of ten years and they are generally tied to projects.[14]

In the last few years, Italy has allocated to Pakistan over $200 million in grants and soft loans. In the last Consortium meeting in 1986–87, Italy pledged additional resources of $50 million as soft loans and $10 million as grants. Substantial aid has also been made available in the form of export credit. Since 1980, Italy has pledged $170 million as state credit. In 1984, a credit of 100 million Italian liras was given, a major part of which has been utilized for various projects.[15]

A further amount of $4 million has been allocated to state mobile farms extension service project; it is the first of its kind in Pakistan, under a scheme prepared by the Fauji Fertilizer Company.[16] Agricultural machinery worth Rs 150 million was also provided for farmers of Gujrat District, and $66 million was contributed by the Italian government for a five year WHO/UNICEF joint nutrition support programme in Pakistan.[17] Italy is willing to offer an additional line of credit amounting to 100 billion liras. A soft loan of $60 million at a rate of 2.54 per cent was extended by Italy.[18] It is the first time that a soft loan has been extended in such a short time by any country.

Italian industry has contributed in various important development projects like the Tarbela Dam, FIAT tractors plant, the fertilizer plant, the Kote-Addu power plant and electrification of the Sibbi railway section. Italian assistance was instrumental in setting up a centre for training in agricultural machinery, its maintenance, and repairs. Centres for precision machineries and some vocal training centres are to be set up to train technicians for the leather and onyx industries. Italy will grant scholarships for training Pakistani technicians in Italy.[19] Several other joint ventures with Pakistani companies—particularly in the high technology sectors—are currently under consideration.

Netherlands

Pakistan is one of the six 'programme countries' currently eligible for Dutch bilateral aid. In 1985, bilateral aid from Holland was 58 million guilders; in 1984 it was 48 million guilders, showing an increase of 21 per cent. In 1987 it is expected to increase to 60 million guilders.[20] Besides grants, Dutch state loan is extended at 2.5 per cent with repayment within 30 years. Suppliers' credit is at 14 per cent and repayment within 6–11 years.[21]

In the seventies, Dutch financial assistance was aimed at infrastructure projects such as harbours, electricity schemes and telecommunication programmes. Now the emphasis has shifted to agricultural and rural development programmes and to some extent on development of small industry, research, education programmes, and humanitarian aid. About 70 per cent of Dutch aid concentrates on Balochistan and the NWFP, for improving conditions of small farmers, small scale irrigation and drainage projects, and development of livestocks. About 19 million guilders are invested in the Balochistan integrated area development project, 94 million guilders in a ground water investigation programme in the NWFP, and 10.5 million guilders have been given for the development of small scale industries in Punjab and the NWFP. Altogether some nineteen projects have been financed by Dutch bilateral aid.[22] Assistance has also been given for the import of potato seeds, fertilizers, machinery for land reclamation projects of WAPDA, and import of equipments for KESC. Future projects include fertilizer producing schemes, vegetable and food processing and horticultural research, collaboration for control of water-logging and salinity, and agro-based industries. Holland is also keenly pursuing an uplift programme for women in the third world. The first development programme of its kind, aimed at women's betterment, financed by the Dutch is the Allama Iqbal Open university project for women.[23]

Recently the aid to Pakistan and its utilization was under scrutiny in the Dutch parliament. Therefore, a number of Dutch MPs visited Pakistan with a view to survey the effects of Dutch aid to Pakistan. They were satisfied with the way the aid was being utilized by Pakistan and expressed their readiness to continue their aid to Pakistan.[24]

France

France is another important member of the Consortium. French aid is given in the form of commodities and project aid, state credit, suppliers' credit, and financial institutional credits. The state credit is given on an interest rate of nearly 3 per cent and repayment period is twenty-five years with an eight-year grace period. Bank credit is on very harsh terms carrying an interest rate of almost 11 per cent and amortization period of ten years.[25] Suppliers' credits are extended at an interest rate of 8.7 per cent with repayment within 5–10 years.

Uptil 1982, French loans to Pakistan amounted to US$520 million for various projects.[26] In 1983, France agreed to provide 190 million francs for the extension of the telephone system, distilling of canals in Sindh and the Punjab, improvement of irrigational aid, civil aviation, and the completion of Dadu-Jamshoro power stations. France has also contributed towards the construction of Tarbela and Chashma canal projects. It has provided credit facilities worth 470 million francs to Pakistan for the purchase of seven electric locomotives, equipment for the Karachi Airport, and other goods. Out of it, 200 million francs will be utilized, among other things, for the upgrading of the Dadu-Jamshoro sub-station and allocation to the IDBP. France is willing to assist Pakistan in the promotion of a wide range of products and equipment especially in the field of electronics, aviation equipment, oil exploration, heavy machinery, transport industry, and agro-based industry. French credits to Pakistan from 1975–86 amount to FF 2 billion. Recently for the first time France has offered a grant of seven million French francs to the KTC (Karachi Transport Corporation) by way of study of transport organization and development by the French state-owned company, BCOM.[27]

Switzerland

Switzerland is an observer at the Consortium, having contributed substantially to Pakistan's development through state and commercial credits. Switzerland was among Pakistan's first creditors to write-off its entire official aid/credits of $1.133 million outstanding against Pakistan as on 30 June 1977. Recently, Switzerland has offered a soft-term mixed credit of 80 million Swiss francs.[28] Part of the credit will be interest-free and part at a low interest rate for the development of agriculture and industry. Switzerland has financed a $2 million project for the provision of potable water in arid zones of Sindh. Economic assistance was also provided for covering grain shortage, dairy projects, forestry and farming techniques, and commercialization of farm products, and small scale industries. It is participating in the Left Bank Outfall Drain Project, for which a grant of $10 million was extended.[29]

Switzerland has provided Pakistan with valuable technical assistance in a wide range of activities. Pak-Swiss training centres were established, one at Karachi and another one in Lahore. Switzerland has also offered to provide financial and technical assistance to Pakistan for establishing a one-year course in industrial electronics and engineering at the Pak-Swiss training centre.[30]

Switzerland has also offered help for the development of the tourism industry in Pakistan. The Industrial Development Bank of Pakistan (IDBP) is expected to finalize shortly the arrangements for the transfer of technology from a Geneva-based Swiss firm known as the Technology For The People (TFTP). It has offered transfer of technology in such projects as would help to increase productivity in industrial enterprises. The technical assistance will come in capital-intensive industries which need sophisticated technology.[31]

Belgium

Belgium's aid is interest-free and has a repayment time of thirty years. Since 1965, state-to-state credit has been made available on a yearly basis. These credits are tied to soft loans and are advanced for the purchase of capital goods and industrial equipment required for Pakistan's industrialization.[32]

In 1984, a loan agreement between Pakistan and Belgium for 400,000 Belgian francs was made, repayable in thirty years with a grace period of ten years. This is the fifteenth credit extended by Belgium. The loans are to be re-paid in the form of Pakistani commodities.[33]

Belgium has given 100 million Belgian francs during 1985-86 for utilization in various infrastructure projects in addition to the 560 million already extended, bringing the total to 660 million Belgian francs.[34] One third of the loan was tied, and though it was for the public sector, it could be converted for the private sector as well. Belgium is also willing to allocate further soft loans for specific projects. It is cooperating to set up gas turbines to overcome the acute power shortage. However, the

660 million Belgian franc soft loan is still lying unutilized with the Pakistan government since the last five years.[35] Belgium also provides ten scholarships a year to Pakistani students.

Sweden

Sweden has been a major contributor to the Aid Consortium. Of late it prefers to give assistance in the form of technical know-how and manpower services. The latest offer lays emphasis on technical cooperation, training programmes for Pakistani nationals in Sweden and transfer of technology. Swedish consultants are helping WAPDA in water resource development in the north and also the civil aviation authorities to modernize the navigational aid system in the country. They have offered a half-a-million dollar grant and a team of experts for this purpose to the Civil Aviation Authority.[36]

Other Sources

To some extent aid, technical assistance, and transfer of technology is also made available to Pakistan from Ireland, Finland, Norway, and Denmark. The European Economic Community has also provided about $136 million worth of financial aid to Pakistan over the past nine years. This includes $24 million for development projects, $55 million for food, and $3 million for trade promotion programmes. The project aid has focussed largely on the development of Pakistan's rural energy resources. Some projects like the Karachi fish harbour, the Balochistan livestock and water supply scheme, and the rural electrification of 176 villages, promotion of the engineering sector through a series of coordinated measures have also been carried out with the Community's assistance. The EEC, between 1976–81, financed eight development projects for a total of $39 million, but these projects have suffered from major implementation delays and some financial problems. The counterpart funds obtained from the sale of EEC food aid, totalling about $40 million, has not been utilized for the financing of development projects but like the Belgian aid is lying unused in various bank accounts.

According to the findings of the Court of Creditors, in their report published in Brussels, a majority of the projects suffer from delays in implementation because of lengthy local administrative procedures for approval of the proposals. This is due to inadequate preparations at the initial stages of project formulation. Further, since the responsibility for various types of community aid to Pakistan and the various stages of implementation of the aid is divided between some ten divisions at the Commission, and as there is no local EEC delegation in Pakistan and the contacts too, between the Commission and Pakistan are not regular and coordinated, hence the delays. Another cause is unforeseen technical snags during the progress of work.[37] Delays in administrative approval and implementation do not help the case for foreign assistance, therefore the bureaucratic red-tapism needs to be cut, and the approval of projects speeded up.

The new five-year agreement signed in July 1985 between Pakistan and EEC countries provides for greater aid links and broader technical co-operation. EEC financing will be available for joint ventures in the field of applied research and sciences. Latest technology is also to be made available in agriculture, industry, fisheries, and animal husbandry. Assistance will be made available for the development and expansion of Pakistan's leather, engineering, fresh fruits, vegetable, gems and jewellery sectors. The EEC officials have also been urged to increase their current annual aid programme for Pakistan and continue its direct and indirect aid efforts for Afghan refugees.[38] The prospects that the EEC might be willing to step-up its aid in coming years are bright.

TABLE 1

**Outstanding External Indebtedness of Pakistan
as on 30 June 1983**

(Payable in Foreign Exchange) (Million dollars)

Lending Country/Agency	Debt Outstanding as on 30-6-1983		
	Disbursed and Un-disbursed outstanding		Total Debt
1	2	3	4
A. Consortium including outside Consortium Arrangements.			
Belgium – Capital Aid	... 20.7	6.4	27.1
– Export Credit	... 2.3	0.1	2.4
Sub-total (Belgium)	... 23.0	6.5	29.5

France	– Capital Aid	...	13.8	–	13.8
	– State-cum-Bank Export Credits		167.4	50.6	218.0
	– Financial Institutions	...	40.7	–	40.7
	Sub-total (France)	...	221.9	50.6	272.5
Italy	– Capital Aid	...	17.4	–	17.4
	– Export Credit	...	109.0	17.4	126.4
	– Sub-total (Italy)	...	126.4	17.4	143.8
Netherlands	– Capital Aid	...	122.3	29.9	152.2
	– Export Credit	...	8.2	2.1	10.3
	Sub-total (Netherlands)	...	130.5	32.0	162.5
U.K.	– Export Credit	...	2.6	2.5	5.1
	– CDFC	...	1.0	–	1.0
	– Tenant Guaranty Ltd. NGB Loan	...	–	–	–
	– UK Financial Institutions	...	97.8	51.8	149.6
	Sub-total (UK)	...	101.4	54.3	155.7

B. Non-Consortium Sources

Austria	– Capital Aid	...	–	1.7	1.7
	– Export Credit	...	1.3	–	1.3
	Sub-total (Austria)	...	1.3	1.7	3.0
Denmark	– Capital Aid	...	26.5	0.6	27.1
	– Suppliers' Credit	...	0.3	–	0.3
	Sub-total (Denmark)	...	26.8	0.6	27.4
Switzerland	– Export Credit	...	26.8	–	26.8
	– Guaranteed Credit	...	5.1	4.3	9.4
	Sub-total (Switzerland)	...	31.9	4.3	36.2

Source: *Pakistan Year Book 1984-85*, pp. 420–21.

TABLE 2
**Terms of Foreign Loans and Credits
Contracted by Pakistan**
(Million dollars)

Lending Countries/ Agency	1982-83			1983-84 (July-March)		
	Amount	Interest Rate Commission%	Amortization year	Amount	Interest Rate Commission%	Amortization year

1	2	3	4	5	6	7
A Consortium						
1 Belgium-Capital Aid	–	6	–	7.5	–	30
Export Credits	0.1	–	2	–	–	–
2. France-State Credits	13.1	3	17	14.4	3	25
Bank Credits	13.1	10.9	10	14.4	10.9	10
Suppliers' Credits	–	–	–	–	–	–
Financial Institutions	–	–	–	–	–	–
3. Germany-Capital Aid	47.9	0.8	50	77.9	0.75	50
Export Credits	–	–	–	–	–	–
Financial Institutions	4.7	10.5/10.75	9.5	9.4		
4. Italy-Capital Aid	–	–	–	–	–	–
Export Credits	23.4	7/7.75	10	13.3	7.5/10	10
5. Netherlands-Capital						
Aid	11.0	2.5	30	9.0	2.5	30
Suppliers' Credits	1.8	8 to 9	10	3.9	14	6 to11
6. UK-Export Credits	2.5	7.5	7	–	–	–
Financial Institutions	63.6	7 to 10	6 to 10	13.5	1.25	7
B. Non-Consortium						
1. Spain	–	–	–	1.7	11.4	7
2. Switzerland						
Guaranteed Credit	4.3	0 to 1	3.4	–	–	–

Source: *Pakistan Year Book 1984-85*, pp. 422–3.

TABLE 3
Grant Assistance Agreements Signed
(Million dollars)

Lending Country/Agency	1979-80	1980-81	1981-82	1982-83	1983-84 (Jul-Mar)
1	2	3	4	5	6
A. Consortium including outside					
Consortium arrangements					
Netherlands	9.683	10.359	–	7.2	2.7
Norway	14.813	12.692	12.349	11.9	11.5
Sweden	9.128	8.187	6.099	–	–
Switzerland	–	–	7.530	–	–
U.K.	28.951	–	8.904	15.5	29.4
E.E.C.	8.700	6.532	26.393	–	–

Source: *Pakistan Year Book 1984-85*, p. 425.

TABLE 4
Total Loans and Credits Contracted
(Million dollars)

Lending Country/Agency	1979-80	1980-81	1981-82	1982-83	1983-84 (Jul-Mar)
1	2	3	4	5	6
A. Consortium including outside Consortium arrangements					
(a) Bilateral :-					
Belgium	5.2	—	—	0.1	7.5
France	58.5	60.2	—	26.2	28.8
Germany	92.6	35.3	20.5	52.6	87.3
Italy	32.8	16.6	15.0	23.4	13.3
Netherlands	19.4	14.9	15.8	12.8	12.9
UK	53.0	31.4	23.8	71.1	15.5
B. Non-Consortium					
Austria	1.2	—	—	—	—
Denmark	0.6	5.4	—	—	—
Switzerland	2.7	—	0.1	4.4	—
Spain	—	—	—	—	1.7

Source: *Pakistan Year Book 1984-85*, pp. 426–7.

Nuclear Technology

West European countries have generally been willing to transfer modern technology in various fields but Pakistan's desire to acquire nuclear technology for peaceful purposes has met with considerable opposition and controversy. In 1976 Pakistan entered into an agreement with France for the supply of a nuclear reprocessing plant. This deal was approved by the IAEA board of governors and Pakistan's need was established at 8600 MW reactors between 1982–1990. Thereafter, Pakistan was to build 9600 MW and 7800 MW units to meet its energy requirements.[39] However, under tremendous US pressure France decided to discontinue the export of reprocessing facilities until further notice though it was announced that this decision would not affect the contract.[40] Instead France offered to replace the reprocessing plant producing pure plutonium with a co-processing plant producing mixed plutonium and uranium. This was not acceptable to Pakistan. In 1978, the French government suggested fresh talks as it found it difficult to honour the old agreement. This failure of France to honour the 1976 contract was a serious loss to Pakistan both financially and technologically. The fuel reprocessing plant was to be the key factor in the country's nuclear power programme; it could alone have satisfactorily solved the energy crisis. Failure to meet the target has caused a serious power shortfall, putting back Pakistan by ten years. Apart from energy considerations, Pakistan cannot afford to lag behind in nuclear technology, as its usage has also greatly increased in the fields of agriculture, medicine, and in the exploration of underground water resources. Therefore, Pakistan is determined to develop nuclear technology for peaceful purposes. In November 1985, the Paris based International Chamber of Commerce, in a judgement ruled that France should pay compensation to Pakistan to the tune of $300 million, for failing to deliver a 50–100 metric tons per year capacity reprocessing plant at Chashma, contracted by the Pakistan Energy Commission with Messers SGN of France.[41] The terms and conditions of the compensation have yet to be negotiated with France. As a compensation for the breach of the reprocessing agreement, France has offered a power plant to Pakistan. However, it is hoped that if no definite plan is worked out for the nuclear plant then France will provide funds for generation of thermal power.[42]

At present various European firms, including a French firm Framatone, have been maintaining interest in the set-up of a 900 MW nuclear power plant at Chashma. The most attractive offers are from West German and Belgian firms. It is now for Pakistan to decide whom to give the contract.[43]

West European countries have by and large upheld the right of every country to acquire nuclear technology for peaceful purposes. At the IAEA general conference at Vienna in 1977, the French and German representatives upheld Pakistan's view that nuclear preparation could not be prevented by placing an embargo on the transfer of nuclear technology and assistance.[44] Where Pakistan is concerned, the West has shied away from transferring nuclear technology, but their attitude is totally different towards India and Israel. France who had caved in under US pressure, was allowed by the USA to take over the contract for the supply of enriched uranium for the Indian Tarapur Nuclear Plant, as the US under its rules could not supply the fuel to India because India had refused to accept the safeguards for the facilities provided. France has also agreed to supply two nuclear reactors to Israel.

Foreign Investments

Pakistan needs to attract foreign investments in various sectors of the economy, which is profit motivated on the basis of full partnership and ultimately aiming at transfer of technology and mobilizing Pakistani indigenous resources.

Britain is the biggest foreign investor in Pakistan, accounting for nearly 60 per cent of all foreign investments. Most of the private British equity investments had their origin in pre-independence days, whereas other investors came in after 1947. Direct British investments amount to Rs 1209 million, while joint ventures account for Rs 365.5 million. Apart from this there are also the non-repatriable investments of overseas Pakistanis living in Britain amounting to Rs 429 million in a variety of projects.[45]

The total British investment amounts to £7000 million[46] of which the polyester plant near Shaikhupura is the largest investment. Most of the private British investment is in the vital and profitable fields of energy (natural gas and petroleum), chemicals, pharmaceuticals, food and beverages, and construction and engineering. Some important British companies operating in Pakistan are Glaxo, Fisons, Reckitt & Colman, etc. Possibilities of Ford and Morris undertaking joint ventures with Pakistani companies exist. A British firm was awarded a major contract in connection with the rehabilitation of the 54 year-old Sukkur Barrage.[47] Five large British companies have formed a Consortium to take part in the bid for the construction of the Kalabagh Dam, if and when decided by Pakistan.[48] Here a note must be made of the fact that remittances made to Britain from Pakistan by British investors were far more than the remittances made to Pakistan by Pakistani workers in Britain, thereby tilting the balance in favour of Britain. However, a number of pharmaceutical companies in Pakistan have re-invested the profits in the much needed manufacture of basic ingredients and chemicals for the production of drugs and medicines, thus reducing the imports of Pakistan.

A conference was held in Karachi in January 1986 under the auspices of the CBI (Confederation of British Industries) which was largely attended by British firms, who showed an interest in investments in the area of Pakistan's greatest need, i.e. power generation. BASATA (British and South Asian Trade Association) was also generating interest among British industrialists for investment in Pakistan.[49] The UK-Pak overseas Chamber of Commerce has also approved 450 projects to be launched in Pakistan in the coming years.

German foreign investments in Pakistan are in the form of direct equity participation, suppliers' credit, and transfer of technology investments, accounting for 3.0 per cent of the total foreign investments in Pakistan. It covers more then two dozen projects. The main fields of investment are electro-chemicals, ceramics and grinding equipment, chemical and pharmaceutical industries, machine building, and banking. Uptil March 1985, direct German investments amounted to DM 64 million, while re-investment was in addition to this. Between 1974–84, German equity investments were more than Rs 19 million and the suppliers' credit for purchase of machinery and equipment is over Rs 422 million.[50] Similar amounts have been invested in fifteen other sectors which include iron, steel production, extraction and processing of stones and gems. DEG of Cologne, which is West Germany's financing corporation for participation in developing countries, has helped in securing German industrial investments in Pakistan. Other German enterprises like BASF, Bayer, Hoechst, Siemens, etc. and some prominent German banking concerns have also made investments in Pakistan. Compared to other countries, especially India, German investment in Pakistan is very low. In November 1985, an industrial delegation from the FRG visited Pakistan to study the investment opportunities. Six German firms have shown interest in joint projects with Pakistani entrepreneurs in different fields. German investors are looking for long term investments in Pakistan.

Swiss investments in Pakistan account for 5.4 per cent of all foreign investments, being second highest. During the period of 1983-84, Swiss investment amounted to Rs 130 million, mainly in the field of pharmaceuticals.[51] French private investments are negligible. Until recently French companies operating in Pakistan were May & Baker and Roneo Alactel. In 1986, two new investments have been made: Prepac Pakistan (Pvt.) Ltd. with 25 per cent French interest and Generale Biscuit who have a 27 per cent holding in Continental Biscuits.[52]

A number of Dutch firms are already present in Pakistan and some have also set up Pakistani subsidiaries bringing the Dutch investment to 3.0 per cent.[53] With the signing of the new Economic Co-operation and Investment Protection Agreement small and medium-size Dutch firms will seek out partners and markets in Pakistan.

West European investments, it is hoped, will greatly improve with the insertion of an investment promotion clause in the new Pakistan-EEC agreement. It will create favourable conditions for stimulating and encouraging increased participation by foreign private firms, thereby increasing foreign financial investments in Pakistan.

In the past, foreign investment was mainly in the consumer goods industry sector, but now the trend is for capital and intermediate goods sector like steel, fertilizer, agricultural machinery, light and heavy equipment, transport equipment, oil and gas industries, cement and construction material, pharmaceuticals, chemicals, agro-processing, and textiles.

A number of West European countries are showing interest in investment in Pakistan. To better acquaint themselves with the investment climate, a delegation of investors from Europe under the aegis of the International Public Affairs Centre, Europe, visited Pakistan. The present investment policy of Pakistan is very liberal, there being many fields which are now open to foreign investors. The most important sectors are power generation and distribution, and agro-based industries. Another important sector in which foreign investment is welcome is petroleum, as 80 per cent of the oil-bearing areas still lie unexplored. Other areas being opened up for foreign investment, in order to bring about substantial change in Pakistan's economy, are banking and telecommunications.[54] With a view to attract foreign investments, an Export Processing Zone (EPZ) was set up. Originally it was meant for non-Pakistani foreign investors, especially well-known American, European, and Japanese firms to utilize this area for the assembly and manufacture of their products and then export or shipment to nearby Gulf markets and other destinations of the world. But the foreign investors did not respond favourably and since non-expatriate Pakistani residents' investments are insufficient, the EPZ authorities must find ways to attract foreign investors.

Now with a liberal policy, and new sectors open for investment what is most needed is to publicize these concessions available to foreign investors. Dr Langmann, head of the German investment delegation, who visited Pakistan in November 1985, suggested that good financial journalists (from abroad) be invited to Pakistan and told about the investment opportunities. In addition, Pakistan should also publicize in foreign newspapers through advertisements.[55]

Establishment of commercial centres in various European countries would greatly help in securing the much needed foreign investments. Agreements with European countries, like the agreement with Sweden to avoid double taxation, could make investments in Pakistan attractive. It is felt that despite the opportunities available, foreign investments in Pakistan are much lower than they should be. There are certain formidable barriers responsible for this lack of investment, as felt by foreign investors. Among them are 'confused' economic policies, recent changes in the banking and financial structure in Pakistan, and the general social and political uncertainty and inadequate safeguards.[56] The political instability and the nationalization programme although not directed at foreign firms have, nevertheless, discouraged private investors. The reluctance of British businessmen to invest in Pakistan is (as pointed out by Mr Paris, Director BASATA advisory group) because Pakistan is basically an agricultural country and industrialization, unlike India, has been slow. Foreign debt and its rescheduling is considered another impediment in the way of foreign investments, and there is also the problem of continued power failure and the uncertainty over the Sixth Five Year Plan. There is no doubt that Pakistan is an agricultural country with economic infrastructure constraints, especially in the field of energy. Therefore, there is all the more reason to seek foreign investment to tide over these difficulties. The most formidable barriers in the way of foreign investment is bureaucratic red-tapism, as government approval for projects takes an extremely long time to be forthcoming. To give impetus to foreign investments it is necessary that bureaucratic control be relaxed and obstacles minimized and general conditions made congenial.

Trade

In the process of economic development, trade plays a key role. Pakistan's greatest need has been to expand her exports and to sustain the development programmes at a satisfactory pace. This could have been possible only if liberal access was available to Pakistani products in the markets of advanced countries and her imports were less than her exports, or at least balanced. Unfortunately, Pakistan's overall balance of trade with Western Europe, especially the enlarged EEC, has been adverse all along; this imbalance is characteristic of the trade between highly developed countries of the West and a developing country like Pakistan. Pakistan's trade with Western Europe consists of an exchange of Pakistan's primary raw materials and some finished consumer products (Rice, cotton yarn, cotton fabrics, grower gum, rugs, mats, leather and leather goods, garments, surgical and sports goods) with West European development goods (machinery, machine parts, transport equipment, chemicals, metals, fertilizers, semi-finished industrial raw materials, edible oil, and pharmaceutical raw materials and finished medicines).

In Western Europe, the EEC is a major trading partner of Pakistan, accounting for nearly 20 per cent of Pakistan's trade. Relations between the EEC and Pakistan were governed by a commercial cooperation agreement entered into on 1 July 1976. In addition, the export of textiles is governed by the textile agreement of January 1983 under which textile items from Pakistan are subject to annual quota limits. It covers the export of products made of cotton, wool, and man-made fibres. Voluntary restriction has seriously hurt the export of Pakistani textiles into the EEC market. It has not only aggravated the existing trade imbalance but has adversely affected the Pakistani textile and clothing industry which in turn affected economic growth. Recently the EEC has given an additional textile quota to Pakistan as a result of invoking the 'carry-over and swing clause'. The export of cottage industry fabrics woven on hand or foot-operated looms, garments or other articles obtained manually from such fabrics, and traditional folk-lore handicrafts are, however, exempted from quantitative limits.

To allow greater share to the export of developing countries into the EEC market than would otherwise be possible amidst fierce international competition, the system of General Scheme of Preference (GSP) was devised in 1971. Under it, there is duty concession on items but they are quantitatively restricted. Pakistan's export to the EEC countries under the GSP increased from US$225.26 million in 1981–82 to $315.37 million in 1982–83. The highest utilization of GSP was in the FRG with $102.77 million followed by Italy with $51.32 million. Principal items exported under GSP cover in 1982–83 were carpets, cotton cloth, leather, skin, ready-made garments, cotton yarn, sports goods, surgical instruments, bedsheets, and shrimps, etc.[57] Though Pakistan has benefited from GSP, her experience is not a very happy one. The GSP system is very complicated, rigid and in favour of the European imports which cannot satisfactorily be utilized in favour of Pakistan. The reasons being that our main manufactured items like textile, leather and leather products are either excluded or subject to restrictive quotas and ceilings. Important agricultural export products like basmati rice are excluded from GSP cover and other items have been subjected to heavy import duty.

Though trade with the EEC has grown over the years from $140 million in 1973 to $2.1 billion in 1984, the balance of trade has remained adversely tilted against Pakistan. In 1983-84 imports from the EEC were $1170 million against which Pakistan's exports to the EEC for the same period were $500 million.[58] Pakistan's exports to the EEC are nearly half of her imports from the EEC, thus resulting in a huge trade deficit. Evaluating it critically, the 1976 agreement narrowed down the legal, administrative, and financial frame for the EEC to discharge its commercial responsibilities. It was discriminatory in terms and conditions as the reluctance of the EEC to extend certain elements of its developmental cooperation policy to 'non-associates' was obvious. The EEC's advocacy of 'Organised International Trade' was really meant to increase the quantitative and other restrictions on international trade, especially with the developing countries. This wave of protectionism and hardening of the Community's attitude was attributed to the economic depression sweeping over Europe.

With the end of the economic depression and signing of the new five-year agreement[59] between Pakistan and the EEC on 23 July 1985, it is hoped that trade conditions will improve and the trade imbalance will be rectified. The EEC should now be in a position to lower the protective barriers and liberalize the import policy, enabling Pakistan to substantially increase her exports to the Community. Pakistan's products like textiles, carpets, basmati rice, canvas shoes, etc. enjoy a good market in the EEC but their imports to the EEC had been restricted. It is also hoped that (i) quota restrictions on Pakistan's main export products—textiles—will be relaxed or where they are subject to quota limits, they should be allowed duty-free; (ii) basmati rice would be allowed duty-free under the GSP for this special type of rice is so priced that it does not need further duty and its export to the EEC would not affect the domestic market for its own rice; (iii) the country quota applied on the export of canvas shoes be eliminated and brought under GSP by which quota restrictions will be waived;[60] (iv) the EEC would further liberalize trade by allowing the transfer of member countries' quotas, where it has been exhausted, to the countries where it has not been fully exhausted.[61] The EEC is also considering the modificaiton of the GSP to make it simpler and more in tune with the needs of the developing nations. With the broadening of its scope, duty-free import of more products could be allowed. The developing countries are looking forward to the EEC lowering the protective barriers and liberalizing its import policy, bringing trade to normal GATT rules.

Bilaterally, of all the EEC countries, Britain is the biggest market for Pakistani products and third biggest non-oil supplier of goods to Pakistan. It is followed by Germany and France. With all West European countries bilaterally too, Pakistan suffered a huge trade deficit as is evident from Table 5.

Pakistan's trade with other West European states too is grossly imbalanced. With Austria, Pakistan's imports are double its exports. Norway too enjoys a favourable balance of trade and has also decided to impose a quota limit on textile imports from Pakistan. This Norwegian imposition does not make sense as the marginal increase in textile exports was offset by an 80 per cent import rise. Pakistan's exports to Scandinavian countries has doubled since the inception of the Copenhagen Trade Centre. It has shot up from Rs 250 million to Rs 500 million. Export of textile items from Pakistan to Finland and Sweden too are subject to annual quota limits.

Pakistan should make efforts to bridge the gap between its imports and exports by not only increasing her exports but by reducing the imports. It is not fair entirely to blame the EEC policy for our huge trade deficit; our business community too is partly responsible for it. Many avenues of trade and commerce have either remained unexplored or inadequately exploited. Important amongst them are the leather goods, gem stones, jewellery and onyx industries. To bridge the trade gap, the export base should be broadened and in the face of an uncertain quota system, a long term policy be evolved to boost textile exports to non-traditional markets. Trade would be further augmented by encouraging exchange of visits between businessmen from West Europe and Pakistan, thus lessening the communication gap. Setting up trade centres and chambers of commerce like the Pakistan Trade Centre in Rotterdam, Copenhagen Trade Centre and the Pak-UK Trade Centre, etc.; participation in trade fairs and regional exhibitions (organised in different countries, from time to time), and aggressive marketing by Pakistan can serve to popularise Pakistani products in European markets. Pakistani exporters must also bear in mind that to compete in international markets, it is very essential that the quality of goods must be very good and at the same time prices competitive.

TABLE 5
Direction of Trade
(Rs Million)

Year	(a) Consortium						(b) Other than Consortium								
	Belgium	France	West Germany	Italy	Netherland	U.K.	Norway	Sweden	Denmark	Austria	Portugal	Switzerland	Spain	Greece	Malta
	1	2	3	4	5	6	7	8	9	10	11	12	13	14	15
1971-72															
Exports	28	62	105	125	50	260	2	15	11	2	4	37	18	12	5
Imports	41	76	344	192	63	353	4	26	9	8	1	37	3	2	—
1972-73															
Exports	175	183	306	434	132	631	7	44	46	8	12	103	94	30	13
Imports	101	113	749	233	196	683	25	69	21	23	35	76	12	2	—
1973-74															
Exports	135	266	463	491	159	687	18	73	50	8	8	217	114	18	30
Imports	256	252	1051	300	515	950	105	110	40	59	33	61	17	5	—
1974-75															
Exports	148	195	462	250	136	687	20	92	59	12	10	131	123	57	15
Imports	387	501	1558	599	392	1230	80	211	64	73	32	100	44	17	—
1975-76															
Exports	82	229	598	431	151	711	41	93	76	20	9	146	275	56	18
Imports	315	548	1242	669	260	1551	68	71	54	84	31	205	25	25	—
1976-77															
Exports	109	262	648	421	215	808	40	94	100	19	5	167	242	10	13
Imports	256	501	1463	717	516	1861	69	109	84	45	310	187	43	4	1

| Year | | (a) Consortium | | | | | (b) Other than Consortium | | | | | | | | |
| | Belgi-um | France | West Germany | Italy | Nether-land | U.K. | Nor-way | Swe-den | Den-mark | Aus-tria | Portu-gal | Swit-zerland | Spain | Greece | Malta |
	1	2	3	4	5	6	7	8	9	10	11	12	13	14	15
1977-78															
Exports	97	253	732	377	233	861	24	65	119	25	4	180	162	15	12
Imports	368	808	2174	783	700	2306	74	238	70	50	16	227	58	23	1
1978-79															
Exports	161	423	1037	678	335	1289	18	126	123	28	5	347	322	17	8
Imports	389	1061	2084	1254	1862	2279	159	220	147	72	37	279	256	47	1
1979-80															
Exports	318	581	1430	882	376	1128	38	162	150	46	26	411	230	77	17
Imports	615	2149	2309	1854	1094	2878	134	291	369	122	42	431	141	65	—
1980-81															
Exports	226	623	1260	750	375	1163	45	159	115	62	34	398	158	60	14
Imports	592	1509	2694	1590	1041	3297	207	332	210	105	31	510	807	51	—
1981-82															
Exports	239	607	1018	873	307	1350	47	202	130	46	13	328	236	30	2
Imports	539	986	3497	1565	1080	3769	159	519	172	142	42	654	412	34	—
1982-83															
Exports	384	617	1545	1041	316	1659	90	218	133	64	31	378	236	49	8
Imports	621	1173	3885	2245	901	4379	166	442	440	148	47	852	327	62	11
1983-84															
Exports	332	767	1778	1309	457	1632	116	352	199	79	56	396	264	28	2
Imports	727	1425	4940	2189	856	5116	192	544	187	139	98	1182	959	184	6

Year	(a) Consortium							(b) Other than Consortium							
	Belgi-um	France	West Germany	Italy	Nether-land	U.K.	Nor-way	Swe-den	Den-mark	Aus-tria	Portu-gal	Swit-zerland	Spain	Greece	Malta
	1	2	3	4	5	6	7	8	9	10	11	12	13	14	15
1984-85															
Exports	482	978	2163	1564	581	2538	107	473	185	59	123	385	387	93	3
Imports	923	1582	5163	2164	947	5277	344	805	168	113	38	1257	570	192	54
1984-85 (Jul-Mar)															
Exports	332	760	1599	1181	427	1931	83	341	140	48	74	323	296	51	1
Imports	649	1122	3347	1582	662	3590	306	602	104	70	29	789	395	120	35
1985-86 (Jul-Mar)															
Exports	400	931	2015	1516	566	1911	95	761	217	52	177	290	306	154	4
Imports	546	935	5485	2101	901	4461	271	456	173	169	20	1195	413	90	21

Source: *Economic Survey, 1985-86* (Islamabad Government of Pakistan, Finance Division, Economic Adviser's Wing), pp. 134–35 (statistical section).

Military Ties

In order to meet the requirements of its armed forces, Pakistan has been importing arms from some West European countries, namely: Britain, France, Italy, Sweden, and recently West Germany.

Pakistan has been offered two new combat helicopters; one by West Germany called *BO-105-SL* and another made by France and Britain named *Gazelle*.[62] Britain also hopes to sell £175 million worth of tank turrets and armaments to Pakistan initially, followed by further purchases totalling about £420 million.[63]

Pakistan now seeks to upgrade, modernize, and streamline its old and widely mixed military equipment and at the same time is striving on self reliance; thus needing transfer of technology from the West to develop a modest defence production capability through indigenization of its equipment and weapon systems.

However, until Pakistan's nascent arms industry is sufficiently developed, there is a short-term requirement to buy arms and West European countries are some of the potential suppliers.

Political Relations

Pakistan enjoys good political relations with all the West European countries. Islamabad has identity of views on a large number of international issues and the irritants, if any, are very few. With a majority of West European states, Pakistan maintains contacts at official level and there is frequent exchange of visits. With Britain, Pakistan's relations are historical, and though over the years its role in Pakistan has declined, the relations are good. Britain looks at our domestic and foreign policy initiative with favour and approval. Britain respects Pakistani membership of the Non-Aligned Movement and the OIC. Britain had asked Pakistan to use its good offices to resolve its dispute with Libya.

Germany has no traditional or colonial interest nor any political ambition in the region; its interest is basically economic or in the East-West context. Therefore politically, Bonn prefers to keep a low profile. Initially because of its membership of Western military alliances, Pakistan received great importance, thereafter the relationship cooled off a bit. However, Pakistan has once again acquired strategic importance because of the Russian presence in Afghanistan. Bonn feels that though the Russians would not march into Pakistan, they would definitely try and influence the policy of Pakistan vis-a-vis the West by promoting pro-Moscow elements. Islamabad's stand on the Afghan issue is considered pro-West and viewed with favour in Germany.

Relations with France, despite the bitter nuclear controversy, have remained cordial and friendly for contacts were not allowed to be severed. Similarly relations with other European countries are excellent and efforts are continuously being made to foster better understanding and relations. The visit of Sahabzada Yaqub Khan in January 1984 to Belgium was the first ever visit by a Pakistani Foreign Minister to that country.[64] With a desire to further improve relations with Pakistan, Greece has decided to open its resident diplomatic mission in Islamabad.[65] Relations between Pakistan and Greece were strained to some extent when Greece sought to block the negotiations for a new EEC pact because of Pakistan's close relations with Turkey and the northern Turkish Republic of Cyprus. However, Greece was pursuaded by the Irish government—incharge of EEC foreign policy—to lift the reserve.

While emphasizing the economic and political aspects of the relationship, the social and humanitarian side should not be missed.

Assistance for Afghan Refugees

The Russian occupation of Afghanistan has greatly influenced the attitude of Western Europe towards Pakistan. Seen in the East-West context, Islamabad's stand on the Soviet military presence in Afghanistan and the presence of three million Afghan refugees within Pakistani borders and their handling are viewed with concern and favour. It has brought in its wake not only aid for the refugees but has also greatly enhanced Pakistan's strategic importance.

Since 1979 Western Europe has re-directed development aid of Afghanistan to the relief of refugees in Pakistan. Generous financial aid has been given by individual states which is channelled through the UN High Commission for Refugees (UNHCR). A number of humanitarian relief organizations and charities based in Western Europe are donating relief aid and providing trained personnel. These funds were being made available to the International Aid Committee and Inter-denominational Christian Organisation in Pakistan. Other

West European charities active from an early stage in providing relief to the refugees are the German Red Cross; the Austrian Relief Committee for Afghanistan; Norway Church Aid and Refugee Council, and two British based organizations: OXFAM and the Save the Children Fund. Besides financial aid, large quantities of food, clothing, tents, blankets, and medicines have been supplied by Western Europe and valuable training imparted to Afghans as medical workers. A large number of schemes to help provide Afghan refugees with skills and materials for weaving, etc. have been undertaken.

Many West European dignitaries visiting Pakistan have visited the refugee camps and appreciated the difficulties of the Pakistani government in handling such a large number of refugees, and also the threat it poses to Pakistan's security. Aid from Western Europe has greatly helped Pakistan in dealing with the problem. However, of late, the aid flow for the refugees has declined due to multiplication of crises around the world. Mr Jean Pierre Hocke, the new UN High Commissioner for Refugees, has said that the question of increasing aid for the Afghan refugees would be taken up with the donor countries. He hoped that they would agree to his request as it was necessary to carry out the programme in the best possible way.[66]

Politically, West European states have strongly condemned the Soviet intervention and assured Pakistan of all possible help to bring about an acceptable permanent solution to the Afghan problem and help the Afghan refugees return home. The Afghan problem has sparked off debates and made an undeniable impact throughout Western Europe. While West European countries have varied considerably in their emphasis and consistent interest in the issue of Afghan independence, there has been virtual unanimity over the condemnation of Soviet action as an act of aggression. There were few defenders of Moscow even in the European socialist circle. The members of the EEC have also shown unanimity on this score. The European Council has called in its declaration for respect for the sovereignty and territorial integrity of Afghanistan and for an end to all interference in the internal affairs of that country.

During his visit to Pakistan in January 1980, Lord Carrington assured British and Western support to Pakistan in its determination to safeguard its integrity and independence. In 1983, British Prime Minister Mrs Thatcher assured President Ziaul Haq of all possible support. In January 1981, the French Prime Minister Giscard d'Estaing proposed an international conference on Afghanistan, but it was rejected by both Kabul and Islamabad. Pakistan felt that France was seeking to undermine Pakistan's efforts to negotiate a political settlement.[67] In 1981, the European Council also proposed a plan towards political solution of the issue by convening of an international conference. In pursuance of this plan on 6 July 1981, Lord Carrington, the British Foreign Secretary, visited Moscow but Russia eventually did not approve the plan. In November 1983, a resolution sponsored by 45 Third World countries and presented by Sahabzada Yaqub Khan found strong support from the EEC states. The resolution re-affirmed the right of the Afghan people to determine their own form of government, called for immediate withdrawal of foreign troops, and requested all parties to come to a political solution and to create conditions which will enable Afghan refugees to return in safety and honour.

Despite their various efforts the West European countries have not responded as strongly as should be expected. Their half-hearted pressure tactics have uptil now failed to achieve the desired result. Sir Frederic, MP from UK, who visited Pakistan in April 1980 admitted that the united will was lacking on the part of the US and Western Europe in meeting the Soviet invasion in Afghanistan. He believed that enough pressure was not being brought to bear on the Russians to withdraw from Afghanistan, though world pressure had persuaded Russia to withdraw from West Iran.[68] This may be because, seen in the context of East-West conflict, the Russian action in Afghanistan did not directly affect the areas vital to Western interest. West European reaction to the Afghanistan crisis had, however, helped in bringing Pakistan and Western Europe closer. West European countries have made a major contribution to the Pakistan-Aid-Consortium, besides helping with the cost of relief for Afghan refugees in Pakistan.

Help to Eradicate Drug Menace

The most important social and humanitarian problem facing the world is drug abuse, its trafficking and control. Pakistan is closely cooperating with the Western countries to eradicate this growing menace. West Germany is extending its help to curb drug abuse by improving Pakistan Narcotic Control Board's mobility to check the transportation of narcotics at important points, modernizing the telecommunication network, linking it with different parts of the world and establishing laboratories where the drugs can be analysed. Training is also being provided to personnel and dogs to help in drug detection. The UK is also helping Pakistan to eradicate the unlawful production and trafficking of narcotics. Under an agreement, the UK will increase its contribution to Pakistan via UN funds for drug abuse control. The combined crop substitution, rural development, and enforcement projects are designed to eradicate poppy cultivation in the Dir district, and also provide necessary technical equipment and training for drug detection. This 'most threatening global crisis' has been further aggravated for Pakistan with the flood of Afghan refugees. As Afghanistan has always been foremost in the illicit opium trade, opium trafficking and new heroin producing labs have sprung up in the tribal areas and the NWFP, where Afghan refugees mostly reside. Despite Pakistan's efforts to control the abuse of drugs, some West European states have subjected Pakistan to adverse propaganda.

Cultural Relations

Pakistan also maintains cultural links with Western Europe. In the UK Pakistani residents have formed a cultural foundation to promote understanding between the two countries. There exist cultural pacts with some West European states for enabling greater cultural contacts but there is great scope for improving bilateral ties. For greater understanding, exchange of cultural delegations and cultural foundations in various European countries should be encouraged.

In the archaeological field too, various European countries are taking keen interest in Pakistan. The Italian Institute for Middle East and Far East has made pioneering efforts in the excavation and exploration of the ancient Gandhara civilization in Pakistan. Under the leadership of Prof. Guiseppe Tuici, an Italian archaeological mission carried out excavations in Swat. A French archaeological mission has been working at Mehrbagh near Sibbi, Balochistan. A Cambridge University archaeological mission, in cooperation with the Department of Archaeology, is carrying out further investigations at Taxila. German archaeological missions are carrying out the documentation of Mohenjodaro. Berlin Museum of Indo-Pak arts has on display some of the specimens of earliest settlement of man in South Asia. The museum has thus helped the Europeans to comprehend the intricacies of

Gandhara culture and the versatility of Muslim arts and craft in the region.[69]

Pakistanis in Western Europe

The Pakistanis settled in Western Europe form an important economic, social, and cultural link between Pakistan and the host countries. A large number of skilled, professional, and educated Pakistanis are employed in Western Europe to the mutual advantage of Pakistan and the host countries. Pakistani labour and technicians are less expensive as compared to the locals, and they in turn remit a considerable amount of their earnings to Pakistan by way of foreign exchange. Pakistanis abroad are to some extent responsible for the flow of foreign investment into Pakistan as they are interested in investing at home. Pakistan should further explore possibilities to export skilled and semi-skilled labour to West European countries where local population is low. One such example is Austria, where there were only 100 Pakistanis in 1982.

Pakistan should actively and consciously look after the welfare of its nationals settled abroad and also tap avenues for export of skilled labour to Western Europe as it is an important source of foreign exchange earnings. The table below shows the number of Pakistanis in major West European countries in 1982.

1. United Kingdom	350,000
2. West Germany	24,412
3. Holland	10,000
4. Denmark	9,334
5. Greece	9,000
6. France	6,417
7. Italy	250
Total:	409,413

Conclusion

In a nutshell, Pakistan enjoys cordial and friendly relations with all West European countries. Because of the Afghanistan issue Pakistan has acquired strategic importance and fresh interest is being generated in maintaining its sovereignty and national integrity. Europe also seeks Pakistan's goodwill because of her being a moderate state in the Islamic bloc. Western Europe has been ready and willing to extend aid and also re-schedule Pakistan's debts, but it is in our own interest that dependence on foreign aid be reduced. Foreign investments should be sought with a view of full partnership and aiming at the transfer of modern technology to Pakistan. It is hoped that the Western attitude towards Pakistan for acquiring nuclear technology for peaceful purposes (especially in the much needed energy sector) would become unbiased and more realistic. Pakistan should improve its trade performance by expanding its trade base and seeking out new avenues[70] for export, and also cutting down on its imports to correct the perpetual adverse balance of trade with Western Europe.

NOTES

1. *Dawn*, Karachi, 14 March 1986.
2. Abdul Majid Khan 'EEC's Prosperity provides scope for increasing Pakistan Export', *The Muslim*, Islamabad, 26 February 1985.
3. Tufail Ahmed Khan, 'Third Biggest Creditor of Pakistan', *Dawn*, 30 December 1985.
4. *Pakistan and Gulf Economist*, Karachi, 12–18 April 1986. p. 13.
5. *The Muslim*, Islamabad, 3 August 1985.
6. *Morning News*, Karachi, 21 February 1986.
7. Tufail Ahmed Khan, 'No. 4 Buyer of Pakistan Products', *Dawn*, 24 April 1986.
8. Rafique Akhtar (ed.), *Pakistan Year Book 1980*, Ma'airf Printers Ltd, Karachi, p. 252.
9. *Dawn*, 6 April 1986.
10. Ibid., 22 April 1986.
11. Ibid., 7 October 1983.
12. Ibid., 6 April 1986.
13. *Pakistan Year Book* 1983, op. cit., p. 241.
14. *Dawn*, 16 January 1986.
15. Ibid., 6 May 1986.
16. *The Pakistan Times*, Lahore, 13 September 1985.
17. *Morning News*, 15 February 1985.
18. *Dawn*, 6 May 1980.
19. Ibid., 16 January 1986.
20. Ibid., 30 April 1986.
21. Abdul Majid, op. cit.

22. *Dawn*, 30 April 1986.
23. *Morning News*, 11 February 1986.
24. *Dawn*, 30 April 1986.
25. Abdul Majid, op. cit.
26. Editorial *Dawn*, 31 March 1983.
27. *Dawn*, 14 July 1986.
28. *Morning News*, 25 June 1985.
29. *Dawn*, 30 April 1985.
30. Ibid., 3 April 1985.
31. *Business Recorder,* Karachi, 25 February 1985.
32. Abdul Majid, op. cit.
33. *Dawn*, 13 April 1985.
34. *Morning News*, 12 April 1986.
35. *Dawn*, 22 April 1986.
36. Ibid., 20 December 1983.
37. Ibid., 14 January 1983.
38. Ibid., 25 July 1985.
39. Samina Ahmed, 'France Pakistan Relations—II'. *Pakistan Horizon,* Karachi, XXXI: 1 (1st Qtr. 1978), p. 37.
40. See *Tehran Documents* in *The Muslim*, 1 and 2 August 1985.
41. *The Pakistan Times*, 17 January 1986.
42. *Dawn*, 11 March 1986.
43. Ibid., 12 March 1986.
44. *The Pakistan Times*, 29 September 1977.
45. Asif Huda, 'The Growing but British Investment is Slow', *Dawn*, 16 March 1985.
46. *The Pakistan Times*, 1 March 1985.
47. *Dawn*, 12 February 1986.
48. *Morning News*, 19 February 1986.
49. *Dawn*, 6 April 1986.
50. Ibid., 30 December 1985.
51. Ibid., 25 January 1985.
52. Ibid., 14 July 1986.
53. Ibid., 12 May 1986.
54. *Morning News*, 4 November 1985.
55. Sultan Ahmed, 'The Problem Facing Foreign Investors', *Dawn*, 28 November 1985.
56. Iqbal H. Hussain, 'Barriers in way of Foreign Investors', *Dawn*, 4 August 1985.
57. Rafiq Javed, 'Pak EEC Trade—Need for Greater Co-operation', *Pakistan and Gulf Economist*, 10-16 August 1985, p. 23.
58. *Dawn*, 30 July 1985.
59. The socialist group of the European Parliament held up the ratification of the new pack. They called for a full assessment of the lifting of martial

law as regards the political parties and the respect for human rights in Pakistan. It was finally ratified on 13 March 1986.

60. *Dawn*, 30 July 1985.
61. Rafiq Javed, op. cit.
62. *The Muslim*, 17 March 1986.
63. *Dawn*, 10 March 1986.
64. *Morning News*, 14 April 1985.
65. *The Pakistan Times*, 29 September 1985.
66. *Dawn*, 3 April 1986.
67. Anthony Hymen, 'Afghan Crisis and European Responsibility', *Europe and the Third World*, Dr A.A. Kadeer and Naveed Ahmed (eds.), Area Study Centre for Europe, University of Karachi, 1985, p. 237.
68. *Pakistan Year Book—1990*, op. cit., p. 253.
69. Ibid., 1984–85, pp. 59–64.
70. It would be very beneficial to develop the tourism industry since in the last few decades tourism has become a major source of foreign exchange earnings. In Western states viz France, Italy, and Spain revenues earned from tourism had even surpassed the profits from big industries.

20

Strategic and Military Dimensions in Pakistan-China Relations*

Mohammad Ahsen Chaudhri

In a world prone to violence, relations between the friendliest of countries sometimes become stale, especially when the countries adhere to different ideologies.[1] Astonishingly, the relations between Pakistan and China,[2] despite many political changes within the two countries, have remained stable during the past thirty-five years. China gave economic and military aid to Pakistan whenever it was badly needed and it continues to flow to this day on a regular basis. The motivating force behind their friendship is their common objective to promote world peace and stability by maintaining the regional geopolitical balance.

Ever since the war between India and Pakistan in 1965, the situation in South Asia has remained in a state of flux. After the dismemberment of Pakistan in 1971, India, with Soviet support, could have established its hegemony in the region. But China's political and military support to Islamabad prevented India from realizing her ambitions. China denounced aggression and supported the just struggle of the people of Pakistan to defend their sovereignty and territorial integrity. The joint communique issued at the end of former Prime Minister Bhutto's visit to China in 1972 clearly stated that friendship between Pakistan and China was based on principles that are in accord with the basic interests of the two countries.[3]

---

* Vol. xxxix, No. 4, 1986.

Pakistan and China are close neighbours. The history of relations between the two countries goes back to the period when merchants, pilgrims, scholars, and diplomats travelled on camel or on horseback through the silk route from one country to the other. During the period of colonialism, however, contacts between the people of China and Pakistan were restricted at both official and unofficial levels. Following the first British aggression against China in 1856 or the Opium War, as it is better known, China's foundation as a state was sapped. As a result chaos and confusion prevailed in China for a long time.

The condition of the Muslims of the subcontinent in the nineteenth century was no better than that of the people of China. They were badly treated by the British for taking an active part in the so-called mutiny of 1857. It was after a long and bitter struggle against both the Hindus and the British that Muslims of the subcontinent succeeded at last in establishing a state of their own. China was then still in shambles. More than eight years of Japanese invasion and three decades of civil war had almost wholly disrupted the economic life as well as peace and order in the country. In 1949 the Communists emerged victorious. Pakistan was the first Muslim country to recognize the new regime and to establish diplomatic relations with her. Obviously there was nothing new in this. It was formal official expression of a position that Pakistan took with regard to the new regime in China, which under the leadership of Mao Zedong, was likely to play an important role in world affairs.

Probably strategic and political considerations did more to influence the course of relations between China and Pakistan than any other factor. Pakistanis were intrigued by Chinese domestic politics and soon it became clear to them that China is not an expansionist power. Pakistan supported the admission of China to the United Nations and other international bodies and opposed the claim of Chiang-Kai-Shek to speak for China. It was a position officially avowed and firmly held by all governments in Pakistan that the People's Republic was the rightful representative of 700 million Chinese as opposed to the American policy of non-recognition of the Communist government which was unrealistic.[4]

In 1951 when China entered the Korean war to safeguard her security, Pakistan abstained from voting on the General Assembly resolution branding China as an aggressor. The Chinese leaders appreciated Pakistan's stand. When following the Korean war there was a big slump in world trade, China imported a big portion of

Pakistan's raw cotton and jute, thus helping the latter to avert the economic crisis.[5]

Much has been written on China's reaction to Pakistan's entry into regional alliances sponsored by the United States. However, it may be mentioned here briefly that Pakistan had joined these alliances to seek security against the danger of war with India; they were in no way directed against China. Speaking in the political committee at the Bandung Conference, Prime Minister Chou En-Lai referred to his meeting with Prime Minister Mohammad Ali and said that the latter had assured him that Pakistan had no fear that China would commit aggression against her. As a result of that 'we have reached mutual understanding.'[6] Of course, there was never any quarrel or friction over any matter between China and Pakistan, nor did they ever look upon each other with suspicion.

China is a big country, having many neighbours. To have peace within as well as around her is a part of the strategy for the continuing development of China. History has taught the Chinese people that they cannot live in peace so long as there is no peace in the neighbouring countries. Pakistan also subscribes to the view that peace in neighbouring countries will make her feel more secure.

Nevertheless, China, despite an agreement with New Delhi over Tibet embodying the five principles of peaceful co-existence, had to face increasing tension on the border with India. It was not a congenial situation. When the rebellion in Tibet broke out in 1959 China saw India's hand in it.[7] At this time China's relations with the Soviet Union had also taken a turn for the worse. The Soviet technicians were withdrawn from China and economic assistance withheld. While China's relations with India and the Soviet Union were worsening, President Ayub Khan offered India a joint defence arrangement. The Chinese might have asked Pakistan against whom such an agreement would be directed. But the Chinese leaders took no interest in this matter. Perhaps they knew that President Ayub Khan was not serious about his proposal. The relations between India and Pakistan, without a settlement of the Kashmir dispute, were bound to remain in a state of flux for a long time to come.[8]

In 1962 China was compelled to go to war with India to prevent Indian territorial encroachments on its territory. Pakistan could have taken advantage of this situation and grabbed Kashmir, but the American influence on Pakistan's foreign policy prevented her from adopting this course. China acted alone but prudently. After pushing the Indians back from her territory, China unilaterally proclaimed a cease-fire and offered to settle the boundary dispute with India through negotiations.[9] So far as Pakistan was concerned she was content with assurances that India will soon enter into negotiations with Pakistan to resolve the Kashmir dispute peacefully. The first round of discussions on Kashmir took place in December 1962 but produced no result. The fact is that after the fighting with China stopped, India's attitude towards Pakistan became adamant again. It was now a chasm. Pakistan and China, treated by New Delhi as enemies, moved much closer to each other. And India moved closer to the Soviet Union in accordance with the saying that if you are not friendly with your neighbour, be friendly with your neighbour's neighbour.

With the posting of Major General N.A.N. Raza as Pakistan's ambassador to Beijing in August 1962, the process of negotiations between Pakistan and China over the frontier demarcation was accelerated. Time was the principal determinant in bringing negotiations to their successful conclusion. China wanted to show to the world that it is considerate and reasonable in its dealings with neighbouring countries. United States military aid to India had disillusioned Pakistan with the policy of alignment; she was trying to adopt an independent course in world affairs. Moreover, Pakistan was convinced that Western military aid to India would be used against her as well as against China. On 2 March 1963 Pakistan and China, having a keen desire for peace on their borders, signed the boundary agreement in Beijing. As a result Pakistan gained 750 square miles of territory containing grazing lands and salt mines which had been under the actual possession of the Chinese.[10]

Pakistan's former Foreign Minister, Z.A. Bhutto, who had gone to Beijing to sign the border agreement was given a rousing reception. Not long after his return, he hinted in his address to the National Assembly that an attack on Pakistan by India would involve the 'largest state in Asia'. He was obviously referring to China with whom Pakistan's relations had grown markedly with the increasing military assistance from the United States and the Soviet Union to India after the outbreak of Sino-Indian hostilities.[11]

Moreover, a trade agreement between Pakistan and China signed on 4 January 1963 provided for commercial exchanges on the basis of the most favoured nations treatment. Soon after this, an air agreement of 26 August 1963 established the PIA Dhaka-Canton-Shanghai air service.[12] Although basically a commercial deal, its importance was noteworthy because China, by acquiring access to the world by a major air link, frustrated the efforts of some countries to isolate her. On 13 February 1965, direct radio and telecommunications links between Pakistan and China were also established.[13]

Perhaps the most important development in the Pakistan-China friendship both from the military and commercial point of view was the reopening of the silk route, linking Xinjiang with the Hunza valley in Pakistan, to traders in 1967. A year and a half later, work on an all-weather road, the Karakoram highway, was started jointly by Pakistani and Chinese engineers. It was a hazardous job. About 15,000 Chinese and Pakistanis took twenty years to build the 774 km long highway through the 16,072 ft. high mountains. The construction of the highway was worth the cost because it has provided an all-weather and motorable link between the two neighbouring countries. Commenting on this highway, a writer remarked, 'it gave China greater influence in Pakistan and access to the Arabian sea port of Karachi'.[14] It may be so, but the opening of the highway boosted trade between Pakistan and China, and created an important link between the two countries to be used in case of any emergency.

The strategic importance of the Karakoram highway is very obvious. It links Xinjiang with Tibet through the Aksai Chin. In case of an attack on Pakistan by sea, military aid from China can reach Pakistan through this route. The bridges on the Karakoram highway are capable of carrying light-weight tanks. To protect the highway from subversion, small military bases along the highway have been constructed. Despite the apparent vulnerability of the road, its usefulness in time of peace and war is conspicuously apparent.

Nevertheless, the real test of Pakistan-China friendship came during the 1965 Indo-Pakistan war. China condemned India's unbridled aggression against Pakistan and rejected India's claim that the attack on Lahore was a defensive measure.[15] Apart from this, China accused the United States and the Soviet Union of showing partiality towards India.[16]

China was concerned about the outcome of the war because any shift in the balance of power in the subcontinent was likely to be exploited by the superpowers to grind their own axe. When the danger of attack on East Pakistan was mounting, China made an important move. It gave an ultimatum to India on 16 September to dismantle all military installations on or over the China-Sikkim border within three days or face 'grave consequences'.[17] This timely Chinese support to

Pakistan not only foiled the Indian plan to attack East Pakistan but also led to the easing of military pressure on the Sialkot front in West Pakistan.

On 19 September China issued a second ultimatum to India demanding that kidnapped men, sheep, and yaks must be returned; besides India's subversive activities in Tibet, the occupation of 92,000 square kilometres of Chinese territory and armed provocation must come to an end.[18] Three days after the ultimatum a cease-fire was agreed upon by India and Pakistan, and the Soviet Union offered its good offices to the parties to settle the conflict.

By risking a war with India, China brought about a change in the attitude of the United States and the Soviet Union. To avoid the conflict from expanding, they urged India and Pakistan through the Security Council to accept a cease-fire. Thus China rendered a valuable service to the cause of peace in South Asia.

Moreover, following the US arms embargo, sizeable amounts of Chinese equipment arrived in Pakistan. Some MiG 15s, tanks, and some other weapons were displayed at the Pakistan Day parade in 1966. Over the years China became Pakistan's principal arms supplier. It may be noted that after the Tashkent conference, the Soviet Union had agreed to sell arms to Pakistan, while she was already supplying arms to India and her influence in India was rapidly growing. The Chinese, therefore, had a cause to worry not only about strengthening of Soviet-India ties but also about a developing Soviet rapprochement with Pakistan. The Soviet-Pakistan arms deal, however, did not go through probably because the Russians were afraid of Indian sensitivities on this issue and were not prepared to take the risk of annoying India. China, which had assiduously courted Pakistan ever since the outbreak of Sino-Indian hostilities, decided to supply arms to Pakistan. The first agreement for military assistance of the value of $120 million was signed by Pakistan and China in July 1966.[19] Within two years China supplied Pakistan with 100 T-59 tanks, 80 MiG-19's (F-6), and 10 Ilyshin-28 bombers. 'By 1970', as a writer puts it, 'the tanks supplied by China already constituted 25 per cent of the entire tank force at Pakistan's disposal. The aircraft supplied by China constituted 33 per cent of the Pakistani air force's 270 planes, 65 per cent of all interceptor-bombers, and 99 per cent of its first-line modern fighter planes.'[20] China proved to be a reliable source of arms supply, while the flow of arms from American and other Western sources dried out for some reasons.

In 1971, when Pakistan had lost much of its military hardware during the war with India, China came to Pakistan's rescue and made up a major portion of the loss despite the fact that China was then recovering from the impact of the Cultural Revolution. In the 1970s Pakistan shared China's perception of the world situation. The Soviet invasion of Czechoslovakia in 1968 had disillusioned the Chinese as well as all other freedom-loving nations. The Chinese not only denounced the invasion as an act of social imperialism but also felt the need to have rapprochement with the United States. There was also a change in the US attitude towards China. The policy of containment and hostility was overshadowed by threats from the Soviet Union. The Russian efforts to gain control of the world's sea lanes was causing concern in Washington as well as in Beijing. By arranging Henry Kissinger's secret trip to Beijing in 1970, Pakistan played an important role in the normalization of relations between China and the United States. India and the Soviet Union disliked Pakistan's role in this episode. As a reaction they moved closer to each other and signed the twenty years Treaty of Peace and Friendship which is virtually an alliance for all practical purposes.[21]

During the Indo-Pakistan war in 1971, the Soviet Union backed India, while China courted Pakistan because it was opposed to the policy of domination or hegemony over South Asia by either superpower and of a state or states aligned with them. Unfortunately China could not act in 1971 the way it did in 1965 to relieve pressure on Pakistan, as Soviet troops equipped with nuclear weapons were concentrating along the Chinese border and the Soviet retaliatory attack could not be easily deterred. China, however, continued to supply arms to Pakistan on easy terms. In 1971 Pakistan received, apart from tanks and guns, nine Shanghai-class motorboats of which four could be converted for firing missiles.[22] It may not be impertinent to point out here that the Chinese weapons to Pakistan, so far as their quality and quantity were concerned, could not match the Soviet weapons to India, but their political impact was much the same.

The most significant contribution of China to Pakistan's defence needs has been the establishment of a heavy mechanical complex and heavy foundry and forge near Taxila. This is the first industrial complex of its kind established by China in a non-Communist country. Now Pakistan can produce ammunition and spares for Chinese equipment. A tank-rebuild factory and arms plant with facilities for repairing MiG-19/F-6 have also been established with Chinese assistance at Kamra near Attock. The foundation stone of the Heavy Electrical Complex to be built with Chinese financial and technical assistance was laid down in April 1986 at Hattar in Haripur in the NWFP. It will produce 500 kv power transformer and associated equipments.[23] China has been sending experts to Pakistan on training missions and a few licenses have also been granted for the production of Chinese weapons. These are commendable steps to make Pakistan self-sufficient in defence products.

Since 1965 all the three branches of the Pakistan military have received Chinese weapons. The arms supplied in the 1970s were older models, but as production increased, the design of Chinese weapons and aircraft improved. The F-6 fighters (MiG-19) were produced in large numbers.[24] Pakistan received 24 F-6s with T-59 trainers from China in 1978. With an increase in China's air force strength, the production of F-7 (MiG-23) went up. Military assistance to Pakistan also increased in proportion to the increase in China's defence products. The terms of assistance were reported to be generous. In 1981 China delivered 25 F-6s[25] to Pakistan and by the end of 1982 the total number of planes delivered to Pakistan rose to 300. The F-6 was specially built to meet Pakistan air force requirements. In 1985 China supplied 50 Q-5/A-5 fighters to Pakistan, and this was in addition to 60 already in service. The Q-5 Fantan-A were first supplied to Pakistan in 1978 and their deliveries continued at the rate of 50 a year.[26]

Apart from planes, Chinese military aid to Pakistan from 1970 to date includes almost 1000 tanks, more than 30 naval vessels, surface-to-air missiles, batteries, gun boats, light weapons, and ammunition. The Chinese tanks, like aircraft, are improved copies of Soviet battle tanks of the 1950s. Although China's capacity and resources to produce tanks for export is limited, it supplied Pakistan with a considerable quantity of Type-59 tanks with a provision for mounting a 12.7 mm anti-aircraft gun.[27] Pakistan was reported to have ordered 1000 Type 59s in 1975. It received 50 annually beginning in 1978 and by 1983 it had a total of 900 Type-59 tanks.[28]

Pakistan is one of the few third world countries which has been provided with 85 mm anti-tank field guns, 100 mm and 130 mm field guns, 107 mm multiple rocket system, 60 mm and 87 mm mortars, and a limited number of surface-to-air missiles.[29] Warships, patrol boats, and torpedoes do not form a part of China's arms aid to Pakistan. This is partly because they are in short supply and partly because they are not needed as much as the other weapons of war mentioned above.

Nevertheless, Pakistan received from China a limited quantity of large patrol boats.

As regards China's assistance to Pakistan in the nuclear field, all that has been said about it by the Western and the Indian mass media is not only incorrect but also misleading. China lags behind the West in the field of nuclear technology and is not yet in a position to assist other countries. In 1981 when the Chinese Prime Minister visited Islamabad, reports were published in the Western press that if Pakistan exploded an atomic bomb on Chinese territory, US military and economic aid to Pakistan will be cut off immediately.[30] The US Secretary of State, George Shultz, during his visit to Beijing in February 1983, reportedly warned China that assistance to Pakistan in the nuclear field would retard the progress toward a bilateral agreement on nuclear cooperation between the US and China. Keeping in view the close ties between Pakistan and China, it has been assumed that China must have provided Pakistan with information about the design of nuclear bombs. Thus, as a writer puts it, 'Pakistan could then develop a "bomb-in-the basement-option" without risking a confrontation with the US'.[31] Pakistan has repeatedly stated, however, that it does not intend to produce a nuclear bomb; it is interested only in the peaceful use of nuclear technology. Lately, Prime Minister Mohammed Khan Junejo, speaking at a seminar in Nathiagali stated that Pakistan's nuclear programme was solely directed towards meeting its needs for socio-economic development.[32] 'Pakistan', he said, 'believed in non-proliferation of nuclear weapons both at the international and regional levels.' Since the people of South Asia were impoverished, their requirements for development must receive top priority. Pakistan, therefore, was genuinely interested in the denuclearization of South Asia and had repeatedly proposed a nuclear-weapon-free-zone in this region.[33] China had endorsed the Pakistani point of view, while India failed to do so.

Both China and Pakistan are interested in minimizing the possibility of a conflict in South Asia. Since the Soviet invasion of Afghanistan, the situation in South Asia has taken a turn for the worse. The danger of encirclement of China has reappeared. Besides, danger to the security of Pakistan, especially the threat of Soviet backed incursions across the Afghan border, has become imminent. Beijing perceives the events in Afghanistan not only as a threat to the security of the neighbouring countries, but also a threat to peace and security of the region. The permanent occupation of Afghanistan will give Moscow a free hand in gaining control of the world's sea lanes running like an arc from the Gulf through the Indian Ocean to the Pacific.[34] Soon after the invasion, China had told the Soviet ambassador in Beijing that Afghanistan is China's neighbour and so long as Soviet troops do not withdraw from Afghanistan the relations between China and the Soviet Union will remain estranged. China regards the Soviet incursion into a neighbouring country as an obstacle to the improvement of her relations with Moscow. Two other obstacles in the view of the Chinese leaders are the presence of Soviet combat troops on the Chinese border and the occupation of Kampuchea by Vietnam.[35]

China has assured Pakistan that in case of foreign aggression the Chinese people and the government would stand by Pakistan.[36] Although China has not broken diplomatic relations with Kabul, it had recognized the Organization of Islamic Conference as an important force against the Soviet advances. China, which has a large Muslim minority, is in favour of a powerful Islamic movement that could play an important role in world affairs. The purpose of support for the Organization of Islamic Conference and the Islamic movements is to counter the influence of the USSR and its allies in Asia.[37]

It is important to note that China increased its military assistance to Pakistan soon after the Soviet armies entered Afghanistan. Besides, China is ready to join in giving international guarantees demanded by the Soviet Union as a part of the deal to resolve the Afghanistan conflict. But China considers the demand for international guarantees before troop withdrawal is like putting the cart before the horse. The Foreign Minister of China, Wu Xuequian, said in a statement given during his visit to Islamabad on 29 July 1983 that the Russians had created the problem which resulted in the exodus of Afghans from their homeland, only they could resolve it by pulling out of Afghanistan. He cited the Chinese proverb that 'he who ties the bell around tiger's neck should untie it'.[38]

China fully agrees with Pakistan that the Afghan people are entitled to have the right to determine their own destiny. Whether China is supplying arms to the Mujahideen (freedom fighters) is not known. Some Western journalists had reportedly seen Mujahideen using Chinese mortars and rocket launchers in 1981. In subsequent years more sophisticated Chinese weapons were seen such as 82 mm recoilless rifles and anti-tank cannons.[39] This does not mean that China is supplying arms to the Mujahideen. Today weapons of any type could be bought in the international market. Nevertheless, Beijing is supporting Pakistan's efforts to find a political solution of the Afghanistan crisis, and gives military and non-military aid to Pakistan as a part of her broader international strategy to prevent a superpower from exercising control over a neighbouring state.

All told it seems that relations between Pakistan and China are built on the basis of enlightened self-interest. When the interests of nations coincide, there is greater cooperation, and when their interests clash, there is less cooperation or no cooperation at all. The contingencies of international politics and geopolitical compulsions have brought China and Pakistan closer to each other. They have developed a more or less common outlook on world affairs despite their adherence to different ideologies. They are especially opposed to the establishment of hegemony by any superpower or its allies in any part of the world. When states have a common enemy they make a common cause against it.

Moreover, Pakistan and China have learnt from one another's experience. Integrative relationship between the two countries is built around their common interest and experience. As a big power, China could be unreceptive to Pakistan's needs but it has not followed this course. It stood by Pakistan in every crisis and proved that a friend in need is a friend indeed. The friendship between Pakistan and China provides an excellent example of integrative relationship. It has proved not only useful but indispensable in promoting regional security and the cause of world peace.

NOTES

1. There are, wrote Prof. Keeneth Boulding, three types of relationships between persons and organizations. These are the threat relations, the exchange relations, and the integrative relations. In the first type of relationship threat is used to influence the role of the other party, while in the second type of relationship goods are given in return for goods. In the integrative relationship parties display understanding and friendship, use aid and trade, both military and economic, to realize their common goals and to promote peace. The relationship between Pakistan and China falls under the third category. Keeneth E. Boulding, 'Integrative Aspects of International System', *Proceedings of the International Peace Research Associations* (Van Gorcum, Assen, 1966), p. 27.
2. People's Republic of China is referred to as China in this paper.

3. See Z.A. Bhutto, 'Pakistan Builds Anew', *Foreign Affairs*, New York, 12: 2 April 1973, pp. 541–54.
4. Hafeezur Rehman Khan, 'Pakistan's Relations With the People's Republic of China', *Pakistan Horizon*, Karachi, Third Quarter 1961, p. 215.
5. See Mohammad Ahsen Chaudhri, *Pakistan and the Great Powers,* Mirror Press Ltd., Karachi, 1970.
6. Ibid.
7. Ibid., p. 81. Also see John Rowland, *A History of Sino-Indian Relations,* London/Toronto, 1967, ch. 10.
8. Mohammed Ayub Khan, *Friends Not Masters,* Oxford University Press, Karachi, 1967, pp. 127–30.
9. For a detailed background of this war see Neville Maxwell, *India's China War*, Jonathan Cape Ltd., London, 1971.
10. W.M. Dobell, 'Ramifications of the China-Pakistan Border Treaty', *Pacific Affairs*, Vancouver, 37: 3 (Fall 1964), p. 290.
11. *Dawn*, Karachi, 18 July 1963.
12. *Morning News*, Karachi, 9 July 1963.
13. Ibid.
14. G.W. Choudhury, 'China's Policy Towards Pakistan', *Current History*, Philadelphia, April 1979, p. 181.
15. *Beijing Review*, Beijing, 24 September 1965, p. 11.
16. Ibid., 17 September 1965, pp. 12–13.
17. John Rowland, op. cit., p. 201. Also *Dawn*, 17 September 1965.
18. *Dawn*, 20 September 1965.
19. Yaacov Verezberger, 'The Political Economy of Sino-Pakistan Relations: Trade and Aid 1963-82', *Asian Survey*, Berkeley 23: 5 (May 1983), p. 647.
20 Ibid., also see W. Howard Wriggins, 'Pakistan's Search For a Foreign Policy After the Invasion of Afghanistan', *Pacific Affairs*, 57: 2 (Summer 1984), p. 295.
21. Mohammad Ahsen Chaudhri (ed.), *Pakistan and Regional Security,* University of Karachi, Karachi, 1985, p. 17.
22. Anne Gelks and Gerald Segal, *China and the Arms Trade,* Croom Helm Australia Pty. Ltd., Sydney, 1985, p. 70.
23. Mohsin Ali, 'Thirty-five years of Sino-Pakistan Diplomatic Relations', *Dawn*, 21 May 1986.
24. Anne Gelks and Gerald Segal, op. cit., p. 63.
25. Yaacov Vertzberger, op. cit.
26. *SIPRI Year Book, 1985*, Stockholm, p. 63 and 399.
27. Anne Gelks and Gerald Segal, op. cit., p. 64.
28. Ibid. p. 66.
29. Ibid., p. 69.
30. Yaacov Vertzberger, op. cit., pp. 648–9.
31. Ibid.
32. *Dawn*, 23 June 1986.

33. Ibid.
34. Lillian Craig Harris, 'China's Third World Courtship', *The Washington Quarterly*, Washington, Summer 1982, p. 129.
35. For a detailed discussion on China's policy towards Afghanistan see Gerald Segal, 'China and Afghanistan', *Asia Survey*, 21:11 (November 1981), pp. 1158–73.
36. *Dawn*, 30 July 1983.
37. Lillian Craig Harris, op. cit., p. 181.
38. *Dawn*, 30 July 1983.
39. Anne Gelks and Gerald Segal, op. cit., pp. 47–8.

21

Impact of the Afghan War on Pakistan*

Pervaiz Iqbal Cheema

The Gorbachev initiative clearly indicates that the Soviets have realized that they underestimated the strength and determination of the Afghan resistance and that their continuous involvement in Afghanistan has placed visible restraints on their behaviour elsewhere, particularly in third world countries.[1] While the decade of the seventies witnessed many third world countries signing treaties of friendship and cooperation with the Soviet Union, the decade of the eighties seemed to have not only put a stop to the continuous enlargement of the Soviet network of such treaties but it has also been consistently tarnishing its image because of the Afghanistan crisis. Gorbachev seems extremely keen to work towards a solution that would not only end the war but would also preserve the socialist government in Afghanistan. Simultaneously the Sovietization programme through educational institutions, coupled with a systematic propaganda campaign to reach the general population, is well underway.[2] Moscow gradually understood that the mere military approach has not really paid the desired dividends despite having incurred a huge monetary cost for maintaining roughly over 120,000 troops in Afghanistan and after having antagonized many countries. The basic pillar of Soviet military strategy was to concentrate around the major urban centres and attempt not to control the countryside but to destroy it with the view that if there was nothing left in the countryside, how would

* Vol. XLI, No. 1, 1988.

resistance get support from the inside sympathizers. The carpet bombing, destruction of crops and irrigation systems, use of chemical weapons of various sorts, the toy booby traps, crippling mines, levelling of villages, were all employed in order to terrorize and cow down the population.[3] Having been somewhat frustrated over the results of the military approach, the new man in the Kremlin seems to support the notion that the political approach to the problem is equally important. This, of course, does not mean the abandonment of the adopted military strategy to destroy resistance gradually. The political strategy implies the intensification of the 'Hearts and Minds' campaign inside Afghanistan, promoting the notion of national reconciliation, since January 1987, undertaking a diplomatic initiative to avoid further isolation and to arrest the ongoing process that was adversely tarnishing its image among the world community.[4] While the outcome of intensification of the political approach inside Afghanistan and the Soviet diplomatic offensive remains to be seen, the war is making things difficult for Pakistan domestically as well as influencing considerably its foreign policy pursuits.

Today the Durand Line is groaning under the combined weight of the Soviet and Afghan soldiers' heavy boots, tanks, guns, missiles, and aircrafts. Frequent violations of its sanctity amount to making a mockery of the border line between the two countries. Repeated warnings have had no effects on the violators. The motivating compulsions that induce the violators to undertake the undesired course of action are not so simple to decipher. Simplistic analysis would easily conclude that on one side of the Line are the foreign Soviet troops and on the other side exists the great reservoir of the resistance groups. An in-depth analysis would point towards many other complexities that are hidden underneath the simplistic facade. However, the purpose of this paper is not to analyse the above mentioned compulsions but to discuss the impact of the ongoing war on Pakistan.

Undoubtedly, the recent developments in Afghanistan effected Pakistan more deeply than any other country. Pakistan had never really enjoyed friendly relations with Afghanistan because of Kabul's irredentist claim for the so called 'Pakhtunistan'. Until 1976 more than once the 'Pakhtunistan' issue reached its crescendo when Pak-Afghan relations deteriorated to the point where the border closure became inevitable. However, the years 1976–78 saw a significant rapprochement between Afghanistan and Pakistan, with Daud visiting

Pakistan twice and Pakistan leaders paying return visits.[5] The results of these visits were that Kabul dropped its insistence on Pakhtun self-determination, hostile propaganda in both countries ceased, and an active search towards the resolution of the 'Pakhtunistan' issue was well underway. But the Marxist takeover in April 1978 not only reversed the trend but the birth of resistance movements and the subsequent violent clashes between the Afghan forces and the resistance groups led to a large scale refugee influx into Pakistan. Since April 1978 the refugees' exodus has fast reached the mammoth proportion of 3 to 4 million.[6] By any yardstick it is a massive number to cater for their basic needs. The size of the influx itself threatens to overwhelm the hard pressed Pakistani authorities who are neither used to nor equipped to play host to such a large number of refugees. A sizeable chunk of the refugees are not registered and do not live in supervized tent villages.[7] They are scattered all over the country, living in rented accommodations and indulging in different types of commercial pursuits.

It may be noted that following Daud's *coup* in 1973 the first major group of refugees, roughly numbering around 2000 loyalists, had sought asylum in Pakistan.[8] Since then the influx of refugees has not stopped. The overthrow of the Daud regime in April 1978 increased the number of refugees (mostly political dissidents). By the middle of June 1978 the number of Afghan refugees in Pakistan was around 109,900.[9] The enthusiastic attempts of Tarahki-Amin to quickly transform the orthodox-traditional Afghan society into a modern socialist progressive society accelerated the refugee movement and multiplied their number rather rapidly. Just before the Soviet invasion, Pakistan had provided asylum to 386,916 Afghan refugees.[10] The Soviet invasion and the consequent intensification of resistance activities opened the flood gates and since then a steady stream of refugees, ranging form 20,000 to 90,000 per month, began to pour into Pakistan. By the middle of 1986 the number was often reported to be around four millions. A comparative analysis of migration within the above mentioned timeframe clearly indicates that the Soviet invasion and the birth of the resistance movement accompanied by the consequent civil war are the major factors that induced almost one-fourth of the entire Afghan population to leave their homeland.

The Afghanistan crisis, in general, and the large concentration of refugees on Pakistani soil in particular, have given birth to many complex problems which are perhaps less obvious but quite disturbing.

For analytical discussion these problems could be broadly grouped into five categories—economic, social, political, strategic, and foreign policy—with allowances for overlapping and inadvertent linkage.

Economic

According to one source, the cost of maintaining the registered refugees is a little over a million dollars a day.[11] This, of course, is the minimum version of the cost entailed as this does not take into account the newcomers and the unregistered refugees. However, most sources agree that almost half of the cost involved in the maintenance of Afghan refugees is borne by Pakistan and the other half is met by many donor states, agencies, and international organizations.[12] It may be true that almost 50 per cent of the cost is borne by the donors, but when invisible expenditures are added it would seem reasonable to assume that Pakistan is sharing the major burden of the cost involved.

Another dimension of the economic problem is the issue of providing fodder to the animals and cattle that came along with their masters. The provision of grazing grounds and water for the Afghani live-stock is a cause of consistent headache for the Pakistan officials. In both provinces of the NWFP and Balochistan, the grazing lands are somewhat limited. In the NWFP most of it belongs to private land owners but in Balochistan part of the green pasture land belongs to the government. Obviously the private owners guard their land with all the care they could muster while the government land is not sufficient enough to cater for all the cattle. Consequently the pressure on land compelled the Pakistan authorities to disperse them to other provinces; a necessity not particularly favoured by the government as such dispersement would make the eventual repatriation of refugees difficult.

The large concentration of refugees in certain areas has also caused ecological problems. Many forests have suffered because most of the refugees use wood for cooking and heating purposes.[13] Refugees, who are generally poor and not familiar with the use of modern cooking and heating gadgets that were provided to them, prefer the traditional method of using wood. Recognizing the inadvertent damage being done to environmental and ecological resources, particularly in the NWFP and Balochistan, the government took many remedial measures including portable water supplies, digging of tube wells and open surface wells, mono pump and hand pump, etc. in order to alleviate the situation.[14]

More affluent Afghan refugees, after their arrival, began to invest their wealth in varied types of commercial pursuits including real estate and the transport business. The purchase of immovable property caused a boom in the real estate business especially in and around the areas of refugee concentration. Realizing the dangerous implications of such a trend the government expressed its determination to curb this development.[15] Although the Afghan refugees were not allowed to purchase the immovable properties, the shrewd Afghans continue to manage to evade the operative rules and regulations either through capitalizing over the incumbent loop-holes within the system or through employment of unfair means.[16] They found ways to get around the law restricting their right to purchase property by obtaining national identity cards, domicile certificates, and at times even passports through agents who charged handsome fees for such procurements.[17] These developments not only raised the property prices but also encouraged corruption. In addition, the house-rents have also soared in cities mainly because city-dweller Afghans were willing to pay higher rent which, in turn, pushed the rent ceiling beyond the capacity of the local lower middle and low classes.[18] In order to check the refugees' unauthorized pursuits in various urban centres of Pakistan and to make things difficult for the Khad agents operating in the guise of refugees, the government of Pakistan has recently decided to recheck all the identity cards issued since 1979. In addition, the procedure to issue a passport has been made a little lengthy, enabling the issuing authorities to satisfy themselves with thorough investigation of the applicants.

Some of the refugees also got involved with the transportation system of the NWFP and gradually managed to own part of the transport business. The Afghan transporters not only offered relatively less rates in order to secure a portion of this business but also operated without immunity. It is also alleged that since the Pakistanis treated them more like guests and gave them facilities that were not available to the local transporters, the Afghanis were able to establish a foothold in this business.[19] Besides, the presence of a large number of refugees has also increased the unemployment problems.[20] Not only did the refugee concentrated areas have their own unemployment problems, but the arrival of many young refugees looking for jobs and willing to work for lesser payment escalated the local unemployment problem. Many Afghanis managed to secure employment in the agriculture and construction industry which implied that those opportunities would have been available to the locals in the absence of the refugees. In addition, the Afghanis have also secured a reasonable position of odd jobs in urban centres. Since the Afghanis were and still are willing to work for lower wages and employers are likely to give preference to them over the locals, the friction has become inevitable.

Social

Many economic issues are, in many ways, linked with social problems and have contributed enormously towards the existing tension. For example transport, grazing land, property purchase, deforestation and unemployment have all contributed considerably towards increasing the tension between the natives and the foreigners. In urban centres not only the increased rents ceiling caused frictions but also the 'privileged position' of the refugees for whom the refugee administration systematically provided all sorts of facilities raised many questions among the local population.[21] Since many poor Pakistanis do not enjoy most of the facilities that had been extended to Afghan refugees and the government is unable to provide similar facilities to all Pakistanis, tension becomes a natural outcome of such a situation. In some areas the refugee settlements have upset the existing sectarian balance. The refugee settlements in the Kurram Agency not only altered the existing sectarian balance and increased tension between the two sects but it is also alleged that the refugees fully participated in the recent sectarian war which left more than 200 dead.[22] The involvement of the refugees in local sectarian clashes was strongly condemned by the leaders of the region.[23]

Another significant social problem that was hitherto non-existent in Pakistan is the drug problem. Until the advent of the eighties, drug addiction was relatively unknown to most Pakistanis. Although poppy was never cultivated on a very high scale in Pakistan and General Zia's concerted efforts further reduced Pakistan's opium harvest from a 1979 high of 800 tons to a low of 45 tons in 1984, in Afghanistan even after the advent of civil war, poppy remained the most attractive cash crop.[24] Before the Islamic revolution in Iran, most of the poppy crop was exported to Iran but with the advent of the new regime, exports to Iran altogether stopped. With the virtual vanishing of the Iranian market, the growers began to set up labs in both Afghanistan and Pakistan with the objective of making more profitable heroin for export to Western countries.[25] With Pakistan welcoming the Afghan refugees and Iran depriving the poppy growers of its market, the former became an obvious route to the West. One dangerous by-product of heroin smuggling through Pakistan was the massive increase of heroin consumption among the Pakistanis within a short span of time. In 1982 it was reported that out of 1.3 million addicts in Pakistan, roughly about 100,000 were heroin hooked and in 1986 the number of heroin addicts exceeded 450,000.[26] In 1987 the official count of addicts rose to 1,901,225 which included 657,842 heroin addicts.[27] Since the advent of the Afghan crisis, the number has been steadily on the rise despite the government's earnest efforts to curb its consumption and to retrieve the hooked persons. However, it must be asserted here that addiction to such a dangerous drug cannot be solely assigned to the Afghans. Perhaps the increased consumption could also be attributed to the shifting centres of heroin activities and its easy availability in local markets.

Another social problem confronting the Pakistanis is the enormously increased crime rate during the last few years. It is alleged that the easy availability of large quantities of smuggled and unauthorized weapons and ammunitions has contributed substantially towards the increased rate of crimes.[28] Three factors seemed to have caused a tremendous increase in weapons inside the country. First, the Afghan rulers have continuously supplied arms to certain tribes in Pakistan with a view to establishing a sympathetic tribal militia that would act as a restraint on resistance activities in and around the tribal belt.[29] Second, since both Pakistani territory and the Afghan political leaders are serving as a conduit for weapon supplies to resistance field commanders, it is alleged that both Pakistani officials as well as Afghan political leaders are peddling weapons for personal profit.[30] While accusing the CIA (Central Intelligence Agency) of gross mismanagement of the arms pipeline to the Mujahideen, the US Congressmen emphasized that 40 per cent of the total arms aid is syphoned off along the way by corrupt officials, Afghan leaders and mujahideen.[31] Third, in a crisis situation, it is inevitable that local arms manufacturers would increase production in order to generate sufficient profit. Conscious of increased smuggling of arms that flooded the market, the indigenous producer was left with limited options; either to employ the economy of scale principles or to indulge in smuggling. A combination of these factors have not only increased the availability of weapons but have also reduced the prices. Thus cheap weapons are now easily attainable which, in turn, seemed to have contributed its share towards increasing the crime rate.[32]

Political

The presence of a large number of Afghan refugees has also caused many political problems in Pakistan. The Pakhtun tradition of *Panah* and Pakistanis' known hospitality faced the dilemma. Two factors seemed to have taxed their patience; the number and the time-span. The number of refugees have swollen to four million and the time-span has already covered eight years with no visible signs of early return of the refugees. The dilemma is how to continue offering them the best of our traditional hospitality and coping with the already surfaced dangerous implications effectively.

The political problems that are in some way directly connected with the refugees which need to be highlighted are the growth of terrorism, and sharp cleavage among the political parties regarding the Afghan refugees and their eventual return. Until the advent of the eighties, organized terrorism was virtually never experienced by Pakistanis. Acts of terrorism are varied and many. The NWFP has been particularly at the receiving end of terrorism. The Kabul regime has managed to penetrate the great reservoirs of resistance, namely the refugee camps. In fact, it is commonly believed in Pakistan that many Afghan saboteurs have come into Pakistan in the guise of refugees with the object of spying and creating tensions between the refugees and the locals. Two factors seemed to have contributed considerably towards the increasing terrorism. First, the agents of the Afghan intelligence service have been extremely active in creating not only the potential for riots in refugee villages and generating antagonism between the refugees and the locals, but have also been responsible for periodic bomb blasts in areas of civilian concentration as well as attempting to destroy targets of tactical importance. Both the Pakistan government and mujahideen sources firmly place the blame on the Khad agents for causing various successful acts of terrorism.[33] Perhaps that is why Khad, in the recent past, has been promoted for its good performance and elevated to cabinet level as the Ministry of State

Security.[34] In fact, Khad has grown as large as the Afghan army and works in close collaboration with the KGB.[35] Second, the internal feuds between various resistance groups and factions have also been manifested in the form of irresponsible terrorist acts.[36] Perhaps that was one of the major considerations to influence the government's decision to order, in August 1984, all Peshawar based resistance groups to move out of Peshawar.[37]

One of the most serious political problems arising from the continuing presence of a large number of refugees in Pakistan is the impact on domestic politics. Normally most external crises tend to have a unifying effect on domestic politics but, in the case of Pakistan, the impact of the Afghan crisis has sharply divided political opinion about the refugees and the eventual settlement of the problem. It all started when one of the political parties gained access to the refugee camps mainly through the Peshawar based Afghan resistance groups.[38] The humanitarian work of that particular party created goodwill among the 'cultivated refugees' which, in turn, generated apprehensions among the other political parties and they began to wonder what would happen if the refugees did not leave and form a large vote-bank for the privileged political party.[39] Besides, until recently, it was not all that difficult, as stated above, to obtain national identity cards, or domicile certificates enabling the cultivated refugees to form a strong political base for the involved party.[40] This simmering fear surfaced in 1986 when the Movement for Restoration of Democracy (MRD) passed a resolution alleging the growing involvement of the Afghan refugees in the politics of Pakistan.[41] In addition, it was also alleged that refugees were being made an instrument to create dissension and disorder in academic institutions to serve the political objectives of a particular section.[42] Indeed these were very serious charges. Some political parties also disagreed with the government's approach towards the Afghan crisis and insisted that direct talks with the Kabul regime should be initiated.[43]

Another sensitive political problem relates to the augured ethnic imbalance in Balochistan that may generate dangerous results, provided the Afghan crisis continues to persist and the flow of the refugees into Pakistan does not stop. Assuming that no change takes place in the operative rate of refugee influx and the conflict remains unresolved for a few more years,[44] the concentration of the refugees could gravely disrupt the socio-economic life in the provinces bordering Afghanistan. Not only have the refugees increased the population of those areas by

10 to 15 per cent but in the case of Balochistan, the inflow of Pakhtun refugees could begin to erode the Balochi predominance. Many Baloch leaders have already expressed fears that the continuous inflow of the refugees could upset the existing delicate balance between the Balochis and the Pakhtuns, and might even cause a situation in which the Balochis may find themselves in minority in their own province.[45]

Politically, the Balochistan situation could be quite easily exploited by the Russians if they so decide. Not only had Balochistan remained a troubled province, specially during the last regime which resulted in the flight of many dissidents who took refuge in Afghanistan, but the Baloch minority problem is extremely sensitive and prone to exploitation. The Soviet Union has many compelling reasons to play the Baloch card in order to coerce, if not undermine, the Pakistan government. Among the reasons that seemed to have annoyed the Soviet Union are Islamabad's linkage with the US and China, the use of Pakistan territory for sanctuary purposes by the Afghan resistance groups, the supply of men and material for the resistance forces from and via Pakistan, Pakistan's repeated refusal to talk directly to the Kabul regime, and recently the unenthusiastic response to the Gorbachev initiative.[46] In fact, according to an American writer, the Soviets have already carefully and actively cultivated support among the Balochis to increase their leverage against the regime in Islamabad.[47]

Finally, among the political circles many questions are repeatedly debated. Would all the refugees go back if the Geneva process is able to produce a settlement? What would be the status of those refugees who opt not to go back to Afghanistan? Will they be allowed to become Pakistani citizens? If no settlement is agreed upon in the near future, would the aid be stopped? What would happen if the refugees refuse to accept the settlement? Would Pakistan force them out? Would there be a war within the bordering provinces between the refugees and the Pakistanis? Such questions not only reflect the apprehensions of those who are directly affected by the presence of the refugees but also communicate indirect fears for future harmony, stability and peace for Pakistani society.

Strategic

Strategically, threats emanating from the Afghanistan crisis did not acquire threatening proportion until the arrival of Soviet combat troops in Afghanistan. The Soviet invasion has dramatically complicated the security situation on Pakistan's western border. Afghanistan, on its own, has never been able to pose much of a problem as Pakistan's military strength was regarded more than sufficient to cope with Afghan threats. It is the Soviet backed and protected Afghanistan which has adversely affected Pakistan's security scenario. For Pakistan the dangers are manifold. First, the invasion has generated fears and apprehensions among many Pakistanis that their country would be the next target. Many Pakistanis believe that, after having consolidated its position in Afghanistan, Moscow will then try to extend its influence beyond the Afghan borders. The argument that Russia is likely to use Afghanistan as a spring-board to destabilize Pakistan in order to gain much desired access to the warm waters of the Indian Ocean, is still held valid by a sizeable section of Pakistanis. Sandwiched between Soviet occupied Afghanistan and the Soviet Union's ally, India, such anxieties do not appear too far-fetched, especially if viewed within the context of past Soviet attitude towards Pakistan.

Second, because of the presence of a large number of Afghan refugees on Pakistani soil and the continuing resistance inside Afghanistan, it cannot be overruled that Pakistan may be drawn into the Afghanistan cauldron willingly or unwillingly. Given the nature of the Afghan resistance, it is difficult to say that it would be a short war. Assuming that the civil war persists and the Soviet casualty rate registers dramatic increase over time, there may come a point where the Soviet Union might seriously contemplate active hot pursuits and sanctuary busting operations. Once this happens, Pakistan would be dragged into the Afghan crisis unwillingly. Such eventualities look real when one realizes that the Soviet leaders and officials already regard Pakistan in a state of undeclared war with the Soviet Union.[48] Undoubtedly the Pakistanis are involved in the Afghan crisis but not the way the Russians are interpreting it. The day Pakistan decided to accommodate a large number of refugees on compassionate grounds, it became involved, though this involvement is of a very different nature. What the Soviet Union appears to have so far failed to recognize is the fact that the massive refugee influx has presented the government of Pakistan with an irreconcilable dilemma. If it organizes help and provides the bare minimum facilities to these refugees on humanitarian grounds, then Moscow begins to accuse Pakistan of aiding, abetting, and encouraging what it terms as counter-revolutionary elements. If it does not look after them, then the danger of refugee camps becoming hot beds of intrigue appears to be even more threatening.

Third, the Soviet Union may be tempted to exploit the internal problems arising from the activities of the dissident elements in the provinces of Balochistan and the NWFP. More than once the substantial internal security capacity of Pakistan's military has been tested in these turbulent provinces. It has often been reported that the Balochis feel that 'they never had a fair deal and are still not getting one'.[49] The Punjabi dominated army and bureaucracy is unable to understand the gravity of the Balochi problem. Similar kinds of feelings also exist in other minority provinces. The problems of the NWFP and Balochistan have been further compounded by the influx of the Afghan refugees. The danger of possible fall-out of Afghanistan's political instability and re-emergence of subversion by dissident elements cannot be underrated. There exists sufficient evidence to support the contention that in the past, the subversive activities were actively encouraged and materially supported by the Afghans as well as the Russians. The situation as it exists today is much more prone to Soviet inspired subversion primarily because of the presence of a massive number of refugees in these provinces and the ongoing civil war in Afghanistan than what was the case in the past.

The final major source of threat to the security of Pakistan primarily emanates from the internal situation but has been exacerbated by the continuing Afghan crisis and an age old unfriendly state of relationship with India. When there exists threats on borders, the internal threats often assume alarming proportion. Because of Soviet involvement in the Afghan crisis and its extremely friendly and stable relationship with India, the emergence of a dangerous Moscow-Kabul-Delhi axis can not just be brushed aside. Even if they decide not to directly invade Pakistan individually or collectively, the exploitation of internal problems could sufficiently weaken Pakistan.

Among the host of domestic problems that seem to have haunted the minds of scholars and leaders alike are the continued search for a viable political system, lack of national cohesion, and the operative inequalities and disparities among the federating units that form Pakistan. The continued inability of the Pakistanis to evolve a viable political system in which the political legitimacy is ultimately sought by a reference to people of Pakistan, has not only consistently impeded the development of nation building institutions, but has also generated a number of complex problems. Excessive political experimentation at various periods of Pakistan's history by different leaders have not yet conclusively provided a panacea for the political problems of Pakistan. An equally potent problem is the lack of national cohesiveness. Economic disparity is the third and perhaps the most important source of tension. Because of the ill-advised and badly planned Harvard Group's developmental strategies during the early post-independence period, the economic disparities were allowed to grow unnecessarily. These disparities were much more visible in the regional distribution of industrialization programmes over the years.[50] Despite the rectification processes undertaken in recent years, the effective removal of these incumbent social and economic disparities is likely to take some time in fading into oblivion.

Foreign Policy

With the advent of the Soviet troops in Afghanistan and the consequential permanent transformation of the regional geopolitical situation, the implications for Pakistan's foreign policy are significantly serious and varied. To begin with, it seems pertinent to mention that while the Americans think in terms of years, the Russians think in terms of decades which means that they play their game of geopolitical chess with no time-limit on their moves.[51] Assuming that the Russians in Afghanistan are there to stay, Pakistan's initial strong and instant reaction seemed reflective of more emotionalism than calculated wisdom. Without having done its own cost-benefit calculus, the anger over the Soviet invasion of Afghanistan was unleashed. Total objectives like unconditional and immediate withdrawal of the Soviet troops were demanded.[52] Such a reaction clearly indicated a somewhat nervous contemplation of possible future Soviet advances. Perhaps two good reasons for such pessimistic thinking were that Pakistan never enjoyed friendly relations with the Soviets whereas its main enemy India maintained enviable cordiality of relationship with them, and the disappearance of the Afghan buffer state that made them acutely conscious of their own vulnerabilities. Pakistan's response to the socialist takeover of April 1978 was much more balanced. It responded in accordance with the principles of non-interference.

The immediate impact of the Soviet invasion was that it frightened the Pakistan decision-makers to reconsider their foreign alignments.[53] While the Afghan crisis provided an opportunity to Pakistan to restore its links with the West which were damaged rather badly because of Pakistan's suspected pursuit of the nuclear path, Pakistan did not rush to friendly overtures of the West immediately and calculated whether or not it should accept arms from the West that would automatically and may even irreconcilably annoy the Soviet Union. In mid-January 1980 President Zia expressed that geography dictated accommodation with our new superpower neighbour as well as with Iran and India.[54] However, after the Islamic Foreign Ministers' emergency meeting in January 1980 and the announcement of Carter's punitive measures, Pakistan decided to press for withdrawal of Soviet troops through the OIC, NAM, and the UN.[55] Apart from the initial outburst, Pakistan exercised restraint throughout the year 1980 and opted for what its President called the 'third option', meaning the China option.[56] However, in the next year, Pakistan, feeling the pinch of the refugee influx along with acute need for replacement of aging weaponry, began to move closer to the USA. This, of course, pushed the Soviets further away and closer to India. While in the late seventies, Pakistan's foreign policy was truly non-aligned (apart from its inherent bias in favour of the Islamic world), the decade of the eighties witnessed a re-emergence of closer ties with the West. The Muslim bloc, torn apart by a multitude of local conflicts, was hardly in a position to shake the Soviet grip on Afghanistan.[57] This of course, does not imply that they readily accepted the *fait accompli* and condoned the Soviet intervention. On the contrary they supported Pakistan's view of the situation and provided some financial contributions to Afghan freedom fighters.

Pakistan is confronted with three threats to its security: direct Soviet military pressure through Afghanistan; indirect Soviet efforts to exploit the internal Pakistan situation; and direct as well as indirect pressures from India, both in its individual capacity or in concert with the Soviet. Despite facing a nightmarish security threat scenario Pakistan took almost a year in evolving its response to the altered geopolitical environment. The hallmark of the new policy was to move even closer to both the US and China and simultaneously try to normalize relations with India with a view to at least minimize, if not defuse altogether, threats on its eastern border.

In an attempt to normalize relations with India, Pakistan made many positive overtures. Among the positive steps undertaken by Pakistan were the no-war pact offer of September 1981; Zia's repeated visits to India that resulted in the Zia-Rajiv peace initiative of December 1985, announcing verbal agreement not to attack each others' nuclear installations; and Pakistan's demonstrated keenness to evolve the South Asian Association for Regional Cooperation (SAARC).[58] Apart from responding constructively to the establishment of SAARC, the Indian response towards Pakistan's sincere overtures was generally skeptical and disappointing, especially on the no-war pact which was not only offered by a military regime but at the cost of some Chinese irritation. However, one positive development of the concerted efforts was the establishment of a joint commission. Although so far the performance of the joint commission has not been all that commendable, its very existence is a source of hope for the future in some strange way.

Equally frustrating had been the Indian reaction over the Afghanistan crisis. Being a founder member of the NAM, the reaction from India was expected to be much more vociferous and critical than what had been expressed by the Indians. However, if the Indian reaction is viewed in the context of India's special relationship with the Soviet Union and its overall foreign policy objectives, then one could easily comprehend its attempt to repay the Soviet gratitude that had been incurred over the years in one go.

Compared to the Indians, the American reaction was not only predictably strong, vociferous and in correspondence with its global pursuits, but was perhaps more reflective of its own inability to correctly perceive the Soviet daring move (invasion) than any great love for Pakistan as it had already cut off all aid to Pakistan by 1979 on mere suspicion that Pakistan was treading on the forbidden path to nuclear bombs. After the change in American administration, the new President took a much tougher line over Afghanistan and offered Pakistan a $3.2 billion economic-cum-military sales package spread over a number of years. The package offered the Pakistanis a chance to buy modern weapons and improve the economic situation; an offer that was difficult to refuse in view of the rapidly increasing Indian military might, complex economic problems with the added refugee burden, aging weaponry and equipment of its armed forces and the real threats perceived from the situation on its western borders. Consequently both the US and Pakistan moved closer to each other; each believing to serve its own national interests.

Similarly China and Pakistan further strengthened their mutual ties. The Chinese reaction to the Afghanistan crisis must also be viewed in the context of its own set of relationships with the Soviet Union and India. The commonality of interests pushed them further closer to each other. However this does not imply that China-Pakistan relations were not all that good. In fact, Pakistan and China have been enjoying cordial relations, Beijing has been a great source of encouragement for Pakistan. In short it could be succinctly stated that because of the Afghan crisis Pakistan moved even closer to China, closer to the US, and attempted to improve ties with India.

Conclusion

In recent times no other crisis has so profoundly affected Pakistan as the ongoing Afghanistan conflict has done so far. The forcible takeover of Kashmir by India and the separation of East Pakistan were the great tragedies of the past that had befallen Pakistan. The effects of the Afghanistan crisis and the consequent influx of refugees are far-reaching. Not only has the proverbial patience of Pakistanis already been stretched to its maximum limits, but the implications are now adversely impinging on our precarious harmony. One suggestion to alleviate the situation is to respond or appear to respond to the Gorbachev initiative even though the initiative appears hollow in some ways. Not only has the violence level inside Afghanistan considerably increased and the border violations rapidly multiplied, but the frequency of the acts of sabotage and terrorism within Pakistan has accelerated to an alarming level. Retaliating to the successful mujahideen operation inside Afghanistan, the Khad agents and local collaborators tend to intensify their nefarious activities in Pakistan.[59] It may be purely coincidental that since the advent of Gorbachev's diplomatically couched peace offensive which started last year, the violence level both inside Afghanistan as well as in Pakistan has touched hitherto unattained new heights. Most Pakistani leaders are quite clear in their perceptions of the current situation and regard the increased acts of terrorism as the direct outcome of Pakistan's Afghan policy.[60] The Moscow-Kabul diplomatic offensive appears to be paying propaganda dividends but not making any contribution towards the much desired settlement of the crisis. The withdrawal of the much publicized six regiments did not weaken the Soviet military strength in Afghanistan in any meaningful sense. Instead the move was loaded with considerable propaganda value. Similarly Najib's reconciliation policy that offered a power sharing formula with the Afghanis in Pakistan and the monarchists, who had left Afghanistan during the earlier part of the last decade, is attracting much attention. Undoubtedly the Moscow-Kabul diplomatic offensive needs to be effectively countered at least to minimize the propaganda dividends with a proposal that the Afghans in Pakistan should now be allowed to directly participate in the ongoing Geneva peace processes. Secondly, Pakistan should communicate to the Kabul regime its willingness to talk with it directly provided it agrees to the participation of the Afghans living in Pakistan in the desired direct talks and assures that such direct talks would lead to some tangible conclusion. These suggestions neither imply that undue importance is accorded to the Afghans living in Pakistan nor mean acceptance of indigenous political pressures. In order to reduce the impact of large concentrations of the refugees and to secure their successful and comprehensive withdrawal, it would be better if they become part of the process that would not only secure the withdrawal of the Soviet troops from Afghanistan but also of the Afghans from Pakistan. In addition it seems desirable to make an attempt to neutralize the propaganda dividends that Gorbachev-Najib are consistently and successfully attaining through their well-planned political strategy.

Ostensibly Gorbachev seems anxious to secure a kind of a settlement that would favour the safeguarding of the Soviet interests. Equally interested in a settlement on similar lines are the Afghan leaders in Pakistan, the government of Pakistan, and the United Nations. Despite the expressed willingness of the most concerned parties to resolve the dispute, the resolution seems far away. Why? Obviously there seems to be some joker clauses operative somewhere that are taking a heavy toll on the peace process and impeding the negotiations. Perhaps it would be useful to make all Geneva negotiations public enabling all of us to understand what the real hurdles are. Maybe a public debate will produce a constructive solution and help the negotiators to arrive at an early resolution. The longer the crisis persists, the more chances are that its effects would gradually acquire dangerous proportions which, in turn, could indeed pose a very serious threat to Pakistan. Even if no solution is agreed upon after such an exercise, at least the world would know whose joker clauses are impeding the peace process.

NOTES

1. Gorbachev initiative refers to his decision to unilateral withdrawal of six regiments consisting of almost 8000 men, his encouragement of Najibullah to express willingness to talk to Pakistan and mujahideen, and to attempt to win hearts and minds of the people of Afghanistan by launching a campaign to obtain popular support of the people of Afghanistan, see 'Afghanistan: Winds of change' by Colonel Edgar O Ballance in the *Asian Defence Journal*, September 1986, pp. 76–86. Also see *The Muslim*, Islamabad, 11, 19 July 1986, *Far Eastern Economic Review*, Hong Kong, 3 July 1986.

2. The propaganda campaign not only aims at projecting ethnic linkage between the tribes of northern Afghanistan and Soviet Central Asia but also trains the Afghans how to present the Soviet system in rather attractive terms. See *The Christian Science Monitor*, Boston, 26 March 1985.

3. Elie D. Krakowski, 'Defining Success in Afghanistan', *The Washington Quarterly*, Washington, Spring 1985, pp. 37–46.

4. The 'Hearts and Minds' approach means to win over the mullah. Mullahs are now well paid, new mosques have been constructed and old ones repaired. The Soviet troops have been ordered to refrain from referring to Afghans as *Bashmatis* (the bandits). The resistance fighters who wish to cease fighting and want to come back are not to be punished but pardoned and rewarded. Many concessions were announced to attract the exiles to return. Promises were made of tribal autonomy provided the resistance groups were kept out. Home Defence Units were supported etc. See O'Ballance, op. cit., p. 82. In January 1987, Najibullah appealed for an end to Afghanistan's eight-year-old guerrilla war and called for open contact with the Mujahideen and the formation of a coalition government that would include not only members of the incumbent government but also representatives of previous government, the monarchists and the mujahideen. He also announced a unilateral cease-fire from 15 January 1987 in order to promote his policy of national reconciliaiton. See *The Muslim*, 3,4,7 January 1987. Also see *The Nation*, Lahore 3–7 January 1987.

5. See 'Red Flag over the Hindu Kush Part II: The Accidental Coup of Taraki in Blunderland' by Louis Dupre in *American Universities Field Staff Reports*, 1979/No. 45 Asia.

6. According to UN sources the number of refugees that have been registered account to just about three million out of which 2.1 million (74% of the total refugee population) is in the NWFP, 580,000 in Balochistan and 123,766 in Punjab. See *UNHCR Bulletin*, No. 2, September 1986.

7. This writer recently visited Balochistan's Afghan refugee camps along with the members of a visiting study group of Webster University (in Geneva, Switzerland) and discovered that a sizeable chunk of the refugees in Balochistan were unregistered and were living in and around urban centres of Balochistan. Most of them were living in and around Quetta.

8. Hafeez Malik, 'The Afghan Crisis and its Impact on Pakistan', *Journal of South Asian and Middle Eastern Studies*, Villanova, Vol. No. 3 (Spring 1982), pp. 40–51.

9. Ibid.

10. Ibid.

11. The administrative cost of 2.4 million registered refugees was put around a million dollars a day in 1985. See, Debra Denker 'Along Afghanistan's War-Torn Frontier', *National Geographic*, Washington, June 1985, p. 788.

12. Ibid. Among the external donors, UNICR, WFP, UNICEF, WHO, FAO are the prominent international organizations. The other group of external donors are individual states that have been giving aid for the refugees. See 'Afghan Refugees in Pakistan: Influx, Humanitarian Assistance and Implications' by Hasan-Askari Rizvi in *Pakistan Horizon*, Karachi, (First Quarter 1984), pp. 40–61. Also see *Humanitarian Assistance Programme for Afghan Refugees in Pakistan*, a publication of the Chief Commissionerate for Afghan Refugees, Government of Pakistan, July 1984, p. 17.

13. Zafar Samdani, 'The Afghan Refugee: The Human Aspect', *Pakistan and the Gulf Economist*, Karachi, 9–15 October, pp. 24–5.

14. Malik, op. cit., p. 46.

15. *The Muslim*, 8 December 1981.

16. See *South*, London, October 1982. p. 24.

17. Rizvi, op. cit., p. 54.

18. Ibid. Also see *The Nation*, 2 June 1987.

19. Ibid., p. 52.

20. Beverly Male, 'A Tiger by the Tail: Pakistan and the Afghan Refugees' in *Refugees; Four Political Case Studies*, Milton Osborne, Beverly Male, Gardon Lawrie, and W.J.O. Maliey, The Australian National University, Canberra, 1981, p. 39.

21. Malik, op. cit., p. 46.

22. Rizvi, op cit., p. 53. Also see *The Muslim*, 29 July 1987; *The Nation*, 29 July 1987.

23. *The Muslim*, 29 July 1987.

24. Denker, op. cit., p. 788.

25. Ibid., also see *The Newsweek*, New York, 6 October 1986.

26. See 'Pakistan's Heroin Problem' by Yameen Mitha in *The Muslim*, 14 August 1986.

27. *The Muslim*, 2 July 1987.

28. See Inspector General's (Punjab Police) Statement in *Jang* (Urdu Daily), Karachi, 7 November 1986. Also see *The Nation*, 31 July 1987.
29. O'Ballance, op. cit., p. 80.
30. *Time*, New York, 9 December 1985.
31. *The Nation*, 31 July 1987.
32. A Chinese Kalashnikov is now available in the booming arms markets of the tribal areas for Rs 15,000 whereas the Russian version costs a little bit more. Local Pathan manufacturers sell the exact copy of a Kalashnikov for Rs 7000 only. One Kalashnikov bullet costs just one rupee. Even anti-tank rocket launchers are available for Rs 25,000. See *The Nation*, 31 July 1987.
33. Denker, op. cit., p. 785. Also see 'Hazards of the Afghan Crisis' by Khalid Akhtar, *The Muslim*, 20 July 1986. Also see *The Muslim*, 29 July, 4 August 1987.
34. Craig M. Karp, 'The War in Afghanistan', *Foreign Affairs*, New York, Summer 1986, pp. 1026–47.
35. Ibid.
36. Denker, op. cit., p. 785.
37. Ibid.
38. Rizvi, op. cit., pp. 56–7.
39. Ibid. It was also reported that a large number of refugees had already managed to enlist themselves as regular voters on Pakistan's electoral roll. See *Jang*, 28 June 1986.
40. Recently the government of Pakistan announced that all identity cards issued since January 1979 would be verified and reissued. This is a measure introduced to check the liberal policy of issuance of such cards. See *The Nation*, 31 July 1987.
41. See *The Muslim*, 4 February 1986.
42. Ibid.
43. Both Wali Khan and Asghar Khan have been supporting this view. See *The Muslim*, 7 May 1985.
44. The influx of refugees continues at the rate of 5000 to 8000 per month even after the passage of over seven-and-a-half years of the Afghan crisis. See *The Nation*, 20 July 1987.
45. See *South*, op. cit., p. 24.
46. See 'In Afghanistan's Shadow' by Arthur Ross in *The Washington Quarterly*, Autumn 1982. Also see Soviet Ambassador Smirnov's speech to the Press Club in Karachi on 18 November 1984, *The Muslim*, 19 November 1984. Also see *Times of India*, New Delhi, 13 April 1984.
47. Ibid., Ross.
48. See 'Pakistan: Nation on Tightrope' by Rowland Evans and Robert Novak in *Reader's Digest*, New York, October 1982, pp. 22–5.

49. See Selig S. Harison in *Afghanistan's Shadow: Baloch Nationalism and Soviet Temptations,* Carnegie Endowment for International Peace, New York, 1981.

50. Khalid Bin Sayeed, *Politics in Pakistan: The Nature and Direction of Change,* Praeger, New York, 1986, pp. 113–30.

51. Amaury de Reincourt, 'India and Pakistan in the Shadow of Afghanistan', *Foreign Affairs,* Vol. 61 (Winter 1982-83), pp. 416–37.

52. *Far Eastern Economic Review,* 11 January 1980.

53. *The Economist,* London, 12 January 1980.

54. *Newsweek,* 14 January 1980.

55. *Time,* 28 January 1980. Also see *Newsweek,* 11 February 1980.

56. *Newsweek,* 14 January 1980.

57. Riencourt, op. cit., p. 429.

58. See *The Muslim,* 2 March, 28 July 1986.

59. Although Pakistan has been experiencing bomb blasts in various cities throughout the last eight years of the crisis, the recent campaign was not only initiated on KGB instruction but its specific objectives include destabilization of Pakistan, encouraging ethnic and sectarian violence, promoting hostilities between the Afghans and the locals and generating pressures against the government's adopted Afghan policies. See *The Nation,* 2 August 1987.

60. See *The Nation,* 31 July 1987. Also see *The Pakistan Times,* Lahore, 29 July 1987. *The Muslim,* 4, 5, 19 and 26 July 1987.

22

The Superpowers and SAARC*

Hamid H. Kizilbash

The South Asian Association for Regional Cooperation has to serve a community of seven states ranging from tiny Bhutan and Maldives to sprawling India. Populated by nearly a billion people, SAARC states are at different stages of political and economic growth and contain a multitude of languages, cultures, and religions. Although all are uniformly poor, the elite class of many of the South Asian states maintain a first world standard of living and outlook. It is this group which has so far determined how the community of South Asian states should develop.

In the last forty years of independence these states have had many disagreements with each other, some of which led to the outbreak of wars. The smaller states of the region feel threatened by the enormous size and the outlook of India towards its neighbours. All of them have therefore sought support and friendship from other world powers and in the process contained the ability of India to establish an exclusive sphere of influence in the region.[1]

I

Although all the South Asian states achieved independence sometime ago, the process of discovering their regional context began only

* Vol. XLII, No. 1, 1989.

recently. The initiative was taken by the late President Ziaur Rahman of Bangladesh in May 1980 and proceeded by stages involving consultations between the foreign secretaries, foreign ministers, and eventually the heads of government of the seven South Asian states culminating in the setting up of SAARC in December 1985.[2] It may be useful to try to summarize the thinking behind this initiative. Was regional cooperation seen as a first step to the development of an effective regional organization with its own institutions or was it simply to be a nocturnal gathering of states with no collective will or identity? Since regional movements have produced both kinds of communities, it is not obvious from the intentions expressed at Dhaka, what shape the association will take.[3]

Clearly the Ziaur Rahman initiative, which was inspired by ASEAN, did not come at the end of a long process of gestation involving greater realization of the need for collective action in the region.[4] If anything, most of the states of the region were looking away from each other: Sri Lanka towards Southeast Asia, Pakistan towards the Middle East, Nepal towards China, and to different degrees, almost all of them, away from India.[5] The Tamil question in Sri Lanka, the Assam (India)/Bangladesh open border problem, the question of greater autonomy for Sikhs in India, Sindhi agitation in Pakistan, were all sources of bilateral difficulties between South Asian states. The post-1979 events had also increased the regional problems because of the Soviet presence in Afghanistan and America's gleeful pursuit of leverage with which it sought to bleed the Russians there. These developments further diverted the attention of the South Asian states away from the region and, at least, engaged Pakistan squarely on the north-western frontiers of the subcontinent.

The concept of regional cooperation did not attract the attention of regional states in 1980; it was dealt a severe blow by the differences that had arisen on the nuclear issue after the explosion of a 'peaceful' nuclear device by India in 1974. It was one thing to see a distant world madly pursuing nuclear technology and it was another to live in a neighbourhood which had gone 'nuclear'. When Pakistan tried to develop nuclear energy for peaceful purposes, it was accused of seeking to join the nuclear club. India and the United States launched a drive to restrain Pakistan and deny her access to technology or parts that may be used for fabricating a nuclear device. Thus one more seed of discontent planted in 1974 began to flower into a major obstacle to unity in South Asia.[6]

In these circumstances, the position taken by the representatives who met to design a regional organization for South Asia could hardly be very radical. They decided to proceed step by step, testing the ability to cooperate in chosen fields like agriculture or telecommunications before embarking on more ambitious projects.[7] It was not till July 1983 that the New Delhi Declaration was adopted by the foreign ministers to launch the Integrated Programme of Action for SAARC in nine identified areas.[8] Developments involving bilateral differences were not allowed to enter into the deliberations of SAARC and at times, it took considerable exercise of restraint for delegates to avoid bringing up bilateral conflicts. A very good illustration is the situation that arose during the SAARC meeting in 1987 at New Delhi. Taking place soon after Indian planes had violated Sri Lankan airspace to drop supplies to Tamil areas in the North, it is remarkable that Sri Lanka's Foreign Minister could be persuaded to desist from bringing up the matter in the meeting.[9] The Indian Prime Minister put this principle into the following words: 'We have evolved modalities which do not allow bilateral stresses and strains to impinge on regional cooperation.'[10]

Moving forward on the basis of consensus, avoiding issues which divide and keeping to a timetable of scheduled preparatory meetings, SAARC seems to have moved forward cautiously. No ideologue has emerged to suggest that the South Asian states should join together to form a tighter union, but a Secretariat has been established in Nepal and recent meetings of the foreign secretaries and foreign ministers have begun to raise issues on which a common policy can be formulated. The North-South dialogue had captured the imagination of representatives to SAARC meetings and some basic identity of views is beginning to emerge.[11]

The Pakistani Prime Minister inaugurating a SAARC ministerial meeting on International Economic Issues in 1986 expressed the views of many when he said that,

> the unilateral and limited measures adopted by the major industrialized countries in response to crisis situations cannot resolve the fundamental problems of the world economy which are structural and interdependent in nature...SAARC countries should consider the feasibility of jointly negotiating agreements with the industrialized nations.[12]

That there is substantial support for such joint activity to promote a rational international economic order cannot be doubted. Almost every member of SAARC has endorsed these views, but the nature of the North-South struggle being what it is, this has not kept member countries from negotiating individual agreements with the big ten for their own advantage. Also, the European powers and the United States have worked hard to take the wind out of the sails of the South. It would not be unfair to say that the following statement of India's Foreign Secretary, Mr Rasgotra, expresses more hope than reality. 'One of the important objectives of SAARC is,' he said, 'to strengthen cooperation among countries of South Asia in international forums on matters of common interest.'[13]

What is yet to be achieved in terms of cooperation in international forums and what is dividing South Asian states on matters concerning bilateral relations suggest that the states have realized that the time for regional cooperation is here but are unable to fully rise to the occasion.

From the point of view of superpowers-SAARC relations, we can anticipate a great deal from the above discussion:

(1) Superpowers should not worry for sometime that SAARC will transform the region into an alternate centre of power, likely to threaten their interests in the region.

(2) Inspite of the establishment of SAARC, South Asian countries remain available for individual bilateral relations both to the Soviet Union and the United States.

(3) Existing advantages enjoyed by the superpowers in the SAARC countries are not threatened by the present outlook of the organization.

(4) While many kinds of programmes have been launched, it seems unlikely that they will wipe out poverty and backwardness from South Asia or seriously threaten the ruling elite that serves superpower interests.

II

The superpowers have not behaved as outrageously in South Asia as in other parts of the world. They have neither acquired any bases on the mainland nor interfered in the politics of the states of the region.

Gunboat diplomacy has not been attempted and the subcontinent has so far escaped being a theatre of Soviet-American confrontation. And yet, both the superpowers have been active in the region to establish relationships of dependence and strategic advantage while reducing the influence of the other power.

Until recently the competition between the two superpowers in South Asia was carried out at a level where the failure of one or the success of the other was not seen as having any serious impact on the existing strategic balance.[14] In the aftermath of the Islamic revolution in Iran and the stationing of Soviet forces in Afghanistan, the region has become more vital in superpower calculations. American strategists consider Pakistan crucial to their interests in the Persian Gulf and the Arabian Sea and India is seen as having a special role as the predominant power in South Asia and the Indian Ocean.[15]

To speculate on the attitude of the superpowers towards SAARC, it is necessary to examine their interests, plans and practices in South Asia. As we have already mentioned, these interests and plans are not static and can undergo a change with new developments in regional and global politics.

The interests of the two superpowers differ in the South Asian region. The United States is basically concerned with the Middle East oil and the expansion of Soviet influence, while the USSR has a more permanent interest in securing its south-western flank against aggression and reducing Western influence in a region with which it has a common border.

South Asia remained of peripheral interest to the United States as long as the Shah of Iran was available to serve as a surrogate. The oil was secured and a low level of aid activity was sufficient to keep communist gains to a minimum. The 1959 bilateral treaty with Pakistan and the CENTO/SEATO alliances gave the impression that America was active and had secured its interests in the region.[16] In fact, so sure was it of its position and so uncertain of the importance of the region that in 1965 the United States decided to place a ten-year embargo on arms sales to both India and Pakistan. Once détente had become a reality in the mid-1970s, the US further reduced its involvement in South Asia.

US plans for the area underwent a complete change in 1979. Having discovered that the Russians were not allowing détente to stand in the way of securing Afghanistan, Pakistan in particular and South Asia in general came in for priority attention. Aid was restored in a big way, traffic of influential Americans increased and military hardware began to pour into Pakistan like it had in India in 1962. A special military command established for the Gulf began to seek support from Pakistan and the Afghan issue was 'adopted' as a free world priority in all international forums. Pakistan was urged to give up its nuclear programme and India was told to make peace and settle differences in the interest of a joint front against Soviet expansionism.

The Soviet Union had achieved a major breakthrough in South Asia with the signing of the 1971 treaty with India. By encouraging substantial Indian dependence, the treaty assured a less strident Indian voice in international forums where Soviet behaviour was under attack.[17] Joint consultation on matters of military strategy and cooperation in the exploration of outer space are other visible signs of Soviet-Indian solidarity.[18] During the sixties, the Soviet Union had achieved considerable leverage in South Asian relations by its mediation between India and Pakistan at Tashkent in 1966. Although the Asian collective security proposal did not go very far, the Soviets could derive satisfaction from the fact that India and other countries of the region stayed out of SEATO and CENTO. Soviet economic aid on very favourable terms also helped to gain the goodwill of South Asian states. The highpoint of Soviet diplomacy was reached with the liberation of Bangladesh and the emergence of India as the pre-eminent power in the region.

It was not until 1979 that the Soviet Union experienced any serious challenge to the position it had established for itself in South Asia after 1971. Its efforts to neutralize the reaction in Pakistan to developments in Afghanistan did not meet with success but the Indians were more obliging. The rapidity with which the Islamic Conference and the larger global community were mobilized against the Soviet action in Afghanistan has tended to overshadow the fact that India could not be persuaded to play any significant role.[19] The protracted nature of the struggle in Afghanistan, the inability of the Soviet Union to win a decisive victory against the Mujahideen and a reactivated America have adversely affected the Soviet position in South Asia. Although a substantial section of people in the region reject the view that Soviet entry into Afghanistan is a first step to Islamabad and Delhi, the image of the Soviet Union as a less aggressive or meddlesome superpower has suffered.[20] Nearly all the South Asian states including India have had increased contact with the United States during this period and the Russians have had to work hard to keep a foothold in Pakistan. The peace initiatives of Gorbachev and his conciliatory remarks during the 1986 visit to India, suggest an awareness of the damage that has been done to the Soviet Union's South Asia policy in the eighties.

Having become an active area of superpower competition, South Asia's regional politics is likely to be viewed in Washington and Moscow primarily in terms of the opportunity to reduce the influence of one power while increasing that of the other. The United States is presently on an influence-gaining offensive which once again aims at winning over Pakistan without losing India.[21] The Soviet Union wants to consolidate its position in India and at the same time counteract the US gains in Pakistan and the rest of South Asia after 1979. Both superpowers are actively offering economic and military assistance and the latest technology to India and Pakistan on the premise that the way to the heart of a third world power is through its military-industrial appetite. More sophisticated weaponry has arrived in South Asia in the last eight years than in the entire period after independence. At least in India, Pakistan, and Sri Lanka, a Kalashnikov culture is in the making which threatens to replace the old values of peace and non-violence.[22] In short, South Asia is acquiring all the characteristics of a superpower battleground.

The United States also has to contend with the Iranian factor when dealing with South Asia. Here is a country which threatens American interests in the region without necessarily serving the interests of Moscow. Gains in South Asia are therefore seen in Washington as also a way of isolating and weakening the Khomeini regime. With the Arabs and China already on their side, Americans are hopeful that the Soviet global challenge as well as Islamic resurgence, can be contained through the new strategic offensive in South Asia.[23]

The Soviet response to the American initiative is complicated by the nature of the Iranian regime, their Arab interests and the slow progress in Afghanistan. A great deal of reliance is being placed on India and its ability to harass Pakistan, thereby preventing the US strategy from succeeding in South Asia.[24] The Russians may be reluctant to side openly with Iran but they know that it is in their interest that the anti-American, anti-imperialist Khomeini revolutionaries remain in power.

Americans have been in favour of a regional movement in South Asia as a bulwark against Soviet expansion. They welcome it because they hope that it would end Indo-Pakistan rivalry, a rivalry which

Washington believes, has led to the misuse of the arms that they supplied, and provided the Soviets with an opportunity to establish themselves in the region. SAARC is expected to free Pakistan and India to worry about the real enemy and to help Washington deal with the problems created by the Iranian revolution and the Soviet move in Afghanistan.

The Soviet Union has to take into account a different set of factors when faced with the movement for regional cooperation in South Asia. The exclusive and substantial relationship which it has established with India gives it an edge in South Asia so far as competition with the other superpower is concerned. A friendly Pakistan, Bangladesh, or Sri Lanka might be a bonus but not much more.[25] Accordingly SAARC cannot play as central a role in improving the prospects for the Soviet Union in South Asia as it is expected to do for the United States.

The basic difference between the United States behaviour in South Asia as compared with that of the Soviet Union is that while Moscow has given complete and unwavering support to its ally, this has not been possible for Washington.[26] Only an arrangement which makes it possible to help India without annoying Pakistan and vice versa would give the Americans the edge that they desire in South Asia. A South Asian regional organization is viewed in Washington as a step in that direction.

III

The role that India defines for itself in South Asia can have a decisive impact on SAARC-superpower relations. Not only is India by far the largest and most powerful member of the South Asian community, it has also the potential for great-power status. America and India have already clashed on the establishment of the Diego Garcia base in the Indian ocean, and the Soviet Union has had to be content with a secondary role for the pro-Moscow Communist Party of India. Whatever plans the two superpowers may have for South Asia they will have to contend with the plans India has for this region. Let us examine a little more closely the role of India in South Asia.

South Asia as India's exclusive sphere of influence

There can be very little doubt about the fact that India desires that all the six neighbouring states of South Asia should let her determine the policies and goals of the region. India would also like them to turn to her for help in solving their problems and meeting their needs for technology. The movement of Indian forces into Sri Lanka in 1987 with reference to the Tamil problem is an illustration of the role India hopes to play in the region.[27] When a small neighbour cannot handle its domestic problem, Delhi will be happy to do so for it, if necessary, by the use of the great military machine which India is building.

India as China's contender for the leadership of Asia

While not immediately ready to match the strength of the superpowers, India has attempted to build its military and industrial strength with a view to compete with China. The 1974 nuclear explosion, the Indian space programme, and the import of supercomputers from the United States are all part of the efforts to establish a status equal to China. The experience of the Sino-Indian conflict in 1962 has left scars which will only vanish if India can demonstrate an ability to surpass the Chinese in technology and military strength. Sino-Soviet differences make this an ambition to be supported by at least one superpower if not both.[28]

India as the largest democracy of the free world

The emergency of 1975 notwithstanding, India has the best track record in the third world for building up democratic institutions and processes. Its particular brand of secularism, socialism, and democracy is now viewed as a model for the rest of South Asia to follow. At present two (Pakistan and Bangladesh) South Asian states are attempting to return to some form of democracy, two (Nepal and Bhutan) are monarchies, and two others (Sri Lanka and Maldives) are struggling with democracy. Indian policy-makers are justifiably proud of their achievements and anxious to see the same practices adopted in the rest of South Asia.

Although the secular and socialist image of India has suffered a little in recent times, there is, at least in Congress Party governments, an equal commitment to selling these ideas to the rest of South Asia. In short, South Asia is to develop in the image of India.[29]

India as South Asia's nuclear umbrella

India clearly has the ability to build nuclear weapons and is equally opposed to any other South Asian power acquiring that capacity. In a world which has shown no serious inclinations towards disarmament, the threat of a nuclear attack on the South Asian region is therefore either going to be met with the help of one of the superpowers or India. Policy-makers in Delhi are preparing to play that role.[30]

India's plans for South Asia appear to involve an approach not too dissimilar to the Monroe doctrine, except that it is to be implemented in the closing years of the twentieth century: a time when even the smallest states prize their independence, want an equal voice in matters of concern to them and want to be free of dependence and exploitation. The superpowers are viewed as a threat to the aspirations of small states and unless India changes its policies, it is likely to be viewed in the same way.

The United States as well as the Soviet Union seem to be prepared to accommodate India upto a point. Difficulties arise where American or Soviet interests in the Gulf and the Indian Ocean clash with those of India. The strategic exploitation of South Asia by the superpowers is a matter on which India would like to have greater control. SAARC is not going to be allowed to interfere with India's grand design for South Asia but at the same time India would like it to present a united front to the outside world. If India can take its neighbours along, SAARC could become a forum of resistance against the superpowers.

That some common strategies can be worked out to deal with the outside world is a view which has already been expressed in SAARC circles. As General Ziaul Haq of Pakistan put it,

Actuated by a deep sense of solidarity, the South Asian countries, acting in concert, could exercise a collective influence far greater than the sum of their individual contributions.[31]

A great deal will depend on the way India decides to implement its grand design. As long as the states of the region have to fear for their territorial integrity and way of life from India, it will not be possible to promote a unanimity of views regarding the superpowers. On the other hand, if territorial and other disputes with neighbours are solved on an amicable basis and a climate of tolerance for diversity within the region can become established, a basis exists for the South Asian states to limit superpower involvement in the region.

IV

The superpowers have played an important role in South Asian politics and continue to do so. Many states of the region are dependent on them for military and economic assistance and both the United States and the Soviet Union are presently contending for greater influence in the subcontinent. SAARC was established in 1985 by the states of South Asia, as King Birendra Shah Dev of Nepal put it,

> not to pitch ourselves against any power or blocs but to win peace for ourselves by agreeing to augment contacts and seek cooperation in a spirit of good neighbourliness.[32]

Events in Afghanistan and the Gulf suggest that the vows of the San Francisco Conference of 1945 'to save succeeding generations from the scourge of war' are fast being replaced by a new recklessness of the superpowers. Lebanon, the Gulf of Sidra, Grenada, Afghanistan, have all demonstrated that resort to the use of force is becoming increasingly acceptable as a means of achieving foreign policy objectives. In this environment small developing states face a crisis which one writer has described by reference to the events in Grenada in 1983 in the following words:

> Grenada shows that small states must conform to the ideology of the powers, and particularly the superpowers, in whose sphere of influence they are located; or at least they ought to keep a low profile if they do not.[33]

The problems of dependency and underdevelopment, instability and recession were bad enough, but the new mood of the superpowers threatens the very existence of small states. To reduce their vulnerability these states will have to strengthen defence, provide an underpinning for economic growth, maximize internal cohesion and manage foreign affairs with prudence. South Asian states can accomplish this through SAARC, but only if certain conditions are met and some bold steps taken to overcome the obstacles.

The future of SAARC is tied up with the containment of superpower activity in South Asia, and the success or failure of that effort depends on the climate of security that can be established within the region. The establishment of a climate of security, in turn, depends on the Indian role in the region and the response of the smaller states.

The presence of superpowers in a region usually undermines sovereignty while regional organizations are supposed to reinforce it. South Asia in the eighties is in the forefront of Soviet-American relations. The urgency for concerted action by the SAARC countries to prevail upon the superpowers to keep their conflicts outside the region cannot be overstated. General Ziaul Haq referred to this kind of possibility in his statement that, 'Our success in this endeavour (SAARC) could serve to inhibit great power rivalry and restrain their action in South Asia and the adjacent regions of the world'.[34]

But this does not seem to be happening. Superpower activity is on the increase in South Asia and SAARC appears to be quite helpless to put a stop to it. Only a fairly radical transformation in the present cautious approach of SAARC can bring about a change in the situation. The conditions that need to be created are:

(i)   The climate of suspicion and distrust will have to be replaced by a sense of oneness based on the struggle for a better life. The variety of cultures and languages in South Asia does not take away from the unity of experience of all groups with exploitation, poverty, disease and neglect. The region must focus more on the unity of experiences rather than the differences.

(ii) South Asians must learn to distinguish between technology for peace and technology that spreads hunger and death. Nuclear weapons in particular and armament in general must be discouraged so that the region can have a greater sense of security from the threat of a nuclear holocaust and save the resources that are being wasted on armament.

(iii) South Asian newspapers and media must be encouraged not to promote the climate of misperception and negative images of one ethnic or religious group against another. A positive role can be played by the media in promoting the philosophy of SAARC so that the people of the various states become more receptive to the tasks of regional cooperation.

(iv) Economic cooperation that benefits all the states of the region is equally essential for self-reliance. Water and power resources, food and technology, properly shared, can change the destiny of many regions of South Asia which suffer from one shortage or another. Together, South Asian states have a large enough domestic market to absorb goods and services at a level with which a few regions can compete.

If conditions of security, economic well-being, and trust can be created within South Asia, SAARC can play an important role in limiting the involvement of the superpowers in the region. These conditions will make possible such bold steps as:

(i) Putting bilateral differences on the agenda of SAARC instead of seeking help from a superpower.

(ii) Use of economic and other sanctions by the community against members who threaten or resort to the use of force.

(iii) Setting up of a regional 'panchayat', court and other institutions to protect the rights of all citizens and states and provide access to peaceful means of settling disputes.

(iv) Collective action to deal with threats from outside the region such as the Sino-Indian conflict or the Afghanistan situation and agreement on a basic line of action *vis-à-vis* the superpowers.

In the past South Asian states have relied a great deal on the superpowers; it is time they boldly test their ability to rely on each other.

NOTES

1. India's desire for a more influential role in the affairs of Pakistan has certainly been made difficult by the United States and China.

2. For background and other details see, *SAARC, First Meeting of Heads of State or Government, Background Material and Basic Documents*, Ministry of Foreign Affairs, Islamabad.

3. The records of the preparatory meetings of SAARC Foreign Secretaries, Foreign Ministers, and the Standing Committee suggest that the

Association of South Asian states could move in either direction but the less ambitious view has prevailed for the moment. See for example the Reports of the sessions of the *Standing Committee of the South Asian Regional Cooperation*, New Delhi, February 1984, Male, July 1984, Male, February 1985, Thimpu, May 1985.

4. As the background note explains, during 1977-1980, President Ziaur Rahman visited Nepal, India, Pakistan and Sri Lanka for talks and then sent a letter in May 1980 to the Heads of Government of all South Asian states following that up with a paper containing the proposal for regional cooperation in November 1980. Meetings between the Foreign Secretaries began in April 1981.

5. Although only Pakistan has had major conflicts with India, there is little doubt that all the South Asian states tend to be uneasy about an exclusive dependence on India and seek links with China, Southeast Asian states, or the Middle Eastern countries.

6. The difference in approach between India and Pakistan on the nuclear question has intensified after the explosion of 1974 in Rajasthan. Prior to this time Pakistan's interest in nuclear technology was not considered of any serious importance.

7. The list grew from five in April 1981 to thirteen in September, sixteen in November 1981 and seventeen by the time of the third meeting of Foreign Secretaries in August 1982 in Islamabad.

8. These included Agriculture, Rural Development Meteorology, Telecommunication, Scientific and Technological Cooperation, Health and Population, Transport, Postal Services and Sports, Arts and Culture, see the *Joint Communique issued at the Conclusion of the First Meeting of Foreign Ministers*, New Delhi, August 1983.

9. For details see newspaper reports, *The Muslim*, Islamabad, 18–20 June 1987.

10. *Address of Prime Minister Rajiv Gandhi to the First South Asian Regional Cooperation Summit*, Dhaka, 7 December 1985.

11. See the Report of the *SAARC Ministerial Meeting on International Economic Issues*, Ministry of Foreign Affairs, Islamabad, March 1986.

12. Ibid., pp. 7–11.

13. See Report of the *First Session of the Standing Committee of SAARC*, 27 February 1984.

14. This is described as traditional geostrategic rivalry, part of the great game of the superpowers. The opposite is nodal point rivalry. See Richard P. Cronin, 'U.S. Policy Toward the U.S.S.R.: South Asian Issues,' in Rose and Husain (eds.), *Pakistan-US Relations*, Berkeley, 1988.

15. Ibid., p. 141.

16. This is significant because the alliances as well as the treaty failed to establish a meaningful relationship with Pakistan because the objectives of the two countries were different. Pakistan wanted US support against

India and the US wanted Pakistan to be concerned with the threat from the Soviet Union.

17. This matter has been raised with respect to the late Indira Gandhi's denunciation of the US invasion of Grenada in louder tones than the criticism of the USSR for sending its forces into Afghanistan.

18. The 1971 treaty of friendship provides for joint consultation on matters of military strategy between India and the USSR.

19. As Richard P. Cronin puts it, '...India could not be relied upon to lead any regional coalition against the Soviet move' in *Afghanistan*, Cronin, op. cit., p. 149.

20. Former Ambassdor Sajjad Hyder of Pakistan has expressed the view that the Soviets wish to enter South Asia proper, see Sajjad Hyder, *Foreign Policy of Pakistan*, Lahore, 1987, but most other observers feel that by sending its forces into Afghanistan the Soviet Union has interfered in the domestic politics of a third world state.

21. The greatest problem for the US in the sixties as well as the eighties is how to keep India happy while providing economic and military aid against the Soviet Union to Pakistan. The failure of the earlier effort seems to have taught the United States nothing.

22. For some interesting material on the situation in Pakistan, see 'The Long Road To Peace', February 1987 and 'Karachi: Apocalypse Now?', January 1987, *The Herald*, Karachi.

23. It appears that the Americans are hopeful of persuading Pakistan to be more supportive of their problems in the Gulf, particularly since the Arab governments are also critical of Iran's Khomeini regime.

24. As long as Pakistan has a hostile neighbour to the east (India) that the United States does not wish to displease, the Soviets know that the United States' strategy cannot succeeed.

25. The smaller states of South Asia even with their combined population and resources cannot match the power of India.

26. Washington is considered by Pakistanis to have betrayed their interests in the East Pakistan crisis, on the nuclear issue, and even with respect to Afghanistan.

27. For some Pakistani views on this question see editorial comments in *Dawn*, Karachi, 22 September 1987, and *The Muslim*, 22 October 1987.

28. The military build-up in India has been supported by the Soviet Union as well as the United States. The Soviet views it as a counterweight to the rise of China as a great power.

29. Secular socialist and democratic propaganda is regularly aired on All India Radio and Television for South Asian audiences.

30. Prime Minister Rajiv Gandhi has made the announcement that India is reconsidering the decision to not build nuclear weapons.

31. Address by General Mohammad Ziaul Haq at SAARC Summit meeting, Dhaka, 7 December 1985.

32. *Closing Address from His Majesty Birendra Bir Bikram Shah Dev, King of Nepal to the Cenference of Heads of State or Government of the Countries of South Asia*, Dhaka, 8 December 1985.

33. See Colin Clarke, 'Third World Small States: Fragile and Dependent', *Third World Affairs*, London, 1987, pp. 207–215.

34. Address by General Ziaul Haq at SAARC Summit meeting, Dhaka, 7 December 1985.

23

Foreign Aid and Indebtedness in Pakistan*

Mohammad Uzair

World War II gave to the world several new phenomena and institutions; inflation, rationing, black marketing are well known to us. However, before the war ended the four leading countries, known as Allied powers, charted the new shape of the world as well as shares for themselves. Formation of the United Nations was decided towards the end of the war. The Bretton Woods Conference decided in 1944 to establish the International Bank for Reconstruction and Development (IBRD) or (World Bank) and the International Monetary Fund (IMF). Needless to say, the United States was the richest country in the group. It assumed the role of political and economic leadership for most of the world. It offered to be the host country for all the three important international organizations, and provided the necessary facilities. In the post war period the US government offered aid under Point Four Programme and Marshall Plan, especially for Europe.

Economists in the post-war period found a new field of Development Economics. The Keynesian concept of 'autonomous' investment leading to more employment, income and 'induced' investment was handy. This could be done best by economic aid to promote economic development of relatively poorer countries. In a way there was enlightened self-interest. The countries getting aid would buy things from the US or other aid giving countries. Sometimes there was 'tied aid' to ensure the benefit to aid givers when economic

---

* Vol. XLVI, No. 1, 1993.

aid was being given to countries which needed and desired it. Needless to say, the US and other donor countries had their angles of choice in deciding which countries should be helped. Anyway we may like to see how much foreign aid was received by Pakistan and from whom. IBRD and its affiliates were active and so were rich countries like the US. The two most important affiliates of IBRD are International Development Association (IDA) and International Finance Corporation (IFC). The first one, IDA, gives very soft loans carrying a nominal rate of interest like service charges. The second affiliate, IFC, channels private sector investment from developed countries to private enterprises in developing countries. For convenience, we have taken two benchmark years, 1970 and 1991. There are thus two phases, one upto 1970 and the other after 1971, i.e. the loss of East Pakistan. The period upto 1970, or the first phase, is divided according to Five-Year Plan. Pre-plan (July 1955) is the first subdivision, then there are First Five-Year Plan, Second Five-Year Plan, and the Third Five-Year Plan.

Let us now look at the first phase. It may be mentioned that in the initial years aid really meant aid or grants. However, some loans were also given. These loans were considered a part of aid. IBRD was meant to be a 'bank' for development. It, therefore, granted loans as a bank would normally do. Needless to say, its decisions were indirectly influenced by the priorities and thinking of the host country (USA). This is perhaps inevitable. Loans of IBRD were also considered as a part of aid. In the early years of Pakistan, there was a greater proportion of grants, and a smaller portion was loans. Gradually the position was reversed. Grants became a nominal component of aid, while loans were a larger component. The position was like this:

Pre-Plan Period (upto July 1955)	First Five-Year Plan (1955-60)	Second Five-Year Plan (1960-65)	Third Five-Year Plan (1965-70)
Grants $251.1m	$575.9m	$345.4m	$193.1m
Loans $121.0m	$417.0m	$2023.3m	$52507.0m

The total grants upto 1970 added to 1365.6 million US dollars. Out of the total grants upto 1970, the US gave 955.1 million dollars. In terms of percentage, the share of the US was 70 per cent. Other donor countries were Canada, UK, Australia, New Zealand, etc. In the pre-plan period (upto July 1955) the ratio of grants in total aid was 70 per cent, and the ratio of loans was 30 per cent. By the Third Five-Year Plan (1965–70) the ratio was 31 per cent for grants.

As far as loans are concerned, the loans disbursed and outstanding in the year 1952–53 amounted to only 1 million US dollars. By 1959–60, the loans outstanding were 145 million US dollars. By 1969–70 the loans outstanding amounted to 2959 million US dollars. Naturally, a good part of loans outstanding was from IBRD and its affiliates. International agencies provided 21.3 per cent of the total debt outstanding on 30 June 1970. Loans from IBRD amounted to 332 million US dollars. Loans given by IDA were 269 million US dollars. Loans given by IFC stood at 10.7 million US dollars. The total loans from IBRD and its affiliates added up to 612.2 million US dollars. However, loans given by individual countries were also important. Loans from the US government and its agencies outstanding as of 30 June 1970 were 1212.5 million US dollars. The American share in the foreign aid or loans accounted for 41.5 per cent of the total foreign loans. This is a rather high share in foreign aid or loans. Political friendship is linked with economic dependence. The borrowing countries, or recipients of foreign loans or aid, have to make adjustments in their policies or actions according to the wishes of aid giving or lending countries. The lending countries or aid giving countries give preference to 'friendly' countries, which conform to the thinking and policies of the aid giving countries. These aid giving or lending countries treat the lending as a 'political favour'. A favour has to be reciprocated. Ironically, the recipients of foreign loans or foreign aid are highly indebted. Any new dose of loan or aid means increase in the accumulated indebtedness as well as debt servicing, which is a burden on the budget besides a foreign exchange outflow. If we add up the loans from international agencies and loans from the US and its agencies, the total of these two sources constitutes about 63 per cent of the total loans outstanding. After these two sources, other important lenders or aid givers would be Germany, UK, and Japan.

During the first phase (upto the middle of 1970) Pakistan was admired at the international level as one of the best users of foreign aid. International agencies cited Pakistan as a model to be followed by other developing countries. Economic management was efficient during the decade of the 1960s. Misuse or leakages of funds received as aid, corruption and even graft did not constitute a serious problem during that decade. Even inflation as a problem almost did not exist. There was a reasonably good stability in the economic field in the sense that price rise was under control. There was also political stability which helped in economic development and efficient economic management. It is a common observation that countries get good results in economic development during dictatorships and undisturbed continuity of system. However, when there is too much of 'democracy' or 'parody of democracy' and intense politicking, there is not much progress in economic development. Korea is a good example. It is an unfortunate 'trade off'. However, if there is a genuine democracy, and leadership is in the hands of sincere, devoted, and competent people for a long period, there may be sound and solid economic results. Malaysia is a good example. In brief, the foreign debt (or foreign aid) outstanding in 1952–53 was 1 million US dollars. By 30 June 1970, at the end of the Third Five-Year Plan, the amount was 2917.8 million US dollars. This is a substantial rise in seventeen years. However, the burden was not as high as in later years.

In the second phase starting from the mid-1970s there was a much more substantial rise in foreign indebtedness or foreign aid. For the second phase, the benchmark we have taken is 1974–75. This was in a way a normal year, after the loss of East Pakistan in December 1971, massive devaluation of the rupee (May 1972) and large-scale nationalization. Foreign aid or indebtedness in 1974–75 was 4796 million US dollars. By 1991–92 (again a period of 17 years) it stood at 16,481 million US dollars. In the table below we have given comparative figures of 30 June 1970 and 30 June 1991. The table also shows the names of aid givers or lenders.

Foreign Aid Loans Outstanding

Donors	(Million Dollars) 30 June 70	30 June 91
Total All Sources	2917.8	151,470.8
I. International Agencies	623.3	6502.8
IBRD (World Bank)	332.5	1808.7
International Development Association (IDA)	269.0	2171.9
International Finance Corporation (IFC)	10.7	39.3
International Fund for Agricultural Development (IFAD)	—	88.4
Asian Development Bank (ADB)	11.1	2394.5

II.	US Govt. and Agencies	1212.5	2974.9
	US AID	1087.1	1499.3
	US EXIM Bank and Others	67.7	409.6
	PL 480	57.5	1066.0
III.	Other Countries		
	Canada	78.3	516.1
	USSR	63.8	242.8
	UK	201.0	35.1
	Germany	268.1	1263.8
	France	49.3	394.4
	Japan	188.9	2137.8
	China	49.1	171.3
IV.	Muslim Countries and Institutions	NA	617.6
	Saudi Arabia	—	265.0
	Abu Dhabi	—	103.0
	Kuwait	—	101.9
	OPEC Fund	—	50.1
	Islamic Development Bank (IDB)	—	39.9

Source: Government of Pakistan Central Statistical Bureau '25 Years of Pakistan in Statistics 1947-72', pp. 305-308, and Government of Pakistan, Ministry of Finance, Economic Survey 1991-92, Statistical Appendix, pp. 223–4.

It may be interesting to have a look at the sources of foreign aid in the form of loans. International agencies accounted for 21.3 per cent of total loans in 1970, while the US share was 41.5 per cent. In 1991 the position was reversed. International agencies provided 42 per cent of the total, while the share of the US was only 19 per cent. The reasons for this reversal were three. One reason was gradual reduction in growth rate and overall economic strength of the US economy. The other reason was that certain new international agencies developed and expanded their operations. The International Fund for Agricultural Development (IFAD) was a new source. Then, IDA and IFC expanded their operations as affiliates of IBRD. Figures of June 1991 indicate a substantial loan from the Asian Development Bank (ADB). In fact, ADB's loans (2394.5 million US dollars) exceeded the loans from IBRD (World Bank). ADB had been liberal. The third reason was that several countries, especially Japan, experienced a higher rate of growth and better balance of payments as compared to the US. Japan's loan (or aid) amounted to 2137.8 million US dollars. The aid from this source constituted 15 per cent of the total aid. Finally, an interesting thing is that during the late 1970s and almost the entire 1980s, Muslim countries and agencies (OPEC Fund and Islamic Development Bank) were aid givers both in the form of grants and loans. In the sphere of loans the share of Muslim countries was 4 per cent.

As discussed earlier, the 'grants' component of foreign aid gradually tapered off, and foreign aid came to mean foreign loans. A concession that the US made was that certain loans, especially PL 480 for obtaining wheat, were repayable in Pak rupees instead of dollars. Grants are now known as relief. We did get some grants or relief (e.g. for help to Afghan refugees). The implication of aid in the form of loans is 'indebtedness' and 'debt-servicing' which means payment of interest and instalments to donor or lending countries or agencies. The burden of debt-servicing gradually becomes heavy as inflow of aid or loans continues. This fact creates two problems. The first problem is that every time a new dose of aid or loan is given, debt service due is adjusted or deducted. Thus, the net transfer is low and limited. The other problem is that the governments of the borrowing countries or recipients of loans, inevitably have to pay large amounts to donor countries. Provision for 'debt servicing' has to be made in the budget. Budget deficit is greater. As for Pakistan, we know that debt servicing is now the largest component of the budget, even higher than defence expenditure. Similarly, the net transfer from foreign loans has declined with the passage of time. The position has been given below:

Year	Gross Disburse-ment	Debt Servicing	Net Transfer Amount	Percentage
1960-61	$342 m	$17 m	$325 m	95 per cent
1971-72	$612 m	$182 m	$430 m	70 per cent
1980-81	$861 m	$603 m	$258 m	30 per cent
1990-91	$2045 m	$1316 m	$729 m	36 per cent
1991-92 (Est.)	$2163 m	$1488 m	$675 m	31 per cent

Source: *Government of Pakistan, Ministry of Finance, Economic Survey 1991-92, p. 59.*

Foreign aid or indebtedness is really a great burden. A net transfer of 31 per cent means that debt servicing consumes 69 per cent of new aid or loans. It is especially a great burden when we compare the position with 1960–61, when net transfer was 95 per cent. Debt servicing took only 5 per cent of aid or loans received. Even 1971–72 was not nearly as bad as 1991–92. Net transfer in that year was 70 per cent, and debt servicing was only 30 per cent. It may be mentioned that a prudent limit or amount of borrowing for individuals, companies, and countries is that the borrower can generate, with the help of borrowed funds, additional income adequate for repayment and interest without any new burden and yet get a net increase in profit or net income. In case of countries, net income means improved standard of living of the people and per capita income. We have not kept this principle as a guideline for economic policies and management. A good part of aid or loan received is wasted or bungled during utilization of borrowed amount or aid. Presently, the debt outstanding is 33.9 per cent of GNP. Debt servicing constitutes 3 per cent of GNP and 14.5 per cent of foreign exchange earning.

The question of foreign aid is an intricate issue. There are paradoxes. It is supposedly needed for promoting economic development. Yet the burden is high, with implications discussed above. Moreover, a good deal of aid is linked with political policies of the donor countries. But we may not be able to meet some of the conditions in view of our own political considerations. Our politicians have shown a paradoxical behaviour. When the aid (or loans) is flowing through 'kindness' of lenders, they keep quiet. In fact they proudly herald it as a success. When aid is not coming easily we talk of self-reliance. Economic management has to be conducted with great sincerity, integrity, imagination, skill and care—almost like determining and conducting a strategy of war against economic backwardness.

24

Pak-Afghan Relations, 1958–1988*

Anees Jillani

One of the first reactions of Mohammad Ayub Khan after coming to power in 1958 was to express his apprehension about the extensive road building and airfield construction in Afghanistan. He opined that this massive activity would enable sizeable military forces to march into West Pakistan at short notice and that the time was not far off when these roads in Afghanistan would prove to be a real threat to the entire subcontinent. Ayub Khan was a staunch anti-communist and he thought that the Soviet Union might be building up Afghanistan as a spring-board for its own expansion southwards. Again in 1959, President Ayub expressed his apprehensions about a possible goal for world domination.

Ayub Khan came from the NWFP. He thus repeatedly challenged Afghanistan's concern for the Pakhtuns in Pakistan. The Afghans had been expressing this interest in the welfare of the Pakhtuns as early as 1942 when the Cripps' Mission came to India to discuss constitutional proposals with Indian leaders. Ayub Khan argued that if the Afghans' interest is based on the historical fact that Afghanistan, at one time in history, ruled over some parts now constituting Pakistan, then they should not forget that there were also times of much longer duration when Delhi's sovereignty extended up to Kabul and beyond. Despite such altercations, the Ayub government continued to make efforts aimed at reconciliation with Kabul. In early 1959, it invited the Afghan

* Vol. XLVI, No. 1, 1993.

Foreign Minister, Sardar Naim, to visit Pakistan. Ayub Khan directly appealed to Naim to abandon the policy of hostility towards Pakistan as it would be to the mutual advantage of both the countries to live as friendly neighbours.

Sardar Naim visited Pakistan. But the incompatibility of views led to the failure of talks. No communique was issued. Nevertheless, Pakistan Foreign Minister, Manzur Qadir, said that the talks had been 'very frank and cordial and that it was agreed that there should be more frequent contacts between leaders of the two countries'. Privately, however, irritated by the persistent Afghan irredentism, Manzur Qadir is said to have made a suggestion to his counterpart during the talks, that 'it is reasonable to assume that Pakhtuns whether they live in Pakistan or Afghanistan belong to generally the same stock and that they want to be together and under the same flag of Afghanistan or Pakistan. Since a referendum had already been held among the Pakhtuns of Pakistan, it is logical that we should ask the Pakhtuns in Afghanistan what their wishes are'. According to Foreign Office officials, at this point the Afghan Foreign Minister went red. The Afghan rulers apparently were not willing to concede the same right of self-determination to tribesmen living within their country.

Subsequent to these abortive talks, police surveillance increased on the Pakistan diplomats in Kabul. On 18 July 1960, the British Foreign Office confirmed that the British and the US embassies in Kabul were no longer able to retain Pakistanis on their staff because the Afghan government was refusing to renew visas of Pakistanis living in Afghanistan. On 11 August 1960, Manzur Qadir disclosed that Pakistan had sent a number of notes protesting against maltreatment of Pakistanis in Afghanistan.

In September 1960, Qadir alleged that the Afghan troops, supported by a few tanks, had concentrated on the border west of Bajaur that the Afghan government organized nearly 70,000 reservists; and that the Afghans were claiming to have the support of a certain big power in the execution of their designs. In March 1960, Khrushchev visited Kabul, openly supported Afghanistan's claims, and extended transit facilities to Afghanistan. He also offered to finance the entire Afghan five year plan for 1960-65 on the condition that Soviet advisers be placed at the highest levels in all Afghan ministries.

On 23–24 September 1960, an Afghan *lashkar* (contingent) supported by Afghan army units crossed into the Pakistani territory of Bajaur to intervene in a local dispute between the Khan of Khar and the Nawab of Dir and his son. The Bajauris resented this outside interference in a private quarrel and repelled the Afghans before any Pakistani troops or scouts could arrive to deal with the invasion. Kabul Radio denied this version, and claimed that the government of Pakistan by levelling such allegations was intending to divert public opinion and to cover the fact that Pakistani troops had been sent in the areas against the wishes of the local population. On 5 October 1960, the government of Pakistan lodged a protest with the Kabul regime against this intrusion, and the hostile concentration of Afghan regulars and irregular forces on its border.

The Afghan regime responded to Pakistan's protests by declaring that Pakistani forces were carrying out repressive operations against the Pakhtuns, including repeated and extensive bombing attacks in the Bajaur area. An article published in *Pravda* on 13 April 1960 under the signature 'observer', believed to be the pseudonym of a high Soviet official, claimed that eight Pakistani divisions supported by tanks and aircraft were active in the bombing of villages causing substantial casualties to Pakhtun areas of Pakistan. The article reaffirmed the Soviet government's support for the Afghan demand for Pakhtuns' self-determination and declared that the situation emerging in the direct proximity of its frontiers was not a matter of indifference to the Soviets.

Finally on 6 April 1960 the government of Pakistan admitted that bombing operations had taken place in the Bajaur area in early March 1960. Lt.-General K.M. Sheikh, Pakistan Minister for States and Frontier Region, said that 'two houses had been bombed 24 hours after the residents of the area had been warned to leave', because they were being used as headquarters and for dumping ammunition by an Afghan agent, Badshah Gul. The Afghan agent had been distributing arms, ammunition, and money amongst the tribesmen. The agent fled to Afghanistan. On 4 April 1961, Daud Khan arrived in Moscow for talks with Khrushchev. And in May, shooting took place between Afghan and Pakistan troops at various border points with each side claiming that the other was using arms supplied by the United States or the USSR. Pakistan asserted that Afghan forces had attacked two Pakistani posts at Mishinai and Sangpura in the Bajaur area on 19-20 May, and PAF planes on 21 May were ordered to destroy machine guns and mortar positions from which these attacks had been carried out. Pakistan claimed that some Afghan agents were arrested in Peshawar and Mardan districts, who had confessed during investigations that they had been commissioned by the Afghan government to kill Pakistani officials and start terrorist activities in Pakistan. In a statement on 23 May, Ayub Khan claimed that Afghanistan had received large quantities of Soviet arms. As a result of these arms, Ayub Khan explained that the Afghans were now employing army troops in border incidents unlike using irregulars in the past.

By August 1961, relations deteriorated to such an extent that Pakistan informed the Afghan government that it intended to close its consulates at Jalalabad and Kandahar, and asked it to withdraw its consulates at Peshawar and Quetta. Afghanistan asked Pakistan to withdraw this note by 6 September, failing which it would sever diplomatic relations with Pakistan. Pakistan dismissed the Afghan threat. Diplomatic relations between the two countries for the second time were snapped in September 1961. Pakistan also refused entry to 200,000 *Pawindas* who trek down to Pakistan in winter for seeking employment and pasture for their cattle.

Transit trade facilities were also again suspended which proved to be a severe economic blow for Afghanistan, particularly in the sphere of its fruit trade. The Soviet government expectedly came to the rescue of Kabul by purchasing the entire stock of fruit, otherwise the suspension could have resulted in an internal strife against the Kabul rulers. This move also affected US AID projects inside Afghanistan. The United States deputed Livingstone Merchant as the special emissary for reconciliation as it perhaps wanted to avoid Afghanistan going totally into the Soviet camp. The Livingstone mission, however, failed. An attempt was made by the Shah of Iran in 1962 to conduct reconciliation but he too could not bring a thaw as Afghanistan insisted on the prior reopening of its consulates in Pakistan.

It was during this time that King Zahir Shah came to appreciate the futility of his country's policy of hostility towards Pakistan as pursued by his premier Daud Khan. Accordingly, in March 1963 he dismissed Daud, the most powerful individual in Afghanistan behind the Pakhtunistan movement. He accused Daud Khan of bringing the Afghan economy to the brink of collapse, and exposing the country to growing Russian pressure against the avowed Afghan policy of neutrality. Daud's dismissal also signified increasing Afghan sensitivity to the danger that massive aid, whether from the United States or the Soviet Union, might alter Afghanistan's traditional policy of non-alignment.

Daud's removal made it easy for the new rulers to reorient Afghan foreign policy. It was decided to resume diplomatic relations in a meeting of the representatives of both the countries in Teheran in May 1963. Consulates were reopened and transit facilities restored. Pak-Afghan trade also increased substantially.

During the Indo-Pakistan war in September 1965, Afghanistan followed a policy of strict neutrality despite 'external pressures'. Pressure was exerted on King Zahir Shah during his visit to the Soviet Union in the course of the Indo-Pakistan war of 1971 to follow a more pro-Indian policy but Afghanistan again took a neutral course. On 30 December 1971, an Afghan Foreign Ministry spokesman declared that the Afghan government extended categorical assurances to Pakistan of its good will, non-interference and support to Pakistan's territorial integrity during the recent Indian aggression on Pakistan. Afghanistan also did not follow the Soviet Union's pro-Indian voting pattern at the United Nations. The sober reality of political pulls and pressures made King Zahir Shah also avoid the hostility of global powers by keeping his country away from Brezhnev's Asian security plan.

Afghanistan was one of the first countries which Zulfiqar Ali Bhutto visited after becoming the President of Pakistan in December 1971. Later his wife, Begum Nusrat Bhutto, also paid a three-day visit to Kabul in May 1972. During the visit, the Afghan Foreign Ministry in a statement said that 'Afghanistan values its brotherly and cultural relations with Pakistan and desires further strengthening of these relations between the two countries'. But the very next day, on 21 May, the Afghan government declared that it had made it clear to Begum Bhutto that 'it will support the Pakhtuns and its relations with Pakistan would depend on that issue'.[1]

The government of Pakistan, however, remained silent on the issue as it did when the subcontinent was classified as the 'Hindustan Peninsula' in a joint communique issued at the end of King Zahir Shah's visit to Moscow in March 1972.[2] In fact, Pakistan during this period was so conciliatory as to grant Afghanistan in August 1972 the facility to send sixty trucks loaded with fruit and other items to India through Pakistan's checkpost at Wagah. Despite this friendly gesture, 'Pakhtunistan Day' of the hypothetical state was officially celebrated throughout Afghanistan on 1 September 1972. In his speech at the United Nations in October 1972, the Afghan Foreign Minister repeated the earlier insinuations and argued that the 'inclusion of NWFP and Balochistan in Pakistan in 1947 constituted a violation of Pakhtuns' right of self-determination, and areas which were never part of undivided India were included in the new state'. It was also contended that Pakistan's attitude on the Durand Line as an established frontier was rather inconsistent with its stand on the McMahon Line, and with its demand for reopening and rectifying of India's borders with China. Pakistan in 1963 had re-negotiated the traditional boundary in Kashmir with the People's Republic of China, and ceded 2050 square miles of territory to the Chinese. In 1958, it agreed to redemarcate its borders with Iran that had been established under the Anglo-Iranian treaties of 1871, 1896, and 1905. Under this new 1958 Agreement, Pakistan had transferred in July 1963 over 300 square miles to Iran and received 95 square miles in return. The Afghans asserted that these new border agreements between Pakistan and two of its neighbouring states illustrated that borders established during the British times were not sacrosanct and were negotiable.

In January 1973, Afghanistan recognized Bangladesh. Soon after the visit of the Afghan Defence Minister, General Muhammad Khan, to Moscow in February 1973, and following the removal of the National Awami Party provincial government in Balochistan and the resignation by the National Awami Party government in NWFP in reaction, Afghanistan intensified its hostile propaganda for what it described as the 'restoration of the rights of Pakhtuns'.

The seizure of power by President Sardar Mohammad Daud through a *coup* on 17 July 1973 exacerbated the already deteriorated relations. President Daud, a former prime minister of the country from 1953 until his dismissal in 1963, ousted his brother-in-law, King Zahir Shah, from the throne and proclaimed the country a republic. In his first policy broadcast, he singled out Pakistan as the only country with which Afghanistan had differences over the 'Pakhtunistan issue'. This hostility was displayed in an international forum when the 'Pakhtunistan' issue was raised by the Afghan envoy in the non-aligned conference at Algiers in September 1973.

In the meantime, in Pakistan, the political situation in Balochistan and the NWFP worsened as the Bhutto government failed in its attempts to silence the political dissident, Wali Khan, or to disband his militant group 'Pakhtun Zalme'. Wali Khan, in October 1973, made the sinister remark that 'just as Bengalis were grateful to Yahya Khan for showing them what to do, so for the same reasons, were Pakhtuns and Balochis grateful to Bhutto'. On 2 December 1973 a leader of the Pakhtun community living in Balochistan was assassinated in his Quetta home.

The adoption by the government of Pakistan in 1973 of the High Treason Act and the Prevention of Anti-National Activities Act suggested the continued presence of fissiparous forces in the country. President Daud Khan was accused in Pakistan for supporting some of these forces.

Daud's stance on Pakhtunistan hardened after his visit to Moscow in June 1974 and the subsequent return visit of the Soviet President, Podgorny, to Kabul in December 1975. Despite the hostile attitude and propaganda of the Daud regime, Bhutto paid his second visit to Kabul as President of Pakistan. After the talks, both countries in a joint communique resolved to settle their differences through the application of the five principles of peaceful coexistence. President Daud paid a return visit to Pakistan and was given a historic welcome. Nothing substantial came out from the talks but both the countries reiterated their determination to resolve their differences by peaceful means.

However, political upheavals in Pakistan prevented further negotiations. The Bhutto regime was toppled by General Muhammad Ziaul Haq in July 1977. Zia visited Kabul in October 1977 soon after assuming office, and President Daud paid a return visit in March 1978, which was his second to Pakistan within nineteen months, 'during which the thread was picked up from where it was left'.

President Daud said in Islamabad that 'during the present round of talks, we have been able to take a big step forward in our relations'. He ended his visit on a happy note by stating that 'Afghanistan and Pakistan were passing through a phase of progress in which any kind of bitterness or tension could become an impediment in the way of development. Both the countries were fighting against poverty and exploitation and the greatest objective before them was the creation of an exploitation-free prosperous society. They could work for the objective only if they single-mindedly implemented their development plans.' He also observed that at one stage the colonial forces had put obstacles between the two peoples through their policy of divide and rule. If 'there was any bitterness or tension it was because of the policies of the time'.[3]

Before the visit of Bhutto and Zia to Kabul and the visit of Daud to Pakistan could facilitate any substantial change in the pattern of Pak-Afghan relations, a major upheaval took place in Afghanistan. In April 1978, the People's Democratic Party of Afghanistan (PDPA) overthrew the Daud government. Nur Muhammad Tarahki, leader of the *Khalq*

faction of the PDPA, was installed as the new President. Unlike the
1973 *coup*, this was a violent change of government as hundreds were
killed, including President Daud, his brother Sardar Naim, and other
members of his family. An estimated 350 Soviet advisers were present
in the country at the time. Pakistan perceived this Afghan 'revolution'
as an expression of Soviet expansion. A Pakistani official commented
that 'the Soviet Union now has a border with Pakistan and the United
States must realize and act accordingly'.[4]

Pakistan started extending support to the Afghan resistance,
popularly known as Mujahideen after this upheaval in Kabul. And one
Afghan regime after another started to face armed opposition.
Thousands of Afghan affectees started coming to Pakistan. By July
1978, the number of Afghan refugees had reached 124,000. An eight
Afghan Islamist parties alliance was formed in Islamabad to oppose
the PDPA regime. In Kabul, the new Tarahki government could not
properly consolidate itself. Dissent developed soon within the Afghan
army which manifested itself firstly in March 1979 in the form of the
Herat garrison rebellion, followed by a mutiny in the Kabul garrison.
In September 1979, President Tarahki resigned and his Prime Minister,
Hafizullah Amin, took over as the new President.

President Amin, however, did not last for long. In December 1979,
Soviet airborne troops led an attack on the presidential palace which
resulted in the death of the President. Babrak Karmal, leader of the
Parcham communist party faction of the PDPA, who had been Afghan
ambassador in Czechoslovakia, was installed as the new President.
The situation drastically changed within a few months. A massive
number of Soviet troops were moved to Afghanistan which became a
household word all over the world. The United States announced trade
embargo and later boycotted the Moscow Olympics for the Soviet
invasion of Afghanistan. While the United Nations General Assembly,
by a 104-18 vote, passed a resolution calling for 'immediate,
unconditional and total withdrawal of foreign troops' from
Afghanistan, Islamic foreign ministers meeting in Pakistan's capital
Islamabad, also passed a resolution calling the Soviet invasion of
Afghanistan a 'flagrant violation of international law'.

Pakistan had now become the frontline state against the Soviet
dominated Afghanistan. International organizations were adopting
Pakistan-sponsored resolutions condemning the Soviet intervention in
Afghanistan. Massive numbers of Afghan refugees started to move to
Pakistan, so much so that by April 1982, the UN High Commissioner

for Refugees reported that the number of Afghan refugees in Pakistan had passed the 2.5 million figure. As a consequence of all these developments, unprecedented foreign aid started to pour into Pakistan against the Soviet might now present next door in Afghanistan. In June 1982 at Geneva, the UN Under-Secretary for Political Affairs, Diego Cordovez, conducted the first round of indirect peace talks between the Kabul regime and Pakistani officials. The parties agreed to discuss 'the withdrawal of foreign troops, non-interference in the internal affairs of states, international guarantees of non-interference and the voluntary return of refugees to their homes'. Nothing concrete took place after these talks until April 1983, when Cordovez opened a second round of talks in Geneva on Afghanistan settlement with representatives of Pakistan and the Kabul regime. Iran also participated in these talks for the first time. In July 1983, US Secretary of State Schultz visited Pakistan, followed by Secretary of Defence Weinberger's visit in September. And in August 1984, for the third consecutive year, the UN sponsored talks took place in Geneva without tangible evidence of progress. The Americans at that stage were reportedly not happy with these peace talks. According to one analyst, in order to sabotage these talks, there were inspired leaks in the American media, including *The Washington Post*, *The New York Times*, and *Time* magazine on the eve of each round of Geneva talks on how the American CIA was supplying arms to the Afghan Mujahideen through its Pakistani counterparts.[5]

Things appeared brighter, however, in June 1985 when the US and Soviet foreign affairs officials met in Washington DC to discuss Afghanistan in their first formal exchange on the issue in three years. However, the very next month, the US State Department announced that 'in response to repeated violations of Pakistan's airspace and territory by communist aircraft operating from bases in Afghanistan', President Reagan has approved immediate delivery to Pakistan of Sidewinder air-to-air missiles and Stinger surface-to-air missiles as well as technical assistance. Earlier in March 1985, Pakistan's General Zia had a one hour meeting with Gorbachev during Chernenko's funeral in Moscow. He described it as a good meeting. The State Department sources, however, stated otherwise and said that the meeting went off badly and that Gorbachev had given Zia a warning.[6]

General Zia in Pakistan again took a hard line on the settlement of the Afghan question perhaps for fear of losing American support after Benazir's return in April 1986. In May 1986, the Afghan President,

Babrak Karmal, stepped down as head of the PDPA. Dr Najibullah, Secretary to the Revolutionary Council Committee, succeeded him as the new President. Dr Najib reiterated that his country's ties with the Soviet Union would be strengthened further. The same month, a Soviet-Afghan plane was shot down by a Pakistani F-16 when it intruded 20 miles into Pakistan's airspace. This was the first time that a Soviet-Afghan plane was shot down in Pakistan since the Soviet invasion. Another SU-22 was hit over Pakistan but it went down in Afghan territory.

In July 1986, Pakistan Premier Muhammad Khan Junejo visited Washington and the Soviet leader, Mikhail Gorbachev, announced the withdrawal of six Soviet regiments from Afghanistan by the end of the year. The withdrawal involved about 6000 men, mostly from anti-aircraft units not being used in Afghanistan. However it was seen by many as a conciliatory gesture. In August the same year, Pakistan and Afghanistan suspended their latest round of UN sponsored indirect negotiations in Geneva without reaching an agreement or setting a date for the next meeting. The impasse continued because of failure to reach agreement on a definite timetable for Soviet withdrawal and the means to monitor compliance with the agreement.

In October 1986, Defence Secretary Weinberger again visited Pakistan. He said that he would not rule out providing AWACS (Airborne Warning and Control System surveillance planes) to Pakistan in view of continuous Soviet-Afghan violations of Pakistan airspace. As if challenging Weinberger to fulfil his pledge, in March 1987, about 10 to 12 Soviet-Afghan warplanes violated Pakistan airspace over the Kurram tribal agency and bombed Teri Mangal, killing at least 51 people and injuring more than 100.

In July the same year, two car bombs, believed to have been planted by the Kabul regime's saboteurs, went off in a busy shopping area in Karachi, killing at least 72 people and injuring more than 250. While inside Afghanistan, the Mujahideen killed more than 1000 Soviet-Afghan troops in three days in a major offensive against Soviet-Afghan bases on a 654 kilometre stretch of highway between Kabul and Jalalabad in an operation, code named 'Operation Avalanche'. In January 1988, Soviet Foreign Minister, Eduard Shevardnadze, paid a three-day visit to Kabul, and stated that the Soviet Union would like 1988 to be the last year that its troops remain in Afghanistan. And later, Gorbachev offered to withdraw Soviet troops beginning 15 May and ending ten months later, provided a Geneva agreement is reached by 15 March. The withdrawal, according to him, would take place without any preconditions for an interim government in Kabul.

At the conclusion of two days of talks in Washington with the Soviet Foreign Minister Shevardnadze, Secretary of State Shultz said in March 1988 that the United States has suggested that if and when Soviet troop withdrawal starts, both sides should be ready to agree to a 'moratorium on military assistance'. In April, Gorbachev met with Afghan President Najibullah in Tashkent and declared that all obstacles to the signing of the Geneva accords were removed, including the question of allowing the United States to continue aiding the Mujahideen.

Finally on 14 April 1988, the Geneva accords on Afghanistan were signed by the Foreign Ministers of Afghanistan, Pakistan, and the Soviet Union, and the US Secretary of State. The United States and the Soviet Union signed as co-guarantors of the main agreement between Afghanistan and Pakistan (representing the Mujahideen). The agreement provided for the withdrawal of the estimated 115,000 Soviet troops from Afghanistan beginning 15 May 1988 and ending nine months later; the voluntary and safe return of some five million refugees and a bilateral agreement between Afghanistan and Pakistan pledging non-intervention and non-interference in each others' affairs. The obligations undertaken by the guarantors were 'symmetrical' allowing the United States to aid the Mujahideen if the Soviet Union continued to aid the Kabul regime.

At a rally at Peshawar two days after the signing of the accord, leaders of the seven parties of the Islamic Alliance of Afghan Mujahideen vowed to continue the *jihad* against the Soviet puppet regime in Kabul until an Islamic government is installed there. The Soviet government, however, completed its withdrawal by 15 February 1989. And thus ended a tragic era in a war in which, according to international observers' estimate, over one million Afghans died as a direct consequence.[7] After the Soviet troop withdrawal, the Kabul regime gradually weakened, so much so that eventually its control was reduced to Kabul and some major population centres.

However, it survived for another three years mainly due to disunity amongst the resistance groups. In February 1989, an Afghan interim government (AIG) was formed, based in Peshawar to oversee a transfer of power. But its component groups could hardly agree on anything substantial. A Mujahideen led government was finally installed in

Kabul in early 1992 when Najibullah stepped down. But the strife in Afghanistan continues.

NOTES

1. *The Pakistan Times,* Lahore, 24 May 1972.
2. *Morning News,* Karachi, 21 May 1972.
3. *The Sun,* Karachi, 10 March 1978.
4. William Borders, 'New Afghan Regime Worries Pakistanis', *The New York Times,* New York, 20 March 1978, cited by Ali T. Sheikh in 'Pak-Soviet Relations and the Afghan Crisis', in L. Rose and N. Hussain (eds.), *Pakistan-US Relations,* Berkeley, 1988, p. 58.
5. Mushahid Hussain, 'Will America let Pakistan settle Afghan question?', *The Muslim,* Islamabad, 10 January 1987.
6. Ibid.
7. US Department of State, 1989, 'Human Rights Report on Afghanistan', p. 1.

25

Prospects of Cooperation with Central Asian States*

S. Amjad Ali

The Central Asian States stretch over a vast expanse of territory from Volga in the west to the Altai mountains in the east, about 1200 miles, and from the Siberian plain in the North to the border of Afghanistan in the south, a distance of 1350 miles. The total area is about 1,542,241 square miles, larger than the area of Pakistan and India combined. The population is, however, only 50 million (as on 1 January 1991) compared to Pakistan's population of 117 million.

Of the five states, Kazakhstan is by far the biggest with an area of one million square miles, more than double the area of all the other four. The smallest, which is nearest to Pakistan, is Tajikistan with only 55,000 square miles. North of that is the slightly bigger Kyrghystan which is spread over 76,000 square miles. Turkmenistan, which shares its southern borders with Iran and Afghanistan, is 188,000 square miles and north of it is the cultural and historical heart of Central Asia, Uzbekistan, stretching over 172,000 square miles, in which lie the fabled ancient cities of Samarkand, Bukhara, and Tashkent. It is also the most populous, with 20 million inhabitants, compared to the 16 million of the six times larger Kazakhstan. Turkmenistan has a population of only 3.6 million, Kyrghystan 4.2 million, and Tajikistan 5.3 million.

Central Asia is a region with rich resources and an advanced economy. The total GNP of the Central Asian states is 156.3 billion

* Vol. XLVI, No. 2, 1993.

dollars compared to Pakistan's 40.9 billion dollars, Turkey's 79.1 billion dollars, and Iran's 81.3 billion dollars. The GNP of Kazakhstan is the highest at 62.2 billion dollars while next comes Uzbekistan with 55.8 billion dollars. The other three have about the same GNP— Kyrghystan 13.3 billion dollars, Tajikistan 12.4 billion dollars, and Turkmenistan, the lowest, at 12.2 billion dollars.[1]

The per capita income is highest in Kazakhstan (3720 dollars) and the lowest in Tajikistan (2340 dollars). Turkmenistan has a per capita income of 3370 dollars, Kyrghystan 3030 dollars and Uzbekistan 2750 dollars.

These cold statistics are confirmed by the personal observation of recent visitors to these lands. Sardar Assef Ahmed Ali, Minister of State for Economic Affairs, noted: 'The people are well off. They have a standard of living much higher than what is generally seen in the subcontinent. Every single citizen has access to this standard of life...Everyone is provided with telephone, electricity and gas.'[2] Another observer, Naeem Sarfraz, has this to say about the infrastructure:

> Broad avenues, tree-lined, with broad pavements, beautifully laid out, surgically clean towns like Alma-Ata, Dushanbe, Baku and Tashkent, where every home has central heating, electricity, gas and telephone, where only trams, trolleys, buses and cars are seen, where there is 100 per cent education, where hospitals are adequate for the needs of the people, where academies of science, libraries, museums, art galleries, theatres and opera houses flourish...The people are highly disciplined. Communism had provided these countries with an incredible infrastructure.

Historical Background

Before the Russians advanced into Central Asia, the northern region, roughly the present day Kazakhstan, was ruled by many Kazakh Khans who were grouped into the greater, the middle, and the lesser hordes. In 1758 the Russians deposed the Khans and this was followed by large scale settlement of Russian peasants on these lands. The Russian rule lasted 233 years, up to 1991. Now the Russians form 38 per cent of the population, against 40 per cent of the Kazakhs. In the south lies the area between the Syr Darya and the Amu Darya (Oxus). Before the coming of the Russians, this was under the rule of three major Khanates—Khiva (Khwarazm), Bukhara, and Kokand (Koh Qand).

The last lies east of the headwaters of the Syr Darya. All three cities are at present in Uzbekistan.

The Russians began their rule by capturing Tashkent in 1865, which was under the Khan of Kokand, and made this their base for further advance. In 1868, they captured Samarkand and Bukhara but allowed the Emir to remain a nominal ruler until 1920, when he was removed by the communists. Khiva was taken in 1873 but the Khan was allowed to remain there till 1920, and last of all, they took the mountain-girt, Kokand, in 1876. This region was ruled by the Russian Czar as one territory called Turkestan. When the communists came to power after the Russian Revolution of 1917, they broke it up into ethnic regions, though as a matter of fact they are all Turkic people. But the division was done in such a way that mutual tensions should continue. For example, large sections of Uzbeks were made part of Tajikistan and vice versa. In this way the region comprising Central Asian states remained under Russian rule for about 115 years, from 1876 to 1991. The last major rebellion against the Russian rule took place in 1916 which was brutally put down.

During the forty-five years of Czarist rule and the seventy years of communist rule, the peoples of Central Asia suffered much political repression and economic exploitation. But by the time the mighty Soviet Union broke up, they had come to enjoy a degree of peace and prosperity that was far greater than that of the peoples of the colonies ruled by the Western imperialist powers, Britain, France, Netherlands, and others (India for 200 years and Indo-China 80 years, Indonesia 400 years, respectively). As a result, we see the strange phenomenon of a people who have been forced to become independent nations, which is precisely what happened to the five Central Asian states after Russia, Byelorussia and Ukraine—the three original signatories of the 1922 constitution which founded the Soviet Union—met in Minsk on 8 December 1991, and created a new Commonwealth of Independent States (CIS).

That action by the three Slavic presidents left Central Asian leaders with an unpleasant choice: they could go it alone—either singly or as a group—or they could shrug off the intended snub by their Slavic counterparts and agree to join the Commonwealth. After a hurried meeting in Ashkhabad, Turkmenistan's capital, they chose the latter course. If independence had to occur, it was best achieved gradually; the new Commonwealth structures, they conceded, would make it easier to regulate their interdependent economies.[3]

Central Asian States' Need for Cooperation

However, willy-nilly, the Central Asian states have been catapulted into a new world of political democracy and free market economy. As for the first, the enthusiasm for democracy is there among the masses, but all the top leaders are the same old communist bosses (except Askar Akaev, a physicist who has been elected the new President of Kyrghystan). Few understand what is meant by a civil society, let alone the ideals of national and religious toleration upon which stable, multinational democracies are based. Abdul Rahim Pulatov, leader of the Birlik Party in Uzbekistan, put it succinctly:

For a hundred and thirty-five years we've been a colony and now we've got independence. Democracy is the first step but what comes after that, is a big question...Every normal and sane politician thinks that turning only to Asia is impossible because, especially in the cities, Europe has had an impact. But we have to think what ties will be most profitable. We have to broaden our contacts with Islamic and Asian countries. We have to communicate with neighbours with whom we have been cut off for seventy years. This is the future.[4]

These are the views of an Uzbek leader. He thinks they must turn to the West. But what does a Westerner say? An American professor of political science, Martha Olcott, wrote very recently:

Central Asia's presidents are not skilled international actors, but they are shrewd politicians. Each understands that their region is not a priority for the United States. US recognition notwithstanding, they know that America cannot be relied upon as a major source of foreign investment nor as the primary conduit of technological expertise. Such help is more likely to come from their neighbours and from states that have traditional interest in Central Asia.[5]

This is exactly what is happening. For example, in the past if a man from Tashkent, the heart of Central Asia, wanted to fly to any of the neighbouring states in the south, he had to fly 1700 miles north-west to Moscow and then fly back over the same territory on an international carrier. Now Pakistan, Iran, and Turkey have started flights of their respective national airlines from Karachi, Teheran, and Ankara direct to Tashkent.

However, these new states are still fully dependent on the old Moscow-based communication grids, which control international mail, telephone and telegraph links, and most international travel. The nearby countries, again, are helping the Central Asian states to emerge from this physical isolation. Pakistan has hastened to open a satellite communications system, via Japan, for semi-automatic telephone and facsimile services between Tashkent and Islamabad, after commissioning the Tashkent ground station. Iran has promised to aid neighbouring Turkmenistan and Persian-speaking Tajikistan with new satellite-based communication systems. Turkey is negotiating with Kyrghystan and has announced plans to provide satellite television transmission to the entire region.

The urgent economic needs of the Central Asian states are many, but mainly these are:

1. To break out of their physical isolation that has been forced upon them by their landlocked geographical position and dependence on Russia;
2. To dismantle the cumbersome and self-defeating centralized planning apparatus in which an army of management personnel set the production targets and prices for millions of production items, and replace it with a free market mechanism without making the change-over a disaster;
3. To establish direct trade relations with the outside world on the basis of barter to begin with, and on normal basis in the future.

The Central Asian republics did not control the hard currency reserves because all exports, if any, made outside the then USSR by them earned foreign exchange which was retained in Moscow and they were paid in roubles. They want barter trade because they cannot pay in hard currency and the exporters will not accept roubles whose value is constantly falling. Some like Kazakhstan are being forced to melt their gold bars to pay for imports. The urgency of their needs can be gauged from the following incident which was reported in the daily *Dawn* of Karachi. During the visit of the Pakistan delegation to the Central Asian states, Sardar Assef Ahmed Ali, Minister of State for Economic Affairs, made an offer to Kazakhstan of 10 million dollars suppliers' credit. The Kazakh Prime Minister, Alexandervich, broke the protocol to interrupt him in his speech to ask if that credit, which was being offered for engineering goods was also available for other goods. Sardar Assef replied, 'Your Excellency, the offer is only for engineering goods but if you permit Pakistani banks to open branches in your country, they will take care of your other credit needs; they will arrange it.' At once the Kazakh Prime Minister replied, 'I allow Pakistani banks to open branches in Kazakhstan here and now but I need 300 million dollars today, for importing fodder and medicines.' Sardar Assef turned towards the members of the Pakistani delegation and asked 'Can you do anything about this?' Instantly, Sultan Arfeen of Instaphone replied that it would be no problem and further stated: 'Would the Prime Minister or his aides discuss details with me after the meeting'.[6]

Cooperation Offered to Central Asian States by Pakistan

The Pakistan delegation which visited all the Central Asian states in November - December 1991 led by Sardar Assef Ahmed Ali, Minister of State for Economic Affairs, comprised government officials, private businessmen and industrialists, journalists, and scholars. They were able to meet their counterparts and to arrive at an understanding for cooperation in a wide variety of fields. Memoranda of Understanding were exchanged with each of the five states at the official level. A brief summary of the Memoranda of Understanding is given below:

Kazakhstan

1. Construction of a five star hotel in Alma-Ata.
2. Establishment of branches of Pakistani banks in Kazakhstan.
3. Establishment of telecommunications system in Kazakhstan.
4. Establishment of joint ventures in pharmacology, light industry, etc.
5. Cooperation between the State University of Kazakhstan and Quaid-e-Azam University, Islamabad.
6. Cooperation between the Kazakh Academy of Sciences and Quaid-e-Azam University and Peshawar University.
7. A Letter of Intent was signed for barter trade with Tabani Corporation, Karachi.

Uzbekistan

1. Cooperation with Ministry of Higher Education of Uzbekistan to exchange students and scholars.
2. Building a five star hotel in Tashkent by the Pakistani private sector.

3. Opening branches of Pakistani banks in Uzbekistan.
4. Cooperation with Pakistan's Institute of Management and Policy and the Quami Youth Convention (private sector) to provide management education and training in youth affairs.

Turkmenistan

1. Agreement with Tabani Corporation for barter trade.
2. Another agreement with Tabani Corporation for a joint venture to manufacture cotton yarn in Turkmenistan.
3. Cooperation with Quami Youth Convention in Youth Affairs.

Kyrghystan

1. Cooperation between the State University of Kyrghystan and Quaid-e-azam University and Peshawar University.
2. Cooperation between the Kyrghystan Academy of Sciences and the Quaid-e-Azam and Peshawar Universities.
3. Agreement with the Institute of Management and Policy and with Quami Youth Convention for management education and youth affairs.

Tajikistan

1. Cooperation in a number of fields.
2. Barter agreement with Tabani Corporation for supply of wheat, rice, tea, and meat in exchange for cotton and aluminium from Tajikistan worth 50 million dollars.
3. Joint venture with Tabani Corporation for international chartered transportation between Dushanbe and Karachi.
4. Arfeen International of Pakistan to establish telecommunication system.
5. A Pakistani private party to set up a five star hotel in Dushanbe.

Besides the above, Pakistan offered 30 million dollars suppliers, credit to Uzbekistan and 10 million dollars each to the other four Central Asian states, immediate despatch from Pakistan of 5000 tons of rice each to Russia, Azerbaijan, Kazakhstan, Turkmenistan, Kyrghystan, and Tajikistan; gift of medicines worth 100,000 dollars to each of the Central Asian states; a donation of 5000 dollars to the *madrassas* and religious boards in each of the Central Asian states; to open consular offices on reciprocal basis in the Central Asian states.[7]

Hurdles in the Way of Cooperation

1. Competition in cooperation with the Central Asian states

As Sardar Assef Ahmed Ali said in an interview:

> All the states seem very keen to deal with Turkey. That is where their natural affinity seems to be. They seem to be looking more to Turkey than to Iran and Pakistan.

Turkey's Prime Minister, Suleyman Demirel, visited the Central Asian states in April-May 1992, the first Western leader to do so. At Tashkent airport, he described Uzbekistan as the 'homeland of our ancestors'. His host, President Islam Karimov, said that Turkey had been the first country to recognize Uzbekistan's independence and that the republic was determined to follow a Turkish role model in its development, that means secular, westernized, democratic development. All the five Central Asian states and Azerbaijan are changing the script of their respective languages from Cyrillic (Russian) to Latin and that will bring them closer to Turkey. Azerbaijan and Kyrghystan have already done so and others are likely to follow, except Tajikistan which is likely to revert to the Persian script. In the economic field Turkey cannot hope to compete with Iran because the Turkish economy is crippled with high inflation, flagging state industries, high unemployment, and the eight-year old Kurdish insurgency in southeast Turkey. Bankers are doubtful if Turkey and Azerbaijan will be able to raise the 1.4 billion dollars needed to build a 663 mile long oil pipeline from Baku across Iran to the Mediterranean coast of Turkey, for which the two signed an agreement in March 1993. Turkey's contribution to the Central Asian states will be mainly in the cultural field. Thus Turkey hosted 10,000 Central Asian students in its universities in 1992.[8] Also, Turkey offered to train officers in the Azeri army. But so far investment has been in predominantly cultural fields. Scholarships have been offered to visiting students. Typewriters, printing presses, and textbooks have been exported to the states.[9]

Turkey does not share land borders with the Central Asian states nor with Azerbaijan while Iran does with Turkmenistan and Azerbaijan. Ashkabad, the capital of Turkmenistan, lies just on the border of Iran and is connected with it by road. It is only 100 miles north of the Iranian railway that runs east-west from Mashhad to

Teheran and Tabriz. This 100 mile spur of the railway will be built by the end of 1993 with the full support of all five Central Asian states.

Turkey's role is seriously handicapped by the strong national belief in the Kemalist doctrine that the mistake of over-reaching abroad should be avoided which was the undoing of the Ottoman Empire. Iran, on the other hand, is enthused with a sense of mission to bring the Muslim Ummah as close together as possible. Iran has thought of another way to come closer to the Central Asian states. President Rafsanjani of Iran has announced the formation of a Caspian Sea Cooperation Zone in which four former Soviet states—Azerbaijan, Kazakhstan, Russia, and Turkmenistan have joined hands with Iran. This organization is unrelated to the Economic Cooperation Organization (ECO) and will act independently.[10] Since 1990 Iran has signed nine bilateral agreements with Turkmenistan for joint development of some of Turkmenistan's oil and gas reserves.[11]

Tajikistan's President Rakhman Nabiyev has opted for a 'Persian model'. 'Iran has provided Tajikistan with financial infrastructure, air links and satellite communications, as well as textbooks written in Persian script. Iran says it has no interest in missionary work among Tajikistan's overwhelmingly Sunni population.'[12]

Pakistan does not share land borders with any of the Central Asian states, thanks to the wedge driven between Pakistan and Tajikistan in the shape of the Wakhan strip by the British imperialist map makers who wanted to insulate the British Indian Empire from Czarist Russia (1895). However, there are two excellent land routes from Pakistan to the Central Asian states that have been used since ancient times by caravans. Both pass through Afghanistan. The shorter one is Peshawar-Jalalabad-Kabul-Kunduz-Hairatan-Termez (in Uzbekistan). It is 500 miles long. On this route an excellent road has been built by the Soviets over the Solangi Pass (in Afghanistan) and a four-lane bridge over the Oxus at Hairatan over to Termez. This was the main route used by the Soviets for bringing supplies and troops to wage war in Afghanistan.

The second route through Afghanistan is Chaman-Kandahar-Herat-Torghundi-Kushka (in Turkmenistan). This route is 513 miles long and is open throughout the year. It was extensively used by Pakistani businessmen and industrialists during 1969-80 for export and import but has remained abandoned for the last thirteen years due to the war and disturbed conditions in Afghanistan. Both these routes can be used after conditions there return to normal.

However, for Pakistan to do business with the Central Asian states, there are two other land routes that pass though Iran:

i) Quetta-Koh-i-Taftan-Zahidan-Birjand-Mashhad-Badjgiran-Ashkabad (in Turkmenistan).
ii) Quetta-Koh-i-Taftan-Zahidan-Kerman-Kashan-Teheran-Qazwin-Rasht-Ardabil-Astara (in Azerbaijan).

At present both these routes can be used, but for this, sufficient warehousing facilities should be provided to accommodate the import and export of goods. Special railway wagons too should be made available for Central Asian transit cargo so that goods can be moved quickly form Zahidan and Chaman to Karachi and vice versa.

2. Lack of Railway connection with the Central Asian states

The lack of a railway connection between Pakistan and the Central Asian states is a serious hindrance. If the 372 mile distance between Zahidan and Kerman is covered with railway track, the Pakistan railway system will be linked with that of Iran and with the Central Asian states (after the 100 mile long spur between Soltanabad in Iran and Ashkabad in Turkmenistan is laid by the end of 1993, as planned). Another possible railway line can be extended from Chaman, which is the last station of Pakistan Railways in northwest Balochistan. It can lead through Kandahar on to Kabul in Afghan territory and then to Ashkabad in Turkmenistan.

Sardar Assef Ahmed Ali, Pakistan's Minister of State for Economic Affairs, discussed this project with the relevant authorities during his official visit to the Central Asian states in December - January 1991-92. He stated in an interview:

> They (the Central Asian states) also want a railway that will connect the Central Asian railway system with either Karachi or elsewhere on the Mekran coast. The Russians also are prepared to help in this. So, it would be a seven or eight nations enterprise, once the Afghan problem is solved. The enterprise will cost an estimated three to five billion dollars but when you have seven or eight nations sharing the expenses, it will lighten the

burden on the individual countries. In seven years we could have a railway line stretching from the northern borders of Afghanistan down to the Mekran coast.[13]

3. Afghan problem hindering import of gas and electricity

As in the case of building a railway line, so for importing gas and electricity from the Central Asian states, the Afghan problem is a big hurdle in the way because the gas pipelines and the electricity lines will pass through Afghanistan. However, at long last peace has been achieved, hopefully, for, on 7 March 1993, the top Mujahideen leaders signed an agreement at the Prime Minister's House in Islamabad according to which President Burhanuddin Rabbani will continue as President for 18 months and Engineer Gulbadin Hekmatyar will become the Prime Minister immediately and later name his cabinet.

The Turkmenistan authorities stated that they have 85 billion cubic meters of natural gas and desired the establishment of joint ventures for supply of gas to Pakistan through Afghanistan. They are very keen on this because Pakistan is the only market for Turkmenistan gas.

The Minister of State highlighted Pakistan's interest in obtaining energy from the Central Asian states. As regards the supply of gas through Afghanistan, he suggested that they may wait till the settlement of the Afghanistan issue.[14]

Similar is the situation with respect to the import of electricity from Tajikistan which has a big surplus. In the whole of the former USSR, Tajikistan occupied the second place, after Russia, in the production of electricity. Electricity output of Tajikistan in 1989 was 15,000 million KW and there are eighty hydroelectric power stations in the country. Two new power projects are in hand for which finance is required. When completed these will have a generating capacity of 4000 MW.

According to the report prepared by the Economic Affairs Division about the visit of the Pakistan delegation to the Central Asian states in November-December 1991, Tabani Corporation signed another protocol for the supply of electricity from Tajikistan to Pakistan and to create a joint venture for this purpose. It was agreed to provide finances for the two proposed power generation projects of Tajikistan.

4. Continuing disturbances and civil war in Tajikistan

Of all the Central Asians states, Tajikistan is nearest to Pakistan and would be sharing land borders if the Wakhan strip was not wedged between the two. Even then a road leads straight north from Kabul to Baghlan and on to Nizhniy Pyandzh in Tajikistan right on the Oxus, where a ferry provides the crossing. Another road leading slightly northwest from Kabul goes to Hairatan on the Oxus where a concrete bridge connects it with Termez in Uzbekistan. But Termez is just on the border of Tajikistan. However, all these facilities of access have been rendered useless for the present because of continuing unrest and civil war in Tajikistan. This is the one Central Asian state where the change-over from the old to the new dispensation has been most turbulent.

After the declaration of sovereignty by the Tajik Supreme Soviet on 25 August 1990, election of the president of the republic was held but due to public protests and upheavals, three presidents changed office in quick succession. At the end of 1992, the last ousted president, Rakhmon Nabiyev, the former communist head, was engaged in armed conflict with his opponents which included the Islamic Renaissance Party. The opposition forces also attacked the Russian troops stationed in Dushanbe, the republic's capital. Tajikistan is the only Central Asian republic in which the Islamic Renaissance Party is functioning legally. Elsewhere it exists only covertly. On 31 March 1993, Tajikistan declared a state of emergency in the republic after two powerful warlords, Sangak Safarov and Faizuli Saidov, killed each other in a big shoot-out. They had installed a pro-communist government after defeating the Islamic rebels.

5. Economic dependence of the Central Asian states on the Slav Republics

When Kazakhstan carved out a degree of financial independence for itself in December 1991, Russia began to boycott it. A month later, with many of Kazakhstan's key industries standing idle, 'Nazarbaev caved in'. The two neighbouring states signed an agreement calling for full cooperation in their trade and financial policies.[15]

It is therefore safe to assume that at this stage and at least for another ten years, their urge to be politically independent would be greatly circumscribed by their compulsion to continue their economic dependence on the Slav republics. The economic interdependence among the former Soviet republics over the last 70 years has acquired a marked depth because of the fact that the lingua franca all over the former Soviet republics has been the Russian language, and it will continue to remain as such for many years to come, despite attempts by the republics of the region to use their local languages for official purposes. And also a good proportion of the population in each republic is Russian. They have largely been manning the administration of these republics. And if ethnic conflicts do not assume a serious proportion, these Russians are likely to continue working and are likely to influence the policies, which naturally will be tilted in favour of continuing with interdependence.[16]

Factors for Cooperation

1. Our dynamic businessmen

One could go on counting the hurdles in the way of cooperation, such as scarcity of hard currency in the Central Asian states, and also of hotels, banks, and insurance companies and economic data and statistics, but where there is a will there is a way. Above all, Pakistan has dynamic and resourceful businessmen who take all these problems in their stride. Stressing this point Sardar Assef Ahmed Ali said in his interview to daily *Dawn* after his visit to the Central Asian states:

> Amjad Tariq of International Multifoods, a member of the delegation, pushed aside these problems and began talking business straight away with the city administration of Samarkand for setting up joint ventures for manufacturing fertilizers, garment stitching and food processing. Negotiations on these projects are going apace...Mr Yaqoob Tabani, a young businessman from an old business family of Karachi, seemed to have performed miracles in the region, as, wherever he went, we heard the presidents and prime ministers mention his name in their official addresses, with warmth bordering on gratitude. At some places I even felt that his name opened doors for our official delegation. I assume he has strictly met delivery deadlines, without worrying much about the payment.[17]

2. Role of the Government of Pakistan

Explaining the role of the government of Pakistan in promoting trade with Central Asian states, Sardar Assef Ahmed Ali said: 'We in Pakistan, in our customs and foreign trade rules and regulations, have already made provisions to facilitate trade and transit with our neighbouring countries, the Central Asian states, the Russian Federation and the Commonwealth of Independent States (CIS). We have also the basic infrastructure and the know-how to handle such transactions...In the wake of the State Bank of Pakistan's latest amendment to the foreign exchange regulations (F.E. Circular No. 23, dated 29 February 1992), a forwarding group in Pakistan is working with some overseas forwarders, on the possibility of routing Pakistan import and export shipments to the Central Asian states and Russia through sea-land-sea routes.'[18]

3. Karachi *vis-á-vis* Odessa

To enter international trade through shipping, the three states of Tajikistan, Uzbekistan, and Kazakhstan can at present use the Black Sea port of Odessa, which is approximately 1860 to 2170 miles from their capitals (Dushanbe, Tashkent, and Alma-Ata). But Karachi port, by comparison, is only about 1500 miles. This will be further reduced by 250 miles when the planned road is completed from Termez to Mazar-e-Sharif-Herat-Kandahar-Quetta-Karachi. Karachi and Qasim ports are being expanded while work has started on a deep sea port at Gwadar. Already a mini-port and fishing harbour have been completed at Gwadar.

4. Haven for joint ventures

Pakistan is offering all facilities and generous concessions to foreign investors by providing export processing zones, freedom to remit earnings in foreign exchange, and, of course, infrastructure. Skilled labour and managerial staff are plentiful and cheap. The Central Asian states are also attracting many foreign investors and Pakistani businessmen too are taking advantage of the opportunities available there. Israel has set up a factory to produce 15,000 denim jeans a day.

President Bush urged US corporations to seize the opportunity to do business in the former Soviet republics, and a federal agency offered unlimited insurance to companies willing to take the risks.[19]

Similarly, Pakistani businessmen are finding it profitable to set up industries in the Central Asian states. 'An average Kazakh worker earns 350 to 400 roubles a month. The dollar-rouble exchange rate in the open market is almost 125 roubles to a dollar. However, once the exchange rate stabilizes, the wage rate is expected to increase. Thus the average Kazakh worker, skilled and educated, is available for only Rs 100 a month. With ample electric power and excellent infrastructure (in comparative terms), Kazakhstan presents itself as a haven for textile industry.

5. Economic Cooperation Organization (ECO)

In February 1992, four of the five Central Asian states—Kazakhstan is still an observer—joined Iran, Turkey, and Pakistan in the broader Economic Cooperation Organization, nicknamed the Islamic Common Market. The new Asian states are slowly but steadily moving away from the Commonwealth of Independent States (CIS). If the pace continues, one of the frontiers between Europe and Asia may run right through the Commonwealth (CIS).[20]

6. Islamic connection

It is said that the Islamic connection should not be emphasized in our economic relations with the Central Asian states. But if according to the impressions brought back by the first official delegation to these states, some of them are not at the moment much concerned with their Islamic identity, so be it. In any case, the emergence of a vibrant Central Asian community need not give rise to a confrontation with any other community. Rather, it should be an opportunity for more purposeful, creative interaction...The strategy should be to evolve economic collaboration and safeguard their political and security interests.[21]

Sardar Assef Ahmed Ali put it very succinctly when he said:

They are Muslims, no doubt about this. They are proud of it. But we should not overplay this hand. If we let loose any ideological movement there, we will be badly rejected by them...We found that religion as a nationalistics force was far greater than as an ideological force.[22]

NOTES

1. 'Prospects and Potential of Air transport in the Central Asian Republics', published by Pakistan International Airlines, Karachi, 1992.
2. *Dawn*, Karachi, 15 January 1992.
3. Martha Brill Olcott, 'Central Asia's Catapult To Independence', *Foreign Affairs*, New York, Summer 1992, p. 108.
4. *New Yorker*, New York, 6 April 1992.
5. Olcott, op. cit., p. 129.
6. *Dawn*, 15 January 1992.
7. Economic report of the visit of the Pakistani delegation to Central Asian States (24 November 1991 to 15 December 1991), *Economic Affairs Division*, Government of Pakistan, Islamabad.
8. *Dawn*, 26 February 1993.
9. Olcott, op. cit., p. 127.
10. *Pakistan & Gulf Economist*, Karachi, 29 February - 6 March 1992.
11. Olcott, op. cit., p. 116.
12. Ibid., p. 127.
13. *Dawn*, 15 January 1992.
14. Economic report of the visit of the Pakistani delegation to Central Asian States (24 November 1991 to 15 December 1991), op. cit.
15. Olcott, op. cit., p. 117.
16. *Christian Science Monitor*, Boston, 21 March 1991.
17. *Dawn*, 15 January 1992.
18. Ibid.
19. *Dawn*, 23 April 1992.
20. *New Yorker*, 6 April 1992.
21. *Pakistan & Gulf Economist*, 29 February–6 March 1992.
22. *Dawn*, 15 January 1992.

26

Reorientation of Pakistan's Foreign Policy after the Cold War*

Marvi Memon

The end of the cold war, with the demise of the Soviet Union, has led to a drastic restructuring of superpower priorities in the international system. The move from a bipolar world with competing ideologies and economic systems has given way to a multipolar system, if not a unipolar system, due to the victory of the dominant Western ideology—liberal capitalism. The question arises, how is a developing Muslim country like Pakistan affected by global changes of such great magnitude?

Due to Pakistan's geostrategic position during the cold war, its foreign policy direction was determined by global conflicts within a system shaped by the victor states of the Second World War. With the dawn of the post cold war system, the constraints and opportunities for Pakistan's foreign policy have changed. The purpose of this paper is to examine how the disintegration of one superpower (or unit in the system) has led to a change in the system, from bipolarity to unipolarity, and how this has affected Pakistan's foreign policy.

It will be argued that during the cold war there were some obvious constraints on Pakistan's foreign policy which have not changed with the end of the cold war; the geostrategic regional environment with neighbours like India, Afghanistan, and the former Soviet Union, imposed certain restraints which intensified Pakistan's insecurity.[1] However, the global environment in the cold war made up for this

* Vol. XLVII, No. 2, 1994.

regional handicap. The cold war offered opportunities to Pakistan through which it was able to solve its security dilemma. It was able to use the global rivalry to its advantage like some other third world countries.[2] It found a geopolitical niche under the global policies of containment, alliances, arms races, and interventions. To compensate for its regional insecurity, Pakistan chose alliance participation in the western camp, non-alignment, and then active alignment as a frontline state in the fight against communism. In this way, it was able to protect its territorial integrity to a certain extent and pursue a foreign policy which allowed military modernization in the form of building the nuclear and conventional options.

With the end of the cold war the constraints have increased. The threat from Pakistan's regional environment lives on in the form of a perceived Indian dominance, only this time the global environment is not able to compensate for its regional weakness. The 1990s have brought a lack of foreign policy options. Faced with the threat of being branded a terrorist state, the continuing Kashmir problem, the end of US aid, and the problems in Afghanistan, the need arises to reassess Pakistan's foreign policy. Is the independent nuclear policy an economic liability? Can it resolve the global constraints by solving its regional constraints? Does the answer lie in solving regional problems through a greater degree of self-reliance and a usage of regional organizations like the South Asian Association for Regional Cooperation (SAARC) and Economic Cooperation Organization (ECO)? Pakistan's objectives have not changed with the transformation of the international system from bipolarity to unipolarity; in fact, it is Pakistan's very inability to adapt to the post cold war order, with its new mechanisms, that has restrained Pakistan's foreign policy.

Pakistan's Security Dilemma

During and after the cold war, the basis of Pakistan's foreign policy has been its security concerns. These exist due to the way the system is formed, due to Pakistan's relations with its neighbours, and due to their relations with the superpowers who shape the sytem. They are the basis for Pakistan's reliance on superpower involvement in the region which imposes constraints and opportunities on Pakistan's foreign policy, making Pakistan vulnerable concerning superpower behaviour. 'The major focus of Pakistan's interaction with the international community has been security against internal and external challenges to its national identity, territorial integrity and independence.'[3]

How is Pakistan's security dilemma unique? Being a relatively new state, having acquired independence in 1947, its security concerns are dependent on the regional and global environment. The external challenge to its territorial integrity which influences its foreign policy has come from Pakistan's immediate geostrategic environment. Firstly, neighbouring India poses the biggest threat to Pakistan. It is perceived to have had problems coming to terms with Pakistan's existence; the two countries have gone to war on three separate occasions (1948, 1965, and 1971). Secondly, Afghanistan has been of some concern to Pakistan's strategists due to its irredentist claims on Pakistan territory. Afghanistan refused to accept Pakistan's North-West Frontier Province (NWFP) as Pakistan's part and as a result, voted against Pakistan's admission to the UN and kept reiterating its position on various other occasions.[4]

Pakistan itself suffers from a number of geopolitical security handicaps.[5] Firstly, it lacks strategic depth; there are no natural barriers on its borders with India and its communication lines and one of its provincial capitals lie too close to this border. Secondly, Pakistan perceives India's superiority in manpower, weapons, industrialization, and defence industry as a threat. This leads to the third handicap which is India's insistence on dominant leadership in South Asia—the natural role of a regional hegemon. This creates problems for Pakistan since its vision of peace and stability is not based on India's dominance in the region; nor does it agree with India's principle of no extra-regional interference to maintain that stability.

More specifically during the cold war, in addition to Afghanistan and India, the third country contributing to Pakistan's feeling of insecurity was the Soviet Union. This insecurity can be explained by the Soviet Union's interest in accessing Pakistan's warm waters. Three actions of the former Soviet Union instilled this fear: firstly, deployment of Soviet troops on Pakistan's border; secondly, Soviet support to two of Pakistan's provinces, namely NWFP and Balochi secessionists; and thirdly, the spillover of civil strife in Afghanistan in the shape of three million Afghan refugees, the use of Pakistani territory for Afghan resistance groups, and its detrimental socio-economic implications. Thus, during the cold war, Pakistan saw the Soviet Union's invasion of Afghanistan as a direct threat to its security. It must be noted that the latter threat from the Soviet Union has subsided with the end of the East-West conflict.

It can be argued that it is Pakistan's location, its geopolitical value to powers who are interested in acquiescing or denying access to lands south of the Indian Ocean, that adds to its insecurity. 'To compensate for the insecurity borne of conventional military inferiority in South Asia, successive Pakistani regimes have attempted to turn geographic position into external political, economic and military support', making extra-regional interference an integral part of its foreign policy requirements. Underpinning Pakistan's security dilemma is the need to augment its strength through extra-regional affiliations; this has made the impact of global conflict more immediate. While India is the cause of Pakistan's insecurity and of Pakistan's extra-regional affiliations, it is these very affiliations that annoy India and, in turn, are the cause of Pakistan's insecurity. India views Pakistan's military links with external powers as a disruption of its natural hegemony in the subcontinent; thus Pakistan's military ties with the US and China have resulted in heightened Indo-Pakistan tensions. Essentially, India insists on bilateralism in the region. Pakistan has always justified extra-regional interference due to the Indian, Afghan, and Soviet threats to its territorial integrity.

How has Pakistan tried to deal with this particular predicament? To understand Pakistan's sense of insecurity (which leads it to a reliance on the superpowers), it is important to appreciate the nature of the arms race and the Indian superiority in it. As long as India continues its ambitious military programme, Pakistan's quest for advanced arms will not stop. If one was to examine the military expenditure in the two countries, India can be observed as superior. In 1948, while India was spending $443 million, Pakistan was spending $160 million. In 1955, despite Pakistan's military alliances with the West (SEATO), India was still spending more: $524 million as opposed to Pakistan's $200 million.[6] At the height of Pakistan's front-line status the country was spending less than India: in 1982, India's spending was at $6.3 billion versus Pakistan at $1.8 billion. In 1990, with the end of the cold war, India stands at $9.6 billion and Pakistan at $2.9 billion.[7] Thus Indian superiority in the arms race further accentuates Pakistan's security dilemma.

Furthermore, losses in conventional wars (India's defeat by China in 1962, and Pakistan's division and defeat by India in 1971) convinced both India and Pakistan to take the nuclear route. This was to provide them with the ultimate guarantee of regional security. The arms race in the form of conventional and nuclear weapons has thus become a matter of national interest and security. Its *raison d'etre* has been: insecurity from the extended aid given to India and secondly, the insecurity felt due to India's dominance. To counter these kinds of insecurities during the cold war, Pakistan flirted with formal alignment, non-alignment, and proxy alliances. With the end of the global conflict, its principal concern has still been to counterbalance and contain its regional threats with active diplomacy. Its foreign policy during and after the cold war is thus underlined by a search for security which is unique, since it is influenced by the global conflict.

Cold War Politics

To understand the politics of bipolarity, it is important to understand that states like Pakistan are inevitably involved in the global conflict, thus increasing the interdependence in the system. Waltz has argued that 'a war or threat of war anywhere is a concern to both of the superpowers if it may lead to significant gains or losses for either of them. As a result, superpowers respond to unsettling events'. Moreover, the influence of the superpowers on states like Pakistan has been even more acute in a bipolar world, since here 'there are no peripheries, with only two powers capable of acting on a world scale, anything that happens anywhere is potentially of concern to both of them. Bipolarity extends the geographic scope of both powers' concern'. Having established that superpower behaviour affected Pakistan during the cold war, an analysis of how it did so will be undertaken.

Superpower behaviour during the East-West confrontation was underlined by a network of alliances and doctrines against each other. As far as alliances are concerned, there were two kinds used by the superpowers to contain communism and capitalism: formal military alliances (written in a form of treaty, giving precise commitment) and informal military alliances or proxy alliances (an understanding without formal commitment). Informal alliances became popular during the time of the second cold war in the 1980s as soon as the threat of direct Soviet aggression had subsided. Moreover, foreign policy disasters such as the Vietnam war made US public opinion wary of any formal kind of military alliances. Furthermore a proxy alliance was easier to dissolve when conditions no longer warranted its presence. Considering the zero-sum contest of the cold war, proxy alliances were safer than formal alliances because they did not require a high degree of commitment. In formal alliance participation it was easy to see any gain or loss of the opponents as shifting the global balance, thus requiring immediate rectification in terms of military action. The objective was to be prepared to halt and reverse the geographic expansion of one's opponent's control and military presence. Needless to say, informal alliances also generated a variety of international commitments to supply military and economic assistance to countries helping with containment.

Apart from the balance of threat doctrines and formal and informal military alliances, the ideological conflict and the bipolar world of the cold war demonstrated itself through political doctrines like the Truman doctrine and the Brezhnev doctrine. The objective was to gather support for capitalism and communism through extended aid and encouragement to potential allies like Pakistan, especially since there was a fear of the 'domino theory' which meant that once a state had fallen to communism other neighbouring states would also follow. The Truman doctrine which was formulated in order to avoid this danger expressed the following beliefs: 'At the present moment in world history nearly every nation must choose between alternative ways of life. The choice is too often not a free one'. President Truman stated: 'I believe that it must be the policy of the US to support free people who are resisting attempted subjugation by armed minorities or by outside pressure'. This doctrine secured a 'foothold...by a combination of economic aid and military alliances embodied in the Marshall Plan and the North Atlantic Treaty'. What came later was the Reagan doctrine of selected intervention in the third world: the objective was to resist communist expansion through doctrines in all arenas of the world.

As far as South Asia is concerned, the area in itself was mainly of serious concern to US policy makers in the context of the East-West conflict. Containment of communism and capitalism was a primary aim in the cold war and to do this the US and USSR moved to different theatres of the cold war. The South Asian threatre became a possibility with four distinctive events: the beginning of the Soviet naval activity in the Indian Ocean, the Sino-Indian conflict of 1962, the Iranian revolution, and the Soviet occupation of Afghanistan in 1979.[8] Superpower policies in the region, in the context of alliance and containment policies, affected the balance of power in the region, and Pakistan's foreign policy in turn.

How did the renewed cold war in the 1980s, especially the policies of the US such as the Reagan doctrine (which encouraged involvement in third world affairs), affect Pakistan's foreign policy? It incorporated Pakistan's foreign policy with the US, making Pakistan geostrategically invaluable against the communists; thereafter changes in US foreign policy were to have a direct impact on Pakistan's foreign policy.

Post-Cold War Order

With the end of the cold war there has been a reassessment of the terms multipolarity, bipolarity, and unipolarity. From the familiar bipolarity of the cold war, where two ideologically opposed systems kept a balance of threat or power in the international system, the world has moved on to unipolarity or, arguably, multipolarity. Thus with the dissolution of one of the poles, it is tempting to see the US as the only pole. The following perspective on the New World Order[9] (NWO) seems reasonable: 'It is a tri-polar world economically, but it's a uni-polar world militarily'.[10] It would be presumptuous to call the new international system as one dominated by multipolarity, since unlike the nineteenth century model of a Concert of Europe, the international system is not made up of roughly equal powers.[11] Thus it becomes difficult to assess the order or disorder in the NWO with the end of the cold war. Furthermore, there is uncertainty in terms of balance of power theories, since unlike the last multipolar system, the current system offers few incentives for the great powers to engage in any balancing role.

In an anarchic international system, a balance of force is necessary to maintain peace and stability. The bipolarity after the Second World War maintained a semblance of stability due to a clear balance of terror. It has been argued by international theorists like Waltz that it was nuclear weapons and not bipolarity that maintained a relative degree of stability in the cold war. Whatever the case, it is clear that a world with two identifiable threats, each balancing the other, is safer than a multipolar world with no identifiable threats. Thus the Soviet nuclear arsenal was safer in Western eyes since it was identifiable, whereas the nuclear arsenal in the Central Asian republics is more dangerous due to the ambiguity in its control.

How has the new correlation of forces (or the disappearance of a pole and the concentration of power on the US) affected the use of force in the NWO? The winners of the cold war claim that the new structure of the international system has brought about responsibilities for the states in the core who are willing to support international law and regimes. The peripheries are still bound by the theories of structural realism where nations use force in zero-sum games.[12] The reason being that nations in the periphery have not been engaged in a massive nuclear arms race; for them an absolute deterrence against military aggression does not exist. Conventional force is still being used in the periphery for greater stability, especially because of the dilemma to project the power of the NWO to solve problems.

Apart from the theoretical aspect, what is the NWO? The first reality of the NWO is the fact that the 'US has attained an international pre-eminence beyond challenge'. According to President George Bush, the NWO is a set of challenges and opportunities for a more harmonious and cooperative international system; international progress through triumph of liberalism and the rule of international law; an era of peace and prosperity, where the UN is to take a more active and important role in global management. If this is the NWO established in the international system, it is obvious that there will be problems with the sudden disappearance or merging of the Soviet pole with the West; there will be nothing to attract those states once oriented in its direction; there is no counter-pull for those states hitherto suspended somewhere between East and West. They will be forced to reorient towards the West by default and not by choice. However, the problem with this is that the West may not be strong enough or willing enough to provide a sense of direction to these states. Moreover, there has been an emergence of regional magnets (Japan, US, EC), thus the responsibility is shared. In the cold war there was a tendency for the great powers to enhance their continental balance through intervention, thereby producing the deadly combination of active alliance formation and political instability. With the end of the cold war, there is no incentive to forge new alliances or take on extra security commitments in any serious form.

A systemic change has taken place. From bipolarity the international system has moved to unipolarity or multipolarity. With the end of the cold war, the dependency of the periphery has increased on the core, but that of the core on the periphery has decreased. This is the major shift in global politics which has affected Pakistan. The next section will analyse Pakistan's security dilemma in the NWO in the regional and global context.

Regional Constraints in the New World Order

Decline in the superpower competition in the developing world has exerted powerful effects on Pakistan and South Asia. Although most of Pakistan's security problems remain, a gradual superpower disengagement will encourage developing countries to make alternative arrangements and create independent regional security associations. 'As these states have always been more concerned with local conditions than with the global balance of power or the ideological competition between US and USSR, the changing world order will affect the resources upon which they can draw and the restraint that other states will be able to impose.' The US in the post cold war era has realized the low strategic value of much of the developing world. Thus global superpower shifts of power, or in this case the end of the Soviet state, has had profound affects on Pakistan's neighbours which, in turn, have affected the regional correlation of power and Pakistan's position in it. As a result of the collapse of the Soviet Union, Pakistan's neighbour, India, has lost an ally. It is important to understand India's options in the post cold war era since considering the close interrelation of Pakistan's foreign policy with India's, this is bound to affect Pakistan's options. India's traditional foreign policy has become irrelevant.[13] It cannot play off the Soviet Union against the West to extort financial, military and trade concessions; the Non-Aligned Movement is dead since third world solidarity is dead. It seems that Third World countries need international institutions like the IMF more than they need each other.

India cannot count on Moscow's support since 60 per cent of its supply of military weaponry is threatened with the end of the Soviet Union.[14] It has thus tried to get US support by discussing joint naval exercises in the sea lanes of the Indian Ocean. This affects Pakistan's relations with the US. Apart from that, since India can no longer be seen as a Soviet proxy in South Asia, China has less incentive to give clandestine help with nuclear weapons and missiles to Pakistan which means that Sino-Pakistan military relations are under strain; especially since territorial disputes between China and India remain unresolved. India's good relations with China represent a zero-sum game. Pakistan is at a disadvantage since India is no longer worried about Himalayan border clashes with the Chinese and can concentrate on Kashmir. Despite the loss of an ally, India has been able to cope by insisting on no extra-regional interference.

How does Afghanistan, a contributing factor in Pakistan's regional insecurity, figure in Pakistan's reoriented foreign policy with the end of the cold war? Firstly, if Pakistan wants to develop its relations with the Central Asian states, it must seek a solution of the Afghanistan problem, thus opening the land route to Central Asia. In preparation for this, Karachi Port and Port Qasim are being expanded; a new modern port is being built at Gwadar, the Indus Highway, and the link between Gwadar and the Indus Highway at Ratodero via Khuzdar is being taken up on a high priority basis. Pakistan's involvement in Afghanistan was acceptable during the cold war but with the end of the cold war and the Soviet withdrawal from Afghanistan, Pakistan cannot follow the same policy in the region. At the moment it feels cut off from Central Asia because of instability in Afghanistan. It needs Kabul as a route; the western route via Iran is too long and the eastern route via China is mountainous. Thus if it wants influence in the Central Asian states, then peace is necessary in Afghanistan.

A complete shift in Pakistan's post cold war foreign policy towards Afghanistan is apparent. Instead of backing the Mujahideen as it had done during the Soviet occupation, it was speculated in January 1992 that Pakistan was more interested in promoting the King to undermine the Mujahideen radicals and encourage the country's silent majority. Pakistan cut support to seven Mujahideen groups. Pakistan was willing to support the five-point UN peace plan. In April 1992, it was reported that Pakistan was willing to send emergency food supplies to Afghanistan, designed to shore up Najibullah. It realized by May 1992 that it had been backing the wrong horse. For cold war purposes, Hekmatyar was adequate but in a NWO he did not fulfil Pakistan's objectives. Therefore, despite domestic repercussions, Pakistan withdrew help to Hekmatyar. Though the will to solve the problem is there, Pakistan did make mistakes. Pakistan's Afghanistan policy was doomed to fail as it never conceptualized operationally the possible dismantling of the Soviet-backed regimes; front-line status meant more than working towards a quick political solution. During the cold war, front-line status had brought in more economic and military largesse, forcing Pakistan's allies to turn a blind eye to illegal nuclear and narcotics activities. With the end of the cold war, Pakistan's discomfiture is noticeable as it has lost the opportunity to fashion the political future of Afghanistan. Overtaken by events, it is now merely reacting to issues concerning its security interests. Thus it is clear that Pakistan followed short-sighted policies in the cold war era, without any vision of a post cold war situation prompted by rewards of a cold war proxy alliance with the US. Having established that Pakistan's regional constraints have continued, the next section will examine how Pakistan has been unable to take advantage of global changes due to its reduced geostrategic position.

Global Constraints

The end of the cold war had brought about a lack of superpower involvement in the region. It has also proved the futility of global conflict in a nuclear age and the limits to their ability to assert authority on regional conflicts. Involvement in Third World affairs is becoming anachronistic since it is not useful or beneficial to the superpower anymore; precisely because 'the most uncertain of all the relationships between the two superpowers are those that occur not in their direct encounters over strategic weaponry or over Europe, but in their relations to other countries, most of them in the third world'.[15]

The end of the cold war has brought an end to vigorous ideological conflicts, though not an end to the US crusades aimed at 'making the world safe for democracy'. There is no ideology threatening the dominant Western ideology anymore. Within a unipolar international system, Pakistan's geostrategic importance has been destroyed, which means that concessions made on its nuclear policy for the sake of alignment will be stopped.[16] It was because of the cold war that South Asia never really had to pay the full price for its challenge to the nonproliferation regime, but donor states are now on the way of making their continued aid (including their votes in international lending institutions) dependent on the non-nuclear status of the recipients. Buried issues such as nuclear non-proliferation, human rights abuse, and narcotics will resurface since there is no forward policy of the US for which Pakistan is needed anymore.

How did the US impose constraints on Pakistan after it became geostratgically redundant? During the spring 1990 crisis over Kashmir, the US believed that Pakistan was able to assemble its nuclear device at the Kahuta enrichment plant. The F-16s were modified to carry nuclear payloads. This perceived behaviour in the post cold war era proved to be unacceptable to the US, and the Pressler Amendment followed in October 1990 which required the President to certify annually to Congress that Pakistan did 'not possess a nuclear explosive device'. Aid became dependent on the stopping of the nuclear programme. This carrot-and-stick approach failed to get Pakistan to stop its programme which it maintained, being peaceful in purpose. This should be considered as a US foreign policy failure. By pursuing nuclear non-proliferation too aggressively, the US drove Pakistan into other nuclear powers' arms. Pakistan, after the end of its aid from the US, had tried to diversify its arms purchases. The 300 megawatt nuclear reactor from China was negotiated. Italy and Germany have been approached and Mirage 2000 fighter bombers from France were being obtained.[17]

In 1991, Pakistan proposed a five-power conference (with the US, China, USSR, India, and Pakistan as participants) to make South Asia a nuclear free zone. This can be considered as a viable policy since the benefits of declaring nuclear capability without actually building the weapons and obtaining a measure of deterrence without attacking penalties of possession is useful. It is, in fact, an important issue since Pakistan's integration with global markets is dependent on it. With this as background, it is not surprising that India and Pakistan have signed agreements prohibiting the use of chemical weapons, setting out a code of conduct on the treatment of diplomats, and giving advance notice of military exercises. Thus the end of the cold war has led to Pakistan's insistence on pursuing its nuclear policy, and an effort to create a regional atmosphere to allow that.

As a result of Pakistan's nuclear policy, its aid has been threatened. The US decision to cut aid to Pakistan has made it a devalued ally. The $564 million aid from October 1990 to September 1991 was frozen.[18] With the Kahuta plant's (in Pakistan) resumption of its enrichment of uranium to the quality required for nuclear weapons, Congress was willing to jettison Pakistan's alliance due to the end of the cold war. It was in the US national interest to cut down expenditure in the form of aid to geostrategically devalued allies (to deal with the recession). For aid to be cut off, Pakistan had fulfilled the criterion of being a state which was at the nuclear threshold. Since this kind of pressure was not successful in forcing Pakistan to abandon its nuclear policy, the US even tried to brand Pakistan a terrorist state due to Pakistan's alleged help to Muslim freedom fighters in Kashmir, and its relaxed narcotics control. This could have had drastic effects on Pakistan's economy which it could not have afforded; it could have meant that trade to all countries would become illegal. Even though Pakistan succeeded in getting the US to recognize Kashmir as a trouble spot, the tug of war on the nuclear and aid issues is bound to continue as long as Pakistan insists on the Pressler Amendment being discriminatory, and the US continues to ignore this reality. Therefore, with pressures of this kind, Pakistan's foreign policy options can be seen as being torn between a sovereign independent foreign policy and a continued subservience to international regimes.

Regional Opportunities in the NWO

To counter the global disinterest in its affairs, Pakistan has to examine its regional options. The Central Asian states and regional organizations like SAARC and ECO provide Pakistan with this opportunity.

The end of the cold war in the form of the political collapse of the Soviet Union has led to the emergence of new independent states which want to strengthen their cultural and historic ties with South Asia and West Asia due to geographical proximity and cultural affinity. Pakistan, due to these reasons, and in order to make up for regional insecurity, sees relations with the Central Asian states as an important foreign policy option. Thus, in a regional context, the transformation of the Soviet Union into a loose association of independent states, at a time when Pakistan has virtually lost its frontline status, (following the Soviet withdrawal from Afghanistan and the end of the cold war) is important; especially, since from a geostrategic point of view, close relations of these states with Pakistan make economic sense. At least for Tajikistan, Uzbekistan, and Kazakhstan the most economical seaport will be Karachi or Gwadar. By comparison, the Black Sea port of Odessa is 3000-3500 km from Tashkent and Dushanbe. Apart from a political will in Pakistan to develop its relations with these states, it is important to understand how likely this will be in reality, considering the historical connections, political will and potential, and regional competition from the ECO states.

Historically, it is interesting to note that this relationship has deep-rooted historic connections. Islam reached Central Asia in the seventh century; Islamization of the population continued for another twelve centuries. Despite the persecution of Muslims, their faith survived in the Russian empire; the survival of a large number of historic mosques and universities is a tribute to this. Even Khrushchev's attempts to Sovietize Muslim society in 1953 were largely unsuccessful. Despite such evidence, it would be a mistake to presume, as Saudi Arabia and Iran have presumed, that the Central Asian states are ready for Islamization. There is evidence which suggests that, due to a significant percentage of the population being Russian, secularization is *l'ordre du jour* in these states. Pakistan should be aware of the discouraging potential of using Islam. Trade, on the other hand, is what these countries want; and Pakistan's historic connections to the silk route ought to be exploited. Before colonization, there was regular trade between the ancient cities of Samarkand and Bukhara and the subcontinent.

Moreover, it needs to be considered whether the political climate in the Central Asian states encourages trade with Pakistan. Is cooperation with Pakistan possible, considering the internal problems in these states? There are four basic problems here. Political fragmentation is one of them. Three main groups are competing for political control everywhere in the region: plutocracy, democratic forces, and Islamic clergy. Secondly, the Central Asian states are tied completely to the former USSR due to the one-sided Soviet strategy of economic development. Cotton growing is a good example of this: how is it possible to get rid of the mono-culture and simultaneously update cotton production for the allocation of substantial resources and investments, which cannot be generated in the region itself? Thirdly, the loss of union subsidies and disruption of material and food supplies pose a major challenge to these states' current economic development. Fourthly, the rapid growth of population in Muslim Central Asia exacerbates the heavy burden of economic transformation.

Furthermore, it is clear from statistics that the Central Asian states will not be junior partners in their relationship with Pakistan since they have a 90 per cent literacy rate, a highly developed infrastructure and a per capita income of $2500 (seven times that of Pakistan). The leadership due to the communist system is secular, as was seen from their readiness to help Najibullah in Afghanistan.

Despite these political handicaps in the Central Asian states, what are the opportunities that Pakistan could exploit? To answer this question, it is important to understand how they show basic characteristics of third world economies. They are richly endowed with natural resources but most of these resources are utilized and processed in the more developed parts of the former Soviet Union. This immediately increases their dependence on Russia, thus posing a problem for closer trade links with Pakistan. For example, it is interesting to note that though Uzbekistan is the third largest producer of cotton in the world, it processes only 15 per cent of the crop within its territory. Azerbaijan produces oil, Turkmenistan natural gas, Tajikistan has potential for hydroelectricity and oil, while Kazakhstan has rich agricultural and mineral resources of iron ore and gold (70 m. tonnes or 13 per cent of the former USSR's iron ore refining capabilities). Uzbekistan has 15 per cent of its gold production capacity and gold reserves. Turkmenistan has large deposits of natural gas (annual production of 83 million cubic meters). Tajikistan, Uzbekistan, and Kyrghyzstan have great potential for hydroelectricity which could help Pakistan. They are further advantaged by the inheritance of a good infrastructure, like roads and buildings, and a 90 per cent trained manpower; but having been developed as hinterland to the Russian mainland they mainly provided raw materials with limited industrial activity. Capacity for sophisticated planning and the preparation and implementation of large projects was centralized in Moscow or in Moscow-controlled institutions; that layer has disappeared, leaving local offices for such activities with enormous responsibility but limited expertise and no resources. This is where Pakistan could help. The Central Asian states do not have experience of collecting revenues, running banks, or conducting international trade. The fall of the rouble has added to their problems. Agro-based industries like theirs, need service industries, insurance, and management markets for raw materials which Pakistan could provide.

What are the concrete measures undertaken by the Pakistan government to promote its relations with the Central Asian states in order to provide an alternative to its global and regional constraints? Pakistan was the first country to recognize all six republics and sent delegations to encourage agreements of various kinds. Aid was also sent though the quantity was insufficient. Pakistan promised $30 million to Uzbekistan and $10 million each to the other states. Furthermore, 5000 tonnes of rice was offered to Azerbaijan, Uzbekistan and Russia. In addition to this, accords have followed. The Pakistan-Azerbaijan accord for cooperation was signed with a capital of $10 million; oil exploration, road construction, and power generation commenced in January 1992. There was an agreement with Tajikistan for the purchase of electricity in March 1992. However, this example shows the shortcomings of

Pakistan's potential; it lacks the foreign exchange needed to fund such projects, thus forcing the Central Asian states to look towards Pakistan's competitors. The discovery of oil in Uzbekistan provides another avenue of cooperation (March 1992), considering that Gwadar in Pakistan could serve as a port for its transportation. As far as the cultural contacts are concerned, Pakistan is faced with the handicap of unfamiliarity with the Russian language unlike its competitors like India, which has an advantage in this area due to its long-standing links with the Soviet Union and due to its size in terms of resources and markets. Moreover, the instability in Afghanistan as well as competition from other states for influence, reduces Pakistan's chances for success in Central Asia.

What kind of competition does Pakistan face in its quest for influence in Central Asia? The fact, that these states are favourably disposed towards the Commonwealth of Independent States (CIS) in terms of military and political alliances with Russia, does put other countries in second position. Each republic initially found a favourite ally. Uzbekistan was looking at Turkey for a model of government. Kyrghyzstan and Kazakhstan seemed to be more interested in the Far East (South Korea and China rather than South Asia). Kazakhstan, with its aspirations for leadership, will need to deal favourably with Pakistan as shown by the visit of Nazarbayev. Kazakhstan does not have any Islamic aspirations as declared by its president during his visit to India and it desires to be a part of the European Community. Turkmenistan is interested in Iran, Turkey, and Saudi Arabia. With Turkey cut off from Central Asia by instability in the Caucasus and Pakistan cut off because of a similar problem in Afghanistan, Iran with its route to the sea stands a better chance of cooperation with Central Asia.

SAARC is another organization which could, in the future, provide Pakistan with an international forum. At the moment, India's insistence on dominance in its activities seems to block all efforts towards regional cooperation. In any case, the fact that there is so little trade between its core members (India and Pakistan) reduces SAARC's effectiveness at the functional level. If it could achieve a functional quality, it might be able to move towards cooperation in military as well as economic fields: that would only be possible with a major political reconciliation between its core members.

Conclusion

Pakistan's security concerns imposed certain constraints on its foreign policy which led it to depend on extra-regional interference in its affairs, as a result, it became involved in cold war politics. Any change at the global level had a direct impact on Pakistan's foreign policy options. It was argued that during the cold war, Pakistan perceived regional threats which were met by participation in the global cold war. With the end of the cold war and the disintegration of the USSR, the regional threats continue to exist; the difference being that Pakistan is no longer a part of the Western alliances. This leads to a reduced opportunity of foreign policy options at the global level. The way Pakistan seems to be reorienting itself is through increased regional involvement in the Central Asian states and regional organizations like SAARC and ECO. It realizes that any success in foreign policy is dependent on a political consensus with its natural enemy, India, without which any move to secure its territorial integrity and promote its socio-economy would be futile. In retrospect, can reduction of Pakistan's foreign policy options be reasoned as Pakistan's insistence on hostility with India?

The underlying feature of Pakistan's foreign policy has been the commitment to its security (especially its perceived threat from India). In its quest for such commitments, it has perhaps avoided the actual security problem and has instead emphasized the need for guarantees of security. The reorientation which has taken place needs to be questioned. Will the Islamic card with 'Islamic states' in Central Asia provide it with security and prosperity? This depends on the anticipation of future stability expectations. In order to adapt to the changing world order, Pakistan needs to stabilize itself internally and consequently become a model for the region. The perception of security in its broad sense is mainly dependent on a stable domestic environment, which can be achieved through democracy. The development of a democratic society ought to be supported by economic development and an element of continuity in the domestic setting rather than through a reliance on superpower politics.

NOTES

1. Hasan-Askari Rizvi, *Pakistan and the Geostrategic Environment*, St. Martin's Press, New York, 1993, p. 10.
2. K.P. Misra, *Non Aligned Movement: India's Chairmanship*, Lancers Books, New Delhi, 1987, p. 20.
3. Hasan-Askari Rizvi, op. cit., p. 9.
4. Mehrunnisa Ali, 'Jinnah's Perception of Pakistan's Foreign Policy and the Kashmir Issue', *Pakistan Horizon*, Karachi, Vol. 43, No. 2, April 1990, p. 63.
5. Hasan-Askari Rizvi, op. cit., pp. 9–11.
6. *Sipri Yearbook of World Armaments and Disarmament (1968–1969)*, Stockholm, p. 206.
7. Ibid., (1992), p. 260.
8. Kreisberg, 'The US, South Asia and American Interests', *The Journal of International Affairs*, New York, Summer 1989, p. 83.
9. By NWO the writer is not referring to Bush's rhetorical vision; instead it refers to the post cold war era.
10. Chomsky, 'The New World Order', *Open magazine*, Pamphlet Series, p. 19.
11. Joseph S. Nye, Jr., 'What New World Order', *Foreign Affairs*, New York, Vol. 71, No. 2, 1992, p. 86.
12. James M. Goldgeier and Michael McFaul, 'A Tale of two worlds: core and periphery in the post-cold war era', *International Organization*, South California, Vol. 46, No. 2, 1992, p. 486.
13. *The Economist*, London, 30 Novemebr 1991.
14. However, it has been argued that Russia's armed capability is not obsolete yet. In fact, it may become an American competitor in arms export in the future.
15. McGeorge Bundy, 'From Cold War Toward Trusting Peace', *Foreign Affairs*, Vol. 69, No. 1, 1990, p. 211.
16. *Sipri Year Book 1992*, p. 102.
17. *The Independent*, London, 3 January 1992.
18. J. Bray, 'New directions in Pakistan's foreign policy', *The World Today*, London, April 1992, p. 65.

27

Advantages and Disadvantages for Pakistan in the Post-Cold War World*

Thom A. Travis

In the last few years, the Soviet Union has disintegrated, the cold war has ended, and the structure of the international political system has shifted from bipolarity to unipolarity. Less change has occurred in the international economy, although the capitalist world system, modified by the recent GATT accord, has penetrated every corner of the globe and countries world-wide are rushing to liberalize their economies. As the international system is altered, the distribution of global wealth, status, power, and benefit is affected. Some countries will be relatively more advantaged and others more disadvantaged.

The purposes of this essay are to discuss the main features of the post-cold war system and the effects on Pakistan foreign policy. First, the salient characteristics of the world system likely to exist through the remainder of the century will be sketched. Second, the advantages and disadvantages for Pakistan in this international system will be discussed. Last, implications for Pakistan's foreign policy will be drawn.

The Post-Cold War System

The main characteristics of the international system likely to exist through the end of the century are described below.

---

* Vol. XLVII, No. 3, 1994.

Values

The liberal ideology of democratic-capitalism has largely superseded that of socialist dictatorship and will continue to be incorporated in one form or another into Eastern Europe, Russia, some of the former Soviet republics, and a growing number of third world countries, including former Marxist states like China and Vietnam. Capitalism is more likely to be successfully introduced than democracy in many of these nations.

Western, particularly American values and attitudes of individualism, materialism, consumption, and self-gratification in an urban, industrial, high technological context will continue to be rapidly spread across the world by American, European, Australian, and Japanese media and transnational corporations. To some extent, there has been a return culturally to the nineteenth century in terms of the global scope and influence of liberalism, at least among the elite classes of most countries.

Socialism has been replaced by religious orthodoxy, whether in an Islamic, Hindu, or Christian form, as the main counter-ideology. For the time being, this movement will be a minor global competitor to liberalism. However, if liberalism should fail to provide personal and spiritual satisfaction or to spur rapid and equitable development, then anti-liberal ideologies—socialistic, fascistic, or religious—could gain wider appeal and become major challenges to liberalism in the early twenty-first century.

Objectives

The dominant objectives will be those of the G-7 powers and their financial institutions and will largely emphasize the status quo—global capitalism and free trade, Euro-North American international law and rules, and inequality in wealth, status and power.

There is little new about these goals. What is different is that the number of states advocating revolutionary aims has substantially shrunk, given the disappearance of the Soviet Union and Eastern bloc and the moderation of former revisionist states like China, Syria, Vietnam, and Cuba. For the remainder of the century, the main opposition to G-7 objectives will not be revolutionary, but reformist, emanating from some third world governments which will strive to modify global rules to ensure less unequal benefits. In the early twenty-first century, if a greater number of states become deeply resentful about inequalities of global wealth and power and/or adopt anti-liberal ideologies, a revolutionary challenge to G-7 objectives could reappear.

Power

The bipolar system has been replaced by a weak unipolar, oligarchical, concert system of the G-7, led on most dimensions by the United States. Power is reminiscent of the nineteenth century concert system (expanded to include North America and Japan), although the United States does not hold full hegemonic power as Great Britain did at the time. While Washington will exert disproportionate influence on most issues, it will have to consult regularly with its G-7 allies, sometimes with Russia, and occasionally with leading third world states in an effort to build support for its world order agenda. On some issues, such as Bosnia, trade, and nuclear non-proliferation, Washington will have to make concessions, and at times it will not get its way. On balance, the G-7 powers, led more often than not by the United States, will act in concert to manage the world system in ways consistent with their ideological preferences and pragmatic interests.

There will be no other country of coalition capable of matching the power of the G-7. The main past challenger, the Soviet bloc, has disappeared. Russia will remain too preoccupied with internal problems and reliant on G-7 support for its liberal experiment to exert independent power on most issues outside its region. If Russia should gain admission to the G-7, then it would become a part of the oligarchical coalition, not a competitor.

Certain non-state actors, including transnational corporations and banks, UN financial institutions, economic and environmental regimes, and the UN Security Council will experience some increase in power, but will largely operate within the confines of G-7 (particularly American, French, and British) guidance and control. The same is true for the UN Secretary-General, whose global leadership and diplomatic initiatives will have to conform to the wishes of the G-7.

NGOs will continue to grow in number and will exert some influence over states and international organizations, largely on issues of human rights, poverty relief, and the environment. Their activities will centre on education and lobbying at the national and international levels to forge attitudinal consensus and collaborative action on global problems, and on the supply of emergency services in natural disasters and civil wars. However, NGOs will have limited influence where their agendas clash with the key interests of the major powers.

Most third world governments will have less global power in the unipolar system then in the past. They have lost sources of influence they possessed in the bipolar period. They can no longer practise non-alignment in terms of manoeuvring between the blocs to gain diplomatic latitude. In the post-bipolar world most developing countries have become less important geostrategically. As a result, they will have diminished opportunity to link strategically to a major power in exchange for reciprocal benefit.

Southern states will sometimes be able to exert negative power, resisting the demands of the G-7 powers, as Pakistan, India, China, Libya, North Korea, and Haiti have recently done. However, they will run the risk of incurring sanctions from G-7 powers, as has happened to the countries above. Third world governments will rarely be able to exercise positive power to convince the major powers to alter their agendas or demands. The G-7 will be more tolerant of regional power of key southern states, as long as the main interests of the northern powers are not jeopardized. As a result, the G-7 will be more accepting of regional power for Brazil, Egypt, South Africa, Saudi Arabia, India, and Indonesia than for Iraq or Iran. China is the developing country with the highest global power potential, but it is likely to remain a 'sleeping giant' for at least the next decade. Its global aims remain modest and it has shown little inclination to project major world power or to challenge the G-7 governments on most key issues.

The United States has become the single military superpower in terms of capability. Russia remains militarily powerful, but less so than the former Soviet Union, and it probably lacks the will to use force outside its immediate boundaries. As a result, there is no longer a credible military balancer against the United States or its military alliances which will allow them to use force largely as they wish against non-nuclear states. When Washington chooses to exert military leadership, it will usually be able to mobilize a coalition to employ military force as it did in the Persian Gulf.

Despite its high military capability and frequent use of force in the last half century, the United States will not often resort to warfare in the post-cold war period. Bipolarity, the main source of past US military intervention has ended; the United States has learnt from bitter experience about the difficulty of using force in civil conflicts; the US government is preoccupied with domestic concerns, and Congress and the public oppose an active American military role. As a result, Washington will probably lack the will and commitment to frequently use force as a foreign policy instrument. The United States will find that diplomatic and economic sanctions will sometimes be sufficient to get its way. Where such sanctions fail, Washington will likely restrict its use of force to countering blatant acts of aggression or to furnishing relief to peoples ravaged by terrible civil wars, provided, in each case, that some tangible American interests are involved. Furthermore, the United States will be reluctant to act unilaterally, preferring, instead, to coordinate its actions with its military allies or the UN Security Council.

Indeed, the UN Security Council has renewed its collective security role and has expanded its peace-keeping activities. However, it will operate mainly as an instrument of the G-7 powers, particularly the United States, Britain, and France, which will preclude independent authority.

International Economy

The world economic system will become increasingly interdependent as economic linkages and sensitivities among state and non-state actors proliferate across the globe. However, this interdependence will remain asymmetrical and hierarchical with power concentrated in the G-7 and associated financial non-state organizations. The United States has increasingly had to share economic power with Germany, the European Union, Japan, and large transnational firms, and this trend will continue. These actors, reaching common decisions through competitive bargaining, will jointly manage the world capitalist system which has extended throughout the globe and is more powerful today than ever before.

With exceptions, such as some of the NICs, southern states will continue to lose economic power relative to northern states and become increasingly marginalized, asymmetrically interdependent, or dependent. Most developing countries will have little say in economic decisions that will affect them. They will be under great pressure to comply to the trade, investment, debt, and intellectual property regimes that the G-7 establishes to guide the world economy.

International Rules

The rules of behaviour manifested in international law and custom, will remain almost entirely northern-centric and serve the interests of the core states as they have for centuries. The number of authoritative regimes, on trade, investment, intellectual property, the environment, telecommunications, and weapon transfers will grow. However, these regimes will continue to be shaped largely by the needs of the G-7 states and will be monitored carefully by these powers to ensure that their interests are preserved.

With the disappearance of the Soviet bloc which followed somewhat different rules and was attempting to revise global norms, the northern rules have become fully global. The preponderance of power of the G-7 coalition will enable its members to enforce these rules much of the time, again reminiscent of the nineteenth century. The G-7 states are assertively demanding that their preferred rules on weapon non-proliferation, human rights, intellectual property, and economic liberalization be followed and expect their calls to be heeded. As mentioned previously, where states refuse to follow these rules, they are liable to be sanctioned. Any revisionist or revolutionary states that emerge in the near future will try to alter these rules, but will lack the power to do so.

Positive and Negative Effects of the Post-Cold War System

The effects of the liberal, unipolar system will be diverse and cannot be discussed in detail here. Only the main military and economic implications will be briefly presented.

Warfare

The elimination of bipolarity, a major source of warfare of the past half century, coupled with unipolar military power, the increased reluctance of the United States (and Russia) to unilaterally employ force, and a more credible threat of UN collective security action, should diminish (but not end) inter-state warfare. Such warfare will be mainly between third world states and among former Soviet republics over territorial and irredentist issues.

If the result of armed force should be the elimination of the sovereignty of a long-term state (Kuwait but not Bosnia or Georgia), a collective security response of the UN Security Council, supported by the United States, will probably be a deterrent in itself. After the Persian Gulf, would-be aggressors, other than nuclear powers, will have to be cautious about their military ventures, particularly when the interests of the major powers are threatened.

The rise of ethnic and religious nationalism, socio-economic inequality and illegitimate government will increase intra-state secessionist and revolutionary wars, particularly in Eurasia and the third world. Internal conflict will become the primary form of warfare. In the absence of bipolarity, domestic wars are more likely to remain free from great-power intervention and to be contained locally.

The UN Security Council will probably become more selective about its peace-keeping intervention in civil wars, given the difficulty of ending such conflicts and of raising sufficient finances and troops. If the UN campaign in Somalia should fail and the civil war in Cambodia should resume, it will be difficult to sustain enthusiasm for peace-keeping in the future.

Particularly in the north, military spending will decline and military industrial complexes will be down-sized. However, despite G-7 efforts to strengthen weapon non-proliferation regimes, advanced weapons will continue to spread which will make warfare, domestic and international, more bloody. The victims will mainly be citizens of Eurasia and the third world. It is unlikely for at least the next two decades that third world states possessing advanced weapons would target northern powers and risk devastating retaliation.

International Economy

With the decline of inter-state warfare and the preoccupation of states with economic growth, the economic dimension of international relations will become even more important. Economic issues will be addressed in frequent conferences, particularly among the G-7, OECD, and GATT organizations, in an effort to shape and enforce global, liberal economic regimes.

Whatever economic interdependence, integration, and benefit occur, will be concentrated in the OECD states, particularly the G-7, and in a set of semi-peripheral states in the south, including the oil rich, low populated states of West Asia, the Asian and Latin American NICs, and China. The majority of third world states will be more marginalized, dependent, and disadvantaged in the free trade world economy.

This inequality is built into the nature of the world capitalist system whose institutions, regimes, and rules serve the interests of the core states more than the periphery. For the next decade at least, the more developed countries, many of which are financially strapped and face domestic problems, will be unlikely to accept ameliorative international economic reforms, such as an NIEO, nor to act generously to ease the plight of the least developed countries. Many of the trends of the international economy that have been unfavourable to most third world states, such as falling raw material commodity prices, mounting debt, and rising capital outflow will continue. Also, the international economy will intensify some of the internal impediments to development in many third world states, such as corruption, wasteful spending, economic dualism, and ecological decay.

As a result, the economic prognosis for the majority of southern states seems dim. Indeed, economic regression with falling standards of living are likely for much of the population of most African and Latin American states. A small minority of third world states will fare better in the world economy. These countries include petroleum producers with a small population, such as Saudi Arabia and the Gulf Emirates, and ones with well-educated, low wage, disciplined labour pools, declining population growth, and efficient, stable governments, such as the Asian NICs and China.

In sum, the world will consist of a small number of privileged, powerful states, largely those of the OECD, favoured by considerable peace, prosperity and ecological quality, and a much larger number of marginalized, weaker states, mainly in the third world and the former Soviet Union, affected to different degrees by warfare, civil unrest, unstable government, economic stagnancy, or environmental decay. A set of states in the semi-periphery will be in-between.

Effects of the Liberal, Unipolar System on Pakistan

The discussion so far suggests that Pakistan will be more disadvantaged than advantaged in the international system of the late twentieth century. Generally, that is true. However, as analysis moves from the general to the specific, the picture becomes more complex. The specific advantages and disadvantages for Pakistan at the regional and global levels will now be examined.

Advantages for Pakistan

Pakistan will be advantaged to some extent in the post-bipolar world. In the unipolar system, the United States has become the leading world power, not the former Soviet Union or Russia. This is fortunate for Pakistan, since it has a history of friendship with Washington. Pakistan has built up a network of personal and organizational ties inside the US foreign policy bureaucracy and Congress, and numerous American foreign policy routines, some still intact from the cold war period, are favourable to Islamabad. Many American officials believe Pakistan should be rewarded for its past loyalty and favours to the United States. As such a foundation of good will and positive attitudes exists on which to build American-Pakistani amity. If Islamabad and Washington can find a way to diminish their dispute over nuclear issues, then close ties should resume.

A key American concern in the post-cold war world has been Islamic 'fundamentalism'. The United States is concerned about anti-liberal, nationalistic, revisionist Islamic states like Libya, Iran, and Sudan, and about revolutionary Islamic movements like Hamas and the Moslem Brotherhood which seek to overthrow westernized governments, such as Egypt or Algeria.

This concern can benefit Pakistan in two ways. Islamabad can offer to play a 'moderating' role in the Organization of Islamic Conference and the Islamic world in exchange for American favours. It can also try to deflect US pressure on Pakistan by manipulating the American fear of Islamic 'fundamentalism.' For example, Islamabad can warn the United States that sanctions, such as those against Pakistan's nuclear programme, risk undermining the Bhutto government and instigating an Islamic backlash in the country.

The emergence of new Islamic states in Central Asia after the disintegration of the Soviet Union has opened new opportunities for Pakistan. Islamabad can offer its regime type—a moderate. Islamic democracy—as a model for these governments to emulate, increasing Pakistan's status. Pakistan should be able to exert influence over these new, vulnerable countries. If these states can be incorporated into an enlarged Islamic coalition, stretching across North Africa, Western and Central Asia into Southeast Asia, Pakistan's global influence, as an integral part of this bloc, would be strengthened. Pakistan should be able to benefit from increased trade with these states and from access to their advanced weapons.

The Clinton administration's enhanced human rights policy will sometimes work in Pakistan's favour. Pakistan's restoration of democracy has satisfied an American aim and Washington has an interest in nurturing this government. Islamabad can argue that its democracy would best be nourished by the removal of American sanctions and by American help in solving the Kashmir problem.

Indeed, US human rights policy has involved Washington in Kashmir in ways conducive to Pakistan's interests. In autumn, 1993, Assistant Secretary of State Robin Raphel questioned the original accession agreement of Kashmir to India and called for the wishes of the Kashmiri people to be taken into account in a settlement of the conflict. In a constituency letter President Clinton expressed concern about the rights of the Kashmiri people. These statements could be construed as support for Kashmiri self-determination. Even if that is not what Raphel and Clinton really meant, their remarks at least temporarily strengthened Pakistan's efforts to internationalize the Kashmir issue.

The American emphasis on controlling the proliferation of nuclear weapons, advanced weapons, and missile technology could work partly to Pakistan's long-run advantage. Faced with resistance from Pakistan and India to a nuclear roll-back, Washington seems to be shifting its immediate priority to a nuclear cap. Washington claims that Islamabad has given assurance that Pakistan's nuclear programme was frozen at the 1989 level which ostensibly meets a key American condition. If Islamabad and Washington can work out a satisfactory arrangement to verify this cap, the nuclear dispute between the two countries could be eased. Indeed, Pakistan might be able to drive a hard bargain with the United States, which could include the resumption of American aid in exchange for such a verifiable cap. The details of such a bargain will be discussed later.

The Pakistani and American positions on regional nuclear non-proliferation, a nuclear-free South Asia, the signing of the NPT, and the convening of a security conference on non-proliferation in South Asia are much closer than those of the United States and India. Moreover, Washington is concerned more about Indian than Pakistani violation of the Missile Technology Control Regime and testing and deployment of long-range missiles. Skilful Pakistani diplomacy might be able to curry favour for Pakistan with US officials and complicate relations between Washington and New Delhi over these issues.

The disintegration of the Soviet Union, reduction of Russian power and global activity have improved Pakistan's regional security in certain respects. Islamabad no longer has to be concerned about a Soviet security threat to its northwest; indeed, the new Islamic states in Central Asia provide a buffer zone against the Russian military. As a result, Pakistan can concentrate more fully on establishing security against India. In addition, Russia is unable to supply India with as much military, economic, and diplomatic support as the Soviet Union did in the past. The erosion of the Indo-Soviet 'alliance' has helped to compensate for the decline in American support to Pakistan and has removed a past source of instability from the balance of power between Pakistan and India.

Finally, Pakistan might benefit in some ways from the modified, liberal world economy. With fewer barriers to free trade, the skilful development of comparative advantage should enable Pakistan to find niches in the world economy for boosting exports and export earnings. If Islamabad can selectively incorporate foreign investment, some benefits might accrue. Foreign capital might be invested in under-financed economic sectors, advanced technology could be transferred, and new employment opportunities could develop. Certainly, Pakistan's upper classes will gain from the country's involvement in a liberalized world economy.

Disadvantages for Pakistan

Despite these advantages, Pakistan will also be disadvantaged by the post-cold war system. Pakistan has become less geostrategically important in the unipolar system. It is no longer needed by the United

States as an ally against the Soviet Union or as a conduit for supplies into Afghanistan. Washington is no longer obsessed by the communist threat and the need to contain the Soviet Union, a preoccupation that Pakistan was able to manipulate to its advantage. As a result, Islamabad has lost an important source of influence over Washington, and the United States has less need to favour Pakistan diplomatically, militarily, and economically. Indeed, it has become easier politically for Washington to press Islamabad on issues of disagreement, such as Pakistan's nuclear programme and to impose and maintain sanctions, such as the Pressler Amendment.

Pakistan has less room to manoeuver diplomatically in the unipolar system. With the passing of bipolarity, relations have improved between China and Russia, China and India, the United States and Russia, and the United States and India. In the past, Pakistan was able to insert itself into each of these relationships, turning them into triangles where it could play a card to its benefit. This strategy has become far more difficult in the unipolar system.

With less geostrategic significance and fewer triangular options, Pakistan has become more vulnerable to the demands of the United States and the G-7 coalition. Pakistan will be able to resist American demands on some issues, such as on nuclear roll-back, but only at the risk of incurring sanctions like the Pressler Amendment. These sanctions have hurt Pakistan economically and militarily. On other issues, Pakistan will have to give in, as it has on the Dunkel Draft, including the multi-fibre agreement and TRIPS. It will be difficult in the unipolar system for Pakistan to exert positive influence to convince the United States or other G-7 powers to alter their positions on issues central to their world order agenda.

Indeed, the post-cold war agenda of the United States and its G-7 allies has become less favourable to Pakistan in several respects. The United States has become preoccupied with nuclear non-proliferation which has produced a dispute between Washington and Islamabad over Pakistan's nuclear programme. Until Pakistan agrees to a verifiable nuclear cap or the United States removes this demand, this disagreement will continue to hamper American-Pakistan relations. Pakistan has gained some temporary advantage (with regard to Kashmir) from the American human rights campaign, but American human rights pressure on Pakistan could mount if democracy should fail or the government should need to use force to quell unrest in any of its provinces. In addition, aspects of American liberal economic agenda, such as the multi-fibre agreement and the proposed social and environmental clauses, are inimical to Pakistan's interests.

A serious consequence of the unipolar system for Pakistan has been the decline in Islamabad's capacity to counter India militarily and diplomatically. The end of the cold war and disintegration of the Soviet Union removed a major source of discord between the United States and India. The animosity between Washington and New Delhi over India's alleged tilt towards the Soviet Union and India's shrill criticism of American interventionist policies has ended. India's economic liberalization and its designation by the United States as a 'big emerging market' indicate that the Indo-American economic relationships will boom. Military cooperation between Washington and New Delhi has been growing. As a result, Indo-American ties seem destined to improve, despite the temporary set-back in autumn, 1993.

This relationship will be reinforced by the fact that on most geostrategic indicators, including landmass, population, GNP, market size, military might, technological sophistication, and scientific expertise, India ranks high, making it one of the most important third world states, more so than Pakistan. As a result, it will become increasingly difficult for Pakistan to convince the United States and the G-7 to treat it on an even plane with India and to favour its stands where they conflict with those of India.

The nuclear issue and Kashmir are examples. Despite the fact that there is more congruence between the positions of Pakistan and the United States than India and the United States on nuclear proliferation and arms control issues, Washington has concentrated on curbing Pakistan's nuclear programme more than India's and has imposed the Pressler sanctions on Pakistan, not India. Following a stiff Indian protest against the Raphel and Clinton statements about Kashmir, US officials have become more cautious about pressing India on this controversial issue.

Pakistan's position *vis-à-vis* India has also deteriorated in other respects. As noted earlier, the Sino-Indian relationship has improved, Islamabad's ability to play its China card against New Delhi and to secure Chinese support on issues of contention with India have diminished. For example, to Islamabad's disappointment, China did not back Pakistan's proposed resolution on human rights violations in Indian-held Kashmir at the UN Commission on Human Rights.

Furthermore, the North-South dimension of international relations has become more important. India is a major third world power and plays a key leadership role in three third world coalitions—the Non-Aligned Movement, Group of 77, and G-15. Third world governments will be reluctant to take stands that will disrupt their relationship with New Delhi. As a result, it will be increasingly difficult for Pakistan to convince developing countries, including many in the Islamic world, to support its stand against India. Islamabad's inability to gain much third world backing for its resolutions on Kashmir in the UN General Assembly and Human Rights Commission is indicative of this difficulty. The same problem exists in the South Asian region. India is the most powerful country in the region and each regional state has reason to fear New Delhi's displeasure. Under these circumstances, Pakistan cannot easily garner support from South Asian states or SAARC for its disputes with India.

Some of Pakistan's military gains in the post-bipolar system have been offset by military costs. While Pakistan can concentrate more of its security force on India as the military threats from the Soviet Union and Afghanistan have eased, India can focus more forces on Pakistan as Sino-Indian relations have improved. Russia is less able than the former Soviet Union to aid India militarily; however, the United States is prohibited by the Pressler Amendment from supplying weapons to Pakistan, including the F-16s. Furthermore, it is unlikely that Washington can succeed in restricting India's nuclear and missile programme, but the Untied States still hopes to curtail those of Pakistan.

Any benefits that Pakistan derives from the liberal economic order could be outweighed by losses. Pakistan will continue to be largely excluded from decisions to fashion the rules of this economic order and has had little choice but to accept the provisions of the new GATT accord. Pakistan will be under strong external pressure to further privatize its economy and to open its domestic market to foreign competition. Foreign corporations have so many advantages in capital, technology, advertising, management, marketing and finance, that it could be difficult for domestic businesses to successfully compete against them. There is a danger that the most dynamic sectors of the Pakistani economy could be bought up by foreign firms and that its market could be flooded with foreign products that out-compete domestically produced goods. TRIPS could significantly boost the price of certain products, such as pharmaceuticals, adding to the hardships of the poor. If the United States should succeed in inserting social and environmental clauses into the free trade regime, some of Pakistan's national comparative advantage could be eroded. While the Pakistani upper classes should benefit from the liberal economic order, the majority of the population could be bypassed or harmed.

On balance, Pakistan will be more disadvantaged than advantaged by the post-cold war system. The costs are particularly serious in terms of Pakistan's disrupted relationship with the United States, the world's most powerful country and a key historical ally; its shrunken geostrategic significance; its smaller diplomatic latitude and manoeuvrability; its decreased capacity to influence the major world powers, and its diminished ability to counter India diplomatically.

Most of Pakistan's advantages in the post-bipolar system are limited or negated by corresponding disadvantages. Its historically close ties with the United States cannot be adequately exploited until the nuclear dispute has been eased. The considerable congruence in the American and Pakistani positions on the nuclear question has been partly countered by the American reluctance to coerce India into making concessions on nuclear and arms control issues. The favourable statements on Kashmir by American officials have not been reaffirmed due to the declining importance of human rights in American foreign policy and to a reluctance to further antagonize India. The end of the Soviet military threat to Pakistan ironically has diminished Pakistan's geostrategic significance to the United States and made it easier for Washington to cut off military aid. The diminished military support to India from the former Soviet Union has been off-set by the end of American military aid to Pakistan. It is premature to determine whether the benefits of the modified international economic order will outweigh the costs.

The main benefits not countered by negative factors are the importance of the Islamic world to the United States and G-7, and the formation of new Islamic states in Central Asia amenable to Pakistani influence.

Implications for Pakistan Foreign Policy

There is little that Pakistan can do to alter the characteristics of the liberal, unipolar international system that constrain its foreign policy. What Islamabad can do is to adroitly take advantage of what opportunities exist to enlarge its benefits and diminish its costs. This would require serious re-evaluation of past policy and creative, flexible policy adaptation.

Pakistan needs to repair its relationship with the United States. To accomplish this, Islamabad must resolve the nuclear dispute with Washington in a way that would satisfy the United States without jeopardizing Pakistan's national security and domestic political needs. Washington greatly needs a success in its nuclear non-proliferation campaign in Asia. This need can be manipulated.

Pakistan might try to drive a hard bargain with the United States consisting of mutual concessions. Islamabad could offer to accept a verifiable cap on its nuclear programme for a defined period of perhaps five years. This period could be extended if India also agreed to cap its nuclear programme. The bargain would require the United States to rescind the Pressler Amendment, complete the sale of F-16s to Pakistan, and resume military and economic aid.

Such a deal would handsomely benefit Pakistan. Its security would not be undermined, since the verification would only cover something the government says has already occurred. Pakistan would not have to roll back or eliminate the nuclear resources it already possesses. Therefore, its nuclear deterrent, whether actual or potential, would remain intact. Its conventional military security would be improved by the resumption of an American flow of arms.

The diplomatic benefits would also be considerable. American pressure on Pakistan's nuclear programme would cease; the onus would shift to India which Washington would press to follow Pakistan's example. The congruence in the stands of Pakistan and the United States on other areas of arms control in South Asia would now work more in Islamabad's favour. If India continued to resist American proposals, as it might well do, then Pakistan could profit from increased strain in Indo-US relations over this issue. With the easing of the nuclear dispute, the historical and bureaucratic factors conducive to the American-Pakistani friendship could have a more positive effect.

The nature of the bargain with the United States should help to counter domestic Pakistani opposition to the deal. Prime Minister Benazir Bhutto would be able to demonstrate that Islamabad had not caved in to the United States because Washington would have also made important concessions to Pakistan. She could argue that the many benefits from the arrangement would outweigh the minor costs.

Critics might counter that the Clinton administration would be unwilling or unable to make so many compromises; that given India's increased importance, Washington will be loathe to antagonize New Delhi by pressing it further to make nuclear concessions; that inevitably once Pakistan accepts a nuclear cap, Washington will next demand a nuclear roll-back.

Pakistan must adroitly play its nuclear card. If the United States wants a verifiable nuclear cap badly enough, then Pakistan should be able to extract major concessions from the Clinton administration. The wisdom of the Pressler Amendment is already being seriously questioned in Washington. Clinton might be able to convince the supporters of the Amendment that this legislation will have had a positive effect—gaining a nuclear cap from Pakistan—and that, otherwise, it has outlived its usefulness. The military industrial complex and the Pentagon would like to resume military sales and aid to Pakistan and are already trying to move the White House in this direction.

Once Pakistan agrees to a verifiable cap, Washington would probably increase pressure on India to do the same, regardless of New Delhi's reaction. Nuclear non-proliferation is too important to the United States not to try to secure an Indian cap. Even if Washington could not convince India to budge, the effects should be favourable for Pakistan. Any increase in tension between Washington and New Delhi works to Pakistan's advantage. If India should refuse to cap its programme then it would be extremely difficult for Washington to ask Pakistan for a unilateral roll-back. If the United States in the future should press for a roll-back, Pakistan could choose to adamantly resist at this point. After all, it is a nuclear roll-back more than a cap that is crucial to Pakistan's security. Furthermore, after a five year period of warmer American-Pakistan relations, the US government would be loath to reinstitute sanctions against Islamabad to curb its nuclear programme.

Next, it is important for Pakistan to improve its relationship with India and to pursue new approaches to ease tension over Kashmir. Current trends in Pakistani and Indian policy towards Kashmir threaten to head the rivals towards a fourth war. While it is difficult to predict the outcome of war, it is unlikely that either country could achieve a decisive victory. With advanced weapons on both sides, a war could have devastating consequences for India and Pakistan, including Kashmir. It is even possible that Pakistan could lose territory, such as part of Azad Kashmir, in the war, undermining Pakistan's security. If the war were to go badly for Pakistan, the government could be ousted and democracy ended. Moreover, the continuing conflict with India and potential for war have inflated Pakistan's military budget. This large defence budget might be good for the military, but inhibits the social and economic development of the country. Insufficient attention to development could undermine the legitimacy and stability of future Pakistani governments.

The key global imperative for third world countries today is the need for southern states to revise the rules of the liberal order in ways more favourable to themselves and to increase their power, status, and wealth relative to the north. This quest requires unity and mutual support among developing countries. Pakistan's attempt to internationalize the Kashmir issue has caused unfortunate friction in third world bodies, including the Islamic Conference. India and Pakistan have a great deal in common on most North-South issues and need to build a relationship of greater trust and accord to work collaboratively in this area. Greater cooperation between Islamabad and New Delhi is also necessary to strengthen SAARC and boost the status and influence of South Asia in the world system.

Furthermore, Pakistan's strategy towards Kashmir has not met with great success. Its campaign to internationalize the Kashmir issue has won scant support from key northern powers; has harmed Pakistan's image with some third world governments, and has sowed discord in third world forums. While the Kashmir issue might bolster short-term domestic support for the Pakistani government, in the long run the government could be destabilized if it proves unable to deliver on its promises to secure self-determination for the Kashmiris.

The Pakistani call for a plebiscite in Kashmir might be just, but seems infeasible. It is inconceivable that India would grant a plebiscite to the Kashmiris with an option to accede to Pakistan. India's vital national interests, as it interprets them, would be violated. It is improbable that Pakistan could convince the United Nations or major powers to coerce India into accepting a plebiscite. A prolonged resistance by the Kashmiri people, whether abetted by Pakistan or not, will try India's patience, but would be unlikely, again, to convince India to accept a plebiscite, and could provoke a fourth war. Pakistan lacks the military might to 'liberate' Kashmir by force, so this is not a viable option.

For all of the above reasons, Pakistan needs to rethink its approach to Kashmir. Pakistan's preoccupation with Kashmir has diverted its government from attending to other important concerns—global, regional, and domestic. This essay is not the place to propose alternative policies for Kashmir. The new approaches must come from the Pakistani people and government instead.

Finally, Pakistan should try to reap maximum benefits from its ties with the Islamic world. The greater the cohesion and power of the Islamic coalition, the more influential Pakistan can be at the global, third world, and regional levels. Pakistan will play a key role in the Islamic world, given its large population, central geographical location, Islamic government, and military might, and it should strive to reinforce its leadership in Islamic coalitions. As long as the United Sates and G-7 governments remain concerned with developments in the Islamic world, Pakistan can transfer its influential role there into enhanced status and influence with the northern powers.

Conclusion

In the last five years, the international political system has shifted from loose bipolarity to a unipolar, oligarchical, concert system. The international capitalist economy has extended across the globe and has been modified by the recent GATT accord. The international system is dominated by the United States and the G-7 coalition which have fashioned a liberal agenda and set of rules which disproportionately benefit themselves. Generally, third world countries have declined in relative power, wealth, and status in this system, although there are exceptions.

An analysis of specific advantages and disadvantages of the post-cold war international system for Pakistan demonstrates that the losses exceed the gains. The benefits of Pakistan's leadership role in the Islamic world and of a reduced security threat from its northwest are outweighed by Pakistan's lessened geostrategic importance; restricted diplomatic flexibility and manoeuvrability; heightened vulnerability to great-power influence, and diminished capacity to counter India. Even most of the ostensible advantages are partly or fully offset by corresponding disadvantages. For example, Pakistan cannot adequately exploit the factors conducive to a close relationship with the United States until the nuclear disagreement is eased. It is uncertain whether or not Pakistan will gain more than it loses from the modified free market world economy.

The Pakistani government needs to review its foreign policy and adapt it creatively and flexibly to deal with these new circumstances. In particular, Pakistan needs to improve its relations with the United States by striking a bargain on Islamabad's nuclear programme; reduce tension with India and build third world unity by contributing to a solution of the Kashmir conflict; and strengthen the Islamic movement, where Pakistan's leadership can be translated into enhanced global status and influence. If Pakistan can make progress in these areas, then its position in the international system will be improved.

28

Central Asia in the New Eurasian Geopolitics: Implications for Pakistan and Russia*

Vyacheslav Ya Belokrenitsky

The end of the current century (AD) marks a watershed in the history of international affairs. It saw the withering of the bipolar system of world relations which came into being after the end of the Second World War. Some people, observers, and analysts as well as common men, still believe that the cold war is not over, but the majority perceives that the former division of the world into two military-political camps and socio-economic-cum-ideological systems has ceased to exist although a carry-over from the late period can be detected in the form of nuclear strategical bipolarity. This by itself has manifested the breakup of the more or less homogeneous geopolitical field into several distinct non-orthogonal groupings, such as nuclear-strategical, military-conventional, trade-economic, socio-cultural, etc. The growing complexity of the interaction of forces in the international arena has given rise to new interpretations of world politics and international relations and re-evaluation of the heritage of classical geopolitics.[1]

The major shift in geopolitical thinking has occurred along the lines of attributing lesser weight to military-cum-ideological factors than to economic-cum-cultural or humanitarian aspects. This change is in line with the trend which had become evident since the mid-50s when nuclear disaster was largely averted. With the passing of the rather artificial and speculative outcry of nuclear superpowers' confrontation in the beginning of the 80s, the attention of the world

*   Vol. XLVIII, No. 3, 1995.

community concentrated more decidedly on manifestations of the deep multifaceted crisis facing humankind in the course of rapid economic growth accompanied by the demographic explosion and technological breakthroughs.

The confluence of two tendencies, i.e., growing unipolarity in the international power structure and increasing realization by the world community of the overall crisis, as reflected primarily in the monographs sponsored by the Rome Club, has resulted in the aforementioned alteration in the agenda of international politics. Geoeconomics and geoculture have largely replaced geopolitics, meaning power politics, although this substitution does not imply the end of the chief actors of the political game. States and nations are still there, growing in number and making the scene look, occasionally, desperately unusual. One such development which caused bewilderment was the breakdown of the giant Soviet power and the sudden birth of independent states in the middle of continental Eurasia.

The breakdown of the Soviet Union released the energy which has since been modifying several spheres of human interaction, geopolitics being one of them. As in the above-mentioned case of the termination of the cold war, the significance and irreversibility of changes can be questioned. The European advancement into Asia, which began in the sixteenth century, had eventually divided Asia into northern and southern parts. The Tsarist (Muscovite) and then imperial (St. Petersburg's) Russia moved along the northern land channels of expansion while the Portuguese and the Dutch, and afterwards, the British and the French colonizers took the southern maritime routes. By the beginning of the nineteenth century, the Asian territories, which were near to Europe and those being in the middle between Europe and the Far East or Pacific region, had been politically controlled or claimed by the major European powers. After the breakup of the post-Napoleon European concert, the 'Great Game' of the British and Russian colonial ambitions had transformed the middle (heartland) Asian landscapes into the primary centre of world politics. As a result of the exploration of the Asian steppes, deserts, and mountainous areas by the Europeans, the notion of the fundamental geographical, historical, and cultural unity of Euro-Asia received great momentum. The notion of Eurasia helped to internalise the attitude of Europeans towards Asia. The great geographers of the nineteenth century, Alexander von Humboldt, Kari Ritter, Friedrich Ratzel, and some others, had played an important role in this respect.

The division of Eurasia into a northern and southern half had not only survived the cataclysm of the First World War but obtained the additional rigidity of a politico-ideological boundary. The first major war of the twentieth century, raging mainly in Europe, was superseded by the second which reached northern Asia's western outposts and engulfed the southern portion of the Eurasian continent along the perimeter of its sea shores. During the first few years after the end of the Second World War, the dreadful image of the possible great continental liaison, which obsessed the British and American political and scholarly minds, seemed materializing in an 'eternal brotherly' union of two land giants, the USSR and the People's Republic of China. The menace evaporated rather quickly, although the North-South division of the continent remained. The solid land borders in the southern belt of the Soviet Union contrasted sharply with the strategic pressure exerted by Moscow through its 'blue water' navy, air and missile forces in the Mediterranean, Atlantic and Pacific directions. The exhaustion of resources maintaining the momentum of the superpowers' encounter misled the leadership in Moscow into the trap of the Afghan invasion. Multiplied by internal embroilment, this had produced the explosion (or implosion) of the Soviet Union's self-destruction. The end of the rigid boundary between the Soviet and the non-Soviet Eurasia constitutes one of the consequences mentioned above as caused by the recent release of social energy. This particular result has modified the geographical-political configuration of the largest and the most populous continent of the planet.

Eurasia in-between Two Poles

The international system of the cold war period is justly labelled bipolar, i.e., having two poles, or centres of attraction and control. Both poles geographically were located in the northern hemisphere which was the major arena of military, political, and ideological actions being divided into West and East. The latitudinality of the main geopolitical axis characterized the entire period of global (outgrowing the regional borders of Europe, the Middle East, and Far East) political history.

The gradual shift of accents from military-ideological to economic and humanitarian in the last two or three decades has paralleled a change in the geopolitical configuration of the world. After a long pause, the longitudinal axis has sprung into being. The disintegration of the Soviet Union and the termination of the West-East confrontation had furthered the end of the former domination of the latitudinal geopolitical axis. In the first half of the 90s, several longitudinal (meridional) political-economic groupings with the prevailing consultative and recommendational functions were created, enlarged, or strengthened. These are the Asian-Pacific community incorporating and relying upon a set of sub-regional organizations, and the much less mature, just emerging, American trading commonwealth. In between these two huge longitudinal zones which border each other in the Western hemisphere, a still broader meridional belt is spread in-between them, overlapping the Eurasian and African continents. The process of economic integration has taken root here too. More so, West Europe gave an example of the most advanced system of supergovernment interaction. There is much truth, of course, in looking at West Europe as a part of greater American, Euro-American or Atlantic pan-region. However, West Europe is also decisively moving in the direction of East Europe and Asia.

Some experts underline the limited usefulness of strictly regional approaches to the present day puzzles of world geopolitics, stressing the cohabitation of regional and metaregional factors.[2] Agreeing with these considerations, we should not underestimate regional aspects as they are definitely of importance, especially when we deal with the geoeconomical side of geopolitics.

The geographical or physical proximity is crucially significant for surface transport, railroad as well as highway, and in pipeline transportation. In all these respects, continental Eurasia can be seen as a very prospective area, destined to serve as a carrying ground for goods and passengers moving from the Atlantic to the Pacific coast and from Siberia to the Persian Gulf, Arabian Sea and Indian Ocean ports. Of no smaller importance are the reverse directions, as the flow of commodities and population from south to north and from east to west can be substantial at present and increase tremendously in the future.

Eurasia might become in the distant future the backbone of the third longitudinal trading and political zone. Although for the time being it is in the grip of deep economic and social crisis, a number of well-known bleeding points have emerged recently in the middle of Eurasia. Topographically this middle zone consists of hilly and semi-deserted areas, spreading from the Balkans in Europe to the Caucasus and Central Asian high mountainous countries, the Tian Shan, Hindukush, and Himalayas. This crisis chain cuts into hemispheres the mainland Eurasia and threatens to perpetuate the division of the continent, turning it into a battleground or a conflict-ridden land. As one of the leading analysts, Zbigniew Brzezinski has noticed, the zone of crisis has shifted to the north, from the Middle East and Horn of Africa to the Balkans, the Caucasus, and Central Asia.[3]

The threat is real, though it is not unavoidable. Much depends upon decisions and concrete actions of the governments and agencies dealing with the problems of the continent.

Central Asia, Eurasia's Heart

There are a number of contenders for the title of the 'continent's heart'. Afghanistan was often mentioned as such. The high mountainous regions of Central Asia were called the heartland too.[4] This image helps to illustrate the significance derived from the focal geographical position. The changed character of the Eurasian continent, its turning from a desolate area inhabited by nomads and semi-nomads, with few oases, towns, and cities into a much more densely populated region having vast tracts of irrigated agriculture and many centres of modern industry and culture, altered the notion of its heartland. The central portion of the continent ought nowadays to be much larger in size and more developed economically. The post-Soviet Central Asia can justly claim to fulfill these requirements.

It can also be regarded as a linking-ground between different parts of the continent. If a known metaphor of alternating 'continental' and 'maritime' periods in world history holds true,[5] mankind is probably approaching a shift from the post-Colombian maritime to a continental epoch. The much talked about restoration of the ancient silk route can be a harbinger of such a rotation. The land means of transport and communications coupled with the air and space facilities may produce a full-fledged revolution in the depth and intensity of man's exploitation of continental riches. The natural resources of continental Eurasia are already quite evident for the contemporary economic agents. And Central Asia occupies undoubtedly a leading position in this respect.

Perhaps the most exciting prospects are opened by the energy resources. The estimated quantity of oil in Turkmenistan alone exceeds

6 billion tons and natural gas 15.5 trillion cubic meters. Hydrocarbonate reserves alone put Turkmenistan in third place in the list of the world's largest holders of oil and gas deposits, having an estimated 25 billion tons of oil equivalent, after the Arab-Iranian oil and gas fields of around 120 billion and the West Siberian (about 40 billion).[6] In addition, vast tracts of hydrocarbonate reserves are spread along the northern half of Central Asia crossing the Caspian Sea and the Kazakhstan steppes. The estimated quantity of oil in Kazakhstan is also close to 6 billion tons and that of natural gas exceeds 10 billion cubic meters.[7] The combined potential of the region, counting the Uzbekistan fields would be only a trifle less than that of Siberia. Needless to say, the prospects of exploration attract world investors. The US Chevron Oil's intention to spend more than 20 billion dollars on the Tenghiz oil project is only one and oft-cited example.

The region has a considerable quantity of other energy resources, i.e., coal and hydropower. The uranium deposits are there too; the ore capacity being estimated differently, as equal from 10 to 25 per cent of the overall world reserves. While the bulk of uranium is believed to belong to Kazakhstan, the largest uranium enriching plant was located in war-torn Tajikistan. This illustrates not only the natural riches of the region but its geopolitical significance for global and continental security.

Gold is also found in abundance in a number of Central Asian republics. Uzbekistan occupies the leading position in the region with reserves estimated to exceed four thousand tons and annual production estimated differently from 65 to 120 tons. This makes Uzbekistan eighth in the world and fifth according to the per capita production.[8]

Copper and chromium ore deposits constitute another source of natural advantages of the region. Mercury, aluminium, and some other metals have been explored too. In sum, the region is well-endowed with practically all minerals needed for industrial development.

Heavy industry production has been on the increase since the 1930s. The rate of growth was at par and in many branches ahead of the pace experienced in other economic regions of the former Soviet Union, especially during the 50s and 60s. In the last two decades the industrial base of Central Asia has widened by including places to the south from the previously exploited belt of eastern and north-eastern Kazakhstan. The south-Tajikistan territorial-cum-production complex (TPC) has been initiated. The hydel power projects on the Vakhsi and Nurek rivers and energy-consuming aluminium production make up the backbone of the TPC.

The large-scale centrally-planned irrigation carried over through the 30s and 70s in the Amu-Darya and Syr-Darya basins resulted in the three-fold increase in the arable land of the region (Kazakhstan excluded) from 2.5 million hectares to more than 7.5 million.[9] The growth of cultivated acreage corresponded to the rise in cotton production. Uzbekistan alone, in the beginning of the 80s, boasted of crop exceeding 5 million tons of raw cotton or 1.5 million tons of cotton lint. After independence, there was a change in emphasis which has started altering the structure of agricultural crops. Though food production has received priority, cotton is still grown in big quantities. Uzbekistan's crop in 1993 was equal to 1.4 million tons. Adding to this, Turkemenistan's crop of about 0.5 million tons and other republics' produce came to be more than 2 million tons of lint for Central Asia as a whole.

Pakistan and Central Asia

Pakistan is in many respects connected with Central Asia. First of all culturally, Islam has been adopted in Sindh, Balochistan, and Western Punjab through the land routes originating in Afghanistan, Khorasan and Maverannahr (i.e., Central Asia) rather than via the sea route connecting the Arabian Sea coast with Makkah and Baghdad. Historically as well, both regions have many common links, right from the invasions of Sultan Mahmud Ghaznavi and other Turkic warlords of Afghanistan who had political links or direct control over portions of Central Asia.[10]

A peculiar link exists in the ethnic and ethnocultural fields. Some groups among Pakistani people claim that their ancestors resided in Central Asia. Foremostly, the Gujars are believed to have changed their habitat in the valley of Amu-Darya (the Oxus) for the Indus Valley and western belt of deserts stretching from the valley up to the Malabar coast. The imprint of these migrations is quite evident from the modern geographical names like the state of Gujrat in India and the cities of Gujranwala and Gujrat in the Pakistani Punjab. One more, though much less known, name, is a place called Guzar in the Kashka-Darya division in Uzbekistan.

More important geopolitically is the common Pushtun ethnicity of the native and predominant population of Pakistan's north-western and western parts and of Afghanistan, particularly southern Afghanistan and common Central Asian (Tajik and Uzbek) nationality of northern Afghanistan and the newly formed republics of Tajikistan and Uzbekistan. This double link makes Pakistan neatly connected with Central Asia. The core zone of this ethnic interaction is supplemented by the periphery as the Pushtun (Pakhtun) belt stretches as far as Karachi while Uzbeks and Tajiks reside in many places of the Central Asian region.

Against all these factors promoting close relationship is the physical geography of the area. High mountains and huge deserts separate Pakistan with its heart, the Indus valley, from the Central Asian Mesopotamia. The two centres of ancient civilizations remained far apart for centuries due to the distances and natural obstacles. Now that technological progress has caused distances to shrink, the air routes are quite short. It takes less time to reach Tashkent from Islamabad and Peshawar than Karachi.[11]

As air transport is uneconomical and its cargo-carrying capacity remains limited, the real prospects for trade and economic infrastructure lie with expanding land routes. The highway system of Central Asia is the only outlet to the south, i.e., Afghanistan. The political turmoil there prevents the commercial exploitation of these roads but this situation will definitely not last forever. Afghanistan is one of the rare cases of a country denied the luxury of railroads. Several schemes were proposed at different stages of its history though nothing practical came out of those schemes.

While political instability in Afghanistan makes it still difficult to pave the shortest way between Pakistan and Central Asia, there are certain other routes linking the two via Iran and China.[12] In the former case the linkage can be easily achieved through the ECO Highway while in the latter with the help of the Karakorum Highway. The railroad systems can be linked also via Iran and Turkmenistan.

The natural gas and oil pipelines as well as hydel electricity transmission lines should also be considered as important channels of land traffic. The gas pipelines have attracted the predominant attention because of the enormous reserves of gas in Turkmenistan and the acute need to find lucrative outlets for it. Iran, by all calculations, will be a conduit for gas from Turkmenistan. Pakistan should be looked upon as the natural terminal of a southeastern spur as well as a hypothetical conduit leading to India.

The plan of bringing hydel electricity from Tajikistan to Pakistan remains on paper and does not look feasible for the time being because of the current political situation and techno-economical difficulties. However, the construction of transmission lines connecting Central Asia with Pakistan via Afghanistan cannot be excluded in a more distant future.

The development of new technologies of communication open a promising avenue for bringing Pakistan and Central Asia closer to each other. Radio and television broadcasts can help build a cultural bridge.

While assessing the possibilities of cooperation between the two economic, political, and cultural entities, one should bear in mind a very low starting point. Except very remote cultural and historical affinities and commonality of basic religious beliefs, there is practically nothing which, in one way or another, unites the peoples of Pakistan and Central Asia. Almost a millennium has passed since the population of these regions intermixed, and for almost a century they were effectively separated by solid political borders. To this should be added the difference of the prevailing 'second language' used in Pakistan and Central Asia for purposes of international communications. Being parts of correspondently northern and southern Eurasia, Central Asia and Pakistan remained almost absolutely closed to each other. The joining of the two halves of the Eurasian continent has made its modest start only quite recently. The achievements thus far accomplished ought to be therefore gauged against the background of the initial conditions.[13]

Russia and Central Asia

In sharp contrast to Pakistan and other countries of southern Eurasia, Russia has one definite advantage *vis-à-vis* Central Asia, which lies in the same physical geography. Through 'great steppes' sometimes called a 'land sea', Russia had easily reached the north-western extreme of Central Asia by the beginning of the seventeenth century. Although culturally alien, it managed to infiltrate and absorb the vast steppes populated by nomadic and semi-nomadic hordes of Turkic origin with an admixture of Mongol element. From there it moved to overcome the resistance of the state formations in more advanced regions of western Turkestan, i.e., the Khanates of Bukhara, Kokand, and Khiva. Since the 1860s, the Russian empire politically dominated the whole region which, after the civil war of 1918-1921 came to be known as Soviet Central Asia and Kazakhstan. Thus geography played an important role in the historic fate of the Central Asian region, separating it from the advancement of the maritime West European (British) imperialism while opening up to the land borne East European (Russian) expansion.

Geography is still on the Russian side. Land communications, so badly in need for the southern neighbours of the Central Asian states, are quite developed in the direction of Russia. Railroads enter the Central Asian region from the north-west, north, and north-east. The first connects the southern Ural (the city of Orenburg) via Kzyl-Orda in Kazakhstan with Tashkent. The second encompassing north Kazakhstan is one transport corridor with west Siberia and the third is the once famous Turksib (Turkestan-Siberia) line linking Novosibirsk with Almaty and Tashkent. Turkmenistan has the oldest railway connection with the Caspian sea port of Krasnovodesk (now renamed Turkmenbashi after the Turkmenistan President Niyazov) and further on with the Uralsk-Atyrau in Kazakhstan and the Russian city of Astrakhan.

The highway network geographically follows the same pattern, thus ensuring another possibility of 'transparent borders' between the Russian Federation and Kazakhstan as the huge northern member of the Central Asian community. The latter's territory totals 2.7 million square kilometers which is only a little less than India's, almost twice larger than Iran's, and more than three times that of Pakistan. The overall distance of the paved automobile roads in Central Asia was 237,000 kilometers in 1990 while the railway mileage stood at 21,000 kilometers.[14]

The pipeline system of Central Asia had been thus far oriented to the north and west as well. The natural gas produced in Turkmenistan and Kazakhstan was to a large extent consumed in Russia and taken from there to Ukraine and the Caucasus. The production and consumption of gas and oil were often not confined to the territorial limits of one republic but extended to the whole region. The high-capability pipeline facilities existed for carrying the Kazakhstan crude to the Volga region cities of Russia.

The air links of Central Asia remained until recently one-dimensional. On the same pattern, the telecommunication system works incapsulating the informational space of the region.

With all these geographic-cum-infrastructural advantages, Russia possesses a unique opportunity to preserve her presence in Central Asia on a renewed and revised basis. The main hindrance is, at present, the economic crisis and continuing industrial slowdown in Russia (the industrial production in 1995 is expected to constitute only 40 per cent of the 1991 volume). The recovery of Russian economic vitality would gradually save the relationship between Central Asia and Russia from fission and decay.

A certain ambivalence of the Russian political elite in their attitude to ties with Central Asia is another important factor. The duplicity is rooted in the approach of the Soviet era's bureaucracy.[15] The Central Asian elites have their own blurred perceptions. Both sides don't want to throw away the heritage of their relationship. At the same time both have reservations. Moscow is reluctant to accept again the burden of sole responsibility for the development in the region. Its potential resources are sometimes viewed in Moscow with suspicion as a trap. Strategic considerations aside, Russia at the moment is devoid of capabilities for the massive re-entry into the Central Asian market, with the possible exception of the energy producing sector. The Central Asians realize the dangers of a one-sided orientation and wish to diversify their external contacts. They prefer to remain under the Russian security umbrella and engage in restructuring of the foreign trade patterns and fields of economic cooperation. Already in 1992-93, the share of Russia in the volume of foreign trade in the Central Asian States has declined to 40-60 per cent from the level of 80-90 per cent in the last years of the Soviet Union.[16] Recently it has evidently diminished further. The countries of the post-Soviet Commonwealth have ceased to be the main trading partners for Russia as well. In the beginning of 1995, the share of the CIS in the trade volume of the Russian Federation was only slightly more than 20 per cent.[17] One can guess that the Central Asian countries now claim about 10 per cent of the Russian foreign trade. In spite of the abrupt change in the trade links, Russia and Central Asia would remain major partners in future. The in-built infrastructural facilities can, at any moment, give a push to their trade and economic relations.

The well-established cultural affinity should be regarded as another asset in the Russian-Central Asian relationship. Realistic observers do not expect the upsurge of radical or fundamentalist Islam in the former Soviet Central Asian republics.[18]

Conclusion

Since the beginning of the 1990s, the world has entered into a new phase of geopolitical process. Two crisis zones, the Middle East and Southeast Asia, known as 'shatterbelts', have ceased to function as pivotal areas, passing on the baton to the continental regions of the Euro-Asian continent. The geopolitical tension in the 'heartland' can assume different forms like inter-state, inter-ethnic, and ethno-religious conflicts of varying intensity as well as rivalry in the economic field coupled with the struggle for accumulation of 'symbolic capital' in the shape of ideational and military-strategic power.

Central Asia should be considered the centre of continental Eurasia from the geographical and political angles. The disintegration of the Soviet Union has turned the region into a 'shatterbelt' characterized by the arbitrariness of the existing state boundaries and immaturity of 'national societies'. These weaknesses of internal composition ought to be assessed in correlation with the attractiveness of the region for external actors, belonging to both state and non-state political and economic entities. It does not necessarily mean that this combination of factors prompts the unavoidability of socio-political explosions or military clashes. However, the complex nature of interaction of internal and external interests makes the future of the region highly unpredictable. What is certain is that it will command the attention of global and regional actors for quite some time.

Russia can, no doubt, be regarded as one of the major components of continental Eurasia. According to Arnold Toynbee, it belongs to east and west, being a unique combination of both. The Russian civilization is separate and composite. It changes periodically in a zigzag manner while maintaining certain constants of the civilizational code. Constituting the northern half of the Eurasian continent, it 'embraces' Central Asia from the north. Due to these geographical factors multiplied by the socio-cultural, demographic, humanitarian, and economic legacy of the recent past, it will continue to play a role in the future of the newly born Central Asian States.

The peculiarity of the geopolitical place of Pakistan is widely recognized. Born as a part of the South-Asian geopolitical 'platform', it was drifting gradually towards the Middle East. Climatically, Pakistan belongs mostly to the arid and desert belt stretching from northern Africa via the Arabian peninsula to Iran and Central Asia. The belt is sometimes called Afrasia. In contrast to India, whose geopolitical inclination lies in the Indian Ocean and further to the east in the Asian-Pacific region, Pakistan seems to be destined to follow the land rather than maritime module in her geopolitical future.

Historical and political realities always differ from theory. The latter is needed to understand long-term trends and alternatives. In a theoretical perspective, Central Asia occupies the focal role in the new geopolitics centered around continental Eurasia. Whether the whole macro-region and its 'heart' turns into a zone of economic contest and cooperation or plunges into a hotbed of clashes and conflicts is there to be seen. By the same token, relations of Russia and Pakistan are certainly of importance to both countries but no one can predict the main features of these relations. Adhering to a more optimistic outlook of peaceful development, for which there are ample reasons, one can conclude by stating that Russia and Pakistan, with their respective positions to the north and south of Central Asia, have a good chance to develop beneficial relationships so that their foreign policy lines converge more often than collide.

NOTES

1. See, J.O. Loughlin and H. Heske, 'From Geopolitik to Geopolitique: converting a discipline for war into a discipline for peace', N. Kilot and S. Watermans (eds.), *The Political Geography of Peace and War*, L. Belhaven Press, 1991, pp. 37–59.
2. I refer in particular to the theoretical proposition made by a Russian analyst, Alexander I. Neklessa, 'The Third Rome' or 'The Third World: global shifts and national strategy for Rusia', *Vostok/Orient*, No. 1, 1995, pp. 5–19.
3. Zbigniew Brzezinski, *Out of Control: Global Turmoil on the Eve of the XXI-st Century*, New York, 1993.
4. See, Sir Francis Younghusband, *The Heart of a Continent*, 1896.
5. See, Owen Lattimore, *Inner Asian Frontiers of China*, Beacon Press, Boston, 1962, pp. 4–5.
6. These estimates contain a classified report of the Russian Ministry for Cooperation between the CIS countries.

7. *Central Asia: Ways of Integration into the World Community,* Institute of Oriental Studies, Moscow, 1995, pp. 43–4.

8. Islam Karimov, *Uzbekistan: Own Model of a Transition to Market Economy,* Tashkent, 1993, p. 32.

9. *Central Asia: Ways of Integration into the World Community,* op. cit., p. 27.

10. See, e.g., Hafeez Malik, *Moslem Nationalism in India and Pakistan,* People's Publishing House, Lahore, 1980, pp. 9–15.

11. Shamim Akhtar, 'Strategic Significance of Central Asia', *Pakistan Horizon,* Karachi, Vol. 45, No. 3, July 1992. pp. 49–50.

12. See the discussion of these routes in S.M. Haider (ed.), *Pakistan, Central Asia and the Region: Prospects of Regional Cooperaiton,* Lahore, 1994.

13. One of the first authors to discuss the issues of a bigger region comprising countries belonging to Central Asia, West Asia, and South Asia was Robert L. Canfield, 'Restructuring in Greater Central Asia: Changing Political Configuration', *Asian Survey,* Berkeley, Vol. XXXII, No. 10, October 1992, pp. 875–87.

14. Narodnoye Hozyaistvo, *The USSR National Economy in 1990,* Finans Statistika, Moscow, 1991, pp. 620–23.

15. See Vyacheslav Ya Belokrenitsky, 'Russia and Greater Central Asia', *Asian Survey,* Vol. XXXIV, No. 12, December 1994, pp. 1093–6.

16. Calculated from *International Financial Statistics: Supplement on Countries of the former Soviet Union,* Supplement Series No. 16, Washington, 1993, pp. 20–24, 40–46.

17. Finansovye Izvestiya, *The Financial News,* Moscow, 23 May 1995, p. 1.

18. See, e.g., special issue of *Pakistan Horizon* on Central Asia, Vol. 45, No. 3, July 1992, particularly contributions by Ahmed Rashid and Mutahir Ahmed. See also the latter's article, 'Radical Islam and Central Asia', *Eurasian Studies,* Ankara, No. 3, Fall 1994, pp. 54–60.

29

Nuclearization of South Asia and the Kashmir Dispute*

Farzana Shakoor

India and Pakistan conducted underground nuclear tests on 11 and 13 May and 28 and 30 May 1998 respectively thus giving a new dimension to the security situation in South Asia. India which first tested its nuclear capability in 1974 related the latest nuclear tests to the concern that it had over the 'nuclear environment in its neighbourhood'. New Delhi further linked these tests to the establishment of the fact that India had a 'proven capability for a weaponized nuclear programme.'

Pakistan's nuclear tests coming in response to India's nuclear explosions were triggered as a matter of fact by the Bharatiya Janata Party (BJP)'s policy of using the nuclear option. Its pro-active stand on Jammu and Kashmir asking Pakistan to vacate Azad Kashmir proved to be the key factor in Pakistan's decision to go nuclear. The Indian Home Minister, Lal Krishan Advani right after the nuclear tests by New Delhi went to the extent of suggesting that 'Islamabad should realize the change in the geo-strategic situation in the region and the world (and) roll back its anti-India policy, especially with regard to Kashmir, India's bold and decisive step to become a nuclear weapon state has brought about a qualitatively new stage in Indo-Pak relations, particularly in finding a solution to the Kashmir problem. It, signifies, India's resolve to deal firmly and strongly with Pakistan's hostile designs and activities in Kashmir.'[1]

---

* Vol. LI, No. 4, 1998.

This arrogance on the part of the BJP leadership to seek a military solution of the Kashmir dispute left Pakistan with little choice but to show India that it would not hesitate to put to test its nuclear capability in order to have an equitable resolution of the Kashmir question. The nuclearization of South Asia once again brought into focus the linkage between the Kashmir dispute and the proliferation of nuclear arms in South Asia.

This paper seeks to examine this very linkage which has neither been acknowledged by India, nor appreciated by global powers like the United States of America with the result that today the two South Asian rivals, i.e., India and Pakistan stand on the precipice of a nuclear conflagration over a dispute, which involves a very basic right granted to all the peoples of the world under the United Nations (UN) Charter, i.e., the right of self-determination. The denial of the right of self-determination to the people of Kashmir by India over the years has added to the complexities of the issue, the most dangerous and latest being the nuclear connotation that the dispute now carries. Apart from exploring the reasons behind Pakistan and India's nuclear tests, the study also takes into account the attempts of the United States to address the Kashmir issue and nuclear proliferation separately, thus leading the two states to indulge in a nuclear arms race to settle their old scores.

Though India regarded the security environment in its neighbourhood as the principal reason for going nuclear the second time, the fact of the matter was that there existed no threat to India either from its big neighbour China, or from smaller states like Nepal, Bhutan, Sri Lanka, Maldives, and Bangladesh neighbouring the country. This leaves out only Pakistan with which India had irritants like Wular Barrage, Sir Creek, and Siachen Glacier; these issues, however, in no way posed a serious threat to India's security. India's dispute with Pakistan over Kashmir however, had been the source of two earlier wars between the two countries in 1948 and 1965 respectively in the cold war era and caused almost a war-like situation in 1990 in the post-cold war era. At the same time, however, it must be acknowledged that despite an indigenous uprising in Kashmir, Pakistan never considered a military solution of the dispute and always placed confidence in the bilateral dialogue knowing fully well that every time India's willingness to hold talks had been nothing more than an exercise to buy time so that it could turn the situation in Kashmir to its advantage. India's perception of a threat from Pakistan particularly in the post-cold war era stems from its insecure position over Kashmir.

Though India had not succeeded in bringing the Kashmiris into its fold through its forceful annexation of the state in October 1947, its hold over the state became all the more tenuous after the uprising in Kashmir in 1989. Having exhausted the political means to quell the uprising in Kashmir, which ranged from the dissolution of the state Assembly to the imposition of the governor rule in 1990, India embarked upon a course aimed at the revival of a political process in Kashmir by staging the state elections in September 1996. However, even after two years of a so-called democratic set-up in Kashmir headed by the National Conference (NC) leader Farooq Abdullah, things have not returned to normal in Kashmir.

The Kashmiris remain as alienated from the central as well as the state government as they were at the time of the uprising despite Farooq Abdullah's pledges of improved security and more autonomy for Kashmiris which he made prior to the elections. As far as the improved security is concerned, pitched battles are still being fought in the state between Indian security forces and those demanding freedom from Indian rule. There has been no withdrawal of the security forces from the state. In fact, soon after the assumption of office by Farooq Abdullah, a tussle had started between the high command of the security forces in the state and the civil administration over who would have an upper hand in the security arrangements for the state. In this conflict, New Delhi seems to be taking sides with the former, thus exposing the credibility of the democratic process that it initiated in Kashmir apart from betraying a lack of confidence in the state government. As Farooq Abdullah made attempts to replace the army units in Kashmir with a local police force, strong reactions were witnessed from the army which appeared dead against the move.[2] Similarly the state chief minister's attempts to scrap the Disturbed Areas Act 1992, had met with little success.

The central leadership as well as the Indian army high command have adopted the line of reasoning that 'increase in the activities of militants combined with large inflows of foreign militants from across the LoC necessitates its presence in anti-militancy operation or internal security duty in Kashmir'.[3]

The logic behind the above-mentioned strategy is enough to bear testimony to the fact that things have not returned to normal in Kashmir. Despite Farooq Abdullah's claims that insurgency in Kashmir has died down, the truth of the matter is that uprising is very much there and even senior Indian security officials admit this. As it has been put, 'insurgents have grown in number, gained in strength and are operating over a much wider area than ever before'.[4] Many analysts of the Kashmir situation seem to agree with the simple fact that things have not changed in Kashmir after the induction of an elected government. As it has been observed, 'In the backdrop of high-profile security arrangements and continued existence of massive number of troops, the ground realities for an average Kashmiri remain the same. The security forces continue to engage in frequent crackdowns and search-and-cordon operations. Going by the daily official handouts, the death toll throughout 1997 has not fallen below five per day and lately it had gone up to above 10'.[5]

The human rights situation in the state has further deteriorated, a fact acknowledged by the US State Department and Amnesty International. The two agencies admit that human rights violations have not subsided with the assumption of office by Farooq Abdullah.[6]

Autonomy was another issue which Farooq Abdullah had assured the masses in Kashmir he would work for, so that the respect and honour of the Kashmiris could be restored.[7] He had pledged to restore autonomy of Kashmir to the pre-1953 status. This, however, proved to be wishful thinking as the central government in New Delhi after the state Assembly elections of 1995 tried to divide the state into three regions on communal lines. As a matter of fact, BJP's stand on the issue of autonomy has been more rigid than its predecessors. Although it has deferred its stand of scrapping Article 370 of the Indian constitution which gives special status to Kashmir, the BJP would very much like to see the integration of the state with the Indian Union. For instance, when in June 1996, the then United Front (UF) government indicated its plan to hold an all-party meeting to discuss the issue of quantum of autonomy for Jammu and Kashmir, the BJP made it clear that it would strongly oppose any move to give the pre-1953 status to Jammu and Kashmir and demanded that the government should spell out what it had in mind on the issue of autonomy for the state.[8] The BJP had always stood for complete integration of the state with the Indian Union.

The result of all this had been that the Indian government remains unable to win the masses as well as the militants to its side even after the revival of the so-called democratic process. As it has been put, 'It was widely acknowledged that the problem had not been solved by the

1996 elections in the state of Jammu and Kashmir and the resultant installation of a new government headed by Farooq Abdullah'.[9]

With the BJP strongly opposed to autonomy and the Kashmiri leadership no longer interested in being ruled by India, autonomy has become a matter of indifference to Kashmiris. The Kashmiris have made it explicitly clear that they want freedom from Indian rule. Thus India's hold over the state is still through its occupation force symbolized by the Indian army and the security forces.

Another reason for India's going nuclear is the conclusion, which the BJP leadership has arrived at, that any Pakistan-India dialogue would ultimately lead to a discussion of the Kashmir dispute. This is contrary to BJP's assertion of Kashmir being an integral part of India. Pakistan feels that Kashmir must form the most urgent part of any negotiations with India. The BJP leadership is also fully cognizant of the fact that it could not make Pakistan drop or even assign a low priority to the Kashmir dispute in any Indo-Pakistan dialogue. Although the recent foreign secretary level talks between Pakistan and India carried the approval of the BJP, it had been only after assurances from the then UF government that talks would focus on Azad Kashmir that the BJP gave its endorsement.[10]

The BJP is also convinced of the fact that the Kashmir issue could be resolved only through the exercise of military muscle. Its manifesto for the 12th Lok Sabha elections held in March 1998 was quite vocal with regard to India's foreign policy. As it has been put, 'The foreign policy section in the BJP election manifesto was probably the most detailed in comparison with those of other political parties in outlining the party's vision on several key issues including the nuclear option'.[11]

A cursory look at the BJP's poll manifesto and the national agenda that it chalked out for the country reveals a firm commitment to the induction of nuclear weapons into India's defence system. It sought to 're-evaluate the country's nuclear policy and exercise the option to induct nuclear weapons; expedite the development of the Agni series of ballistic missiles with a view to increasing their range and accuracy'.[12] The then designate Indian Prime Minister Atal Behari Vajpayee defended the party's tough line on the nuclear issue in these words: 'My government will pay, highest priority to defence and security issues and I am not at all worried about anyone's annoyance or perception on this issue'.[13]

The cost of maintaining a huge security setup in Kashmir and its subsequent failure to quell the uprising there has added up the pressure that the Indian army as well as the establishment are faced with. This failure has led the Indian army officials to blame Pakistan for the proxy war in Kashmir on the one hand and on the other to justify a pro-active policy on Kashmir. As a senior Indian army official put it, 'the country has exercised restraint against Pakistan's proxy war and shown enough tolerance. We must make the costs unbearable for Pakistan. Why is the nation shying away from exercising the military option? Is there not provocation enough'.[14] Furthering the above line of reasoning, an Indian scholar writing in a leading Indian daily, *The Indian Express,* urged the BJP to be firm while dealing with Pakistan. As it was put:

> The BJP government must undo Inder Gujral's infamous tilt towards Pakistan. His Chamberlain Pakistan policy has done little good for the country but heightened tension in Kashmir and demoralized the military. The Pakistani problem must be dealt firmly. Experience has taught us that military strength keeps Pakistan on good behavior....A tough Pakistan policy is called for. One which will change the present defensive posture to an offensive one. It is only military might which will ensure peace in the region.[15]

The BJP seems to have taken its cue from the above-mentioned logic as its leadership soon after taking the reins of power exercised the nuclear option. Contrary to the Indian assertion of Pakistan waging a proxy war in Kashmir, Pakistan since the beginning of the uprising has urged India to tackle the issue politically and refrain from resorting to force.

Pakistan has never conceded the Indian argument of Kashmir being its integral part, but is appreciative of the fact that non-resolution of the dispute has heightened the tension between the two countries. The possession of nuclear capability by Pakistan acted as a deterrent in preventing war between the two countries after the outbreak of uprising in Kashmir. However, the recent Indian nuclear tests and Pakistan following suit have further enhanced the danger of Kashmir emerging as a flashpoint of nuclear catastrophe in South Asia.

Pakistan's policy on Kashmir needs no elaboration here; suffice it to say that it has always stood for the Kashmiris' right of self-determination. To achieve this end it has always called for the resolution of the dispute in accordance with the UN resolutions. The uprising has made Pakistan's case stronger over Kashmir, as it is not only Pakistan, but the Kashmiris also who have been demanding the right of self-determination. Pakistan's strategy over the issue has not changed; instead, a realization has come about that Kashmiris do constitute a party to the dispute. Realizing fully well that a show of military strength would lead the two countries nowhere, Pakistan has not shirked a dialogue over the issue.

The dialogue however, failed to yield positive results simply because at first India failed to acknowledge the existence of the dispute and even when it did so, the emphasis was always placed on bilateral talks excluding third party mediation or even the involvement of international organizations like the United Nations. Even the bilateral dialogue was not conducted with, sincerity of purpose but was used as a means to buy time by the Indian side. The foreign secretary level talks between the two countries, i.e., from 1992–97 bears evidence to this fact. This Indian policy led Pakistan to internationalize the issue by taking it to various international forums during this period.

Apart from this, Pakistan also tried to make India and the international community realize the link between nuclear proliferation and the Kashmir dispute. It also tried to emphasize the point that the Kashmir issue and nuclear non-proliferation could not be addressed in isolation. India's failure to see the linkage between the two and its uncompromising attitude over Kashmir has made Pakistan more vulnerable to a nuclear catastrophe. It is interesting to note that India insisted on seeing the problem of nuclear proliferation in an international setting. However, it remained unwilling to admit that Kashmir, a territory under its control, carried the dangers of a nuclear conflagration in South Asia.

Although Pakistan remained concerned over the induction of nuclear weapons into the Indian defence system, it exercised utmost restraint, not giving India any chance of provocation. It placed confidence in the bilateral talks, hoping for a breakthrough, yet the Indian side not only failed to keep its commitments, but also made it clear that it would not hesitate to use its nuclear prowess in order to shift the strategic balance in the region in India's favour. A warning was also issued to Pakistan that this nuclear option might be used in settling India's dispute with the country over Kashmir.

Pakistan's nuclear tests have been in response to India's nuclear designs and its so-called pro-active policy on Kashmir aimed at liberating what it calls Pakistan occupied Kashmir. Pakistan's alleged military help to those fighting against the Indian rule in Kashmir has been termed as a proxy war by India and is being used as a pretext by the Indian establishment to instigate violations along the LoC.

The crunch came when India, after exploding the nuclear device, asked Pakistan to change its policy over Kashmir. The Indian establishment in alliance with the state government of Farooq Abdullah started a series of statements threatening Pakistan with dire consequences if it did not reverse its policy over Kashmir. For instance, the state Chief Minister, Farooq Abdullah, advised the government of India to launch a very strong and decisive battle against Pakistan and 'taunted Pakistan to detonate its nuclear device if it had one'.[16]

To Pakistan, this was open aggression; Kashmir being so vital to its security, the country was left with little choice but to detonate its own nuclear device. The nuclear tests had also become unavoidable because of the security threats that Pakistan faced had India attacked Azad Kashmir. Pakistan's exercise of its nuclear option apart from dispelling the impression that its nuclear capability is nothing more than a bluff also restored the strategic balance in the region.

The tests not only eased the pressure that Pakistan had to face on the Kashmir front because of India's provocative stand but also helped in raising the morale of the Kashmiris on both sides of LoC. Fireworks crackled around streets in Indian-held Kashmir after Pakistan's nuclear test.[17] The gesture was symbolic of the fact that Kashmiris, despite the indigenous nature of their uprising, look towards Pakistan for help. A more sombre reaction came from the Chairman of the All Parties Hurriyet Conference (APHC), Ali Shah Geelani who said, 'It is to be pondered that why both conducted nuclear explosions. Our view is that the unfinished Kashmir issue after partition is the reason for blasts'.[18]

Another reason for Pakistan's going nuclear right after the Indian nuclear blasts was the lack of support which the country faced over the Kashmir issue from the international community. Although after the end of the cold war, the issue of nuclear proliferation dominated the foreign policy agenda of the United States of America, the linkage between the Kashmir issue and the nuclear proliferation was never acknowledged.

Instead attempts were made to address the two issues separately. As a matter of fact, pressure was put on Pakistan to delink its nuclear programme with that of India and sign the Nuclear Non-Proliferation Treaty (NPT) unilaterally. For instance, the then US Secretary of State, Robin Raphel, came up with the strange logic that unilateral capping of Pakistan's nuclear programme would be in the interest of the whole region including India; as she put it, 'We are working very hard now with Pakistan to persuade them to cap their programme. We've realised to try to get Pakistan and India to move simultaneously didn't seem to be working, we are trying a new tact. If we can get Pakistan to cap their programme, it is very much in the interest of everybody in the region, including India'.[19] The same line of reasoning was adopted by the US Deputy Secretary of State, Strobe Talbott during his visit to Islamabad in April 1994. Delinking the issue of nuclear proliferation in South Asia with the conflict in Kashmir, Strobe Talbott emphasized the need to deal with the issue 'in its own terms'.

The US strategy of delinking the Kashmir issue with nuclear non-proliferation proved counter-productive. On the one hand, it emboldened India to induct nuclear weapons into its defence system with impunity, on the other it made Pakistan realize that it could not forgo its nuclear option as long as the Kashmir dispute persisted.

Despite Pakistan's best efforts to make the international community realize the linkage between the Kashmir issue and the nuclear proliferation, its response remained confined to a mere expression of concern over the situation in Kashmir. This concern failed to register the fact that the Kashmir dispute carried the implications of a nuclearized South Asia. On the contrary, it restricted the dispute to the framework of human rights violations, revival of the political process in Kashmir, apart from urging Pakistan to stop the alleged interference in the state.

For the same reason, the leading world powers like the US and the United Kingdom (UK), without giving explicit endorsement to the state elections in Indian-held Kashmir in September 1996, placed confidence in the electoral exercise staged there believing that it would lead to some kind of a resolution of the dispute. Related to this approach had been the perception of global powers like the US that there was much to talk about with India on other issues like trade and Siachen and that Pakistan should not put everything on halt in its relations with India in pursuit of a better outcome of the Kashmir dispute.[20]

The then US Assistant Secretary of State for South Asian Affairs, Robin Raphel while speaking at a seminar in Washington, argued, 'India and Pakistan can get together and come up with some kind of negotiating process whereby the political status of Kashmir is not first on the agenda...'[21] The strategy was aimed at delinking the Kashmir issue with other irritants in Pakistan-India relations. The US policy makers have in fact resigned to Indian obduracy over Kashmir and believe that India is never going to change its policy over Kashmir and that there is little the United States could do in this connection. As a US think tank in a recent report maintained, 'Unfortunately there is no 'right' or plausible solution to the conflict in sight. India, Pakistan and Kashmiris themselves each have claims that cannot be reconciled. The government does not have a great deal of leverage in regard to the Kashmir dispute and the time is not ripe for Washington to launch a new major initiative'.[22]

Not only this, but the report further suggested, 'And India should be urged to continue and accelerate moves to resurrect the political process in Kashmir...and conduct discussion with the newly elected Kashmiri government about the degree of autonomy for the state within the Indian constitution'.[23] Furthermore, the United States also assured India that it would not concern itself with the Kashmir dispute but would leave it to Pakistan and India.[24]

The US insistence on a Pakistan-India dialogue coupled with its non-committal approach overlooked the fact that dialogue could not be sustained in a vacuum. For a dialogue to be successful, some substantive gains are required, particularly when the defence of a country is at stake. The confidence building could not be based on trivial matters leaving aside the significant ones. This US policy encouraged India to think in terms of a militarist solution of the dispute. As it has been put, '...What the situation calls for is plain speaking. There is no way Pakistan can wrench Kashmir out of India. It has done all it could and failed. Should some frustrated trigger happy hotheads or jackboots decide to attack the state again, they should realize that this time it will mean the end of Pakistan as we know it today'.[25]

Such had been India's attitude towards Pakistan prior to the nuclear tests, the tone became all the more belligerent after India conducted the tests. The Indians were also under the impression that Pakistan did not possess nuclear capability and that its declaration of being in possession of the capability had been nothing more than a bluff. The renowned Pakistani physicist, Dr Pervez Hoodbhoy, confirmed this impression and quoted one of the Indian leaders as saying that 'you (Pakistanis) don't have the bomb'.[26]

Apart from this kind of Indian attitude, Pakistan was also dismayed at the reaction of the world community over the Indian nuclear tests, which in the case of most of the countries did not go beyond mere condemnation of the nuclear tests. Pakistan was in fact very much disappointed in the G-8 countries, who after the Indian nuclear tests urged Pakistan to exercise restraint and failed to take any punitive action against India.

Pakistan's nuclear tests to a great extent have restored the strategic balance in the region. They have also made Azad Kashmir less vulnerable to Indian threats of war. However, the danger of nuclear war over Kashmir is still there, given the militarist strategy of the BJP. Its policy of a complete integration of Kashmir into the Indian Union, the subsequent failure of the Indian governments including the BJP to put to rest the uprising in Kashmir despite the revival of the so-called political process, all have added to the frustration of the BJP government which does not have any previous experience of conducting the country's foreign relations. The situation has been made worse by the religious bigotry that is reflected in the BJP's foreign policy agenda which tends to view even the issues of international and regional concern from the perspective of religion.

In its pursuit of integrating Kashmir into the Indian Union, the BJP has not hesitated from embarking upon a nuclear adventure. The escalation in violations along the LoC after the Indian nuclear tests has made the situation more volatile, which could erupt into a nuclear conflagration any time. As it has been put, 'Islamabad genuinely fears that New Delhi would not hesitate in dismembering Pakistan if it feels the military adventure will pay off. India, on the other hand, is afraid of losing its hold on Kashmir if Pakistan becomes too strong'.[27]

However, India's intransigence with regard to Kashmir during the recent negotiation has convinced Pakistan that it could no longer play the role of sole peacemaker. With no positive initiative coming from India, it needs to bolster its defence capability in nuclear terms as it would not be able to match India's superiority in conventional arms.

Despite all this Pakistan is also cognizant of the holocaust that a nuclear war could bring to South Asia. For the same reason, having conducted the nuclear tests, Pakistan still feels that a solution to the Kashmir dispute should be through peaceful means. The peaceful means could involve several kinds of mechanisms. The option of bilateral negotiations having been tried, it is perhaps time to initiate a tripartite conference on Kashmir involving the three parties to the dispute, i.e. India, Pakistan, and the Kashmiris. India must realize that it cannot force the people into an arrangement against their will, no matter how superior it might be in terms of conventional and nuclear strength.

Pakistan is appreciative of the fact that the Kashmiris' point of view must also be accommodated, as in the final analysis it is they who count most. However, this appreciation must be coupled with a pressure on India to include Kashmiris in any future Indo-Pakistan dialogue. The Kashmiri leadership doesn't seem to approve of the bilateral negotiations that have taken place between the two countries over the Kashmir issue. They, like Pakistanis, are also apprehensive of a nuclear conflagration in South Asia which would be catastrophic not only for their state but for the entire region. They genuinely believe that Kashmir is the unfinished agenda of the partition which has led to a nuclear arms race between the two countries. At the same time it is also their belief that a peaceful *modus operandi* involving the three parties to the dispute could be evolved. In the given circumstances, it is the best option available to Pakistan and India. However, the key to the solution of Kashmir issue lies with India if it really wants to avoid a nuclear war in the subcontinent.

NOTES

1. *The Nation,* Lahore, 19 May 1998.
2. 'Reviving Political Process in IHK: Problems and Prospects', *Spotlight on Regional Affairs,* Islamabad, Vol. XVII, Nos. 4 and 5, April-May 1998, p. 29.
3. Ibid., p. 30.
4. Quoted in ibid., p. 37.
5. Ibid., p. 39.
6. Ibid., p. 53.
7. *Time,* New York, 21 October 1996.
8. For details see, *Spotlight on Regional Affairs,* op. cit., Vol. XVII, April-May 1998, p. 76.
9. Ibid., p. 87.
10. *India Today,* New Delhi, 7 July 1997.
11. *The Telegraph,* Calcutta, 19 March 1998.
12. *The Pioneer,* New Delhi, 21 March 1998.
13. *The Hindu,* New Delhi, 19 March 1998.
14. *The Times of India,* New Delhi, 25 March 1998.
15. *The Indian Express,* New Delhi, 27 March 1998.
16. Kamal Matinuddin, 'Nuclearisation of South Asia: Implications and Prospects', *Spotlight on Regional Affairs,* Vol. XVII, Nos. 7 and 8, July-August 1998, p. 33.
17. *Dawn,* Karachi, 29 May 1998.

18. Ibid.
19. *India Today*, 15 April 1994.
20. Michael Krepon, 'US Perception of Pakistan's Security', *Pakistan Horizon*, Vol. 50, No. 2, April 1997, pp. 13–14.
21. *Dawn*, 28 February 1997.
22. 'A New US Policy Toward India and Pakistan', report of an Independent Task Force, Council on Foreign Relations, New York, 1997, p. 5.
23. Ibid., p. 39.
24. *Dawn*, 24 September 1997.
25. *The Hindustan Times,* New Delhi, 27 March 1997.
26. *Dawn, Tuesday Review*, 5–11 November 1998.
27. Kamal Matinuddin, op. cit., pp. 43–4.

List of Selected Articles*

Ahmer, Moonis, 'Security Perceptions in Indo-Pakistan Relationship', First Quarter, 1984.

Ahmed, Samina, 'Franco-Pakistan Relations-I: Political, Economic and Cultural Ties (1947-1977)', Third and Fourth Quarters, 1977.

_____, 'Franco-Pakistan Relations-II: The Issue of Nuclear Reprocessing Plant', First Quarter, 1978.

Ahmed, Syed Salahuddin, 'Pakistan-Nigeria Relations: A Study in Bilateral Relations', Second Quarter, 1987.

Ali, Mehrunnisa, 'East Pakistan Crisis: International Reactions', Second Quarter, 1971.

_____, 'Pakistan's Withdrawal from the Commonwealth', Fourth Quarter, 1972.

_____, 'The Attitude of the New Afghan Regime Towards its Neighbours', Third Quarter, 1974.

_____, 'Pakistan: Aftermath of the March 1977 Elections', Third and Fourth Quarters, 1977.

_____, 'Pakistan-United States Relations: The Recent Phase', Second and Third Quarters, 1978.

_____, 'Pakistan-Indonesia: Ties of Amity', First Quarter, 1981.

_____, 'Geneva Accords and the Superpowers', Third Quarter, 1988.

_____, 'Jinnah's Perception of Pakistan's Foreign Policy and the Kashmir Issue', Second Quarter, 1990.

---

* Published in *Pakistan Horizon* during 1971–1998.

Burke, S.M., 'India's Offer of a No-War Declaration to Pakistan: Its History and Import', Third Quarter, 1972.

Chaudhri, Mohammad Ahsen, 'Pakistan and the Changing Pattern of Power Relations in South Asia', First Quarter, 1978.

————, 'Geo-Political Factors in Pakistan-India Relations', First Quarter, 1987.

Hasan, Sabiha, 'Pakistan and the Socialist-Republic of Romania', Fourth Quarter, 1979.

————, 'Pakistan-Sri Lanka Relations', Second Quarter, 1985.

Iqbal, Mehrunnisa, 'Pakistan-Foreign Aid and Foreign Policy', Fourth Quarter, 1972.

Kanjilal, Tanmey, 'Improving Pakistan-India Relations: The US Role', Third Quarter, 1997.

Mahdi, Nilofar, 'Sino-Pakistan Relations: Historical Background', Fourth Quarter, 1986.

Mahmood, Tehmina, 'Pressler Amendment and Pakistan's Security Concerns', Fourth Quarter, 1994.

Mehdi, Syed Sikandar, 'The New Pakistan and the Asian Pacific Region', Fourth Quarter, 1974.

Mustafa, Zubeida, 'Pakistan-Afghanistan Relations and Central Asian Politics (1973-1978)', Fourth Quarter, 1978.

Razvi, Mujtaba, 'Pak-Saudi Arabia Relations; An Example of Entente Cordiale', First Quarter, 1981.

Rizvi, Hasan Askari, 'Afghan Refugees in Pakistan: Influx Humanitarian Assistance and Implication', First Quarter, 1984.

————, 'Geneva Parleys on Afghanistan', First Quarter, 1986.

Sherwani, Latif Ahmad, 'Review of Sino-Pakistan Relations (1981-85)', First Quarter, 1986.

————, 'Kashmir's Accession to India Re-examined', Second Quarter, 1990.

Index